KU-077-373

# THE EAST EUROPEAN ECONOMY IN CONTEXT

## Communism and transition

*David Turnock*

London and New York

First published 1997
by Routledge
11 New Fetter Lane, London EC4P 4EE
Simultaneously published in the USA and Canada
by Routledge
29 West 35th Street, New York, NY 10001

© 1997 David Turnock

Typeset in Times by
Ponting–Green Publishing Services, Chesham,
Buckinghamshire

Printed in Great Britain by
MacKays of Chatham PLC, Chatham, Kent

All rights reserved. No part of this book may be
reprinted or reproduced or utilized in any form or by
any electronic, mechanical, or other means, now
known or hereafter invented, including photocopying
and recording, or in any information storage or
retrieval system, without permission in writing
from the publishers.

*British Library Cataloguing in Publication Data*
A catalogue record for this book has been requested

*Library of Congress Cataloging in Publication Data*
Turnock, David.
The East European economy in context: communism and
transition / David Turnock.
p.    cm.
Simultaneously published in the USA and Canada.
Includes bibliographical references and index.
1. Europe, Eastern–Economic conditions–1989–  2. Post-communism–
Europe, Eastern.   I. Title.
HC244.T825  1997
338.947–DC20                          96–41556

ISBN 0–415–08626–4

HOUSE OF COMMONS LIBRARY

LOCATION  ML  Europe  (49)

AUTHOR

ACC DATE          2 2 MAY 199...

TO BE
DISPOSED
BY
AUTHO

House of Commons Library

54056000384807

# THE EAST EUROPEAN ECONOMY IN CONTEXT

Since 1989, the former communist countries of Eastern Europe have witnessed a profound and dramatic upheaval. The economic coherence of this region, formerly maintained through the adoption of the Soviet system of government, has fractured. In *The East European Economy in Context: Communism and Transition*, David Turnock examines the transition from Communist to free-market economies, both within and between the states of Eastern Europe. He offers a comprehensive discussion of the background to this change, as well as detailing the variations which have taken place in each country.

Beginning with a review of the historical background, David Turnock considers Eastern Europe in relation to the imperial systems of the rest of Europe in the eighteenth and nineteenth centuries. He also examines the region in relation to the global perspectives of growth.

As well as containing an informative survey of the impact of Communism, *The East European Economy in Context* provides:

- political profiles of individual countries
- a clear study of the contrasts between northern and Balkan groups
- summaries of regional variations in the transition process
- an exploration of the new state structures and resources
- discussion of political stability, inter-ethnic tensions and progress in economic change

David Turnock argues that the differences found in the economic transition process in each of these countries arise from a host of issues including resources, public attitudes, local government, settlement patterns, power and the environment. *The East European Economy in Context* is a timely and authoritative survey for all those interested in the politics, economy and history of the region.

**David Turnock** is Reader in Geography at the University of Leicester and author of *The Romanian Economy in the Twentieth Century*.

i

# CONTENTS

# TABLES

# MAPS

# ABBREVIATIONS

## MEASURES

| | |
|---|---|
| bn. | billion |
| cu.m. | cubic metre |
| DM | Deutschmark |
| Ft | Forint |
| ha | hectare |
| hl | hectolitre |
| kg. | kilogram |
| km. | kilometre |
| m. | metre |
| mg | milligram |
| mn. | million |
| MW | megawatt |
| pc | per capita |
| ptp | per thousand of the population |
| sq.m. | square metre |
| sq.km. | square kilometre |
| t. | tonne |
| US$ | United States Dollar |
| Zl | Zloty |

## ORGANISATIONS, ETC.

| | |
|---|---|
| CAP | Common Agricultural Policy |
| CEFTA | Central European Free Trade Agreement |
| CIS | Confederation of Independent States |
| CoE | Council of Europe |
| Comecon | Council for Mutual Economic Assistance |
| CSCE | Conference on Security and Cooperation in Europe |
| EBRD | European Bank for Reconstruction and Development |

| | |
|---|---|
| ECE | Economic Commission for Europe |
| EEWP | Enterprise Economic Work Partnership (Hungary) |
| EIB | European Investment Bank |
| EFTA | European Free Trade Association |
| EMBO | Employee-Management Buy-Out |
| EU | European Union |
| FAO | Food and Agriculture Organization (United Nations) |
| FCSFR | Former Czechoslovakian Federal Republic |
| FFRG | Former Federal Republic of Germany (West Germany) |
| FFRY | Former Federative Republic of Yugoslavia |
| FGDR | Former German Democratic Republic (East Germany) |
| FSU | Former Soviet Union |
| GDP | Gross Domestic Product |
| GOP | Gornoslaski Okreg Przemyslowy (Poland) |
| IMF | International Monetary Fund |
| LCY | League of Communists of Yugoslavia |
| MFN | Most Favoured Nation |
| NATO | North Atlantic Treaty Organization |
| NEM | New Economic Mechanism (Hungary) |
| OECD | Organisation for Economic Cooperation and Development |
| Phare | Pologne Hongrie Actions pour la Reconversion Economique |
| SOE | State-Owned Enterprise |
| SOF | State Ownership Fund (Romania) |
| SPA | State Property Agency (Hungary) |
| TEM | Trans-Europe Motorway |
| TER | Trans-Europe Railway |
| UN | United Nations |
| UNESCO | UN Educational Scientific and Cultural Organization |

# 1

# INTRODUCTION
## Eastern Europe to 1945

This book deals with the former communist countries of Eastern Europe apart from the successor states of the Former Soviet Union (FSU). A total of thirteen states (including the eastern part of the now reunified Germany) embrace an area of 1.27mn.sq.km. and a population of 137.8mn. (1985) and with an overall density of 102 persons/sq.km. respectively. The maximum longitudinal spread of Eastern Europe is almost twenty degrees (about 1,300km.) and the distance from the Italian/Slovenian border to the Black Sea at 45 degrees north is some 1,200km. However, at its narrowest (in Hungary) the east–west extent is only 360km. North–south distances tend to be greater, from 40 degrees north in southern Albania to 55 degrees in northern Poland, a distance of some 1,650km. As was also the case before 1989, the region borders on Austria, Greece, Italy and Turkey. However, the unification of Germany means that the northwestern limits are now expressed through the boundaries of the 'New Lander', comprising the Former German Democratic Republic (FGDR). In the east, the breakup of the FSU means that Eastern Europe's neighbours are Belarus, Lithuania and Ukraine, along with Russia by virtue of the Kaliningrad enclave. (See map 1.1.)

Eastern Europe may be regarded as a region with some coherence arising from the adoption, by monopoly communist parties, of elements of the former Soviet system of government, including socio-economic evolution through development of a command economy guided by central planning. There was some relaxation after Stalin's death in 1953 through Red Army withdrawals from the Balkans, though not from FGDR and countries needed for transit purposes. Maintenance of communist power was guaranteed by the Brezhnev doctrine which legitimised Warsaw Pact intervention in Former Czecho-slovakia (FCSFR) in 1968 on the grounds that a threat to the system in one country was a challenge to the alliance as a whole. It was only the declaration by Mikhail Gorbachev (leader of the FSU in the late 1980s) that Eastern Europe was independent which led to radical change throughout Eastern Europe in 1989. It seems that a phase of world war, which has dominated the twentieth century, has at last come to a close, thanks primarily to the Russian decision to abandon a system which arose primarily as a response to the

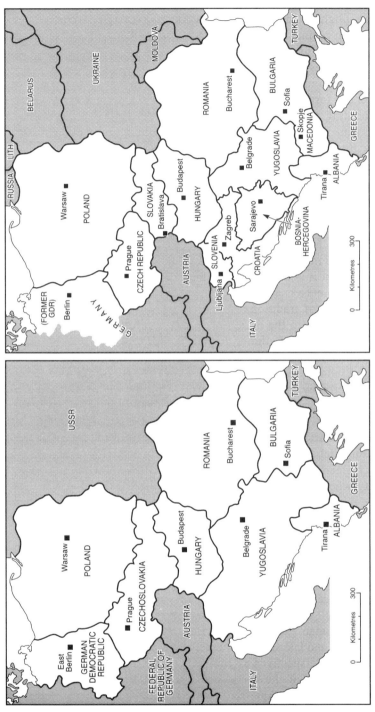

*Map 1.1* Countries of Eastern Europe 1989 and 1996, showing capital cities and neighbouring states

desperate plight of the Russian Empire during the First World War: a more authoritarian regime to draw the ethnic groups together and to provide for the development of priority sectors.

Revolution has robbed Eastern Europe of part of its unity and without the FSU's power to impose stability the future of the region becomes uncertain. However, the former '[state-] socialist countries' still have a common interest in negotiating the transition to a market economy and integrating more closely with Western Europe and the European Union (EU). In this sense Eastern Europe is a region of great importance for the socio-economic progress and political cohesion of the continent (Michalak and Gibb 1992). It is very much in the interest of the EU that there should be stability following the adoption of pluralist systems of government and some major changes in territorial arrangements through the reunification of Germany and the demise of Eastern Europe's two federations: FCSFR and the Former Federal Republic of Yugoslavia (FFRY). Further changes cannot be ruled out, such as the union between Romania and Moldova which once seemed a clear possibility. But it is important that disputes are resolved by peaceful means and ethnic violence is avoided.

The renewal of traditional links with Austria, Germany and Italy may restore credibility to the notion of 'Central Europe' or 'Mitteleuropa' as a region of cultural and ethnic diversity in which Germans (and to a lesser extent Italians) have played a key role in the spread of technology and the growth of industry and trade (Basch 1944). At the same time the tension between Germany and Russia points to the idea of a Marchland Europe (balanced historically between the Habsburg and Prussian states in the West and the eastern empires of Byzantium, the Ottoman Turks and Russia). Independent Eastern Europe disappeared, apart from a few limited instances where imperial power was exerted indirectly through suzerainty (Palmer 1970). Instead there was colonialism, with much instability and ethnic diversity where imperial frontiers were in state-of-flux boundary changes. Historic rivalries still complicate relations, most clearly since the demise of FFRY which has thrown into sharp focus the conflicting aspirations of the leading ethnic groups.

Consideration of the political map for the middle decades of the nineteenth century would show Eastern Europe falling to the Habsburg, Ottoman and Russian empires along with the German states, among which Prussia was gaining ascendancy. This imperial framework had its origins in the medieval period although significant frontier modifications were made with the gains from the Ottoman Empire by the Habsburg Empire in Croatia, Hungary, Transylvania (and later Bosnia-Hercegovina) and also by the Russian Empire in Bessarabia. Perspectives extending further back into history would cover the dynasticstates of the early medieval period reflecting the ethnic quilt arising out of the Dark Age migrations and the potential for autonomy in the marchlands between Russia and the Byzantine and Holy Roman empires.

They would also include both the ultimate imperial precedent in the shape of the Roman Empire and an inspiration for nationhood through the romanisation of Iron Age tribes, a process which provides a cultural foundation for the Albanian and Romanian states.

Eastern Europe's political history can only be described as tumultuous because state formation has been seen as a highly competitve business in which the more successful systems have been able to exert and maintain power over large areas of land. Coercive policies have required economic strength linked with the accumulation of wealth by urban-based merchants and manufacturers. It was Eastern Europe's fate for the medieval dynastic states to be eliminated by strong imperial systems with economic cores that lay outside the region, apart from the Czech Lands and Saxony which played important roles in the growth of the German and Habsburg empires respectively. In the nineteenth century it became common for cohesion to be fostered by cultural programmes based on nationalism as well as religion, but the 'state-led nationalism' of Western Europe contrasted with the 'state-seeking nationalism' in Eastern Europe, where the contraction of the Ottoman Empire led to 'Balkanisation' and a tier of new nation states, and the Habsburgs agreed to a share of power between Budapest and Vienna (Tilly 1989). The process was then completed by self-determination at the end of the First World War which left many Germans stranded by the collapse of the imperial structures (Jaworski 1991).

The Western powers have generally supported self-determination in Eastern Europe but their ideological solidarity has been compromised by the need to coexist with other great powers. The British geographer H.J. Mackinder appreciated the strategic importance of Eastern Europe to both Germany (seeking eastward expansion into the Eurasian heartland) and Russia (looking for security on her western frontier). He advocated a security system for the new democracies of Eastern Europe to be supported by the West, but this was only achieved to the limited extent of the "Little Entente" in view of major foreign policy differences between the East European states themselves (Mackinder 1962). By the late 1930s Germany was casting a shadow, and substantial territorial changes were made to create a Greater Germany (*Grossdeutschland*) and a larger stake in the region for Bulgaria, Hungary and Italy. Measures were taken to simplify the ethnic structure through resettlement (including population exchanges). Then, in 1945, the FSU's security requirements meant that the eastern territories of FCSFR, Poland and Romania were lost (with compensation for Poland at Germany's expense) while several changes were made in border regions: minor transfers in the cases of the Austrian-Hungarian and FCSFR-Polish frontiers (in the Burgenland and Klodzko areas respectively) but more substantial in the case of the Italian-FFRY border, thereby reflecting the political strength of the Yugoslav idea under Tito's leadership at the time.

A German geographer (J. Partsch) once suggested that Central Europe could be recognised in landscape terms through the juxtaposition of 'Alpine' mountains (like the Carpathians and Dinaric Alps), 'Hercynian chains' (referring to the broken hill and plateau country of the Czech Lands and its border regions) and major lowlands like the North European, Hungarian/ Pannonian and Romanian/Wallachian plains). These landscapes have much significance for human geography. The concept of 'ecumene' (a nursery for the nation state) could be considered with reference to Bohemia, Kosovo or Transylvania. There are complementary resource regions: the mountains are important for pastoralism and have a long history of mining activity. Meanwhile, in addition to their potential for intensive agriculture, the lowlands have yielded several important minerals in recent times including oil, gas and lignite, as well as copper and sulphur (Pearton 1971). Moreover, the growth market-oriented manufacturing in the capital cities and the expansion of the ports on the Adriatic, Baltic and Black Seas has also helped to reverse this historic imbalance.

There are significant constraints in the mountains however. Just over one-fifth of the land is higher than 500m. and subsistence farmers must concentrate on the hardiest cereals, such as rye in the Carpathians. But in a commercial context the mountain grazings provide a sound base for pastoralism to complement the arable emphasis of the low ground. High sunshine levels in the southern mountains enhance the potential and in the past remarkably large agricultural communities were supported, although remoteness from marauding armies and feudalising landowners were also significant factors, as was the high incidence of disease in the lowlands in early modern times. The mountains are still heavily forested and the woodlands are very important commercially, for exports of raw timber have been diversified by other products such as board, plywood and furniture requiring a greater degree of processing. Meanwhile the scenic attractions of the mountains with cultural landscapes indicative of settlement continuity and pluriactivity have become important resources for tourism. Within the major structures like the Carpathians there are distinct local characteristics such as the inselberg-like hills in the Jelenia Gora basin of southwest Poland – the result of subtropical morphogenesis going back to the Middle Miocene (Migon 1992).

The lowland areas, particularly the North European Plain and the plains associated with the Danube (the Pannonian Plain – known to Hungarians as Nagyalfold – and the Lower Danube or Wallachian Plain), comprise fertile land interspersed with less tractable sands. The latter have often supported only poor grazing (the *puszta* of Hungary) or woodland, although more recently the supply of irrigation water has opened the way to more intensive use. The southern lands have the advantage of high summer temperatures (all the low ground south of Budapest in Hungary and Iasi in Romania has a mean July temperature exceeding 20°C). However, conditions are very dry in the far southeastern parts of Eastern Europe: Moldavia, Dobrogea and eastern Wallachia (Baragan steppe) have an annual rainfall below 50cm. and irrigation is therefore a critical matter. In the past much of the land was used to rear livestock and grow cereals for export, but the growth of population and industry has meant that more land is needed to feed the population and to generate agricultural raw materials. The trade surplus has been turned into a deficit and by the 1980s there was a considerable net import of cereals. On the farms cereal crops are complemented by sugar beet and fodder, while additional areas are devoted to textile crops, oil plants such as sunflowers, tobacco and a range of medicinal and aromatic plants. There are also vegetable gardens, orchards and vineyards with considerable export potential. Livestock rearing has become more intensive (contributing to the cereal deficit) since meat production is an important indicator of rising living standards. Fish are also more important: they are caught by trawlers in distant waters to supplement the traditional fisheries along the coasts, the inland rivers (the Danube delta and floodplain lakes) and fish-ponds which are particularly numerous in FCSFR.

However, the development of the region's resources has not been straight-forward (Bierman and Laboda 1992; Pounds 1969). Eastern Europe was certainly congenial for settlement and agriculture in prehistoric times, for the relatively warm and dry Balkan lands played their part in the diffusion of crops from the Middle East to Western Europe (Turnock 1988). Prehistoric settlers discovered that the Danube and the Morava–Vardar corridors gave easy access to the better farming lands, and forest was cleared, especially on the light loess soils. The amber routes exemplify the transit role of Eastern Europe, transmitting cultural influences from the Balkans to the North European Plain. The northern coniferous and deciduous woodlands posed a severe challenge, but nevertheless, German and Slav colonists initiated economic developments which eclipsed the Balkans in medieval and modern times. With access provided by such rivers as the Elbe, Oder and Vistula, surpluses could be marketed through the Hanseatic trading system. Yet Eastern Europe lost out when the historic trading axis from the Mediterranean to the East was eclipsed by the great discoveries which stimulated economic advance and technological innovation in Western Europe. During the Industrial Revolution with its coal-based technology, it was impossible to escape from a largely colonial relationship with the West because few large industrial regions were developed (Pounds 1958a, 1958b). Meanwhile, imperial structures imposed severe constraints on enterprise; and wars brought enormous losses and required repeated infrastructural overhauls (Berend and Ranki 1979).

It is usual to divide the region into two halves: a northern tier comprising the relatively well-developed states of FCSFR, Hungary and Poland with considerable democratic experience; and a southern group to take in the FFRY along with Albania, Bulgaria and Romania (Turnock 1989). In the north there was considerable involvement with the core areas of the Habsburg and Prussian/German states (Berend and Ranki 1974a). The Habsburgs kept

6

Hungary in a state of feudal subjection as the empire's breadbasket (for the warmth of the Great Plain gives Hungary an agricultural potential comparable with that of the Balkan states) and industrialisation took off only after the famous compromise *Ausgleich* in 1867 (Berend and Ranki 1974b); but the Czech Lands were developed as the main industrial base (Kaser and Radice 1986). Saxony played a similar role in the German Lands with the great trading emporium at Leipzig and a major centre of manufacturing in Chemnitz, where the textile industries of the Erzgebirge were consolidated on the basis of cotton manufacture and related engineering industries during the nineteenth century. Use of cotton (initially obtained from Macedonia) and production of machines by firms like Richard Hartmann made Chemnitz the 'Manchester of Saxony'. Basic to all this industrial activity was the Elbe waterway and the web of railways which was plainly taking shape from the 1850s on. There were lines to Berlin (via Elsterwerda and Juterbog) as well as a coal supply route from Lugau and Zwickau, and railways advanced up the Erzgebirge valleys to strengthen links with the immediate hinterland. German enterprise extended to Silesia and was drawn over the border into Russian Poland through the concessionary regime established in the city of Lodz.

Meanwhile the Balkans were relatively remote, with a long sea journey required to reach the Danube delta, while penetration from the Adriatic was constrained by the towering Dinaric Alps. Moreover, the trading monopoly maintained by the Ottoman authorities limited the options available until well into the nineteenth century (Carter 1977). The system was initially efficient, with a command economy maintained through administrative and military hierarchies working through a market system of towns interconnected by trading caravans (Stoianovitch 1989). But it failed to modernise in the era of factory industry and growth was stifled as intermediaries intercepted the flow of wealth heading for Istanbul. The Ottoman administration had little to offer the Christian peoples of the Balkans at a time of increasing national awareness (Sugar 1977). It was only after the Treaty of Adrianople (1828) that the Danubian principalities of Moldavia and Wallachia could begin to trade with Western Europe through the ports of Braila, Galati and (after 1878) Constanta. The Balkan states started to gain their independence from the Ottoman Empire in the late nineteenth century and the process was completed by the creation of Albania in 1912 (Augustinos 1991). Romania became one of the world's leading cereal exporters with rail as well as sea transport available. However, despite the proximity of the Danube the lack of irrigation made cereal farming vulnerable to severe summer drought. Feudal obligations were swept away but the peasants remained dependent on the large landowners who paid only low wages while imposing burdensome labour contracts (Chirot 1989). This prompted governments to combine industrialisation with a politically motivated land reform programme to give peasants greater security and independence.

The historic imbalance was addressed by the governments of inter-war Eastern Europe and until 1945 there was some evolution along Western lines (Pasvolsky 1971; Polonsky 1980). But labour intensive methods reflected the limited employment opportunities outside agriculture where the peasant character of farming was enhanced by share cropping arrangements to supplement the produce from the peasants' own land, some of it arising out of land reforms implemented after the First World War. Thus the agricultural emphasis persisted (Zagoroff *et al.* 1955) amidst acute problems of rural overpopulation (Moore 1945). Meanwhile the northern regions were expanding and diversifying. Chemnitz was active in the familiar industrial progression from cycles to motorcycles and cars, emerging as capital of the German Auto Union in 1932. There was much sub-contracting throughout the area. Urbanisation levels increased and growing prosperity led to an expansion of leisure interests. The growth of domestic tourism stimulated measures for the protection of nature. In 1919 the Polish Minister of Education set up a committee which grew into the State Council for the Protection of Wild Nature in 1925. In 1934 a law gave practical effect to their activities particularly with regard to national parks. Six parks were laid out by the end of the 1930s: Bialowieza Forest (4,634ha) was first laid out in 1921 and planning eventually focused on the Tatra Mountains, covering fine mountain scenery on the Polish-Czechoslovak frontier and the distinctive cultural landscape of the Gorale region. A national park was eventually set up in this area in 1954.

Economic development and nationalism reinforced each other, complicating the position of ethnic minorities stranded by the demise of imperialism (Brown 1988; Thomas 1987). Population exchanges were sometimes possible but most minorities chose to remain, unaware of the dangers that would arise through xenophobia associated with the depression years of the 1930s and the rise of Germany as a focus for revisionism. Both themes tended to politicise ethnic issues and some groups were readily perceived as fifth columnists even though they had no subversive intentions of their own, given any attempt at protection by the mother country. Although there was no threat from a Jewish state the Jews in Eastern Europe were particularly vulnerable, with a history of employment as estate stewards and businessmen, maintaining striking group identification through language, religion, dress and food at a time when these manifestations were not as provocative because there was no dominant national force to perceive a challenge (Abramsky *et al.* 1986). But continued identification caused resentment among the dominant groups, especially when minorities (like the Jews) were perceived as being privileged and so became obvious targets for right-wing political parties in the 1930s. The Second World War was a disaster for ethnic harmony through widespread nationalist excesses although it is the holocaust, which accounted for three million Jews in Poland alone (98 per cent of the country's Jewish population), that stands as the most appalling outrage (Nahon 1990; Steinberg 1990).

The degeneration into communism in the late 1940s was in a way a prolongation of the war economy in the Soviet interest, with some additional momentum through perceived benefits in national reconstruction and co-hesion. Yet now, once again, Eastern Europe is faced with the task of restructuring and, with the existence of relatively open frontiers and free trade, it is possible to see the scope of regional specialisation in a range of industries concerned with the processing of food, timber, ores and other raw materials; also in tourism, given the climatic profile of the Balkans and a cultural landscape appropriate to many specific recreational themes. The markets of Eastern Europe are large enough (especially with the spur of import tariffs) to justify investment in modern industry even if each country may be too small to attract the full range of manufacturing capacities. And the commercial experience of East Europeans in dealing with the CIS and Middle Eastern countries lends credibility to the idea of Eastern Europe as a forward base for export-related manufacturing. In broadly the same category is the notion of industrial development at the approaches to Scandinavia. Moreover, the general increase in mobility should impact particularly on border regions which can extend trading hinterlands across frontiers. This could be very beneficial to Hungary whose frontiers were determined only after 1918 and which saw many functional links being severed, leaving rural areas isolated from market centres or undermining vibrant towns through the partitioning of their hinterlands and the consequent loss of local trade. But there could also be scope in areas like southern and western Bohemia where Cheb (Eger) could once again realise its potential as a route centre; and again in southwestern Silesia with the tradition of German tourism in the Sudeten Mountains at resorts like Sklarska Poreba.

In realising these potentials Eastern Europe can take advantage of easy lines of communication such as the Black Sea and Mediterranean route to the Middle East and the railways and waterways linking the region with Western Europe. However, a great deal of new investment will be needed to ensure that passenger and freight traffic flows smoothly across frontiers which until recently have experienced only limited activity. New energy supply arrange-ments will be needed as the traditional dependence on the FSU is modified by greater use of oil pipelines from West European terminals. Eastern Europe also has a growing population which can provide a cheap and adaptable workforce, though one that will have to gear up to productivity levels closer to those in the West and accept a new work ethic in which individuals identify fully with the enterprise and contribute to its success. There needs to be greater homogeneity in terms of societal values, a point which may seem strange after years of state propaganda about the norms of socialist society. But in fact there are considerable social and ethnic divisions (Greenbaum 1988). However, the most serious problems arise in the Balkans and it is here where further territorial change is most likely. By contrast, in the north the present frontiers are much more stable and economic policy is the central issue.

# REFERENCES

C. Abramsky *et al.* (eds) 1986, *The Jews in Poland Between the Two World Wars* (Oxford: Blackwell).

G. Augustinos 1991, *Diverse Paths to Modernity in Southeastern Europe* (New York: Greenwood Press).

A. Basch 1944, *The Danube Basin and the German Economic Sphere* (Kegan Paul Trench Trubner).

I. Berend and G. Ranki 1974a, *Economic Development in East Central Europe in the Nineteenth and Twentieth Centuries* (New York: Columbia University Press).

I. Berend and G. Ranki 1974b, *Hungary: A Century of Economic Development* (Newton Abbot, Devon: David & Charles).

I. Berend and G. Ranki (eds.) 1979, *Underdevelopment and Economic Growth: Studies in Hungarian Social and Economic History* (Budapest: Academy of Sciences).

D.E. Bierman and J. Laboda 1992, *East Central Europe: The Land and its People in Historical Perspective* (Cincinnati, Ohio: Nordic).

J.F. Brown 1988, 'National minorities and their problems' in *Eastern Europe and Communist Rule* (Durham: Duke University Press), 415–44.

F.W. Carter (ed.) 1977, *Historical Geography of the Balkans* (London: Academic Press).

D. Chirot (ed.) 1989, *The Origin of Backwardness in Eastern Europe: Economics and Politics from the Middle Ages until the Early Twentieth Century* (Berkeley, California: University of California Press).

A. Greenbaum (ed.) 1988, *Minority Problems in Eastern Europe Between the World Wars* (Jerusalem: Hebrew University of Jerusalem).

R. Jaworski 1991, 'The German minorities in Poland and Czechoslovakia in the interwar period', in R. Smith *et al.* (eds) *Ethnic Groups and International Relations* (Aldershot: Dartmouth), 169–85.

M.C. Kaser and E.A. Radice (eds) 1986, *The Economic History of Eastern Europe 1919–1975* (Oxford: Clarendon Press).

H.J. Mackinder 1962, *Democratic Ideals and Reality* (New York: Norton).

W.Z. Michalak and R.A. Gibb 1992, 'Political geography and Eastern Europe'. *Area* 24, 341–9.

P. Migon 1992, 'Inherited landscapes in the crystalline area of the Sudetes Mountains'. *Geographia Polonica* 60, 123–36.

W.E. Moore 1945, *Economic Demography of Eastern and Southern Europe* (Geneva: League of Nations).

M. Nahon 1990, *Birkenau: the camp of death* (Atlanta: University of Alabama Press).

A. Palmer 1970, *The lands between: A history of East-Central Europe since the Congress of Vienna* (London: Weidenfeld & Nicolson).

L. Pasvolsky 1971, *Economic Nationalism in the Danubian States* (New York: Macmillan).

M. Pearton 1971, *Oil and the Romanian State* (Oxford: Clarendon Press).

A. Polonsky 1980, *The Little Dictators: The History of Eastern Europe since* 1918 (London: Routledge & Kegan Paul).

A. Polonsky 1991, *The Jews of Warsaw* (Oxford: Blackwell).

N.J.G. Pounds 1958a, *The Upper Silesian Industrial Region* (Bloomington, Indiana: Indiana University).

N.J.G. Pounds 1958b, 'The spread of mining in the coal basin of Upper Silesia and Northern Moravia'. *Annals Association of American Geographers* 48, 149–63.

N.J.G. Pounds 1969, *Eastern Europe* (London: Longman).

J. Steinberg 1990, *All or Nothing: The Axis and the Holocaust 1941–1943* (London: Routledge).

T. Stoianovitch 1989, 'Cities' capital accumulation and the Ottoman Balkan command economy 1500–1800' in C. Tilly and W.P. Blockmans (eds) *Cities and the Rise of States in Europe AD1000–1800* (Boulder, Colorado: Westview Press), 60–99.

P.F. Sugar 1977, *Southeastern Europe under Ottoman rule 1354–1804* (Seattle: University of Washington Press).

C. Thomas 1987, 'Ethnic minorities in Yugoslavia'. *Irish Slavonic Studies* 8, 59–85.

C. Tilly 1989, 'Entanglements of European cities and states' in C. Tilly and W.P. Blockmans (eds) *Cities and the Rise of States in Europe AD1000–1800* (Boulder, Colorado: Westview Press), 1–27.

D. Turnock 1988, *The Making of Eastern Europe from the Earliest Times to 1815* (London: Routledge).

D. Turnock 1989, *Eastern Europe: An Historical Geography 1815–1945* (London: Routledge).

S.D. Zagoroff *et al.* 1955, *The Agricultural Economy of the Danubian Countries 1935–1945* (Stanford, California: Stanford University Press).

# 2

# EASTERN EUROPE UNDER COMMUNISM

## IDEOLOGY, POLITICAL STRUCTURES AND POPULATION

Communism in Eastern Europe is now being regarded as an aberration; an unfortunate survival of global conflict as a cold war played out by opposing power blocks (Dockrill 1988). Wartime cooperation among the allies quickly broke down as the Soviets worked to separate their zone of influence from the rest of Europe and to emphasise the coherence of the new alliance through the national communist parties and more formal institutions like the Warsaw Pact (Holden 1989). The changes were most dramatic in Germany where the zonal division (Sharp 1975) crystallised into two German states with their separate economies (Wilkens 1981) and a highly fortified inner boundary (Ritter and Hajdu 1989). The city of Berlin became a microcosm of the German problem (Elkins and Hofmeister 1988; Francisco and Merritt 1985) as the Soviet Zone (East Berlin) was completely separated from the combined American, British and French zones (West Berlin) by the Berlin Wall in 1961 (Elkins 1989; Smith 1961); and the infrastructure was revamped to isolate West Berlin as far as possible from the FGDR (Merritt 1973). But an Iron Curtain was imposed throughout, with only a few tightly controlled border crossings and international trade internalised within the bloc as far as possible. Between the member states there was an equally comprehensive border administration.

It was in Stalin's interest to impose authority on Eastern Europe to gain security and access to East European resources, initially attractive though later to become problematic where economic matters were concerned. But the establishment of communist regimes also demonstrated 'the readiness of a determined minority of communists in each country to use coercion, deception and manipulation of their fellow countrymen in order to secure a monopoly of power', taking advantage of 'the physical exhaustion and political disorientation of the war-ravaged population' (Batt 1991, p.3). Elite penetration of all facets of government and international coordination made legitimation difficult (Neumann 1988), but power was effectively con-solidated and the propaganda war created an image of purposeful progress.

Although his words were soon undermined by the flow of events, G. Schopflin had some justification for his assertion (1988, p.147) that the Stalinists 'actually succeeded in constructing a political system that was and remains superbly efficient at concentrating power and at ensuring that this is never seriously diluted' (ibid.). It was even possible for Stalinist uniformity to be followed by growing national diversity and limited reform, provided that the communist monopoly was not imperilled (Stokes 1991). Such rivalry is thought to have killed off any idea of a Balkan Federation that was discussed in the early post-war years (Shoup 1990).

The communists were not by any means bereft of ideas when it came to countering Western charges of dictatorship, combined with manipulation of public opinion and persecution of opponents. There was much grass-roots idealism for a new order in Eastern Europe that would boost employment, accelerate the transition to an industrial economy and offer a better future for all sections of the population including the peasantry and the poorer people generally. The military-industrial establishment would provide, both nationally and internationally, a steady flow of orders and there would be sufficient raw materials within the bloc to maintain a high level of self-sufficiency without the need to take account of world market prices or the profits of foreign investors. A growing urban proletariat would constitute a growing demand for food, and as rural infrastructure improved, factory industry could spread through the central hierarchy and take root in the more backward regions. There was great enthusiasm in FFRY, where pride in the wartime resistance movement and the new federal system (Pavlowitch 1989) helped to generate energy for reconstruction, including the heroic 'youth railways' (Casson 1950). Cooperatives were set up in Bulgaria with the help of weekend migrations by urban dwellers to educate the villagers: 'in these bands there is perhaps the compulsion of a social conscience but for the most part the work is done enthusiastically and voluntarily' (Edwards 1947, p.547). While intolerance was manifest in the treatment of Germans (and in the disturbance of certain other ethnic groups like the Ukrainians in Poland) ethnic tension was reduced, perhaps partly through Jewish influence in the party in early days. Federalism could provide some encouragement for minorities coupled with the stability provided by a monopoly party (Leff 1988).

Objective Western appraisal of communist-inspired change was always complicated by the tension between the heroic voluntarism of traditional societies working flat out for modernisation and the coercive state apparatus working to a 'secret agenda' that had much more to do with the great power pretensions of the FSU than with the cause of prosperity for the masses (Mellor 1975; Pounds 1969). It was possible to herald a 'new' and unique way forward (Hamilton 1971) as long as the environmental costs were minimal and the large population of forced labourers could be explained away in terms of 're-education' for criminals and wartime collaborators. Some authors continued to applaud the social objectives and the spatial policies of equalisation well into the 1980s (Rugg 1985). But the realities of coercion could be seen at the international level by the threat to FFRY after Tito's expulsion in 1948 from the Cominform (a Soviet-led political association of ruling communist parties) when it seemed that many of the country's major centres of population might be exposed to a tank assault from Hungary, Romania and Bulgaria (perhaps even from Albania), possibly requiring another retreat to the mountains (Maclean 1951) and a consequent dispersal of development projects (Hamilton 1964). The 'forced march' to modernisation involved heavy social costs through long hours of factory work and persistent shortages in housing, transport and consumer goods. Although agriculture was mechanised and intensified through irrigation and fertiliser production, the farming population remained relatively poor and in this sense an anti-agrarian bias was deliberately maintained to ensure a flood of migrants for the towns. The demands of the military-industrial complex left a legacy through an 'outdated distorted economic structure that was too intimately bound up with the equally distorted political structure' (Schopflin 1988, p.146). Stalin's communism certainly constituted a 'highly contradictory even counterproductive modernising revolution' (ibid., p.126).

## Population

The gender ratio is 51:49 in favour of females, though there is a male majority in Poland, Romania and FFRY. There is also great regional imbalance, as in some rural areas like Poland's northeast where the male:female ratio reached 7:1. The working population is 61 per cent with the highest proportions in FCSFR, Poland and Romania, reflecting relatively high birth rates. Overall, annual growth declined to only 0.5 per cent per annum in the early 1980s after running at roughly 0.8 per cent per annum over the previous three decades. The ageing of the population suggests that this trend will continue and that the forecasts for 2000 calculated in the 1970s will be missed by a considerable margin. However, demographic performance has varied considerably among individual countries. Albania's population increased 2.4 times between 1950 and 1985; and a group of three countries occupy an intermediate position with substantial increase overall (Poland 50 per cent, FFRY 41.4 per cent and Romania 39.4 per cent). Bulgaria (23.4 per cent) and FCSFR (18.4 per cent) showed an increase, with Hungary registering 8.6 per cent and FGDR −7.0, the latter reflecting a pronounced ageing of the population exacerbated by selective out-migration. In density terms FGDR registered 154 people per sq.km, with FCSFR, Hungary and Poland clustered close to 120 and all the southern states below 100 except FFRY (Table 2.1).

Population was of central importance to the governments of communist Eastern Europe. Whether the policy objectives are construed specifically in relation to the FSU's military-industrial complex or national defence or long-

Table 2.1 Population of Eastern Europe 1950–2000

| Country | Area sq.km. | 1950 | 1970 | 1980 | 1985 | 2000 | Growth[1] A | B | Density sq.km. 1985 |
|---|---|---|---|---|---|---|---|---|---|
| Northern tier | 641.9 | 65.65 | 72.73 | 78.46 | 80.06 | 85.7 | 0.8 | 0.7 | 125 |
| FCSFR | 127.9 | 13.09 | 14.47 | 15.28 | 15.50 | 16.8 | 0.6 | 0.7 | 121 |
| FGDR | 108.3 | 17.94 | 17.26 | 16.74 | 16.69 | 16.6 | – | – | 155 |
| Hungary | 93.0 | 9.80 | 10.31 | 10.71 | 10.64 | 10.9 | 0.3 | 0.3 | 114 |
| Poland | 312.7 | 24.82 | 30.69 | 35.73 | 37.23 | 41.4 | 1.7 | 1.6 | 119 |
| Southern tier | 632.9 | 41.15 | 51.27 | 55.97 | 57.78 | 64.6 | 1.4 | 1.4 | 102 |
| Albania | 28.7 | 1.22 | 2.16 | 2.59 | 2.96 | 4.1 | 4.9 | 5.9 | 103 |
| Bulgaria | 110.9 | 7.27 | 8.49 | 8.88 | 8.97 | 9.7 | 0.8 | 0.8 | 81 |
| Romania | 237.5 | 16.31 | 20.35 | 22.20 | 22.73 | 25.6 | 1.4 | 1.4 | 96 |
| FFRY | 255.8 | 16.35 | 20.37 | 22.30 | 23.12 | 25.2 | 1.4 | 1.3 | 90 |
| Eastern Europe | 1274.8 | 106.80 | 124.00 | 134.43 | 137.84 | 150.3 | 1.0 | 1.0 | 108 |

Note 1  A1950–85 trend in relation to Eastern Europe = 1.0; B Ditto 1950–2000.

Source:  United Nations Statistical Yearbooks

term prosperity goals, an active, motivated, skilled and increasing population was fundamental. Population growth (with particular reference to active participation) was crucial for economies that needed to be labour-intensive, at least in the short and medium term, and also for expansion of the armed forces despite the priority given to matching the increasing technical sophistication of NATO. Technical skills were needed for the anticipated explosion in factory employment: hence the emphasis on science and technology in the secondary schools, polytechnics and universities. Motivation was crucial for the acceptance of disciplined work routines and, more generally, tolerance of party and government edicts. So there was a propaganda emphasis on socialism to achieve prosperity for all, with particular reference to 'the workers' as the main prospective beneficiaries of the command economy. There was an implicit need for greater homogeneity to maximise support for the ideology of modernisation under the guidance of the communist party. And since nationalism was used as a motivating factor (albeit in the context of fraternal association with the Soviet bloc), nonconformist ethnic-cultural groups like the Gypsies needed special encouragement to accept a sedentary way of life and full participation in the socialist labour market.

In order to generate the labour required for socialist construction, obvious priorities were the education and health services, the former to provide appropriate training and the latter to maximise natural increase by reducing deaths, particularly among young children (Besemeres 1980). Much funding went into health care (Valentine *et al.* 1987), although inequalities remained (Orosz 1990) and research in Poland pointed to problems of funding (especially for health care), access (dependent on economic status and connections and the quality of local medical centres), and patients' ability to cope with the professional language of doctors. The problem of low pay in the medical and educational professions made recruitment of staff difficult (Grochowski 1990). However, there was considerable waste of labour because of security considerations which resulted in a large prison population (and indeed many deaths through the elimination of political opponents and others concerned with commerce, industry and the churches). Political prisoners were relatively few by the 1960s (although persecution and intimidation continued up to 1989); yet the forced labour that was used extensively for public works (justified to some extent in terms of re-education) could hardly qualify as efficient use of manpower. Furthermore, there was a contradiction for women between participation in the economy and child-bearing. In the early years the immediate needs of the labour market were paramount and hence women were given easy access to abortion (beginning in Bulgaria in 1956) and only Albania found it unnecessary to introduce this facility.

Yet abortion depressed the birth rate and forced a shift to pronatalist policies by the late 1960s. These combined severe checks on abortion with the positive encouragement of child-bearing through various welfare benefits (allowance, maternity benefits and housing concessions) and propagandist exhortation like the 'heroine mother' distinction bestowed on those Romanian women who bore ten or more children (Berelson 1974, p.376). But despite the most coercive policies in Romania after 1966, imposing prison sentences on doctors performing illegal abortions and (eventually) subjecting young women to regular gynaecological testing, the birth rate continued to fall because of family planning that was usually carried out 'in its most rudimentary form: unskilled induced abortion' (Puia and Hirtopeanu 1990, p.5). This created many complications and in such cases the women concerned, fearing legal punishment, sought help from specialised clinics too late. Those who were saved 'have remained infirm for the whole of their life, crippled both physically and psychologically' (ibid.). Small families have become traditional in many areas like Transdanubia (Vasary 1989). However, the more draconian aspects of population policy generated much concern from the standpoint of human rights (Bahro 1978; Kortus 1985).

Communist population policy enhanced the role of women in positions of leadership (Siemienska 1985; Sokolowska 1981). Women became more effective in the workplace, even bargaining over pay when the organisations that were supposed to represent their interests were insufficiently supportive: hence the significance of crises as a factor shaping women's awareness and behaviour in Poland (Siemienska 1983, pp.26–33). Successful efforts were also made during the 1950s and 1960s to proletarianise the peasantry for service in industry and the armed forces (Kolankiewicz 1980) and bring about social structural change in the rural areas (Huszar et al. 1978; Szelenyi and Manchin 1986). However, it is doubtful if the new working class was highly politicised, in contrast to the small pre-war working class who expected the new regimes to be 'theirs'. Instead they became a minority, given the large numbers of unskilled migrants and commuters from the villages, and there was much worker disenchantment when the communist dream remained unfulfilled (Volgyes 1989, pp.259–304). A further distinction of population policy was the conspicious success of East European countries and FSU in international sport. Heavy investment in sport helped to stimulate young people into healthy activity acceptable to communist governments and good performances in the international arena helped to demonstrate the superiority of the system. Despite some questionable use of drugs, there is little doubt that effective training and coaching methods were built in the 1960s (Arthur 1992).

But Eastern Europe failed to match the enormous productivity gains achieved by the West. The social desirability of full employment was a major tenet of communist ideology (replacing the initial political imperative of maximising participation in socialist construction and the growth of the proletariat) and this helped to sustain the hoarding of cheap labour as an alternative to capital investment (Galasi and Sziraczki 1985). There was

17

much wasteful use of labour which transferred *de facto* underemployment from the fields to the factory floor and ensured that production targets could nearly always be met despite any hold-ups in movement of raw materials and intermediates. However, higher productivity had implications for investment and worker initiative in terms of decision-making and initiative which was always problematic in the context of communist power hierarchies. Arguably, large groups of manual workers employed in industries with smokestack technology were most likely to be potential bastions of communism. Hence, there was little creative destruction and new capacities were almost invariably geared to net increases in output rather than to the replacement of obsolete technology. When large enterprises did retool, their discarded machinery often filtered down to small industries under the control of local authorities or cooperatives in the rural areas. Yet in spite of caution there was much worker dissatisfaction.

The post-war period has seen a massive redistribution of population in favour of the towns (Musil and Rysavy 1983). The link between migration and urbanisation was very close (Thomas 1982) and, except for FCSFR and FGDR which were already highly urbanised, an urban transition was achieved (Dawson 1983; Ronnas 1982). There was active recruitment in the case of major economic projects such as the uranium industry in the Erzgebirge and, later, the copper industry in the Glogow-Legnica area of Poland (with incentives to cover the cost of transport and settling in) but most of the rural-urban transfers occurred spontaneously, overwhelmingly involving young people (Sarfalvi 1970). Only in Albania were there sustained efforts to control internal migration (Sjoberg 1991b). There was an absolute population increase in all altitudinal zones between 1945 and 1979, although the high ground settlements (at over 300m.) declined in relative terms. There was improved social security, extended to cooperatives in 1972 to 1976; yet migration was allowed to towns and mining areas especially in southern Albania, which of course meant lower natural increase compared with the northeast (Sjoberg 1989). But there was sustained depopulation in most rural areas of Eastern Europe (Stasiak 1992). During the 1970s the rural areas of Poland lost two million people aged between 18 and 29 (Korcelli 1990, p.319). This was at a time of particularly heavy migration when net rural-urban transfers averaged 250,000 per annum, compared with 120,100 between 1961 and 1970 and 91,000 between 1952 and 1960 (between 1981 and 1985 the average fell back to 137,200 (ibid., p.312). These calculations do not include many cases of daily commuting to work in towns and temporary transfers by students and young people conscripted into the armed services. However, it has been suggested that Eastern Europe remained underurbanised in relation to the overall distribution of economic activity, with serious housing shortages in cities like Budapest (Hegedus and Tosics 1983; Sillince 1985).

## International migration and ethnicity

Planning was upset by out-migration from Eastern Europe which was age- and skill-selective with a disproportionate number of skilled and professional people. Permanent migration was significant in some countries well before 1989, in addition to temporary migration in connection with education, training or work in various parts of the Comecon bloc (and sometimes Western Europe). But although international movement was, for the most part, strictly controlled, there was a steady loss through escapees who were able to use ingenious methods to evade frontier security. East European governments discovered emigration as a way of removing dissidents without attracting protests from the international community. It was also a way of solving the problem of conflict between ethnic groups (especially when there were economic gains through allowing Germans to resettle in the FFRG). However, Yugoslavs were allowed to work abroad under their own individual arrangements: usually it was only leading celebrities who were granted this privilege, except in the case of state contracts involving joint projects in the FSU and programmes of military and economic assistance in the Third World (particularly Africa and the Middle East). Emigration seems to have involved some 259,000 people per annum betweem 1950 and 1985 (some 7mn. in all), but there were striking variations between countries with Albania and the FGDR showing the two extremes (Table 2.2). Security was generally tight but in the latter case the sealing of borders came only after the Berlin Wall was built; while liberalisation in 1989 followed another flood of out-migration to the FFRG indirectly through third countries (Hungary and subsequently FCSFR and Poland) which accelerated the demise of the FGDR government when the closure of the borders precipitated demonstrations. Of course, the FGDR was always prone to the loss of population given the cultural affinity between the two Germanies (maximised by the availability of West German television in all parts of the FGDR except the so-called 'Valley of the Innocents') and the big differences in per capita incomes ($US8,900 against $US5,400). But the FFRG was also a popular destination for migrants from the other East European countries, with 38.2 thousand per annum arriving in the 1950s, 20.3 thousand in the 1960s and 29.6 thousand in the 1970s before soaring to 80,700 in the 1980s (when there were also 54,700 *Ubersiedler* coming annually from the FGDR) (Jones 1990).

Ethnicity has been a factor in international migration and while some groups have moved into the region, such as Greek revolutionaries displaced by the failure of the insurgency (Wojecki 1977), the dominant movement has been in the other direction. After the trauma of the holocaust the number of Jews in Eastern Europe was reduced still further by emigration to Israel which was facilitated by the permissive policy of the FSU, reflecting the prominence of Jews in the communist movement. The number of Jews in Eastern Europe is now very small and although most of those who remain have avoided group identification in favour of assimilation, anti-Semitism has not entirely

Table 2.2 Inferred migration 1950–92

| Country | 1950–1970 | | | 1965–1974 | | | 1975–1984 | | | 1985–1992 | | 1950–1992 | |
|---|---|---|---|---|---|---|---|---|---|---|---|---|---|
| | A | B | C | A | B | C | A | B | C | A | B | C | D |
| Albania | 75.4 | 75.4 | 0.00 | 29.4 | 29.4 | 0.00 | 23.4 | 23.4 | 0.00 | 14.7 | 13.8 | 0.03 | 0.7 |
| Bulgaria | 19.3 | 16.8 | 0.18 | 6.4 | 5.9 | 0.01 | 3.9 | 3.1 | 1.10 | 0.3 | 0.1 | 0.02 | 9.7 |
| FCSFR | 17.0 | 15.7 | 0.17 | 4.8 | 3.7 | 0.16 | 5.5 | 5.0 | 0.07 | 1.6 | 1.5 | * | 9.9 |
| FGDR | 6.3 | -7.2 | 2.49 | 0.1 | -0.5 | 0.11 | 0.6 | -2.1 | 0.28 | 0.0 | -5.5 | 0.92 | 113.1 |
| Hungary | 12.5 | 10.8 | 0.16 | 3.2 | 3.1 | * | 1.8 | 1.0 | 0.06 | -1.1 | -2.4 | 0.13 | 10.2 |
| Poland | 33.2 | 31.1 | 0.53 | 8.4 | 7.0 | 0.45 | 10.4 | 9.5 | 0.28 | 4.0 | 3.2 | 0.32 | 39.6 |
| Romania | 25.7 | 24.2 | 0.25 | 11.1 | 10.5 | 0.11 | 8.2 | 7.6 | 0.13 | 3.2 | 0.1 | 0.70 | 30.3 |
| FFRY | 32.4 | 24.6 | 1.28 | 9.6 | 8.9 | 0.13 | 8.6 | 8.2 | 0.10 | 4.2 | 3.6 | 0.13 | 49.6 |

Notes: A Percentage change based on natural increase with no migration; B Actual percentage change; C Inferred net out-migration (mn.); D Estimated annual average net out-migration (000s).

Sources: For 1950 to 1970 The population debate: dimensions and perspectives (New York: UN Department of Economic and Social Affairs) I, 237–48. Other calculations are based on UN demographic yearbooks

disappeared from the political programme (Kovacs 1992). Meanwhile, 10.2mn. Germans migrated from within the new boundaries of Poland, including those moved by Hitler in 1944 (Landau and Tomaszewski, 1985 pp.183–4) and 2.8mn. Germans had been expelled from FCSFR by 1948 (Bicik and Stepanek 1994). There were some exchanges of minorities as 489,000 Ukrainians and 36,000 Belorussians went east from Poland while 1.5mn. Poles went west. Exchanges also took place between FCSFR and Hungary where it was always difficult to draw a frontier line (Macartney 1947). FCSFR was particularly keen to implement the exchange and Hungary agreed to allow Slovak propagandists to operate in Hungarian villages and for representatives of Slovak communities to make inspections before repatriation documentation was undertaken (Davidson 1947). Hungary would then accept the same number of Hungarians from Slovakia.

However, some major ethnic groups remain undisturbed, despite continuing prejudice through historical experiences with minorities that have played an exploiting role or posed a perceived threat to national security (Klein & Reban 1981) (Table 2.3). Despite many years of activity to establish Auschwitz as a major national monument (absorbing more investment by the Ministry of Culture than any other project), the Poles still find anti-Semitic grudges embedded (indeed nourished to some extent by Jewish prominence in the Communist Party until the purge in the late 1960s). However, in order to enhance stability under communism some use was made of FSU autonomy systems (King 1973). Experimentation with a 'Magyar Autonomous Region' for Hungarians in Transylvania probably reflected the prominence of Hungarians in the Romanian Communist Party at the time (Illyes 1982; Kovrig 1986). However, the region was modified after 1956 (both in extent and

*Table 2.3* Principal minorities *c.* 1990

| Country | Population (000s) | Principal minorities (mn.) |
| --- | --- | --- |
| Albania | 3,202 | Greeks 0.30 |
| Bulgaria | 8,991 | Turks 1.20; Yugoslavs 0.18 |
| FCSFR | 15,638 | Hungarians 0.60; Poles 0.07; Germans 0.05; Ukrainians 0.05 |
| FGDR | 16,614 | Sorbs 0.11 |
| Hungary | 10,552 | Germans 0.20; Czechoslovaks 0.11; Yugoslavs 0.08; Romanians 0.02 |
| Poland | 37,850 | Germans 1.20; Belorussians/Ukrainians 0.40 |
| Romania | 23,272 | Hungarians 2.50; Germans 0.20; Ukrainians 0.05; Yugoslavs 0.04; Russians 0.04; Turks/Tatars 0.04; Czechoslovaks 0.03; Bulgarians 0.01 |
| FFYR | 23,807 | Albanians 1.73; Hungarians 0.43 |

*Note*: Many of these figures are estimates, given the frequent lack of detailed census coverage. Nationalities have been grouped where the federations are concerned (the 0.18mn. Yugoslavs shown under Bulgaria are in fact Macedonians)
*Source*: *Statesman's Yearbook 1991–2*

degree of autonomy) and it disappeared altogether in the 1968 administrative reform (Verdery 1983, 1991). Hungarians also believed that their position deteriorated as a result of the mini cultural revolution of 1971, which placed a greater emphasis on the Romanian language, and the 1974 law providing for confiscation of privately-owned artefacts of cultural value (Knight 1987). Yet in view of the sophistication of the Hungarian population and its relatively high living standards, there was bound to be dissatisfaction with austerity policies even when there was no intentional ethnic content. Moreover, it is a fact of life that the Romanian majority, conditioned by the historical legacy of Hungarian rule in Transylvania, is always sensitive to Hungarian assertiveness.

Ethnic tensions continued under communism when the homogenising concept of 'new socialist man' made for conflict with groups (both cultural and religious as well as ethnic) maintaining their own value systems. Several groups appeared to resist the modernising ethos of the majority. The Muslims of FFRY were relatively poor, constituting a majority group in most of the poorest districts in Bosnia-Hercegovina, Montenegro and Serbia (both Kosovo and Serbia Proper). The Albanian Muslims did not participate in migration to the towns in the north of the country partly because of strong ties with their own region but also because of 'linguistic barriers, inadequate qualifications and technical skills required in an industrial environment' (Thomas 1987, p.72). Many Muslims both in Bosnia-Hercegovina and Kosovo had only menial jobs and they tended to extend their kinship networks in a situation where intermarriage was complicated by Croat, Serb and Slovene discouragement. Moves were made against Islam in Bulgaria in the 1950s. There was rapid deterioration in relations between the Turkish minority and the Bulgarian authorities with the Kurdzhali area being kept in 'enforced isolation' for long periods. The government tried to forcibly assimilate the Turks in 1984 through changing their names from forms reminiscent of the Ottoman period to Bulgarian equivalents. The new policy was allegedly based on Bulgarian national consciousness and voluntary reactions by individual Muslims to forcible Turkicisation in the past! It implied that all people in Bulgaria could be only Bulgarians. There was pressure on both Turks and the Islamicised Bulgarians (or Pomaks) to conform in dress, religion and language. Schooling in Turkish was stopped, while newspapers and broadcasts in Turkish were also affected, as was everyday use of Turkish in public places. Even the names on cemetery memorials had to be changed. When the Turks staged Labour Day demonstrations in areas like Shumen and Razgrad, mass expulsions amounted to some 370th people of whom only 155th later returned (Hellier 1989; Todorov 1991). The Turkish minority declined from 848th to 633th as a result of these upheavals (Carter 1995, p.67) and it would appear that as many as 85th Turks left Bulgaria voluntarily after 1989.

Similar problems were seen on a larger scale with Gypsy communities across Eastern Europe (Crowe and Kolsti 1991). They have been present since at least the early fifteenth century and follow a largely itinerant existence as 'service nomads', staying in an area for as long as their skills in repairing domestic equipment, horse trading or rodent control were required. Under communism great efforts were made to assimilate the Gypsies through the offer of employment and accommodation, working on the assumption that they had been stranded by the loss of their old itinerant occupations and that with the availability of regular work they would 'grow up from their child-like attachment to the sudden and spectacular earnings of the dealer and the profligate consumption that goes with that life-style' (Stewart 1990, p.143). But while some embraced mainstream community values and took steady employment, others maintained their independent lifestyle (Fraser 1992). Further, it must be said that enterprise managers were rarely sympathetic towards the idiosyncracies of the Gypsy lifestyle: Gypsies were engaged in the context of full employment and corresponding labour-hoarding mentalities for unskilled, uncongenial and low-paid work. Quite remarkable job-hopping resulted, condemned in the Hungarian media through sarcastic references to *vandormadarak* (wandering birds). Greater stability was achieved when factories helped with housing, and many rural Gypsies travelled by special trains for a week's labouring on Budapest building sites in order to earn money for 'open plan' cottages specially sanctioned in a bid to wean families away from traditional forms of contingency housing. However, Gypsies naturally sought every opportunity to move back into commerce and the reforms of the 1980s gave them greater scope through the encouragement of the second economy (McCagg 1991). Studies in FCSFR showed that the Gypsies lagged way behind the majority groups in education standards, infant mortality and life expectancy (Davidova 1971). In some cases this reflected an inevitable lag in the demographic response to social and economic change; although it is also true that perhaps one-third of all Gypsies in FCSFR lived below the poverty line in the mid-1980s (Kostelancik 1989; Ulc 1988).

## ECONOMY

As already noted, the post-war development of Eastern Europe was organised along Soviet 'command economy' lines, given the FSU's inassailable position in the region in 1945. The central planning system eventually produced a pattern of Five Year Plans, which provided for growth and structural change while also ensuring that industrial projects were supported by the necessary buildings, machinery, raw materials and labour (Wilczynski 1982) (Table 2.4). Where international trade was needed, coordination was provided through the Comecon organisation (discussed below). Growth rates were high in the 1950s and 1960s, when national economies were relatively small, domestic raw materials could be fully used (with some imports from

*Table 2.4* Employment 1985

| Country | Agriculture & forestry | | Industry | | | Services | | Total |
|---------|------|------|------|------|-----|------|------|-------|
|         | A    | B    | A    | B    | C   | A    | B    |       |
| Bulgaria | 939 | 21.1 | 2028 | 45.6 | 2.2 | 1481 | 33.3 | 4448 |
| FCSFR   | 1048 | 13.6 | 3615 | 46.9 | 3.4 | 3044 | 39.5 | 7707 |
| FGDR    | 944  | 10.6 | 4082 | 50.9 | 4.7 | 3484 | 39.1 | 8910 |
| Hungary | 1114 | 22.7 | 1897 | 38.6 | 1.7 | 1902 | 38.7 | 4913 |
| Poland  | 5360 | 29.6 | 6537 | 36.1 | 1.2 | 6210 | 34.3 | 18107 |
| Romania | 3059 | 28.9 | 4711 | 44.7 | 1.5 | 2816 | 26.4 | 10586 |
| FFRY    | 2931 | 27.7 | 3235 | 31.2 | 1.1 | 4303 | 41.1 | 10469 |

*Notes*: A Numbers employed (000s); B Percentage of total numbers in employment; C Jobs in industry for each one in agriculture.
*Source*: European Conference of Ministers of Transport 1991, p.199

FSU) and surplus labour could be released from agriculture. Progress was initially rapid by European standards: Eastern Europe accounted for 12.3 per cent of European production in 1950 but 14.4 in 1970; and per capita growth increased by 2.4 times the European average during this period. There was priority for manufacturing, and industry's contribution to national income (where agriculture = 1.0) rose in Bulgaria from 1.3 to 3.4 between 1965 and 1983; 5.5 to 7.3 in FCSFR, and 5.0 to 8.8 in the FGDR. Values for employment were much lower (because of the great differences in productivity and the artificial pricing which discriminated in favour of manufacturing): Bulgaria 0.5 and 2.2; FCSFR 1.9 and 2.8, and FGDR 3.1 and 4.1; but all show the same trend.

Once installed, the system was difficult to change, given the importance of politically reliable management and the prestige value of very large enterprises. Factories were sometimes inefficiently located, incurring high transport costs, while poor organisation within the plant could result in production hold-ups, with knock-on effects in other industries dependent on monopoly suppliers of intermediates. High costs passed down the line boosted the 'value' of production on which wage increases might be based, but made exports less competitive. Old factories were rarely closed even when new capacities came on stream elsewhere. Thus the Polish steel industry retained plant in the heart of the Upper Silesian conurbation despite the opening of modern integrated units on the periphery. Only in 1986 was the last Siemens-Martin furnace (installed in the nineteenth century) closed down. Performance declined during the 1970s and 1980s due to inefficiency at a time when industry's inputs were becoming increasingly costly (high cost energy at subsidised prices) while Western loans for technology transfer failed to boost productivity in state-owned enterprises (SOEs) used to hoarding labour (Winiecki 1986).

The 'forced march' to modernisation involved heavy social costs and left a legacy through an 'outdated distorted economic structure that was too intimately bound up with the equally distorted political structure' (Schopflin 1988, p.146). Central management detracted from enterprise flexibility (Laki 1985). In the end some major sectors of industry were operating at a loss, sustaining exports to the West at prices below the real value of the raw materials and justifying the view that Stalin's communism was a 'highly contradictory even counterproductive modernising revolution' (Schopflin 1988 p.126). Hungarian steel costs were double those in Western Europe (where there are also inefficiencies) and in 1985 a quarter of the state budget was spent on supporting inefficient enterprises. Output in Bulgaria stagnated after 1983 in spite of a generous allocation of resources for the rest of the decade: there was an 'unfailing intensive saturation of industry with capital resources' (Minassian 1992 p.710) which gave rise to gloomy predictions for the 1990s because tight planning built around industry's special status generated continual shortages elsewhere in the economy (Kornai 1980a, 1980b).

Meanwhile, the proletariat became dissatisfied with low incomes and reduced social mobility, though some expectations of higher living standards were satisfied by higher wages without a commensurate improvement in either productivity or the supply of consumer goods. There were long waiting periods for certain goods – including an estimated fifty-seven years for an apartment in Warsaw! In Poland it became common to buy hard currency to get access to the black market and dollar shops opened in 1987. Generally, communist governments discouraged the use of Western currencies in order to maximise holdings in the national bank, but in Poland the use of dollars prevented inflation and helped to compensate for neglect of the tertiary sector due to the priority for industry (especially large enterprises), discouragement of private enterprise and an autarkic approach which severed links with the world economy (Bicanic and Skreb 1991). However, the dollar price collapsed in September 1989 when government bonds were issued. This led to zloty hyperinflation, with notes for Zl1mn. coming into circulation in 1991 compared with Zl1,000 as the highest denomination in 1967. By contrast, Hungary allowed inflation in the 1980s and was less embarrassed by it when the transition began.

## Comecon

This economic organisation for the communist states arose out of the FSU's desire to minimise Western influence in Eastern Europe. France and the UK could not pose any real threat (despite their commitment to democracy in Eastern Europe) but the US produced the European Recovery Programme (or 'Marshall Plan') in which FCSFR, Hungary and Poland all expressed interest. The FSU signalled its unease by boycotting the Paris peace conference which led some commentators to suggest that a master plan for the division of Europe was already in existence. But it seems unlikely that Stalin wanted to extend the system of Soviet Socialist Republics to Eastern Europe even though Bulgaria and FFRY may have aspired to such status in 1945–6. However, the Council for Mutual Economic Assistance (Comecon) appeared in due course as a reaction to the Marshall Plan's perceived incompatibility with Soviet security requirements (Kaser 1965; Sobell 1984). Stalin probably wanted to marginalise the USA by 'strengthening groupwide economic cohesion with the explicit purpose of fostering economic growth within the group' (van Brabant 1989, p.18) and the new arrangement may have been introduced under the pressure of the Yugoslav crisis and the need for a concerted offensive to deny Tito all economic assistance; and indeed to cut off all normal trade in essential goods and services (Mendershausen 1959). Comecon was the brainchild of the Gosplan chairman N.A. Voznesenskiy, who was subsequently removed from the office of Chief Soviet Planner in 1949 and has been regarded as a powerful instrument of Soviet expansionism; providing for a solid economic block (*Grossraumwirtschaft*) paralleled by the Cominform which ensured unity in ideological and political matters (Marer 1984; Marer and Montias 1982).

Stalin may not have welcomed the sophistication of the Voznesenskiy plan, preferring direct links with other party chiefs. So although the founding treaty was signed in 1949 Comecon's role was somewhat ambigious in the early days (van Brabant 1974, 1979). Despite discussion of socialist economic integration before 1949 (also consideration of plan coordination between 1949 and 1950), the organisation seems to have played no significant role in the planning of economic development in individual countries throughout the 1950s. Efficient economic linkages through plan coordination to produce an international division of labour were evidently ruled out, along with the possibility of supranational organisations. It seems clear that Stalin was unwilling to countenance any transfer of power to Comecon, given the cold war, the actual warfare in Korea 'and the imminent danger of a new, possibly final, global conflagration' (van Brabant 1989, p.42). However, the organisation had great symbolic importance in underpinning the notion of a Soviet economic sphere, even though elite penetration of the organisation and limited bargaining power for East European member states made legitimation difficult (Neumann 1988). The organisation provided a cloak of respectability for Soviet plundering after the war and the imposition of joint companies which gave the FSU a major stake in the economic development of Eastern Europe in return for only limited investments (sometimes no more than confiscated German assets). An outstanding example was the Wismut uranium company in the Erzgebirge region of FGDR (van Brabant 1987, 1988). Later there were plans for greater coordination, for example, in machinery and transport equipment (Montias 1968), with international division of labour envisaged between 1991 and 2005 (Brada and Mendez 1988).

However, the balance changed to one of net Soviet subsidy to Eastern Europe amounting to US$20–80bn. by the late 1970s with low cost raw materials and fuels delivered in return for shoddy manufactures (Volgyes 1989, p.235). The Balkan countries especially could benefit from access to the FSU's huge and relatively undemanding market. Romania could develop her heavy industry using imported raw materials because of the scope for exports within Comecon and to a much lesser extent the Third World (Montias 1980). By the mid-1980s several economists were emphasising the shift in Eastern Europe's economic value from asset to liability (Bunce 1985) and several authorities offered their own calculations on the extent of the subsidy (Brada 1985; Desai 1986). Because of its exclusive approach which denied Eastern Europe the opportunity of exploiting its comparative advantages in world markets (Csikos-Nagy 1973), Comecon has been seen as an organisation that 'destroyed' trade (Holzman 1965, 1985) or at least diverted it into the Soviet sphere (Pelzman 1977). However, links with a wider world were never broken off completely, although trade in essential items was handled by state companies which effectively maintained bureaucratic control (Csaba 1983). Lack of hard currency or knowledge of value led to a preference for barter deals which were not popular with Western companies. However, under Hungary's 'New Economic Mechanism' (NEM), direct dealing was allowed for a total of 211 enterprises by 1983. By this time the West was deeply involved in Eastern Europe through the investment of OPEC petrodollars which produced indifferent results. After 1988 individual Comecon members could negotiate directly with the EU as a result of the FSU decision to grant it official status in 1988. In 1989 exploratory steps were taken to formalise the EU's position with Eastern Europe.

## Economic reform

Declining growth rates generated pressures for reform (Sandstrom and Sjoberg 1991; Szamuely 1986). Since foreign trade failed to respond adequately to foreign loans and international technology transfers, indebtedness increased. It was essential that production should be made more efficient and that there should be appropriate incentives to encourage greater output (Jeffries 1992). In the mid-1970s a combination of low prices and propaganda against private enterprise succeeded in reducing meat production from small farms in Poland. Market incentives were therefore offered and the farmers responded (Gomulka 1986). In Hungary the more radical NEM was introduced to allow greater enterprise autonomy. Hungary also appreciated the need for improved technology, with in-house research and development linked to imported technology and with new technology diffused throughout the system in order to establish compatibility (Hare et al. 1981, pp.153-4). This helped to modify the Stalinist war economy approach with 'scientism' and the encouragement of a kind of labour aristocracy (Korbonski 1989). Reference has also been made to Hungary's relatively early concern for marketing, with university courses on the subject in 1967 (Mueller et al.

1993) and some radical treatment of inefficient SOEs which had lost much of their local resource advantages (Okolicsanyi 1988). In 1986 and 1987 the Ozd steelworks phased out its oldest furnaces and rolling mills and reduced its payroll from 14,000 to 11,500: the greatest job losses ever to occur within one of the country's socialist establishments. The mining industry was also in crisis in the same frontier area where the population of both the town and its surrounding villages was heavily dependent on basic industries. Many people had migrated into the area when employment increased in the early post-war years, but this process went into reverse during the 1980s under the 'Ozd Model', which was to be a blueprint for the other problem areas. But the Ozd experience revealed the problem of attracting new light industry in an area where enterprise managers had discouraged diversification in the past to avoid competition in the local labour market. It also revealed the limited scope for alternative work with local government (like seasonal work in gardening), farming on the Great Plain during the harvest or daily commuting across the frontier for work in Slovakia. With job-hopping Gypsies (as well as unskilled Magyars with low educational attainment) often being singled out for dismissal, it was clear that employees needed proper union representation and a more generous financial cushion.

However, the Hungarian reforms were always constrained by the communist monopoly on power which prevented significant decentralisation. Little was done to stimulate competition and enterprises continued to take advantage of their monopoly position in a seller's market by setting prices as they chose. It was still difficult to make rapid technical progress and to achieve product innovation but initiatives were being taken and there was 'better adjustment of production to domestic and external market demand' (Csaba 1989, p.25). Even so, the Hungarian record was significant when compared with those 'extremist' regimes that retained a high level of centralisation (Pecsi 1989). Klaus (1989) sees the first steps to reform in FCSFR coming as late as 1987, but even then changes were carried out 'almost exclusively by representatives of various government institutions' rather than by economists. Despite talk of a mixed system there was great reluctance to accept the market forces (Bogomolov 1990). Limitations in FGDR have also been emphasised (Bryson *et al.* 1991). Vested interests may have formed the major barrier, rather than ideology which had in some respects become trivialised by the 1980s. It is interesting that housing reforms were relatively far-reaching within an expanding private sector (Szelenyi 1989).

There was greater scope for individual initiative through the 'second economy' which was openly encouraged in some countries, like Hungary, and tolerated in others (Bauer 1983). Gabor (1989) defined the second economy as a field of economic activity where income was gained legally or illegally outside the socialist sector. While the first economy was made up of large scale production units directly controlled by the planners (with an unlimited appetite for absorbing capital labour and materials), the second was small-scale and entrepreneurial and well able to overcome shortages and bottlenecks.

As part-time work became available to supplement income from a full-time job in the first economy, households would try and combine two first economy salaries with additional income from the second economy and, perhaps, access to a private plot through the family home. Small enterprises became prominent in Hungary (Tardos 1983) and by the mid-1980s 70 per cent of Hungarian households had some second economy income which in many cases provided between one-third and one-half of the total income. It offered scope to Gypsies and others with an aptitude for dealing rather than labouring. It demonstrated enough success to convince virtually everybody that the only way forward lay with private enterprise and a free market, although political constraints were not removed until 1989.

The vast majority of private businesses were in agriculture. Peasant farms were already prominent in Poland and FFRY (Rostowski 1989), but elsewhere more diverse organisational forms came into existence and generated the stimulation of competing paradigms (Vasary 1990). Individual enterprise generated a significant social movement ('embourgoisement' in Hungary) in sharp contrast to the collective stereotype (Szelenyi 1988). Meanwhile, enterprise economic work partnerships (EEWPs) introduced in 1982 made a significant contribution to manufacturing (Hann 1990). Some of these partnerships involved merely a group of SOE elite workers brought together in an EEWP to cope with various tasks delegated to it, but some workers avoided such a satellite relationship by finding work with other enterprises. A third category consisted of 'wholly independent full-time participants in the second economy whose only link with the socialist sector is via the market' (Swain 1990 p.104). Some EEWPs in the computer industry grew to become dynamic small cooperatives, the industrial equivalent of the private plot in agriculture. The partnerships were of considerable social and political significance in transcending manual-intellectual and blue collar-white collar barriers but they seemed to attract those who were already successful in the first economy. Consequently, it did not seem 'that the second economy might offer opportunities to those who were disadvantaged in the first economy' (Hann 1990, p.28).

## INDUSTRIAL LOCATION

Manufacturing was the priority sector under the command economy and great increases in output and employment were registered (Fallenbuchl 1970). The result was a dramatic structural change in the economy, particularly in the more backward Balkan economies (Minassian 1992). Heavy industry had priority because of its importance for the military-industrial establishment and for the engineering sector which produced the machinery for use in consumer industries. Rapid growth occurred particularly in the iron and steel industry (Stefanovic 1994) and in non-ferrous metallurgy including aluminium (Kostic 1983). The priority for heavy industry meant exploitation of virtually all known reserves; hence the importance of the resource base, augmented by further mineral prospecting (Pounds and Spulber 1957). Disparities in levels of production between countries and between regions narrowed but did not disappear. It would appear that Weberian ('least cost') location principles retained their relevance. After all, the central planners were looking for the highest possible growth rates in each country overall and inappropriate locations would harm this objective. Little is known of the decision-making processes which must have involved meetings and discussions within the various ministries with considerable input through the party hierarchy. No doubt the criteria taken into account were similar to those relevant in a Western situation, although a different set of transport costs and commodity prices would have applied. It may be assumed that there was a good deal of lobbying within party circles so that influential local officials could attract industry which might otherwise have gone elsewhere. But there are few documented cases although commentators within Eastern Europe have confirmed the disproportionate influence of party leaders projecting their own brand of political expediency.

There has been widespread articulation of an 'equity' principle to prevent concentration and achieve greater decentralisation than was normal under capitalism. This has led some Western writers to emphasise a distinct 'ideological' component in socialist decision-making over industrial location, bringing out a geography of production quite different from the capitalist counterpart. But the argument is complex and the strength of the ideological factor remains obscure. In the first place, propagandist claims for the equity principle as a tenet of ideology are no proof of successful implementation. They merely point to the hope of improved living standards everywhere and a determination to avoid one of the perceived contradictions of capitalism. Furthermore, it should be remembered that East European planners worked in an environment that favoured very high levels of concentration. Given the central planning system there were powerful arguments in favour of large projects which were relatively easy to supervise and impressive as national achievements. Moreover these large projects would naturally tend to gravitate towards the national capitals and the centres of administrative regions with the best infrastructure, including the higher echelons of the party command hierarchy. Meanwhile, allowance must be made for the initial increase in concentration through the expropriation, consolidation and relocation of small-scale industry (much of it in rural areas) through nationalisation and discriminatory fiscal policies. Hence the ideological pressure of equity as a counterweight to the bureaucratic instinct in favour of concentration.

In any case, there is no way in which the operation of the equity principle can be demonstrated in opposition to classical economic logic, since the politicians have never attempted to present statements of comparative costs to show how a 'least cost' location was rejected in favour of an economically less attractive choice on the grounds of equity. All investment in backward areas could well have been guided by a clear Weberian logic unrelated to ideology. Thus when Polish planners hailed the decision to build a new iron and steel works at Nowa Huta on the eastern side of Krakow as a contribution to the prosperity of working people in what was seen at the time as a 'bourgeois' city, they merely found some political advantage in one particular location on the edge of the Upper Silesian industrial region where the expansion of the metallurgical industry would logically occur in the twin interests of decongesting the conurbation and improving opportunities for rural workers. The Kosice iron and steel complex in eastern Slovakia was naturally hailed as a milestone in the economic advance of the formerly backward Slovakia. Yet it was conceived in rational economic terms as a supplier of Slovakia's engineering industry using local ore combined with coking coal from Ostrava in Moravia. And although the local ore proved unacceptable the revision of the project on the basis of imported ore from the FSU maintained this essential, rational base. Again, when the FGDR decision to build a blast furnace at Calbe was applauded as a gesture to rural employment, the planners were again massaging an economically logical decision in terms of the flow of commodities and the transport facilities available. Strategic considerations made for dispersal in FFRY in the early 1950s, while industrial linkages with the FSU often sustained locations close to the eastern frontiers of East European states.

## Dispersal of industry

It is undoubtedly true that factory industry became more dispersed under socialism than had previously been the case under capitalism. But it is hardly appropriate to compare one system in the 1950s to 1980s with another for the period 1900 to 1950. The technological environments were quite different for these two periods, not least in the sense that electricity became widely available (and railways more extensive) in the Balkans as well as the northern part of Eastern Europe during the later period. In the north, where the infrastructure was in a relatively good state before the Second World War, factories were quite widely distributed. Dispersal was further increased through intense mineral prospecting and heavy investment in resource-based industries. There was therefore certainly a greater dispersal of industry across the region under socialism (Hamilton 1970). Prior to 1945, metallurgy, food-processing and wood-processing were often located outside the major cities. However, since 1945 further cases of dispersal have arisen in metallurgy through the priority given to iron and steel in the 1950s, reinforced by strategic considerations in Yugoslavia (Caesar 1962; Hoffman 1956). Reference may also be made to the use of some locations close to the eastern frontiers on account of linkages with Soviet raw materials (Hamilton 1971).

But despite regional spread there was an underlying preference for mature industrial regions as in Poland (Dawson 1969; Lijewski 1985). Regional centres emerged as growth poles (Dobrowolska 1976) but the links with smaller towns were weak compared with the intense commodity links between Upper Silesian cities including Krakow and Opole: this conurbation remained the country's main industrial establishment with an increasing intensity of commodity links (Debski 1980). There were also strong links between the shipbuilders in the ports and inland engineering centres (Adrjanowska 1972; Debski 1974). In Hungary there was again a spatial structure that focused on the regional centres (Bora 1976) but with Budapest retaining a clear dominance despite some decentralisation (Dienes 1973b). On the other hand, local government could be a force for decentralisation. To be sure, the party hierarchy in each region would project a 'regional interest', drawing attention to unused potentials (raw materials, labour, linkages), and attracting certain new projects known to be seeking suitable locations while trying to keep potentially troublesome and disruptive projects well away from the 'backyard'. But regional planning remained weak because the local authorities had only limited initiative promoting new ventures and resisting what was considered harmful. However, some meaningful local initiative in economic planning was also possible through self-financing. Reforms in Romania allowed commune leaders to finance small-scale developments in tourism (like a motel) or in manufacturing, perhaps using second-hand machinery (secured from a large enterprise through personal contacts) for sub-contracting.

From the large enterprise point of view sub-contracting could be very beneficial in facilitating expansion where labour was relatively scarce. The Cervena Zastava car factory was a case in point. The venture started in Kragujevac in 1954 after the Federal Office for Economic Planning selected the city's Military Technical Institute to take responsibility. There was an engineering tradition in the town (*Fabrika Motora 21 Maj* which manufactured the engines for the new factory) and a decade of reconstruction after the war paved the way for the new enterprise which began with the assembly of the 1400 model under licence from Fiat of Turin (following detailed study of ten possible candidates drawn from France, Italy, the UK and USA). Production of the 600 model began the following year on a limited basis (for lorry production was a higher priority at the time) but the scale of business increased to the level of 200,000 cars per year and 30,000 employees. Additional capacities employing new production technology were installed between 1963 and 1970 (during which period car production increased gradually from 27,000 to 46,400), leading to large-scale assembly of the 101 in addition to the 750, 1300 and 1500 models introduced between 1960 and 1964 (replacing the older types which had ceased production by this time), respectively. However, Zastava expanded in other locations; so the Fabrica Aotomobila and Komponente organisations in Kragujevac were complemented by Heroj Toza Dragovic in Ohrid and Ramiz Sadiku in Pec; to say nothing of 280 sub-contractors (over a hundred supplying car parts) from 130 factories all over FFRY (and some abroad).

The sub-contractors became responsible for all the components apart from transmission, suspension elements and car bodies which continued to be produced at Zastava's own plants. The company also diversified its foreign contacts between 1966 and 1984 through arrangements with two Polish firms for mutual deliveries of parts and finished cars; also with a Hungarian firm for parts in return for finished cars; and another with *Transportmaschinen* in the FGDR for tools and parts. Zastava also went into production of Lada cars under a cooperation agreement with VAZ of the FSU (Antanaskovic and Djekic 1986). In the 1980s links between Zastava and two other vehicle producers in FFRY – Industrija Motornih Vozila of Novo Mesto (Slovenia) and Tvornica Automobila of Sarajevo (Bosnia-Hercegovina) – allowed for better utilisation of capacity. Unfortunately the industry went into decline by 1985 because of balance of payments difficulties and raw material/energy shortages. Yet Zastava had shown that it could perform all the operations required for large-scale production, with modern technology assembly and a range of domestic component suppliers. It was a pity that not all the producers have achieved a high level of efficiency, for the Ramiz Sadiku factory (opened in 1968) was mismanaged on a grand scale with absenteeism, poor organisation and low quality production, which has resulted in hold-ups on the Kragujevac production line (Palairet 1992). Hence while there was decentralisation some of the dangers of this process were highlighted. They seemed to reflect a lack of interest that may have been politically motivated by Kosovo's loss of republic status and its ultimate loss of autonomy within Serbia.

Finally, party leaders were known to intervene in favour of their home areas especially when a location decision might involve a multiplicity of near-equal choices (Mihalyi 1992). Romania's two principal leaders of the socialist era (Gh. Gheorghiu-Dej and N. Ceausescu) were well known for their support of Moldavia and Oltenia respectively, and especially their home districts of Barlad and Scornicesti. Such input was also significant in terms of both siting and implementation. Ceausescu was especially disposed to interfere in decisions at all levels, and the working visit (*visita de lucru*) would always include a good deal of instruction to local officials as to how developments should be carried out. Such directions were fuelled by an acknowledged fascination with the built form of socialism, especially integrated industrial complexes. Thus the economic logic of siting the Anina power station in a river valley (with cooling water readily available), some distance from the bituminous schist quarried on the higher ground, was firmly ruled out by the president who wanted the quarries, stockyard, power station and new town to form a single integrated complex despite pollution hazards and the need to pump cooling water to the top of a mountain! Yet in other instances Ceausescu is reputed to have supported local interests trying to resist the centralising urges of regional authorities. The local *primar* took advantage of a presidential visit to the Nehoiu sawmill in the Buzau Mountains to make successful representations against the county administration's plans to consolidate the timber industry on the edge of Buzau City.

## SOCIALIST AGRICULTURE

Eastern Europe's agricultural resources remained substantial (Dawson 1982), especially in the south, where areas like Hungary's Great Plain offered good soils and a warm climate during the growing season (Ando 1980). They were fully exploited because communist industrialisation rested on an assured supply of cheap food and raw materials. So agriculture was reorganised in order to proletarianise the peasantry and control production at prices determined by the state (Francisco 1980). State farms comprised former experimental units and crown domains while cooperatives (or collectives, as they were usually labelled in the early days) arose through coercion to pool peasant land, livestock and equipment without compensation apart from a right to work for the new organisation and retain a small private plot (Francisco *et al.* 1979). This enabled the state, through the party hierarchy, to secure food deliveries from communally farmed land while leaving each peasant with the option of additional work to secure a measure of self-sufficiency for the family and to create small surpluses for sale at local markets. In theory the old system could have achieved similar results through compulsory deliveries on a quota basis, and the disruption experienced in the FSU in the 1930s (and on a less dramatic scale in Eastern Europe in the l950s and 1960s) could have been avoided. But the ethos of revolution prevailed, supported by economic arguments concerned with the overall planning of investment and production over large areas without the complications of individual peasant decision-making. With state control of prices and capital investment (including the supply of farm machinery through special depots) there could be effective coordination and development. There was also an element of welfare because, although the profits of the more successful cooperatives were checked by loan repayments and the charges levied by the machine and tractor stations, the weaker cooperatives could usually generate some income for their members through the periodic writing-off of debts. But the strong peasant links with the land through private ownership were broken and many young people left for careers in industry. Moreover, the highly formalised cooperative system (going far beyond traditional forms of mutual assistance) generated a small corps of salaried officials who, as party members as well as farm managers, became part of the village elite; while the scope for security police activity among this group (and other sections of rural leadership concerned with commerce, education and even the church) effectively neutralised the villages politically.

Despite some decreases in the amount of agricultural land, evident in the Sudetenland through a decline in arable farming and an increase in woodland after the Germans were expelled (Bicik and Stepanek 1994), communist agriculture achieved significant intensification (Dohrs 1971). Farm production increased, but as a result of the growth of population (with a demand for higher living standards) and the need for more agricultural raw materials in industry, there was a change from net exports to net imports. Between 1934 and 1938 the surplus was equivalent to the production of 3.74mn.ha (6.4 per cent of a total agricultural area of 58.3mn.ha) but between 1962 and 1966 there was a net import of food equivalent to 2.97m.n.ha (5.9 per cent of a total agricultural area of 50.6mn.ha) (Borgstrom and Annegers 1971). The high cost of cereal imports (much of it from hard currency countries) brought great efforts to increase self-sufficiency during the 1980s. In 1985 cereal imports were only 1.8mn.t. (on top of domestic production of 108.9mn.) whereas in 1980 the figures were 18.1mn. and 97.4mn. However, the picture varied considerably in different countries: in 1985 there were net exports in Hungary (2.1mn.t.), FFRY (0.8) and Romania (0.1) and net imports in Bulgaria and FCSFR (both 0.4), FGDR (1.7) and Poland (2.4). The cereal question is complex and should be seen in the context of demands from the pastoral sector, the reduction in cereal land through allocation to other crops, and inefficiency in production, harvesting and storage. On the other hand the fisheries help to reduce pressure on agriculture.

Eastern Europen farming retained considerable diversity under socialism; with many variations on the basic logic of combining cereal farming with stock rearing and fattening. The mountain districts certainly specialised most heavily in stock-rearing (cattle, sheep and pigs) and much of the remaining cereal production (especially rye and maize) was undertaken in the interest of local self-sufficiency. But the main arable zones in the lowlands also expanded their herds and raised whole complexes of buildings for the purpose. The arable sector provided the fodder and the finished animals were conveniently situated in relation to the domestic food market and the international trading system. There was, however, a danger that such a strategy pursued by the state farms and cooperatives would ignore the full potential of the mountain grazings and that the individual farmers prominent in such areas would lack the incentives to maximise output. In Romania the state farms began to show more interest in the mountain grazings during the 1980s, in some cases as a result of permission to clear woodland. Meanwhile, industrial crops (flax, hemp, sugar beet and sunflowers) appeared in the most suitable areas, as did orchards, vegetable gardens and vineyards. Intense specialisation was discouraged by the inefficiency of inter-regional trade which perpetuated traditional emphasis on self-sufficiency. But there were some outstanding specialities (some of long standing). Bulgaria retained its reputation for tobacco and also for oleaginous roses yielding rose oil or attar of roses for the manufacture of perfumes (the latter specialism was prominent in the Kazanlik Valley). Specialisation was also noticeable in connection with local market demand, sometimes providing a base from which successful entry into longer-distance commerce has been possible. Horticulturalists at Turany near Brno in FCSFR enjoyed a strong local market for flowers and then started trading with Western Europe. Other centres of horticulture arose in the vicinity of the northern cities of Eastern Europe since flowers are widely appreciated as presents when there may be few obvious alternatives. There was (and still is) a massive output of carnations in the immediate surroundings of Warsaw, especially Jablonna, where many families success-fully changed from mixed farming to the production of flowers under glass, benefiting from a pure water supply underground and carefully prepared manures. A good local organisation was created for an industry that could employ one person full time for every 250sq.m. of glass.

Greater attention was given to fertiliser production and pest control as well as both animal and plant breeding. Each country behaved as an autonomous unit but there was some cooperation. Bulgarian sheep were crossed with the Soviet Romanov breed and Soviet Bezostaya 1 was widely used in Bulgaria as a basis for new low-stalk varieties of wheat like Ogosta, Trakia and Vratsa. Fertiliser applications were increased in step with output from the chemical industry but some heavy dressings proved counter-productive. More effort went into the improvement of farm machinery (including machines suitable for use on small farms) and storage facilities. Irrigation was quite successful despite some cases of salt accumulation through poor water management. Bulgaria's irrigated area increased from 0.13mn.ha in 1950 to 0.72mn. in 1960 and almost 1.0mn. in 1968 (but well short of the target of the 2.0mn.ha target which a 1959 decree had set for 1965). Romania eventually exceeded this level as the steppelands of Baragan and Dobrogea were transformed. But costs were high when artificial water storages and distribution systems were taken into account and two harvests each year were necessary to justify the investment. But output rarely met this target, despite cooperation between Bulgaria and the FSU to establish optimum watering rates for different crops and to establish computerised control systems. River floodplains were protected by the construction of dykes so that former permanent grasslands could be drained and converted for arable farming. Much of the Lower Danube was improved in this way, though the artificial confining of a river could be dangerous without large areas of storage in the mountains (geared perhaps to hydro-electricity generation or navigation facilities) to prevent a sudden rise in river levels after heavy rain or snow melt. There was some success in terracing eroded hill slopes, a strategy that was often combined with the establishment of orchards and vineyards linked with enhanced capacity in the food-processing industry.

## Limited reforms

Over the years the Stalinist model was subjected to overhaul. Mere organisational changes did not secure the increased output that was expected and
higher investments have been needed to secure the fertilisers, machines and
irrigation waters required to boost output from a dwindling workforce
(becoming more elderly and more highly feminised as the young male
population opted for work in the towns). Regular wages and improved welfare
benefits were introduced and the importance of economic rather than ideological incentives led to the allocation of specific tasks to individuals and
groups in return for payment by results. During the 1980s reforms (which
were particularly far-reaching in Hungary) encouraged individuals to expand
output from their gardens and plots through various forms of collaboration
with the state sector. Improved coordination measures brought together
cooperatives, state farms and private plotholders so as to make the fullest use
of land and labour. In Hungary, where the NEM reduced the role of the state
in price fixing in favour of free market forces, competition could develop
between different farming systems (Vasary 1990). Small farms gained both
economic and social significance as suitable machinery became available,
with the option of loaning additional equipment from the state farms where
there was spare capacity (Szelenyi 1985;1988). The cooperative at Ocsa
near Budapest allocated private plots according to the number of cows
each member agreed to look after (0.75ha for each animal) while at Pastzo
(Nograd County) vineyards were leased to responsible individuals in units
of 1,500sq.m. In some villages in northeastern Hungary (for example,
Szabolcs-Szatmar county) cooperative farms planted orchards and arranged
for periodic spraying while contracting out the other routine work (including
the harvesting) to individuals who knew there was a guaranteed market at
the end of the day. Another cooperative near Sopron collaborated with several
hundred individual gardeners and smallholders to produce grapes, vegetables
and poultry for sale in Austria under 'small border traffic' arrangements
(Swain 1985).

But mainstream thought was more conservative and tended to rely on
gigantism through larger farms in FCSFR and FGDR (Brezinski 1990): the
average size of a state farm in FCSFR increased from 490ha in 1950 to
10,500ha in 1980 (collectives from 310ha to 2,500ha) and during this period
socialist agriculture increased its share of the land from 27.1 to 92.7 per cent.
Some very large organisations emerged as groups of state farms (Korbonski
1965). In Poland one such organisation was set up in the Masurian Lakeland;
providing a model for a similar approach to the development of agriculture
in the Sudeten Mountains. However, *Agrocompleks Sudety* was a failure due
to over-centralisation. The livestock herds failed to expand as expected and
frustrated local managers were forced to 'borrow' animals from private farms
to impress visitors from Warsaw (a not uncommon strategy in all countries

affected by central planning). Meanwhile, in Bulgaria there was some emphasis on small enterprises (MacIntyre 1988) but the main innovation was the agricultural-industrial complex, formed through the combination of state farms with units in the food-processing industry (Wyzan 1989). For example, vertical integration was secured through combining farms that grew sugar beet with the processing factories. This made for efficiency in the use of transport and helped to overcome anomalies evident in Poland where potato processors sometimes drew supplies from distant parts of the country (Stryakiewicz 1985). These large units gained considerable political clout because they were represented by people with expertise and local knowledge, often subsidised local councils and became responsible for some industrial-isation in the villages. Thus, 'it has been exceptional for local councils to seek to limit the activities of large scale farms and their associated industries even if they are environmentally hazardous' (Persanyi 1990, p.42). But some investment was illogical because pig-rearing required imported protein and domestically produced feed sustained by artificial fertilisers, while meadow land and cattle pasture was left underused and the environment was damaged by disposal of slurry from the pig farms (ibid., p.43).

However, despite some flexibility under the command economy, private peasant farming was heavily constrained. Individual farms were retained in small areas (usually the mountain districts) where settlement patterns and field systems made cooperation very difficult logistically. Elsewhere there were usually restrictions on amalgamation and the use of non-family labour, and in any case, state control of distribution and prices gave little en-couragement to private enterprise. The main exceptions were Poland (Korbonski 1967; Tomczak 1990) and FFRY (Halpern 1967; Stipetic 1982) where there was no political will to persist with coercive policies. But private peasant farming needed a stimulative regime to increase production and this was not always in place (Morgan 1989; 1990). Moreover, in mountain areas the infrastructure needed attention, in addition to the regimes of subsidies and tax concessions recommended in Slovenia (Meze 1983); and diversifica-tion was often crucial in maintaining family incomes (Stasiak 1977). In some cases the peasants could take significant initiatives. Pine and Bogdanowicz (1982) have shown how Carpathian farming communities in southern Poland were able to diversify on the basis of pluriactivity extending to light industry, tourism and even temporary migration to the USA on the basis of family ties with migrants who left the area at the beginning of the twentieth century. In the case of the remote community of Tymova in the Nowy Targ area, once slated for evacuation and resettlement in Silesia, villagers were able to use their connections with the administration to undertake a number of communal projects which cumulatively had a great effect on developing the infra-structure. In 1954 the villagers built a railway station with their own funds and labour. Improved communications helped to stimulate a growth of tourism while links with industrial enterprises brought in finance for a new school in return for summer holiday camp facilities. Moreover, the village found ways of maintaining control of its own farm equipment when the government tried to enlarge the 'agricultural circles' intended to secure machine services for small farmers. Thus by operating in a politically correct way the villagers took action which the authorities did not intend but could not prevent. As a result, the village community was safeguarded and living standards improved as large modern houses were built to accommodate both tourists and extended families.

## INFRASTRUCTURE

Both transport and power are crucial for industrial development but with 'tight' central planning, investment in transport advanced only slowly in the wake of increased demands exaggerated by a high level of transport absorptiveness caused by a policy of specialisation and by long hauls for many raw materials and intermediates (Ciesielaki and Kaczmarek 1989; Taylor 1989). There was enhanced passenger mobility, especially in urban areas and their commuter zones (Fuchs and Demko 1978). There was a great increase in capacity in all transport modes and although the railway was dominant, its share of all Comecon freight handling (including FSU) declined sharply from 89.3 per cent in 1950 to 66.1 per cent in 1970 and an estimated 47.4 per cent in 1990. Meanwhile, sea/river transport increased from 9.7 per cent to 17.3 per cent and 24.8 per cent; pipelines from less than 0.1 per cent to 16.4 per cent and 27.4 per cent; and road transport from the same low level to 0.2 per cent and 0.4 per cent. Within Eastern Europe, however, it is likely that the 1990 rail and road shares would have been higher than the overall Comecon figures, while sea/river and pipeline figures would have been lower.

Despite Comecon coordination of the production of locomotives, trams, motor vehicles, aircraft and ships, the lines of communication themselves were frequently deficient in the border areas because of the relatively limited importance of international trade and travel. However, Western involvement became more important, especially with regard to motor vehicles in the 1970s and 1980s (Ambler *et al.* 1985; Tismer *et al.* 1987). Meanwhile, electricity generators provided another crucial support for industry, again with heavy price subsidies which helped to compensate for the use of heavy and energy-inefficient machinery. Power station capacities were greatly increased but domestic supplies in winter were often inadequate. Moreover, large thermal power stations (especially those burning lignite) became notorious polluters, while some hydro-electric schemes performed badly on account of dry seasons and silt accumulation in reservoirs. Meanwhile, nuclear power projects were prone to long delays in commissioning. Overall, Eastern Europe ran up a heavy energy deficit which was burdensome, even in the context of concessionary prices for Soviet crude oil.

## Transport

There was much new investment in railways, although, as always, the decisions made through central planning did not involve a lot of market research. Railway lobbies were politically powerful, so the hoarding of labour kept productivity low and there was little 'creative destruction' so characteristic of market economies (Winiecki 1988). Some narrow gauge lines were dispensed with, but while some standard gauge lines have lost their passenger services, few were closed completely. The northern countries inherited a dense railway network including many industrial lines (Webster and Garret 1984). There was investment in new equipment, including electrification and double-tracking (including some restoration second tracks on lines initially singled out to meet Soviet demands for war reparations in the FGDR) (Holocek 1988). A ring railway was built around Berlin (avoiding transit through West Berlin) and at Eisenach the route over the inner German frontier was realigned to create a single crossing. In Poland a new 160 km. east–west line was built to the south of Warsaw for transit traffic (especially between the FSU and the FGDR) in 1954. A 'Central Trunk Line' connecting Upper Silesia with Warsaw (225km.) was completed in 1977 with potential for 200km/h running; and the 'Steel/Sulphur' line from the Soviet border to an iron ore stockpile near the Katowice steelworks at Dabrowa Gornicza (410km.) was opened in 1979. The latter was broad gauge throughout to avoid the problems of transfer from the Soviet broad gauge to the European gauge. Even so, the Polish-Soviet border boasted the largest rail trans-shipment stations in the world (especially at Terespol/Brest and Medyka/Mostiska) with Soviet traffic boosted by the growing traffic between Japan and Western Europe (Lijewski 1982).

In the south there was a greater element of new construction, especially in Albania where the country's entire railway network originated in the post-1945 period. Albania's first external rail link was built between Shkoder and Titograd and was opened between 1985 and 1986. The main projects in FFRY were the Belgrade–Bar line (Wilson 1971) and projects to convert the Bosnian narrow gauge lines (Suscevic 1987). In the latter case an early priority was the conversion of the railway across the Sava to Sarajevo. The narrow gauge line from the interchange at Brod was replaced in 1948 by a new standard gauge line of 177km. from Samac (on the Sava downstream of Brod). It involved five major bridges (including one of 550m. across the Sava) and four tunnels. It was built with the help of the National Youth Movement and some other young people from Eastern European (Smith 1948). With the infrastructure improved, Doboj (an intermediate station on the line) was identified as the location of a new iron and steel plant. In the mid-1960s the conversion extended southwards through Mostar to a new port on the Adriatic coast at Ploce.

Road transport gained ground with the surfacing of the main roads and the introduction of road freight and passenger services. However, while some duplication of road and rail did arise, integration was the overriding principle. So bus services were prominent in urban areas (Carter 1980) and in more backward rural districts, while road freight services were provided for short hauls to feed the railways. And while most national road systems had good surfaces by the 1980s there was little dual carriageway or motorway available: in FGDR the autobahn from Berlin to Rostock and the Berlin Ring (avoiding West Berlin) was the only addition to the inherited system. Likewise there were few purpose-built urban ring roads and bypasses. Private car ownership remained low by Western standards although the 1970s and 1980s did see considerable increases, especially with the production of relatively inexpensive vehicles like the Trabant and Wartburg cars manufactured in FGDR. Even so, people had been waiting ten years for the Trabants distributed in Berlin in 1987 and up to fifteen years in the case of Lada and Skoda cars imported from FSU and FCSFR respectively. However, traffic from the West became an important factor in the summer months, supplemented by a growth of 'shopping tourism' across frontiers within Eastern Europe.

Air services expanded on international routes which operated only out of the capital cities, with domestic services to cover the main provincial cities at distances in excess of some 200km. With few exceptions (such as the one-eleven planes used in Romania), fleets consisted entirely of aircraft from the FSU. Meanwhile, there was more shipping business for the Adriatic, Baltic and Black Sea ports and particular expansion at Rostock when in 1957 the FGDR decided to minimise its dependence on West German facilities. Some of the traffic was linked with the FSU because of ferry services to reduce pressure on the railway routes through Poland and Romania. In the Baltic the Klaipeda-Rostock freight service was replaced by the Klaipeda-Mukran (near Sassnitz) train ferry which was a precaution against mounting political instability in Poland in the Solidarity era (Elkins 1986). In the Black Sea theatre the Ilichevsk (Odessa)-Varna ferry connected the FSU directly with Bulgaria. Pipelines were built to deliver oil and gas from the FSU, while other systems served the domestic oil and natural gas workings of Albania and Romania and distributed imported crude from non-Soviet sources: for example, the Adria system in FFRY based on a terminal near Rijeka. But most of the expansion in ports and shipping was to handle the growing trade with non-European communist countries and the rest of the world. A growth of East European merchant shipping ensured that imported fuels and raw materials should not involve transport costs in convertible currencies.

In Poland there were sudden increases in transport absorption in the years between 1965 and 1968 with the extension of exports of coal and iron to Asia (Korea, Japan, Pakistan and Vietnam) and the Americas (Brazil and USA); and again during 1973 and 1978 with a further growth of trade in these theatres, including Canada, China and Middle Eastern countries (Iran and

Iraq) which became important for oil imports (Ciesielski and Kaczmarek 1989). Fleets were built up through the construction of new ships, usually built in East European yards; for example, the socialist era thus saw the FGDR endowed with a substantial and relatively modern merchant fleet (Cranfield 1991). Activities began in 1953 with the construction in Rostock's Neptun yard of *Rostock* and *Wismar*, two of a class of vessel built mainly for the FSU. Later in the decade, and again in the early 1960s, further ships (comprising two new classes) were delivered from the Warnowerft yard in Warnemunde; and additional vessels were acquired second-hand (mainly from Sweden). By the mid-1960s the fleet was large enough for the shipping company Deutsche Seereederei Rostock to enter the Conference-dominated liner trade linking Europe with Africa and Asia, with some services operated jointly with Polish companies. Further vessels were acquired second-hand (along with three new ships from a Dutch yard in 1967), leading to a replacement programme involving eighteen Poseidon vessels built by Warnowerft between 1975 and 1980. Tankers and ore carriers joined the fleet from the late 1950s and at the end of the 1960s bulk operations were taken over by a new organisation, Deutfracht, whose operations included the Klaipeda-Rostock service mentioned above.

There was much discussion about the scope for greater use of the waterways which were grossly neglected in some countries (note the prohibition on the ownership of boats in Poland which effectively brought the maintenance of river navigation facilities to an end). This situation was balanced further south by speculation about improvements on the Danube and possible linkages by canal with the main rivers of the North European Plain. Romania and FFRY have collaborated over hydro-electricity and navigation facilities at the Iron Gates (along downstream at Iron Gates II) although FCSFR and Hungary failed to implement a similar joint project for Gabcikovo-Nagymaros. However, much store was attached to the prospect of through transport from the Black Sea to the North Sea and Romania pressed ahead with a Danube-Black Sea canal to connect the Black Sea port of Constanta with Cernavoda and provide a much more direct route to avoid the Danube delta where the navigation facilities were improved after the Crimean War by the European Danube Commission. However, the critical Rhine-Main-Danube Canal in Germany was not finished until after 1989, though this new facility will be of greater potential value now that the transition is underway.

On the whole, transport in Eastern Europe was characterised by poor infrastructural maintenance, especially for the road network with its inadequate load capacity, poor surfacing and deficient roadside servicing (Hall 1993, pp.6–9). Inferior technology was most evident in the case of Soviet-built aircraft with high fuel consumption and heavy maintenance demands; not to mention obsolete motor vehicles, continued heavy dependence on animal power and overloaded telecommunications. Organisational deficiencies were evident in relations between government departments (mirrored by imbalances in investment programmes) and in the regulation of joint ventures which inhibited Western investment), as well as neglect of human resources with overmanning combining with poor productivity and low morale. Environmental problems arose in most spectacular fashion through traffic congestion in the cities, aggravated by the pollution generated by poorly maintained vehicles and only belatedly relieved by the construction of metro systems. Fuel seepage at airports (especially some FSU airfields like Stara Kopernia in Poland and Tokol in Hungary) was serious enough to threaten water supplies and require reclamation by measures which included well-digging and pumping by local residents.

Most significant perhaps were the mobility constraints arising partly from the inadequacy of the transport system but also from bureaucratic measures. While internal movements became largely free of regulation (apart from Albania), the stringent controls on the issue of passports, visas and foreign currency made foreign travel difficult, even in the case of socialist countries. It is also striking that Comecon did not make a greater impact, considering the crucial importance of transport for the bloc as a whole. In theory, the programmes introduced by the Standing Committee for Transport should have produced a rational system, but investment strategies were too modest in scale and inappropriately organised, with insufficient emphasis on the reduction of costs and improvement in the quality of service. Comecon member nations were inured to isolation and the emphasis on economic autarky introduced into central planning in the early post-war years tended to marginalise the international dimension and restrict functionaries to domestic perspectives orchestrated by the propaganda of each national regime (Korbonski 1990). There were ambitious plans for north-south Trans-European motorways (TEM) and railways (TER) but these were never finalised, although some national transport programmes did involve *ad hoc* contributions to these grand designs. Once again a critical breakthrough was delayed until after 1989.

## Power

There have been great increases in the production of electricity, reflecting the growth of industry and the use of relatively heavy machinery consuming large amounts of power by Western standards. National grid systems, which did not exist outside Germany before the Second World War, now assure a power supply for domestic and industrial consumers almost everywhere. Moreover, international connections organised through Comecon's 'Mir' grid allowed surpluses and deficits to be balanced out. However, each country tried to be self-sufficient in electricity (even if some of the necessary fuels were imported) and the result was the development of large power stations on the principal domestic fuel bases such as the lignite fields: more than 5,000MW of capacity was built in areas like Cottbus in FGDR and at Maritsa Iztok in

Bulgaria; and more than 2,000MW at Belchatow/Konin in Poland and Craiova/Rovinari in Romania. The pollution problems arising from the burning of lignite were very serious, but there were few alternatives. FGDR installed pumped storage hydropower capacity in the Harz Mountains (Rubeland) and also at Saalfeld, following an earlier project in the Dresden area in the 1930s. But there was only limited potential in the northern countries, and in the Balkans too the most attractive sites like the Iron Gates developed within a few decades (Hall 1972; Hamilton 1963). A substantial energy gap (Kramer 1990) had to be filled through increasing dependence on FSU (Hoffman 1983; Kramer 1985). But the need for self-sufficiency became more acute in the 1980s because of the rising cost of Soviet oil and gas which was formerly supplied at concessionary rates. The level of future demand (Dienes 1976; Saunders 1980) introduced the nuclear option which was increasingly adopted during the 1970s and 1980s, particularly in Bulgaria and FCSFR where Soviet technology was used (Carter 1988). But costs were still high and commissioning delays were common. More seriously, the Chernobyl disaster swung public opinion against further nuclear projects, even when non-Soviet technology was involved: for example, Poland's Zarnowiec project was opposed by the Freedom and Peace Movement.

## Tourism

Services were typically underdeveloped given the endemic shortages in the planned economic systems of Eastern Europe (Kornai 1982). There were also anomalies because, although the cities were main service centres, the relationship between urban hierarchy and tertiary functions became increasingly irregular due to industrial developments (Korcelli and Potrykowska 1979). However, tourism did attract some major investments in order to build up the international side of the business. Tourism and recreation opportunities were of course in place well before the Second World War, but by 1945 most hotels were in a run-down state and many of those which were not converted for other uses under the central planning process were maintained largely for domestic use (Casson 1950). State companies were set up to arrange for travel and accommodation: Bulgaria's Balkantourist State Enterprise for Travel and Tourism dates back to 1948. During the 1960s it became common for state enterprises to provide recreation centres for the use of their employees in the coastal areas or mountain regions (Rogalewska 1978), and many families were able to secure simple second homes on the edge of large cities and in major recreation areas like Poland's Tatra Mountains and lake country (Rogalewska 1980). Meanwhile, the larger towns provided facilities for sports and recreation in their immediate vicinities on the basis of surveys indicating needs and potentials, as indicated by studies of Bydgoszcz (Niewiarowksi 1976) and Lodz (Dubaniewicz 1976).

International tourism was neglected, but there was potential for rapid growth (from a low base level) to provide summer holidays for people from other communist countries, and by the 1960s there was a substantial movement from FCSFR, FGDR and Poland to the Balkan countries. Later, investments were made in facilities and marketing to attract Western visitors and earn hard currency needed to buy machinery and technology and also to repay loans. Tourism helped to boost Eastern Europe's image and it offered benefits through regional income and employment; while investments in infrastructure improved the quality of the environment for the population as a whole. The greatest growth occurred in FFRY (Allcock 1986; Gosar 1989; Sallnow 1985) where the number of foreign tourists increased from 2.6mn. in 1965 to 8.4mn. in 1985 (with particularly rapid growth in the late 1960s and early 1970s); and registered foreign exchange from tourism grew from US$81.1mn. to just over US$1.0bn during the same period. FFRY accounted for 4 per cent of Europe's tourist arrivals but only two per cent of foreign exchange earnings in 1985. Elsewhere in the Balkans there was development in the coastal areas, although it was relatively modest in scale by the standards of FFRY (and Greece). By 1971 Western tourists accounted for just over 30 per cent of international tourist nights in Bulgaria (Pearlman 1990, p.104). But levels in the 1970s and 1980s were modest by comparison with FFRY (and Greece). There was also rapid growth of international tourism in Hungary during the 1960s and 1970s after the tourist 'ice age' in the aftermath of the 1956 rising. With a stagnating population at home 'Hungary became one of Europe's numerically most tourist-saturated countries' (Borocz 1990, p.21). Business with Austria was particularly brisk and a 'mini city' opened on the Austrian border at Hegyeshalom in 1988 to attract further spending. Hungary was the only communist country where the number of foreign visitors exceeded the number of domestic tourists (Table 2.5).

However, after considerable efforts in the 1970s to improve facilities (with substantial hotel building programmes) and attract package-tour companies to the Adriatic and Black Sea coasts, momentum flagged in the 1980s in the absence of long-term strategies to ensure 'improvements in the environment for tourists including freedom of movement and exchange problems and upgrading the quality of tourist products' (Buckley and Witt 1990, pp.17–18). Bulgaria tried to remain competitive by abandoning compulsory currency exchange (in force between 1974 and 1977) and providing premium exchange rates. But the bulk of the foreign visitors were always from socialist countries. The total income from tourism was high in some countries (6.5 per cent of total exports in Hungary and 18.6 per cent in FFRY) but should be seen against even higher figures for Austria (20.1 per cent), Greece (20.8 per cent) and Spain (25.8 per cent), leading to the conclusion that the potential, arising through climate and scenery along with cultural attributes and traditional hospitality, was not being fully exploited. There was also a lack of excellence in marketing and training and problems of coordination between East European countries which complicated joint development of holiday pack-

Table 2.5 International tourism 1983–7

| Country | 1983 | | | | | | 1987[1] | | | | | |
|---|---|---|---|---|---|---|---|---|---|---|---|---|
| | A | B | C | D | E | F | A | B | C | D | E | F |
| Bulgaria | 16.9 | 20.6 | 105.6 | 271 | 1.1 | 0.5 | 19.1 | 24.3 | 113.4 | n.a. | n.a. | 0.5 |
| FCS | 9.2 | 28.6 | 95.2 | 299 | 0.8 | 6.0 | 11.0 | 27.8 | 118.7 | n.a. | n.a. | 7.5 |
| FGDR | n.a. | n.a. | 67.8 | n.a. | n.a. | 0.9 | n.a. | n.a. | 67.8 | n.a. | n.a. | n.a. |
| Hungary | 14.1 | 13.9 | 34.7 | 426 | 2.0 | 4.8 | 17.5 | 12.8 | 42.7 | 827 | 3.2 | 7.2 |
| Poland | 1.9 | 79.9 | 91.0 | 85 | 0.1 | n.a. | 3.3 | n.a. | 91.5 | 136[1] | 0.2[1] | n.a. |
| Romania | 5.0 | n.a. | 164.7 | 202 | 0.4 | 1.7 | 4.7 | n.a. | 169.8 | 178[1] | 0.3[1] | 1.0[1] |
| FFRY | 35.4 | 55.3 | 302.6 | 929 | 1.6 | 9.3 | 52.3 | 57.7 | 351.4 | 1668 | n.a. | 20.0[1] |

Notes: A International tourist nights in registered accommodation (mn.); B Ditto Domestic; C Beds in hotels and similar establishments (000s); D International tourism receipts (US$mn.); E. D as a percentage of national product; F Departures abroad (000s)
1 Figures for 1986.

Source: Buckley and Witt 1990, pp. 11–13.

ages. Even in the major complexes there were problems of seasonality and the recruitment of skilled manpower. Moreover, poor and unreliable equipment affected the quality of catering, and black market activity was liable to take off when home-produced goods were inferior to the stocks in the foreign currency shops (Pearlman 1990). But in both Bulgaria and Romania there were many customer complaints (with the limited availability of evening entertainment being a particular issue in the case of Romania), although the winter sports resorts fared better. Some progress was made through joint ventures with Western equity participation, particularly in Hungary, Poland and FFRY. Hotels could be run by Western chains and new accommodation was provided, especially in Budapest. But quality control remained difficult with a shortage of trained staff and visa complications for personnel selected for training in the West (Buckley and Witt 1987; 1990).

There were also problems of concentration. Large complexes on the Adriatic accounted for much of FFRY's tourist beds during the decade 1978 to 1988, one-fifth falling to the Dubrovnik and Makarska areas and one-tenth to the Sibenik and Zadar areas. In such areas large organisations ran much of the industry, with Union Dalmacija in Split employing 4,000 people. Concentration arose because of the need for a good infrastructure: hotels; roads, airports and ferry links; museums and monuments. The larger centres were also the places where further growth could most easily be accommodated; thus tourism made a significant contribution to urban development (Vukonic and Tkalac 1984). But ecological conflicts became more acute. Tourists visiting the ecologically endangered areas helped to 'make the problem of environmental degradation a nationwide issue and, with respect to foreign tourism, an international concern' (Kruczala 1990, p.77). Pressure on Bulgaria's Black Sea coast was eased by various conservational projects, including nature reserves and conservation areas like Nessebur. But arguably it was always difficult to cope with Western tourism under the socialist system with its controls on small private businesses which usually provide the best standards of service in the industry. In FFRY encouragement of small businesses should have allowed for a greater spread of tourist activity away from the coast, but although some investment did come from private funds (generated by migrants who spent time working in Germany), most capital came from industry and other sectors of the Yugoslav economy.

Catering for foreign visitors was beneficial in complementing the provision of facilities for the domestic sector, but the two involved very different standards of provision, and the relatively high-quality infrastructure in complexes receiving Western tourists could not easily be replicated in different areas despite the desirability of a more even distribution in terms of regional development. In the case of Albania, 'the desire to preserve ideological discipline and to minimise the demonstration effect of the presence of numbers of (usually richer) foreigners have led to a common strategy of segregation' (Allcock and Przeclawski 1990, p.5). Albania's

Stalinist government was always concerned about the subversive effect of the tourist industry and business was restricted to 6,000 visitors a year (Hall 1984). Further conditions were imposed through the ban on citizens of four countries (Israel, South Africa, the USA and FSU) and only organised tour groups were accepted: individual travellers were not allowed in. Foreigners also had to meet the regime's sartorial standards and were banned from using public transport. However, Hall (1990, p.51) believed that Stalinist tourism in Albania could only be a transient phenomenon: either tourism would contribute to the breakdown of conservative forces or else the latter would 'eventually react against the wide range of social, psychological and ideological impacts that tourism brings in its wake'.

## SETTLEMENT PATTERNS

### Urban settlement

The post-war period saw a massive redistribution of population in favour of the towns (Bourne *et al.* 1984; Sarfalvi 1975) (Table 2.6). The capital cities grew with particular speed between 1950 and 1980, often accompanied by substantial suburban development that called for spatial planning across the whole agglomeration (Grocholska 1989). Then there were progressively smaller rates of growth at lower levels of the hierarchy (Toth 1994). This took in regional administrative centres like Pecs in Hungary (Kolta 1980), other towns with substantial resources for industry, and small towns, which in some cases actually declined (Hajdu 1993). Despite these increases Eastern Europe remained 'under-urbanised' because housing shortages induced high levels of commuting. The situation cannot be related directly to 'counter-urbanisation' in the Western sense because dependence on the

*Table 2.6* Urban population 1950–2000

| Country | 1950 | | 1980 | | | 1991 | | 2000 | |
|---------|------|------|-------|------|-----|------|-----|------|-----|
|         | A    | B    | A     | B    | C   | B    | D   | B    | D   |
| Albania | 0.25 | 20.5 | 0.90  | 33.6 | 2.6 | 35   | 2.8 | 39   | 2.6 |
| Bulgaria | 2.00 | 27.5 | 5.51 | 62.1 | 1.7 | 68   | 2.4 | 73   | 0.9 |
| FCSFR   | 6.35 | 52.5 | 10.16 | 66.4 | 0.6 | 77   | 2.1 | 83   | 1.1 |
| FGDR    | 13.04 | 72.0 | 12.75 | 76.2 | –  | –    | –   | –    | –   |
| Hungary | 3.55 | 38.6 | 5.70  | 53.2 | 0.6 | 61   | 1.6 | 68   | 1.0 |
| Poland  | 9.61 | 39.0 | 20.29 | 56.8 | 1.1 | 62   | 1.7 | 66   | 1.2 |
| Romania | 3.71 | 23.4 | 11.01 | 49.6 | 2.0 | 53   | 2.2 | 58   | 1.4 |
| FFYR    | 3.27 | 21.9 | 10.00e | 44.8 | 2.0 | –   | –   | –    | –   |

*Notes* A Urban population (mn.); B Percentage share of total population; C Growth between 1950 and 1980 in relation to the average for Eastern Europe; D Average growth per annum (absolute) for 1960–91 and 1991–2000.
*Source*: *UN Demographic Yearbooks*

city remains high and the home in the countryside is retained largely out of necessity rather than choice. Note the bureaucratic controls on migration which have led to large-scale growth in 'villages' close to city boundaries. It remains to be seen whether urban growth rates will increase (with the relaxation of migration controls) or if they are reduced (through unemployment resulting from the restructuring of industry and the improved prospects in privatised agriculture).

The largest of the capitals was Budapest, which also registered the highest level of dominance over the second city (Table 2.7). This situation arose because of an industrial history based on engineering and food processing in the centre of nineteenth-century Hungary (which then included Croatia, Slovakia and Transylvania) (Zovanyi 1986). Budapest's dominance was then increased by the territorial changes after 1918: 27.7 per cent of all industrial workers in 1910 but 65.3 per cent in 1920 (38 per cent in 1970, with frontiers the same as in 1920). Under communism, attempts were made to limit the city's growth in the context of the National Settlement Plan of 1971 (which tried to strengthen the five largest provincial cities – Debrecen, Gyor, Miskolc, Pecs and Szeged – and five others of intermediate size (Bekescsaba, Kekskemet, Szekesfehervar, Szolnok and Szombathely) (Compton 1984; Dienes 1973a). But Budapest's position was subsequently boosted by the NEM with enterprise self-financing from profits (note the research and development spending by successful Budapest companies like Videoton), as well as high spending on infrastructure in the stronger regions by government and local authorities, and the political clout of Budapest and the whole northern industrial region. However, there was some change within Budapest through displacement of industry from the inner city associated with slum clearance, and the growth of peripheral housing estates extending the rail/river-based complexes of Csepel and Obuda (Berenyi 1986). There was also some relocation in the wider region, affecting such areas as Godollo, Jasbereny and Torokszentmiklos (Compton 1979).

Provincial cities also experienced rapid growth, especially those places identified as centres for administrative regions (Ianos 1993). The tendency to concentrate investment in such centres resulted in considerable distortion of the inherited central place systems (Enyedi 1980). The regional towns advanced rapidly, especially in the Balkan countries, while the second towns remained weak (Dziewonski *et al.* 1977; Regulaska 1987). Even so, in FGDR some cities were permanently weakened by the Second World War and the immediate aftermath. In the case of Chemnitz there was heavy damage caused by the UK air force which ravaged the residential areas, after which the Soviets were able to extract booty from the largely intact industrial areas where much of the equipment was dismantled. However, Chemnitz derived some benefit from being renamed Karl Marx Stadt (despite the fact that Marx had never visited the city) and becoming the capital of one of the new administrative regions (Bezirken). Moreover, the city was the base of the

Table 2.7 Population of capital cities 1950–90

| Country | City | Capital city population (000s) | | | Percentage of national pop. | | | Multiple of second city pop. | | |
|---|---|---|---|---|---|---|---|---|---|---|
| | | 1950 | 1980 | 1990[1] | 1950 | 1980 | 1990[1] | 1950 | 1980 | 1990[1] |
| Albania | Tirana | 40 | 198 | 245 | 3.3 | 7.6 | 7.4 | 1.4 | 3.2 | 2.9 |
| Bulgaria | Sofia | 437 | 1057 | 1313 | 6.1 | 11.9 | 14.6 | 3.4 | 3.0 | 3.0 |
| FCSFR | Prague | 933 | 1193 | 1210 | 7.5 | 7.8 | 7.7 | 3.3 | 3.2 | 2.8 |
| FGDR | East Berlin | 1090 | 1146 | 1285 | 5.9 | 6.8 | 7.9 | 1.8 | 2.0 | 2.4 |
| Hungary | Budapest | 1600 | 2061 | 2047 | 17.2 | 19.2 | 19.5 | 12.5 | 9.8 | 9.1 |
| Poland | Warsaw | 804 | 1617 | 1656 | 3.2 | 4.5 | 4.3 | 1.3 | 1.9 | 2.0 |
| Romania | Bucharest | 1042 | 1861 | 2068 | 6.6 | 8.4 | 8.8 | 8.8 | 6.1 | 5.9 |
| FFYR | Belgrade | 389 | 911 | 1168 | 2.5 | 4.1 | 5.4 | 1.3 | 1.4 | 1.6 |

Notes 1 FGDR 1988.
Source: UN Demographic Yearbooks

huge uranium mining joint company Wismut: uranium ore from the Erzge-birge 'was able to provide the Soviets with by far the most important source of raw materials from their entire sphere of influence'. Indeed, had the value of this resource not been greatly reduced by the 1980s, German reunification might have been further delayed (Bockmann *et al.* 1995, p.543). The mining industry meant that there was considerable purchasing power in the city and its vicinity, while the massive ore shipments protected the railway to Dresden from being dismantled: it retained its two tracks and was eventually electri-fied. Meanwhile, the city was rebuilt so that it could be presented as a socialist showcase. But there was a great loss of population 'due to politically motivated flight' (ibid., p.546): loss of businessmen, entrepreneurs, the engineering/technical elite and intellectuals, compounded in the run up to unification by massive migration to the West. The airport disappeared under a new housing estate with 'almost nonexisting infrastructure'; meanwhile historic buildings were neglected as part of a 'traumatization of cultural history that can be seen throughout the FGDR' (ibid.).

Some attempts were made to limit the growth of large cities by controlling migration, but in the case of Poland's Upper Silesia industrial region (Gornoslaski Okreg Przemyslowy (GOP) an elaborate decongestion pro-gramme was drawn up in the 1950s, following a long industrial history concerned with metallurgy and coalmining (Fisher 1962). The 1950 to 1953 plan sought to transfer industry and population from 'Zone A' (area 700sq.km. and population 1.85mn. in 1950) to 'Zone B' (area 1,700sq.km. and population 0.31mn.), with new towns like Tarnowskie Gory/Miasteczko Slaski to the north and Mikolow/Tychy to the south (Szczpanski 1993). Between 1950 and 1975 the urban population of Zone A increased by 48 per cent, from 1.29mn. to 1.91mn. (clearly it was not possible to stop natural growth), while Zone B grew four fold (0.09mn. to 0.36mn.) and the Rybnik Coalfield six fold (0.06mn. to 0.36mn.). This latter area continued to grow rapidly in the 1970s and 1980s, with in-migration by young people from all parts of Poland in the context of the 50 per cent rise in GOP coal production to 150m.n.t anticipated in 1980: new towns are emerging at Jastrzebie-Zdroj and Zory (Abrams and Francaviglia 1975). The high proportion of young migrants has produced particularly radical attitudes among the workers in contrast to a more conservative approach in the old centres: this was apparent in strong support for Solidarity in Rybnik in the 1980s (and again in strike calls by new labour unions faced with austerity and a contraction of mining in the early transition years).

GOP has also experienced a decentralisation of industry, along with a change in structure. Fuel, power and metallurgy registered a fall in employ-ment share from 74.6 per cent in 1946 to 59.9 per cent in 1970 while engineering, chemicals and food increased their share from 16.9 per cent to 29.4 per cent. Locational shift emphasised the fringes of the region: this was evident in coalmining (already mentioned); lead-zinc workings (shifting from

Bytom to Olkusz and Siewierz-Zawiercie; steelmaking at Dabrowa Gornicza (Huta Katowice), and chemicals at Alwernia, extending the wartime expansion in the Vistula valley at Oswiecim/Auschwitz. But there has been too much emphasis on new capacity and not enough on modernisation. Thus the enormous investment at Dabrowa Gornicza (including a broad gauge railway link with FSU) was not undertaken as part of a comprehensive modernisation of the Upper Silesian steel industry and old obsolete plant remained in the Katowice area: the percentage of new industrial plants (built after 1945) was much lower in GOP than in Poland as a whole. The planners also failed to modernise the infrastructure of the core and coordinate the growth of the periphery (which has led to a substantial improvement in living standards in the Olkusz and Rybnik areas) with plans for the adjacent industrial regions of Bielsko-Biala, Czestochowa and Krakow so as to ensure an adequate protective band of forest and farmland (Forster and Kortus 1989). A motorway and express railway for the conurbation remained a priority to complement the electrified railway and dual carriageway links with Warsaw.

The smaller towns were, relatively speaking, neglected. Planning at the county level under communism meant the sudden growth of some small towns that lacked an industrial economy, intellectual society and traditional town–country relations. Meanwhile, the other small towns tended to stagnate. The situation was anomalous because the cities continued to draw in migrants and, although large, they had a more diversified industrial economy; with agglomeration economies and a mix of large enterprises (Begovic 1992), it would have been logical for them to have concentrated on higher productivity to avoid labour shortage (Korcelli 1990). Consequently, some planners thought it better to expand smaller towns where land was more readily available and costs were lower. According to Perger (1989, p.102), 'the most favoured type of settlement was the medium-sized town consisting of an industrial plant and a housing estate. This was the cheapest way of providing infrastructure facilities'. Moreover, country people perceived a move to a medium-sized town as offering greater probability of advancement than a move to the city. Hence the argument advanced in Poland that the regions (*voivodships*) should try and stem the decline of district (*powiat*) towns by strengthening their sub-regional servicing and avoiding concentration in *voivodship* capitals where too much competition was being generated among the higher order economic and cultural centres (ibid., p.233).

Concentration was felt to be most obvious in the northwest of Poland (with the problem of backward rural areas most evident in the centre and east); whereas small towns had a stronger role in the west and southwest. However, in Hungary some small towns grew too quickly because of socialist industry, without adequate services and 'small town society' (Becsei 1993; Csatari 1993). Urban centres on the Hungarian Plains were strongly supported under communism, but they were less dynamic than the urban centres in the hill country and in-migration played a less important role (Toth 1980). There were even references to the 'ruralisation' of the towns 'both because of the large numbers of people who migrated to towns from rural regions and also because of low standards of infrastructure in these towns' (Perger 1989, p.102). Critical functions for town–country integration were secondary school, hospital, department store, law court (prosecutor's office) and a police station (Csatari 1993). Links with the rural hinterland could be difficult, emphasising the isolation of some rural labourers in the fringe areas. However, the scope for work in small-scale farming offered some compensation for the remoteness of the urban infrastructure and communal services. By contrast, some small town labourers could not get involved in the second economy, though generally the newer migrants to the towns did better in small-scale agriculture than their second-generation peers. 'Amenities are plentiful in the urban centres but a lack of additional income sources delays the rise from social marginality in the case of people still coping with serious housing and income difficulties' (Karpaty 1986, p.132).

## Socialist cities

Town planning, as in FFRY (Simmie 1989), was inspired to some degree by the notion of the socialist city as an urban system quite clearly different from its Western counterpart (French and Hamilton 1979). Socialist cities have been associated with monumental buildings with an ideological inspiration. An example is Warsaw's Palace of Culture in a once densely built up area lying in ruins at the end of the Second World War. A 22ha site was levelled to receive a 'gift' from the FSU, built between 1952 and 1995: 234m. high and 817,000cu.m. in volume. To maintain the dominance of the palace other buildings in the vicinity were not to exceed 32m. until the 'Eastern Wall' (built along an adjacent shopping street between 1962 and 1970) brought about a 'counter-revolution in space' (Grime and Weclawowicz 1981). But, in any case, this theme of monumentalism can be exaggerated. All totalitarian regimes tend to seek expression through buildings but scarce resources must limit the scale of ostentation. As regards morphology there was no sustained adoption of a linear city model once considered by the FSU.

However, it might be claimed that there was an emphasis on collective functions (parks and parade grounds) rather than increased living space for individual apartments (Hegedus 1987; Morton 1979); also public transport rather than private car ownership (the latter was explicitly banned in Albania) (Machon and Dingsdale 1989). And certainly under socialism there was only limited evidence of a Western-style central business district since residential functions were retained in the central area through lack of any land value gradient (and the limited development of services above the level of the neighbourhood unit). The inner city remained functionally mixed (a legacy of nineteenth-century railway-related growth) with redevelopment featuring opportunity sites, especially the main boulevards where facades were transformed. Suburban development occurred on greenfield sites with large apartment complexes linked with community facilities and industry (Pickvance 1988). The near-total emphasis on large apartment blocks was a common feature of the socialist city in the 1970s and 1980s (following the smaller buildings of the 1950s and 1960s) (Musil 1987). But some low density rural-type housing intruded as the cities expanded to take in formerly separate villages; and it was also encouraged through the reforms in Hungary in the 1980s which brought an increase in the private sector for housing (Sillince 1990).

Some changes in urban areas during the later years of the socialist era so closely resembled Western experience as to suggest a gradual process of convergence between the once separate socio-economic systems. Some of the housing in Eastern Europe was managed in the context of a mixed economy (Szelenyi 1989), allowing a measure of privatisation (Tosics 1987). Inequalities in cities were emphasised (Hegedus 1988; Szelenyi 1983, 1987; Tosics 1988), including the contrasts in services between neighbourhoods (Abonyi-Palotas 1991). Differentiation in housing also became more apparent (Zaniewski 1989) especially in Hungary, concentrating in Budapest (Hegedus and Tosics 1983; Kovacs 1990; Sillince 1985) and Poland (Zaniewski 1991), and with particular reference to Warsaw's social differentiation (Dangschat 1987; Dawson 1971; Prawelska-Skrzypek 1988). Yet some aspects of socialist cities continued to be emphasised right up to the 1989 revolutions. In the FGDR the perceived cost advantages of large apartment blocks led to a rash of post-Stalinist architecture on the edge of large cities continuing into the 1980s: cramped apartments in concrete buildings 'which leaves one with a cold and grey impression when viewing the broadly lined streets' (Bockmann et al. 1995, p.546). And although East Berlin was favoured with relatively high shopping and residential standards, new housing was still restricted to vast suburban complexes like Neubaugebiet Hellersdorf (Pensley 1995). Moreover, strict controls on rents meant that not even the traditional town houses 'gifted' to local authorities (by private owners lacking the resources to continue maintaining them) were refurbished and offered to tenants. This now leaves a tremendous backlog of property repairs, although at the same time it offers the promise of an eventual revival in historic centres with entire ensembles of traditional building. Furthermore, the late president of Romania, N. Ceausescu, decided to reinforce the role of the state in the late 1980s by comprehensively redeveloping the inner city Uranus/Piata Unirii district. The 'Victory of Socialism Boulevard' was built across the Dambovita flood plain where extensive demolition of private housing was undertaken. The scheme was part of a policy of minimising the loss of agricultural land by high density housing but the Ceausescu epoch's obsession with 'National Stalinism' should also be noted: enhanced security; social engineering to create the 'new socialist man' and eliminate private property; also the former president's personal fascination with the built form of socialism arising from the earthquake of 1977 and the economic crisis of the 1980s which restricted alternative forms of development.

## Rural settlement

Under communism the villages retained their traditional agricultural functions, although there was considerable social change because of socialist farms which eliminated the differences between rich and poor peasants (Szelenyi and Manchin 1986; Vasary 1987). However, it has been pointed out that in the poorer countries the relatively low level of mechanisation and continued dependence on carts driven by the *conductori* of Romanian villages, in contrast to the working peasants (*maistri*) gave the remnants of the kulaks a grip on the cooperatives' affairs (Kideckel 1993). There were some radical changes, most notably through resettlement in Poland's 're-covered territories' where Germans were expelled to make way for Poles displaced further east (Gawryszewski and Ksiezak 1977; Hamilton 1975). There was some immediate post-war rebuilding after war damage, as in the case of Lucimia in the Gura Pulawska area of Poland (Harris 1948). Houses were gradually replaced by new structures in more modern styles. Some small apartment blocks were provided for state employees but most rural housing remained owner-occupied with the emphasis on single-storey cottages. There were some new functions, for investment occurred not through the development programmes of cooperative and state farms but through the plans of silvicultural and woodcutting enterprises.

There were also mining and manufacturing companies (particularly those with interests in light engineering, food-processing and textiles). Rural industries multiplied in the 1970s at a time of labour shortage in the towns (Barta 1986). It was a spontaneous process, not targeted in regional planning. Many units were poorly equipped with obsolete machinery, but some rural growth areas emerged and improved rural living conditions often resulted. There was some rural development through tourism; with 'resort villages' attracting investment from the state (road-building and hydro-electrification); cooperatives (camp sites and motels) and the individual household (second homes and bed and breakfast accommodation). In the Slovene Alps craft workshops were prominent and by the 1980s increasing use was made of the mountain pastures (compared with the situation in the 1960s and 1970s) as livestock numbers started to grow again (Thomas and Vojvoda 1973). This was because of improved accessibility, as the number of second homes increased, and the less favourable situation in non-agricultural activities. Pollution from Jesenice and other industrial centres made only a slight impact (Senegacnik *et al.* 1983).

Services improved as the budgets of education and health ministries impinged on rural services but rural education was often deficient (Ciecho-cinska 1989b). Public transport was particularly sensitive to the needs of the commuter because falling employment in agriculture gained some compensation from commuting to work in the cities, particularly the regional centres where light industry was promoted. Small commercial developments provided additional shopping and catering facilities. Yet there were clear deficiencies by the standards of the towns. In FGDR an average telephone provison of ten phones per 100 of the population (compared with fifty in FFRG) worked at one phone per two apartments in East Berlin compared with one in ten in Dresden and Rostock; while at the other extreme 2,000 villages had no connection with the telephone network at all. Depopulation became a universal feature of rural change (Enyedi 1976), except in Albania where internal migration controls were maintained (Sjoberg 1991a) (Table 2.8). On the whole, it could be said that villages remained surprisingly traditional in character and the countryside of Eastern Europe retained advantages in terms of human contacts and physical conditions while suffering many material and cultural disadvantages such as lack of employment and poor services. So the urbanisation of the countryside is still far from complete.

These various strands of development tend to affect the larger, best-placed villages and to introduce increasing differentiation between the 'key villages' and the outlying settlements which have relatively few facilities. The individual farmsteads (*tanyak*) and dwarf villages of the Great Hungarian Plain faced an uncertain future (Sarfalvi 1971). This was because the dispersed patterns of settlement appropriate under a system of small, largely self-sufficient peasant farms were not so satisfactory in the context of large commercial farms with labour deployed from central points (Timar 1989). A population of some 2,000 marked the threshold for key village characteristics (Lacko 1986). Socialist agriculture could have a bearing on growth trends (Held 1980) as studies in FGDR have shown (Berentsen 1982; Freeman 1979). In Poland, the state farms and agricultural schools played an important role in the expansion of villages (Kwiatkowska 1976). In Pomerania (north-west Poland) state farms took over manorial farms in some villages and absorbed many of the peasant farms. The whole village might be taken over where the settlement was small, remote and constrained by poor soil conditions. Enlargement of state farms might then in effect amalgamate several villages. There would be less consolidation where fragmented peasant holdings remained or where collectives were subsequently dissolved (Szulc 1978). Key villages have been favoured by investment in light engineering, food-processing and textiles, services and an intensified agriculture. However, rural industry was initially discouraged through nationalisation and the concentration of capacity in large urban-based units. Small-scale enterprise also tended to be more prominent in the larger villages (Kovach 1991) although diversification was common throughout the mountain regions

Table 2.8 Rural population 1900–90 (mn.)

| Country | 1897–1900 | | 1939–41 | | 1961 | | 1980 | | 1988–90 | |
|---|---|---|---|---|---|---|---|---|---|---|
| | Rural | Total | Rural | Total | Rural | Total | Rural | Total | Rural | Total |
| Bulgaria | 3.00 | 3.71 | 4.08 | 4.90 | 4.95 | 7.90 | 3.35 | 8.88 | 3.06 | 8.97 |
| FCSFR | 7.05 | 12.15 | 7.15 | 14.43 | 5.84 | 13.65 | 4.18 | 15.31 | 3.81 | 15.62 |
| Hungary | 4.25 | 6.85 | 5.00 | 9.32 | 5.23 | 9.96 | 4.66 | 10.71 | 4.33 | 10.60 |
| Poland | 17.21 | 23.42 | 20.25 | 32.05 | 15.25 | 29.73 | 14.76 | 35.75 | 14.62 | 38.04 |
| Romania | 9.18 | 11.20 | 13.06 | 16.75 | 12.49 | 18.40 | 11.19 | 22.20 | 10.48 | 22.94 |
| FFYR | 9.12 | 10.60 | 12.67 | 16.00 | 13.30 | 18.55 | 12.09 | 22.42 | 11.24 | 23.41 |

Source: Eberhardt 1994

(Stasiak 1977). The larger villages usually had much better services. Electrification failed to reach the smaller places, like the hamlets and medium-sized settlements on the Hungarian Plain (Sarfalvi 1971); commercial facilities were sparse and there were few kindergarten/nursery places in many areas). Variations in the employment structure were also related to population size (Enyedi 1980) and levels of educational attainment were similarly structured with respect to settlement groups (Sarfalvi 1980).

Some efforts were made by the planners to bring the town closer to the remoter rural areas (Hajnal 1989). This could be done by creating new towns through a change in the administrative status of villages enjoying some nodality of location and established market functions. In some cases large-scale industrial development led to the emergence of a completely new industrial centre. This occurred where new mineral resources were found, for example, Dimitrovgrad in Bulgaria and Gh. Gheorghiu-Dej (now Onesti) in Romania; alternatively at new assembly points for manufacturing like Eisenhuttenstadt in FGDR and Leninvaros in Hungary; and again at de-congestion points on the edge of conurbations, as at Tychy in Poland (already noted). However, gradual urbanisation based on well-situated villages seems to offer the best way forward, although no absolute equality will be feasible (Leszczycki 1976). The range of services required will depend on the local environmental profile (Werwicki 1982). On this basis some radical programmes evolved to consolidate rural settlement: notably in Hungary in the 1950s (when there was a plan to eliminate *tanyak* and consolidate population in agrogorods on the Soviet model) and Romania in the 1980s (with Ceausescu's plan for agro-industrial towns and the destruction of 'non-viable' villages) (Ronnas 1987, 1989). But the Hungarian project was not pressed too strongly and consolidation was often frustrated when people from small settlements chose to migrate directly to the towns (Csatari and Enyedi 1986). The Romanian plan seemed more likely to succeed (Sampson 1984). Ceausescu claimed that his personal hobby was the building of socialism, recalling Stalin's boast that there was no fortress the Bolsheviks could not storm. The 'unbridled voluntarism' of the rural programme has been linked with a personal inferiority complex and a wider perception of communism's inferiority in Romania in the inter-war years (Tismaneanu n.d.). But the plan was overtaken by the revolution in 1989. In fact, most cases of village abandonment have resulted from the extension of lignite quarries in FCSFR and the FGDR and soil contamination in the Glogow 'Copper Basin' of Poland. In Bohemia, sixty-five villages were destroyed to make way for the expansion of huge lignite quarries: eventually five separate complexes evolved, each covering around 25sq.km., and these required resettlement of some 180,000 people. This was a far greater upheaval than the much-publicised programme of *sistematizare* in Romania in the late 1980s where only a handful of villages were destroyed before the revolution.

## REGIONS

Under the central planning system investments were arranged spatially through a network of administrative regions (Fisher 1966). Regions were therefore important for economic management (Hajdu 1987; Horvath 1987). Major changes were normally undertaken by communist governments at the outset (Berentsen 1981) and each national system was overhauled from time to time, as the Romanian experience demonstrates (Helin 1967). However, the centre made the decisions and the regions were passive recipients of plan directives (Bachtler 1992; Berentsen *et al.*, 1989; Mihailovic 1972), but regional authorities could exercise their limited influence (Bennett 1989). Thus in Poland, the existing planning organisations were abolished in 1949, yet their influence was still apparent in the first medium-term plans and a law on spatial planning was passed in 1961 to ensure 'adequate development for particular parts of the country' (Stasiak 1993, p.9). Equalisation was a goal frequently mentioned in policy statements (Koropeckyj 1972) and each country had its own particular strategy as suggested by studies of Hungary (Sillince 1987) and Poland (Hamilton 1982).

However, there was some increase in local independence through administrative reforms in the 1980s (Palne Kovacs 1988). Local authorities could exercise greater initiative and were more accessible to lobbying by local societies (Maurel 1989). In FCSFR the administrative reform of 1983 gave more power to 'basic-level national committees that are closest to the citizen and are in the best position to judge the legitimacy of citizens' needs and interests' (Vidlakova and Zarecky 1989 p.179). The 1978 reform in Bulgaria provided for an elected mayor (*kmet*) whose duty was to manage public services and organise social and cultural activities, though with inadequate finance and administrative power until 1988. Provision was made for merging municipalities to create 'associated municipalities' in order to find more efficient solutions to local problems concerned with infrastructure and the assimilation of new economic activities. There was probably most substance in the reforms in Hungary where there was an attempt to revive local democracy by providing a new administrative body (*eloljaroszag*) in villages that did not have their own administrative functions due to the merging of councils. Their role was to defend local interests and mobilise local initiatives (Maurel 1989, p.121). This measure was one of several important changes in the administrative reform of 1984 (Hajdu 1989). There was also local economic management by councils in 1986 and the responsibilities of local government were expected to increase further, even under the communist system. Finance was always a sticking point however, and it is significant that in the FGDR after 1980 some plan targets were handled by local authorities resourced by lump sum payments. This gave them 'direct access to the financial resources derived from the economic enterprises in their localities' (Brauniger 1989, p.201) and, with it, the stimulus to use the money as efficiently as possible, perhaps carrying out more building work (such as dwelling units) than the sum was notionally geared to do. In Poland there was a new regime of regional autonomy through the subordination of some 1,800 enterprises to *voivodship* administration and a wider reintegration of society at the individual settlement level as well as the *voivodship* (Ciechocinska 1989a). There was more finance for small towns and villages in the 1980s but the budget was tight everywhere. Hence thinking moved towards tax-raising powers for local government (Nagy 1993).

There were considerable contrasts between regions. Broadly, a distinction can be made between 'urban regions', where the regional centre was a large city with half a million population or more and where the urban population in the region as a whole was relatively large; and 'rural regions' where urbanisation was much restrained and where population was lost by migration to stronger regions. In the case of Poland there was a net loss of population to Warsaw from the surrounding regions of Lomza, Plock, Siedlce and Radom; also to Poznan from Gniezno, Konin and Pila (Zurek 1975; Zurkowa and Ksiezak 1980). Governments showed ambivalence over regional equality for, although the equity principle implied strong support for rural regions, economic factors (economies of scale in export-orientated industry, with strong linkages) and 'political clout' have tended to limit decentralisation (Ianos 1988). Low productivity and inefficiency in some backward areas also made for caution (Palairet 1992), although the importance of international trade gave some advantage to the use of coastal locations and sites on the Soviet frontier (Ghenovici 1985). Kortus and Adamus (1989) have explained how the Polish state experienced problems in trying to industrialise the Carpathian region of the country; long neglected under the Habsburgs (with the exception of Bielsko's weaving traditions and the oil of Krosno, Jaslo and Gorlice) and only modestly favoured by factories built between the wars (as at Jaslo and Sanok). Hydropower projects built after 1945 were successful but factories were too big, creating oppressive commuting and environmental problems and generating conflicts with the region's tourist industry. It was particularly difficult for the Podhale peasants to come to terms with the shoe factory at Nowy Targ and there was a heavy turnover of workers as a result. The carbon electrode plant at Nowy Sacz infringed planning regulations and caused pollution which again conflicted with local tourism. Small, clean industries were much preferred and a broad-based strategy was needed instead of the fetishising of industry.

There was some use of migration controls (especially where there were perceived congestion costs and severe housing shortages) and some re-location of industry (especially for polluting and labour-intensive industries) but vested interests were strong. Hence the literature made considerable mention of the problems of backward areas (Farago and Hrubi 1988). Regional disparities narrowed to some extent although problems remained (Demko 1984; Szelenyi 1978). Studies of regional inequality became numerous in the late 1970s and 1980s (Fuchs and Demko 1979; Kende and Strmiska 1987; Nelson 1983). In the case of Poland, insufficient attention was given to the problem between 1950 and 1975 (Kuklinski 1976). The country seemed to split into two halves (Gorzelek and Szuk 1989), with polarisation between the urbanised areas (Kowalski 1986) and the more backward rural regions (Zimon 1979).

The federal states evolved relatively strong regional policies. FCSFR made a major effort to accelerate the development of Slovakia because of the extent of the inherited differences which Slovak politicians wished to see eliminated (Burghardt 1975). The factory system developed late in Slovakia, although several staple industries were established by 1914 and further factories were built in the inter-war years, like the hosiery factory at Svit and the shoe-making started by Bata at Batavany (renamed Partizanske). Infrastructure was also improved, notably by developments to the railway system. After Slovakia had enjoyed some years of independence as an ally of Germany during the Second World War, autonomy was enshrined in the 1945 'Kosice Programme' which restored the union while asserting that 'Slovaks should be masters in their Slovak land'. This agreement was not fully honoured until a federal system was adopted in 1969, but great efforts were made to accelerate Slovakia's industrial growth. There was much plant relocation from the Czech Lands while FSU raw materials supported major projects like oil refining and petrochemistry at Bratislava (Slovnaft) and the iron and steel at Kosice. Great attention was also given to defence industries in Western Slovakia, backing up the Warsaw Pact troops deployed in the Bohemian 'diamond'. In 1980 Slovakia accounted for 33 per cent of the country's population and 28 per cent of its industry; a much smaller deficiency than in 1938 when the figures were 25 per cent and 8 per cent respectively. Unfortunately, Slovakia continued to lag in terms of efficiency when allowance was made for subsidies and the prominence of new machinery. These deficiencies continue to trouble Slovak politicians who seek independence as a means of achieving faster growth; particularly in the light of reduced aid to Slovakia in the 1980s when lignite quarrying in Bohemia became a critical area for new investment.

In the case of FFRY there was regional autonomy for both administrative and economic organisations. Indeed, 'the spheres of authority granted to the regional level made it possible for the administrative agencies in each of the republics to become the major redistributional centres' (Perger 1989, p.105). But regional development was of great political importance in a multinational situation (Milanovic 1987; Pleskovic and Dolenc 1982) and reference should be made to the special fund of 1965 for 'insufficiently developed areas'. This involved the allocation of up to 2 per cent of the social sector economy's gross material product to the less-developed regions as well as an inter-regional reallocation of resources. However, despite some convergence in the proportions of workers in relation to population, there were widening gaps in investment and GNP per capita when the 1955 situation is compared with 1988 (1987 for investment). If the average level is reckoned as a 100, then the stronger republics of Croatia and Slovenia registered 140 for investment and 148 for GNP per capita in 1955 with comparable figures of 166 and 165 for 1988; while the three weaker republics of Bosnia-Hercegovina, Macedonia and Montenegro registered 129 for investment in 1955 and 76 for GNP; but 65 and 68 respectively in 1988. The situation in Serbia was intermediate: 81 for investment and 86 for GNP in 1955 compared with 95 and 90 respectively in 1988 (Flaherty 1988). It was clear that despite many new ventures in the southern republics (Vriser 1981), the stronger position of Slovenia was hardly compromised (Vriser 1992).

Border regions attracted some special attention on account of the lack of integration through tight security (Kovacs 1989). In the FGDR an elaborate control system was introduced at the time the Berlin Wall was built in 1961 (Shears 1971). It was not possible for FGDR citizens to enter a strip of territory extending back for several kilometers from the frontier with the FFRG. Many villages were cut off from normal circulation and some sensitive areas were cleared altogether with the exception of 'reliable' families. Consequently the frontier areas had to be supported with their own closed economies and light industries were extended at this time, including a textile factory at Tanne which employed a hundred workers. Some modifications to the regime allowed a revival of the tourist industry in such Harz Mountain villages at Schierke and Tanne, but post-1989 free circulation has been possible. This has been good for tourism but disastrous for many of the protected manufacturing industries. Hungary took particular interest in the development of border regions where there were large cities isolated from much of their historic hinterlands (Toth 1993). Szeged's growth was impeded by the proximity of the frontier but the city benefited through the policy of establishing counter-poles for Budapest (Krajko 1980). Some local cross-border arrangements were made: Hungarian agricultural products were processed at Beli Monastir in Croatia and a customs-free area was established at Sopron to encourage Austrian enterprise (Toth 1993). Hungary also became involved in the Alps-Adria Working Community (Horvath 1993).

## ENVIRONMENT

There can be no doubt about the environmental damage which occurred during the socialist era as a consequence of the rapid rate of economic growth (Volgyes 1974). What was widely seen as an environmental crisis (Carter 1989; Kramer 1987) included a number of components such as noise, scenic damage, soil deterioration and cultural pollution but the two critical indicators were air and water pollution. For long dismissed as phenomena to be associated only with capitalism, pollution increased rapidly in the 1960s and 1970s with industrial growth, increased electricity generation, urban development and the intensification of agriculture. Damage was to some extent imported as 'transboundary pollution' but only in a few cases, for example, the forests of southwest Poland and the beaches and fisheries of the Baltic coast, could the bulk of the damage be attributed to this source. At home the difficulties were magnified through insufficient attention to the installation of filters, water purification, sewage treatment and the proper planning of fertiliser applications and irrigation schemes.

Urban areas were badly affected because very high levels of pollution occurred in the main industrial regions along with the artificial heat phenomenon (Kraujalis 1972). Examples include the state capitals like Prague (Carter 1984) and provincial cities like Krakow, covered by a stationary cloud of smog on 135 days of the year, and Wroclaw, embarrassed by a chrome fog and by the dumping of toxic waste within only 200m. of drinking water supplies. Some small towns suffered severe hardship including those in the border areas of FCSFR, FGDR and Poland which experienced rapid industrialisation in the nineteenth century. In Lower Silesia there were mining projects and a range of industries (chemicals and glass; food and wood processing; metals and textiles) which 'operated in widely-scattered medium-size or small plants with outdated equipment and technology' (Czerwinski 1976, p.274). Water and sewage, transport and communal facilities were 'all factors potentially detrimental in environmental terms' (ibid.). Local problems arose through the dumping of mine waste in areas concerned with coal (Nowa Ruda and Walbrzych), copper (Legnica-Glogow) and lignite (Turoszow), not to mention the surface quarries which extended over 20sq.km. in the case of the Turoszow complex that was expected to reach depths of 200m. Pollution problems in Lower Silesia were also compounded by water shortages, reflecting the high industrial demand and the variable discharge of the rivers. Elsewhere, uranium mining by Wismut in FGDR resulted in a widespread distribution of arsenic-rich radioactive tailings and a rash of tip heaps appeared in the expanding Rybnik coalfield of southern Poland (Wrona 1975). Subsidence in the coalfields was also a problem, as in the Pecs-Komlo area of Hungary (Erdosi 1980).

To be sure, there were many country areas which remained idyllic but land was damaged by excessive and careless use of chemicals, leading to the degradation of soil structure and the pollution of water through nitrification (which gives rise to the blue-baby syndrome). This was especially the case in Hungary where pesticides and fertilisers are applied at high levels by international standards. Agricultural areas also suffered from serious soil erosion (Churska 1976), though some use was made of conservation measures like ploughing across the slope and establishing small plantations (Skrodzki 1972). But measures were also needed to cope with wind erosion which was a significant cause of soil degradation in those parts of the Sudeten Mountains where there is only a thin layer of good soil (Jahn 1972). As a result of copper smelting at Glogow, several villages (including Biechow, Bogomice, Wroblin and Zukowice) had to be evacuated due to contaminated soil, although some farm production continued to come from land polluted in this way (Rosenbladt 1991). There was also acidification (by 1 pH on average across the country), while waterlogging and salinisation have resulted from irrigation, including 125,000ha from the first Tisza barrage which was poorly planned). Farmyard manure is less widely used and this creates further pollution problems, especially in the case of the large quantities of liquid manure generated by intensive livestock rearing units. Large monocultures (for wheat and maize) also have environmental disadvantages. Many hedges and spinneys were removed and streams canalised so that natural habitats were eroded while protected areas were far too limited: indeed, the protected areas in Hungary were mostly cultivated by agro-industries, leading to conflict between conservationists and farm managers. On the positive side closed borders in FCSFR, often devoted to military training areas, did have ecological advantages with high natural and environmental values in contrast to the Jablonec/Liberec area and other parts of the northern border (with FGDR) where there were fewer restrictions.

The decline of woodlands has been taking place over the long term and there are cartographic and statistical sources that trace the process through the nineteenth and twentieth centuries (Szymanski 1978). However, during the socialist period there was damage through the spruce monoculture and restructuring to emphasise other fast-growing species. Meanwhile, the effects of pollution were very evident in the forests exposed to emissions from power stations not only in Poland (Turoszow) but also in FGDR (Cottbus area). On exposed sections of the higher ground defoliation became very evident, for example, around Sklarska Poreba (south of Jelenia Gora). Some damage to forests arose from insect attacks (also drought, frost and strong winds) but the consequences were all the more serious because the trees were already in a poor condition. Between 1981 and 1987 11,000ha of pine forest were damaged in the Sudeten Mountains, mostly in the west (Gory Izerskie and Karkonosze), and overall only 65 per cent of the Sudeten forests were still in a healthy state in 1983. There was a significant fall in the density of woodland (wood mass per unit of area) and the amount of wood produced.

Further rural problems arose from the mismatch between piped water supplies and sewerage. Because of the greater priority given to piped water supplies, 88 per cent of rural dwellings in Hungary had piped water in 1987 but only 49 per cent had sewerage (in 1945 the figures were 25 per cent and 18 per cent). The dwellings with running water but no sewerage (which increased fourfold between 1972 and 1987) generated almost 150mn.cu.m. of sewage per annum, but only one-sixth of this was collected by tank trucks leaving the rest to seep into the soil. Drinking water became so polluted that over 700 villages had to be supplied by tanks, bottles and plastic bags. The situation over solid waste was also bad because garbage collection was usually restricted to the towns and the more urbanised villages. As a result, 'throughout the countryside the margins of villages and the edges of towns and watercourses are strewn with rubbish'(Persanyi, 1990 p.46). Recycling schemes made an appearance but up to 1989 there were insufficient collection points.

Pollution was in many respects counter-productive, leading not only to ecological problems but also to wasted resources (reduced farm/forest yields; dwindling pure water stocks and depression in tourism) and ill health among the population. NGOs became active in the campaign for a better environment. In the Solidarity era pressure of the Polish Ecological Club (founded in 1980) was effective in securing the closure of Skawina aluminium plant in 1981 because of its damaging fluorine emissions (Rosenbladt 1991). Environmental groups also monitored new developments including power station projects. A case in point was the Opole power station on which construction began in the mid-1970s at the same time as the Katowice steel works was set up. However, the diversion of hard coal into exports led to a preference for lignite-fired power stations and the 4,300MW Belchatow station was built instead between 1977 and 1988. Therefore, Opole was still under construction in 1989 and the decision to proceed followed from the abandonment of the Zarnowiec nuclear project when the environmentalists saw it as the lesser of two evils. So controversy at Opole then focused not so much on construction *per se* as the need for sulphur dioxide abatement by flue gas desulphurisation (FGD) and a chimney of adequate height (300m. eventually). Meanwhile, 'environmental consciousness' was born in FFRY when the federal government planned to dam the Tara River canyon (Jancar 1992, p.180), and in 1983 the Danube Circle was created in Hungary to oppose the Gabcikovo-Nagymaros hydropower project agreed in 1977 by FCSFR and Hungary. The government was forced on the defensive by protest letters and had to coerce the Hungarian Academy of Sciences to provide a favourable evaluation of the scheme. It also had to act against Hungarian and Austrian demonstrators staging a 'Danube Walk' in 1986. Eventually in 1989 a demonstration brought 100,000 people into Budapest's Kossuth Square demanding an end to the project. Free elections were promised and the project was abandoned the following year.

Chernobyl was a flashpoint for environmental action and there were protests in Serbia in 1986 against a proposed second nuclear power station for FFRY. By the time a moratorium was declared in 1988, 'nuclear power had become the symbol of what was perceived as an entrenched, uncaring and deaf bureaucracy' (Jancar 1992 p.169). Even though the anti-nuclear movement had split into separate factions in the various republics by 1989, it was very significant in terms of the erosion of support for the communists. But by the late 1980s people were also galvanised into action by persistent air and water pollution. Indeed, the socialist era ended with increasing protests about environmental problems. These sometimes involved urban dwellers defending scenic features in the countryside against both the threat of mining or industrial development and the ambivalence of country dwellers. But rural people became more environmentally aware during the 1980s and started to protest about the large-scale dumping of hazardous waste. They might accept their own contribution to environmental degradation but were sensitive to the damage when additional waste was imposed on them (Persanyi 1990, pp.50–1). In 1989 Czech mothers protested in Prague about polluted drinking water while the citizens of Chomutov demonstrated against high levels of air pollution. In Ruse, Bulgaria, people objected to toxic gases emitted from a Romanian chlorine factory at Giurgiu on the opposite side of the Danube. And although many groups were just concerned with specific local issues, others looked at ecological matters more generally (like the environmental sector of the Academy of Sciences' biological section in Prague) and some went on to form green parties, although this led to polarisation between 'ecodemocrats' waging a political struggle and those who merely wished to apply pressure on those in political power (Jancar 1992, p.171). The results were substantial in terms of plant closures and new economic policies. Transboundary pollution helped people to mobilise across closed frontiers.

Increased exposure by East European governments to international standards on pollution control (notably the Stockholm Conference of 1972) led to a flurry of legislation, even before public opinion became politically significant. There was also greater attention given to research to monitor pollution levels and examine landscapes through cartography and photography (Czeppe 1976). In Poland's flysch Carpathians there was a need for a structure of climatically determined vegetation belts (reflecting inversions); also to predict environmental change and clarify the nature of water circulation and soil denudation under different types of land use. In eroded areas of the Polish flysch Carpathians it was recommended that cultivation should be reduced in preference for woodland, grassland and orchards (Gerlach 1976). It was argued that forest should be established on all slopes of over 30 degrees and parts of the interfluves as well as zones adjacent to river channels. Arable was acceptable only on slopes of up to 15 degrees (Gil and Starkel 1976). The scheduling of protected areas and national parks became more common (Singleton 1987) and there was more emphasis on environmental management generally, as indicated by the literature on FCSFR (Carter 1985), Hungary (Compton and Pecsi 1984; Pecsi and Probald 1974), and FFRY (Jancar 1987). However, while action demonstrated an awareness of the problem, it did not necessarily indicate a firm political will to ensure improvements. For even when legal pollution limits were clearly set, enterprises responsible for excesses were not always prosecuted; still less were they confronted by financial penalties adequate to ensure compliance with regulations. Understandably there were conflicts within governments between ministers seeking a cleaner environment and others who gave top priority to meeting the plan targets.

However, some notable successes in conservation arose through the restoration of some historic town centres. Warsaw was the outstanding example through the rebuilding of the old town square after wartime destruction (Dziewulski and Jankowski 1957; Jankowski 1990), but provincial cities were also restored. The rebuilding of Wroclaw (reduced to a state of near-total devastation through the German strategy of 'Fortress Breslau') involved restoration of much of the old fabric. The famous Market Hall regained its familiar exterior despite internal reconstruction involving massive concrete beams. Elsewhere in the city, redevelopment involved appropriately sensitive architectural styles while some redundant public buildings like the Swiebodzki railway station (superseded by the main station Wroclaw Glowny) were put to new uses. Meanwhile, in FCSFR, where a Trust for Reconstruction of Urban Historical Reserves and Monuments was created in 1956, protected urban areas were designated in the historic cores of thirty towns in the Czech Lands and ten in Slovakia. Moreover, in Prague the whole nineteenth-century city was effectively made an urban reserve in 1971, with protection extended to some 1,400 monuments and one-third of the housing stock (Sykora 1995). In FGDR, Dresden's Frauenkirche was preserved as a ruin (and is now to be rebuilt in all its Gothic splendour following German reunification) while the Zwinger Palace (an eighteenth-century royal playground for dances, tournaments and opera) was largely reconstructed. There was also some sensitive building in Hauptstrasse and the early twentieth-century garden city of Hellerau was retained (Paul 1990). Finally, in Hungary the Buda Castle project was outstanding (Harrach 1990). However, despite much good work it has to be said that conservation areas received only limited investment and, of course, they could not be protected from the pollution that affected the environment generally.

## CONCLUSION

The communist era left an indelible impression on Eastern Europe. In terms of human effort the achievements were in many respects heroic and Western literature reflects an element of the triumphalism that marked some of the early development projects. Social scientists appreciated that the West was not typical of the world as a whole and that Soviet ideology must inevitably generate a distinctive economic system. But at a time when source material was very limited and travel complicated by bureaucratic restrictions it was difficult to separate reality from communist party propaganda claims which were the nearest approximation to 'official publications'. It was only in the 1980s in the context of the Western offensive over human rights, fortified by the structuralist movement seeking greater political awareness in social science, that the unbalanced nature of the system became widely understood. Even so, there continued to be a mismatch between some Western scholarship alluding to elegant models of socialist construction and the thrust of underground literature from Eastern Europe pointing to human rights abuses, environment crises and, above all, a priority for personal goals in policy implementation. The East European material may have been high on reports of insensitive bureaucracy (not necessarily restricted to communist systems), but Western assessments remained all too circumspect where the behavioural aspects were concerned. It was as though a veil could be drawn across the Stalin period, leaving central planning to be legitimated as a corrective to a wayward capitalism and authoritarian rule a precondition for prosperity over the longer term. Yet nobody could see the books and appreciate how much economic activity was unprofitable as politically motivated management strategies continued to operate in a semi-feudal environment where progress depended primarily on personal connections within the nomenclature hierarchy. Ideology was being trivialised, but vested interests were a stumbling-block for change, above all in the FSU. Thus when the Polish Communist Party reformists sat down with radical intellectuals early in 1989 both sides appreciated that the Soviets would not allow the ruling party to relinquish ultimate control. It was Gorbachev's crucial concession on this point that opened the way towards the present post-socialist era.

## REFERENCES

J. Abonyi-Palotas 1991, 'The inner spatial differentiation by neighbourhoods of infrastructure in Szeged'. *Foldrajzi Ertesito* 40, 297–316. In Hungarian with an English summary.

I. Abrams and R. Francaviglia 1975, 'Urban planning in Poland today'. *Journal of the American Institute of Planners* 41, 258–69.

E. Adrjanowska 1972, 'Interregional links in the shipbuilding industry in Poland'. *Geographia Polonica* 21, 5–16.

J.B. Allcock 1986, 'Yugoslavia's tourist trade: pot of gold or pig in a poke?' *Annals of Tourism Research* 13, 565–88.

J.B. Allcock and K. Przeclawski 1990, 'Tourism in the centrally-planned economies: introduction'. *Annals of Tourism Research* 17, 1–6.

J. Ambler et al. (eds) 1985, *Soviet and East European Transport Problems* (London: Croom Helm).

M. Ando 1980, 'Natural resources and economic development in the South Hungarian Plain' in G. Enyedi and J. Meszaros (eds), *Development of Settlement Systems* (Budapest: Hungarian Academy of Sciences), 151–7.

S. Antanaskovic and D.Djekic 1986, 'The passenger car industry'. *Yugoslav Survey* 27(2), 89–104.

C. Arthur 1992, 'Why the gold went east'. *New Scientist* 135(1831), 32–5.

J. Bachtler (ed.) 1992, 'Socioeconomic situation and development of the region in the neighbouring countries of the Community in Central and Eastern Europe' (Brussels/Luxembourg: Commission of the European Communities Directorate General for Regional Policies, Regional Development Studies 2).

R. Bahro 1978, *The Alternative in Eastern Europe* (London: New Left Books).

G. Barta 1986, 'Rural industry in Hungary' in G. Enyedi and J. Veldman (eds), *Rural Development Issues in Industrialized Countries* (Pecs: Hungarian Academy of Sciences, Centre for Regional Studies), 34–44.

J. Batt 1991, *East Central Europe from Reform to Transformation* (London: RIIA/Pinter).

T. Bauer 1983, 'The Hungarian alternative to Soviet-type planning'. *Journal of Comparative Economics* 7, 304–16.

J. Becsei 1993, 'Settlement morphological features of Mezohegyes'. *Foldrajzi Ertesito* 42, 193–223.

B. Begovic 1992, 'Industrial diversification and city size: the case of Yugoslavia'. *Urban Studies* 29, 77–88.

R. Bennett (ed.) 1989, *Territory and Administration in Europe* (London: Pinter).

B. Berelson 1974, *Population Policy in Developed Countries* (New York: McGraw-Hill).

W.H. Berentsen 1981, 'Regional change in the GDR'. *Annals Association of American Geographers* 71, 50–66.

W.M. Berentsen 1982, 'Changing settlement patterns in the GDR 1945–1976'. *Geoforum* 13, 327–37.

W.H. Berentsen *et al.* (eds) 1989, *Regional development: Processes and Policies* (Budapest: Hungarian Academy of Sciences).

I. Berenyi 1986, 'Conflicts in land use in suburbia: the example of Budapest' in G. Heinritz and E. Lichtenburger (eds) *The Take-off of Suburbia* (Stuttgart: Steiner Verlag), 125–34.

J.F. Besemeres 1980, *Socialist Population Politics: The Political Implications of Demographic Trends in the USSR and Eastern Europe* (White Plains, New York: M.E. Sharpe).

I. Bicanic and M. Skreb 1991, 'The service sector in East European economies: what role can it play in future development?' *Communist Economies and Economic Transformation* 3, 221–33.

I. Bicik and V. Stepanek 1994, 'Post-war changes of land-use structure in Bohemia and Moravia: case study Sudetenland'. *GeoJournal* 32, 253–9.

A. Bockmann *et al.* 1995, 'The city of Chemnitz in Saxony (Germany): building its new economic profile'. *GeoJournal* 37, 539–56.

O. Bogomolov 1990, *Market forces in planned economies* (London: Macmillan)

G. Bora 1976, 'Changes in the spatial structure of Hungarian industry and the determinants of industrial location' in P.A. Compton and M. Pecsi (eds), *Regional Development and Planning* (Budapest: Hungarian Academy of Sciences), 91–108.

G. Borgstrom and F. Annegers 1971, 'Eastern Europe: an appraisal of food and agriculture in the thirties compared with the sixties'. *Tijdschrift voor Econiomische en Sociale Geografie* 62, 114–25.

J. Borocz 1990, 'Hungary as a destination'. *Annals of Tourism Research* 17, 19–35.

L.S. Bourne *et al.* (eds) 1984, *Urbanisation and Settlement Systems*: international perspectives (Oxford: Oxford University Press).

J.C. Brada 1985, 'Soviet subsidization of Eastern Europe: the primacy of economics over politics'. *Journal of Comparative Economics* 1, 80–92.

J.C. Brada and J.A. Mendez 1988, 'An estimate of the dynamic effects of economic integration'. *Review of Economics and Statistics* 2, 163–8.

J. Brauniger 1989, 'The German Democratic Republic' in R. Bennett (ed.) *Territory and Administration in Europe* (London: Pinter), 191–202.

H. Brezinski 1990, 'Private agriculture in the GDR: limitations of orthodox socialist agricultural policy'. *Soviet Studies* 42, 535–53.

P.J. Bryson *et al.* 1991, *The End of the East German Economy: From Honecker to Reunification* (London: Macmillan).

P.J. Buckley and S.F. Witt 1987, 'The international tourism market in Eastern Europe'. *Service Industries Journal* 7(1), 91–104.

P.J. Buckley and S.F. Witt 1990, 'Tourism in the centrally-planned economies of Europe'. *Annals of Tourism Research* 17, 7–18.

V. Bunce 1985, 'The empire strikes back: the evolution of the eastern bloc from a Soviet asset to a Soviet liability'. *International Organization* 39, 1–46.

A.F. Burghardt (ed.) 1975, *Development Regions in the Soviet Union Eastern Europe and Canada* (New York: Praeger).

A.A.L. Caesar 1962, 'Yugoslavia: geography and postwar planning'. *Transactions Institute of British Geographers* 30, 33–44.

F.W. Carter 1980, 'Public transport in Eastern Europe: a case study of the Prague conurbation'. *Transport Policy and Decision Making* 1, 209–30.

F.W. Carter 1984, 'Pollution in Prague: environmental control in a centrally planned socialist economy'. *Cities* 1, 258–73.

F.W. Carter 1985, 'Pollution problems in postwar Czechoslovakia'. *Transactions Institute of British Geographers* 10, 17–44.

F.W. Carter 1988, 'Czechoslovakia: nuclear power in a socialist society'. *Environment and Planning: Government and Policy* 6, 269–87.

F.W. Carter 1989, 'Air pollution in Poland'. *Geographia Polonica* 56, 155–77.

F.W. Carter 1995, 'National minorities and ethnic groups in Bulgaria: regional distribution and cross border links'. *Region and Regionalism* 2, 61–85.

F.R.C. Casson 1950, 'Yugoslavs and the seaside'. *Geographical Magazine* 23, 298–301.

Z. Churska 1976, 'Tentative evaluation of the intensity of soil erosion as determined by natural conditions and type of land use: a case study of the valleys of the Drweca and the Lower Vistula'. *Geographia Polonica* 34, 176–93.

M. Ciechocinska 1989a, 'Poland: searching for increasing economic effectiveness' in R. Bennett (ed.), *Territory and Administration in Europe* (London: Pinter), 138–53.

M. Ciechocinska 1989b, 'The level of educational achievement in Poland: a town–countryside comparison'. *Geographia Polonica* 56, 213–25.

M. Ciesielski and W. Kaczmarek 1989, 'Transport absorptiveness of Polish foreign trade' in T. Bartkowski *et al.*, *Papers on Spatial Economy* (Poznan: Akadernie Ekonomiczna w Poznanin Zeszyty Naukowe Zesyt 182), 35–52.

P.A. Compton 1979, 'Planning and social change in Budapest' in R.A. French and F.E.I. Hamilton (eds), *Socialist City* (Chichester: John Wiley), 461–92.

P.A. Compton 1984, 'Hungary: the national settlement strategy'. *Cities* 1, 374–86.

P.A. Compton and M. Pecsi 1984, *Environmental Management: British and Hungarian Case Studies* (Budapest: Hungarian Academy of Sciences).

M Cranfield 1991, 'East German deep sea shipping 1953–1990'. *Ships Monthly* 26(7), 20–3.

D.M. Crowe and J. Kolsti 1991, *The Gypsies of Eastern Europe* (White Plains, New York: M.E. Sharpe).

L. Csaba 1983, 'Integration into the world economy and the cooperation of the CMEA countries in planning'. *Osteuropa-Wirtschaft* 2, 105–22.

L. Csaba 1989, 'Some lessons from two decades of economic reform in Hungary'. *Communist Economies* 1, 17–29.

B. Csatari 1993, 'Crisis signs of Hungarian small towns' in A. Duro (ed.) *Spatial Research and the Social-Political Changes* (Pecs: Hungarian Academy of Sciences, Centre for Regional Studies), 97–102.

B. Csatari and G. Enyedi 1986, 'The formation of new clustered rural settlements in Hungary' in G. Enyedi and J. Veldman (eds), *Rural Development Issues in Industrialized Countries* (Pecs: Hungarian Academy of Sciences, Centre for Regional Studies), 96–105.

B. Csikos-Nagy 1973, 'Mutual advantage in the economic cooperation' in T. Kiss (ed.), *The Market of Socialist Economic Integration* (Budapest: Academy of Sciences), 179–90.

Z. Czeppe 1976, 'Mapping of the geographical environment in the West Carpathians'. *Geographia Polonica* 34, 69–71.

J. Czerwinski 1976, 'Problems of protecting the natural environment against the background of the economic development of Lower Silesia'. *Geographia Polonica* 34, 273–7.

J. Dangschat 1987, 'Sociopolitical disparities in a socialist city: the city of Warsaw at the end of the 1970s'. *International Journal of Urban and Regional Research* 11, 37–59.

F. Davidova 1971, 'The Gypsies in Czechoslovakia'. *Journal of the Gypsy Lore Society* 50, 40–54.

W. L. Davidson 1947, 'A village goes to Hungary'. *Geographical Magazine* 20, 295–301.

A.H. Dawson 1969, 'The changing distribution of Polish industry 1949–1965'. *Transactions Institute of British Geographers* 50, 177–98.

A.H. Dawson 1971, 'Warsaw: an example of city structure in free-market and planned socialist environments'. *Tijdschrift voor Economische en Sociale Geografie* 62, 104–13.

A.H. Dawson 1982, 'An assessment of Poland's agricultural resources'. *Geography* 67, 297–309.

A.H. Dawson 1983, 'Poland: thirty year rural-urban transition'. *Cities* 1, 175–84.

A.H. Dawson (ed.) 1986, *Planning in Eastern Europe* (London: Croom Helm).

J. Debski 1974, 'The spatial influence of the Gdansk agglomeration'. *Geographia Polonica* 28, 127–44.

J. Debski 1980, 'The integration of Poland's big cities through commodity links'. *Polish Academy of Sciences Geographical Studies* 135 (in Polish with an English summary).

G. Demko (ed.) 1984, *Regional Development: Problems and Policies in Eastern and Western Europe* (London: Croom Helm).

P. Desai 1986, 'Is the Soviet Union subsidizing Eastern Europe?' *European Economic Review* 1, 107–16.

L. Dienes 1973a, 'Urban growth and spatial planning in Hungary'. *Tijdschrift voor Economische en Sociale Geografie* 64, 24–38.

L. Dienes 1973b, 'The Budapest agglomeration and Hungarian industry: a spatial dilemma'. *Geographical Review* 63, 356–77.

L. Dienes 1976, 'Energy prospects for Eastern Europe'. *Energy Policy* 4, 119–29.

M. Dobrowolska 1976, 'The growth pole concept and the socioeconomic development of regions undergoing industrialisation'. *Geographia Polonica* 33(2), 83–101.

M.L. Dockrill 1988, *The Cold War* 1945–1963 (London: Macmillan).

F.E. Dohrs 1971, 'Nature versus ideology in Hungarian agriculture: problems of intensification' in G.W. Hoffman (ed.), *Eastern Europe – Essays in Geographical Problems* (London: Methuen), 271–97.

H. Dubaniewicz 1976, 'An appraisal of the natural environment of the Lorz region for the needs of economic development and recreation'. *Geographia Polonica* 34, 265–71.

K. Dziewonski *et al.* 1977, 'Distribution migrations of population and settlement system of Poland'. *Polish Academy of Sciences Geographical Studies* 117.

S. Dziewulski and S. Jankowski 1957, 'The rebuilding of Warsaw'. *Town Planning Review* 28, 209–21.

P. Eberhardt 1994, 'Distribution and dynamics of rural population in Central Eastern and Eastern Europe'. *Geographia Polonica* 63, 75–94.

L.F. Edwards 1947, 'The new Bulgaria'. *Geographical Magazine* 19, 540–9.

T.H. Elkins 1986, 'The island of Rugen and new Baltic ferry links with the USSR'. *Geography* 71, 358–9.

T.H. Elkins 1989, 'The wall: a way of life'. *Geographical Magazine* 51(4), 27–30.

T.H. Elkins and B. Hofmeister 1988, *Berlin: The Spatial Structure of a Divided City* (London: Routledge & Kegan Paul).

G. Enyedi (ed.) 1976, *Rural Transformation in Hungary* (Budapest: Hungarian Academy of Sciences).

G. Enyedi 1980, 'Regional types of living conditions in Hungary' in G. Enyedi and J. Meszaros (eds), *Development of Settlement Systems* (Budapest: Hungarian Academy of Sciences), 205–17.

F. Erdosi 1980, 'The geographic evaluation of the environment of an industrial town' in G. Enyedi and J. Meszaros (eds), *Development of Settlement Systems* (Budapest: Hungarian Academy of Sciences), 159–69.

European Conference of Ministers of Transport 1991, *Prospects for East–West European Transport* (Paris: ECMT Publications).

Z.M. Fallenbuchl 1970, 'The communist pattern of industrialisation'. *Soviet Studies* 21, 458–84.

L. Farago and L. Hrubi 1988, *Development Possibilities of Backward Areas in Hungary* (Pecs: Hungarian Academy of Sciences, Centre for Regional Studies).

J.C. Fisher 1962, 'Planning the cities of socialist man'. *Journal of the American Institute of Planners* 28, 251–68.

J.C. Fisher (ed.) 1966, *City and Regional Planning in Poland* (Ithaca, New York: Cornell University Press).

D. Flaherty 1988, 'Plan market and unequal regional development in Yugoslavia'. *Soviet Studies* 40, 100–24.

H. Forster and B. Kortus 1989, *Social-geographical Problems of the Cracow and Upper Silesia Agglomerations* (Paderborn: Ferdinand Schoningh).

R.A. Francisco 1980, *Agricultural Policies in the USSR and Eastern Europe* (Boulder, Colorado: Westview Press).

R.A. Francisco and R.L. Merritt (eds) 1985, *Berlin Between two Worlds* (Boulder, Colorado: Westview Press).

R.A. Francisco et al. (eds) 1979, *The Political Economy of Collectivised Agriculture* (New York: Pergamon).

A. Fraser 1992, *The Gypsies* (Oxford: Blackwell).

V.D. Freeman 1979, 'Agricultural development and rural change in the GDR'. Sheffield City Polytechnic Department of Geography and Environmental Studies Occasional Paper 1.

R.A. French and F.E.I. Hamilton (eds) 1979, *The Socialist City: Spatial Structure and Urban Policy* (Chichester: John Wiley).

R.J. Fuchs and G.J. Demko 1978, 'The postwar mobility transition in Eastern Europe'. *Geographical Review* 68, 171–82.

R.J. Fuchs and G.J. Demko 1979, 'Geographic inequality under socialism'. *Annals Association of American Geographers* 69, 301–18.

I.R. Gabor 1989, 'Second economy and socialism: the Hungarian experience' in E.L. Feige (ed.) *The Underground Economies: Tax Evasion and Information Distortion* (Cambridge: Cambridge University Press), 339–59.

P. Galasi and G. Sziraczki 1985, 'State regulation enterprise behaviour and the labour market in Hungary 1968–1983'. *Cambridge Journal of Economics* 9, 203–19.

A. Gawryszewski and J. Ksiezak 1977, 'The natural increase and migrations of Poland's population in 1974'. *Przeglad Geograficzny* 49, 453–79. In Polish with an English summary.

T. Gerlach 1976, 'Present-day slope development in the Polish flysch Carpathians'. *Geographical Studies Polish Academy of Sciences* 122.

A. Ghenovici 1985, 'Seashore location of industry: a new phenomenon in the Romanian industry distribution'. *Revue Roumaine: Geographie* 29, 39–45.

E. Gil and L. Starkel 1976, 'Physico-geographical investigations and their importance for the economic development of the flysch Carpathian area'. *Geographia Polonica* 34, 47–61.

S. Gomulka 1986, *Growth Innovation and Reform in Eastern Europe* (Brighton: Wheatsheaf).

G. Gorzelek and R. Szuk 1989, 'Spatial order and Polish disorder: problems in the Polish space economy'. *Geoforum* 20, 175–85.

A. Gosar 1989, 'Structural impact of international tourism in Yugoslavia'. *GeoJournal* 19, 277–83.

K. Grime and G. Weclawowicz 1981, 'Warsaw' in M. Pacione (ed.) *Urban Problems and Planning in the Developed World* (London: Croom Helm), 258–91.

J. Grocholska 1989, 'Spatial policy in the Warsaw agglomeration'. *Geographia Polonica* 56, 55–61.

M. Grochowski 1990, 'Myth and reality in the availability of free medical care: the case of Poland'. *GeoJournal* 22, 445–53.

Z. Hajdu 1987, *Administrative Division and Administrative Geography in Hungary* (Pecs: Hungarian Academy of Sciences, Centre for Regional Studies).

Z. Hajdu 1989, 'Hungary: developments in local administration' in R. Bennett (ed.) *Territory and Administration in Europe* (London: Pinter), 154–67.

Z. Hajdu 1993, *Settlement Network Development Policy in Hungary in the Period of State Socialism* (Pecs: Hungarian Academy of Sciences, Centre for Regional Studies).

B. Hajnal 1989, 'The role of small towns in the development of an under-developed region: the case of Szabolcs-Szatmar county' in P.A. Compton and M. Pecsi (eds) *Theory and Practice in British and Hungarian Geography* (Budapest: Hungarian Academy of Sciences), 257–72.

D.R. Hall 1972, 'The Iron Gates scheme and its significance'. *Geography* 57, 51–5.

D.R. Hall 1984, 'Foreign tourism under socialism: the Albanian "Stalinist" model'. *Annals of Tourism Research* 11, 539–55.

D.R. Hall 1990, 'Stalinism and tourism: a study of Albania and North Korea'. *Annals of Tourism Research* 17, 36–54.

D.R. Hall (ed.) 1993, *Transport and Economic Development in the New Central and Eastern Europe* (London: Belhaven Press).

J.M. Halpern 1967, 'Farming as a way of life: Yugoslav peasant attitudes' in J.E. Karcz (ed.), *Soviet and East European Agriculture* (Berkeley, California: University of California Press), 356–84.

F.E.I. Hamilton 1963, 'Yugoslavia's hydroelectric programme'. *Geography* 48, 70–3.

F.E.I. Hamilton 1964, 'Location factors in the Yugoslav iron and steel industry'. *Economic Geography* 40, 46–64.

F.E.I. Hamilton 1970, 'Changes in the industrial geography of Eastern Europe since 1940'. *Tijdschrift voor Economische en Sociale Geografie* 61, 300–5.

F.E.I. Hamilton 1971, 'Decision making and industrial location in Eastern Europe'. *Transactions Institute of British Geographers* 52, 77–84.

F.E.I. Hamilton 1975, *Poland's Western and Northern Territories* (Oxford: Oxford University Press).

F.E.I. Hamilton 1982, 'Regional policy for Poland: a search for equity'. *Geoforum* 13, 121–32.

C.M. Hann 1990, 'Second economy and civil society'. *Journal of Communist Studies* 6(2), 21–44.

P. Hare *et al.* (eds) 1981, *Hungary: A Decade of Reform* (London: George Allen & Unwin).

E.C. Harrach 1990, 'The reconstruction of Buda Castle after 1945' in J.M. Diefendorf (ed.) *Rebuilding Europe's Bombed Cities* (London: Macmillan), 155–69.

L. Harris 1948, 'Lucimia restituta: rebuilding a Polish village', *Geographical Magazine* 20, 438–43.

J. Hegedus 1987, 'Reconsidering the roles of state and market in socialist housing systems'. *International Journal of Urban and Regional Research* 11, 79–97.

J. Hegedus 1988, 'Inequalities in East European cities'. *International Journal of Urban & Rural Research* 12, 129–32.

J. Hegedus and I. Tosics 1983, 'Housing classes and housing policy: some changes in the Budapest housing market'. *International Journal of Urban and Regional Research* 7, 467–94.

J. Held (ed.) 1980, *The Modernization of Agriculture: Rural Transformation in Hungary* (Boulder, Colorado: Westview Press).

R. Helin 1967, 'The volatile administrative map of Rumania'. *Annals Association of American Geographers* 57, 481–502.

C. Hellier 1989, 'Turmoil in the Balkans'. *Geographical* 61(10), 18–21.

G.W. Hoffman 1956, 'Yugoslavia in transition: industrial expansion and resource base'. *Economic Geography* 32, 294–315.

G.W. Hoffman 1983, 'Energy dependence and policy options in Eastern Europe' in R.G. Jensen *et al.* (eds), *Soviet Natural Resources in the World Economy* (Chicago: Chicago University Press), 659–67.

G. Holden 1989, *The Warsaw Pact: Soviet Society and Bloc Politics* (Oxford: Blackwell).

M. Holocek 1988, 'The electrification of Czecho-Slovak railways: a contribution to the reduction of negative influences upon the natural environment'. *Historicka Geografie* 27, 291–305.

F.D. Holzman 1965, 'More on Soviet bloc trade discrimination'. *Soviet Studies* 17, 44–65.

F.D. Holzman 1985, 'Comecon: a "trade-destroying" customs union?' *Journal of Comparative Economics* 4, 410–23.

G. Horvath 1987, *Development of the Regional Management of the Economy in East Central Europe* (Pecs: Hungarian Academy of Sciences, Centre for Regional Studies).

G. Horvath (ed.) 1993, *Development Strategies for the Alpine-Adriatic Region* (Pecs: Hungarian Academy of Sciences, Centre for Regional Studies).

T. Huszar *et al.* (eds) 1978, *Hungarian Society and Marxist Sociology in the 1970s* (Budapest: Corvina).

I. Ianos 1988, 'Geographical mutations in the territorial distribution of industry in Romania in the second half of the twentieth century'. *Revue Roumaine: Geographie* 32, 85–9.

I. Ianos 1993, 'Comparative analysis of urban and industrial hierarchies of Romanian towns until 1990'. *GeoJournal* 29, 49–56.

E. Illyes 1982, *National Minorities in Romania* (New York: Columbia University Press).

A. Jahn 1972, 'Niveo-eolian processes in the Sudetes Mountains'. *Geographia Polonica* 23, 93–110.

B. Jancar 1987, *Environmental Management in the Soviet Union and Yugoslavia: Structure and Regulation in Communist Federal States* (Durham, North Carolina: Duke University Press).

B. Jancar 1992, 'Chaos as an explanation of the role of environmental groups in East European politics' in W. Rudig (ed.) *Green Politics* Vol.2 (Edinburgh: Edinburgh University Press), 156–84.

S. Jankowski 1990, 'Warsaw: destruction secret town planning 1939–1944 and post-war reconstruction' in J.M. Diefendorf (ed.) *Rebuilding Europe's Bombed Cities* (London: Macmillan), 77–93.

A.C. Janos 1996, 'What was communism: a retrospective in comparative analysis'. *Communist & Post-Communist Societies* 29, 1–24.

I. Jeffries (ed.) 1992, *Industrial Reform in Socialist Countries: from Restructuring to Revolution* (Aldershot: Edward Elgar).

P.N. Jones 1990, 'Recent ethnic German migration from Eastern Europe to the FRG'. *Geography* 75, 249–52.

Z. Karpaty 1986, 'Peripheral settlement in Hungary: the example of Baranya County' in G. Enyedi and J. Veldman (eds.) *Rural Development Issues in Industrialized Countries* (Pecs: Hungarian Academy of Sciences, Centre for Regional Studies), 128–33.

M. Kaser 1965, *Comecon: Integration Problems of the Planned Economies* (Oxford: Oxford University Press).

P. Kende and Z. Strmiska 1987, *Equality and Inequality in Eastern Europe* (Leamington Spa: Berg).

D.A. Kideckel 1993, *The Solitude of Collectivism: Romanian Villagers to Revolution and Beyond* (Ithaca, New York: Cornell University Press).

R.B. King 1973, *Minorities Under Communism: Nationalities as a Source of Tension Among Balkan Communist States* (Cambridge, Massachusetts: Harvard University Press).

V. Klaus 1989, 'Socialist economies, economic reforms and economists: reflections of a Czechoslovak economist'. *Communist Economies* 1, 89–96.

C. Klein and M.J. Reban 1981, *The Politics of Ethnicity in Eastern Europe* (New York: Columbia University Press).

G.D. Knight 1987, 'The nationality question in contemporary Hungarian-Romanian relations'. *Nationalities Papers* 15, 215–27.

G. Kolankiewicz 1980, 'The new "awkward class": the peasant worker in Poland'. *Sociologia Ruralis* 20, 28–43.

J. Kolta 1980, 'The development of the city of Pecs' in G. Enyedi and J. Meszaros (eds), *Development of Settlement Systems* (Budapest: Hungarian Academy of Sciences), 141–7.

A. Korbonski 1965, *The Politics of Socialist Agriculture in Poland 1945–1960* (New York: Columbia University Press).

A. Korbonski 1967, 'Peasant agriculture in socialist Poland since 1956: an alternative to collectivisation' in J.E. Karcz (ed.) *Soviet & East European Agriculture* (Berkeley, California: University of California Press), 411–35.

A. Korbonski 1989, 'The politics of economic reform in Eastern Europe: the last thirty years'. *Soviet Studies* 41, 1–19.

A. Korbonski 1990, 'CMEA economic integration and perestroika 1949–1989'. *Studies in Comparative Communism* 23, 47–72.

P. Korcelli 1990, 'Poland' in C.B. Nam *et al.*, *International Handbook on Internal Migration* (New York: Greenwood Press), 305–22.

P. Korcelli and A. Potrykowska 1979, 'The development of tertiary functions and the administrative hierarchy of places in Poland'. *Przeglad Geograficzny* 51, 209–33. In Polish with an English summary.

J. Kornai 1980a, *Economics of Shortage* (Amsterdam: North Holland).

J. Kornai 1980b, 'The dilemmas of a socialist economy: the Hungarian experience'. *Cambridge Journal of Economics* 4, 147–57.

J. Kornai 1982, 'Shortage as a fundamental problem of centrally planned economies and the Hungarian reform'. *Economics of Planning* 18(3), 103–13.

I.S. Koropeckyj 1972, 'Equalization of regional development in socialist countries: an empirical study'. *Economic Development & Cultural Change* 21, 68–86.

B. Kortus 1985, 'Towards a more humanistic-social approach to Polish industrial geography'. *Geographia Polonica* 51, 207–11.

B. Kortus and J. Adamus 1989, 'Characteristic traits of industry in the Polish Carpathians'. *Zeszyty Naukowe Uniwersytetu Jagiellonskiego Prace Geograficzne* 76, 95–100.

D.J. Kostelancik 1989, 'The Gypsies of Czechoslovakia: political and ideological considerations in the development of policy'. *Studies in Comparative Communism* 22, 307–21.

B. Kostic 1983, 'The aluminium industry 1975–1981'. *Yugoslav Survey: Record of Facts & Information* 24, 51–8.

I. Kovach 1991, 'Rediscovering small-scale enterprise in rural Hungary' in S. Whatmore *et al.* (eds) *Rural Enterprise: Shifting Perspectives on Small-scale production* (London: Fulton), 78–96.

M.M. Kovacs 1992, 'Jews and Hungarians: a view after the transition'. Woodrow Wilson Center East European Studies Occasional Paper 35.

Z. Kovacs 1989, 'The effects of a national border: human geographical approaches' in P.A. Compton and M. Pecsi (eds) *Theory and Practice in British and Hungarian Geography* (Budapest: Hungarian Academy of Sciences), 75–91.

Z. Kovacs 1990, 'Rich and poor in the Budapest housing market'. *Journal of Communist Studies* 6(2), 110–24.

B. Kovrig 1986, 'The Magyars in Romania: problems of a 'coinhabiting nationality'. *Sudosteuropa* 35, 475–90.

J.S. Kowalski 1986, 'Regional conflicts in Poland: spatial polarisation in a centrally planned economy'. *Environment & Planning* 18a, 599–617.

G. Krajko 1980, 'Main tendencies in the development of Szeged' in G. Enyedi and J. Meszaros (eds) *Development of Settlement Systems* (Budapest: Hungarian Academy of Sciences), 131–9.

J.M. Kramer 1985, 'Soviet–CMEA energy ties'. *Problems of Communism* 34(4), 32–47.

J.M. Kramer 1987, 'The environmental crisis in Poland' in F. Singleton (ed.) *Environmental Problems in the Soviet Union & Eastern Europe* (London: Lynne Rienner), 149–67.

J.M. Kramer 1990, *The Energy Gap in Eastern Europe* (Lexington: Heath).

M.W. Kraujalis 1972, 'Artificial heat over the territory of Poland'. *Geographia Polonica* 21, 41–51.

J. Kruczala 1990, 'Tourism planning in Poland'. *Annals of Tourism Research* 17, 69–78.

A. Kuklinski 1976, 'Strong and weak regions in socio-economic policies'. *Przeglad Geograficzny* 48, 389–400. In Polish with an English summary.

R. Kulikowski 1989, 'Agricultural geography on the current work on the plan of the country's spatial organisation up to 2000'. *Geographia Polonica* 56, 115–9.

E. Kwiatkowska 1976, 'New forms of rural settlement in the voivodship of Torun in the 30 years of People's Poland'. *Przeglad Geograficzny* 48, 635–48. In Polish with an English summary.

L. Lacko 1986, 'The place of village development in the settlement development policy of Hungary' in G. Enyedi and J. Veldman (eds), *Rural Development Issues in Industrialized Countries* (Pecs: Hungarian Academy of Sciences, Centre for Regional Studies), 29–33.

M. Laki 1985, 'Central economic management and the enterprise crisis in Hungary'. *Acta Oeconomica* 35, 195–211.

Z. Landau and J. Tomaszewski 1985, *The Polish economy in the Twentieth Century* (London: Croom Helm).

C.S. Leff 1988, *National Conflict in Czechoslovakia: The Making and Remaking of a State 1918–1987* (Princeton: Princeton University Press).

S. Leszczycki 1976, 'Methods to activate less developed areas'. *Przeglad Geograficzny* 48, 379–88. In Polish with an English summary.

T. Lijewski 1982, 'Transport in Poland', *Transport Reviews* 2, 1–21.

T. Lijewski 1985, 'The spread of industry as a consequence of the location of new factories in Poland 1945–1982'. *Geographia Polonica* 51, 199–206.

W.O. McCagg 1991, 'Gypsy policy in socialist Hungary and Czechoslovakia 1945–1989'. *Nationalities Papers* 19, 313–36.

C.A. Macartney 1947, 'The Slovak-Hungarian frontier'. *Geographical Magazine* 20, 293–5.

P. Machon and A. Dingsdale 1989, 'Public transport in a socialist capital: Budapest'. *Geography* 74, 159–62.

R.J. MacIntyre 1988, 'The small enterprise and agricultural initiatives in Bulgaria: institutional innovation without reform'. *Soviet Studies* 40, 602–15. See also discussion in Vol. 41 (1989), 646–53.

F. Maclean 1951, 'Yugoslavia: the land and the people'. *Geographical Magazine* 24, 22–31.

P. Marer 1984, 'The political economy of Soviet relations with Eastern Europe' in S.M. Terry (ed.) *Soviet Policy in Eastern Europe* (New Haven, Connecticutt: Yale University Press), 155–88.

P. Marer and J.M. Montias 1982, 'The CMEA' in A.M. El-Agraa (ed.) *International Economic Integration* (New York: St Martin's Press), 102–38.

M-C Maurel 1989, 'Administrative reforms in Eastern Europe: an overview' in R. Bennett (ed.) *Territory and Administration in Europe* (London: Pinter), 111–23.

R.E.H. Mellor 1975, *Eastern Europe: A Geography of the Comecon Countries* (London: Macmillan).

H. Mendershausen 1959, 'Terms of trade between the Soviet Union and smaller communist countries'. *Review of Economics & Statistics* 2, 106–18.

R.L. Merritt 1973, 'Infrastructure change in Berlin'. *Annals Association of American Geographers* 63, 58–70.

D. Meze 1983, 'Mountain farms in Slovenia'. *Geographica Iugoslavica* 5, 47–54.

K. Mihailovic 1972, *Regional Development: Experiences and Prospects in Eastern Europe* (The Hague: Mouton).

P. Mihalyi 1992, *Socialist Investment Cycles: Analysis in Retrospect* (Dordrecht: Kluwer Academic Publishers).

B. Milanovic 1987, 'Patterns of regional growth in Yugoslavia 1952–1983'. *Journal of Development Economics* 15, 1–19.

G. Minassian 1992, 'Bulgaria's industrial growth and structure 1970–1989'. *Soviet Studies* 44, 699–712.

J.M. Montias 1968, 'Socialist industrialisation and trade in machinery products' in A.A. Brown and E. Neuberger (eds) *International Trade and Central Planning: An Analysis of Economic Interactions* (Berkeley, California: University of California Press), 130–58.

J.M. Montias 1980, 'Romania's foreign trade between east and west' in P. Marer and J.M. Montias (eds) *East Europe: Integration and East–West Trade* (Bloomington, Indiana: Indiana University Press), 321–54.

W.B. Morgan 1989, 'Recent government policy and private agriculture in Poland'. *Resource Management & Optimization* 6, 291–305.

W.B. Morgan 1990, 'Some aspects of recent improvements in the productivity of private agriculture in Poland'. *Geographia Polonica* 57, 99–110.

H.W. Morton 1979, 'Housing problems and policies of Eastern Europe and the Soviet Union'. *Studies in Comparative Communism* 12, 300–21.

R.D. Mueller *et al.* 1993, *Market Changes and their Impact on the Structure of Food*

*Distribution Systems in the Impaired Economies of Central Europe: A Case Study of Hungary* (Leicester: De Montfort University, Leicester Business School).

J. Musil 1987, 'Housing policy and the sociospatial structure of cities in a socialist country: the example of Prague'. *International Journal of Urban & Regional Research* 11, 27–36.

J. Musil and Z. Rysavy 1983, 'Urban and regional processes under capitalism and socialism: a case study from Czechoslovakia'. *International Journal of Urban & Regional Research* 7, 495–527.

C.K. Nagy 1993, 'Local development strategies' in A. Duro (ed.) *Spatial Research and the Social-political Changes* (Pecs: Hungarian Academy of Sciences, Centre for Regional Studies), 103–7.

D.N. Nelson (ed.) 1983, *Communism and the Politics of Inequalities* (Lexington, Kentucky: Heath & Co).

I.B. Neumann 1988, 'Soviet foreign policy towards her European allies: a model'. *Nordic Journal of Soviet & East European Studies* 5(2), 69–97.

W. Niewiarowski 1976, 'Some problems in the evaluation of the natural environment for the demands of tourism and recreation: a case study of the Bydgoszcz region'. *Geographia Polonica* 34, 241–54.

K. Okolicsanyi 1988, 'Hungarian experiments continue' in V. Mastny (ed.) *Soviet-East European Survey 1986–7* (Boulder, Colorado: Westview Press), 250–63.

E. Orosz 1990, 'Regional inequalities in the Hungarian health system'. *Geoforum* 21, 245–59.

M. Palairet 1992, 'Ramiz Sadiku: a case study in the industrialisation of Kosovo'. *Soviet Studies* 44, 897–912.

I. Palne Kovacs 1988, *Chance of Local Independence in Hungary* (Pecs: Hungarian Academy of Sciences, Centre for Regional Studies).

J. Paul 1990, 'Reconstruction of the city centre of Dresden: planning and building during the 1950s' in J.M. Diefendorf (ed.) *Rebuilding Europe's Bombed Cities* (London: Macmillan), 170–89.

S.K. Pavlowitch 1989, *The Improbable Survivor: Yugoslavia and its Problems 1918–1988* (Columbus: Ohio State University Press).

M.V. Pearlman 1990, 'Conflicts and constraints in Bulgaria's tourism sector'. *Annals of Tourism Research* 17, 103–22.

K. Pecsi 1989, 'The extremist path of economic development in Eastern Europe'. *Communist Economies* 1, 97–109.

M. Pecsi and F. Probald (eds) 1974, *Man and Environment* (Budapest: Hungarian Academy of Sciences).

J. Pelzman 1977, 'Trade creation and trade diversion in the CMEA 1954–1970'. *American Economic Review* 4, 713–22.

C.F. Pennacchio 1995, 'The East German communists and the origin of the Berlin blockade crisis'. *East European Quarterly* 29, 293–314.

D.S. Pensley 1995, 'City planning and state policy in the GDR: the example of Neubaugebiet Hellersdorf'. *International Journal of Urban & Regional Research* 19, 549–75.

E. Perger 1989, 'An overview of East European developments' in R. Bennett (ed.) *Territory and Administration in Europe* (London: Pinter), 93–110.

M. Persanyi 1990, 'The rural environment in a post-socialist economy: the case of Hungary' in P. Lowe *et al.* (eds) *Technological Change and the Rural Environment* (London: David Fulton), 33–52.

C.G. Pickvance 1988, 'Employers' labour markets and redistribution under state socialism: an interpretation of housing policy in Hungary 1960–1983'. *Sociology* 22, 193–214.

F.T. Pine and P.T. Bogdanowicz 1982, 'Policy response and alternative strategy: the process of change in a Polish highland village'. *Dialectical Anthropology* 7(2), 67–80.

B. Pleskovic and M. Dolenc 1982, 'Regional development and multinational country: the case of Yugoslavia'. *International Regional Science Review* 7, 1–24.

N.J.G. Pounds 1969, *Eastern Europe* (London: Longman).

N.J.G. Pounds and N. Spulber 1957, *Resources and Planning in Eastern Europe* (Bloomington Indiana: Indiana University Press).

G. Prawelska-Skrzypek 1988, 'Social differentiation in old central city neighbourhoods in Poland'. *Area* 20, 221–32.

S. Puia and C. Hirtopeanu 1990, 'Coming out of the dark: family planning in Romania'. *Planned Parenthood in Europe* 19(2), 5–6.

J. Regulaska 1987, 'Urban development under socialism: the Polish experience'. *Urban Geography* 8, 321–39.

G. Ritter and J.G. Hajdu 1989, 'The East–West German boundary'. *Geographical Review* 79, 326–44.

B. Rogalewska 1978, 'Tendencies in the location of recreation centres controlled by establishments in Poland until 1971', *Geographical Studies Polish Academy of Sciences* 129.

B. Rogalewska 1980, 'On the spatial structure of summer house building in Poland'. *Przeglad Geograficzny* 52, 575–82.

P. Ronnas 1982, 'Centrally-planned urbanization: the case of Romania'. *Geografiska Annaler* 64b, 143–51.

P. Ronnas 1987, 'Agrarian change and economic development in rural Romania: a case study of the Oas region'. *Geografiska Annaler* 69b, 51–63.

P. Ronnas 1989, 'Turning the Romanian peasant into a new socialist man: an assessment of rural development policy in Romania'. *Soviet Studies* 41, 543–59.

S. Rosenbladt 1991, 'Environmental concerns in Poland' in G. Stokes (ed.) *From Stalinism to Pluralism: A Documentary History of Eastern Europe since 1945* (Oxford: Oxford University Press), 188–92.

J. Rostowski 1989, 'The decay of socialism and the growth of private enterprise in Poland'. *Soviet Studies* 41, 194–214.

D.S. Rugg 1985, *The World's Landscapes: Eastern Europe* (London: Longman).

J. Sallnow 1985, 'Yugoslavia: tourism in a socialist federal state'. *Tourism Management* 6, 113–24.

S. Sampson 1984, *National Integration Through Socialist Planning: an Anthropological Study of a Romanian New Town* (Boulder, Colorado: Westview Press/East European Monographs).

P. Sandstrom and O. Sjoberg 1991, 'Albanian economic performance: stagnation in the 1980s'. *Soviet Studies* 43, 931–47.

B. Sarfalvi (ed.) 1970, *Recent Population Movements in East European Countries* (Budapest: Hungarian Academy of Sciences).

B. Sarfalvi (ed.) 1971, *The Changing Face of the Great Hungarian Plain* (Budapest: Hungarian Academy of Sciences).

B. Sarfalvi (ed.) 1975, *Urbanization in Europe* (Budapest: Hungarian Academy of Sciences).

B. Sarfalvi 1980, 'Regional divergence in the educational level of rural settlements' in G. Enyedi and J. Meszaros (eds) *Development of Settlement Systems* (Budapest: Akademiai Kiado), 219–24.

C.T. Saunders (ed.) 1980, *East and West in the Energy Squeeze* (London: Macmillan).

G. Schopflin 1988, 'The Stalinist experience in Eastern Europe'. Survey: *Journal of East–West Relations* 30(4), 124–47.

G. Schopflin 1993, *Politics in Eastern Europe 1945–1992* (Oxford: Blackwell).

J. Senegacnik *et al.* 1983, *The Direction of Regional Development of Slovenia: Slovene Alps-Northeastern Slovenia-Bela Krajina* (Ljubljana: Institute of Geography, Geographica Slovenica 14). In Slovene with an English summary.

T. Sharp 1975, *The Wartime Alliance and the Zonal Division of Germany* (Oxford: Clarendon Press).

D. Shears 1971, *The Ugly Frontier* (London: Chatto & Windus).

P.S. Shoup (ed.) 1990, *Problems of Balkan Security: Southeastern Europe in the 1990s* (London: University Press of America/Wilson Center Press).

R. Siemienska 1983, 'Women and social movements in Poland'. *Women & Politics* 6(4), 5–35.

R. Siemienska 1985, 'Women work and sex equality in Poland: reality and its social perception' in S.L. Wolchik and A.G. Meyer (eds) *Women, State and Party in Eastern Europe* (Durham, North Carolina: Duke University Press), 344–61.

J.A.A. Sillince 1985, 'The housing market in the Budapest urban region 1949–1983'. *Urban Studies* 22, 141–9.

J.A.A. Sillince 1987, 'Regional policy in Hungary: objectives and achievements'. *Transactions Institute of British Geographers* 12, 451–64.

J.A.A. Sillince (ed.) 1990, *Housing Policies in the Soviet Union & Eastern Europe* (London: Routledge).

J. Simmie 1989, 'Self-management and town planning in Yugoslavia'. *Town Planning Review* 60, 271–86.

M. Simmons 1988, *Berlin: The Dispossessed City* (London: Hamish Hamilton).

F. Singleton 1987, 'National Parks and the conservation of nature in Yugoslavia' in F. Singleton (ed.) *Environmental Problems in the Soviet Union and Eastern Europe* (London: Lynne Rienner), 183–98; see also pp. 169–82 on Czechoslovakia.

O. Sjoberg 1989, 'A note on the regional dimension of post-war demographic development in Albania'. *Nordic Journal of Soviet & East European Studies* 6, 91–121.

O. Sjoberg 1991a, Rural Change and Development in Albania (Boulder, Colorado: Westview Press).

O. Sjoberg 1991b, 'Rural retention in Albania: administrative restrictions on urban-bound migration'. *East European Quarterly* 28, 205–33.

M. Skrodzki 1972, 'Present day water and wind erosion of soils in northeast Poland'. *Geographia Polonica* 23, 77–91.

C.G. Smith 1948, 'The Yugoslav Youth Railway'. *Geographical Magazine* 20, 470–6.

J.E. Smith 1961, *The Berlin Crisis of 1961* (Baltimore, Maryland: Johns Hopkins University Press).

V. Sobell 1984, *The Red Market: Industrial Cooperation and Specialisation in Comecon* (Aldershot: Gower).

M. Sokolowska 1981, 'Women in decision-making elites: the case of Poland' in C. Epstein and R.L. Coser (eds) *Access to Power* (London: George Allen & Unwin), 90–114.

A. Stasiak 1977, 'Changes in the professional structure of the rural population in Poland'. *Przeglad Geograficzny* 49, 677–88.

A. Stasiak 1992, 'Problems of depopulation of rural areas in Poland after 1950'. *Landscape & Urban Planning* 22, 161–76.

A. Stasiak 1993, 'Development of spatial planning in Poland on regional and countrywide scale' in A. Duro (ed.) *Spatial Research and the Social-political Changes* (Pecs: Hungarian Academy of Sciences, Centre for Regional Studies), 7–14.

M. Stefanovic 1994, 'The iron and steel industry 1976–1982'. *Yugoslav Survey: Record of Facts & Information* 25, 97–108.

M. Stewart 1990, 'Gypsies, work and civil society'. *Journal of Communist Studies* 6(2), 140–62.

V. Stipetic 1982, 'The development of the peasant economy in socialist Yugoslavia' in R. Stojanovic (ed.) *The Functioning of the Yugoslav Economy* (New York: M.E. Sharpe), 166–201.

G. Stokes (ed.) 1991, *From Stalinism to Pluralism: A Documentary History of Eastern Europe since 1945* (Oxford: Clarendon Press).

T. Stryakiewicz 1985, 'The relationships between the location of the agricultural processing industry and the produce base of the Poznan region'. *Geographia Polonica* 51, 189–98.

M. Suscevic 1987, 'Yugoslav Railways 1979–1986'. *Yugoslav Survey: a Record of Facts & Information* 28, 61–76

J.S. Sutterlin and D. Klein 1989, *Berlin: From Symbol of Confrontation to Keystone of Stability* (New York: Praeger).

N. Swain 1985, *Collective Farms which Work?* (Cambridge: Cambridge University Press).

N. Swain 1990, 'Small cooperatives and economic work partnerships in the computing industries: exceptions that prove the rule'. *Journal of Communist Studies* 6(2), 85–109.

L. Sykora 1995, 'Prague' in J. Berry and S. McGreal (eds) *European Cities: Planning Systems and Property Markets* (London: Spon), 321–44.

L. Szamuely 1986, 'Prospects of economic reforms in the European CMEA countries in the 1980s'. *Acta Oeconomica* 36, 55–65.

M.S. Szczpanski 1993, 'Planning housing and the community: the case of Tychy, Poland'. *Town Planning Review* 64, 1–22.

I. Szelenyi 1978, 'Spatial inequalities in state socialist redistributive economies'. *International Journal of Comparative Sociology* 19, 63–87.

I. Szelenyi 1983, *Urban Inequalities under State Socialism* (Oxford: Oxford University Press).

I. Szelenyi 1985, *Socialist Entrepreneurs: Embourgeoisement in Rural Hungary* (Cambridge: Polity Press).

I. Szelenyi 1987, 'Urban inequalities, housing inequalities and occupational segregation in state socialist economies'. *International Journal of Urban and Regional Research* 11, 61–78.

I. Szelenyi 1988, *Social Entrepreneurs: Embourgeoisement in Rural Hungary* (Cambridge: Polity Press).

I. Szelenyi 1989, 'Housing policy in the emergent socialist mixed economy of Eastern Europe'. *Housing Studies* 4, 167–76.

I. Szelenyi and R. Manchin 1986, *Peasants Proletarians Entrepreneurs: Transformation of Rural Social Structures under State Socialism* (Madison: University of Wisconsin).

H. Szulc 1978, 'Property structure and types of transformation in the layouts of West Pomeranian villages in the period from 1945 to 1975'. *Przeglad Geograficzny* 50, 87–99. In Polish with an English summary.

B. Szymanski 1978, 'The initial results of investigations concerning the degree of afforestation in the Kielce region'. *Przeglad Geograficzny* 50, 603–19. In Polish with an English summary.

M. Tardos 1983, 'The increasing role and ambivalent reception of small enterprises in Hungary'. *Journal of Comparative Economics* 7(3), 277–87.

Z. Taylor 1989. 'Contemporary trends in the Polish transport system'. *Geographia Polonica* 56, 179–94.

C. Thomas 1982, 'Migration and urban growth in Yugoslavia'. *East European Quarterly* 16, 199–216.

C. Thomas 1987, 'Ethnic minorities in Yugoslavia'. *Irish Slavonic Studies* 8, 59–85.

C. Thomas and M. Vojvoda 1973, 'Alpine communities in transition: Bohinj Yugoslavia'. *Geography* 58, 217–26.

J. Timar 1989, 'New features of the linkages between tanyas (farmstead settlements) and towns in the Great Hungarian Plain' in P.A. Compton and M. Pecsi (eds) *Theory and Practice in British and Hungarian Geography* (Budapest: Hungarian Academy of Sciences), 273–94.

V. Tismaneanu n.d., 'Understanding national socialism: a comparative approach to the history of Romanian communism'. Wilson Center Smithsonian Institution East European Program Occasional Paper 25.

J.F. Tismer *et al.* (eds) 1987, *Transport and Economic Development: Soviet Union and Eastern Europe* (Berlin: Osteuropa Institut an der Freien Universitat Berlin/ Verlag Duncker & Humblot).

S. Todorov 1991, 'Name changes in Bulgaria' in G. Stokes (ed.) *From Stalinism to Pluralism: A Documentary History of Eastern Europe since 1945* (Oxford: Oxford University Press), 232–4.

F. Tomczak 1990, 'Farming and socialism in Poland: towards a new understanding of the peasant question' in K-E. Wadekin (ed.) *Communist Agriculture: Farming in the Soviet Union and Eastern Europe* (London: Routledge), 279–89.

I. Tosics 1987, 'Privatization in housing policy: the case of Western countries and that of Hungary'. *International Journal of Urban and Regional Research* 11, 61–78.

I. Tosics 1988, 'Inequalities in East European cities'. *International Journal of Urban and Regional Research* 12, 133–6.

J. Toth 1980, 'Characteristic features of the development of towns on the Great Hungarian Plain' in G. Enyedi and J. Meszaros (eds) *Development of Settlement Systems* (Budapest: Hungarian Academy of Sciences), 123–30.

J. Toth 1993, 'Historical and today's socio-economic conditions of regionalism in Hungary' in A. Duro (ed.) *Spatial Research and the Social-political changes* (Pecs: Hungarian Academy of Sciences, Centre for Regional Studies), 15–28.

J. Toth 1994, 'Urbanization and spatial structure in Hungary'. *GeoJournal* 32, 343–50.

O. Ulc 1988, 'Gypsies in Czechoslovakia'. *Eastern European Politics and Societies* 2, 306–33.

L. Valentine *et al.* 1987, 'Short notes on health and health care in Eastern Europe'. *Survey: Journal of East–West Relations* 29(4), 105–22.

J.M. van Brabant 1974, 'On the origins and tasks of the CMEA'. *Osteuropa Wirtschaft* 3, 181–209.

J.M. van Brabant 1979, 'Another look at the origins of East European cooperation'. *Osteuropa Wirtschaft* 4, 243–66.

J.M. van Brabant 1987, 'Economic adjustment and the future of socialist economic integration'. *East European Politics and Society* 1, 75–112.

J.M. van Brabant 1988, 'Production specialization in the CMEA: concepts and empirical evidence'. *Journal of Common Market Studies* 3, 287–315.

J.M. van Brabant 1989, *Economic Integration in Eastern Europe: A Handbook* (London: Harvester Wheatsheaf).

I. Vasary 1987, '*Beyond the plain: social change in a Hungarian village*' (Boulder, Colorado: Westview Press).

I. Vasary 1989, 'The sin of Transdanubia: the one-child system in rural Hungary'. *Continuity and Change* 4, 429–68.

I. Vasary 1990, 'Competing paradigms: peasant farming and collectivisation in a Balaton community'. *Journal of Communist Studies* 6(2), 163–82.

K. Verdery 1983, *Transylvanian Villagers: Three Centuries of Political, Economic and Ethnic Change* (Berkeley, California: University of California Press).

K. Verdery 1991, *National Identity under Socialism: Cultural Politics in Ceausescu's Romania* (Berkeley, California: University of California Press).

O. Vidlakova and P. Zarecky 1989, 'Czechoslovakia: the development of public administration' in R. Bennett (ed.) *Territory and Administration in Europe*, (London: Pinter), 168–79.

I. Volgyes 1974, *Environmental Deterioration in the Soviet Union and Eastern Europe* (New York: Praeger).

I. Volgyes 1989, *Politics in Eastern Europe* (Pacific Grove, California: Brooks/Cole Publishing Company).

I. Vriser 1981, 'The distribution of manufacturing industries in Yugoslavia'. *Geografica Slovenica* 12, 5–38. In Serbo-Croat with an English summary.

I. Vriser 1992, 'Industrialization of Slovenia'. *GeoJournal* 27, 365–70.

B. Vukonic and D. Tkalac 1984, 'Tourism and urban revitalization: a case study of Porec, Yugoslavia'. *Annals of Tourism Research* 11, 591–605.

W. Wallace and R. Clarke 1986, *Comecon Trade and the West* (London: Pinter).

L. Webster and C. Garret 1984, 'The other Poland' in R. Chamberlain *et al.* (eds) *Great Little Railways* (London: BBC), 87–114.

A. Werwicki 1974, 'A model of the internal structure of the medium-sized Polish city'. *Geographia Polonica* 28, 117–25.

A. Werwicki 1982, 'Problems of small towns in Maria Kielczewska-Zaleska's research'. *Przeglad Geograficzny* 53, 263–8. In Polish with an English summary.

J. Wilczynski 1982, *The Economics of Socialism* (London: George Allen & Unwin).

H. Wilkens 1981, *The Two German Economies* (Aldershot: Gower).

O. Wilson 1971, 'The Belgrade–Bar railroad: an essay in economic and political geography' in G.W. Hoffman (ed.) *Eastern Europe: Essays in Geographical Problems* (London: Methuen), 365–93.

J. Winiecki 1986, 'Are Soviet-type economies entering an era of long-term decline?' *Soviet Studies* 38, 325–48.

J. Winiecki 1988, *The Distorted World of Soviet-type Economies* (London: Routledge & Kegan Paul).

M. Wojecki 1977, 'Greek emigration in Peoples Democracies'. *Przeglad Geograficzny* 49, 507–13.

A. Wrona 1975, 'Problems of erosive degradation and protection of land surface in the Rybnik Coal Basin'. *Przeglad Geograficzny* 47, 519–37. In Polish with an English summary.

M.L. Wyzan 1989, 'The Bulgarian experience with centrally planned agriculture: lessons for social reformers' in K.R. Gray (ed.) *Contemporary Soviet Agriculture: Comparative Perspectives* (Ames, Iowa: Iowa State University).

R.J. Zaniewski 1989, 'Housing inequalities under socialism: a geographical perspective'. *Studies in Comparative Communism* 22, 291–306.

R.J. Zaniewski 1991, 'Housing inequalities under socialism: the case of Poland'. *Geoforum* 22, 39–53.

H. Zimon 1979, 'Regional inequalities in Poland 1960–1975'. *Economic Geography* 55, 242–52.

E. Zizmond 1992, 'The collapse of the Yugoslav economy'. *Soviet Studies* 44, 101–12.

G. Zovanyi 1986, 'Structural change in a system of urban places: the twentieth century evolution of Hungary's urban settlement network'. *Regional Studies* 20, 47–71.

A. Zurek 1975, 'Spatial structure of urban migrations in the Kielce voivodship'. *Polish Academy of Sciences Geographical Studies* 113. In Polish with an English summary.

A. Zurkowa and J. Ksiezak 1980, 'Elements of spatial structure of internal migrations in Poland'. *Przeglad Geograficzny* 52, 81–102. In Polish with an English summary.

# 3

# THE TRANSITION
## Political and social issues

Eastern Europe has become a region of critical importance for the stability of the continent after half a century of cold war separation from the West (Michalak and Gibb 1992). M. Gorbachev's independence declaration to Eastern Europe, revoking the Brezhnev doctrine which insisted on the primacy of the Soviet-bloc interest, signalled a major change in military strategy. Suppression of the 'Prague Spring' in 1968 blocked any move towards pluralism in Eastern Europe and reformist tendencies including the Hungarian NEM were always constrained by the need to maintain the communist monopoly on power. Yet it was clear to Gorbachev that the FSU could neither win a nuclear war nor sustain an effective *blitzkrieg* capability in Europe. More fundamentally perhaps, the Soviets came to reject the long-held Leninist view that war between the capitalist and socialist worlds was inevitable (Stokes 1991). Belief that war might be averted by political means paved the way for the achievements of the Gorbachev years: arms reductions and more effective independence for Eastern Europe. Reducing military tension and scaling down the ideological cold war was, in turn, fundamental to an integration of the Soviet economy with the capitalist world; very necessary in the light of the faltering performance of the command economy during the 1980s. For the strategy of supplying raw materials at concessionary prices and providing a market for large sections of East European industry could no longer maintain steady growth. Investment in Siberian resource regions was falling, manufacturing industry was not being modernised and large amounts of gold were being sold to pay for essential imports.

At first there seemed little likelihood of immediate political change. Gorbachev anticipated that reform of the governing communist parties would allow them to stay in office. But he failed to appreciate the pressure for change building up as major institutions were undermined, and through his defence of the Communist Party of the Soviet Union he became a victim of his initial success. Hungary and Poland were the first countries to seek reform but their respective leaderships (under J. Kadar and W. Jaruzelski) were hardly contemplating radical departures from communist orthodoxy, while other regimes remained staunchly conservative in outlook. Towards the end of the

1980s there was still repression, with secret police activity in Albania, FGDR and Romania, so that both East Europeans and Western commentators remained gloomy through 1988 and even the early months of 1989. Reform motivated by perestroika began in Poland in 1987 but there was no immediate consensus over economic policy because price rises the following year provoked widespread strikes and it was these that were a prelude to more radical change. The Communist government resigned and Gorbachev accepted the partially free election that ushered in a Solidarity-led administration. Then further peaceful regime change in Hungary led on to effective mass demonstrations in Bulgaria, FGDR and FCSFR (Mason 1992). Finally, against all considered predictions, there was violent confrontation in Romania between demonstrators and the security police in which the army (very significantly) declined to support the Ceausescu regime; while the tentative reform in Albania in 1990 precipitated the removal of communist hardliners early in 1991 (Barany 1992). So the decade ended in explosive fashion as, one by one, the communist parties found their positions untenable (Schopflin 1990). But although several regimes initially used repressive measures to retain their power monopoly the transition was relatively peaceful.

Eventually it will be for the historians to explain the nature and significance of this latest round of revolution. But it is clear that while the FSU was prepared to allow change, given the collapse of supra-national state authority, the population was in some respects proactive (Pearson 1995). Environmental problems associated with Chernobyl produced 'green nationalism', assisted by a media revolution that was also helpful to other opposition groups; while there was 'demographic flux' involving the (often involuntary) departure of minorities from host states. The 'Dallas Complex', yearning for better material conditions, was also a factor. Indeed, the second economy's development in communist Hungary is seen as significant because 'bourgeoisification' resumed among farmers and, even on a small scale, contributed to a silent revolution from below (Gabor 1991). Despite misgivings over the increased prosperity of the peasants (the price of an improved food supply), country people were able to start working for their own benefit and ultimately for the benefit of a new system (Ziolkowski 1993). At the same time Mihalyi (1992) suggests that the economic difficulties were much more serious than most people realised. Politically motivated management strategies were operating in a semi-feudal 'jungle world' of secretiveness and dishonesty where progress depended primarily on personal connections within the nomenclature hierarchy. Thus the progressive legitimation of a second economy that once operated as a disruptive force on the margins of legality could well have sapped morale in a first economy often apparently devoid of economic logic and incapable of rewarding its most successful managers beyond the provision of a house and a car (Volgyes 1989).

So there could be several components to a gradualist approach that would see limited reform gathering an inexorable momentum for further change. J.

Szmatka (1993) refers to a threshold situation when the system is poised to transform itself. To operate smoothly the system must be 'finished' but in such a state that it cannot easily change without the risk of dissolution. Reform to enhance legitimation may be counter-productive if party members lack ideological motivation. Despite a great increase in the proletariat it is doubtful if the new working class was very conscious politically. The small pre-war working class subscribed to a revolutionary political culture and took a proprietorial interest in communism. But they were swamped by a tidal wave of unskilled migrants and commuters from the villages who took a much more pragmatic view and were easily disenchanted when the socialist dream remained unfulfilled. Vested interests remained a stumbling-block for the reformers who, like Gorbachev himself, could hardly conceive of change getting out of hand. Yet as ideology became trivialised, the defensive bastions were being steadily undermined, even within regimes that excluded reform in favour of a continuing 'revolution' against private ownership and enterprise: for example, the 'extremism' in Romania (Pecsi 1989). The result has been a radical transformation from totalitarian regimes to democratic systems with political pluralism to allow civil society to express itself freely.

Political change has certainly been potent. If the toleration of opposition parties and Round Table discussions are seen as the critical events, then the process started in Poland in 1988 was followed by elections in 1989 which allowed opposition parties to contest a majority of the seats. In Hungary new parties were formed late in 1988 with Round Tables in 1989 and elections in 1990. In 1989 Round Tables were convened in the FCSFR and FGDR, followed by Albania, Bulgaria and Romania in 1990 (with the situation in FFYR confused by the trends in individual republics) (Staniszkis 1991). In contrast to the situation in Hungary, Poland and some parts of FFYR, communist parties initially tried to stay in power by employing repressive measures and this made change in the FGDR and Romania especially dramatic. In Romania the option of reform was resisted until the very end of 1989 when the heckling of the president was shown on state television in the immediate aftermath of demonstrations in the provincial city of Timisoara. This led on to the replacement of the Communist Party by the National Salvation Front and execution of the former leader. On the whole, there have been few outbreaks of popular unrest and little sign of mass migration to the West. Political life is generally peaceful with only occasional exceptions. Fascist groups in FGDR have demonstrated against immigration and in Albania in 1994 an opposition Alliance Party meeting was disrupted by pro-government activists in Shkoder: a politically active and independent-minded Catholic stronghold that was a Democratic Party bastion in the 1992 election.

Such an interpretation may be modified by a continuity thesis arguing for a sideways transfer from state capitalism, guided by totalitarian regimes, to market capitalism with a liberal plural political culture, rather than revolutionary change from real socialism to European liberalism. For socialist elites have not necessarily disappeared but have sometimes managed to transform their power base from the political to the economic realm. Such a view would moderate any notion of social disorganisation and institutional vacuum. There are still many conservative elements in political life and in public administration, evident through the survival of some former bureaucratic practices and the retention of security police forces which helped to bring the 'miners' to the streets of Bucharest in 1990 and 1991 and, it is widely believed, had a hand in the ethnic violence in Targu Mures in 1991. As free elections were held throughout Eastern Europe, the former communist parties were reorganised through the adoption of social democratic credentials. Only in the FGDR (and to a lesser extent the Czech Republic) has there been a determined drive against the communist elite and especially those who cooperated with the secret police. In FGDR action against Stasi (with its 100,000 employees and 140,000 freelancers out of a population of 17mn.) extended to people who profited through holding party membership, leading to a comprehensive clear-out of functionaries on the grounds of their unreliability. Business is still affected by the activities of former party activists and security agents with prominent positions in former SOEs. In using their accumulated wealth to set up their own enterprises they may be helped by former party colleagues to secure attractive auction prices. Influence may also be used to get help from conservative bankers who are happy to lend to the managers of former SOEs, thereby helping the least efficient smokestack industries rather than more deserving new companies. Thus any unbounded belief in the consolidation of democracy runs the risk of emphasising voluntarism over 'persistent sociological realities' (Jowitt 1996, p.5). Legacies cannot be ignored, whether they are in the landscape (Rugg 1994) or in the public mind, and therefore stable democratic institutions may seem unlikely in the present climate of global disintegration and in the context of prevailing tensions (Carlton *et al.* 1996).

But despite reservations, the scale of the change should not be glossed over. The market economy is prompting a restructuring of industry geared to meet public demand rather than plan targets (so often attained only through high investment and subsidy) and expectations of a gradual improvement in material conditions seem realistic. More than half the people of Poland are now supported by private business. Throughout Eastern Europe pluralism is evident and there is now scope for all elements in society to influence the future. For people in general are beginning to sample newly won freedoms and to overcome the stark contrasts that once separated them from the party hierarchies. Communist party monopolies have been overcome and as new social systems emerge there is scope for free civil society to exist apart from the state (Kraus and Liebowitz 1995; Rau 1991), owning property and taking initiatives in the transition to a democratic multi-party system and a market economy (Kovacs and Maggard 1993; Mahr and Nagle 1995). Each civil society is adjusting to European democratic values as the basis of legitimation and 'socialisation' of new elites (Agh 1994, 1995). People seem to be behaving positively and to look forward with some optimism (Szabo 1994). Broadly, they are staying with non-extremist parties and so there are relatively few demagogues on the political scene. Leaders have become more accessible (as witnessed by Lech Walesa's reported availability to telephone callers during his presidency in Poland). Reforms continue and governments change through parliamentary decision, rather than a *coup d'état*. Parties have replaced movements (Pridham 1995; Wightman 1994); they have also come to rely on the steady support of sections of the electorate, including formal links with organisations representing major interest groups in the economy (Bergland and Dellenbrandt 1991; Korbonski and Graziano 1993; Roskin 1993). However, the tendency for trade unions to enter politics could detract from their effectiveness in protecting working people and campaigning on behalf of the poorer sections of society (Waller and Myant 1994).

However, an underlying satisfaction with the course of the transition does not imply any easy consensus over domestic and foreign policy goals (Bertram *et al*. 1995). At a time when the political infrastructure is still being laid down there is some disillusionment and apathy over party politics based on philosophies which are sometimes remote from the lives of ordinary people, some of whom may distance themselves from politics as a result. Parties all too often reflect personalities rather than group interests; they tend to generate policies on the basis of internal discussion rather than dialogue with the electorate, so the public may favour a candidate on the basis of good character and administrative capability rather than party affiliation. It is difficult to construct a legitmatory ideology because there are not yet enough 'winners' and early hopes of affluence have been replaced by increasing social uncertainty and a decline in living standards, with extremes of wealth also evident. Conflict management calls for a careful balance to protect the 'losers' while allocating sufficient resources for growth and action must be taken at both local and national levels. 'Small town Poland' seems to be doing rather well, with considerable growth and greater optimism than in large conurbations.

Small business is making a greater contribution in the small towns than in the large cities and local government is becoming more responsive to grass-roots opinion instead of merely carrying out duties handed down from the central planning machinery (Murphy 1991). Indeed, Kolankiewicz (1993) sees authentic local self-government (freely elected and independent of the state administration with its own fiscal and property base) as a principal component of civil society. However, tensions can develop when local government is extensively controlled by parties that are in opposition nationally and the Romanian government has sought to remove opposition mayors and to impose firm controls on local authority finance. Central government will be all the more reluctant to decentralise if local councils back radical (even secessionist) parties as a lever for more state support. And there is further difficulty for democratically based centre–periphery relations when local government reform leads to localised patronage with mafia organisations emerging out of contact between officials, businessmen and other influential local people (Cirtautas 1995).

Of course, the final destination of the transition process cannot be clearly determined, for there is no monolithic Western model and each post-communist civil society is evolving its own form of creative adaptation to and pragmatic incorporation of Western forms. Differences between countries are becoming more evident (Table 3.1), with a north–south division in social and material conditions which is expressed through fast and slow path programmes for economic reform and the enlargement of the EU. Differences can be seen in the stability of new institutions and the levels of foreign investment. FCSFR, FGDR, Hungary and Poland have now clearly embraced parliamentary democracy but in the Balkans democratic institutions are perceived as being less stable and the situation has not been helped by civil war in FFRY. Civil society plainly needs civic virtues: civility, self-reliance, civic culture and education in the rights and obligations of citizenship (Tong 1995). But progress is taking place at an uneven rate. Meanwhile, nationalism is very strong and so the transition is stimulating a rediscovery of history hidden by decades of totalitarian rule. The big question is whether nationalism will generate more energy for reform and reconstruction in the spirit of a wider 'Europe of the regions' or whether it will become a more divisive force opposed to integration (Volten 1990; Webster 1993). There is the possibility of evolution along European lines with a strong middle class grounded in cultural democracy (a willingness to compromise for the wider good); or along Latin American lines with sharper class distinctions and mafia politics. The options have implications for foreign affairs: free trade and international cooperation or 'internalisation' based on xenophobia and protected domestic markets.

## THE STATE SYSTEM

State boundaries have remained largely intact because communism was grafted on to nation states which can now rely on a resurgence of nationalism. In some parts of the Balkans the territorial basis of nationalism has become a critical matter (Carter and Norris 1996; Hall and Danta 1996), yet for the most part economic reconstruction is the main priority. There is a widespread desire to persevere and work with the international community (Jeffery and Sturm 1993). Nationalism could become more extreme if market reforms fail and this could increase inter-ethnic tensions; yet the notion that this would necessarily precipitate war for territorial gain is for the most part implausible because the necessary military strength is not always available, for example, in Albania. Some politicians in Romania and Slovakia, like G. Funar and V. Meciar respectively, have expressed some irritation over the demands of the

Table 3.1 Socio-economic criteria[1]

| Country | A | B | C | D | E | F | G | H | I | J | K | L | M | N | O | P |
|---|---|---|---|---|---|---|---|---|---|---|---|---|---|---|---|---|
| Albania | 72.2 | – | 9 | 6.0 | – | 3.0 | 176 | 86 | 42 | – | – | – | 3.8 | 2.2 | 78 | 90 |
| Bulgaria | 72.6 | 12 | 15 | 7.0 | 340 | 4.7 | 438 | 250 | 451 | 140 | 137 | 38 | 10.8 | 7.6 | 40 | 67 |
| FCSFR | 71.8 | 32 | 18 | 9.0 | 389 | 4.9 | 587 | 412 | 507 | 255 | 200 | 55 | 6.0 | 4.5 | 26 | 49 |
| Hungary | 70.9 | 31 | 41 | 9.6 | 307 | 4.9 | 595 | 410 | 233 | 158 | 169 | 79 | 8.7 | 4.3 | 28 | 52 |
| Poland | 71.8 | 11 | 13 | 8.0 | 487 | 4.2 | 429 | 293 | 127 | 128 | 128 | 27 | 9.1 | 1.8 | 48 | 80 |
| Romania | 70.8 | 20 | – | 7.0 | 567 | 2.8 | 198 | 194 | – | – | 53 | 9 | 8.0 | 8.8 | 77 | 84 |

Notes A Life expectancy at birth (years); B Divorces as a percentage of marriages contracted (1987–90); C Suicides per 100,000 of population (1987–90); D Mean years of schooling; E Population per doctor (1984–9); F Adjusted pc GDP (US$000); G Radio sets (1988–90); H Television sets (ditto); I Daily newspapers (ditto); J telephones (1986–8); K Cars (1985–9); L Titles published annually per 100,000 of population (1988–90); M Library books pc (1988–90); N Cinema attendances pc (1987–90); O Human development index (based on a range of demographic, health, income and social criteria) world ranking; P pc GNP world ranking.

1 ptp 1990 except where otherwise stated.

Source: UN Development Programme 1993, Human Development Report (Oxford: Oxford University Press)

Hungarian minorities, but the rhetoric is geared primarily to winning support from the majority community by allusion to imaginary Hungarian threats. The main exception has been Serbia's response to the disintegration of FFRY (Allcock 1994). Autonomous regions of Serbia have been reincorporated and 'fighting for Yugoslavia' has challenged the independence of Bosnia-Hercegovina and Croatia through attempts to detach the Serb-settled areas from these two successor states.

## Unification in Germany

Resolving the German problem was the first major political development of transition (Jones 1993; Verhayen 1991). A peaceful and rapid revolution was brought about by a crucial collapse of self-confidence marked by protest in the regions where a key role was played by low-ranking officials who no longer believed in their own legitimacy (Friedheim 1993; Jeppke 1993). The outpouring of population from the FGDR continued after the breaching of the Berlin Wall in November 1989 (40,000 left during the following eight months) and made rapid unification essential (Glaessner and Wallace 1992; Terrill 1994). A freely elected Volkskammer appointed a new government which participated in the 'Two plus Four' negotiations in 1990 to combine unification with the full sovereignty after almost half a century of allied occupation (Fritsch-Bournazel 1992; Heisenberg 1991). It was particularly significant that the FSU accepted a united Germany within NATO, although 360,000 Red Army troops were retained in the FGDR for a short transition period and Germany promised economic aid (Paterson 1993; Wettig 1993). July 1990 saw full economic and monetary union, followed by the formal incorporation of the FGDR into the FRG in October 1990. The first all-German elections were held in December 1990 (Breuilly 1992). The regions (Bezirken) of the FGDR were rejected in favour of the traditional provinces (Brandenburg, Mecklenburg-Vorpommern, Sachsen, Sachsen-Anhalt and Thuringen) which now comprise Germany's 'New Lander' (Glaessner 1992). The economic consequences of unification will be considered below. Here it may be noted that the perceived advantages of unification for the Easterners ('Ossies') through better services (including the overhaul of a dilapidated infrastructure) and freedom of movement westwards are tempered by economic restructuring which has brought much unemployment (Fritsch-Bournazel 1988; Roesler 1991). Change has been underpinned by a massive privatisation of state assets (Blum and Siegmund 1993).

*Aufschwung Ost* is bringing improvements in employment, environment and housing with Berlin as the pace-setter, followed by Dresden, Halle and Leipzig which are major urban service centres that were somewhat suppressed under communism (Wild and Jones 1994). But the eastern electorate does not embrace the postmaterialist values (for example, over environment and gender issues). Reorganisation has meant a shock to a people conditioned by FGDR propaganda to associate the lack of a job with 'parasitism' and was especially agonising for those in the armed forces and education who were deemed politically unsuitable for work in the new Germany because of links with the former establishment. There has been some relaxation of policy since the Constitutional Court ruled that FGDR intelligence agents cannot be prosecuted because their actions were in line with their country's constitution (Hamalainen 1995). But the union has delivered some bitter fruit through perception of pseudo-military triumph for the Bonn government and hostility against foreign workers under conditions of high unemployment (Weisbrod 1994). With the Westerners ('Wessies') sensitive to the financial costs of unification and indignant about continued overmanning in the east, the old inter-zonal boundary will evidently linger in the public mind long after it has disappeared from the landscape (Turner 1993). Hence the references to *die Mauer im Kopf* (the wall in the head) to highlight the persistence of a siege mentality behind a symbolic Berlin Wall and the difficulty of coming to terms with the communist past (Torpey 1993).

## Other potential unions

Other unions could arise through the forging of links between Eastern Europe and successor states of FSU: Poland with Lithuania; Romania with Moldova. In both cases there are historic ties, through the Polish-Lithuanian Commonwealth and the Medieval Moldavian Principality respectively, but these associations have been weakened by recent experiences. It is difficult for Lithuania to contemplate joining Poland today in view of the bitter struggle for control of the Vilnius area during the inter-war years, but Lithuania might be interested in some form of association with a grouping of Baltic states including Poland (Burant and Zubek 1993). Meanwhile, Romania is keen to regain the frontiers of the inter-war years when the then Bessarabia (the land between the Prut and Dniester rivers) was one of its provinces (Crowther 1992). Bessarabia was lost in 1940 through the absence of effective international support to resist the Soviet ultimatum. However, thanks to Romania's wartime alliance with Germany the territory was regained in 1941 and although she was forced to surrender it again in 1944, the annexation was never recognised. Following the collapse of the FSU, Moldova did contemplate links with Romania as an alternative to joining the CIS. But the idea of reunification was sharply contested by the Russian minority which is strong in the towns and in the eastern part of the country generally (particularly Transdniestria, east of the Dniester) where an alternative assembly was set up in Tiraspol in 1992.

The Turks of the Gaugaz region (around Cahul) also opposed a merger with Romania and even the Moldavian majority now express a clear preference for independence as the best way to preserve a unitary state and enhance the position of Chisinau which is now a national capital. Part of the problem lies in the frontiers of Moldova which do not coincide with those of Bessarabia. In 1940 (and again in 1944) the southern part of Bessarabia, including the ports of Ismail and Reni, was allocated to Ukraine while Moldova gained additional territory east of the Nistru, absorbing most of the puppet Moldavian state created by the Soviets in the 1920s to destabilise Bessarabia. However, although it is in Transdniestria where most of Russians live and where a large part of Moldova's industrial establishment is located, Soviet cultural policies have contributed to the movement for independence in the country generally. Such policies do seem to have created a Moldovan state identity, in contrast to the situation in the FGDR (Miller 1994). Moldova is seeking to maintain the frontiers of the Soviet period and to perpetuate the rupture with Bucovina and South Bessarabia, and it has been decided that the language is Moldovan rather than Romanian. Meanwhile, Russia has rejected the demands of Transdniestria to join the CIS and there are plans for the withdrawal of the Russian army between 1994 and 1997. Meanwhile, the secessionists under I. Smirnov appear to be conceding Moldovan sovereignty and a compromise may be reached with the Chisianau government of M. Snegur over some form of autonomy. Meanwhile, Romania has not given up on union with Moldova and seeks cooperation for a 'common ethnic and cultural space' through a treaty that is still being negotiated. But there is little doubt that Moldova's short experience with independence has instilled a sense of national identity that few would have anticipated in 1991.

## The collapse of federal structures

Eastern Europe's two federations (FCSFR and FFRY) have broken up. Both states pre-date the communist period, for they emerged out of the peace settlements at the end of the First World War, but the federal structures were introduced under communism and it is arguable that awareness and confidence among the constituent nations (initiated through the Second World War experience with independence in Croatia and Slovakia) was nurtured through limited decentralisation under the umbrella of a monopoly party. Pluralism has not brought a major growth of nationalism, but it has offered the possibility of secession. As irritations have come to the surface, electorates have been able to vote for democratic parties advocating secession: hence the reality of 'pluralist mobilisation as a catalyst for the dismemberment of Yugoslavia' (Mrdjen 1993). At the same time, independence can be taken all the more seriously in view of the security system of the modern world which gives small states a very good chance of survival against external forces. Tensions have arisen largely through economic factors: Slovak dissatisfaction with federal attempts to marginalise the defence industries and introduce sweeping privatisation; and Croat/Slovene pressure for economic reform which the federal government in Belgrade was unable to deliver (Dubravcic 1993; Uralic 1993). Economic reform was less pressing for

Bosnia-Hercegovina and Macedonia but, with the defection of Croatia and Slovenia in 1991, these republics were unwilling to stay in a federation dominated by Serbs. There is a striking contrast between the harmony of the 'velvet divorce' in FCSFR and the violence of the fighting in FFRY. But in the latter case the separation was not negotiated. Instead it offended major vested interests in the *status quo* including the bulk of the former federal army and the political establishment in Belgrade; also the highly dispersed Serb nation for whom Yugoslavia could be regarded *de facto* as Greater Serbia.

## Former Czechoslovakia

Former Czechoslovakia broke up in 1993 following the transitional arrangement for a Czecho-Slovak Federal Republic (subsequently a 'Federal Republic of Czechs and Slovaks') arising out of the velvet revolution of 1989. The Slovaks forced the pace and it seems that several factors were important (Ramet 1994). Historical factors were relevant because, although both the Czech Republic and Slovakia were previously parts of the Habsburg Empire, the Czech Republic was close to Austria while Slovakia was governed from Budapest. Moreover, Slovakia enjoyed some years of independence (with German support) during the Second World War, at a time when the Czech Republic was stripped of its border territories (transferred to Grossdeutschland) and subjected to an occupation regime for the 'Protectorate of Bohemia and Moravia'. Economic issues were also important, for although the relatively backward Slovakia received considerable economic assistance from Prague, the adequacy of this help was always a matter of dispute. Slovaks were dissatisfied over the extent of their influence even after the federal state was first created in 1969, although it certainly brought progress to the city of Bratislava which increased its population much more rapidly than Prague: 173,000 in 1947 to 435,000 in 1989 (151 per cent) compared with 922,000 to 1,211,000 (31 per cent) for Prague. In the process it overtook the two largest provincial cities of the Czech Republic: Brno with a growth of 43 per cent (273,000 to 390,000) and Ostrava which increased by 83 per cent (181,000 to 331,000). However, Slovakia was smaller than the Czech Lands in terms of both area and population: 49.03,000.sq. km. (compared with 78.87 for the Czech Republic) and 5.26mn. in 1989 (10.36 for the Czech Republic).

Economic policy remained a matter of controversy because the Slovaks were embarrassed by unemployment of around 10 per cent in 1991, compared with only 4 per cent in the Czech Republic (Hall 1992). They favoured gradual reform, compared with the more radical stance adopted by the federal government, but until the elections of 1992 it seemed that the majority of Slovaks were aiming at more effective input at all levels of government in the federal state (Olson 1993). However, separation became the only option in view of the 'instability and immobilism often inherent in fragmented plural societies' (Henderson 1993, p.39). There were geographically separate sub-cultures and, although there were no running conflicts apart from economic policy, the federal system always provided the option of separation which it seemed natural to take in the circumstances of the 1990s. Szayna (1993) refers to a centrifugal trend with extremes of view over economic issues which threatened the continuation of the joint state after the 1992 elections endorsed the platform of the nationalists in Slovakia. Negotiations for a divorce were then put in hand (Kirschbaum 1993), but division has become more complete than was originally envisaged with the abandonment of a common currency (Bulir and Charap 1993).

The separation has not created any difficulties in defining the frontier which is long established, though some minor alterations were made in the east after the Second World War to suit the FSU (Luknis 1988). But there have been problems over unofficial names because while 'Slovakia' is an obvious choice the Czech equivalent of 'Cesko' or 'the Czech Lands' is much less satisfactory and the full title 'Czech Republic' is therefore widely used. On the other hand, devising a coded name for use on motor vehicles posed problems for Slovakia because the obvious choice of SL had already been taken by Slovenia and hence the adoption of SK instead. It is also evident that separation has increased the perceived threat of ethnic minorities. In addition to the Czechs in Slovakia and Slovaks in the Czech Republic it is clear that Hungarian minority in the south of Slovakia is a potential source of instability which may result in closer links with Austria and Ukraine. Meanwhile, there may be problems of identity as the Czech Republic draws closer to Germany, for there are some worries for the Czechs in defending their culture in the context of increasing German penetration (including German claims over expropriated property in Sudetenland which are now a serious issue in relations between the two countries).

*Former Yugoslavia: disintegration and civil war (Cohen 1995; Crnobrnja 1994)*

Once the communist party (League of Communists of Yugoslavia (LCY)) lost its monopoly it was possible for the 1990 elections to be contested by nationalist parties (Mircev 1993) (Table 3.2). Four of the six republics have exercised their constitutional right to secede, despite the opposition of Serbia and (to a lesser extent) Montenegro: two states whose union after the 1913 Balkan War formed the basis of the Yugoslav or South Slav state (Glennie 1992). Breakdown now implies rejection of both the centralised government of the 1930s and the federal structure championed by Tito after the Second World War in favour of independence for each the Southern Slav states. The Croats were probably the most ambivalent towards a unified country in view of their Second World War experience with independence and the concessions negotiated with Belgrade in the 1930s (Irvine 1993). By contrast, opinion in Slovenia underwent a major change because prior to 1918 there was admiration for the Serbs and a strong preference for a South Slav union over the concept of a decentralised Habsburg Empire advocated by the Croat Bishop J. Strossmayer. And during the Second World War there was still an absence of Habsburg nostalgia of the kind prominent in Croatia. However, within post-war Yugoslavia the relatively prosperous Slovenes made common cause with some Serb intellectuals against the power of Belgrade (as in 1985) and in the post-Titoist reform climate of the 1980s public opinion swung in favour of independence (Bebler 1993; Ramet and Adamovitch 1995). Slovenia made a successful break for independence after free elections in 1990 and the Yugoslav army was obliged to withdraw after only a few days of hostilities. With no significant Serb minority to create dissention, the new state was able to forge close links with Austria, Hungary and Italy and to take full advantage of its central position on the European transport network (Muller 1993).

*Table 3.2* Ethnicity in Former Yugoslavia

| Republic | Area sq. km. (000s) | Census 1981 (mn.) | |
|---|---|---|---|
| | | Majority group | Principal minorities |
| Bosnia-Hercegovina | 51.1 | 4.12 Muslims | Serbs 1.32; Croats 0.76 |
| Croatia | 56.5 | 4.60 Croats | Serbs 0.53 |
| Macedonia | 25.7 | 1.91 Macedonians | Albanians 0.38; Turks 0.09 |
| Montenegro | 13.8 | 0.58 Montenegrans | Muslims 0.08; Albanians 0.04 |
| Serbia | 88.4 | 9.31 Serbs | Albanians 1.23[1]; Hungarians 0.39[1] |
| Slovenia | 20.3 | 1.89 Slovenes | |

*Note* 1 Albanians are the majority group in the former autonomous area of Kosovo (10.89,000sq. km.); Hungarians likewise in Vojvodina (21.5,000sq. km.).
*Source*: Census of Yugoslavia 1981

However, further disintegration arose with independence for Croatia in 1991 and Bosnia-Hercegovina in 1992. There was a strong majority in favour of this action in Croatia; whereas in Bosnia-Hercegovina the Muslims of the Democratic Action Party (F. Abdic and A. Izetbegovic) had an overall majority when combined with the Croatian Democratic Union but faced a determined opposition from the extreme Serbian National Renewal Party. Rather than accept the uncertainties of minority status, like the Muslims in Bulgaria, the Bosnians showed a readiness to advance their national interests with the precedents of earlier recognition by both the Habsburg Empire and Tito's federation (Friedman 1994; Karpat 1992). In both countries independence sparked off prolonged and extremely bitter hostilities. When the incompetence of the federal army forced an early withdrawal from Slovenia the loss of face seems to have introduced a new volatility into the situation and the army openly took sides when clashes occurred between Croat and Serb militias in the Serb minority areas of Croatia, leading to all-out war in Krajina and Eastern Slavonia by the autumn of 1991 (Klemencic 1996). There is a historic precedent for conflict because of the pre-First World War association of Bosnia-Hercegovina and Croatia (as well as Slovenia and Vojvodina) with the Habsburg Empire, contrasting with Serbia's connections with the Ottoman Empire which made for particularly sharp cultural and economic divisions. It has, for example, been claimed that the Serb tradition lacks a civic political culture (Krizan 1994, p.64), suggesting that a major cultural divide separates Serbia from Croatia and Slovenia. But reference should also be made to dissatisfaction with attempts to form a centralised government in inter-war Yugoslavia and the Second World War experience with independence (and German support) for a large Croatian state at a time when Serbia was subjected to a harsh occupation regime. Thus the civil war in Bosnia-Hercegovina and Croatia has revived memories of the Croat Ustasha and Serb Cetnik militias of a generation ago (Sorenson 1993).

Historic tensions created a situation where all the main groups in Bosnia-Hercegovina sought their clearly defined ethnically cleansed sectors, leaving central government with very limited overall authority. Indeed, Serbs wished to detach the territory they controlled in both Bosnia-Hercegovina and Croatia in keeping with the historic goal of a Greater Serbia (Lukic 1994). It is true that Serbs have most to lose with the breakup of FFRY since they comprise significant minorities in some other republics while not enjoying an overwhelming majority in Serbia itself (Denitch 1994; Ruscinov 1991). Thus they have always had a major vested interest in Yugoslavia through the existence of a state framework within which virtually all Serbs were living together. Yugoslavia has been described as a 'fatal misunderstanding' since there is a 'homogenous Serbia in the frame of Yugoslavia into which [Serbs] will instill their spirit' (Krizan 1994, pp.50–2) which includes the Second World War record of resistance to the Germans. So the government in Serbia has inherited a strong Pan-Serb (Greater Serbian) ideology. Serb intellectuals drafted a Memorandum in 1986 arguing that the traditional goal of Greater Serbia retained its validity. So Milosevic has sought either communist or Serb hegemony and under his leadership Serbs have taken calculated risks in consolidating their position within Serbia (dismantling autonomy in Kosovo and ignoring Albanian claims for republic status in 1981), while simultaneously contesting similar tendencies in other republics (ibid., p.56). Serb predominance in the federal army ensured that military strength could be used to challenge the independence of the seceding republics. If the army could not prevent disintegration then at least the Serbs could be sufficiently well armed to ensure autonomy for the Serb-populated areas of both Bosnia-Hercegovina and Croatia, and hopefully union with Serbia. Thus Greater Serbia would be resurrected out of the ruins of the old federation.

In Croatia the Serb population separated itself from the rest of the population and the situation was stabilised in 1992 by UN peacekeepers operating in three separate zones (Krajina, East Slavonia and West Slavonia). But normalisation was prevented by the Serb refusal to accept that their territories lay within the Croatian state: the option of autonomy for Krajina within Croatia was rejected. But as their military forces gained strength the Croats were able to regain territory inland from Zadar before overrunning the Pakrac area of Western Slavonia early in 1995. During the summer of that year the whole of Krajina was taken in a massive *blitzkrieg* operation which saw almost the entire Serb population displaced. The remaining occupied territory (Vukovar in Eastern Slavonia) was then secured under the Dayton (Ohio) negotiations at the end of 1995. Meanwhile, the ethnic divisions in Bosnia-Hercegovina seemed so complex as to make for a prolonged war, given the balance of power between the three armies. The three communities (Bosnian Muslim, Croat and Serb) were so intermixed that there were few areas without significant minority groups (Friedman 1994) and there were certainly no urban functional regions where one group was totally dominant. This made for complicated supply lines and draconian measures to impose unity by ethnic cleansing during 1991 and 1992. Yet the Bosnian War has also been fought with economic considerations in mind and Serb drives in eastern Bosnia (and previously in Croatia's Dubrovnik/Prevlaka exclave) suggest an attempt to extend the Serb state, with improved access to the sea. The Serbs also attempted to control the heavy industrial base of Central Bosnia although this remains a major Muslim interest.

Bosnian Serbs were greatly assisted by a division of the former federal army which gave them a substantial arsenal of tanks and artillery pieces; also an effective unity of forces which overcame the dichotomy between the army and irregular forces that was evident during the Croatian War. An initially overwhelming weapons superiority enabled them to capture territory to a far greater extent than their population share warranted. However, their advant- age was somewhat reduced by the rapid buildup of the Bosnian (Muslim) Army during 1993 and measures to circumvent the blockade which were crowned by the accord with Croatia after the winter of 1993–4. The overstretched Croats had to renounce their ambition of a Croatian canton for Herceg-Bosna based on Mostar (though tension in the city remained high) and military coordination brought limited territorial gains between 1993 and 1995. But the situation remained tense, for although the Bosnian Serbs controlled far more territory than their population share could justify and could threaten Muslim 'safe areas' which the UN Protection Force estab- lished in Sarajevo and the provincial areas of Bihac, Gorazde, Srebrenica and Zepa, their demands for an independent existence outside Bosnia- Hercegovina were not accepted either by the Bosnian (Muslim) government or the international community. Peace proposals based on an equitable division of territory were consistently rejected by the Bosnian Serbs: notably the Contact Group proposal (France, Germany, Russia, UK and USA) of 1994.

So it seemed that, despite initial military success, the opportunism of the Serb President Milosevic had incurred incalculable costs (Ciger 1993). He was able to harness Serb nationalism, all the more potent through linkage withthe Serb Orthodox Church and the 'paranoid ideology' of a continuing Kosovo struggle (interpreted as the defence of Europe and Christianity) (Krizan 1994). The view was reinforced by a perception of insecurity in the face of both Catholic Europe (personified by Croats) and Muslim Europe (represented by Albanians and Bosnians); while control of the media ensured a degree of ignorance in Belgrade about the true situation in the war zones (especially in Bosnia). Yet while sanctions imposed by the international community clearly imply Serbian (and Montenegran) complicity in the fighting in adjacent republics, it became clear that in Bosnia-Hercegovina the local Serbs could operate quite independently when Belgrade sought to reduce its involvement. Milosevic could no longer directly control the war that he initially did little to prevent, such was the political capital attaching to Greater Serbia as 'a dream too far'. The Serbs seemed threatened by a cordon sanitaire of devastation, 'condemning themselves and their enemies to long years of poverty and isolation' (ibid., p.65).

A decisive change occurred in 1995 when the Bosnian Serbs failed to read the signs of increasing UN irritation over the impotence of their protection force. A series of provocations including hostage-taking of UN soldiers, followed by the capture of the 'safe area' of Srebrenica (with the massacre of the Muslim male population) and the continued shelling of Sarajevo attracted sustained NATO air strikes which eventually forced the removal of heavy weapons threatening the city. Parallel US diplomatic moves in Belgrade secured the cooperation of Serbia's President Milosevic who was able to regain the initiative of the Bosnian Serb authorities in Pale. Meanwhile, the growing military strength of the Bosnian Muslims and especially the Croats enabled massive gains to be made in western Bosnia immediately after Croatia had recaptured Krajina. A string of towns was captured along Bosnia's border with Dalmatia (Gorni Vakuf, Jajce, Mrkonjic Grad, Kljuc, Bosanski Petrovac and Sanski Most), forging a link between the Muslim-Croat heartland in central Bosnia and the isolated safe area of Bihac. It resulted in an equitable balance of territory and even placed the Serb stronghold of Banja Luka under pressure. All these factors made for a readiness to negotiate with Milosevic representing the Bosnian Serbs.

The Dayton agreement of December 1995 acknowledged the sovereign status of Bosnia-Hercegovina while providing for a confederation between the Muslim-Croat state and the Serbs' Republika Srpska, with boundaries that followed the ceasefire lines with two important modifications: the whole of Sarajevo was included within the Muslim-Croat state while the Croats evacuated the town of **Mrkonjic Grad** and the surrounding area (part of the conquests of summer 1995). There have also been some accommodations so that the Serbs can secure the Brcko Corridor, crucial for supplies to Banja Luka although the situation was left for further clarification later. The agreement was implemented in 1996 although Serbs are pressurised by their own leaders to leave areas due for allocation to their enemies. The agreement provides for a return to integration but there is no early prospect of ethnic harmony (even Muslim-Croat relations in Mostar are tense) and the present ethnic structure of the two areas shows the impact of ethnic cleansing. In the federation's territory the population of Muslims and Croats increased from 1.21 to 1.67mn. between 1991 and 1995 while the Serb population declined from 0.21 to 0.04mn. In addition, the eastern enclaves sheltered 0.11mn. Muslims in 1995 (prior to the fall of Srebenica and Zepa) in contrast to a mixed population of 0.08mn. Muslims and 0.02mn. Serbs in 1991. Meanwhile, in Serb territory the Serb population increased from 0.93 to 1.17mn. between 1991 and 1995 while the numbers of Muslims and Croats fell from 0.84 to 0.07mn. But now, although peace has been established, many people are being prevented from returning home and reconstruction has hardly started, despite the fact that some French companies quickly became involved in limited rebuilding in Sarajevo. An end to authoritarian regimes and the removal of elites responsible for war is a distant prospect (Mircev 1993). However, there are some promising signs; for example, the peaceful transfers of property between Croats in the Boka Bay area of Montenegro and Serbs living close to Dubrovnik, although this again underlines the determination of most FFRY citizens to live within their own nation state.

### Former Yugoslavia: problems in Kosovo and Macedonia

Macedonia's decision to opt for independence in 1992 reflects Tito's success in creating national consciousness among the Macedonians as a people distinct from Bulgarians, Slavophone Greeks and Serbs (Perry 1992). Macedonia was able to secede without major conflict, but the country faced problems of internal division (on both ethnic and religious grounds) and economic isolation as a result of UN sanctions imposed against Serbia in connection with the war in Bosnia-Hercegovina (Perry 1991a, 1991b). The major ethnic division is between Macedonians and Albanians, with the latter estimated officially at one-fifth, although Albanians think the figure is almost double. But since fifteen years' residence is required to qualify for Macedonian citizenship, recent immigrants from Kosovo are excluded. Albania wants equal constitutional status for its minority, including the creation of an Albanian university, but Macedonians are reluctant to allow this. Cantonising Macedonia is also resisted, but some easing of tension has been achieved by greater involvement of Albanians in government since 1991 when they were offered five of the twenty-seven portfolios. This has helped Macedonia to concentrate more attention on external problems because tension arises with her other three neighbours (Bulgaria, Greece and Serbia) who partitioned Turkish-occupied territory after the Second Balkan War in 1913 when Macedonian national consciousness was only weakly developed. Serbia has shown ambivalence over accepting Macedonian nationality, for some leading Serbian nationalists would claim the whole of Macedonia or advocate partition between Serbia and Greece. But Serbia also depends on Macedonia for communications with Thessaloniki. Bulgaria also declined to recognise Macedonian nationality because this would have implications with respect to Macedonians within Bulgaria, although she has recognised the Macedonian state and has entered into bilateral economic relations.

Greece has shown extreme belligerence towards Macedonia because the name Macedonia is seen as a focus for a larger state that could have brought the frontiers of Greece into question. There is a fear that the Macedonian minority in Greece (the so-called 'Slavophone Greeks') might secede if there was a Macedonian state in existence (Perry 1992). Greece is also concerned at the impact of Macedonian nationalists on the Turkish minority of 'Greek Muslims' who might also demand secession. For this reason Greece also objected to the Macedonian flag with its fourth-century star, said to be a symbol of Philip II and hence an appropriation of Greek heritage. But in 1992 Macedonia formally denied territorial claims and any policy of interference in the internal affairs of neighbouring states. Greece would accept 'Vardar-Macedonia' or 'Republic of Skopje', but Skopje insists on the name 'Macedonia' although the interim solution of 'Former Yugoslav Republic of Macedonia' paved the way for UN membership and recognition by Russia, USA and major West European states (following earlier recognition by Bulgaria) (Stefas and Kentrotis 1994). It has also enabled the EU to support Macedonian independence with its Phare programme and ensured continued Macedonian support for the sanctions in force against Serbia at the time. But it is not acceptable as a permanent arrangement and early in 1994 Greece imposed an economic blockade to emphasise the lack of effective security and the need for the powers to accommodate Greek sensitivities.

Greece maintained her policy through 1994 and 1995, so activity in the port of Thessaloniki (a major potential business centre for the Balkans as a whole) was much reduced. The loss of business was widely deplored although the port continued to modernise for the future. A Bulgarian–Macedonian union is a possibility if the country fails to be viable, but a worse scenario would be war between Macedonia and Greece that might attract intervention from other neighbouring states, since Macedonia is significant for the balance of power in the Balkans. Serbia would support Greece while Bulgaria might join Albania in seeking a partition of Macedonia, given the historical precedents for Bulgarian control over the western Balkans. Another Balkan War could result, perhaps with Turkish involvement in support of Albania and Bulgaria. A stable Macedonia will help to provide security for the

Balkans as a whole and UN troops have been deployed as a stabilising force. Nevertheless, the experience in Bosnia-Hercegovina shows the extent of a 'crisis waiting to happen'. Economic progress would provide a basis for greater domestic harmony although this in turn requires stable government and international action to improve the infrastructure: either the Morava–Vardar corridor (Belgrade–Skopje–Thessaloniki) or the Durres–Skopje–Sofia–Varna Trans-Balkan axis. In the latter case the section between Kustendil (Bulgaria) and Kumanovo (Macedonia) is currently being developed for rail transport. Fortunately, by 1996 the Greek attitude was softening in the light of moves for peace in FFRY as a whole.

Kosovo as well as Macedonia could easily be destabilised (Gagnon 1991). M. Andrejevich (1991) referred to the possibility of a chain reaction arising out of tension between Muslims and Serbs in the Sandzak (forming Serbia's borderland with Bosnia-Hercegovina and Montenegro) and spreading to Serbia's former autonomous regions (Kosovo and Vojvodina) and ultimately to Macedonia. However, Serbia has been fully stretched in other theatres, while Albanians, Hungarians and Macedonians have been careful not to inflame ethnic tensions. There has been particular restraint on the part of the Albanian government (perhaps reflecting the weakness of their armed forces) although the ethnic map suggests the potential for the annexation of adjacent territories along the lines taken by the Serbs. Yet rather than encourage a 'Greater Albania' or independence for Kosovo, the Albanian President S. Berisha has said that Albanians should work out their salvation where they are. Yet, the situation in Kosovo remains tense because autonomy has been replaced by direct rule from Belgrade (Zanga 1991). There is, for example, a crisis over medical care through the refusal of Albanian families to accept treatment from the Serbian staff who have taken over the health care facilities. Up to 95 per cent of babies born to Albanians have been delivered at home (a much higher proportion than that registered when Albanian medical staff were available). In the face of a polio outbreak Albanians have perceived vaccination by Serb doctors as carrying a risk of sterility and so progress has been made largely through international aid workers establishing relations with Albanian communities through their religious leaders.

A complete resolution of the Yugoslav crisis is a long way off. The complexities have been increased by outside involvement so that German influence in Croatia balanced by Russian interests in Serbia could lead to a Lebanese-style proxy conflict. Meanwhile, Western indecision has imposed the heavy cost of trade sanctions not only on the Serbs, for whom the war has been a disaster, but on other Balkan nations such as Romania which are debarred from decision-making. There have been huge losses in trade and transit estimated at over US$10bn, but the heavy costs of war in Bosnia-Hercegovina and Croatia seem to be reinforcing the determination of other Balkan nations to avoid hostilities. And the domino theory that anticipated an extension of hostilities to the Sandzak, Kosovo and Macedonia (where

Albania and Greece might confront Bulgaria and Turkey in a Balkan War) now seems less relevant. People across the region are becoming wary of endorsing irredentist demands and there is little enthusiasm in Albania, Bulgaria and Romania for adventures dedicated to absorption of Kosovo, Macedonia and Moldova respectively. Instead there are good prospects for economic growth through trade between the Balkan countries on the basis of comparative advantage; and in particular between the former communist states of the Balkans and Greece and Turkey. Bulgaria is trading the products of its heavy industry for foodstuffs and light manufactures. It also offers low energy prices. A recent meeting of the Inter-Balkan Council of Entrepreneurs in Thessaloniki may provide a start for regional initiatives. But for them to succeed there is a need for Western investment to help reverse the calamitous decline in investment since 1989. Investment should not simply target consumer goods for domestic consumption.

## A NEW SECURITY AND ECONOMIC SUPPORT SYSTEM

It is possible that the new nationalism of Eastern Europe will not normally be aggressive because conflict runs counter to the ethos of the EU whose enlargement is widely sought. People want a new society and do not want to remember a past when most were only passively anti-communist, but the future is uncertain because civil society is still in the process of creating a morality and philosophy for the liberal free market economy. The Polish Solidarity movement showed some promise, but after fragmentation it remains as little more than a labour union. While the present society of the transition has only slender roots, security is important and since the Warsaw Pact was wound up in 1991 (Michta 1992) the issue must be considered within the wider Europe (Dalby 1993; Williams 1994). Retention of links through a new grouping of East European states has been raised and there is a compelling logic in rebuilding bridges eastwards in order to consolidate democracy and market reforms in the FSU successor states. However, East European states with a recent history of subjection to the FSU will not countenance a security system in which Russia is the strongest power. Even an eastern trade organisation is complicated by the spectre of Russian dominance when what is most wanted is access to Western capital and technology (Hill and Zielonka 1990). In other words, an eastern grouping could develop as an addition to, but not as an alternative to, a set of relationships linking Eastern Europe with the West (Graubatd 1991; Dawson 1993).

Poland is in the most sensitive position because of its long eastern frontier with FSU. The collapse of the Soviet state brought the advantage of Russian withdrawal, for there is only a limited frontier by virtue of the Kaliningrad enclave. Poland also has frontiers with Belarus, Lithuania and Ukraine, a situation which should be guaranteed by the West European security system

(Kaninski and Kosciuk 1993). Poland appreciates that there is the threat of intimidation of countries which constitute Russia's 'near abroad' and that moves are being made to strengthen links between Russia and her neighbours, especially Belarus and Ukraine (Latawski 1993). It is thus necessary to strengthen democratic forces in Russia and promote regional cooperation to reduce insecurity. The situation is potentially threatening because of the enormous buildup of troops and armaments around Kaliningrad as a result of withdrawals from Germany and elsewhere in Eastern Europe. There is a Russian desire for access to Kaliningrad via Belarus and a road 'corridor' through northeastern Poland. Meanwhile, it is also important for Poland that Germany's new strength is placed in a European system (Kurz 1993). NATO is very important for Eastern Europe's security, so much so that idealists would advocate an open pact that East European countries could join immediately, with the possibility of Ukrainian and even Russian membership at a later stage. However, NATO is unwilling to take the East European states formally under its wing and risk antagonising Russia, but is has offered military cooperation under a 'Partnership for Peace' (Clarke 1991). But military cooperation has been offered under a 'Partnership for Peace' that could be a possible stepping stone towards a pan-European system of collective security (Khalilzad and Brzezinski 1993; Parzympies 1993).

On the economic plane, expectations of assistance on the scale of a Marshall Aid programme have been disappointed; this makes Western commercial advertising a source of some 'cultural misunderstanding'. Flaunting commercial strength can be provocative when East Europeans feel that politically motivated promises of aid have not been kept. However, a more mature and realistic attitude has become apparent since 1992. Eastern Europe has much to learn about a market economy and Western models may be highly relevant. But there is no simple recipe: there are many different ways to manage and organise a market economy. Rather than see their sphere of the continent as 'failing' in the face of Western scrutiny, East Europeans should critically examine the West and consider what is the most acceptable package. This exercise can be facilitated by rediscovery of the past democratic experience in Eastern Europe before the compromising associations with the German Nazi and Soviet Communist regimes. However, there are inevitable complications through differences of cultural tradition among ethnic groups and the changes in state boundaries during the present century which mean that there cannot be a simple return to the past.

There is, however, momentum for cooperation in Central Europe (Kipp 1993; Shumaker 1993). FCSFR, Hungary and Poland have found a common interest in seeking EU membership and lowering trade barriers among themselves (Tokes 1991). The so-called 'Visegrad Group' was formed in 1990 and at a subsequent meeting in Krakow in 1992 a regional trading zone was agreed, with tariffs to be removed on agricultural and industrial goods over the 1995–7 period (cars, textiles and steel by 2001). In 1993 the group expanded from three to four members with the breakup of FCSFR. This has increased contrasts within the group because the Czech Republic is a front-runner while Slovakia depresses the median level of economic development (Perczynski 1993). But trade barriers are being lowered and there are many cases of local cross-border cooperation (De Weydenthal 1992). Meanwhile, developing an economic and security system for the Balkans will remain difficult until stability is achieved in FFRY (Cvijic 1991; Shoup 1990), although Slovenia is uncoupling herself and moving closer to the Visegrad group. Leaders of the Visegrad countries and Slovenia are currently seeking closer cooperation with regional cooperation extending to Austria, Germany and Italy.

## Involvement by individual EU member states

All the EU states have a role in the future of Eastern Europe (Palankai 1991). France and the UK have historic responsibilities as supporters of democracy, although the closest trade relations may develop with the neighbouring states (Brown 1994). German manufactures are much in demand. In a recent assessment of the meaning of Mitteleuropa, W. Tietze pointed out (1989, p.175) how the German language 'functioning as a lingua franca of commerce and culture seems to have been favoured by the general weakness of national politics' and it remained very useful 'so long as world trade was still European or indeed European-dominated'. Obviously the global scope of modern trade patterns, to say nothing of recent conflicts between the Germans and their eastern neighbours, have weakened the traditional community of interests. Yet nobody doubts the key role that Germany can play in future, given the economic resources of the unified state. Despite the expulsion of German communities from FCSFR, Poland and elsewhere there is still arguably a Central European culture. Tietze notes the conservation pro-grammes in Gdansk (the former Danzig) and argues (1989, p.175) that it is here in the Baltic 'where Central European traits left behind by the Order of Knighthood, the Hanseatic League, the Lutherans and the intellectual life of the Enlightenment are still so evident'.

### Austria

Separated from Germany by the Anschlussverbot is the German federal state of Austria, once the core of a Habsburg Empire embracing the whole of FCSFR, southern Poland, western Ukraine, northern Romania (Transyl-vania), Hungary, the northern half of FFRY (Bosnia-Hercegovina, Croatia and Slovenia) and parts of Italy. Destroyed by self-determination in 1918 and apparently split irrevocably by the Iron Curtain after 1945, the historic associations are beginning to reappear. For, although nationalism seemed to reduce the empire to irrelevance, there is a continuing cultural identity and a common economic interest in the Adriatic and Middle Danube area of landscape diversity and ethnic complexity. After the 1956 uprising in Hungary refugees found sanctuary across the frontier in Austria and an outstanding feature of communist Hungary's New Economic Mechanism (NEM) was a closer link with Austria, leading to Austrian investment in Hungary and a project (subsequently abandoned) for the twenty-fifth World Expo in Budapest and Vienna in 1995. Close contacts are well demonstrated by the commercial development on the frontier itself at Hegyeshalom and in the border regions around Gyor and Sopron. Meanwhile, Austria also moved closer to FCSFR after foreign ministers from the two states presided over the demolition of the Iron Curtain and abolished visas. There could also be a more extensive collaboration extending through the Balkans given the Danubian interests of Bulgaria and Romania.

### Italy

Although Italian foreign policy has been rather passive in recent years, the country does have a long history of association with the Balkan and Danubian countries, with roots in the Roman and Venetian empires. There is also a recent history of Italian economic penetration through close links with the Balkan peoples (subsequently extended between 1939 and 1945 through Italy's Second World War role in the Axis camp). A 'Habsburg Reunion' seems implicit in meetings which have taken place between Austria, Hungary, Italy and FFRY, constituting an *iniziativa quadrangolare*. Interestingly, at the end of the 1980s the four states represented the full range of international affiliations for Europe: Italy was a founder member of the EU, while Austria was attached to the then-EFTA, Hungary was involved with Comecon and the Warsaw Pact while FFRY was non-aligned despite its contacts with Moscow. Italy would like to see a zone of trust (*zona de fiducia*) to replace the old fortified frontier and is interested in regional entente to ease the isolation of Trieste, hemmed in by FFRY since the end of the Second World War when the territories of Istria and Zadar were lost. Trieste plays a modest international role as the port from which crude oil is sent by pipeline to Germany, but the reopening of former trade routes would make the city an obvious place for the provision of warehousing and customs-free facilities to enlarge the transit role. The Italians would like to increase capacity on the railway from Trieste to Udine, Tarvisio and the Austrian frontier. The focal importance of Trieste is underlined symbolically by the restoration of the famous Cafe San Marco and its reopening in the presence of representatives from neighbouring countries. Italian investment can be seen in shopping in the southern part of Eastern Europe: Croatia, Hungary, Slovakia and Slovenia, while the Favorittas travel office is one of several expressions of collaboration.

## Greece and Scandinavia

Greece features prominently in the rebuilding of the Balkans with Thessaloniki as a good base for foreign firms to set up their offices. There are already
some 2,000 (generally small) Greek ventures in food and textiles, mostly in
Bulgaria, and there is good potential for Greek businessmen throughout the
northern part of the country. But at the moment there are fears throughout
the Balkans about Greece's reliability, even in Bulgaria and Romania.
Meanwhile, Scandinavian businesses are prominent on the Baltic coast, with
several hundred small businesses in Poland as well as joint projects involving
Denmark, Finland and Sweden: thus there is Finnish involvement in Nestle
oil corporation, with Scania assembling trucks at Koszalin and Volvo
planning bus assembly at Jelcz. Scanbeton (a subsidiary of a Swedish
company) has four cement plants in the Rostock-Stralsund area of FGDR.
And as part of a strategy to penetrate growing markets in Eastern Europe,
Sweden's Skanska construction company has purchased a 50 per cent stake
in the Prague-based construction management company Hakastav, following
its acquisition of the Berlin builder Voigt.

## CIVIL SOCIETY

There was a trend towards pluralism before 1989, although it was seldom
recognised because of Western infatuation with the totalitarian model and the
supposed uniqueness of communist politics (Korbonski 1993). However,
there was some questioning of ideological principles (Poznanski 1993), and
Moran (1994) suggests that an explosive situation built up in the northern
countries where there was no scope for either dissent or emigration. There
was some economic change with the growth of a second economy (Hann
1990), but reform was very limited and the system remained highly damaging
in spiritual terms through regulations that had to be broken in order to survive.
Hence a confusion of moral values between state and private property with
legitimation for theft from the one rather than the other. There will have be
a new concept of what 'private' means: under communism the 'private'
domain was a limited intellectual and spiritual sector outside the influence of
politics, but now the private domain becomes a critical sphere of family
activity (Tos 1993). There will be a partial dependency through institutions
such as the churches which are important for spiritual enlightenment,
education and social functions, for example, rural festivals (Trix 1994).
Communist legacies will gradually fade in the face of activity by a new
generation without a dissident past (Konvicka and Kavan 1994) and the
influence of the young people who tend to be most positive about the
transition (Riordan *et al.* 1995; Tymowski 1994).

In the process, the permanent values of socialism may emerge, for instead
of a simple switch to Western values there is likely to be 'creative adaptation'

or 'pragmatic incorporation' of Western norms (Stark 1989, 1992). There is a need for codification of individual rights (Pogany 1995); links with wider communities through standards of accountability (for example, for representatives in local and national government), and more generally through renewal of the legal system and other state institutions in line with public opinion. While any government may intervene with principles that reflect its own philosophy, consensus is proving difficult to find. There will have to be a community fabric (projected through citizenship) to minimise intolerance for ethnic or religious minorities, abuse of press freedoms or breakdowns in the legal system. Society will also have to find ways of coping with increased inequalities (through the market system) and greater social differentiation; with more self-help (rather than state intervention) and more input by secular rather than religious organisations to avoid unacceptable material contrasts and further polarisation. In general, civil society will have to provide greater mobility than was possible in the later years of communism when there was insufficient scope for people who achieved economic success (Schopflin 1993).

Civil society is influencing not only the fundamentals of economic and social policy but also the political map at the national and local authority level. The isolation of social and economic actors under communism, with salaries and welfare benefits largely unrelated to individual economic performance, delayed the cultivation of attitudes associated with the normal functioning of a market economy and of a consensus over 'expectations of behaviour' (Schotter 1981). More generally the changes in civil society (Lewis 1992) need consideration as the transition proceeds. There may be evolution along European lines with the growth of a strong middle class grounded in 'cultural democracy' (a willingness to compromise for the wider good); or change may follow the Latin American model with sharper class distinctions and mafia politics (Croan et al. 1992). As already noted, these fundamental choices have implications for foreign and trade policy: free trade and cooperation or internalisation and protection. Religion should exert a positive influence, although the coexistence of church and state will be far from ideal while individual churches are preoccupied with their institutional interests and continue to be sensitive about perceived threats from communist and Jewish sources (Grabowska 1994). There is freedom to worship, but some churches, such as the Uniates in Romania, have to hold services out of doors because very little property has been returned since the forced amalgamations of the communist period were overthrown after 1989 (Foldresi 1995; Keleher 1995). It will take a long time for buildings to be put into a state of repair and outside help is needed; for example, the Aromanian church in Korce is supported by members of the community in the USA (Shundi 1994). Churches are also under pressure from a shortage of priests, especially teacher-priests. Yet as the churches regain their establishment role they may lose the refuge function enjoyed under communism (Cantrell and Kemp 1995, p.28). There is a need for a middle ground where the church does not directly participate in policy-making but where its presence and influence can be felt (Pater 1995).

## Population

The demographic transition continues, with higher rural fertility and higher natural increase in the east compared with the west where there are some areas of demographic disaster arising through severe depopulation (Okolski 1992) (see Table 3.3). Despite pronatalist policies under central planning (particularly coercive in some Balkan countries), natural increase declined during the 1980s and there was also net out-migration which makes it very unlikely that the population targets for the year 2000 (projected in the context of the 1970s) will be reached. Ageing is now pronounced, with overall growth now less than 1 per cent per annum (and likely to be still lower in future even assuming nil out-migration). It is not clear how far the revolutions have affected natural increase: it can only be said that the removal of draconian measures to stimulate the birth rate and of bureaucratic controls on migration will have had negative effects on population growth in the short term. The effect may be compounded if the birth rate is adversely affected by the uncertainties of the transition, as seems to be the case in FGDR. Eberstadt (1993, p.512) sees falling rates of natural increase as a serious decline in health policy reflecting 'a constellation of social economic and environmental factors [including] education housing conditions and environmental quality'. Yet while the FGDR's dismal demographic record may stand as an indict-ment, the situation has deteriorated further since 1989 and not only because of an increase in migration with the removal of bureaucratic controls. For despite unparalleled plenty in FGDR there has been 'demographic shock': an upswing in mortality and a collapse of births and new marriages suggestive of a severe reduction in material well-being (Eberstadt 1994). Given very high female unemployment (Quack and Maier 1994), a choice may have to be made between keeping a job and having a child. There is a need for new structures on the jobs market to combine the desire for work with the role of the mother (Fleischacker 1995, p.134).

### *Migration: patterns of movement*

At the domestic level migration since 1989 presents a rather confused picture. Some official figures suggest increased rates of migration but this may reflect recognition of earlier movements that were illegal at the time because of migration controls affecting some large cities (Sjoberg 1994). UN estimates also indicate that rural–urban movement has continued between 1990 and 1995 and only in Albania and Macedonia is the rural population still increasing in absolute terms (Table 3.4). Rising urban unemployment might

Table 3.3 Area and population 1994

| Tier and country | Area sq. km. (000s) | Population Total (000s) | Population Density sq. km. | Capital City Name | Capital City Population A | B |
|---|---|---|---|---|---|---|
| Northern tier | 641.9 | 80.39 | 125.2 | Total | 6,606 | 8.2 |
| Former Czechoslovakia: FCSFR | 127.9 | 15.50 | 121.0 | Prague | 1,210 | 7.7 |
| Czech Republic/Ceska Republika | 78.9 | 10,295 | 131.0 | Prague | 1,210 | 11.7 |
| Slovakia/Slovenska Republika | 49.0 | 5,333 | 108.0 | Bratislava | 438 | 8.2 |
| Former GDR (Germany NL) | 108.3 | 16.21+ | 149.7 | East Berlin | 1,285 | 7.9 |
| Germany/Bundesrepublik Deutschland | 356.9 | 81,278 | 224.9 | Berlin | 3,454 | 4.3 |
| Hungary/Magyar Koztarsasag | 93.0 | 10,266 | 111.0 | Budapest | 2,017 | 19.5 |
| Poland/Rzeczpospolita Polska | 312.7 | 38,544 | 122.7 | Warsaw | 1,656 | 4.3 |
| Southern tier | 633.8 | 58.93 | 93.0 | Total | 6,698 | 11.3 |
| Albania/Republika Shqiperise | 28.7 | 3,414 | 117.1 | Tirana | 245 | 7.4 |
| Bulgaria/Republika Bulgaria | 110.9 | 8,856 | 81.1 | Sofia | 1,313 | 14.6 |
| Romania/Republica Romania | 238.4 | 22,733 | 95.6 | Bucharest | 2,047 | 8.8 |
| Former Yugoslavia FFYR | 255.8 | 23.79 | 93.0 | Belgrade | 1,278 | 5.4 |
| Bosnia-Hercegovina/Republika Bosna i Hercegovina | 51.1 | 3,527 | 85.6 | Sarajevo | 410 | 9.5 |
| Croatia/Republika Hrvatska | 56.5 | 4,504 | 84.2 | Zagreb | 700 | 15.5 |
| Macedonia/Republika Makedonija | 25.7 | 2,142 | 79.0 | Skopje | 445 | 21.7 |
| Slovenia/Republika Slovenja | 20.3 | 1,942 | 98.5 | Ljubljana | 260 | 13.6 |
| Yugoslavia/Savezne Republika Jugoslavija | 102.2 | 10,763 | 104.0 | Belgrade | 1,278 | 12.6 |
| Eastern Europe | 1275.7 | 139.32 | 109.2 | Total | 13,304 | 9.5 |

+ 1992

Source: United Nations 1995, UN Statistical Yearbook (New York: UN).

be a disincentive to new potential migrants and a stimulus for return migration back to the countryside, but the predominant flow seems to be in the other direction. Counter-urbanisation might also be expected in the case of professionals moving to suburban zones with good conditions for high-tech industry, although the scale of such movement seems to be rather small at present (Gawryszewski 1992). However, community attitudes to migration and the transition seem likely to result in regional variations. In some regions like the Podhale in the Polish Carpathians where pluriactivity is traditional, there is a spontaneous increase in entrepreneurial activity when local employment opportunities are limited: people move around the country (at least on a temporary basis) to work in commerce or as temporary wage labourers; some make use of family contacts as far afield as Chicago. In other words, the established patterns of second economy involvement provide knowledge and experience for entering the new capitalist economy. By contrast, in Central Poland there is a deep sense of loss when unemployment rises and people try to get involved in sweat-shop labour and local kinship networks. Only after a few years may other options be considered, like migration to other parts of Poland or abroad. Movement may be discouraged initially by demands of farming and the local family network dependency, and the very slow development of a housing market also places a brake on movement. However, the 'farming constraint' may become less significant over time as the marginality of small-scale farming becomes clear and knowledge about the migration options increase. Suitcase traders from FSU and migrants from other areas (such as agricultural and manual workers from

*Table 3.4* Rural and urban population 1990–5

| Country | Rural population | | | | Urban population | | | |
|---|---|---|---|---|---|---|---|---|
| | 1990 | | 1995 | | 1990 | | 1995 | |
| | A | B | A | B | A | B | A | B |
| Albania | 64.3 | 1.8 | 62.7 | 0.4 | 35.8 | 2.7 | 37.3 | 1.8 |
| Bosnia-Hercegovina | 55.4 | −0.7 | 51.0 | −6.1 | 44.6 | 3.0 | 49.0 | −2.5 |
| Bulgaria | 32.3 | −1.8 | 29.3 | −2.4 | 67.7 | 1.0 | 70.7 | 0.4 |
| Croatia | 40.2 | −2.1 | 35.6 | −2.6 | 59.8 | 1.9 | 64.4 | 1.4 |
| Czech Republic | 35.1 | −0.3 | 34.6 | −0.3 | 64.9 | 0.2 | 65.4 | 0.1 |
| Germany | 14.7 | −1.3 | 13.4 | −1.2 | 85.3 | 0.7 | 86.6 | 0.3 |
| Hungary | 38.0 | −1.7 | 35.3 | −1.9 | 62.1 | 0.4 | 64.7 | 0.3 |
| Macedonia | 42.2 | 0.3 | 40.1 | 0.1 | 57.8 | 2.0 | 59.9 | 1.8 |
| Poland | 37.5 | −0.6 | 35.3 | −1.1 | 62.5 | 1.2 | 64.7 | 0.9 |
| Romania | 46.7 | −0.5 | 44.6 | −1.3 | 53.3 | 1.2 | 55.4 | 0.5 |
| Slovakia | 43.5 | −0.6 | 41.2 | −0.7 | 56.5 | 1.3 | 58.8 | 1.2 |
| Slovenia | 41.0 | −2.0 | 36.5 | −2.1 | 59.0 | 2.2 | 63.6 | 1.8 |
| Yugoslavia | 46.9 | −0.8 | 43.5 | −0.2 | 53.1 | 2.0 | 56.5 | 2.6 |

*Notes* A Percentage of the total population; B Change per cent per annum.
*Source*: United Nations 1995, *UN Statistical Yearbook* (New York: UN)

FFRY) may influence locals as to their own migration decisions. Another factor is the way people will be received in the areas they visit: wealthy Westerners and poor Easterners have both being 'demonised' in Poland where it is also a keen perception that migrating women may be lured into prostitution.

There was considerable international migration before 1989 with movement from FFRY in Western Europe (Malacic 1994) and the use of foreign labour in FCSFR where there were 100,000 people on residence permits in 1990, including many from Vietnam. But migration has increased due to simpler frontier formalities and the removal of stringent movement controls and patterns of movement are now extremely diverse. There is a good deal of temporary movement for work purposes (by people who normally move without their families), with FCSFR and Hungary drawing from Poland and the Balkans. There are also Romanians undertaking harvest work in Serbia. There is also a feeling of vulnerability in Eastern Europe to possible large-scale emigration from FSU, particularly with the instability of 1990–1 which saw East European countries erecting defences along their eastern frontiers (Oberg and Boubnova 1993). There has been some 'shopping tourism' by merchants who arrive in Eastern Europe, sell goods obtained at subsidised prices in FSU shops, and then return home with zloty and other East European currencies changed into dollars. But no great influx has yet occurred and, in any case, measures are now being taken to minimise the risks through changes in legislation (Heyden 1991).

However, Hungary is facing the possibility of return migration by Hungarians from Croatia (due to the civil war), Slovakia and Transylvania (Dovenyi and Vukovich 1994). Camps have been used by refugees from Romania at Bicske near Budapest (along with Hajduszoboszlo and Bekescsaba) while refugees from fighting in FFYR have been accommodated in the Balaton area and the southwest. The influx into Hungary was 13.2,000 in 1988, 17.5 in 1989 and 18.4 in 1990 (predominantly ethnic Hungarians from Romania, with a peak following the Targu Mures demonstrations); increasing to 53.3 in 1991 and 16.1 in 1992 with FFYR citizens (predominantly Croats and ethnic Hungarians from the Baranya Triangle) as the main element when people from Romania were refused entry after October 1991. The numbers are probably underestimates since ethnic Hungarians frequently apply immediately for citizenship, citing discrimination and the political situation as reasons for leaving. Hungary has also experienced some return migration from the West after 184,500 left in 1956: there was a trickle of below 1,000 per annum during the 1970s and 1980s, rising to 3,500 in 1991. There is some ambivalence towards those who return: they are accepted if they work quietly (indeed there is a tradition of respect in rural areas for people who went abroad and did well) but there is some resentment against returnees who subsequently enter politics. For there is a sense of 'opting out' of the hardships of communism. In Poland such sentiments are tinged with suspicion that the returnees may have actually benefited under communism with the 'Polonia' companies of the 1980s which provided for joint ventures under favourable terms when the foreign partner was of Polish origin. However, an element of public disquiet has not discouraged some from entering politics, such as I. Ratiu in Romania (senator and presidential election candidate in 1990) and S. Tyminski in Poland (presidential election candidate in 1992).

However, the predominant flow is still from Eastern Europe to the West which seems destined to enlarge the communities already established (Grecic 1993). At present East Europeans are very unevenly distributed in Western Europe: around 1mn. in Germany (excluding Germans from FGDR or Eastern Europe) comprising large Czech, Hungarian and Polish communities plus some people from FSU and the overwhelming proportion of Yugoslavs who were able to leave without difficulty to become Gastarbeiter. But only a few parts of FGDR have large foreign populations: mainly Chemnitz, Eisen-huttenstadt and Rostock where Mozambicans, Poles and Vietnamese were introduced by the FGDR government. There was some immigration to the Berlin area, but generally little in FGDR: most migrants went to the central and southern parts of West Germany. Meanwhile, France and the UK each have about 150,000 (which again includes migrants from FSU). Today much of the movement is more temporary, and in connection with training programmes linked with the transition. But some stays may become permanent although the migration balance will depend on the development of the labour market within Eastern Europe.

Another special case concerns the 3.7mn. Aussiedler who arrived in Germany between 1950 and 1993, despite attempts to slow the movement by investments to give Germans a higher living standard in the FSU and elsewhere (Jones and Wild 1992). There has been a rising tide of movement of Germans from the east. In the late 1980s the main flow was from Poland (438.9000) compared with 160.2 from FSU and 50.3 from Romania. But in 1990–2 the number from Poland fell to 171.1 and was almost equalled by the number of Germans from Romania (155.5) which was easily exceeded by movement from FSU (490.4). The flow is likely to continue in the latter instance, whereas it cannot be sustained in the other two cases. Another 2mn. are expected from FSU by the end of the century. Aussiedler are allocated to the Lander on an 'equality of burden' principle. But the New Lander have high unemployment and poor job prospects in the short term. Integration is most successful where there are good job prospects and lower than average housing costs. Unfortunately, poor language ability and irrelevant occupational experience often make it difficult for the new arrivals to find employment.

Germany is also a prime target for economic migrants who want to cross the *Wohlslandsgrenze* (prosperity frontier). Germany experienced heavy in-migration from Eastern Europe with 127.5,000 from Bulgaria, Romania and FFYR in the first half of 1991; 30.1 in the second half and 107.6 in the first

113

half of 1992 (compared with 32.0; 13.9, and 18.9 respectively for Turks and Vietnamese) (Kemper 1993; Mihalka 1993). Yet there is no economic need for further migration since Germany has a large (though partly hidden) labour reserve of 7.5mn. people and job creation is now complicated by the wages precipice on the frontiers with FCSFR and Poland. But Germany is revising agreements affording access to its labour market and migrants from Angola, Cuba, Mozambique and Vietnam have been offered free flights home. Large numbers of Romanian Gypsies entered Germany during the months after the revolution but many of them have now been repatriated. Even ethnic Germans (an estimated 100th of whom moved out of Romania after the revolution) are now being encouraged to stay at home. Meanwhile, Austria introduced visa schemes for Poles and Romanians in 1990. Yet such decisions are morally questionable in the context of the CSCE Helsinki Treaty of 1975 when Western countries successfully pressed the communist states over human rights. A more constructive approach would be to improve job prospects within Eastern Europe so that there would be fewer economic migrants.

*Migration: towards a policy*

A sensible immigration policy is needed: perhaps contract-linked migration for skilled and unskilled workers that avoids what Heyden (1991) has described as the curse of illegal status. The pressure of new arrivals can hardly be blunted by the official view that Germany is not a country of immigration, especially in the context of labour market deregulation. There is an ongoing political debate in Germany on identity which is questioning the government strategy of closer ties with the EU. Hence the activity of the Republikaner Party whose support is not related simply to opponents of immigration policy (Jones 1994). In Germany, admission to citizenship is a privilege rarely granted to non-Germans and hence Germanness is anti-pathetic to the development of a multi-cultural society that dilutes a mono-linguistic and mono-ethnic German culture; all the more since most of the foreign population is of non-Western European origin (Blotevogel *et al.* 1993). Pressure for stricter control is quite high in FGDR, because while some youth activities in FGDR espouse left-wing causes there are also right-wing campaigns against asylum seekers which serve to heighten ethnic tension (Stock 1994). Xenophobic attacks tend to be higher in the east although there are few areas with large numbers of foreign migrants.

Greater emigration control has its implications for FFRY since much of the recent movement into Western Europe has arisen through the war which led to some 0.5mn. people seeking refuge abroad by the end of 1992: 260,000 in Germany, 75,000 in Sweden, 70,5,000 in Switzerland, 57.5,000 in Austria, 52,000 in France and 44,000 in the UK. A further 2mn. people have been internally displaced, including 750,000 refugees in Croatia (one-third of thom are from the former UN-protected areas) where food and power shortages have occurred (Black 1993; Grecic 1993). Late in 1992 the EU decided that refugees could be sent back to a third country (through which they had travelled) if that country was safe, i.e. Austria, Croatia, Hungary or Slovenia in the case of refugees from Bosnia-Hercegovina. Visa formalities are also being used to control numbers. This has tended to concentrate the problems within FFYR where 4.24mn. were receiving some form of UN assistance by the end of 1993, mostly in Bosnia-Hercegovina.

Attempts to control movement into EU countries during the early 1990s has also placed stress on neighbouring East European countries which are being used for transit purposes. A migration buffer zone is appearing around Western Europe and since the late 1980s Hungary has become a receiving rather than a sending country, reflecting its situation in the context of less stable areas in the Balkans (Dovenyi and Vukovich 1994). Hungary was prepared to use barracks vacated by returning FSU soldiers to accommodate economic refugees moving in the opposite direction. But there is also movement from south to north through Hungary by people with the urge to escape from rising unemployment (Bobeva 1994) and to take advantage of the relatively easy entry formalities into Germany which used to exist (Jones 1991). FCSFR has also acquired a new role as a destination for immigrants, both legal and illegal. The transit movement is mainly from Romania, Bulgaria and FFRY. There were an estimated 150,000–200,000 illegal immigrants in FCSFR at the end of 1992 (1.5 per cent of the total population), including some from the Third World. Like Hungary, the Czech Republic is attractive for would-be illegal migrants (false tourists and illegal traders) in view of the country's stability and increasing economic strength. And the open frontier with Slovakia makes control more difficult. Another migration route operates through Poland for Afghans and Indians who enter the FSU and reach Poland by way of Belarus or the Baltic states. Already more than 10,000 persons each year are detected trying to cross Germany's frontiers illegally, a situation which demonstrates the need for a wider plan of border control in Eastern Europe to stop would-be migrants while respecting human rights and freedom of movement. Such a plan will have to be part of an agreement clarifying relations and responsibilities of sending, receiving and transit states.

There remains the special case of migration by people from Albania into Greece. Albania's population is still increasing quite rapidly by 2 per cent per annum (compared with the European average of 0.4 per cent) and more than half of the country's 3.4mn. population are under 30. Migration controls were very tight indeed before 1989 but there have been massive upheavals recently because some 300,000 people have left (many of them Greeks); while a similar number have arrived from Kosovo. An accurate balance is difficult to establish since many have returned from Greece and Italy. Initially it seems

115

that people were attracted by the lure of consumer goods but now there is migration to undertake temporary work especially in Greece. There has been an ambivalent response from the Greeks who associated the influx of Albanians with an increase in petty crime, while the government was concerned at the cultural impact of Muslims in an Orthodox state. Some 100,000 Albanians were reportedly deported under 'Operation Scoupa'. It was an unfortunate situation where Greece could have set quotas and given more thought to longer term economic benefits of dealing with Albania; Albania should have shown more sensitivity, bearing in mind xenophobic opportunists in Athens and the regional centres near the Albanian border (Ioannina and Konitsa). Better neighbourly relations have now been established. Meanwhile, within Albania the population should have become more homogenous, but Kosovo Albanians may mix rather uneasily with Albanians who have lived most or all their lives sheltered by the former Hoxha regime, and a north–south migration to take up spare housing capacity in the former Greek villages has been described emotively as ethnic cleansing.

## Welfare, culture and gender

The transition is proving to be stressful for East Europeans. They have escaped from an economy of shortages and from the intimidation of the communist security services, but they have entered an altogether more competitive world that is full of uncertainty. The reality of low incomes was concealed by the limited range of goods available in the shops, but now low spending power is highlighted by exposure to Western consumerism. Communities that previously worked together to maintain a caring environment are now under stress through the uneven distribution of benefits under the various programmes of privatisation. Unemployment has been a serious blow for millions of people across the region, used to believing that a job was in effect a welfare benefit. An evolving civil society is torn between the need for a stimulative business environment in which wealth can be created and the equally pressing necessity for protection against the pressures imposed by recent upheavals. Radical change has been widely accepted, but it is clear that, as wealth increases, improvements in welfare are preferred to further increases in individual incomes.

There should be better protection for workers, a more comprehensive financial cushion (for there is only limited welfare provision outside the enterprise) and more help with retraining (Deacon et al. 1992). There is a need for housing benefit in the public housing sector to limit the fall in real living standards in Hungary (Pudney 1995). Social policy is being restructured (Svetlik 1992) but finding money to maintain and expand social services is a challenge throughout Eastern Europe. The health situation also provides a test for international policy-making in view of the scale of east–west differences as well as the contrasts within and between East European countries, verging on crisis in some cases (Davis *et al.* 1993). Access to health care seems to vary according to economic position and informal connections; also location (in the context of a lack of choice between medical centres, when many local centres have only limited facilities) and inhibitions through the doctor's professional language. World Bank loans have been provided for health care in Hungary where better health education in respect of smoking, drinking and diet is needed to improve performance over heart disease and life expectancy (Grochowski 1990). There are also deficiencies in Poland where cities in the west do not provide health care commensurate with their pollution problems (Okolski 1992).

In education, Poland has responded to the transition with a growth of academic as opposed to vocational education. While jobs in government and in the state-owned factories have in the past been secured through vocational qualifications, graduates from academic secondary schools have been doing better in the labour market recently. At the same time academic courses are relatively cheap from the state's point of view. Appropriate education policies are needed to reduce linguistic isolation which applies to provision for minority languages and also for opportunities for mainstream communities to learn Western languages (Radnai 1994). The CoE launched a scheme in 1993 to twin each of Albania's 2000 schools with similar institutions elsewhere in Europe or North America. This is a follow-up to the CoE emergency relief programme 'SOS Albanian Children' to tackle deprivation in Albanian schools. There has been a growth in higher education in Romania where a buoyant private sector, taking off in 1990, now complements the state-run institutions which are also expanding.

Education for good citizenship requires a better supply of information which the media has a major responsibility to provide (Bellows 1993). Newspapers and magazines have multiplied in numbers and there is wide choice especially in the towns, although most publications provide psychological satisfaction rather than objective information (Deltcheva 1996). There are some continuing supply problems because in Romania state-controlled distribution has been blamed for the limited availability of opposition newspapers which means that opinions sharply critical of the governing Party of Social Democracy are effectively shut out of the rural areas where the regime attracts strongest support. However, there is now real potential for a media bonanza. Several Western companies are active, including Axel-Springer-Verlag, European Media Enterprises and the Swiss-based Ringier. Hungary's daily tabloid *Mai Nap* and the weekly *Reform* have attracted US$4mn. of investment from News International. However, it was reported in 1993 that the stake was conditional on satisfactory profit levels and was to be withdrawn because of poor performance. This seems to be symptomatic of a situation where there is an unsatisfactory compromise between editorial and advertising interests. Meanwhile, a considerable number of national-language editions of titles like *Cosmopolitan*, *Elle* and *Reader's Digest* are now available.

There has been a trend towards liberalisation in broadcasting, despite the problems of finance (broadcasting equipment is often between thirty and forty years old at a time when modern FM technology is in use in most other parts of the world) and political resistance to independent institutions. After major controversy Hungary has made most progress in keeping state television away from the direct control of the ruling party. There is still political resistance to privatisation with political resistance to a liberalised broadcasting system financed heavily by advertising. However, the beginnings of a breakup of state television monopolies are now evident and national commercial television stations have appeared. TV Nova became the first national commercial broadcaster in Eastern Europe in early 1994, backed by both Czech and North American investors led by the Central European Media Enterprises Group. Nova's reporters have trained with staff of the Atlanta USA-based CNN and the station has gained increased advertising time compared with what was allowed to the earlier competitors of state television; it has also developed links with the leading advertising agencies in Prague. Within a year it gained over 70 per cent of the market share while the public broadcaster Czech Television faced decreasing viewing numbers due to limits on advertising much lower than the 10 per cent figure available to TV Nova. So the Italian-owned Premiera, a Prague-based regional broadcaster established in 1993 to serve Central Bohemia, is to develop a national network of regional stations. By contrast, the only national commercial channel in Poland, Polsat, has only a small audience share and foreign media involvement in the other East European countries has also been limited (Giorgi and Pohoryles 1995).

In Bulgaria the Russian television station Ostankino has been replaced by a private channel for which several companies have competed. Local stations are developing: Hungary has allocated over a hundred licences for television and radio frequencies geared to 'local reach' defined as 500,000 people in Budapest and 100,000 in other parts of the country. It remains to be seen how effective this will be in terms of competition for the state MTV. There are plans for commercial television channels in Poland to compete with state channels which will continue to attract advertising. Belgium's FilmNet International has launched Poland's first subscription television film channel; while Canal Plus of France will build and operate Poland's sole subscription television broadcasting operation through a joint venture with Polish investors. There are delays because the Polish military says it is unwilling to release the frequencies needed until 1997. Overall, considerable progress has been made, although foreign intervention over finance and training is limited by some investment restrictions and also by uncertainty over advertising revenue in the transition.

## Gender

Gender issues are relevant to the transition (Corrin 1992; Heitlinger 1996). In Albania women are active in political movements but they have not yet achieved fundamental change towards equality (Emandi 1993). Women bear the brunt of poor services in a country where there is just one nurse for every two to three villages; also where there is much overcrowding and malnutrition linked with alcoholism and domestic violence (Corrin 1995). However, in general, communists went further than Western countries in providing day nurseries and abortion clinics 'but changes came about because the ruling elite deemed they were necessary' to get women on to the labour market (De Silva 1993, p.312) not because of pressure from the feminist movement. Equality on the labour market gave women independence, but meant the forced imposition of unsuitable jobs and neglect of the family. Now, after half a century of dependence on the 'patriarchal state' the situation is changing.

The reduction in jobs and the incidence of unemployment among women has been very noticeable in the FGDR, for women seem to be unemployed for longer periods than men and face greater difficulties getting new jobs (Quack and Maier 1994). Moreover, despite the fact that equal opportunity legislation is now in force, there is concern over the erosion of child care facilities which complicates female employment where young mothers are concerned. In FGDR women could be mothers and also enjoy independence in the context of single-parent families. They enjoyed easy access to nurseries and family planning assistance, although in the West the communist strategy was seen as tantamount to locking women in a traditional reproductive role. Now, with rising costs for nurseries, it is difficult for unmarried mothers in FGDR with more than two children to get a job. Forced to choose between family and career, some women are opting for sterilisation in order to compete for jobs. Families may become more stable if women resist the cyclical pattern of marriage, child-bearing and divorce. However, with the legacy of full integration into employment and economic independence they will be reluctant to accept the West German model of only partial labour market integration.

In Poland too, women carry domestic burdens while bearing the brunt of unemployment, especially in the old industrial areas which have traditionally had high rates of female employment (Ciechocinska 1993). Women have become prominent in business banking and finance; while the feminization of professions like book-keeping has given women an opportunity for entry into accountancy. However, women have shouldered a major share of the burdens of transition, including responsibility for the family budget at a time of economic stringency with reductions in subsidies, social services and real wages (Millard 1995). Initial passivity over the loss of many state-financed day care facilities, deterioration in the health service and rising poverty has given way to the growth of women's movements (Davin 1992). In particular, women have tried to organise to fight legislation that would permit abortion only when the life or health of the mother was threatened and envisaged imprisonment for doctors and patients contravening the regulations (Kozakiewicz 1989). It is evident that women's issues have been much more adequately articulated since a social democrat government came to power in 1993. However, there is an urban–rural divide on this issue. On balance the feminist movement is not strong and most women think they should be in the home. But even so, regrets have been expressed that even with a measure that many would see as progressive (women's right to abortion), the communist regime failed to convince the population as to its merits. However, in Romania the very tough communist abortion laws were relaxed in 1989 and abortion is now available on request up to twelve weeks (and thereafter if medical evidence is supportive). French organisations have been helpful with information on contraception (Puia and Hirtopeanu 1990).

## Ethnicity

This is a major source of instability and one that has become more significant under the transition because nationalism can be openly expressed not only through cultural manifestations but through the political process, with parties to project the interests of mainstream and minority communities (Blank 1994). It is regrettable that ethnicity is widely perceived as a source of stress rather than cultural enrichment (Kovacs 1991) but this situation follows from conflicting aspirations between a majority and minority with respect to the territorial limits of a nation state and the extent of regional autonomy (Cuthbertson and Leibowitz 1994). Despite a decline in the weight of the ethnic minorities through expulsions, exchanges and assimilation (Carter 1993), there are still many instances where minorities inhabit sensitive areas and can (at least potentially) attract support or be adopted as pawns in a nationalist struggle orchestrated in a neighbouring country (Kotor 1993; Poulton 1996). It is this capacity for minorities to identify with 'mother countries' elsewhere in the region that invests inter-ethnic relations with particular significance. There is a potential for subversion which may lie dormant for long periods but which is validated as a threat by historical experience.

Statistics are unsatisfactory because of inadequate coverage of minorities in some census exercises and by some reluctance on the part of individuals to declare their ethnic affiliation, sometimes the result of genuine uncertainty in the case of certain provincial groups (Lieblich 1991). Certainly the ethnic issue has become much more diverse since 1989 because provincial groups have been politicised, as in Cieszyn, Istria and Moravia (Kubik 1994; Markotich 1993b); while the breakup of the federations has resulted in the separate consideration for Czechs and Slovaks (Kocsis 1992; Pehe 1993b) and for the various Southern Slav peoples previously subsumed under the Yugoslav umbrella (Lampe 1994). Thus a small country like Slovenia has become embroiled in ethnic issues through the Croat minority in the south of the country and the claims advanced by Italy on behalf of families expelled from Istria at the end of the Second World War (Gosar 1993). In most cases numbers are small, but free political expression enables all ethnic issues to be discussed much more widely than before, often by partisan political parties. And while claims for cultural autonomy may reasonably be linked with basic human rights (Szepe 1994), there may be difficult questions of resource allocation when cultural facilities for small scattered populations like the Greeks in Albania, Poles in Lithuania or Romanians in Hungary are being considered (Berxholli *et al.* 1994; Zubek 1993).

In the past, the German minorities have been most prominent but they are now greatly reduced through expulsions after 1945 and recent emigration to the FRG (Kosiarski 1992). Significant groups still exist in several countries, especially Poland, where there is some confusion over numbers because of the ethnic ambivalence of the Silesians (Gwiazda 1994). The plight of the Turks in Bulgaria was the most serious ethnic problem during the 1980s (Karpat 1990, 1995) because the communist authorities tried to assimilate this minority and settle Bulgarians in sensitive border regions. However, although former communists in the Bulgarian Socialist Party initially exploited the dilemmas facing Bulgarians in ethnically mixed regions, the situation is now much improved because the Turks are represented by their own party (the Movement for Human Rights and Liberties) which sometimes holds the balance of power. But today the most important issues concern the Albanians in Macedonia and Yugoslavia (especially Kosovo) and the Hungarians in Romania, Slovakia and Yugoslavia (Markotich 1992; Paul 1991, 1993). The Kosovo problem is very delicate because of the Albanian majority in an area that is adjacent to Albania yet vigorously defended by Serbs as an essential part of their cultural heritage (Schmidt 1993). Withdrawal of autonomy has been greatly resented and the status of Albanians stands in marked contrast to the situation in Macedonia where accommodations have been made. It so happens that civil war elsewhere in FFRY and Albania's restraint (a reflection of both military weakness and economic aid from the West) have relegated the issues to the back-burner for the time being. 'Pan-Serb' politics in Bosnia-Hercegovina and Croatia (Hayden *et al.* 1994; Markotich 1993a) and associated refugee problems have been much more in evidence (Dominis and Bicanic 1993; Putaki 1993). But Kosovo remains a critical issue and it is perhaps the part of Eastern Europe where political change is most likely to occur in the future.

The Hungarians in Transylvania have been extensively discussed in recent years (Oltay 1991a). Hungarians want a Romanian Ministry for National Minority Problems (Shafir 1993) and the reopening of the Hungarian consulate in Cluj-Napoca, closed unilaterally by the Romanians in 1988. Above all, they want cultural autonomy and a status of equality for the Hungarian language. But concessions are opposed by the Romanian National Unity Party whose members (many of whom migrated from Moldavia during the communist era) are fearful of Hungarian assertiveness (Shafir 1991). Even moderate Romanian opinion would argue that current provision is substantial and would express reservations over full equality for the Hungarian language (Buza and Ianos 1994). They would certainly insist that minority issues are an internal matter and not an issue on which international pressures should be exerted (Fischer-Galati 1994). On the other hand, right-wing politicians in Hungary (such as L. Csurka's faction within the Hungarian Democratic Forum) support the case for adequate living space (*Lebensraum*) in Transylvania, including cultural autonomy (Oltay 1991b). Unfortunately, what one party sees as a legitimate human right becomes contentious when greater autonomy may become a prelude to separation (Eyal 1989). Neither Hungarians nor Romanians can forget the territorial arrangements in force before the First World War and their partial restoration through the partition of Transylvania between 1940 and 1944. Similar tensions arise in Slovakia where the Hungarians are campaigning for their own local councils (Reisen 1992).

'There is no question that the further we move to the east the greater the number of specific problems caused by nationalism that can be seen today' (Skubiszewski 1993, p.25). These problems are not new, but the recent experience with authoritarian regimes may intensify intolerance as 'a previously ideological state changes into a nationalist one' (ibid., p.26) and intolerant attitudes could be more destabilising than in Western Europe. A human rights agenda is very relevant, but a more realistic view would emphasise the security concerns of mainstream communities and see a way forward in arrangements for an effective international framework evolving through EU membership. The CoE 'framework convention' on the protection of minorities should be adopted in international treaties but with consideration for security to foster a greater sense of trust. This would help to meet the argument put forward by Verdery (1993) that adequate institutions are needed and the understandable cultural aspirations of Hungarian communities could then be more easily met in the context of expanding cross-border collaboration than through entrenched historic attitudes which have cast the Hungarians as fifth column (Kocsis 1994). He argues that the Hungarian communities 'should play an important role as mediators in a political and economic rapprochement of the nations in the Carpathian Basin' (ibid., p. 431). In the meantime the political process will continue to highlight inter-ethnic issues in a partisan fashion with the risk of double standards as states seek regimes for 'their' people in neighbouring countries without a will to reciprocate (Christopulos 1994). The other side of the coin is the peaceful nature of most routine inter-ethnic relations and the wider political processes operating through local government and regional planning that integrate the ethnic issue with other problems of socio-political development (Turnock 1994).

## Jews and Gypsies

National integration is also compromised by cultural or religious groups which have no national programmes but which may emphasise their identity in such a way as to generate discrimination. Although the number of Jews is very small there has been some anti-Semitism in political life (Bergmann 1994; Tucker 1996), although it seems that 'Jews' are merely convenient targets for ultra-nationalist polemics by candidates on the political fringes. Of much greater significance for integration in civil society are the large numbers of Gypsies in Eastern Europe. Accurate information is lacking because many Gypsies, for various reasons, do not declare themselves as such (Crowe and Kolsti 1991). Taking the mean average of figures presented by handbooks as well as information from government sources and Gypsy organisations, it would seem that there are 1.90mn. Gypsies in Romania, 0.75 in Bulgaria and FYR, 0.60 in FCS (predominantly Slovakia) and Hungary, 0.06 in Albania, and 0.02 in Poland. However, Z.D. Barany (1995a) has produced an estimate of 5mn. (2mn. in Romania, 0.80 in Bulgaria and Hungary, 0.40 in Slovakia, and 0.30 in the Czech Republic) which conform reasonably closely to these averages although their provenance is not clear. In the case of Romania the 1992 census recorded only 0.40mn. and although informed estimates would increase the true figure to over 1mn. this is still well below the average estimate and must therefore be treated with the greatest caution.

However, there is no doubt that Gypsies remain a large underclass taking low-paid, dirty jobs. They tend to change their employment frequently and under communism were usually prominent in the second economy. Although denied proper representation they were expected to accommodate to the mainstream work culture (Stewart 1990). With rising unemployment they now face further discrimination. Hence it is likely that anti-Gypsy prejudice may well be on the increase through rising unemployment (linked with the loss of jobs in agriculture and industry through privatisation) and a perceived association of Gypsies with the growth of alcoholism and petty crime. The situation varies between countries and the relatively favourable position of Gypsies in Macedonia (Barany 1995b) is contrasted with the universal hostility felt towards them in Slovakia (ibid. 1995a). This may be an over-statement, because the Gypsies are generally 'tolerated' by the mainstream communities and irritation on the part of local government officials and other members of the public at large is often the result of significant provocation. Therefore, if social intolerance is to be reduced, Gypsies need to play their part and show greater respect for the law and for the interests of others (Pehe 1993a).

After the velvet revolution in FCSFR the crude assimilationist policies of the communist period (including female sterilisation to reduce the birth rate) were abandoned. There have been attempts to improve relations between

Gypsies and the police, while ministries in the Czech Republic employ experts on Gypsy affairs, appreciating their need for social care. But social services are being run down and there is no sign that dismissive attitudes towards education and family planning will be moderated. There is a relatively high birth rate and 43.1 per cent of the Gypsy population in FCSFR was younger than 15 years old in 1980 (48.7 in 1970) compared with only 24.3 for the entire population (Kalibova *et al.* 1993, p.138). Education has improved, but standards are still below the level of the mainstream communities; Barany (1991) sees the Gypsies caught in a vicious circle of inadequate education (with very few schools using Romany languages) and poor employment prospects, even for unskilled labourers. Yet Romany language instruction has started in several schools in Bulgaria, a language faculty has opened in Shumen and a Roma Theatre in Sofia is on the agenda. The Hungarian government has funded cultural organisations and newspapers, while an all-Gypsy secondary school operates in Pecs (as at 1994). Unfortunately, Gypsy parents place little value on formal education and rarely insist that children complete their education, with a resultant high drop-out rate.

Limited life expectancy reflects low health standards which are unlikely to improve because of the link with a poor housing situation. Better access to housing is being sought in Bulgaria and the Slovak authorities are trying to solve this problem, although many private property owners find Gypsy tenants uncongenial and the phenomenon of Gypsy enclaves is likely to grow. Signalling an end to pre-1989 policies of integration, more than four-fifths of Czechs would not like to have a Gypsy neighbour and consider the behaviour of Gypsies to be provocative. As many as one-third are in favour of deportation or isolation in ghettos. Friction has occurred where there are large numbers of Gypsies on the edges of towns in encampments or multi-storey blocks sometimes allocated exclusively to Gypsy families. But even in villages there can be tension: as in Spisska Podhradie in Slovakia where the local authorities imposed a curfew in July 1993 on Gypsies and 'other suspicious persons' in a bid to reduce crime (Fisher 1993). Some Slovak politicians have threatened to withdraw benefits from Gypsies, and the Czechs are drafting legislation to control migration by Gypsies from Slovakia. On the other hand, some Gypsies returning from Germany have resources to build substantial houses for extended families: they may be a good influence for the future in stimulating a greater priority for higher living standards.

Job creation projects are needed, although as the economic transition proceeds Gypsies are likely to find more opportunities in private business. Over the longer term there will have to be more training and welfare, as well as social work among the Gypsies and education to get the birth rate reduced. Representation is being improved (there is a National Gypsy Council in Hungary) and self-administrative bodies have been facilitated in more than 200 localities. In Bulgaria there is an Independent Socialist Democratic

Union of Romanies and a Roma Democratic Union while the Party of Rights and Freedoms attracts Gypsy support. There are several small political parties in Romania where the work of an institute concerned with the quality of life is preoccupied with the Gypsy community. In FCSFR today there is scope for autonomy under the Charter of Basic Rights and Freedoms adopted in 1991. The Slovak authorities have recognised the Gypsies as a national minority although there is little funding to enable them to make much progress with publishing and political activity. Gypsy political parties have been formed where possible (ethnically based political parties are not allowed in Bulgaria), although infighting between rival Gypsy organisations like Romania's Democratic Union of the Roma reduces their effectiveness. Some leaders, like Romania's Gypsy 'emperor' I. Radulescu, have behaved as self-promoting entrepreneurs.

## CONCLUSION

Political change seems inevitable, for just as the old regimes have lost their legitimacy (though the left is regaining public confidence in the context of social democracy) those who have brokered the revolution have also become vulnerable because of deepening dissatisfaction over the short-term impact of radical reform and inadequate levels of welfare provision. People are caught between aggression and helplessness. Although there is no intellectually credible alternative to the market as the key to future prosperity, the short-term problems are providing a platform for anti-market populist forces and forcing a wide-ranging exploration of possibilities for hybrid systems of economic management to provide social protection and worker ownership of enterprises. Alternative political programmes need discussion and thus there is a role for people connected with neither the old communist nor the revolutionary elites. The transition will take much longer than was initially supposed and there may be a complicated legacy through the residue of socialist industry which will be neither sold nor closed.

It will be a slow process for people's incomes to catch up with those in the West on the basis of a resumption of growth in 1994. The EBRD suggests that even in 2025 East European incomes will only run at half the levels prevailing in the West. But since 1994 economic growth has resumed in most countries and East Europeans hope for steady improvement, according to surveys conducted by the Centre for the Study of Public Policy at Glasgow's Strathclyde University and the Paul Lazarsfeld Gesellschaft fur Sozialforschung in Vienna. According to interviews conducted throughout Eastern Europe (excepting FGDR and FFYR, other than Croatia and Slovenia) in late 1993 and early 1994 people feel freer to quite an overwhelming extent (Haerpfer and Rose 1994). Except in Bulgaria, Hungary and Slovakia, post-communist governments have won a far higher approval rating than the old regimes (while approval ratings in five years time are expected to be even higher). In Bulgaria, Hungary and Slovakia there is considerable nostalgia for the old order (with around 75 per cent approval) and even in five years' time the new system will only have regained this level of acceptance, with a continuing discrepancy in Hungary where expectations are obviously very high. However, by 1996 only one-third of respondents in Bulgaria favoured a return to communism compared with one-fifth in Hungary and Slovakia and only one-tenth elsewhere.

Public opinion is certainly not overawed by the political process. While presidents and armies inspire trust, parliaments and political parties (along with most other institutions of civil society) do not; though in the case of the churches there is an even balance between trust and distrust. People are remarkably patient and only in Hungary is there an even balance between those who are prepared to give government time and those who would favour a change if results are not forthcoming soon; though the balance is reasonably close in Romania at 60:40 (compared with 80:20 in the Czech Republic). Incidentally, people see the best alternative to the present pluralist system in greater influence by experts in running the economy (two-thirds' support) or else a strong leader (one-third); although it seems that people want efficient administrators rather than experts in economic theory.

## REFERENCES

A. Agh (ed.) 1994, *The Emergence of East Central European Parliaments: The First Steps* (Budapest: Hungarian Centre for Democratic Studies).

A. Agh 1995, 'The experiences of the first democratic parliaments in East Central Europe'. *Communist and Post-Communist Studies* 28, 203–14.

J.B. Allcock 1994, 'The fall of Yugoslavia: symptoms and diagnoses'. *Slavonic and East European Review* 72, 686–91.

M. Andrejevich 1991, 'The Sandzak: the next Balkan theatre of war?' *Radio Free Europe/Radio Liberty* 1(47), 26–34.

Z.D. Barany 1991, 'Democratic change brings mixed blessings for gypsies'. *Radio Free Europe/Radio Liberty Research* 1(20), 40–7

Z.D. Barany 1992, 'East European armed forces in transition and beyond'. *East European Quarterly* 26, 1–30.

Z.D. Barany 1995a, 'Ethnic politics and the East European Roma'. Woodrow Wilson Center *East European Studies Newsletter* March–April, 2–8.

Z.D. Barany 1995b, 'The Roma in Macedonia: ethnic politics and the marginal condition in a Balkan state'. *Ethnic and Racial Studies* 18, 515–31.

A. Bebler 1993, 'Yugoslavia's variety of communist federalism and her demise'. *Communist and Post-Communist Studies* 26, 72–86.

H.E. Bellows 1993, 'The challenge of informationalization in post-communist societies'. *Communist and Post-Communist Studies* 26, 144–64.

S. Bergland and J.A. Dellenbrandt (eds) 1991, *The New Democracies in Eastern Europe: Party Systems and Political Cleavages* (Aldershot: Edward Elgar).

W. Bergmann 1994, 'Anti-Semitism and xenophobia in the East German Lander'. *German Politics* 3, 265–76.

B. Bertram *et al.* 1995, 'Experiencing Soviet transformation in Eastern Europe'. *Journal of Area Studies* 6, 19–34.

A. Berxholli *et al.* 1994, 'The Greek minority in the Albanian Republic: a demographic study'. *Nationalities Papers* 22, 427–34.

R. Black 1993, 'Refugees and asylum seekers in Western Europe' in R. Black and V. Robinson (eds) *Geography and Refugees: Patterns and Processes of Change* (London: Belhaven), 87–103.

S. Blank 1994, 'The return of the repressed?: post-1989 nationalism in the "new" Eastern Europe'. *Nationalities Papers* 22, 405–25.

H.H. Blotevogel *et al.* 1993, 'From itinerant worker to immigrant?: the geography of guestworkers in Germany' in R. King (ed.) *Mass Migration in Europe* (London: Belhaven), 83–100.

V. Blum and J. Siegmund 1993, 'The politics and economics of privatizing state enterprise: the case of Treuhandanstalt'. *Governance* 6, 397–408.

D. Bobeva 1994, 'Emigration from and immigration to Bulgaria' in H. Fassman and R. Munz (eds) *European Migration in the Late Twentieth Century* (Aldershot: Edward Elgar), 221–38.

J. Breuilly (ed.) 1992, *The State of Germany: The Nation idea in the Making, Unmaking and Remaking of a Modern State* (London: Longman).

C. Brown (ed.) 1994, *Political Restructuring in Europe* (London: Routledge).

A. Bulir and J. Charap 1993, 'The Czech and Slovak Republics: the process of divergence'. *Communist Economies and Economic Transformation* 5, 369–90.

S.R. Burant and V. Zubek 1993, 'Eastern Europe's old memories and new realities: resurrecting the Polish–Lithuanian union'. *East European Economies and Societies* 7, 370–93.

M. Buza and I. Ianos 1994, 'Some geographical remarks on education and prints in the languages of ethnic groups in Romania'. *GeoJournal* 34, 457–65.

B. Cantrell and U. Kemp 1995, 'Eastern Germany revisited'. *Religion State and Society* 23, 279–90.

D. Carlton *et al.* (eds) 1996, *Rising Tension in Eastern Europe and the Former Soviet Union* (Aldershot: Dartmouth).

F.W. Carter 1993, 'Ethnicity as a cause of migration in Eastern Europe'. *GeoJournal* 30, 241–8.

F.W. Carter and H.T. Norris (eds) 1996, *The Changing Shape of the Balkans* (London: UCL Press).

D. Christopulos 1994, 'Minorities protection: towards a new European approach'. *Balkan Forum: International Journal of Politics Economics and Culture* 2, 155–74.

M. Ciechocinska 1993, 'Gender aspects of dismantling the command economy in Eastern Europe: the Polish case'. *Geoforum* 24, 31–44.

N. Ciger 1993, 'The Serbo-Croatian War 1991: political and military dimensions'. *Journal of Strategic Studies* 16, 297–338.

A.M. Cirtautas 1995, 'The post-communist state: a conceptual and empirical examination'. *Communist and Post-Communist Studies* 28, 379–92.

D.I. Clarke 1991, 'Central Europe's military cooperation in the triangle'. *Radio Free Europe/Radio Liberty Research* 1(2), 42–5.

L.J. Cohen 1995, *Broken Bonds: The Disintegration of Yugoslavia* (Boulder, Colorado: Westview Press).

C. Corrin 1992, 'Gendered identities: women's experience of change in Hungary' in S. Rai *et al.* (eds), *Women in the Face of Change: The Soviet Union, Eastern Europe and China* (London: Routledge), 167–85.

C. Corrin 1995, 'Creating change or struggling to survive?: women's situation in Albania'. *Journal of Area Studies* 6, 74–82.

M. Crnobrnja 1994, *The Yugoslav Disease* (London: I.B. Tauris).

M. Croan *et al.* 1992, 'Is Latin America the future for Eastern Europe?' *Problems of Communism* 41, 44–57.

D. Crowe and J. Kolsti (eds) 1991, *The Gypsies of Eastern Europe* (Armonk, New York: M.E. Sharpe).

W. Crowther 1992, 'Romania and Moldavian political dynamics' in D.N. Nelson (ed.), *Romania after Tyranny* (Boulder, Colorado: Westview Press), 239–59.

C. Cvijic 1991, *Remaking the Balkans* (London: RIIA/Pinter).

I.M. Cuthbertson and J. Leibowitz (eds) 1994, *Minorities: The New Europe's Old Issue* (Boulder, Colorado: Westview Press).

S. Dalby 1993, 'Post-Cold War security in the new Europe' in J. O'Loughlin and H. Van Der Wusten (eds) *The New Political Geography of Eastern Europe* (London: Belhaven Press) 71–85.

D. Davin 1992, 'Population policy and reform: Soviet Union Eastern Europe and China' in S. Rai *et al.* (eds) *Women in the Face of Change: Soviet Union, Eastern Europe and China* (London: Routledge), 79–104.

C.M. Davis *et al.* 1993, 'Health care crisis: Eastern Europe and Former USSR'. *Radio Free Europe/Radio Liberty Research* 2(40) 31–62.

A.H. Dawson 1993, *A Geography of European Integration* (London: Belhaven Press).

B. Deacon *et al.* 1992, *The New Eastern Europe: Social Policy Past Present and Future* (London: Sage).

R. Deltcheva 1996, 'New tendencies in post-totalitarian Bulgaria: mass culture and the media'. *Europe Asia Studies* 48, 305–15.

B. Denitch 1994, *Ethnic Nationalism: The Tragic Death of Yugoslavia* (Minneapolis: University of Minnesota Press).

L. De Silva 1993, 'Women's emancipation under communism: a re-evaluation'. *East European Quarterly* 27, 301–15.

J.B. De Weydenthal 1992, 'Cross-border diplomacy in East Central Europe'. *Radio Free Europe/Radio Liberty Research* 1(42), 19–23.

I. Dominis and I. Bicanic 1993, 'Refugees and displaced persons in the Formner Yugoslavia'. *Radio Free Europe/Radio Liberty Research* 2(3) 1–4.

Z. Dovenyi and G. Vukovich 1994, 'Hungary and international migration' in H. Fassman *et al.* (eds) *European Migration in the Late Twentieth Century* (Aldershot: Edward Elgar), 187–206.

D. Dubravcic 1993, 'Economic causes and political context of the dissolution of a multinational federal state'. *Communist Economies and Economic Transformation* 5, 259–72.

N. Eberstadt 1993, 'Mortality and the fate of communist states'. *Communist Economies and Economic Transformation* 5, 499–518.

N. Eberstadt 1994, 'Demographic shock in Eastern Germany 1989–1993'. *Europe Asia Studies* 46, 519–33.

H. Emandi 1993, 'Development strategies and women in Albania'. *East European Quarterly* 27, 79–96.

J. Eyal 1989, 'The Romanian-Hungarian dispute over Transylvania: where nationalism and history meet ideology'. *Slovo: An Interdisciplinary Journal of Contemporary Russian and East European Affairs* 2(2), 5–17.

S. Fischer-Galati 1994, 'National minority problems in Romania: continuity or change? *Nationalities Papers* 22, 71–81.

S. Fisher 1993, 'Romanies in Slovakia'. *Radio Free Europe/Radio Liberty Research* 2(42), 54–9.

J. Fleischacker 1995, 'The impact of deindustrialization and unemployment on family formation in East Germany'. *Geographia Polonica* 64, 117–35.

T. Foldresi 1995, 'The main problems of religious freedom in Eastern Europe'. *Religion in Eastern Europe* 15(1), 18–26.

D.V. Friedheim 1993, 'Regime collapse in the peaceful East German revolution: the role of middle level officials'. *German Politics* 2, 97–112.

F. Friedman 1994, *The Bosnian Muslims* (Boulder, Colorado: Westview Press).

R. Fritsch-Bournazel 1988, *Confronting the German Question* (Oxford: Berg).

R. Fritsch-Bournazel 1992, *Europe and German Unification* (Oxford: Berg).

I. Gabor 1991, 'Private entrepreneurship and re-embourgoisement in Hungary'. *Society and Economy (Budapest)* 13, 122–33.

V.P. Gagnon 1991, 'Yugoslavia: prospects for stability'. *Foreign Affairs* 70(3), 17–35.

A. Gawryszewski 1992, 'Spatial population mobility in Poland 1952–1985'. *Geographia Polonica* 59, 69–77.

L. Giorgi and R.J. Pohoryles 1995, *The Post-socialist Media – What Power the West?: The Changing Media Landscape in Poland Hungary and the Czech Republic* (Aldershot: Avebury).

G-J Glaessner 1992, *The Unification Process in Germany: From Dictatorships to Democracy* (London: Pinter).

G-J Glaessner and I. Wallace (eds) 1992, *The German revolution of 1989: Causes and Consequences* (Oxford: Berg).

M. Glennie 1992, *The Fall of Yugoslavia* (London: Penguin Books).

A. Gosar 1993, 'Nationalities of Slovenia: changing ethnic structures in Central Europe'. *GeoJournal* 30, 215–23.

M. Grabowska 1994, 'The church in times of change' in M. Alestalo *et al.* (eds) *The Transformation of Europe: Social Conditions and Consequences* (Warsaw: IFiS).

S.R. Graubatd (ed.) 1991, *Eastern Europe – Central Europe – Europe* (Boulder, Colorado: Westview Press).

V. Grecic 1993, 'Mass migration from Eastern Europe: a challenge to the West?' in R. King (ed.) *The New Geography of European Migrations* (London: Belhaven Press), 135–51.

M. Grochowski 1990, 'Myth and reality in the availability of free medical care: the case of Poland'. *GeoJournal* 22, 445–53.

A. Gwiazda 1994, 'Poland's policy towards the national minorities'. *Nationalities Papers* 22, 435–44.

C. Haerpfer and R. Rose 1994, *New Democracies Barometer 1994: Mass Response to Transformation in Central and Eastern Europe* (Vienna: Paul Lazarsfeld Gesellschaft).

D.R. Hall 1992, 'Czech mates no more'. *Town and Country Planning* 61, 250–1.

D.R. Hall and D.A. Danta (eds) 1996, *Reconstructing the Balkans* (London: John Wiley).

P.K. Hamalainen 1995, *Uniting Germany: Actions and Reactions* (Boulder, Colorado: Westview Press).

C.M. Hann 1990, 'Second economy and civil society'. *Journal of Communist Studies* 6(2), 21–44.

R.M. Hayden *et al.* 1994, 'The partition of Bosnia-Hercegovina 1990–1993'. *Radio Free Europe/Radio Liberty Research* 2(22), 1–17.

W. Heisenberg 1991, *German Unification in European Perspective* (London: Centre for European Policy Studies).

A. Heitlinger 1996, 'Framing feminism in post-communist Czech Republic'. *Communist and Post-Communist Studies* 29, 77–93.

K. Henderson 1993, *Czechoslovakia: The Failure of Consensus Politics* (Leicester: University of Leicester Discussion Papers in Politics).

H. Heyden 1991, 'South–North migration'. *International Migration* 29, 281–90.

R.J. Hill and J. Zielonka (eds) 1990, *Restructuring Eastern Europe: Towards a New European Order* (Aldershot: Edward Elgar).

J.A. Irvine 1993, *The Croat Question* (Boulder, Colorado: Westview Press).

C. Jeffery and H. Sturm 1993, *Federalism Unification and European Integration* (London: Frank Cass).

C. Jeppke 1993, 'Why Leipzig?: "exit" and "voice" in the East German revolution'. *German Politics* 2, 393–414.

A. Jones 1993, *The New Germany: A Human Geography* (London: Belhaven Press).

D.C. Jones 1991, 'The Bulgarian labour market in transition'. *International Labour Review* 13, 211–26.

P.N. Jones 1994, 'Destination Germany: the spatial distribution and impacts of the Third Wave of postwar immigrants' in W.T.W. Gould and A. Findlay (eds) *Population Migration and the Changing World Order* (Chichester: John Wiley) 27–46.

P.N. Jones and M.T. Wild 1992, 'Western Germany's "Third Wave" of migrants: the arrival of Aussiedler'. *Geoforum* 23, 1–11.

K. Jowitt 1996, 'Dizzy with democracy'. *Problems of Post-Communism* 43(1), 3–7.

K. Kalibova *et al.* 1993, 'Gypsies in Czechoslovakia – demographic development and policy perspectives' in J. O'Loughlin and H. van der Wusten (eds) *The New Political Geography of Eastern Europe* (London: Belhaven Press) 133–44.

A.Z. Kaninski and L. Kosciuk 1993, 'The disintegration of the USSR and Central European security'. *Polish Quarterly of International Affairs* 2(1), 29–54.

K.H. Karpat 1990, *The Turks in Bulgaria: The History Culture and Political Fate of a Minority* (Istanbul: Isis Press).

K.H. Karpat 1992, 'The Muslim minority in the Balkans'. *Polish Quarterly of International Affairs* 1(1–2), 131–46.

K.H. Karpat 1995, 'The Turks of Bulgaria: the struggle for national-religious survival of a Muslim minority'. *Nationalities Papers* 23, 725–49.

S. Keleher 1995, 'The Romanian Greek Catholic Church'. *Religion State and Society* 23, 97–108.

F-J Kemper 1993, 'New trends in mass migration in Germany' in R. King (ed.) *Mass Migration in Europe: The Legacy and the Future* (London: Belhaven Press) 257–74.

Z. Khalilzad and I.J. Brzezinski 1993, 'Extending the democratic zone of peace to Eastern Europe'. *Polish Quarterly of International Affairs* 2(3), 41–54.

J. Kipp (ed.) 1993, *Central European Security Concerns* (London: Frank Cass).

S.J. Kirschbaum 1993, 'Czechoslovakia: the creation, federalization and dissolution of a nation state'. *Regional Politics and Policy* 3, 69–95.

M. Klemencic 1996, 'Croatia rediviva' in F.W. Carter and H.T. Norris (eds) *The Changing Shape of the Balkans* (London: UCL Press), 97–117.

K. Kocsis 1992, 'Changing ethnic religious and political patterns in Carpatho-Balkan area' in A. Kertesz and Z. Kovacs (eds) *New Perspectives in Hungarian Geography* (Budapest: Hungarian Academy of Sciences), 115–42.

K. Kocsis 1994, 'Contribution to the background of the ethnic conflicts in the Carpathian Basin'. *GeoJournal* 32, 425–33.

G. Kolankiewicz 1993, 'Poland' in S. Whitefield (ed.) *The New Institutional Architecture of Eastern Europe* (London: Macmillan), 99–120.

L. Konvicka and J. Kavan 1994, 'Youth movement and the Velvet Revolution'. *Communist and Post-Communist Societies* 27, 160–76.

A. Korbonski 1993, 'The decline and rise of pluralism in East Central Europe 1949–1989'. *Communist and Post-Communist Studies* 26, 432–45.

A. Korbonski and L. Graziano (eds) 1993, 'The emergence of pluralism in East Central Europe'. *Communist and Post-Communist Studies* 26, 339–462.

J. Kosiarski 1992, 'The German minority in Poland'. *Polish Quarterly of International Affairs* 1(1–2), 47–68.

M. Koter 1993, 'Geographical classifications of ethnic minorities'. *Geografica Slovenica* 24, 123–38.

D. Kovacs and S.W. Maggard 1993, 'The human face of political, economic and social change in Eastern Europe'. *East European Quarterly* 27, 317–49.

Z. Kovacs 1991, 'Ethnic tensions in Eastern Europe'. *Geography Review* 4(4), 37–41.

M. Kozakiewicz 1989, 'Locked in battle with the Catholic Church'. *People* 16(3), 13–7.

M. Kraus and R.D. Liebowitz 1995, *Russia and Eastern Europe after Communism: The Search for New Political Economic and Security Systems* (Boulder, Colorado: Westview Press).

M. Krizan 1994, 'New Serbian nationalism and the Third Balkan War'. *Studies in East European Thought* 46, 47–68.

J. Kubik 1994, 'The role of decentralization and cultural revival in post-communist transformation: the case of Cieszyn, Silesia'. *Communist and Post-Communist Societies* 27, 331–56.

H.D. Kurz 1993, *United Germany and Europe* (Aldershot: Edward Elgar).

J.R. Lampe 1994, 'The failure of the Yugoslav national idea'. *Studies in East European Thought* 46, 69–89.

P. Latawski 1993, 'The Polish road to NATO: problems and prospects'. *Polish Quarterly of International Affairs* 2(3), 69–88.

P.G. Lewis (ed.) 1992, *Democracy and Civil Society in Eastern Europe* (London: Macmillan).

A. Lieblich 1991, 'Minorities in Eastern Europe: obstacles to a reliable count'. *Radio Free Europe/Radio Liberty Research* 1(20), 32–9.

R. Lukic 1994, 'Greater Serbia: a new reality in the Balkans'. *Nationalities Papers* 22, 49–70.

M. Luknis 1988, 'The concept of Slovakia and the development of its frontiers'. *Acta Facultatis Rerum Naturalium Universitatis Comenianae Geographica* 29, 3–10.

A. Mahr and J. Nagle 1995, 'Resurrection of the succession parties and democratization in East-Central Europe'. *Communist and Post-Communist Studies* 28, 393–409.

J. Malacic 1994, 'Labor migration from Former Yugoslavia' in H. Fassman and R. Munz (eds), *European Migration in the Late Twentieth Century* (Aldershot: Edward Elgar), 207–20.

S. Markotich 1992, 'Vojvodina: a potential powder keg'. *Radio Free Europe/Radio Liberty Research* 1(46), 13–8.

S. Markotich 1993a, 'Istria seeks autonomy'. *Radio Free Europe/Radio Liberty Research* 2(36), 22–6.

S. Markotich 1993b, 'Ethnic Serbs in Tujman's Croatia'. *Radio Free Europe/Radio Liberty Research* 2(38), 28–33.

D.S. Mason 1992, *Revolution in East-Central Europe: The Rise and Fall of Communism and the Cold War* (Boulder, Colorado: Westview Press).

W. Michalak and R. Gibb 1992, 'Political geography and Eastern Europe'. *Area* 24, 341–9.

A.A. Michta 1992, *East Central Europe after the Warsaw Pact: Security Dilemmas in the 1990s* (New York: Greenwood Press).

M. Mihalka 1993, 'German and western responses to immigration from the East'. *Radio Free Europe/Radio Liberty Research* 3(10), 27–35.

P. Mihalyi 1992, *Socialist Investment Cycles: Analysis in Retrospect* (Dordrecht: Kluwer Academic Publishing).

F. Millard 1995, 'Women in Poland: the impact of post-communist transformation'. *Journal of Area Studies* 6, 60–73.

M.W. Miller 1994, 'Moldova: a state-nation identity under post-communism'. *Slovo: An Interdisciplinary Journal of Contemporary Russian and East European Affairs* 7(1), 56–71

D. Mircev 1993, 'Ethnocentrism and strife among political elites: the end of Yugoslavia'. *Governance: International Journal of Policy and Administration* 6, 372–85.

J.P. Moran 1994, 'The communist torturers of Eastern Europe: prosecute and punish or forgive and forget?' *Communist and Post-Communist Societies* 27, 95–109.

S. Mrdjen 1993, 'Pluralist mobilization as a catalyst for the dismemberment of Yugoslavia' in J. O'Loughlin and H. Van Der Wusten (eds) *The New Political Geography of Eastern Europe* (London: Belhaven Press), 115–31.

E. Muller 1993, 'Slovenia: effects of the new independence on its economic-geographic situation'. *Europa Regional* 1, 16–24. In German with an English summary.

A.B. Murphy 1991, 'The emerging Europe of the 1990s'. *Geographical Review* 81, 1–17.

S. Oberg and H. Boubnova 1993, 'Ethnicity nationality and migration potential in Eastern Europe' in R. King (ed.) *Mass Migration in Europe: The Legacy and the Future* (London: Belhaven Press), 234–56.

M. Okolski 1992, 'Anomalies in demographic transition in Poland'. *Geographia Polonica* 59, 41–53.

D.M. Olson 1993, 'Dissolution of the state: political parties and the 1992 elections of Czechoslovakia'. *Communist and Post Communist Studies* 26, 301–14.

E. Oltay 1991a, 'Minority rights still an issue in Hungarian-Romanian relations'. *Radio Free Europe/Radio Liberty Research* 1(12), 16–20.

E. Oltay 1991b, 'Minorities a stumbling block in relations with neighbours'. *Radio Free Europe/Radio Liberty Research* 1(19), 26–33.

T. Palankai 1991, *The European Community and Central European Integration: the Hungarian Case* (Boulder, Colorado: Westview Press).

S. Parzympies 1993, 'The EU and Central Europe: prospects for security cooperation'. *Polish Quarterly of International Affairs* 2(3), 89–100.

D.K. Pater 1995, 'Grandiose visions: changes in the Catholic Church in Poland after 1989'. *Religion in Eastern Europe* 15(4), 1–16.

W.E. Paterson 1993, 'Germany and Europe' in J. Story (ed.) *The New Europe: Politics Government and the Economy since 1945* (Oxford: Blackwell), 165–84.

L.J. Paul 1991, 'The Hungarians in Romania: portrait of an explosive minority issue' in H. Van Amersfoort and H. Knippenberg (eds), *States and Nations: the Rebirth of the 'Nationalities Question' in Europe* (Amsterdam: Nederlandse Geografische Studies 137), 59–78.

L. Paul 1993, 'The stolen revolution: minorities in Romania after Ceausescu' in J. O'Loughlin and H. Van Der Wusten (eds) *The New Political Geography of Eastern Europe* (London: Belhaven Press), 145–65.

R. Pearson 1995, 'The making of '89: nationalism and the dissolution of communist Eastern Europe'. *Nations and Nationalism* 1(1), 69–79.

K. Pecsi 1989, 'The extremist path of economic development in Eastern Europe'. *Communist Economies* 1, 97–109.

J. Pehe 1993a, 'Law on Romanies causes uproar in the Czech Republic'. *Radio Free Europe/Radio Liberty Research* 2(7), 18–22.

J. Pehe 1993b, 'Slovaks in the Czech Republic: a new minority'. *Radio Free Europe/Radio Liberty Research* 2(23), 59–62.

M. Perczynski 1993, 'The Visegrad Group: cooperation towards EC entry'. *Polish Quarterly of International Affairs* 2(2), 55–72.

D.M. Perry 1991a, 'Macedonia: Balkan problems and a European dilemma'. *Radio Free Europe/Radio Liberty Research* 1(25), 35–45.

D.M. Perry 1991b, 'The Republic of Macedonia and the odds for survival'. *Radio Free Europe/Radio Liberty Research* 1(46), 12–9.

D.M. Perry 1992, 'Macedonians Bulgarians or Slavophone Greeks?: a question of national consciousness'. *Polish Quarterly of International Affairs* 1(1–2), 113–30.

I. Pogany 1995, *Human Rights in Eastern Europe* (Aldershot: Edward Elgar).

K. Poznanski 1993, 'An interpretaton of communist decay: the role of evolutionary mechanisms'. *Communist and Post-Communist Societies* 26, 3–24.

H. Poulton 1996, 'Minorities and boundaries in the Balkans' in F.W. Carter and H.T. Norris (eds), *The Changing Shape of the Balkans* (London: UCL Press), 157–71.

G. Pridham 1995, *Stabilising Fragile Democracies: New Party Systems in Southern and Eastern Europe* (London: Routledge).

S. Pudney 1995, 'Income distribution and the reform of public housing in Hungary'. *Economics of Transition* 3, 75–106.

S. Puia and C. Hirtopeanu 1990, 'Coming out of the dark: family planning in Romania'. *Planned Parenthood in Europe* 19(2), 5–8.

J. Putaki 1993, 'Hungary copes with refugee influx'. *Radio Free Europe/Radio Liberty Research* 2(18), 35–8.

S. Quack and F. Maier 1994, 'From state socialism to market economy: women's employment in Eastern Germany'. *Environment and Planning* A. 26, 1257–76.

Z. Radnai 1994, 'The educational effects of language policy'. *Current Issues in Language and Society* 1, 65–92.

S.P. Ramet 1994, 'The re-emergecn of Slovakia'. *Nationalities Papers* 22, 99–117.

S.P. Ramet and L. Adamovitch 1995, *Beyond Yugoslavia: Politics Economics and Culture in a Shattered Community* (Boulder, Colorado: Westview Press).

S. Rau (ed.) 1991, *The Reemergence of Civil Society in Eastern Europe and the Soviet Union* (Boulder, Colorado: Westview Press).

A.A. Reisen 1992, 'Meciar and Slovakia's Hungarian minority'. *Radio Free Europe/Radio Liberty Research* 1(43), 13–20.

J. Riordan *et al.* (eds) 1995, *Young People in Post-communist Russia and Eastern Europe* (Aldershot: Dartmouth).

J. Roesler 1991, 'Mass unemployment in eastern Germany'. *Journal of European Social Policy* 1, 129–50.

M.G. Roskin 1993, 'The emerging party system of Central and Eastern Europe'. *East European Quarterly* 27, 47–63.

D. Rugg 1994, 'Communist legacies in the Albanian landscape'. *Geographical Review* 84, 59–73.

D. Ruscinov 1991, 'Yugoslavia: Balkan break-up'. *Foreign Policy* 83, 143–59.

F. Schmidt 1993, 'Kosovo: the time bomb that has not gone off'. *Radio Free Europe/Radio Liberty Research* 2(39), 21–9.

G. Schopflin 1990, 'The end of communism in Eastern Europe'. *Foreign Affairs* 66, 3–16.

G. Schopflin 1993, 'The road from post-communism' in S. Whirefield (ed.) *The new Institutional Architecture of Eastern Europe* (London: Macmillan), 183–200.

A. Schotter 1981, *The Economic Theory of Social Institutions* (Cambridge: Cambridge University Press).

M. Shafir 1991, 'Transylvanian shadows: Transylvanian lights'. *Radio Free Europe/Radio Liberty Research* 1(26), 28–33.

M. Shafir 1993, 'The HDTR Congress: confrontation postponed'. *Radio Free Europe/Radio Liberty Research* 2(9), 34–9.

P.S. Shoup (ed.) 1990, *Problems of Balkan Security: Southeastern Europe in the 1990s* (London: University Press of America/Wilson Center Press).

D. Shumaker 1993, 'The origins and development of Central European cooperation 1989–1992'. *East European Quarterly* 27, 351–73.

V. Shundi 1994, Rebuilding the churches of the Aromanians in Albania'. *Romanian Review* 50(6), 87–9.

O. Sjoberg 1994, 'Rural retention in Albania: administrative restrictions on urban-bound migration'. *East European Quarterly* 28, 205–33.

K. Skubiszewski 1993, 'Nationalism in Europe today'. *Polish Quarterly of International Affairs* 2(3), 11–26.

M. Sorenson 1993, 'Major causes of hatred between Serbs and Croats'. *Balkan Studies* 34, 121–45.

J. Staniszkis 1991, *The Dynamics of Breakthrough in Eastern Europe* (Berkeley, California: University of California Press).

D. Stark 1989, 'Coexisting organizational forms in Hungary's emerging mixed economy' in V. Nee and D. Stark (eds), *Remaking the Economic Institutions of Socialism: China and Eastern Europe* (Stanford, California: Stanford University Press).

D. Stark 1992, 'The great transformation?: social change in Eastern Europe'. *Contemporary Sociology* 21, 299–304.

S. Stefas and K. Kentrotis 1994, 'Skopje in search of an identity and international recognition'. *Balkan Studies* 35, 337–77.

M. Stewart 1990, 'Gypsies work and civil society'. *Journal of Communist Studies* 6(2), 140–62.

M. Stock 1994, 'Youth culture in East Germany: from symbolic dropout to politicization'. *Communist and Post-Communist Studies* 27, 135–43.

G. Stokes (ed.) 1991, *From Stalinism to Pluralism: A Documentary History of Eastern Europe since 1945* (Oxford: Oxford University Press).

I. Svetlik (ed.) 1992, *Social Policy in Slovenia* (Aldershot: Avebury).

M. Szabo 1994, 'Nation state nationalism and the prospects for democratization in East Central Europe'. *Communist and Post Communist Societies* 27, 377–99.

T.S. Szayna 1993, 'The break-up of Czechoslovakia: some thoughts about its implications'. *Polish Quarterly of International Affairs* 2(2), 55–72.

G. Szepe 1994, 'Central and Eastern European language policies in transition'. *Current Issues in Language and Society* 1, 41–64.

J. Szmatka 1993, 'In search of the syndrome of threshold situation' in J. Szmatka *et al.* (eds) *Eastern European Societies on the Threshold of Change* (Lampeter: Edwin Mellen Press), 1–14.

D.A. Terrill 1994, 'Tolerance lost: disaffection, dissent and revolution in the GDR'. *East European Quarterly* 28, 343–80.

W. Tietze 1989, 'What is Germany: what is Central Europe (Mitteleuropa)?' *GeoJournal* 19, 173–6.

T. Tiner 1993, 'Regional distribution of motor car coverage in Hungary'. *Foldrajzi Ertesito* 42, 79–91. In Hungarian with an English summary.

R.L. Tokes 1991, 'From Visegrad to Krakow: cooperation competition and coexistence in Central Europe'. *Problems of Communism* 40(6), 100–14.

Y. Tong 1995, 'Mass alienation under state socialism and after'. *Communist and Post-Communist Studies* 28, 215–37.

J. Torpey 1993, 'Coming to terms with the communist past: East Germany in comparative perspective'. *German Politics* 2, 415–35.

N. Tos 1993, 'Social change and shift in values: democratization processes 1980–1990'. *Nationalities Papers* 21, 61–9.

F. Trix 1994, 'The resurfacing of Islam in Albania'. *East European Quarterly* 28, 533–49.

T. Tucker 1996, 'Political transition and the "Jewish" question in Hungary'. *Ethnic and Racial Studies* 19, 290–315.

H.A. Turner 1993, *Germany from Partition to Reunification* (London: Routledge).

D. Turnock 1994, 'Developing a regional approach for studies of ethnicity in Eastern Europe'. *GeoJournal* 34, 521–2.

A.W. Tymowski 1994, 'Youth activism in the East European transformation'. *Communist and Post-Communist Studies* 27, 115–24.

M. Uralic 1993, 'The disintegration of Yugoslavia: its costs and benefits'. *Communist Economies and Economic Transformation* 5, 273–94.

K. Verdery 1993, 'Ethnic relations economies of shortage and the transition in Eastern Europe' in C.M. Hann (ed.) *Socialism: Ideals Ideologies and Local practice* (London: Routledge), 172–86.

D. Verhayen 1991, *The German Question: A Cultural Historical and Geopolitical Exploration* (Boulder, Colorado: Westview Press).

I. Volgyes 1989, *Politics in Eastern Europe* (Pacific Grove, California: Brooks/ Cole Publishing Company).

M.E. Volten (ed.) 1990, *Uncertain Futures: Eastern Europe and democracy* (New York: Praeger).

M. Waller and M. Myant (eds) 1994, *Parties Trade Unions and Society in East-Central Europe* (London: Frank Cass).

A.F.C. Webster 1993, 'Kingdoms of God in the Balkans?' *East European Quarterly* 27, 437–51.

L. Weisbrod 1994, 'Nationalism in reunified Germany'. *German Politics* 3, 222–32.

G. Wettig 1993, 'Moscow's acceptance of NATO: the catalytic role of German unification'. *Europe Asia Studies* 45, 953–72.

G. Wightman 1994, *Party Formation in East-Central Europe: Post-communist Politics in Czechoslovakia, Hungary, Poland and Bulgaria* (Aldershot: Edward Elgar).

T. Wild and P.N. Jones 1994, 'Spatial impacts of German unification'. *Geographical Journal* 160, 1–16.

A.J. Williams (ed.) 1994, *Reorganizing Eastern Europe: European Institutions and the Refashioning of Europe's Security Architecture* (Aldershot: Dartmouth).

C. Zanga 1991, 'The question of Kosovo sovereignty'. *Radio Free Europe/Radio Liberty Research* 1(43), 21–6.

M. Ziolkowski 1993, 'Individuals and the social system: the types of individuality and varieties of its contribution to society' in J. Szmatka *et al.* (eds), *Eastern European Societies on the Threshold of Change* (Lampeter: Edwin Mellen Press), 207–24.

V. Zubek 1993, 'New Poland's old dilemma: the Polish minority in Lithuania'. *Ethnic and Racial Studies* 16, 657–8.

# 4

# TRANSITION TO A
# MARKET ECONOMY

Political change has opened the way for radical economic reform to transform the discredited system of central planning (Havlik 1990; Myant 1993). But economic restructuring requires much more time than revolutionary political upheaval and few East Europeans realised just how challenging the process would be (Somogyi 1993). Perfecting a market economy after decades of central planning is a major task complicated by unemployment and capital shortage (Csaba 1991, 1995). Fundamentally, the switch to a market system requires a relaxation of state controls (evident only just before 1989 through the greater enterprise autonomy allowed under the Hungarian NEM), the breakup of large monopolies and encouragement of private businesses (Batt 1988; Fischer and Gelb 1991). But while there is no doubt about the ultimate objective of a market economy, there is disagreement over the best way to proceed, including the role of the state during the early stages when there are severe problems of unemployment and inflation (Brada 1993). Typically, there has been a fall in GDP (reflected in both agricultural and industrial production) because of the reduced demand when international trade is freed and imports cease to be restricted to state barter agreements (Table 4.1). The effect of free market rejection of much of the old planned production has been accentuated by greatly reduced buying in the FSU (Dawisha 1990). But market incentives are gradually beginning to make an impact and production should eventually rise to higher levels than before. However, much will depend on international competitiveness and the consequent inflow of foreign investment; so policies for restructuring are of crucial importance.

It is a fact of political life that strategies for long-term stability and growth have to be tempered by short-term considerations which are of great significance in electoral terms. The new democratic governments have experienced serious reductions in tax revenue at a time of increasing budget pressure to provide welfare. The early transition years were marked by the particularly weak performance of taxation on corporate incomes (Belanger 1994). The issue was complicated by exemptions, but concessions are being narrowed and economies showing signs of recovery should soon generate more buoyant revenues. At the same time governments have found that their

*Table 4.1* Annual change in Gross Domestic Product 1989–96

| Country | Percentage change during the year | | | | | | | | |
|---|---|---|---|---|---|---|---|---|---|
| | *1989* | *1990* | *1991* | *1992* | *1993* | *1994* | *1995* | *1996[1]* | *1997[1]* |
| Albania | 9.8 | −10.0 | −27.1 | −9.7 | 11.0 | 7.4 | 11.0 | 8.5 | 8.0 |
| Bulgaria | −0.6 | −9.3 | −13.8 | −5.7 | −4.2 | 1.4 | 2.6 | 1.0 | 3.0 |
| Croatia | −1.9 | −8.5 | −20.9 | −9.7 | −3.2 | 0.8 | −1.5 | 3.5 | 4.0 |
| Czech Republic | 1.4 | −1.2 | −14.2 | −6.4 | −0.9 | 2.6 | 4.8 | 4.5 | 4.1 |
| Hungary | 0.7 | −3.5 | −11.9 | −4.3 | −2.3 | 2.9 | 1.5 | 3.5 | 1.5 |
| Macedonia | n.a. | −9.9 | −10.7 | −14.7 | −15.2 | −8.2 | −3.0 | 3.0 | 5.0 |
| Poland | 0.2 | −12.1 | −7.6 | 2.4 | 3.8 | 5.3 | 7.0 | 4.9 | 5.2 |
| Romania | −5.8 | −5.6 | −12.9 | −13.6 | 1.3 | 3.9 | 6.9 | 4.5 | 4.5 |
| Slovakia | 1.1+ | −2.5 | −14.5 | −7.0 | −4.1 | 4.9 | 7.4 | 5.0 | 4.1 |
| Slovenia | −2.7 | −4.7 | −8.1 | −5.4 | 1.3 | 4.9 | 3.5 | 2.0 | 3.5 |
| Yugoslavia GSP[2] | n.a. | −8.4 | 11.1 | 27.0 | −27.7 | 6.5 | 6.0 | 5.0 | 6.0 |

*Notes* 1 Estimate 2 Gross Social Product.

*Source*: Economist Intelligence Unit except where otherwise stated (EC Directorate for Employment Industrial Relations and Social Affairs)

own spending has much more severe inflationary consequences than was the case before 1989. Countries which had invested huge sums in economic development under communism suddenly find themselves in financial crises with the onset of the transition (Winiecki 1993, 1994). However, the wealth of communism was largely illusory, consisting as it did of a series of commands rewarded by only modest levels of consumption and underwritten to no small degree by the natural resources of the FSU. Moreover, the communist system controlled international trade and currency exchange rates. And since, by definition, the end of the command economy means a growth in private trading and market pricing of goods, higher spending linked to the printing of more money has had an immediate inflationary effect as wages stimulate demand and increased imports of Western goods. Table 4.2 shows dramatic changes in the value of East European currencies in the early 1990s: Bulgaria and Poland in 1990–1; Romania in 1992–5; Albania and Croatia in 1992–3. Only FCSFR and Hungary have escaped relatively lightly.

Spending has been reduced and many public projects have been frozen in order to limit inflation and the falling value of the currency as policy moves towards convertibility. However,

> limits on the speed with which public expenditure can be reduced, while retaining popular support for reform has meant that falling revenues have usually been accommodated by wider budget deficits. With only limited sources of non-monetary financing of the deficits, this has meant that, in several cases, somewhat higher rates of monetary expansion and inflation had to be accepted.
>
> (Belanger 1994, p.17)

For example, the rise in unemployment requires spending on social services and further outlays to protect employment in SOEs as far as possible (Gomulka 1994). It may also be necessary to subsidise the prices of some essential goods. This action risks higher inflation through the need to print money without a commensurate increase in goods and services and without public purchase of government bonds to finance budget deficit (Kolodko 1991) (Table 4.3). Admittedly, inflation can be a useful welfare strategy to some extent, since it provides a cushion without involving government in

*Table 4.2* Consumer and retail price inflation 1990–6

| Country | Price increases (%) | | | | | | | |
|---------|------|------|------|------|------|------|--------|--------|
| | *1990* | *1991* | *1992* | *1993* | *1994* | *1995* | *1996[1]* | *1997[1]* |
| Albania | 0.0 | 37.0 | 226.0 | 85.0 | 23.0 | 6.0 | 9.0 | 8.0 |
| Bulgaria | 21.6 | 334.0 | 89.1 | 72.8 | 96.2 | 62.0 | 77.0 | 48.0 |
| Croatia | 609.0 | 123.0 | 665.0 | 1517.0 | 98.0 | 2.0 | 3.5 | 4.0 |
| Czech Republic | 10.8 | 56.6 | 11.1 | 20.8 | 10.0 | 9.1 | 8.9 | 8.5 |
| Hungary | 28.9 | 35.0 | 23.0 | 22.5 | 18.8 | 28.2 | 17.0 | 24.0 |
| Macedonia | 608.0 | 121.0 | 1691.0 | 335.0 | 122.0 | 16.0 | 7.0 | 8.0 |
| Poland | 585.8 | 70.3 | 43.0 | 36.9 | 33.3 | 26.8 | 21.2 | 18.1 |
| Romania | 50.1 | 174.5 | 210.9 | 256.1 | 136.8 | 32.3 | 34.0 | 27.0 |
| Slovakia | 10.4 | 61.2 | 10.0 | 23.2 | 13.4 | 9.9 | 6.2 | 6.0 |
| Slovenia | 548.7 | 117.7 | 201.3 | 32.3 | 19.8 | 12.6 | 10.2 | 8.5 |
| FFRY | 593.0 | 121.0 | 9237.0 | 116.5 | 72.0 | 78.6 | 100.0 | n.a. |

*Note* Estimate.
*Source*: Economist Intelligence Unit

*Table 4.3* Currency exchange against the dollar 1989–96

| Country | Units of currency equivalent to US$1 | | | | | | | | |
|---------|------|------|------|------|------|------|------|--------|--------|
| | *1989* | *1990* | *1991* | *1992* | *1993* | *1994* | *1995* | *1996[1]* | *1997[1]* |
| Albania (Lek) | 6.0 | 5.6 | 5.0 | 80.0 | 110.0 | 94.7 | 94.0 | n.a. | n.a. |
| Bulgaria (Lev) | 0.9 | 2.4 | 18.4 | 23.3 | 27.8 | 54.2 | 67.1 | 170.0 | 177.0 |
| Croatia (Kunar)[1] | 3.5 | 11.2 | 18.7 | 258.0 | 3577.0 | 6.0 | 5.2 | n.a. | n.a. |
| Czech Republic (Crown) | 15.0[3] | 17.9[3] | 29.5[3] | 28.3[3] | 29.2 | 28.8 | 26.5 | 27.7 | 27.5 |
| Hungary (Forint) | 59.1 | 63.2 | 75.7 | 79.0 | 91.9 | 105.2 | 125.7 | 153.0 | 175.0 |
| Macedonia (Denar) | n.a. | 11.3 | 19.7 | n.a. | 42.7[4] | 43.3 | 40.0 | 40.0 | 42.0 |
| Poland (Zloty)[2] | 1439 | 9500 | 10576 | 13626 | 18115 | 22713 | 2.43[2] | 2.71[2] | 2.98[2] |
| Romania (Leu) | 14.9 | 22.4 | 76.4 | 307.9 | 765.0 | 1655.1 | 2033.3 | n.a. | n.a. |
| Slovenia (SLT) | n.a. | n.a. | 27.6 | 81.3 | 113.2 | 128.8 | 118.5 | 137.5 | 143.5 |
| Slovakia (Crown) | 15.0[3] | 17.9[3] | 29.5[3] | 28.3[3] | 30.8 | 32.0 | 29.8 | 30.9 | 31.8 |

*Notes*
1 Kunar replaced the Dinar in 1994 at the rate of 1:1000.
2 From May 1995 1 New Zloty = 10,000 Old Zloty.
3 Situation in FCSFR.
4 Estimate.
*Source*: Economist Intelligence Unit

open-ended commitments to provide specific ongoing benefits. It is a 'grease' allowing relative prices to adjust to market realities more easily. But it undermines confidence abroad and discourages foreign investment. So compromises are needed. There will be a gradual phasing out of subsidies and tighter control of the money supply to balance the budget (Jefferies 1993). Yet governments will also want to avoid social unrest which could drive it from office (Campbell 1994; Siebert 1991).

## THE EAST EUROPEAN WORKFORCE

Eastern Europe has a workforce that is highly skilled and motivated in relation to wage levels but opportunity in the new economy seems to be by no means equal, with major structural contrasts between and within countries (Table 4.4). But entrepreneurship is in short supply after decades of propaganda which portrayed private enterprise as morally reprehensible. The growth of the private sector has been substantial, though relatively slow in the Balkans through delayed privatisation and the scale of the trade shock, along with the accompanying deflation, which discouraged business generally. When it comes to expanding business and employment social capital seems to be a key factor through positive attitudes to risk taking: reflecting family background, occupation and connections. Former communists do not seem to be represented above the average and hence the 'nomenclature model' of entrepreneurship may be questioned. There are certainly spatial differences and enterprise is most likely to blossom in the cities where improvements in living standards are already becoming evident. There are sharp variations in levels of car ownership in Hungary, with Budapest showing the highest level followed by an west–east split (with the western areas having higher levels and smaller differences between town and country) (Tiner 1993). In Poland there are relatively high living standards in urban areas (through the emphasis in investment on the agglomerations) and former German territories (Chojnicki and Czyz 1992). In the last dynamic it may be possible to stimulate greater enterprise and higher employment levels. International Development Association credits are helping to develop the labour market in Albania and reform the social safety net (Ronge 1991).

Trends in real wage levels were negative during the inflation years of the early 1990s (Table 4.5) but the geography of unemployment has become an important line of enquiry, previously marginalised by the traditional role of agriculture as the residual employer (Burda 1993) (Table 4.6). In FGDR 142,000 were out of work in June 1990, rising to 537,000 in October 1990 to reach a peak of 1.7mn. in 1991 (when another 1.75mn. more were in part-time work) (Roesler 1991). Rates of unemployment vary a good deal, not simply due to the decline in jobs but also according to the ease with which people can register as unemployed: many people have ceased to participate in salaried employment and have turned to farming. Thus during the years

Table 4.4 Population and employment 1993

| Country | A | B | C | D | E | F | G | H | I | J | K | L |
|---|---|---|---|---|---|---|---|---|---|---|---|---|
| Albania | 3168 | 1763 | 977 | 590 | 214 | 25 | 110 | 107 | 396 | 29.8 | 32.4 | 23.2 |
| Bulgaria | 8470 | 4737 | 3222[1] | 706 | 1102 | 168 | 518 | 704 | 601 | 15.7 | 17.4 | 9.0[1] |
| Czech Republic | 10330 | 6180 | 4853 | 333 | 1710 | 453 | 1106 | 1251 | 155 | 3.0 | 3.5 | 1.5 |
| Hungary | 10294 | 6064 | 3827 | 349 | 1087 | 207 | 966 | 1267 | 671 | 13.4 | 11.4 | 9.7 |
| Poland | 38459 | 23693 | 14584 | 3763 | 3705 | 903 | 2946 | 3267 | 2737 | 15.5 | 17.5 | 13.5 |
| Romania | 22755 | 12866 | 10062e | 3615e | 3030 | 574e | 1308e | 1535 | 1076 | 9.4 | 11.7 | 6.9 |
| Slovakia | 5325 | 3119 | 2128e | 258e | 682e | 165e | 364e | 659e | 323 | 12.7 | 12.9 | 4.4* |

Notes A Population B Working age population C Employment D Agriculture E Mining, manufacturing and energy F Construction G Trade and transport H Other services I Unemployed J Unemployment rate K Ditto women L Ditto core region with capital

1 indicates capital city alone as a region 2 Estimate.

Source: EU Directorate General for Employment Industrial Relations and Social Affairs

*Table 4.5* Percentage growth in real wages 1990–4

| Country | 1989 | 1990 | 1991 | 1992 | 1993 | 1994 |
|---|---|---|---|---|---|---|
| Albania | 3.0 | 6.2 | –42.3 | 18.6 | 1.1 | 1.1 |
| Czech Republic | 0.8 | –5.5 | –26.3 | 10.3 | 3.6 | 4.5 |
| Hungary | 0.8 | –0.2 | –3.7 | 1.7 | –0.4 | 6.8 |
| Poland | 11.6 | –27.4 | 0.2 | –2.9 | –1.1 | 2.9 |
| Romania | 2.1 | 5.6 | –17.2 | –13.0 | –16.7 | –6.7 |
| Slovakia | 1.4 | –6.1 | –25.2 | 0.7 | –4.3 | 1.7 |

*Source*: EU Directorate General for Employment Industrial Relations and Social Affairs

*Table 4.6* Unemployment rates 1990–6

| Country | 1990 | 1991 | 1992 | 1993 | 1994 | 1995 | 1996 |
|---|---|---|---|---|---|---|---|
| Bulgaria | 1.5[1] | 10.0[1] | 15.0[1] | 16.0[2] | n.a. | n.a. | n.a. |
| Czech Republic | 1.0[1] | 4.0[1] | 3.0[1] | 3.5 | 3.2 | 2.9 | 3.3 |
| Poland | 6.0[1] | 12.0[1] | 14.0[1] | 16.0[2] | n.a. | n.a. | n.a. |
| Hungary | 2.5[1] | 8.0[1] | 12.0[1] | 13.0[2] | n.a. | n.a. | n.a. |
| Romania | n.a. | 2.0[1] | 8.0[1] | 10.2 | 10.9 | 14.5[2] | n.a. |
| Slovakia | n.a. | n.a. | n.a. | 14.4 | 14.5 | 10.5 | 9.5 |

*Notes* 1 Estrin 1994; 2 Estimated.
*Source*: Economic Intelligence Unit

*Table 4.7* Regional unemployment rates 1993

| Country | Regions | Lowest rate | | Highest rate | |
|---|---|---|---|---|---|
| Albania | 3 | 17.8 | Central | 29.2 | North East |
| Bulgaria | 9 | 9.0 | Sofia | 21.8 | North West (Montana) |
| Czech Republic | 6 | 1.5 | Mid Bohemia | 5.0 | North Moravia |
| Hungary | 4 | 9.7 | North West/Budapest | 22.5 | North East |
| Poland | 9 | 10.0 | Poludniowy (South) (Northeast) | 22.0 | Polnocno-Wschodni |
| Romania | 9 | 6.9 | Bucharest | 14.2 | South Moldavia |
| Slovakia | 4 | 4.4 | Bratislava | 15.1 | East Slovakia |

*Source*: EU Directorate General for Employment, Industrial Relations and Social Affairs

1990–2 there were much greater increases in unemployment in Hungary and Poland (over 14 per cent) compared with the Czech Republic (2.5 per cent) although the change in employment has been between 11.5 and 12.6 per cent in all three cases. But in addition 'there appears to be a major imbalance in the distribution of the unemployed and vacancies across regions. This geographic mismatch – exacerbated by constraints on mobility, including a poorly functioning housing market – has led to severe inefficiencies in matching workers with jobs' (Blanchard *et al.* 1994, p.7) (Table 4.7). In Poland unemployment has been most persistent in the north and northeast and is partly the result of low residential mobility: 'the national housing shortage, which affects even the more developed urban agglomerations, serves to maintain the spatial structure of unemployment' (Weclawowicz 1996, p.149). At the local level the range is from 6.2 per cent in Warsaw to 41.1 in Goldap (Suwalki voivodship). However, there is a change of attitude occurring from the socialist perception that jobs should follow labour to the free-market attitude that labour should follow jobs (ibid., p.151). But unemployment trends will also be affected by demography, and the people of economically productive age is increasing by 150,000 per annum through the 1990s: the total increase up to 2010 will be 2.7mn. There is also high unemployment in Hungary on the northeastern border areas while Budapest and the western regions are relatively prosperous (Dovenyi 1994). In other countries too the old industrial areas have suffered badly because their outdated plant is no longer competitive and there may be little experience over problems of diversification when enterprise managers previously discouraged competition within their labour catchments.

Case studies have highlighted the plight of workers in the coal and uranium mines of the Pecs area of Hungary where social security and high salaries were enjoyed under communism. Now there is unemployment and falling real wages. Although enterprises try and minimise dismissals the pauperisation is unmistakable. Clearly there is scope for new economic initiatives such as the creation of enterprise zones and other measures to boost employment on a spatially selective basis; in the case of Pecs there has been some alleviation of poverty through the Alps–Adria network. The case of the Hungarian town of Ozd is also instructive (Sziracki 1990). People who left the area before 1989 often found work elsewhere but now the rising unemployment levels limit the options available. Given the inadequate legislation for worker protection it is possible for dismissals to be disproportionately heavy among minority groups (especially Gypsies), the poorly educated and those who have frequently changed their employment in the past (easy to pick up through the Hungarian *munkakonyv* or employment card system). Such people have found few alternatives apart from seasonal work in municipal parks and gardening and in agriculture. On the other hand, with low unemployment in the Czech Republic, factory managers in the small towns of Moravia try to hold on to labour. Enterprises are getting down to the 'technological minimum' below which reductions will mean a decline in output. This seems to be because skilled workers are leaving to look after their own businesses – usually a lucrative strategy. This means there are fewer people to train the young workers. It is not clear if low unemployment is because of or in spite of privatisation (Szell 1992).

Any sense of national well-being is compromised and, even in the FGDR, which is receiving substantial assistance from West Germany, there is little awareness of improvement since unification. In the longer term there should be benefits through the greater flexibility in the labour market that comes with rising unemployment and widening wage differentials; but for the moment unemployment is in itself a traumatic experience for societies used to full employment with lack of a job construed as parasitism. And the situation is even worse when social security systems are modest (Rupp 1992) and a better welfare system is obviously needed (Gotovska-Popova 1993; Okolicsanyi 1993b; Vinton 1993). Contrasts in well-being have widened; yet resources are limited and there is a dilemma between employment protection (perhaps through subsidies or bank credits to finance labour-hoarding) in the interest of social stability (for high unemployment could undermine democracy) and the encouragement of retraining and mobility for future economic efficiency. Of course, financial supports to the state sector (the 'guaranteed employment' mentality) will put a brake on private sector growth whereas the phenomenon of unemployment driving down wage levels will have the opposite effect. However, in the present situation there has been a general preference for the state sector because wages are seen as being higher and there is a perception of greater job security. Even in countries with most rapid reform there is a fear about the private sector's ability to create employment on an adequate scale.

Meanwhile, the unions are struggling for legitimacy. In some cases there is a continued high level of confidence in shop-floor representatives, sometimes through former brigade leaders who had a role in stimulating individual performance through 'socialist emulation'. Unions also retain some welfare functions, particularly where recreation is concerned. However, despite a cooperative stance some unions seem to be losing the capacity to take effective action through being excluded from bargaining. They should be negotiating greater productivity and flexibility in return for higher pay, but management is not always cooperative and negotiations are often difficult because of individual pay contracts. Meanwhile, workers feel under pressure through authoritarian control and the threat of unemployment if they perform unsatisfactorily. The system should stimulate workers to be 'involved' and creative, and to adopt new attitudes such as smiling at the customers. The environment in the workplace should harmonise with the style of political life, but the management culture is such as to dismiss critics as 'communists'. Fortunately, the well-established multi-nationals are setting high standards, but other private businesses seem interested only in gaining access to the domestic market through cheap (especially female) labour with a short-term view in search of immediate profits. There seems to be a need for compromise between aggressive marketing and worker disillusionment so that modern trade union organisations can appreciate market realities while at the same time protecting workers.

Most people are worse off than before in view of the reduction in the real value of wages and many need 'multiple economies' in order to get by. Only one-fifth are either already content or expect to be so within five years, but most also expect to be better off in the future. Improvements will come slowly, but most people are confident about the direction of change in terms of both government and the economy. There are particular problems of

143

poverty among pensioners, the unemployed and some ethnic minority groups such as Gypsies (Stewart 1993). Low wages in the private sector have given rise to a 'new' group of poor people whose plight contrasts with the 'old' poverty associated with inefficient farming in remote rural areas. More than a quarter of Hungary's population is now considered poor, according to studies of the 'new' poverty arising from closures of factories or mines (Vuics 1992). The links between poverty and crime need investigation because, at Ozd, lay-offs in the metallurgical industry have been associated with both high unemployment and rising crime, such is the feeling of depression in a town where it seems that politicians from Budapest have no answers and local authorities lack the resources to offer meaningful assistance. In some countries it is now common for private security organisations to protect business premises. Yet organised crime, like bribery and sanctions-busting (unrelated to poverty), seem the greater problem. Oil deals for Serbia have been struck in Szeged (Hungary's 'mafia city'), while Kosovo Albanians are active in drug smuggling and Poles steal cars in Germany for sale in Eastern Europe. It is said that police forces are too poorly paid and equipped to check crime and avoid becoming involved in bribery.

## ECONOMIC REFORM AND THE GROWTH OF THE PRIVATE SECTOR

Reform can be postponed if the SOEs continue to serve as an elite vested interest with money from the export of primary produce to finance subsidies for loss-making firms (Bird 1992; Blanchard et al. 1991). States with lucrative mineral deposits can, in theory, earn enough from exports to support inefficient manufacturing industries based on the command system. But this strategy will impose continuing burdens and will be a source of discouragement for foreign investment outside the resource industries (Blejer and Coricelli 1995). No East European countries have the natural wealth to sustain such a conservative policy, so governments must intervene to stabilise the currency, control inflation and encourage investment (Brada and King 1992). The early stages of transition can be accomplished fairly quickly through 'shock therapy' involving macroeconomic stabilisation along with price and trade liberalisation, and with wages policies in the state sector to control inflation (Hare 1990a, 1990b). Government must also discipline the state sector (by limiting borrowing and other forms of subsidy) and should balance the interests of unions and employers' organisations. It must increase experimentation and train natural agents of capitalist development. Other transition policies may come more slowly: privatisation and structural adaptation to the market, along with institutional, fiscal and legal reforms including a greatly enlarged banking system to deal with financial markets. Attention must also be paid to the labour market to ensure mobility, retraining and an adequate social safety net (Murrell 1991).

144

The notion of rapid change is a theoretical one postulating a decisive break with the past on the grounds that a chasm cannot be crossed with two jumps (Murrell 1992b). An argument for rapid change is that reform must galvanise a population and create a new civil society with a voluntarist outlook to legitimate new practices, although they will inevitably be conditioned by some communist legacies. But all reforms cannot be introduced immediately and the notion that there is a choice between shock-therapy and gradualism is illusory. Macrostabalisation could take two to three years, while privatising the SOEs could extend over a decade. And in any case, 'several years must pass before the fruits of reform are widely evident'; in the meantime there is a 'valley of tears' requiring consistency and boldness to negotiate (Sachs 1992, p.17). Government should be strong during this period to avoid wavering and inconsistency, while containing the danger of 'rapacious Western investors intent on profiteering' through the gaps in legal structures, which could then prompt a xenophobic backlash (ibid.). Resolute government is also needed to discriminate against the former elite, control lobbies (representing powerful vested interests) and encourage competition (Estrin and Cave 1993). 'The most successful reforms will occur in those countries that effect change consistently over an extended time period rather than in those that attempt to use economic strategies to create a sudden divide between the past and the future' (Murrell 1992a, p.92). The transition is often made difficult by mistrust of politicians; also by weak law and the lack of restraining powers to complement the market ethos in the early days (Keren and Ofer 1992; Knell and Rider 1992).

For a market economy to operate efficiently a complex array of institutions is needed to encourage enterprise and investment while controlling abuses. The state must of course be proactive, yet too much effort to accelerate the transition can be counterproductive (Poznanski 1992a, 1992b). In addition to the speed of reform there is the matter of sequencing: for instance, should trade and price liberalisation precede or follow the breakup and privatisation of large enterprises? Hasty elimination of the old communist infrastructure may cause excessive dislocation. Encouraged by the collapse of FSU, Comecon was eliminated although it might have served a useful role in the first phase of transition as a club for barter trade. Liberalisation of trade can be too rapid. For a time there were lower tariffs in Poland than in the EU and although they were later revised upwards fiscal revenue was adversely affected (with a worsening revenue:GDP ratio) and bargaining with EU negotiators was complicated. If new institutions (such as an amended constitution, commercial codes, civil law procedures and banking regulations) are not put in place very quickly to control large SOEs it may be necessary to introduce stringent monetary policy with restricted access to foreign currency that will impact heavily on the private sector. In other words, there is a danger of conflict between liberalization of the economy and liberalization of the state sector because SOEs may continue to attract disproportionate funding on the basis of political contacts with banks and parliamentary representatives (Kornai 1990). In the case of cultural institutions like universities, the collapse of party supervision without alternative arrangements can leave the management free to assert their own preferences (favouring particular subjects in the case of university rectors). So ideally there needs to be a trade-off between reform of the old state sector institutions and the creation of others relevant to the new private sector; yet there has often been a significant time gap between collapse and rebuilding; likewise the privatisation of SOEs and the flow of capital and enterprise into new small businesses.

On the domestic front, it is important to create an environment in which both large and small businesses can operate, because there is a danger that large firms in retailing, wholesale, distribution and transport may operate unfairly and stifle competition in what are the most promising sectors for small private enterprises. Large firms stifle competition and make it difficult for small enterprises to gain access to the banking system. Tight monetary policy will tend to favour a bank's largest customers and will delay repayment of trade credit advanced by small firms to large buyers. Wage controls in large enterprises, while there is liberalisation of prices and wages in the private sector, can be stimulative, 'but this advantage may be thwarted if the private sector is discriminated against by the residual power of large firms' (Newbery 1992, p.216). Stiglitz (1992, p.171) refers to the 'disease of soft budget constraints' which leads firms to extend credit to suppliers and customers. 'If there is a widespread belief that the state stands behind state firms and will honour their debts, then any state firm is in the position of being able to create credit.' The difficult question is how to harden the budget constraint. The simplest solution is privatisation because 'once a firm is in the private sector it has no more entitlement to the public purse: it must sink or swim' (ibid.). Privatisation by EMBO is the best way to stimulate labour demand to offset large employment declines in SOEs.

All this points to the benefit of breaking down large enterprises into smaller units. Yet rapid privatisation is not always feasible. Breaking up SOEs to encourage entrepreneurial behaviour could reduce the value of the assets. This would damage the assets of state banks and risk a financial 'melt-down'. At the same time the role of small firms needs to be carefully considered. On the one hand, the success of small-scale privatisation and the 'extraordinary growth of very small firms' suggests that the key to the transition 'may lie less in the privatisation of the very large industrial firms than in the development of new firms and the growth of existing smaller firms' (Fischer 1992, p.243). Yet on the other hand, the small scale private businesses may not always be the critical base for success in the market economy because there are tendencies towards mafia control and the evasion of registration and taxation. The new entrepreneurs may in some cases represent elements of the former nomenclature, well able to create a powerful lobby especially in the case of the military-industry sector. This does not deny a role for private sector business in building an emergent market economy but its potential may be exaggerated. It seems that whatever reforms are implemented a core of powerful SOEs (or former SOEs) will remain prominent in heavy industry and will be crucial for production, employment and exports. And although 'corporatised', they may well remain protected from the full rigours of the market by an uneasy alliance of owners, bankers, managers (with the workers too in some cases) and the state.

It is in this context that Murrell (1992a) sees a critical issue as the freeing of resources for the new private sector; although sudden change is undesirable and a dual system will therefore arise by economic necessity (Zonis and Semler 1992). The growth of small businesses and entrepreneurship was encouraged in some communist states in the early 1980s as part of a growing 'second economy', while the countries which retained more centralised economic systems until 1989 have made a slower start (Gacs et al. 1993). Small businesses are prominent in the craft sector, as well as tourism and transport. Small firms suffer because interest rates are high (subsidies in the state sector) and there is often spare capacity through low demand. There is also limited training for owners and managers, despite the fact that many have state sector experience and feel confident about the future. But small businesses are good for job creation; also for innovation and technological diffusion, which must extend throughout East European industry; in addition they can supply a boost for tax revenue (Sik 1992). By strengthening the economy the new jobs reduce the risk of government by ultra-nationalist parties which could provoke ethnic strife and threaten the stability of the region as a whole. Small businesses are also helpful in terms of decentral-isation because they can operate in rural areas much more easily than large enterprises. Yet, at the same time, small units are springing up around the larger enterprises on the basis of sub-contracting: private traders can get deals done relatively quickly and so large firms may prefer the smaller operators to state trading companies. So, for several reasons it is very important that small businesses should thrive and generate new jobs to compensate for losses through the restructuring of SOEs. Kolodko (1993) points to long-term optimism and opportunity for sustained growth but with more differentiation within Eastern Europe because some countries will be much more successful than others.

Hence the idea of innovation centres which spread from Western Europe to Hungary at the end of the 1980s and have since taken root throughout Eastern Europe as a means of stimulating small business. Thanks to con-cessions by local authorities and large institutions, premises may be made available at low cost, while linkage with universities and polytechnics can add the benefit of technology transfer. In Romania the National Privatisation Agency introduced the concept of business and technology incubation centres in 1991. With the support of the Ministry of Research and Technology momentum gathered and a centre opened in Timisoara in 1993. This reflects local initiative backed up by some government money and foreign co-operation. The incubation centre in Brasov, Romania is connected with the Transilvania University and two major engineering enterprises: Roman and Tractorul. There are now centres in most of the large provincial cities. The only problem seems to be that nobody wants to leave their sheltered environment, which raises the question of unfair competition (Fiedler 1992).

It is significant that a 'bazaar economy' has arisen out of the collapse of state distribution systems. Instead of replacement by large capitalised trading and wholesaling companies there are numerous small operations using cars, vans and even suitcase traders travelling by train or bus. Opportunity costs for labour are low enough to draw many people into small-scale commerce: use of kiosks and private houses and trading on the streets away from the official markets (Pedersen 1993). This creates many jobs but lack of efficient distribution makes for inter-regional differences in prices which can be exaggerated on the international plane by taxation regimes. There is much small-trader activity operating over international frontiers, accompanied by the evils of bribery and outright smuggling.

### Banking and the business infrastructure

Banks are now crucial in matters of business confidence, so they merit government help and supervision. Eastern Europe has abandoned the socialist mono-bank system whereby all banking activity fell under the umbrella of a central bank acting as an arm of government (Brom and Orenstein 1994). Hungary was exceptional in that the national bank split into three commercial banks as early as 1987. Independent commercial banks were formed to take over the central bank's clientele and network, creating a two-tier system with one bank concerned with monetary policy and others active in the high street. In some countries the split has involved a much larger number of units (for example, nine in Poland) with scope for associations with specific regions (Poland) or economic sectors (Bulgaria). The banks have got to attract savings and transfer them efficiently to both existing and emerging enter-prises so that the money supply is enhanced and development is increased. Excessive speculations like the Caritas Pyramid in Cluj-Napoca (Romania), where high interest rates were maintained by new savings, should be avoided and so regulation is very necessary (Lindsay 1992).

Banks also need to be prepared for privatisation which will open the way for foreign participation (generally foreign capital is limited to a 25 per cent stake in a domestic bank). Precedents for activity by foreign banks are available through the US Citibank which is making a good profit in Hungary, but Austrian banks (Creditanstalt, GiroCredit and Raiffeisen) have success-fully penetrated the former Habsburg Empire, while Bavarian banks are active in the Czech Republic. Credit Lyonnais and ING are also prominent, though they do not have a large branch network, and many other new banks have now appeared, especially where only a small initial amount of capital is needed. In the Czech Republic the minimum is only US$18mn. and so, with the national bank maintaining a powerful regulatory role, it is possible that rationalisation will be needed in the years ahead. However, progress is being made and the quality of banking services should reach Western levels in Visegrad countries and Slovenia by the end of the decade (Essinger 1994). Meanwhile, national banks are tending to follow the German model of complete independence from government with the stability of the currency as the prime concern.

However, there is the problem of outdated mentalities through lack of experience in running a profit-oriented banking network. Banks also experience difficulties through bad debts. Massive debts have been inherited from the communist period when SOEs were supported as a matter of course. Banks should be relieved of the burden of debt from the past. They should also be oriented towards new business, otherwise capital may flow to enterprises with the best connections (for example, smokestack industries with managers still supported by the old communist network). The result may be less money for new enterprises, with high interest rates and high levels of collateral necessary. Related to banking is the matter of bankruptcy, for arguably the existence of machinery to close down insolvent businesses and thereby (1) remove poor managers from the system and (2) recycle the assets to create viable units is an indicator of progress towards a market economy. The lack of bankruptcy laws has enabled enterprises to go on getting support through loans, non-payment of taxes or the acquisition of banks and insurance companies. However, new legislation (like Hungary's tough bankruptcy law of 1992) may generate too many bankruptcies in the short term. These laws should not be too harsh to the point where potentially viable businesses are destroyed; though they should not be so accommodating as to allow inefficiency and waste of resources to become excessive.

There can be no investment without confidence and legislative safeguards regarding contracts. The private sector must also work within the framework of conventional accountancy, contractual and property laws. Wider share ownership raises the need for stock exchanges which disappeared completely under the communist system. In the early stages of restructuring there may be insufficient business to justify such institutions because more informal methods of trading were most appropriate for thin volatile markets. But stock exchanges are now operating throughout Eastern Europe, though some are plagued with charges of insider dealing (Lampe 1992; Lindsay 1992). They do not yet function successfully in raising capital for enterprises and, on the other side of the coin, in providing investment opportunities for domestic savers. But they are a force for economic transformation and the creation of shareholding societies. In future they should become more reliable indicators of national economic performance.

## PRIVATISATION

This is a highly significant issue which is widely regarded internationally as a barometer of economic reform (Estrin 1994; Major 1993). Although foreign investment is most likely to come through joint venture capital, privatisation is seen as a critical indicator of political will: it is a highly complex issue, complicated by the pressures of the free market and nomenclature interests (Frydman and Rapaczynski 1994; Rondinelli 1994). Private enterprise can contribute stability, yet governments fear social upheavals and the loss of vested interests (Aslund 1985). International financial institutions want the fastest possible privatisation so that the allocation of capital and the use of labour and machinery will be determined by market forces. Much privatisation concerns the restitution of farmland and other property; also the privatisation of housing where the UK experience with council house sales may have some relevance. But most discussion involves the large SOEs where privatisation involves difficult decisions which take years to implement (Milanovic 1991). Privatisation of the SOEs tends to be piecemeal because it is inevitably prone to political interference: typically, short steps generating feedback for the refinement of policy.

It has taken time to frame privatisation legislation (Peng 1992). In Hungary a legal framework was drawn up in 1989 and some SOEs were put up for sale in 1990, while in FCSFR work on a privatisation and restitution law was completed only in 1991. But among the northern countries Poland has found privatisation particularly difficult, for although a law was passed in 1990 little has yet been achieved. Poland has tilted towards the adoption of the 'German' system requiring a major shareholder, whereas the Czech Republic follows the UK model of diffused ownership (Buck *et al.* 1991). There are various options. There can be public subscription for shares (with or without vouchers) or EMBOs (Stark 1990). And various options arise over the options for foreign capital. The variables that arise in terms of enterprise potential, local willingness to invest small stocks of capital and the ability to attract foreign buyers all contribute to uncertainty. But they also explain why a successful privatisation is seen as a significant achievement. A disappointing response from the public or from the international business community can erode confidence and encourage gradualism. Yet even this strategy can generate worthwhile innovations in the management of enterprises that continue in state ownership. So there may be a trade-off between the speed and cost of privatisation and the quality of resulting process. Rapid progress could be made through limited negotiations which might allow managers to maximise their personal gain at the expense of the future viability of the enterprise. On the other hand, 'a broad-based open and pluralistic negotiating environment could result in a more equitable disposition of the enterprises, but the process could be slow and costly, especially if it involved extensive outside auditing' (Rausser and Simon 1992, p.268).

Van Brabant (1992) argues that privatisation should be brisk and be carried out in a context of a clear legal framework with regard to property rights. But privatisation cannot be achieved overnight (Grosfeld 1991). Yet rapid progress may be hindered by political instability and by the nature of an 'inner structure' within each society which may signal opposition to privatisation through support for populist parties. Market conditions are also crucial and the potential sales available to enterprises following foreign investment may easily be exaggerated. The progress and success of privatisation will depend on previous economic and political circumstances, with advantages for states like Hungary which attempted some devolution under communism, and the adequacy of the institutional infrastructure. Privatisation of the bulk of the economy quickly won majority support as the only way forward (Earle *et al.* 1993). But exceptions were made for 'strategic' industries and utilities. Hungary decided that some enterprises like defence would stay in state ownership indefinitely with a special agency to look after them (and direct subordinate to ministries in some cases). This arrangement covered major infrastructural companies and research institutes. It does not mean total state ownership, but a degree of state control; so there can be part-privatisation as in telecommunications. There is also the risk of failure to realise long-term potential through lack of information about enterprises (such as defence industries) that could potentially be re-profiled. Arguably they should not be vulnerable to immediate closure in the absence of private sector interest, but should attract state support until a new structure evolves.

However, although academic debate has questioned the need for private ownership in a market economy, 'practical experience has convinced East-Central Europeans that the two cannot be separated' (Batt 1991, p.76). It is evident that international financial institutions want the fastest possible privatisation so that the allocation of capital and the use of labour and machinery will be determined by market forces. This is partly because of a tendency to assume a close link between privatisation and restructuring, as though the two are inextricably bound together. This might well be the case if foreign capital was attracted to privatisation programmes on a large scale. There is some evidence to support this assumption; indeed there were joint ventures between Western and FCSFR state companies going back well before 1989 and these are now being complicated by restitution and privatisation. But it is doubtful if foreign capitalists will be interested in many of the assets even if governments do not wish to place limits on their involvement. Foreign capital may well prefer new developments on greenfield sites rather than the takeover of an SOE which may mean battling with bureaucrats to secure what may prove to be a troubled inheritance. So the privatisation process becomes more of a domestic issue and it does not automatically result in more enlightened and progressive management (Kolodko 1993). This is because many privatisations result from the virtual give-away of assets through EMBO or vouchers. The new shareholders may not expect immediate returns and employee shareholders will give the highest priority to continuity of employment. Hence the task of both privatising and restructuring is described by Thomas (1992, p.290) as 'monumental'. There may be resistance from workers and management over the danger of layoffs and plant closures. And even if there is the political will, privatisation faces 'numerous financial, economic and legal hurdles' (ibid.). Foreign capital may be injected at a later stage and then restructuring becomes more critical.

## The political and economic rationale

State ownership gave communist parties their dominant influence over economic affairs and involved the government bureaucracy in resource allocation. So it seems reasonable that the link should now be broken. Privatisation may therefore undercut the entrenched positions of interest groups like the trade unions and former nomenclature elements, buttressing democracy with a property/shareowning middle class to ensure that reform is irreversible (Hughes and Hare 1992). There is a clear distinction between various degrees of state withdrawal from the industrial scene (Smit and Pechota 1994). The state may choose to abandon its interest in the ownership of capital and thereby cease being involved in the appointment of managers and the planning of production; or it may retain ownership of capital (at least in part) and concentrate its decentralising efforts on leaving management to decide on matters of production and distribution. It might even step back from direct control of management and merely commission certain directors sitting on a board to appoint and supervise managers. Although governments can withdraw from day-to-day management and strategic planning and just remain owners of capital, this still leaves liability – and political accountability – in their hands. Hence the powerful advocacy of complete privatisation. Indeed, most discussion about privatisation presumes that it is a transfer of capital that is involved. However, this may well be demanded by an electorate to reduce the state's power and it may be equally sought by a governing party in order to reduce liabilities and spread risk across a variety of organisational forms.

Privatisation also places risk on a commercial basis and helps to create economic growth in the shortest time, with balanced budgets and stable currency. Privatisation can be a possible vehicle for stabilisation if it reduces wage inflation and encourages shareholders to take decisions according to economic considerations. It provides more scope for people in close touch with the market because capital can be borrowed according to economic criteria. This helps to build a capital market and encourages personal saving, while management can organise production according to efficiency criteria, and market discipline will subsequently rub off on the remaining state enterprises. Managers are therefore controlled by the capital market and resources will be allocated to the best uses. As ownership is extended enterprises become more accountable and there is less scope for political decision-making.

However, it does not follow that SOEs cannot be responsive to public demand, with sufficient autonomy to adopt a commercial approach and to diversify. State-owned assets may be leased, or grouped into holding companies pending privatisation, with some competition and a regulatory environment (Van Brabant 1990). For private enterprise is not fundamentally more efficient than state enterprise but there is a tendency for an oversized state sector to make managers comfortable, and so 'to regain competitiveness, deregulation and reactivism' private enterprise may be necessary (Kiss 1991, p. 305). Since progressive and realistic attitudes over capital and profit are crucial, ownership of assets is less important. But empirical evidence tends to support the view that privatisation leads to greater efficiency with improved management, increased capital investment and keener interest in improved technology and market penetration (Hare and Hughes 1991). On balance, private enterprise has demonstrated its superiority in the market system (Winiecki 1991). At the same time, private ownership is of limited value on its own. Privatisation must be complemented by financial institutions and a stimulative legal framework, including controls on monopolies: the industrial structure in the Czech Republic is such that privatisation does not really stimulate competition.

There is a need to balance economic efficiency with social considerations, given the potentially serious impact of any radical reorganisation that might result from transfer out of state ownership (Estrin 1991). Political judgement is needed to gauge the right time to sanction what will be heavy lay-offs to increase productivity. But the IMF, which often presses for accelerated privatisation as a loan condition, does accept welfare risks and allocates part of its loans to cushioning the effects (Szelenyi 1989). Nevertheless, there is often a mismatch between government and IMF approaches since the IMF takes a longer-term strategic view. They want to build confidence and see unemployment positively as a means whereby retraining can generate the skills for which new investments will provide employment. And they can force compromise from governments that may become too sensitive over the unemployment issue (Kemme 1991; Kolankiewicz 1993).

The discussion may also be linked with the allied question of restitution. Deprivation of property rights lay at the heart of communism's destruction of civil society and so it is appropriate that there should now be a reversal of the policy (Feigenbaum and Henig 1993). But there are complications over the rights of former owners who were expropriated under communism; and also the liability of former owners for environmental damage by enterprises at the time the property is regained. Although there is a moral case for restitution, through natural justice and a clear message that wrongs are being righted, practicalities stand in the way. The original owners may no longer be alive and it may not even be possible to trace their families. Further problems arise where property has deteriorated or else undergone major development through state investment. And furthermore, because restitution and privatisation can easily become entangled, it may be best to settle restitution claims by payments to keep the privatisation issue separate and avoid a legal minefield. There are clear limits to what can be simply handed over to individuals to compensate for seizure of assets when the communists came to power.

## Privatisation options

There is a choice between individual privatisation with the transfer to shares to owners – perhaps foreign capitalists or existing managers or employees – and mass privatisation which involves a large number of companies whose shares will be bought in small blocks by members of the public. Hungary has favoured the sale of assets for cash. Initially, its State Property Agency (SPA) set itself up 'on high' and tried to organise Western partners (Okolicsanyi 1991). Little progress was made; so enterprises were given greater initiative and just checked out the arrangements with the SPA (price of shares for example). This worked better, bringing in cash for the government despite criticism that foreign capitalists were making too many inroads (Mizsei 1992). The best assets have now been disposed of, but the selling continues and attracts more interest by domestic buyers through subsidised share purchase and payments against future dividends. There are also some compensation vouchers for former owners.

The approach to privatisation will also be affected by the question of revenue. If the prime objective of privatisation is revenue then assets must be sold at their 'scarcity value' to those with wealth. To charge a realistic price for shares will reduce the national debt. If state property is sold by auction few people will be able to bid and the advantage will normally rest with the former governing elite because they would tend to be the most wealthy elements in society. Potentially at least, there are disproportionate gains for nomenclature (and mafia) elements converted into new business-men. Even so, there may be ambivalence over running private businesses after years of communist propaganda against private enterprise. But to buttress democracy there should be rapid action, 'making assets available to those who reveal themselves to be interested in exercising property rights' (Van Brabant 1991b, p. 516) and giving each citizen an equal share (despite administrative problems). In the same way institutions like pension funds can be created and resourced.

Voucher privatisations have been regarded cautiously as 'large scale speculative schemes' (Murrell 1992a, p.92) which could undermine reform. The state may prematurely relinquish obligations while others take risks. Privatisation is political; likewise the way it is accomplished with socialist parties looking for free distribution of assets (since state assets arose through the efforts of workers in the past). However, there is now growing use of voucher systems whereby a proportion of the shares in former SOEs are virtually given away to the citizens of each country (Hare and Grosfeld 1991). The strategy allows everyone to benefit through the allocation of vouchers, to be exchanged for shares in companies chosen by each individual. However, 'the free distribution of shares would create a wide dispersal of ownership among inexperienced and possibly indifferent shareholders' who would not be expected to scrutinise managerial performance that was supposedly a consequence of privatization (Batt 1991, p.80). Voucher privatisation has been undertaken extensively in FCSFR where it has won a high level of public approval, especially in the Czech Republic.

There is an important difference between 'top-down' privatisation, when government decides on priorities, and 'bottom-up', where enterprises prepare their own programmes (Slay *et al.* 1992). The EMBO option enables managers to mobilise enterprises behind privatisation and negotiate with political allies in government, thereby bolstering management's legitimacy and survival (Bogetic 1993). EMBOs may involve manipulation to ensure the state's readiness to sell; or the formula may allow for 'decentralised reorganisation': under pressure of debt, falling sales and the threats of bankruptcy – or to forestall takeovers or increase autonomy – directors of SOEs may be able to take advantage of legislation to establish joint stock companies and limited liability companies. This effectively breaks up a large state enterprise into as many as twenty satellites. Under EMBO the firm may start to do better because of increased commitment by management and workers and good product sales (especially exports) can then give room for manoeuvre. But the problem of employee ownership is that it creates a conflict of interest because protecting jobs and boosting wages discourages capital seeking a good return. However, if the enterprise is not viable there is always the option of selling out to a foreign company and accepting some redundancy in return for new machinery. Of course, despite its name, which should indicate 'takeover' rather than 'buy-out', EMBO does not generate capital for the state (in sharp contrast to Western privatisations) but it does shift liability and may be further commended on the grounds of communist equity on the grounds that the state does not have title but merely holds in trust. The new economy will be more intensive with capital investment for mass production of consumer goods.

## CONCEPTUALISING THE TRANSITION

The transition is complex but there is an emerging body of concepts which helps to crystallise the general picture. First of all the transition involves a new style of regulation of the factors of production through a mix of institutions, habits and practices. Regulation of the socialist system was operated through a command hierarchy (hence 'command economy') geared to production for the military-industrial complex and operating on an extensive basis with much use of land and labour (including a stimulus to hoard) rather than capital. Resources were exploited in the context of autarky with some modification by Comecon integration but with only a slight impact from East–West trade and technology transfer. The old regulatory system was too inflexible and came to depend on informal networks generated by a second economy operating in some cases on the margins of legality (Gabor 1989; Hann 1990). Indeed, a process of 'deinstitutionalisation' arguably began under communism with the blurring of boundaries between collective/ cooperative and private property. And some economists thought there was so much informal activity in the 1980s that the communist systems had ceased to be organised around a single logic. However, the basic institutions of communist power remained in place and the political force of civil society remained weak.

Under the transition regulation is now being geared to a market economy, with a profit motive and reduced government intervention. Production becomes more intensive with capital investment for mass production of consumer goods. It will be necessary to 'restructure' to concentrate on profitable manufactures with substitution of high cost inputs. But arguably there is a balance between a model code of regulation associated with a conventional capitalist market economy (for example, markets presuppose the regulation of economic activity according to exchange-value) and specific national characteristics which arise out of the transition process. Privatisation may well result in institutional forms unlike those in Western market economies, for organisational change is not necessarily 'replacement': it may amount to a 'transformation' or 'recombination' of existing institutional elements. Potentially, there is a multiplicity of development paths with many contradictory elements when all the economic, socio-cultural and political aspects are considered. 'Paths of extrication' from the Soviet system are therefore unique, each one involving the breakup of the the old patterns followed by civil society's 'search' for a reconfiguration and institutional-isation of the new patterns to regulate the new economy (Stark 1992a, 1992b).

In other words, there is an interactive approach in which institutions are reformed through the persistence of some values inherited from the communist system and selective borrowings from outside: we have 'institutional legacies' rather than an 'institutional vacuum' (Hausner 1995). Thus, privatisation in Hungary means that property is being transformed into hybrid forms which are neither state-owned nor privately owned. The result is recombinant property because of ownership by 'private' companies which are in turn owned very largely by national property agencies. In the Czech Republic investment funds attracted the bulk of the investible points but the founder of seven of the nine largest funds was a state-owned bank. Recombinant property may be seen as a hedging strategy: because the future is uncertain, actors are reluctant to place all their bets on (or use all their resources within) just one organisational form (Nee and Stark 1989). There may be an element of corruption in privatising gain while socialising losses in the short term, but the overall effect is to spread risk across various organisational forms and reduce the state's influence and obligations at a time of great uncertainty. Creation of satellites will identify winners and losers so that the loss-makers can be eliminated. Meanwhile, 'some of the semi-autonomous limited liability companies might more likely become targets for takeovers by foreign firms or indigenous private entrepreneurs whose limited means could not acquire properties left integrated within the large state enterprises' (Stark 1993, pp.17–18). The links with the state are retained through managerial links with high-placed government officials and also through the prominence of state property agencies in shareholding.

So instead of revolutionary change and a transition to a quite different system of regulation heralding a victory for capitalism, there is a process of gradual transformation that may safeguard an interventionist paradigm at the heart of a new political order ((Fischer and Gelb 1991; Weiss 1993). All the East European countries have experienced cuts in production, high un-employment and a hiving off of subsidiary enterprises (set up as separate businesses, including trading companies); also the health and recreation functions. But there have been attempts at work sharing which reflect the ethos of the 'worker collective'. Likewise, there are privatisation formulae which seek to maintain employment levels and organisational forms with worker contributions of capital (as opposed to capitalisation by merchant capital from external sources). But it remains to be seen if these arrangements will be practical and if management will be successful in defending worker interests over the longer term (Dittrich et al. 1995).

While every strategy is unique a broad distinction is being made between neo-liberal and neo-statist approaches. The neo-liberal approach is based on concepts of modernisation based on 'transnational capital' and 'development of the national bourgeoisie'. The free market operates and state intervention is restrained. But private investment often proves to be restrained by comparison with the Asian 'tiger' economies and, since about 1993, neo-statist approaches have started to adopt either a 'transformative model' formulated by technocrats and imposed by decree or a 'developmental' model with intervention to help selected firms solve their problems of increasing quality and productivity (Amsden et al. 1994). The contrasts should not be exaggerated because the neo-statist approach endorses much of the liberal strategy approaches but with greater concern for a Scandinavian model of social democracy approach, acknowledging the central importance of the SOEs and their workers in a new economic structure where the role of the private sector may have been exaggerated. There is clearly a greater readiness to contemplate state intervention in the light of limited foreign investment because state budgets have grown after six years of transition and further state action can be contemplated. Furthermore there is less prejudice against state intervention now that a return to communism is impossible.

## TRADE AND EXTERNAL ASSISTANCE

East European commerce has been upset by the trade shocks of German reunification followed by war and sanctions in FRY (Bekker 1990; Morgan 1992). But there have been further dislocations through the collapse of the FSU and the loss of two-thirds of normal trade for lack of a payments mechanism (Koves 1993). Exports to Comecon exceeded one-third in Bulgaria and were between 10 and 20 per cent in FCSFR, Hungary and Romania with least dependence in Poland and FFYR. Reliance on Comecon had some advantages in terms of delivery of Soviet raw materials at concessionary prices and assured markets for manufacturers without stringent quality controls. Eastern Europe was shielded from the problems of convertibility (Van Brabant 1991a; Williamson 1991a, 1991b). But these arrangements locked industry into a relatively backward technological environment and ultimately posed massive problems of readjustment. Serious trade difficulties arose during the 1980s with a shift in import:export ratio. There was only a marginal change in Bulgaria (99.0 in 1981 to 103.9 in 1989), FCSFR (101.6 to 102.8) and FGDR (98.8 to 103.0), but greater change in Hungary (95.3 to 106.7) and a major transformation in Poland (85.6 to 114.8) and Romania (101.8 to 135.1). The system could not sustain itself without the FSU and it became clear that saving the system was no longer in the FSU's interest (Botsas 1992).

Trade has grown during the 1990s, although deficits arise almost everywhere, in contrast to several cases of surplus in 1989 (Table 4.8). The possibility of a free trade area to follow Comecon has been much discussed (Bakos 1993; Shumaker 1993). The Visegrad free trade zone is a milestone in economic cooperation (Okolicsanyi 1993a) but it looks forward to the enlargement of the EU (Kolankiewicz 1994; Palankai 1991). There was more trade with EU countries than with the CIS in 1992: only marginally in Bulgaria, but 1.5 times in FCSFR and Romania, 2.0 in Hungary and 2.5 in Poland (Rollo and Smith 1993). There has also been a swing towards the West and away from the Third World and Non-European Communist States (Zhong 1994). The EU has a crucial role to play in terms of both free trade and extension of membership to guarantee the independence of Eastern Europe (Gibb and Michalak 1993). Its role is 'decisive because of the attractiveness of its market and the fact that it is the chief course of such productive factors as capital and technology' (Halizak 1993, p.84). So far its involvement has been limited, and many East Europeans feel they are being kept at arm's length (De Weydenthal 1993). The Joint EU/Comecon declaration in 1988 led to diplomatic relations between the EU and Bulgaria, FCSFR, FGDR, Hungary and Poland and 'first generation' trade agreements with Poland in

*Table 4.8* International trade 1989–95

| Country | 1989 | | 1990 | | 1991 | | 1992 | | 1993 | | 1994 | | 1995 | | 1996[2] | |
|---|---|---|---|---|---|---|---|---|---|---|---|---|---|---|---|---|
| | | | | | | | *Exports and Imports (US$bn)* | | | | | | | | | |
| Albania[1] | 133 | 224 | 155 | 262 | 82 | 314 | 82 | 540 | 125 | 583 | 141 | 519 | 187 | 603 | 270 | 850 |
| Bulgaria | 3.1 | 4.3 | 2.5 | 3.3 | 3.7 | 3.8 | 5.1 | 4.6 | 3.6 | 4.3 | 3.9 | 4.0 | 5.1 | 4.7 | 4.1 | 3.2 |
| Czech Republic | 5.4 | 5.0 | 5.9 | 6.5 | 8.3 | 8.8 | 11.5 | 13.3 | 12.6 | 12.7 | 14.0 | 15.0 | 16.9 | 20.8 | 20.7 | 25.8 |
| Croatia | 2.8 | 3.5 | 4.0 | 5.2 | 3.3 | 3.8 | 4.6 | 4.5 | 3.9 | 4.7 | 4.3 | 5.2 | 4.6 | 7.5 | 7.5 | n.a. |
| Hungary | 6.4 | 5.9 | 6.3 | 6.0 | 9.3 | 9.1 | 10.0 | 10.1 | 8.1 | 12.0 | 7.6 | 11.4 | 12.8 | 15.3 | 13.5 | 15.7 |
| Macedonia | n.a. | n.a. | 1.1 | 1.5 | 1.1 | 1.4 | 1.2 | 1.2 | 1.0 | 1.1 | 1.1 | 1.5 | 1.2 | 1.5 | 1.3 | 1.6 |
| Poland | 8.3 | 8.4 | 11.3 | 9.9 | 13.8 | 14.6 | 13.9 | 14.0 | 13.6 | 16.9 | 17.1 | 18.9 | 22.9 | 24.7 | 24.9 | 28.3 |
| Romania | 10.5 | 8.4 | 5.9 | 9.1 | 4.3 | 5.4 | 4.4 | 5.8 | 4.9 | 6.0 | 6.2 | 6.6 | 7.5 | 8.8 | 7.8 | 9.1 |
| Slovakia | n.a. | n.a. | 5.9 | 6.5 | 4.7 | 5.5 | 2.5 | 3.9 | n.a. | n.a. | 6.7 | 6.6 | 8.5 | 8.5 | 8.6 | 10.2 |
| Slovenia | 3.4 | 3.2 | 4.1 | 4.7 | 3.9 | 4.1 | 6.7 | 6.1 | 6.1 | 6.5 | 6.8 | 7.0 | 8.3 | 9.3 | 9.3 | n.a |
| Yugoslavia | n.a. | n.a. | 5.6 | 6.8 | 4.7 | 5.5 | 2.5 | 3.9 | n.a | n.a | 1.5 | 1.9 | 1.4 | 2.4 | n.a. | n.a. |

*Notes*
1 US$mn.
2 Estimate.

*Source:* Economist Intelligence Unit

1989 and FGDR in 1990 (Marrese and Richter 1990). The revolutions of 1989 then resulted in 'second generation agreements' following the initial treaties arising out of the recognition of the EU by Comecon states in 1985. The EU has adopted a protectionist stance with the Maastricht Treaty signalling closer union within limited frontiers. Absorbing the countries of Eastern Europe would complicate further political union, although this is a situation that a minority of members (including the UK) would support. Asymmetric tariff reductions were accepted in recognition of Eastern Europe's weaker position (Nello 1991a, 1991b).

Further access to Western markets is needed to diversify trade (Hamilton and Winters 1992). Some countries have very close ties: Albania with Italy, Hungary and Slovakia with Austria, Poland with Germany and the UK and Romania with France (Mastny 1995; Misala 1993). Increases in exports are seen as a crucial indicator because they indicate that the prevailing prices are appropriate to meet international competition and evolve strategies based on comparative advantage. Eastern Europe's record during the 1980s was extremely poor, apart from FFYR where IMF support and competitive exchange rates (though with very heavy subsidies and high inflation) allowed a growth of exports by one-fifth each year. Hungary also did quite well and it is in Hungary again, along with FCSFR and Poland, where the earliest signs of improved export performance in the 1990s are becoming evident (Kaser 1993). There was much concern over Hungarian trade with Austria when Austria joined the EU, for the tighter regulation of the border for a transitional period was extremely damaging to Hungary's exports although the EU had said it would honour EFTA's export concessions. Wine exports to Finland and Sweden were also held up. Meanwhile, for the EU increasing imports from Eastern Europe are a contentious issue since domestic manufacturers claim unfair competition through dumping (Rollo et al. 1990). But in future there will inevitably be more agricultural produce which will create difficulties for the peripheral states among the present EU membership (Hudson 1984). The challenge arises in both directions since peripheral EU countries close to Eastern Europe (like Greece) are in a strong position, and Eastern Europe may have to raise tariffs against subsidised agricultural imports (Padoan and Pericoli 1993).

Further agreements were negotiated with FCSFR, Poland and Hungary in 1991, followed by Bulgaria and Romania in 1992 (Laffan 1992). This allowed free trade in industrial goods by 2001, but while the East European countries keep their tariffs for ten years the EU reduces them slowly on selected items (steel from 5 per cent to zero between 1992 and 1997; textiles to zero by 1998). There are safeguards against surges in imports such as tubes from Croatia, FCSFR and Poland. Even after this time (2001) there will be restrictions on agricultural produce, coal, steel and textiles so that Eastern Europe's most competitive goods will remain under tight control in order to prevent dumping, and with it the erosion of markets retained by subsidised

EU producers. The standstill in liberalisation favours Eastern Europe with its comparative advantages in agriculture, textiles and steel. On the other hand, encouragement of East–West trade will result in greater exports of manufactures from the EU which will benefit the core countries. Meanwhile, there is growing momentum behind a Central European Free Trade Agreement (CEFTA) involving the Visegrad states and Slovenia, with the probability of extension to include Bulgaria and Romania in 1996. The organisation has promoted an increase in barter (or 'counter') trade conducted among member countries. The Czech Republic is working on separate bilateral agreements with the Baltic States and Israel.

## Local trade situations

There are some interesting trade developments in the region. German trading companies are able to develop exchanges between Poland and Ukraine on the one side and Western Europe on the other. There can be cooperation with Polish agricultural exporters for the export of fruit, meat and vegetables in exchange for food-processing machinery. The case of the family trading company Kulczyk Aussenhandel in Berlin has been noted in this connection. Profits from trading can be invested in further projects which may include food-processing capacity in Poland and projects to improve transport facilities (the Berlin–Warsaw motorway). Links with Ukraine take advantage of Poland's convenience for transit. Many local arrangements operate across the German–Polish frontier. Germans travel across the bridge which separates Gorlitz from Zgorzalec. The frontier has been quite open since 1958 and since the collapse of the FGDR the situation has returned to the relaxed regime previously in force between 1972 and the onset of the Solidarity era. Germans travel to get cheaper goods (with lorry loads of German waste heading for Polish dumps as a less desirable form of commerce) and some Poles work in German factories. However, the local industries (textiles and optics) have been affected by closures and reductions in labour, while EU regulations prevent Poles from getting jobs unless there are no Germans available. But Poles do have scope in the building industry, for there is much restoration work to be done in the town centre after years of neglect. Poles have also been travelling into Ukraine with only a modest visa charge payable at the frontier, when food, petrol and consumer goods could be found at relatively low (controlled) prices. These purchases would then be sold immediately on return to Poland to wholesalers waiting near the frontier post. Ukrainians find some advantages when moving in the opposite direction although travel restrictions (trains and tour buses only in 1991) reflect Ukraine's ambivalence over private enterprise.

Albanians buy food and consumer goods (including vehicles and parts) in Greece and stand to make profits in spite of 10 per cent import taxes. It has been even more lucrative to cross the frontier illegally and work on Greek building sites or drive rustled livestock: in either case the proceeds can be spent on goods in Greece before 'surrender' to the authorities as an illegal immigrant wins free transport to the border and deportation under 'Operation Skoupa'. After sale of the goods in Tirana the cycle can be repeated. Meanwhile, Serb 'tourists' have flocked to Timisoara where prices are lower than in Belgrade – drinks, cigarettes, cosmetics and toiletries are particularly sought after. There is also an export of Romanian labour, stimulated by seasonal contracts for a wide range of activities. Interest is particularly strong in the Romanian border counties where there are South Slav minorities. There was a lively trade in petrol under the sanctions regime, with Romanians driving across the border with full tanks of petrol. Although Romania cooperated over the Serbian blockade there were local activities that could not be adequately controlled. There was a major nocturnal activity at Moldova Veche and surrounding villages, such as Pescari (known locally as Dallas), where small boats with Russian-made outboard motors make contact with Serbs in mid-river and petrol for double the price of 20p per litre paid in Romania. One smuggler might carry a tonne of fuel eight times a night and after paying protection money there is still enough to finance the modern-isation of houses. There was always a danger of explosions, drownings and shootings, but the border police took an easy-going attitude (seizing only a fraction of the oil and equipment), while land-based sanctions monitors made only superficial inspections.

## Aid and investment

Consideration of free movement of labour is seen only as a possibility although it is very much desired by the East European countries. However, the perceived danger of massive migrations has led the EU to introduce quotas. The year 1991 saw Eastern Europe in a state of heavy indebtedness (Bleaney 1990). It was low in Romania at US$2.2bn, followed by 9.8bn. in FCSFR, 12bn. in Bulgaria, 22.8bn. in Hungary and 52.8 in Poland. When calculated with regard to assets in Western banks, only Romania was in credit at the time to the tune of US$1.3mn. (2 per cent of GNP). FCSFR had a burden of US$5.7mn. (5 per cent); FFYR 12.4bn. (13 per cent); Poland 37.8bn. (29 per cent); Bulgaria 9bn. (30 per cent), and Hungary 19.2bn. (35 per cent). Many debts have been inherited from the communist period and repayments have been rescheduled. However, according to the Economist Intelligence Unit (Table 4.9), levels of indebtedness have edged up in recent years except in Poland and Slovenia. Though some schemes are considered effective (Michalak and Gibb 1992), the international financial community is perceived as being less than generous and the limited extent of financial assistance is making it difficult for East European countries to persevere with radical reform. Hence the debate not so much about the need for reform as the speed with which market reforms can be implemented. There is some concern in

*Table 4.9* External debt 1988–94

| Country | External debt (US$bn) | | | | | | | |
|---------|------|------|------|------|------|------|------|------|
|         | 1988 | 1989 | 1990 | 1991 | 1992 | 1993 | 1994 | 1995 |
| Albania | n.a. | n.a. | n.a. | 0.4 | 0.4 | 0.8 | 0.9 | 1.0 |
| Bulgaria | 7.2 | 10.2 | 10.9 | 12.0 | 12.2 | 12.3 | 10.5 | 9.5 |
| Croatia | n.a. | n.a. | n.a. | 2.8 | 2.6 | 2.6 | 3.0 | n.a. |
| FCSFR | 7.3 | 7.9 | 8.1 | 9.3 | 9.5 | n.a. | n.a. | n.a. |
| Czech Republic | n.a. | n.a. | 6.4 | 7.2 | 6.8 | 8.5 | 10.7 | 16.5 |
| Hungary | n.a. | 20.4 | 21.3 | 22.6 | 22.0 | 24.8 | 28.3 | 31.7 |
| Macedonia | n.a. | n.a. | n.a. | n.a. | n.a. | 0.9 | 1.1 | 1.2 |
| Poland | n.a. | 43.1 | 49.4 | 52.6 | 48.7 | 45.3 | 42.2 | 43.9 |
| Romania | 1.1 | 1.2 | 1.2 | 2.2 | 3.5 | 4.5 | 5.6 | 6.8 |
| Slovakia | n.a. | n.a. | 2.0 | 2.7 | 2.6 | 3.5 | 4.1 | 5.8 |
| Slovenia | n.a. | n.a. | 1.4 | 1.4 | 1.2 | 1.2 | 1.3 | 1.4 |
| Yugoslavia | n.a. | n.a. | n.a. | n.a. | 5.6 | 5.6 | 10.8 | 11.2 |

*Source*: Economist Intelligence Unit

the Balkans over discrimination by the West on aid issues and Romanians have felt themselves to be losers through the elimination of foreign debt under previous regimes when Western aid is lavished on the northern countries and on Soviet successor states which constrained the country's option in the past (Murphy 1992; Sjoberg and Wyzan 1991).

However, in the long run it is commercially motivated inward investment that will be critical, rather than foreign aid, and economic growth potential will be the crucial factor (Welfens 1992). Other important criteria are market size, export base and labour (both cost and supply); also the scope for lowering production costs, financial concessions and scope for the re-patriation of profits. Perceived disadvantages include political instability, complex bureaucracy, poor telecommunications and inadequate support facilities such as banking. Spending power in Eastern Europe is limited at the moment, when it is remembered that per capita income in FCSFR fell from 66.1 per cent of the West European average in 1938 (US$2,725; combining figures for France, Germany, Italy and UK) to 16.5 per cent in 1990, while Hungary fell from 40.4 to 14.9, Poland from 36.7 to 9.1, Bulgaria from 25.7 to 11.7, and Romania from 25.7 to 8.5 (Halizak 1993, p.67). Foreign investment levels have therefore been very low compared with the Pacific Rim: Hungary has been in the lead with US$1.5bn in 1990 compared with 0.3 for both the Czech Republic and Poland. Since then the figures have increased and the combined figure for the Czech Republic and Poland had moved up to equal Hungary at US$2.2bn in 1993 (the totals for the four years 1990–3 being US$7.8bn for Hungary and 7.3bn for the Czech Republic and Hungary together). These latter countries may continue to do relatively well because in 1995 monthly wages in the Czech Republic were US$222 (with additional costs for social security, etc. at 36 per cent), compared with US$252 for Poland (48 per cent) and US$342 for Hungary (53 per cent). EBRD finance to the end of 1994 has favoured Poland with investments exceeding ECU750mn. while Hungary has attracted over 500mn. and the Czech Republic lies in the 250–500mn. band with Romania, Slovakia and Slovenia (Smyslov 1993).

Eastern Europe desperately needs outside help (Benson and Clay 1993; Hill and Zielonka 1990). There are objective criteria for need: life expectancy, GNP per capita and economic growth rates, etc. (McGillivray and White 1994). After the 1989 revolutions the 'Group of twenty-four Industrialised Countries' embarked on aid programmes for Hungary and Poland with the European Commissioners playing a coordinating role. There was some support from the USA, happy to see the EU taking a major role. The Commissioners made contact with the IMF, OECD and the 'Paris Club' of creditor nations; and they also undertook fact-finding missions to Hungary and Poland in the first instance and aid was offered against acceptance of five basic values: the rule of law, respect for human rights, free elections, political pluralism and progress towards a market economy (Pelkmans and Murphy 1991). Priorities in the field of trade and technical assistance were identified under the programme of 'Pologne-Hongrie Actions pour la Reconversion Economique' (now widely known as 'Phare' and, despite the specific reference to Poland and Hungary, oriented towards all the East European countries in 1990 and 1991). These were: food aid and the restructuring of Polish agriculture; improved access for Hungarian and Polish goods in Western markets; EBRD investment in such fields as energy, industry and services; also improved environment and vocational training for students and managers, especially in financial and banking services. Part of the financial support has been used to import Western agricultural products and in this sense Phare has been seen as an extension of the CAP. However, it has covered the other fields of interest and the scheme has extended through 'Tempus' (concerned with science and technology, with the first mobility grants becoming available in 1990) and the EBRD which can provide investment capital for large projects (Kostrzewa et al. 1990). The European Training Foundation has a key role. Moreover, these arrangements also make a start on the establishment of compatible legal systems which are a precondition for EU membership and the development of trade (Dobosiewicz 1992; Hunya 1992; Paliwoda 1995).

Eastern Europe cannot absorb limitless amounts of capital, for there has to be a balance between domestic savings and foreign assistance (Van Brabant 1990). Working on the basis of the experience of countries like Spain which have recently joined the EU, foreign investment would run at about one-tenth of the level of domestic savings (Mihaly and Smolik 1991). The injections made into Eastern Europe have not been massive and their effectiveness has been limited in some cases by a donor/recipient syndrome rather than partnerships. Fly-in visits make a poor impression with much of the advantage being restricted to spending in the local economy for the duration of the visit. There is a need for people-to-people contact: donors have to learn partners' needs and abilities in order to achieve harmony between indigenous and external expectations. There is also a need to have East Europeans in the West for a period of months. Western governments initially underestimated the help needed, while Eastern Europe exaggerated expectations of what was forthcoming (Pinder 1990); not to mention further disillusionment through delays between the offer and disbursement of funds. Clearly, innovation in constructing democratic institutions should be applauded at a critical time, but Western aid organisations have started with only limited expertise in dealing with Eastern Europe and with no experience in problems of 'misdevelopment': how to recover the decades of socialism. At the same time East European ministries initially lacked familiarity with protocol and politics of donor organisations (Sazblowski and Derlien 1993).

The UK government's 'Know-How Programme' is widely regarded as effective in the matter of technology transfer (Charles and Howells 1992). But Western donors have tended to concentrate heavily on privatisation despite the complicated nature of this process. The problem is not only money but psychology: a need for popular legitimising of private enterprise. Aid needs to be based on useful and suitable goods and should not result in postponement of government action to create new institutions. There has beensome 'over-assistance' for example, consultants' studies on privatisation in a situation which is rapidly changing and where resources and political will are absent can lead to corruption. Encouragement of pluralism can lead to support of just a few political parties that voters have supported, while assistance to non-governmental organisations may be misdirected where these bodies have strong political connections. There is a tendency for a small number of individuals and organisations to use their influence to get a disproportionate share of foreign aid.

The bulk of the financial assistance comes from global financial institutions like the IMF (with standby loans to secure a balance of payments and advice on macroeconomic policy) and World Bank project loans. There is also OECD technical assistance and a number of banking institutions in Europe like the EIB. The EBRD was first contemplated as a French initiative in Autumn 1989. It was established in 1990 and inaugurated a year later. It is the only Western organisation concerned exclusively with Eastern Europe. It focuses on banking reforms, separating institutions responsible for monetary policy from those making commercial lending decisions. The bank helps Eastern Europe deal with capital markets. FCSFR and Hungary launched bonds: indeed Hungary has a well-developed domestic bond market and McDonald's have raised money in this way. Other states have delayed doing this because they were considered poor risks but the EBRD could help in carrying this risk, for a premium, in order to increase Eastern Europe's access to capital markets. However, the bank is restricted by limited funds and the need to apply the usual banking principles. There are many joint ventures which do not concern the bank but most of these involve only modest investments (Bugajski 1995).

Foreign investors are attracted by good market prospects for consumer goods and some specialised products; also by opportunities in the environmental and energy fields and a well-trained workforce (reflecting high standards achieved by the education system) capable of being motivated to work for wages which are modest by Western standards. Aid may be exaggerated by inclusion of loans and previous grants: new figures do not imply 'new money'. Commitments tend to be higher than disbursements. But they are discouraged by political instability sometimes combined with suspicion over foreign investment and outstanding debts that await agreement on rescheduling. There may be ambiguities over property rights, business law and tax rules. Poor infrastructure, especially in the field of telecommunications, is off-putting, as is any perceived lack of governmenmt commitment to provide a stable operating and regulatory environment (Markowski and Jackson 1994). Western investment companies are starting East European funds. Ivesco have an 'East Europe Development Fund' (covering Russia as well) which has shown higher growth than any Western investment fund. Meanwhile, First Boston's Central European Growth Fund and Baring's Emerging Europe Trust lost some ground early on because they raised money when the stock markets were bullish and invested as they fell back.

## Cultural and aid organisations

Each Western country operates its own schemes of scientific and cultural exchanges. In the UK the British Academy, British Council and Royal Society are all involved while the Centre for International Briefing prepares people for living and working effectively in Eastern Europe. There are many voluntary organisations active in Eastern Europe. Aid workers have been active in Albania, Romania and FFYR, with the Academic Lifeline scheme a notable initiative during the civil war in Bosnia-Herceogovina. Education and health is also a concern of the East European Partnership (EEP), an initiative by Voluntary Service Overseas, with some 300 volunteers active in the region at any one time. Qualified teachers and health care workers are placed in East European countries, working alongside nationals for a sojourn of up to two years. A major concern is the training of teachers of English, recruiting some of the surplus teachers of Russian which is no longer a very popular language. Foreign language teacher training colleges have been opened especially for this retraining function in Poland and elsewhere. EEP also works on an EU-funded programme to develop community care for the mentally disabled. Health and welfare have been particularly important in Romania where EEP works closely with the Romanian Orphanage Trust to stimulate interest in adoption of orphans by Romanian nationals through a Family Placement Scheme. In Albania there is staff training in the four main cities (Korce, Shkoder, Tirana and Vlore) for teachers to look after children in nurseries and other people with learning difficulties. In Macedonia there is small business advice and training in looking after disabled people. EEP activity has been extended to include natural resource protection and advice and training over the running of small businesses: well-qualified business graduates are required for one-year postings to a Small and Medium Enterprise Support Unit in Albania.

There has been a good deal of foreign assistance over advanced training. An American University has been established at Blagoevgead in Bulgaria. And there is support by the Netherlands for an institute in Bratislava for postgraduate studies by students from all over Eastern Europe (fifteen students each year) in subjects linked with economy, environment and social questions. There is also a trust fund set up by the International Finance Corporation and the government of Norway for technical assistance projects in Eastern Europe; while the EU Jean Monnet Project is sponsoring university chairs and courses on teaching European integration. Hungary and Poland will set aside part of their Phare funds for this purpose. There are also cultural organisations with international support, like Academia Istropolitana in Slovakia for courses in public administration, applied economics, environmental planning and conservation. There is also an Osterreichisches Ost- und Sudosteuropa-Institute founded in 1958 which now has branches in Bratislava, Brno, Budapest and Ljubljana; and additional contacts with Albania, Bosnia-Hercegovina, Bulgaria, Croatia, Macedonia, Poland, Romania and Serbia. It has extended cooperation in academic, cultural and scientific matters and has made a major contribution through the *Atlas of Eastern and Southeastern Europe* published on individual sheets issued since 1989 and a pamphlet series *Osterreichische Osthefte* published since 1959.

## CONCLUSION: REGIONAL ISSUES

Enormous economic problems have arisen with the collapse of Comecon, and the transition has certainly proved more complex than was anticipated (Rosenberger 1992). A good environment for private sector growth needs an anti-inflation policy, restructured finances (balanced budgets) and convertible currency. But new structures take time to develop and a shift in enterprise behaviour will have to be bolstered by effective banking, hard budget constraints (i.e. a bankruptcy law), a legal framework for competition and better market information. The mechanics of change are themselves time-consuming with choices to be faced over the methods of privatisation. In the meantime the removal of price controls and trading restrictions has fuelled inflation and reduced confidence abroad. Economies have shrunk and have become plagued by inflation arising from the failure to balance budgets.

People see themselves as worse off, sensing a lack of economic security and dismissing the wider selection of goods and improved opportunities. Although there is no obvious alternative, the adverse effects of reform (in terms of social costs) are providing support to opportunist political parties which are harnessing public ambivalence to oppose the reform process.

Technology transfer is likely to reduce the differences in business efficiency between East and West (Charles and Howells 1992). But a feature of the transition is the 'bazaar economy' which arises through the collapse of state distribution systems and their replacement not by large capitalised trading and wholesaling companies but by small operations using cars, vans and even suitcases (the traders travelling by train or bus) (Pedersen 1993). Lack of efficient distribution makes for inter-regional differences in prices which are sufficient to attract small businesses; internationally the differences may be exaggerated by taxation regimes which small traders can evade by bribery or outright smuggling. Opportunity costs for labour are low enough to draw many people into small-scale commerce: use of kiosks and private houses; also trading on the streets away from the official markets.

Spatial trends are difficult to forecast, but it is evident that economic restructuring has gone ahead more rapidly in the north (FCSFR, FGDR, Hungary and Poland) than in the Balkans (though the Yugoslav successor states of Croatia and Slovenia are taking radical action as well). There was rising GNP for FCSFR, Hungary and Poland in 1987–8 (though Hungary was almost level), falling in 1989–91, bottoming out in 1992 (80 per cent of the 1987 level) to start the upswing in 1993 and 1994. By contrast, GNP in Bulgaria and Romania was starting to level out in 1987 and to decline in 1988, with a steep fall in 1989–91, slowing in 1992 to bottom out in 1993 and 1994 (at some 60 per cent of the 1987 level). Indeed, with heavy dependence on FSU in Bulgaria and Romania, decline in manufacturing output was seen as a possibility to the end of 1993. In 1992 inflation was lower in FCS (9 per cent) Hungary (20 per cent and Poland (40 per cent) than in Bulgaria (80 per cent) and Romania (130 per cent). Most investment has gone into FCSFR, Hungary and Poland, where sectors such as chemicals and pharmaceuticals, construction materials, food and tobacco, hotels and vehicles have proved more popular than heavy industry. It is noticeable that the tourist industry has been doing especially well in the north, although the south would appear to have the better long-term prospects. There seems to be greater interest in the free market in the north, with the Czechs highly supportive of an open society; whereas Balkan countries are more preoccupied with a regulated market and state guarantees. Parties advocating radical market reforms have not prospered, especially in Romania where surveys have revealed more apprehension over market reform than in any other country.

Yet a simple north–south divide is an oversimplification, for within the northern group Slovaks are particularly inclined towards a system that maintains a powerful role for the state. Within the southern group Bulgarians have shown considerable inclination towards individual opportunities within a regulated market. But in all countries there is apprehension over the costs of transition with a 'frustration hypothesis' to account for the 'Lithuania-Poland-Hungary (LPH) Syndrome' of switching back to the left-wing government in 1993–4 through dissatisfaction over the distribution of costs and benefits: too many losers and too few winners. This process was continued in Bulgaria later in 1994 but not in either Albania or the Czech Republic, where elections were held in 1996. The main struggle is clearly between Christian Democrat parties, tending to be nationalistic and veering towards the totalitarian, and the conservative forces regrouping as Social Democrats. This has tended to undermine the synergetic effect that might have been anticipated as a surge of enterprise carried forward by the euphoria of the revolution. Civil society is fragile, with power in the hands of post-communist mafia groups and a stabilising linkage between private property and the market that is no more than embryonic. Yet there is little popular unrest and change is being made by parliamentary debate and not by *coups*; the private sector is growing. Indeed people have shown remarkable constraint, perhaps because of an awareness of the dangers of extremism. There is a danger that failure to effect market reforms and achieve 'results' acceptable to the majority will lead to a re-emergence of intransigent nationalism and various forms of protection and state intervention.

At the same time all countries have regional problems. Within individual states restructuring in industry will adversely affect the towns (especially towns in formerly backward areas where industries tend to be less efficient); by contrast joint ventures (many dealing with consumer industries) are particularly prominent in the capital cities and in the provincial cities with a depth of industrial experience (Vasko 1992). Hungary's 'fertile half moon' covers Budapest and a group of urban regions in the centre and northwest of the country (Gyor, Kecskemet, Pecs and Szekesfehervar) (Ivan 1993). The western parts of the Czech Republic and Poland are doing well, as is the Bratislava area of Slovakia (Czyz 1993); indeed, a preferential banana-shaped axis sweeps across East-Central Europe from Budapest to Bratislava, Brno, Prague, Wroclaw, Poznan and Gdansk (Gorzelak 1996, p.128). In the Balkans the capital cities attract a disproportionate share of inward investment, although some provincial cities are favoured like Timisoara in Romania (Sjoberg and Wyzan 1991). But spread effects are needed to relieve high unemployment in the eastern regions (Csefalvay 1994). Meanwhile in the rural areas there should be great scope in the privatised service sector and in small-scale food-/wood-processing and tourism. Neglected farm machinery stations might be transformed into a new generation of light industrial estates of rural areas. But foreign investors show only scant interest in the countryside and the market for agricultural produce is not yet stimulative enough to enable the rural dwellers to build up significant stocks of capital at the present time.

# REFERENCES

A.H. Amsden et al. 1994, *The Market Meets its Match: Restructuring the Economies of Eastern Europe* (Cambridge, Massachusetts: Harvard University Press).

A. Aslund 1985, *Privatisation in Eastern Europe* (London: Macmillan).

G. Bakos 1993, 'After Comecon: a free trade area in Central Europe?' *Europe Asia Studies* 45, 1025–44.

J. Batt 1988, *Economic Reform and Political Change in Eastern Europe* (London: Macmillan).

J. Batt 1991, *East Central Europe from Reform to Transformation* (London: RIIA/Pinter).

Z. Bekker 1990, 'Response patterns to external shocks in five East European countries'. *European Economic Review* 34, 921–40.

G. Belanger 1994, 'Eastern Europe: factors underlying the weakening performance of tax revenue'. *IMF Working Paper* 94/104.

C. Benson and E. Clay 1993, *Eastern Europe and the Former Soviet Union: Economic Change, Social Welfare and Aid* (London: Overseas Development Institute).

G. Bird (ed.) 1992, *Economic Reform in Eastern Europe* (Aldershot: Edward Elgar).

O. Blanchard et al. 1991, *Reform in Eastern Europe* (Cambridge, Massachusetts: MIT Press).

O. Blanchard et al. 1994, 'Unemployment in Eastern Europe'. *Finance and Development: A Quarterly Publication of the International Monetary Fund and the World Bank* 31(4), 6–9.

M. Bleaney 1990, 'Some trade issues in Eastern Europe'. *World Economy* 13, 250–62.

M.I. Blejer and F. Coricelli (eds) 1995, *The Making of Economic Reform in Eastern Europe: Conversations with Leading Reformers in Poland, Hungary and the Czech Republic* (Aldershot: Edward Elgar).

Z. Bogetic 1993, 'The role of employee ownership in the privatisation of state enterprise in East and Central Europe'. *Europe Asia Studies* 45, 463–83.

E. Botsas 1992, 'Trade and the collapse of central planning in Europe'. *East European Quarterly* 26, 239–59.

J.C. Brada 1993, 'The transformation from communism to capitalism: how far? how fast?' *Post-Soviet Affairs* 9, 87–110.

J.C. Brada and A.E. King 1992, 'Is there a J Curve for the economic transition from socialism to capitalism?' *Economics of Planning* 25, 37–54.

K. Brom and M. Orenstein 1994, 'The privatised sector in the Czech Republic: government and bank control in a transitional economy'. *Europe Asia Studies* 46, 893–928.

T. Buck et al. 1991, 'Post communist privatization and the British experience'. *Public Enterprise* 11, 185–200.

J. Bugajski 1995, *Nations in Turmoil: Conflict and Cooperation in Eastern Europe* (Boulder, Colorado: Westview Press).

M. Burda 1993, 'Unemployment, labour market and structural change in Eastern Europe'. *Economic Policy* 16, 101–38.

R.W. Campbell 1994, *The Post-communist Economic Transformation* (Boulder, Colorado: Westview Press).

D. Charles and J. Howells 1992, *Technology Transfer in Europe* (London: Belhaven Press).

Z. Chojnicki and T. Czyz 1992, 'The regional structure of the standard of living in Poland'. *Geographia Polonica* 59, 95–110.

L. Csaba (ed.) 1991, *System Change and Stabilization in Eastern Europe* (Aldershot: Dartmouth).

L. Csaba 1995, *The Capitalist Revolution in Eastern Europe: A Contribution to the Economic Theory of Systemic Change* (Aldershot: Edward Elgar).

Z. Csefalvay 1994, 'The regional differentiation of the Hungarian economy intransition'. *GeoJournal* 32, 351–61.

T. Czyz 1993, 'The regional structure of unemployment in Poland'. *Geographia Polonica* 61, 479–96.

K. Dawisha 1990, *Eastern Europe, Gorbachev and Reform* (Cambridge: Cambridge University Press).

J.B. de Weydenthal 1993, 'EC keeps Central Europe at arm's length'. *Radio Free Europe/Radio Liberty Research* 2(5), 29–31.

E. Dittrich *et al.* (eds) 1995, *Industrial Transformation in Europe* (London: Sage).

Z. Dobosiewicz 1992, *Foreign Investment in Eastern Europe* (London: Routledge).

Z. Dovenyi 1994, 'Transition and unemployment: the case of Hungary'. *GeoJournal* 32 393–8.

J.S. Earle *et al.* (eds) 1993, *Privatization in the Transition to a Market Economy* (London: Pinter).

J. Essinger 1994, *Eastern European Banking* (London: Chapman & Hall).

S. Estrin 1991, 'Privatisation in Central and Eastern Europe: what lessons can be learnt from the experience?' *LSE Centre for Economic Policy Research Working Paper* 99.

S. Estrin (ed.) 1994, *Privatisation in Central and Eastern Europe* (London: Longman).

S. Estrin and M. Cave (eds) 1993, *Competition and Competition Policy: a Comparative Analysis of Central and Eastern Europe* (London: Pinter)

H.B. Feigenbaum and J.R. Henig 1993, 'Privatisation and democracy'. *Governance: International Journal of Policy and Administration* 6, 438–53.

H. Fiedler 1992, *Innovation Centres in Central and Eastern Europe* (Berlin: Weidler Buchverlag).

S. Fischer 1992, 'Privatization in East European transformation' in C. Clague and G.C. Rausser (eds) *The Emergence of Market Economies in Eastern Europe* (Oxford: Blackwell), 227–44.

S. Fischer and A. Gelb 1991, 'The process of socialist economic transformation'. *Journal of Economic Perspectives* 5(4), 91–105.

R. Frydman and A. Rapaczynski 1994, *Privatization in Eastern Europe: Is The State Withering Away* (London: CEU Press).

I.R. Gabor 1989, 'Second economy and socialism: the Hungarian experience' in E.L. Feige (ed.) *The underground economies* (Cambridge: Cambridge University Press), 339–60.

J. Gacs *et al.* 1993, 'Small scale privatisation in Eastern Europe and Russia: a historical and comparative perspective'. *Communist Economies and Economic Transformation* 5, 61–86.

R. Gibb and W. Michalak 1993, 'The EC and Central Europe: prospects for integration'. *Geography* 78, 16–30.

S. Gomulka 1994, 'Economic and political constraints during transition'. *Europe-Asia Studies* 46, 89–106.

G. Gorzelak 1996, *The Regional Dimension of Transformation in Central Europe* (London: Jessica Kingsley/Regional Studies Association).

T. Gotovska-Popova 1993, 'Bulgaria's troubled social security system'. *Radio Free Europe/Radio Liberty Research* 2(26), 43–7.

I. Grosfeld 1991, 'Privatization of state enterprises in Eastern Europe'. *East European Politics and Societies* 5, 142–61.

E. Halizak 1993, 'Economic cooperation in post-Cold War Europe'. *Polish Quarterly of International Affairs* 2(4), 65–84.

171

C.B. Hamilton and L.A, Winters 1992, 'Opening up international trade with Eastern Europe'. *Economic Policy* 14, 77–116.

C.M. Hann 1990, 'Second economy and civil society'. *Journal of Communist Studies* 6(2), 21–44.

P. Hare 1990a, 'Creating market economies: Eastern Europe in the 1990s'. *The Economic Review* 7(5), 2–7.

P. Hare 1990b, 'Eastern Europe: the transition to the market economy'. *Royal Bank of Scotland Review* 169, 3–16.

P. Hare and I. Grosfeld 1991, 'Privatization: Hungary Poland and Czechoslovakia'. *LSE Centre for Economic Policy Research Discussion Paper* 544.

P. Hare and G. Hughes 1991, 'Competitiveness and industrial restructuring in Czechoslovakia, Hungary and Poland'. *LSE Centre for Economic Policy Research Discussion Paper* 543.

J. Hausner 1995, 'Imperative versus interactive strategy of systemic change in Central and Eastern Europe', *Review of International Political Economy* 2, 249–66.

P. Havlik (ed.) 1990, *Dismantling the Command Economy in Eastern Europe* (Boulder, Colorado: Westview Press).

R.J. Hill and J. Zielonka (eds) 1990, *Restructuring Eastern Europe: Towards a New European Order* (Aldershot: Edward Elgar).

R. Hudson 1994, 'The regional implications within the European Union of political and economic change in Eastern Europe'. *European Urban and Regional Studies* 1, 79–83.

G. Hughes and P. Hare 1992, 'Industrial restructuring in Eastern Europe: policies and prospects'. *European Economic Review* 36, 670–6.

G. Hunya 1992, 'Foreign direct investment and privatisation in Central and Eastern Europe'. *Communist Economies and Economic Transformation* 4, 501–11.

L. Ivan 1993, 'Spatial distribution of joint ventures in Hungary'. *Foldrajzi Ertesito* 42, 67–78. In Hungarian with an English summary.

D. Jefferies 1993, *Socialist Economies and the Transition to the Market* (London: Routledge).

M. Kaser 1993, 'The marketisation of Eastern Europe' in J. Story (ed.) *The New Europe: Politics Government and Economy since 1945* (Oxford: Blackwell), 378–96.

D. Kemme 1991, *Economic Transition in Eastern Europe and the Soviet Union: Issues and Strategies* (Boulder, Colorado: Westview Press).

M. Keren and G. Ofer (eds) 1992, *Trials of Transition: Economic Reform in the Former Communist Bloc* (Boulder, Colorado: Westview Press).

K. Kiss 1991, 'Privatisation in Hungary'. *Communist Economics and Economic Transformation* 3, 305–16.

M. Knell and C. Rider (eds) 1992, *Socialist Economies in Transition* (Aldershot: Edward Elgar).

G. Kolankiewicz 1993, 'The other Europe: different roads to modernity in Eastern and Central Europe' in S. Garcia (ed.) *European Identity and the Search for legitimacy* (London: Pinter), 106–30.

G. Kolankiewicz 1994, 'Consensus and competition in the eastern enlargement of the EU'. *International Affairs* 70, 477–95.

G.W. Kolodko 1991, *Hyperinflation and Stabilization in Postsocialist Economies* (Dordrecht: Kluwer Academic Publishing).

G.W. Kolodko 1993, 'From recession to growth in post-communist economies: expectation versus reality'. *Communist and Post-Communist Studies* 26, 123–43.

J. Kornai 1990, *The Road to a Free Economy* (New York: Norton).

W. Kostrzewa *et al.* 1990, 'A Marshall Plan for Middle and Eastern Europe'. *World Economy* 13, 27–49.

A. Koves 1993, *Central and Eastern European Economies in Transition: The International Dimension* (Boulder, Colorado: Westview Press).

B. Laffan 1992, *Integration and Cooperation in Europe* (London: Routledge).

R. Lampe (ed.) 1992, *Creating Capital Markets in Eastern Europe* (Washington: Woodrow Wilson Center Press).

M. Lindsay 1992, *The Development of Capital Markets in Eastern Europe* (London: Pinter).

M. McGillivray and H. White 1994, 'How much aid should the Balkan states receive?: a utility-maximising model of aid allocation'. *International Journal of Politics Economics and Culture* 2, 155–74.

I. Major 1993, *Privatization in Eastern Europe: A Critical Approach* (Aldershot: Edward Elgar).

S. Markowski and S. Jackson 1994, 'The attractiveness of Poland to direct foreign investors'. *Communist Economies and Economic Transformation* 6, 515–36.

M. Marrese and S. Richter (eds) 1990, *The Challenge of Simultaneous Economic Relations with East and West* (London: Macmillan).

V. Mastny (ed.) 1995, *Italy and East-Central Europe: Dimensions of the Regional Relationship* (Boulder, Colorado: Westview Press).

W.Z. Michalak and R.A. Gibb 1992, 'A debt to the West: recent developments in the international financial situation of East Central Europe'. *Professional Geographer* 44, 260–71.

P. Mihalyi and J.E. Smolik 1991, 'Lending is not enough: assessment of Western support for reforms in Hungary and Poland 1989–1990'. *Communist Economics and Economic Transformation* 3, 210–9.

B. Milanovic 1991, 'Privatisation in Post-Communist societies'. *Communist Economics and Economic Transformation* 3, 5–39.

J. Misala 1993, 'Germany as an economic partner of Poland'. *Polish Quarterly of International Affairs* 2(2), 37–54.

K. Mizsei 1992, 'Privatisation in Eastern Europe: a comparative study of Poland and Hungary'. *Soviet Studies* 44, 283–96.

J.P. Morgan 1992, *Investing in Eastern Germany: The Second Year of Unification* (Frankfurt: J.P. Morgan).

A.B. Murphy 1992, 'Western investment in East-Central Europe: emerging patterns and implications for state stability'. *Professional Geographer* 44, 249–59.

P. Murrell 1991, 'Evolution in economics and in the economic reforms of the centrally-planned economies' in C.O. Clague and G. Rausser (eds) *Emerging Market Economies in Eastern Europe* (Oxford: Blackwell), 35–54.

P. Murrell 1992a, 'An antidote to shock therapy: an evolutionary approach to the East European economic transition'. *Woodrow Wilson Center East European Studies Occasional Paper* 37.

P. Murrell 1992b, 'Evolutionary and radical approaches to economic reform'. *Economics of Planning* 25, 79–96.

M. Myant 1993, *Transforming Socialist Economies* (Aldershot: Edward Elgar).

V. Nee and D. Stark (eds) 1989, *Remaking the Economic Institutions of Socialism: China and Eastern Europe* (Stanford, California: Stanford University Press).

S.S. Nello 1991a, *The New Europe: Challenging Economic Relations Between East and West* (New York: Harvester/Wheatsheaf).

S.S. Nello 1991b, *Eastern Europe and the European Community: A Study in Trade Relations* (New York: Harvester/Wheatsheaf).

D. Newbery 1992, 'The safety net during transformation: Hungary' in C. Clague and G.C. Rausser (eds), *The Emergence of Market Economies in Eastern Europe* (Oxford: Blackwell), 197–218.

K. Okolicsanyi 1991, 'Tungsram: a case study'. *Radio Free Europe/Radio Liberty Research* 1(17), 34–6.

K. Okolicsanyi 1993a, 'The Visegrad Triangle's free trade zone'. *Radio Free Europe/Radio Liberty Research* 2(3), 19–22.

K. Okolicsanyi 1993b, 'Hungary's unused and costly social security system'. *Radio Free Europe/Radio Liberty Research* 2(17) 12–6.

P.C. Padoan and M. Pericoli 1993, 'The single market and Eastern Europe: specialization patterns and prospects for integration'. *Economic Systems* 17, 279–99.

T. Palankai 1991, *The European Community and Central European Integration: The Hungarian Case* (New York: Institute for East–West Security Studies).

S.J. Paliwoda 1995, *Investing in Eastern Europe* (London: Economics Intelligence Unit/Addison Wesley).

J.S. Pedersen 1993, 'The Baltic region and the new Europe' in R. Cappellin and P.W.J. Batey (eds) *Regional Networks, Border Regions and European Integration* (London: Pion), 135–56.

J. Pelkmans and A. Murphy 1991, 'Catapulted into leadership: the Community's trade and aid policies vis à vis Eastern Europe'. *Journal of European Integration* 14, 125–51.

Y. Peng 1992, 'Privatization in East European countries'. *East European Quarterly* 26, 471–84.

J. Pinder 1990, *The EC and Eastern Europe* (London: Pinter).

K. Poznanski 1992a, *Constructing Capitalism: The Reemergence of Civil Society and Liberal Economy in the Post-communist World* (Boulder, Colorado: Westview Press).

K. Poznanski 1992b, 'Market alternatives to state activism in restoring the capitalist economy'. *Economics of Planning* 25, 55–78.

G. Rausser and L. Simon 1992, 'The political economy of transition in Eastern Europe: packaging enterprises for privatization' in C. Clague and G.C. Rausser (eds) *The Emergence of Market Economies in Eastern Europe* (Oxford: Blackwell), 245–70.

J. Roesler 1991, 'Mass unemployment in eastern Germany'. *Journal of European Social Policy* 1, 129–50.

J.M.C. Rollo et al. 1990, *The New Eastern Europe: Western Responses* (London: RIIA/Pinter).

J. Rollo and A. Smith 1993, 'The political economy of East European trade with the EC'. *Economic Policy* 16, 139–82.

D. Rondinelli (ed.) 1994, *Privatization and Economic Reform in Central Europe: The Changing Business Climate* (Westport, Connecticut: Quorum Books).

V. Ronge 1991, 'Social change in Eastern Europe'. *Journal of European Social Policy* 1(1), 49–56.

L. Rosenberger 1992, 'Economic transition in Eastern Europe: paying the price for freedom'. *East European Quarterly* 26, 261–78.

K. Rupp 1992, 'Democracy market and social safety nets: implications for Post-communist Eastern Europe'. *Journal of Public Policy* 12, 37–59.

J. Sachs 1992, 'The economic transformation of Eastern Europe'. *Economics of Planning* 25, 5–20.

G.J. Sazblowski and H-U. Derlien 1993, 'East European transition elites, bureaucracies and the European Community'. *Governance: International Journal of Policy and Administration* 6, 304–24.

D. Shumaker 1993, 'The origins and development of Central European cooperation 1989–1992'. *East European Quarterly* 27, 3510–73.

H. Siebert 1991, *The New Economic Landscape in Europe* (Oxford: Blackwell).

E. Sik 1992, 'From second economy to informal economy'. *Journal of Public Policy* 12, 153–75.

E. Sik 1994, 'From the multicoloured to the black and white economy: the Hungarian second economy and the transformation'. *International Journal of Urban and Regional Research* 18, 46–70.

O. Sjoberg and M.L. Wyzan (eds) 1991, *Economic Crisis and Reform in the Balkans: Albania, Bulgaria, Roumania and Yugoslavia Facing the 1990s* (London: Pinter).

B. Slay *et al.* 1992, 'Privatisation in the post-Communist economy: an overview'. *Radio Free Europe/Radio Liberty Research* 1(17), 1–90.

H. Smit and V. Pechota 1994, *Privatisation in Eastern Europe: Legal, Economic and Social Aspects* (Irvington on Hudson, New York: Transnational Juris Publications).

D. Smyslov 1993, 'Economic problems of Eastern Europe within the context of East–West relations'. *Journal of Regional Policy* 12, 239–50.

L. Somogyi 1993, *The Political Economy of the Transition Process in Eastern Europe* (Aldershot: Edward Elgar).

D. Stark 1990, 'Path dependence and privatization strategies in East Central Europe'. *Eastern Europe Politics and Societies* 6, 17–54.

D. Stark 1992a, 'Path dependence and privatization strategies in East Central Europe'. *East European Politics and Societies* 6, 17–51.

D. Stark 1992b, 'From system identity to organisational diversity: analyzing social change in Eastern Europe'. *Contemporary Sociology* 21, 299–304.

D. Stark 1993, *Recombinant Property in East European Capitalism* (Princeton: Princeton University Sociology Department/Berlin: Wissenschaftszentrum Discussion Paper FSI), 93–103.

M. Stewart 1993, 'Gypsies, the work ethic and Hungarian socialism' in C.M. Hann (ed.) *Socialism: Ideals, Ideologies and Local Practice* (London: Routledge), 227–42.

J.E. Stiglitz 1992, 'The design of financial systems for the newly emerging democracies of Eastern Europe' in C. Clague and G.C. Rausser (eds) *The Emergence of Market Economies in Eastern Europe* (Oxford: Blackwell), 161–86.

I. Szelenyi 1989, 'Eastern Europe in an epoch of transition: towards a socialist mixed economy?' in V. Nee and D. Stark (eds) *Remaking the Institutions of Socialism: China and Eastern Europe* (Stanford, California: Stanford University Press), 208–32.

G. Szell (ed.) 1992, *Labour Relations in Transition in Eastern Europe* (Berlin: Walter de Gruyter).

G. Sziracki 1990, 'Redundancy and regional unemployment: a case study in Ozd'. *Journal of Communist Studies* 6(2), 125–39.

S. Thomas 1992, 'The political economy of privatization: Poland, Hungary and Czechoslovakia' in C. Clague and G.C. Rausser (eds) *The Emergence of Market Economies in Eastern Europe* (Oxford: Blackwell), 279–96.

T. Tiner 1993, 'Regional distribution of motor car coverage in Hungary'. *Foldrajzi Ertesito* 42, 79–91. In Hungarian with an English summary.

J.M. Van Brabant 1990, *Remaking Eastern Europe: On The Political Economy of Transition* (Dordrecht: Kluwer Academic Publishing).

J.M. Van Brabant 1991a, *Integrating Eastern Europe into an International Economy: Convertibility Through a Payments Union* (Dordrecht: Kluwer Academic Publishing).

J.M. Van Brabant 1991b, 'Privatisation in Post-Communist societies: a comment'. *Communist Societies and Economic Transformation* 3, 511–9.

J.M. Van Brabant 1992, *Privatising Eastern Europe: The role of Ownership and Markets in Transition* (Dordrecht: Kluwer Academic Publishing).

T. Vasko (ed.) 1992, *Problems of Economic Transition: Regional Development in Central and Eastern Europe* (Aldershot: Avebury).

L. Vinton 1993, 'Poland's safety net: an overview'. *Radio Free Europe/Radio Liberty Research* 2(17), 3–11.

T. Vuics 1992, 'The "new" poverty in the environment of Pecs' in W. Zsilincsar (ed.) *Zur okonomischen und okologiischen Problematik der Stadte ostmitteleuropas nach der politiischen Wende* (Graz: Karl Franzens Universitat Institut für Geographie), 53–66.

G. Weclawowicz 1996, *Contemporary Poland: Space and Society* (London: UCL Press).

D. Weiss 1993, 'Issues of the economic transformation in the former Comecon countries', *Journal of Regional Policy* 13, 249–66.

P.J.J. Welfens 1992, 'Foreign investment in East European transition'. *Management International Review* 32, 199–218.

J. Williamson 1991a, *Currency Convertibility in Eastern Europe* (Washington DC: Institute for International Economics).

J. Williamson 1991b, *The Economic Opening of Eastern Europe* (Washington DC: Institute for International Economics).

J. Winiecki 1991, 'Theoretical underpinnings of the privatisation of state-owned enterprises in Post-Soviet type economies'. *Communist Economies and Economic Transformation* 3, 397–416.

J. Winiecki 1993, *Post Soviet-type Economies in Transition* (Aldershot: Avebury).

J. Winiecki 1994, 'East Central Europe – a regional survey: Czech Republic, Hungary, Poland and Slovakia in 1993'. *Europa Asia Studies* 46, 709–34.

Y. Zhong 1994, 'The fallen wall and its aftermath: impact of regime change upon foreign policy behaviour in six East European countries'. *East European Quarterly* 28, 235–57.

M. Zonis and D. Semler 1992, *The East European Opportunity: The Complete Business Guide and Sourcebook* (Chichester: John Wiley).

# 5

# NATIONAL PROFILES
## Northern countries

### FORMER CZECHOSLOVAKIA (FCSFR)

Pressure for change was not evident at the very beginning of 1989 when the anniversary of J. Palach's suicide of 1969 (protesting against the suppression of the 1968 Prague Spring) led to the arrest and imprisonment of the dissident dramatist V. Havel. Further demonstrations in the summer were linked with the anniversary of the Warsaw Pact invasion and renewed manifestations in November marked the fiftieth anniversary of the execution of J. Opletal by the Nazis. Police brutality on the latter occasion provoked a massive pro-democracy campaign coordinated by Civic Forum (CF) in which Havel (released from prison in May) and other opposition figures were active, with support from the equivalent Slovak group Public Against Violence (PAV) (Ulc 1992). The entire communist leadership resigned and the Federal Assembly deleted the reference to the Communist Party's leading role from the constitution. At the end of the year a new communist premier (L. Adamec) failed to win opposition acceptance for a majority communist government; so a 'Government of National Understanding' emerged under M. Calfa (a former communist PAV member) allowing a majority for candidates nominated by the non-communist political parties (Wolchik 1993). President G. Husak resigned and was replaced by Havel, while A. Dubcek (the reformist communist leader of 1968) became Chairman of the Federal Assembly. And then the velvet revolution was rounded off by the formation of a CF government in the Czech Republic in 1990, while PAV assumed power in Slovakia (Jehlicka *et al.* 1993). Support for PAV was high, aiming at the progressive urban electorate, while Catholic areas in rural West Slovakia tilted towards Christian Democrats; and Hungarians in the south supported their own party (Mariot 1991). There was a witch-hunt against communists and secret police collaborators in the Czech Republic; this possibly went too far when isolated and trivial indiscretions were used as grounds for dismissal.

## The reform programme

The politicians decided on a new official name for the state (Czech and Slovak Federal Republic) and a modified division of responsibilities between national and federal governments. The economic programme aimed at a rapid transformation with clear rules for foreign capital (Adam 1993). Agreement was reached with the USA whereby FCS was accorded MFN status (Charap and Dyba 1991). Legislation in 1991 provided for restitution of property seized by the state after 25 February 1948, a date meant to exclude the possibility of claims from Sudeten Germans expelled after the Second World War. Czech politicians have emphasised that any return of property to Sudeten Germans is now out of the question (Pehe 1994), but the issue is becoming a highly sensitive one in Germany and there are hints of dialogue (Bren 1994; Obrman 1994). Representatives of the 2.5–3mn. Sudeten Germans want their expulsion declared a crime and the issue is becoming serious enough to complicate the Czech Republic's bid for EU membership. Meanwhile, in 1990 the country joined the IMF and World Bank. Policy clearly favoured a strong central bank, responsible for the preservation of monetary stability. The four established banks developed their own distinctive profiles with Ceska Sporitelna attracting private savings while Komercni Banka specialised in commercial loans. Meanwhile, Ceskoslovenska Obchodni Banka (CSOB) started to target business and the long-established Zivnostenska, backed by the German bank BHF, looked after foreign clients. The banking system developed rapidly as more than fifty new banks moved into the country (Brada 1991). Austria's Raiffeisenbank selected Prague as the hub of its new Central European capital investment division. As a result, the banking system is rapidly coming into line with Western practice and Czech banks have a yardstick against which they can measure their own performance. They also provide access to outside capital.

Industrial production fell but trade increased, especially in the case of the developed market economies, responsible for 31 per cent of imports and 27 per cent of exports in 1988 against 51 per cent and 52 per cent respectively in 1991 (in the case of the Czech Republic, imports from developed market economies rose from 58 per cent in 1991 to 71 per cent in the first half of 1993 while exports increased from 55 per cent to 70 per cent). Germany replaced FSU as the most important trading partner, restoring the situation which had existed before 1948. However, Western trade is not enough to compensate for the decline in former Comecon markets for medium technology engineering products and consumer goods, so there have been high-level contacts with other countries such as Japan, South Africa and South Korea. Trade dependence on former socialist countries used to be higher than in Hungary and Poland and there is still a lot of business with FSU for energy, though it may be reduced in future through the Ingoldstadt–Kralupy pipeline. Privatisation was anticipated early in the 1990s, although there were reservations from Slovakia on the grounds that radical change might have disproportionately negative effects. There were already high levels of unemployment, especially the eastern half of Slovakia where the Gypsies are particularly badly affected (Rajcakova and Kusendova 1993). President Havel expressed concern about the social problems arising from a rapid transition in all parts of the country (Kapl *et al.* 1991; Tomes 1991).

Some 100,000 properties were returned to their owners and an auction system was used to privatise 31,000 small businesses, including shops (Burger 1992). The system was criticised because it favoured people with money in hand, or with the contacts and confidence to get bank loans, but it was nevertheless extended to medium-sized business (Thomas 1992). Meanwhile, foreign investment in FCSFR has involved complex review procedures affecting at least two ministries. Applicants do not always understand what the key criteria are, but government is now trying to clarify the procedure and there is an Office for Economic Competition to review deals involving enterprises with more than one-third of the market. It also provides machinery to resolve the complex matter of environmental responsibilities: buyers were made liable for on-site environmental requirements but half the purchase price could be used for environmental investment. Some state enterprises have been sold to foreign and domestic investors, with an interministerial privatisation commission, which in effect means 'one-stop shopping' for foreign buyers (Wightman and Rutland 1991).

Mass privatisation of SOEs was then envisaged through V. Klaus's voucher scheme which originally involved 947 Czech enterprises and 487 enterprises in Slovakia (Shafik 1994; Svejnar and Singer 1994). It was a great success in 1992 with shares worth US$10.5bn going to 8.5mn. individuals who purchased vouchers at a nominal price (Parker 1993). This was more than double the government's estimate of 3.0–4mn. Each enterprise employing over 500 people produced a plan, with a proportion of the equity to be sold to voucher applicants and the rest to be disposed of through auctions or direct sales. Where demand for equity exceeded supply, prices rose and new applications were invited until a balance was achieved. Many voucher holders placed their assets in the hands of investment funds which made up over 70 per cent of the applications. This has placed fund managers in a key position. But whereas one-tenth of Slovaks invested in Czech firms, only 1 per cent did the reverse (Grime and Duke 1993). Banks are restricted to ownership of one-tenth of privatised property.

In the Czech Republic the 1992 elections brought success for V. Klaus's Civic Democratic Party (CDP) which emerged out of CF (like the Civic Movement and the Civic Democratic Alliance); while in Slovakia the premiership fell to V. Meciar of the Movement for a Democratic Slovakia (MDS), a party emerging out of PAV. Both Dubcek's Social Democrats and the former communists (Party of the Democratic Left) were eclipsed (Olson 1993). Meciar appreciated the importance of nationalist rhetoric as parties

179

competed for public support. This upset the liberal intellectuals who were supportive of Slovak autonomy but found Meciar's provocative behaviour objectionable (Batt 1993, p.43). However, his success clearly reflected public unease over Czech-inspired economic policy favouring rapid privatisation. Furthermore, while the Czechs were becoming more discriminating over foreign capital by the end of 1992 and wary of tax holidays, the Slovaks were keen to maintain incentives for up to ten years and seemed prepared to sell assets cheaply where investment and job creation was likely to follow. There was the prospect of a continuing federation, with an economic and defence umbrella, along with environmental and social policy. But the Slovaks made it clear they wanted their own currency-issuing central bank and the right to borrow, both to support their industry and to maintain social benefits.

When it became impossible to formulate a federal government programme during 1992, complete separation at the beginning of the following year seemed inevitable. Negotiations made rapid progress, despite problems over gold reserves, the armed forces (how to divide the air force when there were few facilities in Slovakia) and international treaties. But, since there was a willingness to settle, the 'velvet divorce' became the sequel to the velvet revolution. The breakup of the federation led to a decline in trade but, after considerable delays, share certificates were sent to Slovaks who had used their vouchers to acquire interests in Czech enterprises before the separation. A customs union (with parity for Czech and Slovak crowns) and coordination of defence was anticipated (Capek and Sazama 1993). However, with strict budget discipline in the Czech Republic and interventionism in Slovakia, parity has not been maintained.

## The Czech Republic

The recession in the Czech Republic was short-lived, with a decline in GDP by 14 per cent in 1991 and a return to stability by 1993. Prague's stock exchange reopened in 1993 after a break of fifty-five years and it remains to be seen how many of the country's 6mn. small investors (a remarkable number considering the total population is only 10.3mn.) will hold on to their shares (Pollert and Hradecka 1994). Some 900 SOEs were drawn into the second round of voucher privatisation. A wave of bankruptcies was expected in the aftermath of voucher privatisation and a consolidation bank was set up to redeem promissory notes of bankrupt companies for 60 per cent of the nominal values. However, this setback has not yet come back, although it is widely believed that major restructuring will eventually occur. Low unemployment is the result of support for unprofitable enterprises by banks and government, a substantial inflow of foreign capital which has created new jobs and the intensity of activity in small private businesses in the service sector. Unemployment is higher in Moravia where the greater importance of agriculture is a factor. Migrants still move towards Prague and Brno but also to the border areas with Austria and Germany, with Ceske Budejovice as a significant growth centre (Nefedova and Trejvis 1994, p.42). The Czech Republic enjoys formidable economic strength and political stability. Withdrawal of Slovak support for V. Havel opened the way for him to become President of the Czech Republic only. Despite its right-wing image the CDP is, in effect, a pragmatic party veering towards social democracy (Kropecky 1995). The unemployment rate is only 3.2 per cent because radical restructuring has been delayed. But, at the same time, Klaus has shown a commitment to the free market which is unique in Eastern Europe and the Czech Republic shows up well in terms of government debt, budget deficit and currency stability. The money supply has been carefully controlled to contain even the smallest inflation, a remarkable success since there has not yet been a massive shakeout of labour from industry.

Paradoxically, there has been privatisation but no extensive restructuring to achieve efficiency gains (Kupka 1992). Yet some SOEs are doing well, with enterprising managements that were elected in some cases even before the revolution. On the other hand there are multinational companies which are not always being run along strict market lines. Some large shops fail to concentrate on the most popular lines and there is still worker and management frustration over lack of input into decisions, reflecting the fact that Czech industry is still burdened by a conservative hierarchy and a lack of competition because of the privatisation of monopolies. Employment levels have been largely maintained, though many people have left state jobs to run their own small businesses, and there seems to be more concern over possible labour shortages than surpluses. Management should be seeking greater productivity, stimulated by higher pay, but retention of individual pay dealing frustrates negotiation on a broad front while government pay restraint measures prevent significant wage increases. The country is not in debt and foreign investment continues to flow, with the USA beginning to catch up on the initial German lead, especially after a very significant investment in Tabak Kutna Hora combined with Volkswagen's scaling down of its stake in Skoda Mlada Boleslav. Canada's Canstar Sports is to open a factory producing roller-skates in Zdar nad Sazavou (Moravia). Bass Breweries have purchased Prazske Pivovary; Philip Morris has acquired Tabak; while Proctor and Gamble have bought a Czech cosmetics factory. Shell has established its Central European headquarters in Prague. Edmund de Rothschild Securities are designing a 'Czech Value Fund' to invest in Czech voucher funds which are considered to be undervalued. Trade continues to be diversified. The Czech Republic is cooperating with Thailand over investments in Vietnam and there is trade with Thailand itself in foodstuffs, machine tools and aircraft in return for rice, electronics, textiles and rubber. Knowledge of the Russian language is seen as an advantage for developing trade links with the CIS. But the poor quality of information and the complexity of bureaucracy were being mentioned as discouragements in 1993. However, the Bank of Tokyo has an agreement with CzechInvest, the country's agency for the promotion of foreign investment, over mutual investment possibilities. Banks continue to flourish with French assistance for Agrobanka and UK advisers Rothchild and Sons attempting to bring CSOB to privatisation within a few years.

The Czech Republic will not offer tax incentives to foreign investors because the country is doing well enough not to need to sacrifice tax revenue. CzechInvest, the Ministry of Trade and Industry's promotional arm, is the only fiscal incentive on offer; it is funded by Phare and the Czech government. The stability of the country has begun to attract Japanese firms: in 1996 Matsushita decided to invest US$66mn. in a new factory in Plzen to produce television sets. Some 1,500 workers will be employed. Automotive and electronics industries are particularly interested in the Czech Republic: following the Volkswagen purchase of Skoda, over forty new joint ventures with foreign partners and fifteen greenfield investments have been established to act as suppliers. Labour is skilled as well as cheap: US auto parts manufacturer TRW found that their Czech plant quickly reached productivity levels achieved in other parts of the world. There is also an Association for Support of Foreign Investment to help with the bureaucracy and the search for suitable partners. Meanwhile, the state trading companies are still doing business: Metalimex can barter with FFRY, exchanging Skoda's engineering products for non-ferrous metals. Skoda could not sell in such a market but they can get money from the trading company which would be reimbursed from the sale of the non-ferrous metals to other Czech companies. Hopes of faster growth are expected in exports in 1996 based on likely restructuring (including new production methods) in industries with the greatest export potential: high quality engineering products, semi-finished products and consumer goods.

ING Bank of The Netherlands has put forward a plan to create a pension fund investment scheme that will target the country's largest industrial concerns. Meanwhile, Investicini Banka has become the first large-scale commercial bank to offer long-term mortgages for home buyers. All round, the Czech Republic is seen as a bright prospect for the future. There is cheap labour and an outstanding export performance comparing favourably with the 'tiger countries' of the Far East. Following the second wave of voucher privatisation in November 1994 the Czech Republic has more than six million small shareholders and at the end of 1995 some four-fifths of the economy was in private hands. Despite neo-liberal rhetoric Klaus believes in gradualism, with government regulatory intervention: creating opportunities for small-scale business is more important than privatisation. He avoids social conflict and wins tolerance for further policy initiatives and a moderate approach to the welfare system that will avoid high costs. Inflation is still coming down, but at 9 per cent in 1995 (and estimates of 8.1 per cent for 1996 and 7.5 per cent for 1997) it remains high in relation to Germany. Lower inflation would mean lower interest rates. Deregulation of housing rents is being undertaken to stimulate the construction industry.

The Czech Republic seems closer to EU membership than any of its Visegrad neighbours. Apart from inflation (which is nevertheless low by East European standards), the country already gives the impression of being part of the West. Unemployment rate is at 3.1 per cent. The most significant international recognition has been admission into the OECD. This was achieved in 1995 at the same time as the Czech crown's external convertibility, tied to a currency basket dominated by the DM and US$. It has a fluctuation range of 15 per cent which has reduced short-term speculative investment. The National Bank uses its own bond issues as a major instrument to control the inflow of capital. However, enterprise restructuring was still to come and there is a widening trade deficit: US$3.7bn in 1995. Much of this applies to sectors such as machinery and transport equipment where there is disappointment that Skoda-Auto's new model will contain almost 70 per cent of imported parts (20 per cent with the current Felicia model). But the growth of imported consumer goods is higher than the growth of retail turnover; though it is an indication of higher purchasing power, and most CEFTA countries ran trade deficits in 1995.

Although the government's position has not been seriously threatened, there have been tensions between the CDP and its coalition partners over financial malpractices. There have also been controversies over the creation of a senate, the formation of large administrative regions (under pressure from Moravia and Silesia) with considerable powers of self-government and the restoration of property belonging to the Roman Catholic Church. There is the prospect of a stronger opposition if the leftist parties were able to build a common platform but the Social Democratic Party cannot cooperate with the Communist Party of Bohemia and Moravia which retains its Stalinist credentials. In the 1996 election the CDP lost ground slightly although Klaus remains in power with the continuing support of the Christian Democratic Union and the Civic Democratic Alliance. M. Zeman's SDP, seeking a socially and ecologically oriented market economy, polled well in the areas of relatively high unemployment in Northern Bohemia and Moravia, where the government's complacency has created resentment. And although the economy has certainly been doing well, with a doubling of the average monthly wage under Klaus (to 8,400 crowns), reduced taxation, widespread privatisation, a balanced budget and steady growth (5.2 per cent in 1995 with industrial production registering an increase of 9 per cent), there is concern over the state of the health service and means-testing of social security benefits.

## Slovakia

Despite high unemployment (rising to 14.4 per cent in 1993), Slovakia has had to impose strict monetary and fiscal controls and inflation has been kept under control. Given the shortage of domestic capital, incentives for foreign capital have been provided and the opening of the Bratislava Stock Exchange in 1993 has improved the possibilities. Austria and the Czech Republic are seen as particularly important sources of investment as well as major export markets. Slovakia also wants to renegotiate some privatisation deals in order to retain the state's controlling interest. The privatisation of Danubiaprint was stopped because all twelve Slovak dailies came from the one complex which, it was felt, should not be under private control. Slovakia is keen to maintain as much as possible of her defence industries. A prototype armoured personnel carrier was sent to Sudan even before the breakup of the federation, evading the federal rules over the licensing of arms exports then in force. Privatisation has been slow (Fisher 1993), but Slovakia has attracted heavy American investment by K-Mart in stores, complemented by the Volkswagen project in Bratislava and investment by Samsung of South Korea at Nove Zamky; also Henkel (Austria) and Molnlycke (Sweden). There is a joint venture between Italy's Enichem Augusta Industriale and Slovakia's Petrochema Dubova. Slovakia's Pozemne Stavby of Banska Bystrica is participating in a German-financed construction project for 1,800 apartments for returning Russian soldiers at Voronezh where work on the service facilities is already under way. Arrangements are being made for training Slovak students abroad; for example, on Wearside in the UK in conjunction with local industries.

Slovakia became a member of the UN, CSCE and CoE, with associate status within the EU. Through agreements with the IMF and World Bank, Slovakia has obtained crucial loans towards the US$700–1000mn. thought necessary for stabilisation. Devaluation by as much as one-third has been proposed although the government has tried to avoid this extremity. Concern has arisen over the rights of minorities and the commitment of Slovaks to liberal democracy; yet the disputes with the Hungarian minority are not simply the result of Slovak intransigence. There is no little indignation that Hungary has refused to sign a bilateral treaty on the inviolability of the Hungarian–Slovak border because of outstanding disputes over the Gabcikovo/Nagymaros hydropower project as well as the Hungarian minority issue. Central to the latter case is the Hungarian minority's aspiration for majority status in some of the restructured administrative regions. Yet the distribution of the Hungarians is such that this cannot be squared with the functional 'city regions' that the Slovaks understandably prefer. Slovaks would therefore argue that legitimate Hungarian demands have already been met and that attention should be drawn to the interests of Slovak minorities within the Hungarian enclaves. However, Hungarians resent the removal of bilingual signs and the policy against the use of Hungarian place-names on state television. They want better cultural provision through Hungarian language schools and a Hungarian university. They also seek greater administrative powers in territories where they are in a majority (Rhodes 1995).

The government has not been stable, and by the end of 1993 there was widespread dissatisfaction with the MDS whose victory in 1992 arose largely out of the desire for gradual reform to keep the lid on unemployment in eastern Slovakia and retain egalitarian principles inherited from communism. Meciar's coalition with the Slovak National Party (SNP) was weakened in 1993 by defections from both parties and his government's failure in 1994 over the matter of amendments to the privatisation law seemed to concentrate too much power in Meciar's hands. Despite success in the international sphere, there was also a feeling of disillusionment with independence and concern about radical nationalism (Fisher and Hrib 1994). A broad-based coalition under J. Moravcik introduced new regulations to help Slovakia's capital market to function properly, while legislation was also enacted to prevent double taxation and to provide greater incentives for investors (Fisher 1994). A stabilisation loan was negotiated with the IMF, with cuts in government spending and accelerated privatisation.

However, elections in Autumn 1994 saw Meciar returned again as the leader of the largest party. He is once more governing in coalition with J. Slota's SNP as well as the left-wing Workers' Party. Policy changes may now make for greater centralisation and a rolling back of privatisation to signal a higher priority for jobs than profitability. Indeed, a delay to the privatisation programme has been announced (pending the clarification of ambiguities) after three million Slovaks had registered to buy vouchers. Although Meciar has tried to reassure the international community over Slovakia's commitment to NATO and the EU, the Slovak Workers' Association is opposed to NATO while the SNP is strongly anti-Hungarian. So neither of Meciar's coalition partners seem to favour ratification of a treaty between Slovakia and Hungary (not to mention dissent within Meciar's own MDS). There is also an attitude of suspicion towards foreign capital. But although Meciar attracts support from rural areas and from eastern Slovakia, where unemployment is relatively high, many Slovaks prefer a more moderate approach involving market reforms and accommodations for the Hungarian minority. Such an outlook is apparently favoured by President Kovac who has a high standing in the country. However, Slovakia should gain more foreign investment in future in view of the saturation of the Czech Republic which has led to rising prices. The growth of the service sector is expected to average 9.5 per cent per annum between 1994 and 1996 (slightly higher than the figure of 9 per cent for the Czech Republic), although unemployment is expected to average 14.7 per cent compared with only 4.1 per cent in the Czech Republic. However, the government is secure to the extent that the main opposition parties cannot cooperate with the neofascist or communist parties and would support Meciar over a Hungarian treaty.

# FORMER GERMAN DEMOCRATIC REPUBLIC (FGDR)

No event surrounding the collapse of communism had more impact in Eastern and Western Europe than the fall of the Berlin Wall (Shingleton *et al.* 1995).

However, this event links back to the early autumn of 1989 when a reforming regime in Hungary began to break down the fortified border with Austria and gave some 2,400 East German holidaymakers the opportunity to reach the West. Alternative routes to freedom were opened up through West German embassies in Prague and Warsaw (eventually allowed passage in special trains), but attempts to stem the flow by closing the country's borders then undermined the legitimacy of E. Honecker's government just when the regime was preparing to celebrate its fortieth anniversary. Political pressure groups began to organise mass demonstrations and, with the FSU clearly seeking reform, the ruling communists of the Socialist Unity Party (SUP) decided to remove Honecker and appoint E. Krenz as a new leader who would introduce change from above. However, the protests continued and concessions culminated in the SUP's gradual relinquishment of power as a reformist regime reopened the frontiers with FCS and Poland and allowed the Berlin Wall to be breached. The floodgates had opened and the existence of the GDR as a separate state was clearly threatened (Osmond 1991).

## Unification

Unification appeared to be the only possible option, given the overwhelming desire of East Germans to travel to the West and the FSU's readiness to negotiate. Although some reservations have since been expressed over policy-making, the necessity of stopping the surge of migrants was a top priority and only rapid and total unification seemed able to do this (Smith *et al.* 1992). It fell to a new prime minister (H. Modrow) to preside over the abolition of the State Planning Commission (replacing it with an Economic Committee composed of economists and representatives of political groups) and to encourage the private sector. Monetary union was needed to stop excessive shopping by people from West Berlin and Poland, and there had to be interim measures to restrict the purchase of goods available at subsidised prices for GDR citizens (Bryson 1991). Free elections in FGDR in March 1990 returned the Christian Democratic Union (CDU) in every region except Berlin, Frankfurt/Oder and Potsdam. In these areas the SPD lead over CDU was between 3.1 and 4.9 per cent, whereas in the other regions the CDU lead over Social Democratic Party (SPD) was at least 9.5 per cent (Rostock) and in four cases exceeded 30 per cent: 30.2 per cent in Dresden, 32.4 per cent in Gera, 34.5 per cent in Suhl and 38.3 per cent in Erfurt. L. de Maiziere formed a broad coalition government which negotiated the country's incorporation into the FRG. Protest organisations like the New Forum did not achieve electoral success because people were in no mood for experimentation with a new hybrid system. 'The proven success of West Germany's stable democracy and flourishing economy enjoyed an authority with which neither the communists nor the newly-formed political groupings could compete' (Henderson 1993, p.59).

The Two Plus Four talks, involving the two Germanies and the four wartime allies, negotiated reunification, with continued (medium-term) presence of Soviet troops and payment in Deutschmarks for both the continuing deployment and the eventual withdrawal (Munske 1995). Germany also provided substantial economic aid to the FSU. This paved the way for monetary, economic and social union in August 1990, when trade between East and West Germany ceased to be foreign. Ostmarks were converted to DM at 1:1, except for large holdings (over 4,000) where the rate of 2:1 was still much more favourable than the black market exchange of between 5–7 Ostmarks for each DM. Complete unification followed three months later (Hall 1990). West German produce flooded the eastern market, while the introduction of the new 'hard' currency complicated trade deals with Eastern Europe. This threatened many of the FGDR's established trading contacts, although a major decline in FSU orders would have occurred in any case (Lipschitz and McDonald 1990). Elections in March 1990 brought the CDU to power in the enlarged Bundestag in Bonn and in most of the New Lander (replacing the communist Bezirken) where the party normally ruled in coalition with the Free Democratic Party. The only exceptions were Berlin and Brandenburg which gave a majority to the SDP. In the 1994 election the CDU majority in the Bundestag was much reduced but members in the East have now become more influential on the party nationally (Clemens 1993). The FGDR transformation is quite unique in Eastern Europe because it is based on financial transfers which do not have to be repaid (Morgan 1992). But there was a thorough reorganisation of government and administration (Konig 1993) with the importation of a complete system of legal-institutional rules and corporate actors. Yet the FGDR continues to be haunted by the problem of *vergangenheitsbewaltigung* (overcoming the past): leading communists lost their privileges (cars and hunting lodges) and there was a sense of defeat throughout society (Schmidt 1991).

The disadvantages experienced since 1989 are attributed to West German interests. The undermining of eastern morale is expressed by low levels of satisfaction and low participation rates for political parties. Alienation is also reflected in right-wing tendencies (Neckermann 1992). However, the 'Wessies' are paying a 'solidarity surcharge' in their income taxes and they are aware of the mismatch between Ossie expectations of high wages combined with low productivity; part of an unrealistic attitude symptomatic of 'Die Mauer im Kopf' (Grosser 1992). The policy of higher taxes in the West to create jobs in the East has been linked with job losses in the West, resulting in reduced investment in the East by companies like Volkswagen. There was only limited opportunity for East German views to make an impact. Some 1,000 civil servants from Nord Rhein Westfalen were seconded to Brandenburg while many Easterners travelled to the West for education and business training. There has been some interest in the possibility of a political grouping for the East to cross party lines, but only the reformed communist party has exploited this opportunity (Padgett 1993). Most FGDR initiatives lost their impact and so 'as a result of greater institutional experience, of superior organizational skills and extensive transfers of personnel from the West, societal transformation of FGDR became a project of external actors' (Wiesenthal 1994, p.12). On the other hand, enormous investments are being made in the East. It was estimated that DM150bn would be needed to bring the infrastructure up to standard and privatisation was costed at a further DM30bn.

Pressure against former *Stasi* (secret police) collaborators was demanded, but many teachers, army officers and diplomats were also dismissed as being unsuitable for work in the new Germany; while outside politicians came in to run three of the New Lander (Hamilton 1992). On balance, the majority seem pleased with the union, for there are many who are now better off. The restoration of local self-government has been a major change in itself (Osterland 1994). There has been a strong revival in Saxony, for the power and privilege of East Berlin was resented in the cities of Dresden and Leipzig. Under the effective leadership of the CDU leader K. Biedenkopf there was a resurgence of medium-sized businesses in Saxony which made for a clear break with the past (Wild 1992).

### Economic policy

Of course, there were serious dislocations through economic and monetary union in July 1990 as prices were freed and subsidies cut (Roesler 1991). There was a need for stabilisation and early introduction of the DM in the East. But contrary to trends elsewhere, currency convertibility involved a massive revaluation of the Ostmark. Wages and social incomes were fixed at one-to-one with the West German mark, but the move to wage equality eroded the FGDR's claim to be a low wage economy and contributed to an initial collapse. Purchases of Western goods without credit restrictionn after the currency reform also helped to undermine eastern industry (Drost 1993). Immediate access to West German products led to an avoidance of local manufactures which were seen as being of inferior quality and even price reductions failed to make a significant impression (Hall and Ludwig 1993). Thus the FGDR policies for economic transformation were 'a strange mixture of market-oriented liberalism and opulent favours granted to the East German electorate for political reasons: to improve chances for party competition and government re-election. This brought about the deepest decline in economic performance that has been observed in East and Central Europe' (Wiesenthal 1994 p.11).

Unemployment averaged 0.91mn. in 1991, rising to 1.17mn. in 1992 and 1.35mn. in 1993: 17.2 per cent, even with retraining and job creation under the *Aufschwung Ost* (Upswing East) investment programme. There was free training for the easterners; also employment promotion companies set to work on the refurbishment and/or demolition of derelict property. By mid-1993 600,000 people had been forced out of agricultural employment and the situation was particularly serious in Mecklenburg-Vorpommern and Brandenburg. There was much urban deprivation in the large estates in the cities with few amenities, and also in small towns: a typical description highlighted the centre of Apolda where 'the coat of lignite is thickest [and where] cobbled streets lead past tumbledown houses and silent factories'. Factories have closed (chemicals, engineering and leather) and the knitting industry has shrunk from 8,000 jobs to 800 (Schutte 1993). But the brewery has been modernised and is finding rising sales in Saxony; there are also some new shops. A core of small modern businesses is needed (note the food-processing potential). Half the people are unemployed although job creation reduces this to a quarter. But environmental improvement and conservation was helped by industrial decline (Jones 1994).

There is uncertainty as to how quickly recovery will come: telephone provision may come into line with the West by the late 1990s but it may be 2010 before per capita GNP comes close to the West German level. At least, the recovery will certainly be quicker than in other parts of Eastern Europe. Investments have been substantial and FGDR industry is now in a unique position of modernisation which should bring dividends through the turn of the century (Pickel 1992). There is much building work which creates jobs and helps to slow East–West migration (and with it the growth in the number of 'Wossies', i.e. Easterners – 'Ossies' – who have moved West). Unemployment is aggravated by high potential activity rates of 85–90 per cent compared with 55–60 per cent in the West, a difference which arises largely from the position of women. Wages were supposed to reach parity in 1994 but if this occurs without productivity gains it will reduce the FGDR's industrial competitiveness further. So, controversially, equality has been renegotiated for 1996 in order to save jobs (Collier and Siebert 1991). Some large investments have been delayed by pollution problems, poor infrastructure and EU competition rules.

## Privatisation

This has been facilitated by the Treuhandanstalt (THA) which took on the task of dismantling the SOEs and disposing of the properties belonging to the secret police and the armed services. THA was given the ownership rights of some 8,000 major enterprises employing more than four million people (Roesler 1994). The number increased to some 13,700 separate units as a result of the break-up of the very large combines in order to encourage EMBO. There was particular difficulty for the large *Kombinate* (conglomerates) like Carl Zeiss and Deutsche Waggonbau which sold 40–60 per cent of their output to FSU. Some cases of very heavy subsidy came to light, such as Zeissoptik Jena and the Practica cameras make by Pentacon in Dresden, which were sold with a 75 per cent subsidy: the business closed in 1990 with the loss of 6,000 jobs. Formerly, the spinning industry was run as a single *Kombinat* but now the various units are separate and a few are surviving, like the Branksa works in Brandenburg which has received some investment and management advice from THA and cut its workforce from 750 to 145 to help in the search for a buyer.

Altogether, some 3,400 units were sold off by the summer of 1991. There was rapid penetration by West German businesses. Thus Staatsbank was bought by the Deutsche and Dresdner banks, with a parcelling out of the branches between them. The state insurance monopoly DVAG passed to the Munich-based Allianz. THA was also active in agriculture through the leasing of state farms and food-processors and the provision of debt relief schemes for farming companies taking over the former collectives. There has been a plea for a rehabilitation policy from THA to allow public support for 'structurally essential industries' by bringing together central and state governments with employers and unions. But THA was not self-financing and incomes from sales did not meet the outgoings through guarantees over the risk of bad debts and allowance for restructuring, compensation and environmental costs. Hence the raising of cash through bonds including a DM10mn. issue in 1992 to meet deficits. THA was disbanded in 1994 since only some 350 enterprises remained and these are now looked after by a department of the Finance Ministry.

Meanwhile, smaller enterprises nationalised in 1972 were returned to their former owners (Southern 1993). Shops and restaurants were privatised quickly, while the larger stores and many hotels had been dealt with by the early months of 1991 (Siebert 1991). However, privatisation has been complicated by *Eigentumsfrage* (the property question) with many claims being submitted on behalf of former owners expropriated by the communists. Assets lost after 1949 have been reclaimed, although where land had been developed (or a business absorbed into a larger enterprise) compensation has been paid instead. Moreover, where FGDR citizens acquired houses, farms or businesses by honest dealing (i.e. before the resignation of the Honecker government in October 1989) they have been left in possession, while the original owners have been given compensation. However, in order to remove controversy and pave the way for secure investment in property it was decided that claims could also be made in respect of expropriation during the years 1933 to 1945. In all, some two million claims could take ten years to settle, even though most involve only compensation (Osmond 1992). Where property is returned it results in rent increases and the danger of eviction when protection ends. Naturally 'Ossies' advocate a more socially oriented capitalism.

# HUNGARY

Hungary established a formidable economic reform record in the 1970s (Hare *et al.* 1981) continuing into the 1980s (Clarke 1989; Revesz 1990; Richet 1989). Despite some major obstacles to reform through an absence of entrepreneurial skills, a lack of financial infrastructure and high interest rates (Angresano 1992), the late 1980s saw an interest in a mixed system that might transcend 'the undemocratic character of both capitalism and existing socialism' (Brown 1988, p.2). Hungarian agriculture did well as a result of Western loans used to increase food exports. But high interest rates were charged to the farms and cheap food resulted from high subsidies. Living standards actually fell and there was much theft from the well-stocked shops. At the same time there was a slow erosion of communist authority which became a landslide at the end of 1988 and the beginning of 1989. The palace *coup* that removed Kadar seemed highly significant initially, yet by the end of 1988 even his successor K. Grosz was tarnished by a 'neo-conservative agenda' (Agocs 1993, p.189). A multi-party system was rejected but there was a fall in party membership and increased public debate with education in a central position (Szekely and Newbery 1993).

Hungary experienced extensive reform in a bid to save the communist system (Lomax 1993, p.83). The political changes marking the end of state socialism have been extensively researched (Csepeli and Orkeny 1992; Horvath and Szakolczai 1992). The year 1989 heralded a new foreign policy by the government of M. Nemeth. This was highly significant because when the Iron Curtain was dismantled along the Austrian border, the refusal to rescind this decision (rather than a positive decision to expedite the movement of FGDR citizens) contributed to the collapse of government in East Berlin. The same government also negotiated the departure of FSU troops by 1991 and implemented further economic reform on top of the NEM of 1968 and the new arrangements for small business introduced during the 1980s. Summarising the progress of the period, Swain (1991, p.126) also refers to enterprise autonomy from the administrative apparatus in 1985, reform of the banking system in 1987 and overhaul of the tax system in 1988. An economic programme for 1989 was unfurled in January, when the Nemeth government's Transformation of Business Organisation Act, authorised the creation of limited liability companies and measures were taken to balance the budget in view of IMF concern over Hungary's heavy external debts (Hieronymi 1989). Food prices continued to rise and housing subsidies were cut (Lorinc 1992). Despite limits to foreign currency entitlement most convertible currency imports did not require special approval (Kornai 1990).

Legislation enabled enterprise managers to become owners and heralded the era of 'spontaneous privatisation' when assets tended to be grossly undervalued (Stark 1990). New legislation governing foreign investment was also passed at the beginning of 1989. This again contributed to the momentum for privatisation when the lighting group Tungsram was acquired by General Electric of USA. Ganz-Hunslet (1989), with 51 per cent British capital,was another development of this period. Some 200 enterprises were privatised, usually by closed tenders involving established partners and organisations capable of offering a secure future. However, there was widespread concern over corruption when companies privatised themselves and there were also cases of asset stripping including the attachment of liabilities to other state enterprises. It was decided in September 1989 that state supervision of the privatization process was needed and so a State Property Agency (SPA)began work in March 1990. But even with SPA in existence there was a controversial case after a Dutch/Swedish company paid US$90mn. for half of Hungar Hotels; only for the deal to be cancelled in the face of a public outcry against the former communist management (Hann 1990).

Political reform began relatively early when the communists reorganised themselves sufficiently to abandon many of the pretensions of political monopoly and contemplate coalition (Korosenyi 1991). Four of the five new parties that eventually entered parliament in 1990 were formed by late 1988 and they were joined by the fifth in March 1989. However, the communists' route to pluralism was somewhat tortuous because it was only after they had first expelled prominent reformers in May 1988 that Grosz (the party leader who succeeded the long-serving J. Kadar at a special conference in 1988) was obliged to accept a praesidium which would group him with three prominent reformers: Nemeth along with R. Nyers and I. Pozsgay. The party congress in October 1989 then agreed to form a new Hungarian Socialist Party (HSP) with Pozsgay as president, committed to democratic socialism and a market economy. Meanwhile, the rump continued to operate as the Hungarian Socialist Workers' Party (HSWP) (Bozoki *et al.* 1992; Bruszt and Stark 1991).

The Hungarian Democratic Forum (HDF) emerged in 1987 as a nationalist party with encouragement from reform-minded communists and began to work towards a coalition with the then HSWP. It won several by-elections in 1989 but the string of revolutions in that year created a new situation in which non-communist parties gained the prospect of governing outright. The centrist HDF was now assailed from the right by the Alliance of Free Democrats (AFD) and the Alliance of Young Democrats (AYD), with origins in the dissident movements of the 1970s and 1980s, sustained by *samizdat* (underground) publishing. These groups took a particularly vigorous line during the Round Table discussions and forced a referendum in November 1989 on the timing of the election of the president which had been arranged to precede the parliamentary elections (McDonald 1993). It was believed that this procedure would allow Pozsgay to be elected, but in the event the referendum decided by a narrow majority that the presidential election should be delayed. This was significant, not only because it boosted the credibility of the right wing, but because it eroded the link between the communists and the HDF and set the latter on a more independent track. The HDF had initially favoured a 'third road' for development (avoiding close alignment with either East or West) but slowly transformed itself, under Antall's leadership, into a Western-style Christian Democratic party. However, the HDF remained prone to nationalist sentiments emanating from its right wing while the AFD has shown some anti-communist extremism, such were the factions created by competing elites (Szablowski 1993).

An opposition Round Table encouraged the communists to discuss transformation of the political system in June 1989 and paved the way for the elections of spring 1990 which produced a decisive change (Bozoki 1993). The HSWP was firmly rejected and failed to get enough votes to enter parliament. Even the HSP gained only 8.6 per cent of the seats. The winner was the HDF with 42.5 per cent, which formed the core of J. Antall's coalition government with the Independent Smallholders' Party (11.4 per cent) and the Christian Democratic People's Party (5.4 per cent) (Kovacs 1993; Racz 1991). All supported a growth of foreign investment (Barany 1990). To the right of the governing coalition were the liberal intellectuals who saw themselves as serious contenders for power, seeking a clean break with the past and rejecting compromise (Lomax 1990). The electorate was probably right in rejecting their free trade policy but nevertheless the AFD took 23.8 per cent of the seats and the AYD 5.4 per cent. It was noticeable that both these right-wing parties (urging faster privatisation and greater scope for foreign investment), along with the HDF, did well in Budapest and other major cities. They also did well in the northwestern part of the country, with the AYD especially strong in the university and college towns. Predictably the Smallholders picked up modest support fairly consistently across the rural areas while the HSWP found most of their strength in the east, especially in the areas of high unemployment (Hars *et al.* 1991).

## The Antall and Horn governments

As already noted, the reform agenda was well under way when the Antall government came to power. The economy was doing well and the Warsaw Pact was not an issue, although relations with former allies (especially Romania and Slovakia) were strained by concern about the fate of Hungarian minorities, formalised by declarations of the Hungarian state's responsibility for their welfare. This approach was driven by the HDF's right wing, reacting to the perceived high level of foreign penetration of the Hungarian economy. For Hungary's 'social market economy' rhetoric led to a rapid state withdrawal after the Nemeth government had for a long time resisted the IMF call for cuts in welfare expenditure. Antall planned for a budget surplus in 1990, requiring a modicum of shock therapy, but some change was needed as manufacturing output fell during 1989 and 1990; while there was an increase in bankruptcies as enterprises dependent on trade with the FSU saw their markets diminish.

Hungary was in a weak technological position through the trade surplus with the FSU which developed through the 1980s, since the government was politically committed to Comecon while enterprise managers appreciated the long-term contracts available in a relatively undemanding market (Swain 1991, p.134). However, change was soon evident in the computer business where production of obsolescent Comecon equipment collapsed in the face of joint ventures by West European and American firms, including IBM which greatly increased its activity, having been connected with Hungary throughout the socialist era. This switch was a microcosm of Hungarian trade in general, which showed a clear reorientation from former Comecon countries to EU countries during 1990 (Palankai 1991).

Trade relations were diversified through business in the West for firms benefiting from new investment; for example, Videoton and Tungsram, with its compact fluorescent lamps. Meanwhile, Ikarus found markets for buses in Iran, Taiwan and Turkey although it failed to find a foreign partner prepared to invest in the Hungarian factories (Richter 1992). There were closer links with Ukraine through a Hungarian-Swiss joint venture envisaging a special economic zone along the Ukrainian border in 1993–4 and plans for a Vienna–Kiev motorway. Hungarian cigarettes were finding favour in Ukraine since Philip Morris acquired the Eger tobacco factory, setting new standards for an industry that could do much better in export markets with new ideas for production and packaging. Meanwhile, farm production fell in 1989 and 1990, with the aggravation of drought in the latter year which depressed the level of agricultural exports. This period was also a time of agrarian change for, as Swain points out (1991, p.131), there was a broad consensus that 'the collective farms should be transformed into service centres for new authentic cooperatives' and that efficiency should be enhanced by creating a land market. However, this approach, reflected in the arrangements for the sale of land drawn up by the Nemeth government, was broken by the Smallholders' Party which used its influence in Antall's coalition to press for a restitution programme implemented through the allocation of vouchers for former owners for use at district land auctions. Meanwhile, agricultural trade continued to be vulnerable to drought, as in 1993 when the overall trade balance was again in deficit.

There have been improvements in infrastructure with the start of the Budapest motorway ring and the beginning of an express parcel delivery service by the Austrian-based TNT after the Post Office's monopoly was abolished. Energy emerged as a problem in October 1990 when reduced oil deliveries necessitated high cost purchases on the open market which forced a sharp increase in domestic prices and helped precipitate the taxi and lorry blockade. Antall survived the strike, but the upheaval led to the promise of more consensus government. By this time Hungary had decided to pull out of the Gabcikovo-Nagymaros hydropower deal with FCSFR. The Budapest Stock Market opened in 1990 and most of the world's leading accountancy and management consultant firms established a presence in Budapest. During 1992 many newspapers fell under foreign ownership (often the German Springer organisation) but the question of government influence over radio and television continued to be controversial (as it had been under the Nemeth government) until it was agreed that the heads of the two services should be appointed by the president on the recommendation of the prime minister.

Relations with the IMF were stabilised, but at the cost of keeping budget deficits down (Bartlett 1996). The economy failed to climb out of recession because, although tourism did well and small businesses made a growing contribution, output continued to fall and unemployment rose (Cukor and Kovari 1991). Antall was able to carry on the reform momentum with a bankruptcy law, signalling hard budget constraints, and with some re-structuring of the administration to cope with differences of economic opinion. But experts have suggested that after a head start the government became complacent with its efforts to restore foreign confidence, and began work on compensation and privatisation measures. The AFD opposition felt that government was too interventionist and nationalistic, frightening away foreign investment in the process (Csaba 1992). Gradualism had been promised on the grounds that Hungarians, with a depressive national psycho-logy and a high propensity for suicide, would not respond well to shock treatment (Hare and Revesz 1992). But the problem was how to combine gradualism with a clear sense of purpose. Painful decisions were postponed through 1990, despite undertakings to implement radical tax reform (with a new income tax and VAT) while reducing inflation and the state sector of the economy.

Nevertheless, in the local elections of September to October 1990 the urban areas (especially Budapest and the county towns) moved strongly to the right with support for the AFD and AYD. The government did better in the rural areas and small towns, but still only won in five of the nineteen counties. A right-wing challenge to Antall in 1993 was overcome by a breakaway of the nationalist extremists under I. Csurka, which at least allowed the HDF to move back to the centre of politics. When Antall died at the end of the year (to be replaced by P. Boross on the right of the HDF) it seemed unlikely that the party would win another term in office at the forthcoming (1994) election (Pataki 1994). Government was blamed for the continuing recession because of its harsh emergency budget and its failure to accelerate reform. The security police revealed a scandal by weeding out foreign speculators taking advantage of inexperienced Hungarian managers desperate for foreign assist-ance. There was nostalgia for the welfare system of communism, though not for the political institutions, and G. Horn's Socialist Party, which grew out of the reformed Communist Party, duly won the 1994 elections with a programme of social democracy, seeking to combine market forces with the security of the old regime (Racz 1993).

Horn's government, based on a coalition of Socialists and Free Democrats which commands 70 per cent of the seats in parliament, has accelerated privatisation, with income redistribution and consideration of social problems (Lomax 1995). A basic treaty between Hungary and Slovakia is anticipated, with acceptance of frontiers balanced by undertakings to protect national minorities by working to European norms. Hungary is also keen to settle the dispute with Slovakia over the Gabcikovo-Nagymaros hydro project and to secure a greater flow of water along the old Danube channel. On the economic front the government considered intervening in the sale of Hungar Hotels (with American General Hospitality gaining a majority stake in competition with Intercontinental of Japan). But it took the view that interference might undermine investor confidence, already sensitive about the government's decision to review privatisation sales over the last two years. The government is redrafting tax codes and withdrawing tax holidays. Higher taxes on agricultural imports and VAT increases on telecommunications (from 10 to 25 per cent) will help to reduce the budget gap. The World Bank is helping Hungary to modernise its tax system to cover the 70,000 or so private businesses which are now operating. The economic position is quite strong with unemployment held at 12 per cent (6 per cent in the capital) and inflation below 20 per cent. But there was a deficit of US$4bn on current account in 1994 and the total foreign debt of US$20.0bn has caused an austerity programme of budget cuts (reversing the original growth strategy) because of the need to raise money for debt servicing.

The AFD want to see a market-oriented economic policy and were disturbed by the resignation of Finance Minister L. Bekesi. His replacement by the much-respected L. Bokros is therefore important for the future of the coalition which may not survive until the next election. However, the government appears all the more secure by the weakness of the HDF whose nationalist platform is no longer popular with several sections of society, including the young. But there was a further resignation when Bokros departed in 1996 and was succeeded by P. Medgyessy. The trouble arose because the ruling socialists strongly opposed austerity and stabilisation measures worked out by Bokros and central bank governor G. Suranyi to bring down the budget deficit from 9.5 per cent of GDP in 1994 to 6.5 in 1995. The situation is now much less certain because industrial output failed to pick up at the end of 1995 and unemployment rose, even though energy prices were raised and inflation was brought down. External debt stands at US$33bn and debt servicing absorbs 40 per cent of export earnings. Meanwhile, privatisation revenues are falling, forecast at US$690mn. in 1996 (mainly from utilities) and a big drop on 1995. Government will have to reduce spending on a large public sector and the welfare system in particular, with the IMF US$300mn. stand-by loan dependent on parliamentary approval of Bokros's final budget. However, although support for the socialists has fallen, the next election is not due until 1998.

## Private and foreign investment

Privatisation has progressed more slowly than expected, despite foreign support for wider share ownership and assistance through the UK Know How Fund (Kiss 1991). The SPA employed a rigorous monitoring policy, working on asset valuation rather than market worth, and showed considerable flexibility in determining prices. But all did not go smoothly and stock market trends were highly variable: the Ibusz travel agency was privatised in 1990 but after shares were initially over-subscribed the price fell by one third after the launch, and purchasers lost money in the short term because of over-optimism about profit levels. A programme of twenty privatisations later in the year featured attractive companies and drew some 250 tenders, with British and French companies the most successful followed by Austria, Belgium and Italy. There was also interest from North America and Japan (Major 1991a, 1991b, 1991c). Privatisation deals in 1991 included the sale of the Lehel refrigerator company to Electrolux of Sweden (the first outright privatisation sale) and consumer goods companies were acquired by Western multinationals: they were a natural target for foreign companies wanting to build up market share, especially where licensing and trading arrangements were already in force. Some four-fifths of the first 200 SOEs to be privatised went to foreign capital. But changes have been made in response to accusations of 'cherry picking' and assets are now being more highly valued (Kiss 1992). Hotels, banks and utilities have now been dealt with, though not without difficulty: the sale of the Danubius hotel chain was cancelled because of taxation problems which affected the valuation. Meanwhile, procedures for small companies were simplified in order to reduce bureaucratic control. There was great public interest in the sale of many small businesses (shops and commercial/catering establishments) which frequently passed into the hands of sitting tenants.

By the end of 1992 it was estimated that more than 15 per cent of state property had been privatised, some of it by EMBO (Karsai and Wright 1994; Lawrence 1993). Meanwhile, another 30 per cent of the SPA's assets were put into corporate form pending privatisation. However, while many privat-isations were eminently successful (like the airline Malev in which Alitalia gained an interest) others were failing. Investment was depressed by high interest rates and foreign demand seemed to fade due to a preference for Czech and Polish assets. However, there were well over a thousand joint ventures with Austrian, German and Swiss companies at the end of 1990 compared with another 650 for USA, UK, Italy and Sweden combined. Important investments in the car industry were announced, while the Ozd metallurgical works was sold as a consortium including Austrian and German firms. Italian companies gained an interest in the Salgotarjan metallurgical works and a French company, Sanofi, took a majority stake in Hungary's largest pharmaceutical firm Chinoin. It already has a stake in Hungary's veterinary medicine producer Phylaxia. At the end of 1992 there were seven foreign firms with investments of US$100mn. or more: the car projects by General Motors (250) and Suzuki (225) followed by General Electric (owner of Tungsram, with 200), the German insurance company Allianz with its holding in Hungaria Biztosito (125), Prinzhorn of Austria (110), Guardian Industries of USA (owner of the Hungard float glass producer) and Siemens of Germany (each 100). However, investment was expected to peak in 1992 and the investment promotion agency ITD Hungary has been set up as an investment and trade development agency looking especially at motor components, food-processing and tourism.

Some firms are doing well: new private companies or large SOEs enjoying a monopoly. But many are drifting because they cannot grow and avoid liquidation by living off assets. Finally, there are others which are bound to disappear unless they are rescued by government. With only slim prospects of profitability they face the threat of bankruptcy. Hungary went for a tough 'big bang' bankruptcy law in 1991 (also legislation on accountancy and banking) which forced one-tenth of the country's companies into liquidation. This was thought necessary to get poor managers out of the system and allow assets to be reallocated. A law should not be too harsh (destroying businesses that could be viable) or too soft (allowing excessive inefficiency). There was some sensitivity towards promising ventures such as Hungaroton, the record producer with a factory in Dorog which was placed under SPA control pending privatisation. One-fifth of the companies under the control of the SPA were vulnerable to liquidation under the 1992 Bankruptcy Law and there has been particular apprehension over the 'Dirty 13' (major enterprises in engineering and chemicals), where closure would result in a considerable increase in unemployment (Keay 1993). The Ministry of Industry and Trade has proposed a government rescue of these enterprises which could become competitive with an injection of working capital (Brada *et al.* 1993). This produced a strong feeling that the Hungarian public should have a greater opportunity through a Czech-style voucher system. It is significant that Hungary has not used the voucher scheme which has proved popular elsewhere (Okolicsanyi 1993). By the end of 1992 there was a clear political direction imposed on the SPA, reflecting public disquiet over the dominance of foreign multinationals. Privatisation through the stock exchange is increasing and, as shown by the case of the meat/salami firm Pick Szeged, it will afford opportunities for small investors through discounts, deferred payments or bonus shares.

During the Spring of 1993 'easy payment' schemes were made available for domestic investors, with discrimination in their favour when allocations were made. Domestic investors can borrow funds at a preferential rate and pay it back over a fixed period (Laki 1993). There is a also a scheme for transferable 'compensation vouchers' for those who suffered under communism (mainly those who had property or business nationalised): an estimated

800,000 will eventually benefit. Another 300,000 will receive benefit for having been unjustly imprisoned. These schemes promise to inject some Ft50bn. into the privatisation scheme. More interest may follow from an upturn in the market, although the private companies seem more likely to lead the recovery. There is also consideration once again of flexible arrangements for small SOEs which might become privatise with the help of consultants. Many businesses could be made profitable however and EMBOs have been advocated. Another strategy could be admission of foreign capital into industries (such as telecommunications) currently controlled by the State Asset Management Company. The liquidation method can also be used: it can reduce debt burdens and enable buyers to deal directly with the creditor banks who become the effective owners.

## Enterprise and regional contrasts

Meanwhile, Hungary continues to stand out as one of the most attractive investment environments in Eastern Europe (Agh 1993; Ivan 1993). After the difficult years of 1991–2, 1993 marked a turning point and 1994 brought a rise in living standards (Mattheisen 1991). Whereas Poland sought rapid change that was potentially destabilising, Hungary's gradual (and somewhat inconsistent) change helped to avoid social tensions (Adams 1995). GDP is now increasing and unemployment is falling. Hungary has a range of financial institutions and a differentiated banking system which can play an important part in the market economy (Estrin 1992). The Hungarian-American Enterprise Fund is helping to boost the dynamic private sector (Audorka 1993). EBRD has agreed a loan to the Hungarian manufacturer of recycled paperboard (PCA Budafok) to improve quality and productivity in order to recapture market sales and boost exports to the Middle East and former Comecon countries. However, it will take time for services to reach Western levels in view of the prevailing level of office technology. 'It is not only the stores and restaurants that are not prepared to accept cheques and credit cards, but consumer habits and lack of experience with the market economy also contribute to the difficulties' (Lengyel 1994, p.391). The German government has enabled the Deutsche Ausgleichbank to become involved in the creation of a fund to help the Hungarian National Bank to support small and medium-sized businesses (Schlegel 1994). Former barrack buildings have been refurbished to create small factory units under a Phare programme for small business incubation. The British-Hungarian Small Business Foundation assisted with a conversion near Kecskemet which, for a period of five years, will help small businesses to avoid the heavy initial costs of starting up. Meanwhile, the informal economy remains important, supporting legal activities through personal contacts and illegal operations, for example, East–West trade in stolen cars through Hungary. The importance of the informal economy and small-scale trading makes for a similarity with Latin America (Sik 1994).

The US computer firm International Business Machines is making a major investment in Szekesfehervar to provide production facilities for computer disk drives for the European market. The UK's International Distillers and Vintners has a 25 per cent stake in the Hungarian spirits producer Zwack. The UK bed manufacturer Slumberland has opened a factory and showroom in Budapest. The Belgian-Hungarian joint venture Buchmann-MOM has a factory on a greenfield site in Hungary for continuous production of contact lenses. Phillips of the Netherlands would like to start a joint venture with Videoton to produce components for cassette players. South African Breweries is to acquire an 80 per cent stake in Hungary's largest brewery Kobanyi Sorgyar to increase capacity for production of the popular Dreher brand. Agrikom at Kecskemet has won a contract to build grain storage installations in Egypt. Regional trends show low unemployment in the northwest: hence a west–east axis for unemployment; but also centre-periphery. According to a range of criteria the backward east and northeast are the worst off. However, there are areas scattered through the country which are either backward (like the frontier areas of both Transdanubia and eastern Hungary) or have been hit by the crisis in FSU or by a crisis in the supply of raw materials. This is revealed by the research of J. Bachtler and R. Downes (quoted by Nefedova and Trejvis 1994, p.39).

## POLAND

After more than a decade of uneasy conformity following the Warsaw Pact invasion of FCSFR in 1968, Eastern Europe was galvanised by the Solidarity strikes of 1980, the ensuing negotiations with government and the subsequent reaction by the military under General W. Jaruzelski. This radical Solidarity movement, born in the Baltic shipyards and Silesian coalmines, was able to maintain a community of interest among a social grouping (*spoleczenstwo*), linking peasants, proletariat and intelligentsia. Such a broad social grouping had previously developed in the nineteenth century and persisted anachronistically up to the First World War (Tymowski 1993). But now it was reconstituted as a national reawakening. Unfortunately, unity has not been maintained through the transition, since more peasants are becoming commercial farmers or are working in rural services, while the factory workers are embittered by the restructuring and dismantling of their enterprises. But there are still flickers of this association in the programme of the present government.

### The Solidarity era

The communist power of the Polish United Workers Party (PUWP) was gravely weakened by Solidarity and martial law failed to restore its fortunes effectively (Kolankiewicz and Lewis 1988). The government was driven back to reform in 1988 through sharp price rises which caused a wave of strikes and subsequent wage increases as labour was able to negotiate with SOE managers. There was further inflation and many consumer goods became unobtainable outside dollar shops. The government of F. Rakowski then set about privatisation in a manner favourable to the nomenclature (Kaminski 1991). There was also an attempt to close the inefficient Gdansk shipyard, although this provoked bitter opposition from Solidarity on the grounds that the move was politically motivated, the Gdansk yard having been the spawning ground of the Solidarity movement and Walesa's political career. There was further reform through the freeing of prices which, again, fuelled inflation (Milanovic 1992).

It was while the food market was stabilising that the first Solidarity-led government came into existence under the circumstance of perestroika in the FSU. The communists (organised as the Polish United Workers' Party (PUWP)) decided to try and bring elements of the opposition into the official political system and, despite some dissension within Solidarity, talks were held early in 1989 at Magdalenka (near Warsaw) between Walesa and Interior Minister C. Kiszczak. These paved the way for Round Table negotiations involving Solidarity and the PUWP (Blaszkiewicz *et al.* 1994). It was agreed that Solidarity should contest just over one-third of the seats in the *Sejm* (parliament), while Jaruzelski would occupy the new presidency in order to reassure the FSU and other Warsaw Pact allies. Although the PUWP was guaranteed a majority, discontent associated with Rakowski's reform policies (with huge price increases following the abolition of rationing and price controls), followed by the failure of the president's nominee (Kiszczak) to form a new government, led to the formation of a Solidarity-led coalition under T. Mazowiecki (Barany 1990). Solidarity ministers looked after the economy while PUWP elements controlled the defence and interior ministries, leaving Foreign Affairs in the hands of an independent body. The PUWP then transformed itself into a new party: the Social Democracy Party of the Polish Republic (Regulska 1993).

## Economic and social reform

Solidarity showed hesitancy over market reform, being aware that elimination of central planning could lead to market uncertainty (Ebrill *et al.* 1994; Gomulka 1991). It was believed that trade could break down and the development of efficient marketing might therefore be delayed (Charemza 1992). Yet the movement could not waste its mandate for reform and it decided on radical action (Rychard 1991). It was fortunate that the government was able to avoid 'violent or uncontrolled labour disruption' (Kramer 1995, p.107) because there was a consensus that communism should be abandoned; and although the labour force was fragmented the workers played a central role in the privatisation process (Taras 1995). After considerable anxiety, the year 1992 marked a turning point. Practically all remaining price controls were removed and imports were also freed (Lipton and Sachs 1990). At the same time there was a strict monetary policy and a move towards limited convertibility. Despite dire warnings, famine did not occur during the winter of 1989–90 and while unemployment increased it did not engulf between one-fifth and one-third of the workforce as had been predicted. Many people who lost their jobs found alternative employment in the private sector. Business was buoyant, with some 700,000 new enterprises triggered by reform during the first three years of transition (Gora 1991). Exports rose from 9.2 to 15.3 per cent of GDP between 1989 and 1991 while imports went up from 13.6 to 22.8 per cent. Great economic advantage was bestowed by the high level of energy self-sufficiency (Blazyca and Rapacki 1991), although uncertainties over oil imports forced a reduction of coal exports. The government has tried to control coal prices to prevent exploitation of a monopoly situation but this has made for difficulty with the miners, despite the agreement worked out by the Round Table.

The radical economic policy of 1989–90 was associated with the Finance Minister I. Belcerowicz and, although policy was widely believed to be extreme, the political climate was conducive to the concept of the 'social market economy' which did include welfare considerations (Dabrowski 1991).

Early in 1990 it was evident that inflation was coming under control (Calvo and Coricelli 1992). Subsidies were cut and a retail revolution was sparked off. Liberalisation of prices eliminated both the queues and the black market (Winiecki 1992). Foreign goods came in and inflation went down: from 5 per cent per month in April 1990 to 2 per cent in July. Major foreign assistance was not required; but a stabilisation fund allowed Poland to peg its currency at the beginning of 1990 and was critical in the decision to go ahead with the reform programme (World Bank 1990). In 1991 currency appreciated against the dollar and this fuelled consumer imports, including some 300,000 new and used cars. However, imports meant competition with domestic industry and agriculture: hence the contrast between the glitter of overstocked shops and the depressed state of the factories consigned to closure or short-time working. There was growing unemployment, while incomes for those in work rose by less than the rate of inflation. It was widely accepted that reform was needed as a prelude to eventual EU membership (Lewis 1993). But a number of financial scandals heightened public unease and encouraged an independent 'go-it-alone' political outlook supposing that rapid reorganisation could be avoided (Kowalski 1993).

There were also changes in social policy in 1990 with abortion permitted only if three doctors agreed. Then in 1992 abortion was stopped altogether, except in cases of rape victims and people whose lives would be endangered by childbirth. Other important reforms effected in 1990 included the abolition of press censorship and provision for optional religious classes in schools. In foreign affairs there was a settlement of the western frontier question and a 'return to Europe' through contacts with the EU. There was also regional collaboration with the Bratislava meeting in 1990, when Polish ministers met their counterparts from FCS and Hungary, creating what later became known as the Visegrad Group. But there was some discord over Soviet troops because of Walesa's preference for immediate withdrawal against Jaruzelski's desire for delay pending new security arrangements. Walesa's presidential campaign (discussed below) meant that negotiations were speeded up. But the issue was complicated by claims and counter-claims: from Poland in respect of environmental damage and housing costs for FSU troops and from Russia (concerned about extricating its troops from FGDR) with regard to assistance in rebuilding Poland after the Second World War. Eventually the Treaty of Friendship was signed in 1992 and this secured the removal of Russian troops by the end of that year. The idea of using former Soviet troop facilities for joint ventures was abandoned.

## Consolidating the reforms

The economic team continued to function, despite the fall of the Mazowiecki government late in 1990 after being in power for just over one year (Sachs 1992). Solidarity influence remained strong, although the next two governments – under J.K. Bielecki and J. Olszewski – were in power for progressively shorter periods. Strong government was bound to be difficult given the system of proportional representation with a proliferation of parties. But in addition, stability was elusive because it seemed that the social consequences of radical restructuring were being overlooked. There was a proposal for selective stimulation of state industries, reflecting the economic policies of J. Eysymontt, yet spending cuts were demanded by the finance minister, aware of the need to accommodate IMF and World Bank requirements. Hard monetarist pressure continued, although after zero growth in 1992 recovery was expected in 1993 led by construction, trade and services. Successful private businesses were created in engineering and foodprocessing, often through links with German technology and FSU markets in Belarus and the Baltics. There was a stimulus to new industry through development of industrial sites near Warsaw Airport and also at Zarnowiec (the site of the abandoned nuclear power project near Gdansk) which offered complete territorial development including buildings of up to 15,000sq.m.

Meanwhile, Walesa stayed out of parliament and maintained his personal standing by advocating greater concern for welfare (Zubek 1991). His demand for Jaruzelski's resignation (when it was obvious that the new order in Poland was acceptable in the FSU) paved the way for a presidential election and a split in Solidarity between the Mazowiecki and Walesa factions. Walesa's election dominated events in 1990 and saw Mazowiecki marginalised by emigré millionaire S. Tyminski who benefited from protest against the government's austerity measures and again, in the second ballot, from the support given by former communist supporters to the strongest anti-Walesa candidate. The 'war at the top' split Solidarity irrevocably and achieved what the communists themselves had never been able to accomplish (Kolankiewicz 1993). It was to some extent a self-destruction scenario, although there were inevitable differences of approach between the intellectual and proletarian wings of the organisation. But Walesa's election was highly significant in other ways. It reflected his determination 'to use his popular charisma and symbolism to get into power before volcanic socio-economic discontent shattered the Polish political scene yet again' (Sanford and Myant 1991, p. 158) and, at the same time, offered the country an effective mediator between government and people. Walesa was keen to increase presidential power given the fragmentation in parliament, and there were particularly difficult relations with Prime Minister Olszewski in the context of a highly fragmented parliament in late 1991 and early 1992 (Donnorummo 1994).

Polish industry was embarrassed by a failure to modernise during the 1980s. Thus the Odra computer was developed during the 1970s but the product was not perfected further because a Soviet design was preferred for Comecon use. There was only limited production for export and domestic use in the modernisation of Polish industry. The Ursus tractor factory was left with much-reduced sales (despite some new export markets) and heavy financial obligations after an inadequate investment programme during the 1980s. But the state sector was generally embarrassed by the fall in demand from FSU and enterprises geared to this market are unlikely to be attractive to Western investors. Hence the grave problems facing some thirty large engineering companies, formerly geared exclusively to the FSU market and cumulatively responsible for well over half of the country's Soviet exports in 1989. Mielec, a recession-hit aircraft factory undermined by the collapse of the FSU market, was reorganised as a Polish enterprise zone in late 1992 and there were further examples in light industry with the textile and clothing companies of Lodz, producing low quality goods from outdated technology which could not be sold in the West. These relatively small firms, lacking any monopoly status, experienced acute competition leading to sharp falls in employment and falling real wage levels. Some state enterprises continued to increase exports. Those that were exporting to the West during the 1980s used their established contacts and knowledge of the market to enter into discussions immediately reforms were introduced.

During the summer and autumn of 1992 the OECD expressed concern over the budget deficit and the persistence of soft loans to state enterprises (one-third of 6,200 such enterprises reported pre-tax losses in late 1991). There seemed to be a need for greater consistency in applying stabilisation measures, with tighter financial management to stimulate investment. In 1992 VAT was introduced to strengthen the budget and the zloty was devalued. Foreign trade was thrown open to private entrepreneurs in 1992 and this contributed to continued export-led recovery, with exports up in the first half of the year by 12.5 per cent to US$6.9mn., while imports fell by 8 per cent to US$5.9mn, creating a trade surplus (Berg and Sachs 1992). Crucial Polish exports of coal, steel and textiles were maintained. But falling real wages brought damaging strikes in 1992, including seven-week stoppages at the vehicle factories at Bielsko-Biala and Tychy, which halted recruitment of additional shift workers to increase output. The coal and copper mines were affected, as was the Mielec aircraft factory. Government refused to intervene and the church remained unsympathetic. However, following the strikes Labour Minister J. Kuron tried to involve unions in restructuring and privatising SOEs.

There was intense interest in Poland in the spatial aspects of crisis with classification of voivodships (administrative regions) and ultimately derived indexes of investment attractiveness (Weclawowicz 1996). Initially, the main urban-industrial centres lost out through supply problems, but they won substantial state credits and took a leading role in restructuring and in attracting foreign investment. The coal and steel economy of Poland has been well protected and the areas experiencing the greatest stress have been in the south but away from the main industrial centres (Czestochowa, Legnica and Walbrzych), though the greatest recession has been in Suwalki in the northeast. Meanwhile there has been growth in places like Gdansk and Poznan which are open to the West through Gdansk port and Poznan's proximity to Germany (Lewis 1995). But in neighbouring regions the importance of the private sector increased rapidly through 1992 and 1993. The net result is four centres of relative prosperity: Warsaw-Siedlce, Poznan, Gdansk and the south (covering Upper Silesia and the adjacent Carpathian zone). However, migration is still dominated by rural–urban flows (Nefedova and Trejvis 1994 pp.40–1).

Olszewski was followed by W. Pawlak, a former member of the PUWP's ally the United Peasant Party. But after he failed to form a government, the Democratic Union leader H. Suchocka was able to win the support of Christian Democrats, free marketeers and right-wing nationalists to obtain a majority. Her government lasted for about one year (from mid-1992 to mid-1993) and dealt effectively with strikes by removing the unpopular *popiwek* tax (on high pay increases) in favour of free collective bargaining. However, the government would not finance wage increases for the SOEs unless they were tied to productivity. The 1993 budget kept within IMF conditions although the opposition tried to get higher social spending. Significant economic growth was evident by 1993 (Kramer 1995) and some 60 per cent of the workforce was engaged in private sector activity by the middle of the year. But during 1993 Suchocka had to struggle to stay in power as Solidarity unions were placed in the dilemma of backing austerity measures that would attract IMF loans but impacted negatively on workers in the short term. There was consideration of a social pact as a labour relations response to strikes through appropriate restructuring and privatisation. But the concept did not make headway in domestic politics and the government fell after failing to win a confidence motion. Since many Polish firms are highly unprofitable it may well be that market forces will have to resolve the matter eventually (Slay 1993).

Even the pace of privatisation has been disappointingly slow. Although shares in seven companies – ready for sale late in 1990 – were over-subscribed, there did not appear to be enough money available to support massive privatisation. Privatisation has been quickest where capital require-ments have been low and the skills obtained in the past can be redeployed: thus domestic and foreign trade has been quickly privatised with many family businesses emerging in premises rented from local councils (Poznanski 1993b). Eighty per cent of shops were privatised in two years and in 1991 46 per cent of imports were handled by the newly privatised trade sector (Mroz 1991). The privatisation law of 1990 provided for Ministry of Ownership changes, following the 1988 decision over enterprise-initiated privatisation which Solidarity denounced as 'nomenclature privatisation' and refused to implement it.

It seemed that anyone with ample resources would try and set up their own business from scratch. But domestic investment was discouraged by declining share prices on the Warsaw stock exchange and the failure of quoted companies to announce dividends in 1992. Privatisation was also slowed by new consultation procedures introduced in 1992: people were becoming less impressed with the necessity to privatise and many thought that the process should not be too rapid. There are industrial interests in parliament and complicated restitution questions (Poznanski 1993a), while many firms are so unprofitable that they could not even be given away. However, Poland seems to be moving towards mass privatisation through public share offers and investment funds. Shares were now to be sold for their full value, although one fifth will be available to employees at preferential rates and employees will also hold one third of the seats on enterprise supervisory boards. The concept of free shares has been ruled out because it would not educate Poles over the rights and responsibilities of ownership. The president wants to see free dollar loans to families wishing to invest with repayment after twenty years. But money is in short supply. However, with nominal sums for shares and competition among fund managers promising rapid appreciation, this is crude speculation (Charemza 1992).

The Suchocka government initiated a programme to privatise between 400 and 600 of the largest state enterprises with transfer to twenty management funds and ultimately to private shareholders. Though initially rejected by parliament it has been reconsidered because it is a crucial IMF indicator; it is critical for the support of the World Bank and international confidence and Suchocka insisted after her government's defeat that the programme would go ahead (Bjork 1995). There must be efficient management to make

enterprises attractive for privatisation and to safeguard their social importance. There is also a World Bank initiative that would restructure and
privatise banks and also restructure those state enterprises that are placing
the greatest burden on the banks. There has been a pact with the unions to
encourage enterprises to convert into joint stock companies which can
subsequently be privatised. Meanwhile, SOEs have been taken off the
government's hands by other methods: there have been over 500 EMBOs,
perhaps incorporating equity stakes by employees and some outside small
business investment (Nuti 1993). For example, management and workers own
much of the Torun clothing firm Torpo. This is a good solution where the
main value of the enterprise lies in staff expertise and capital equipment is
limited. The local authorities may also be involved in this process. The
privatisation is breathing new life into foreign trade organisations which are
starting to purchase industrial plants and turn themselves into holding
companies with sufficient strength to challenge overseas competition (Slay
1994a). The privatised Zywiec Brewery was able to raise wages (freed from
state control) and evaded several taxes affecting the state sector. Profits rose,
even though equipment was outdated and modernisation is needed.

## Foreign investment

Poland is finding capital on the international bond market with the help of
US investment banker J.P. Morgan, but there are numerous foreign invest-
ments being made by private companies attracted by the present price–wage
dynamics in the country (Golinelli and Orsi 1994; Markowski and Jackson
1994). Fiat is undertaking small car production at Bielsko-Biala while
Lucchini of Italy has a joint venture with Warsaw steelworks. ABB, the
Swiss/Swedish power plant producer, acquired a majority stake in Elta (the
Lodz transformer company) while the US food company CPC acquired
Anino, the Poznan dehydrated food producer. Belgium's Cimenteries CBR
has a stake in two cement companies: Zaklady Cementowo-Wapiennicze
Gorazda and Cementownia Strzelce Opolaskie. International Paper has
acquired the Kwidzyn paper-cellulose works. Philips have moved into
electric bulbs and Unilever into detergents. Pepsi-Cola has a majority holding
in the Warsaw chocolate producer Wedel, while Coca-Cola has a large
investment programme with major new bottling plants. The Katowice-based
Bank Slaski now has a stake by ING Bank of the Netherlands. The EBRD
has agreed loans to the Szczecinek chipboard manufacturer Polspan and the
Poznan melamine paper producer Malta-Decor, both of which are owned by
Europe's largest chipboard producer Kronospan. Following success in Hungary, Compact Computer of the USA has opened a subsidiary in Poland and
expects to boost sales and become the leading supplier, overtaking IBM and
staying ahead of Apple, Commodore and Olivetti. Cussons of the UK has
acquired an 80 per cent stake in Pollena, the Polish soap and detergent

manufacturer based in Wroclaw. Sweden's paper producer Trebruk has taken over Poland's Kostrzyn pulp and paper plant. The Daewoo project at Pruszkow where a television plant opened in 1994 has done well; it is to be followed by a consumer electronics complex which will export to both Eastern and Western Europe. British Vita Polymers have opened a factory at Brzeg Dolny, producing polyurethane foam for the furniture industry. The factory has a unique filter system which prevents the emission of harmful substances.

However, it is noticeable that most investment has gone to the Gdansk, Krakow, Poznan and Warsaw areas; while the depressed southeast is relatively neglected, though the Amoco concession of 1992 to search for oil involved the area south of Warsaw and east of Lublin. Sweden's Bofors is renewing old links with Huta Stalowa Wola with a view to getting complete turrets for armoured vehicles manufactured in Poland. Continental Can Europe has started construction on Poland's first factory (in Radom) to produce cans for beer and soft drinks. Meanwhile, territorial claims in the east have been abandoned in the interest of developing stable economic relations with FSU (De Weydenthal 1993). There is a priority to redevelop intense trade contacts as well as collaboration to support democracy and market economies in general (De Weydenthal 1994). Pollene-Ewa, owned by its workers, is to export cosmetics to Belarus.

## Swing to the left

There is now the prospect of stronger government through the decision that parties not gaining 5 per cent of the votes will not be represented in parliament (Jasiewicz 1993; Wade 1995). Hence, unlike the four Solidarity prime ministers, the Pawlak government of 1993, combining the Democratic Left Alliance with the Polish Peasants Party (PPP) started out with a good prospect of running its full term (Bivand 1993). Victory rested on several factors, not the least important of which was the ability of the left to make common cause throughout the election and to stand as effective representatives of those who felt they had lost out in the reform process through unemployment or falling real wages. The shift showed that the public wanted stronger welfare policies. The change was also assisted by the failure of previous governments (especially the outgoing Suchocka government) to 'sell' their policies, and the failure of Solidarity to organise a coalition, aggravated by the new electoral law. Further explanations can be found in the defensive stance of the EU (against Polish exports) and the influence of the Catholic Church (with the abortion law strongly supported by the right-wing Catholic Party) in the formation of social policy in previous governments (Tworzecki 1994). This is to say nothing about political ineptitude, such as the one-member boycott of the vote of confidence which precipitated the Suchocka government's demise (Kawecka-Wyrzykowska 1993).

The Pawlak government succeeded initially because there was genuine coexistence between coalition partners as the urban-based intellectuals forged an alliance with the peasantry (Zubek 1994). It was expected that the new government would boost welfare (and inflation at the same time) rather than stick to a monetarist policy desired by the IMF. It also seemed that nomenclature elements might regain some of their lost status. But the programme was fairly measured despite its left-wing inclination (Lewis 1994), seeking to maintain growth of 4.5 per cent per annum or better (Slay 1994b). But while Western businessmen are impressed by Poland's potential they express concern over unstable tax regimes and uncertain business environment, flavoured by population distrust of foreign investors. However, the government has been taking a number of important initiatives. It has created a Polish Labour Fund to cut unemployment by encouraging unemployed people to go into business on their own account and it is providing funds for an agricultural cooperative bank in order to increase credit for farmers. This is one of several ways in which the PPP's interests have been funded and the supply of capital to agriculture improved (Sabbat-Swidlicka 1994). The government is also considering the idea of an economic super-ministry responsible for both economic policy and the implementation of reforms including privatisation (Zubek 1995).

However, there was friction in Poland between Pawlak and A. Kwasniewski's Left Democratic Alliance (LDA). There were divisions over abortion with the new government producing a more liberal bill which the president would not sign. But privatisation has proved a stumbling-block. The government has been unable to proceed with the 1995 mass privatisation covering 440 medium-sized companies, despite EBRD support for start-ups and other initial costs. A factor here has been the undermining of the pact between trade unions and government which amounted to a precondition for the privatisation deal. The factory workers comprised the working-class aristocracy, disillusioned in the later years of communism (hence support for Solidarity); but now frustrated and suspicious of privatisation. But privatisation of 800 of the largest factories could have been a major factor in repoliticising the Polish electorate and government now appears to be more conciliatory. It may be that the factory workers will settle for privatisation in return for one-tenth of the shares. There is strong support for the LDA from J. Kuron's Union of Freedom with regard to modernising policies.

A further change of government in 1995 has followed Walesa's refusal to approve a budget providing for tax increases to support a financial policy for economic growth. But J. Oleksy retained the coalition of the DLA and the PPP. There was an uneasy understanding between Walesa and the Oleksy cabinet at a time when it was widely reported that, both nationally and internationally, Walesa was no longer being taken seriously and that he would almost certainly fail to win a second term. The LDA leader Kwasniewski seemed best placed, ahead of possible Union of Freedom candidates such as

I. Belcerowicz and J. Kuron. But public opinion remained unpredictable. Paradoxically, Poles may appear alienated from national politics while operating as activists within their own milieux: opposing privatisation in general, while seeking it for their own factory; opposing German capital in the national economy, yet looking for it in their own enterprise, and thinking that things are getting worse in the country, yet improving in their own locality. In the presidential election of 1995 Kwasniewski scored only a narrow victory over a rejuvenated Walesa who remains active in politics. The new president soon had to cope with a change of prime minister because of Oleksy's resignation over spying allegation. The new premier is W. Cimoszewicz who has built a cabinet drawn from the ranks of the LDA and PPP, including some independents. The Finance Minister G. Kolodko produced a 'Strategy for Poland Package 2000', aiming at 5.5 per cent average annual GDP growth until 2000 (it was estimated at 6.6 per cent for 1995), a reduction of the budget deficit to 1.5 per cent of GDP and inflation down to 5.0 per cent by 1999. There are fears in the government that spending on social services will be sacrificed for a low budget deficit and control of inflation. Unemployment is still a problem at 15.4 per cent in January 1996, though slightly down on 16.1 at the beginning of 1995, but there was a growth of 6 per cent in 1995 (10.2 per cent for industrial output) and foreign investment has not been stemmed by the change in the presidency. Forty-seven per cent of the working population is now in the private sector.

## REFERENCES

J. Adam 1993, 'Transformation to a unified economy in the Former Czechoslovakia'. *Europe Asia Studies* 45, 627–45.

J. Adams 1995, 'The transition to a market economy in Hungary'. *Europe Asia Studies* 47, 989–1006.

A. Agh 1993, 'Europeanization through privatization and pluralization in Hungary'. *Journal of Public Policy* 13, 1–36.

S. Agocs 1993, 'The collapse of communist ideology in Hungary 1988–1989'. *East European Quarterly* 27, 187–211.

J. Angresano 1992, 'Political and economic obstacles inhibiting comprehensive reform in Hungary'. *East European Quarterly* 26, 55–76.

K. Audorka 1993, 'Regime transition in Hungary in the twentieth century: the role of national counter-elites'. *Governance: International Journal of Policy and Administration* 6, 358–71.

Z.D. Barany 1990, 'Breakthrough to democracy: elections in Poland and Hungary'. *Studies in Comparative Communism* 23, 191–212.

D.L. Bartlett 1996, 'Democracy institutional change and stabilisation policy in Hungary'. *Europe Asia Studies* 48, 47–83.

J. Batt 1993, 'Czechoslovakia' in S. Whitefield (ed.) *The New Institutional Architecture of Eastern Europe* (London: Macmillan), 35–55.

A. Berg and J. Sachs 1992, 'Structural adjustment and international trade in Eastern Europe: the case of Poland'. *Economic Policy* 14, 117–74.

R. Bivand 1993, '"Return of the new": the regional imprint of the 1993 parliamentary elections in Poland'. *European Urban and Regional Studies* 1, 63–83.

J. Bjork 1995, 'The uses of conditionality: Poland and the IMF'. *East European Quarterly* 29, 89–124.

A. Blaszkiewicz *et al.* 1994, 'The Solidarnosc spring?' *Communist and Post-Communist Studies* 27, 125–34.

G. Blazyca and R. Rapacki 1991, *Poland into the 1990s* (London: Pinter).

A. Bozoki 1993, 'Hungary's road to systemic change: the opposition Round Table'. *East European Politics and Societies* 7, 276–308.

A. Bozoki *et al.* (eds.) 1992, *Post-communist Transition: Emerging Pluralism in Hungary* (London: Pinter).

J.C. Brada 1991, 'The economic transition of Czechoslovakia: from plan to market'. *Journal of Economic Perspectives* 5, 171–7.

J.C. Brada *et al.* 1993, *Firms Afloat and Firms Adrift: Hungarian Industry and the Economic Transition* (Armonk, New York: M.E. Sharpe).

P. Bren 1994, 'Czech restitution laws rekindle Sudeten Germans' grievances'. *Radio Free Europe/Radio Liberty Research* 3(2), 17–22.

D.M. Brown 1988, *Towards a Radical Democracy: The Political Economy of the Budapest School* (London: Unwin Hyman).

L. Bruszt and D. Stark 1991, 'Remaking the political field in Hungary: from the politics of confrontation to the politics of competition'. *Journal of International Affairs* 45, 201–45.

P.J. Bryson 1991, *The End of the East German Economy: From Honecker to Reunification* (London: Macmillan).

J. Burger 1992, 'Politics of restitution in Czechoslovakia'. *East European Quarterly* 26, 485–98.

G.A. Calvo and F. Coricelli 1992, 'Stabilizing a previously centrally planned economy: Poland 1990'. *Economic Policy* 14, 175–226.

A. Capek and G.W. Sazama 1993, 'Czech and Slovak economic relations'. *Europe Asia Studies* 45, 211–36.

J. Charap and K. Dyba 1991, 'Transition to a market economy: the case of Czechoslovakia'. *European Economic Review* 35, 581–90.

W.W. Charemza 1992, 'Market failure and stagflation: some aspects of privatisation in Poland'. *Economics of Planning* 25, 21–36.

R. Clarke (ed.) 1989, *Hungary: The Second Decade of Economic Reform* (London: Longman).

C. Clemens 1993, 'Disquiet on the eastern front: the Christian Democratic Union in Germany's New Lander'. *German Politics* 2, 200–23.

I.L. Collier and H. Siebert 1991, 'The economic integration of post-wall Germany'. *American Economic Review* 81, 196–201.

L. Csaba 1992, 'Macroeconomic policy in Hungary: poetry versus reality'. *Soviet Studies* 44, 947–64.

G. Csepeli and A. Orkeny 1992, *Ideology and Political Belief in Hungary: The Twilight of State Socialism* (London: Pinter).

E. Cukor and G. Kovari 1991, 'Wage trends in Hungary'. *International Labour Review* 13, 177–89.

P. Dabrowski 1991, 'The Polish stabilisation programme: accomplishments and prospects'. *Communist Economics and Economic Transformation* 3, 121–33.

J.B. De Weydenthal 1993, 'Economic issues dominate Poland's eastern policy'. *Radio Free Europe/Radio Liberty Research* 2(10), 23–6.

J.B. De Weydenthal 1994, 'Poland's eastern policy'. *Radio Free Europe/Radio Liberty Research* 3(7), 10–3.

R. Donnorummo 1994, 'Poland's political and economic transition'. *East European Quarterly* 28, 259–80.

H. Drost 1993, 'The great depression in Germany: the effects of unification on East Germany's economy'. *East European Politics and Societies* 7, 452–81

L. Ebrill *et al.* 1994, *Poland: The Path to a Market Economy* (Washington DC: International Monetary Fund Occasional Paper 113).

S. Estrin 1992, 'Banking in transition: development and current problems in Hungary'. *Soviet Studies* 44, 785–808.

S. Fisher 1993, 'Economic development in the newly independent Slovakia'. *Radio Free Europe/Radio Liberty Research* 2(30), 42–8.

S. Fisher 1994, 'The Slovak economy: signs of recovery'. *Radio Free Europe/Radio Liberty Research* 3(33), 58–65.

S. Fisher and S. Hrib 1994, 'Political crisis in Slovakia'. *Radio Free Europe/Radio Liberty Research* 3(10), 20–6.

J. Frentzel-Zagorska and K. Zagorski 1993, 'Polish public opinion on privatisation and state intervention'. *Europe Asia Studies* 45, 705–28.

J.W. Golebiowski (ed.) 1993–4, *Transforming the Polish Economy* (Warsaw: Warsaw School of Economics), 2 vols.

P. Golinelli and R. Orsi 1994, 'Price–wage dynamics in a transition economy: the case of Poland'. *Economics of Planning* 27, 293–313.

S. Gomulka 1991, *Polish Economic Reform: Principles Policies and Surprises* (London: Centre for Economic Performance).

M. Gora 1991, 'Shock therapy and the Polish labour market'. *International Labour Review* 13, 145–63.

K. Grime and V. Duke 1993, 'A Czech on privatisation'. *Regional Studies* 27, 751–7.

D. Grosser 1992, *German Unification: The Unexpected Challenge* (Oxford: Berg).

D.R. Hall 1990, 'Planning for a united Germany'. *Town and Country Planning* 59, 93–5.

J. Hall and U. Ludwig 1993, 'Creating Germany's Mezzogiorno'. *Challenge* 36(4), 38–44.

D. Hamilton 1992, 'Germany after unification'. *Problems of Communism* 41(3), 1–18.

C.M. Hann 1990, 'Market economy and civil society in Hungary'. *Journal of Communist Studies* 6(2), 1–19.

P. Hare and T. Revesz 1992, 'Hungary's transition to the market economy system: the case against a big bang'. *Economic Policy* 14, 227–64.

P. Hare *et al.* 1981, *Hungary: A Decade of Economic Reform* (London: Longman).

A. Hars *et al.* 1991, 'Hungary faces unemployment'. *International Labour Review* 13, 165–73.

K. Henderson 1993, 'The East German legacy' in S. Whitefield (ed.) *The New Institutional Architecture of Eastern Europe* (London: Macmillan), 56–78.

O. Hieronymi 1989, *Economic Policies for a New Hungary: Proposals for a Coherent Approach* (Columbus, Ohio: Battelle Press).

A. Horvath and A. Szakolczai 1992, *The Dissolution of Communist Power: The Case of Hungary* (London: Routledge).

L. Ivan 1993, 'Spatial distribution of joint ventures in Hungary'. *Foldrajzi Ertesito* 42, 67–78. In Hungarian with an English summary.

K. Jasiewicz 1993, 'Polish politics on the eve of the 1993 elections: towards fragmentation or pluralism?' *Communist and Post-Communist Studies* 26, 387–411.

P. Jehlicka *et al.* 1993, 'Czechoslovak parliamentary elections 1990' in J. O'Loughlin and H. Van Der Wusten (eds) *The New Political Geography of Eastern Europe* (London: Belhaven Press), 235–54.

A. Jones 1994, *The New Germany: A Human Geography* (Chichester: John Wiley).

P. Kaminski 1991, *The Collapse of State Socialism: The Case of Poland* (Princeton, New Jersey: Princeton University Press).

M. Kapl *et al.* 1991, 'Unemployment and market-oriented reform in Czechoslovakia'. *International Labour Review* 13, 199–210.

J. Karsai and M. Wright 1994, 'Accountability governance and finance in Hungarian buyouts'. *Europe Asia Studies* 46, 997–1016.

E. Kawecka-Wyrzykowska 1993, 'Poland's trade relations with the European Community'. *Polish Quarterly of International Affairs* 2(2), 21–35.

J. Keay 1993, 'Privatisation at the crossroads (Hungary)'. *Business Europa* August/September, 23–6.

Y. Kiss 1991, 'Privatisation in Hungary'. *Communist Economics and Economic Transformation* 3, 305–16.

Y. Kiss 1992, 'Privatisation in Hungary: two years later'. *Soviet Studies* 44, 1015–38.

G. Kolankiewicz 1993, 'Poland' in S. Whitefield (ed.) *The New Institutional Architecture of Eastern Europe* (London: Macmillan), 99–120.

G. Kolankiewicz and P. Lewis 1988, *Poland: politics, economics and society* (London: Pinter).

K. Konig 1993, 'Bureaucratic integration by elite transfer: the case of Former GDR'. *Governance: International Journal of Policy and Administration* 6, 386–96.

J. Kornai 1990, *The Road to a Free Economy: Shifting from a Socialist System – the Example of Hungary* (New York: W.W. Norton).

A. Korosenyi 1991, 'The decay of communist rule in Hungary: a silent drama in six acts: the phases of transition 1985–1990'. *Slovo: An Interdisciplinary Journal of Russian and East European Affairs* 4(1), 47–57.

Z. Kovacs 1993, 'The geography of Hungarian parliamentary elections 1990' in J. O'Loughlin and H. van der Wusten (eds) *The New Political Geography of Eastern Europe* (London: Belhaven Press), 255–73.

S. Kowalski 1993, 'Poland's new political culture'. *Economy and Society* 22, 233–42.

M. Kramer 1995, 'Polish workers and the post-communist transition 1989–1993'. *Communist and Post-Communist Studies* 28, 71–114.

P. Kropecky 1995, 'Factionalism in parliamentary parties in the Czech Republic: a concept and some empirical findings' in R. Gillespie *et al.* (eds) *Factional Politics and Democratization* (London: Frank Cass), 138–52.

M. Kupka 1992, 'Transforming ownership in Czechoslovakia'. *Soviet Studies* 44, 297–311.

M. Laki 1993, 'The chances for the acceleration of the transition: the case of Hungarian privatisation'. *East European Politics and Societies* 7, 440–51.

P. Lawrence 1993, 'Selling the state: privatization in Hungary' in T. Clarke and C. Pitelis (eds) *The Political Economy of Privatization* (London: Routledge), 391–409.

I. Lengyel 1994, 'The Hungarian banking system in transition'. *GeoJournal* 32, 381–91.

P.G. Lewis 1993, 'Poland and the other Europe' in J. Story (ed.) *The New Europe: Politics, Government and Economy since 1945* (Oxford: Blackwell), 358–77.

P.G. Lewis 1994, 'Political institutionalisation and party development in Post-Communist Poland'. *Europe Asia Studies* 46, 774–99.

P.G. Lewis 1995, 'Poland and Eastern Europe' in R. Gillespie *et al.* (eds) *Factional Politics and Democratization* (London: Frank Cass), 102–24.

L. Lipschitz and D. McDonald (eds) 1990, *German Unification: Economic Issues* (Washington DC: IMF Occasional Paper 75).

D. Lipton and J. Sachs 1990, 'Creating a market economy in Eastern Europe: the case of Poland'. *Brookings Papers on Economic Activity* 1.

B. Lomax 1990, 'Endgame in Hungary'. *Journal of Communist Studies* 6(2), 190–3.

B. Lomax 1993, 'Hungary' in S. Whitefield (ed.) *The New Institutional Architecture of Eastern Europe* (London: Macmillan), 79–98.

B. Lomax 1995, 'Factions and factionalism in Hungary's new party system' in R. Gillespie *et al.* (eds) *Factional Politics and Democratization* (London: Frank Cass), 125–37.

H.I. Lorinc 1992, 'Foreign debt management policy and implications for Hungary's development'. *Soviet Studies* 44, 997–1013.

J. McDonald 1993, 'Transition to utopia: a reinterpretation of economics and politics in Hungary 1984–1990'. *East European Politics and Societies* 7, 203–39.

I. Major 1991a, 'Credibility and shock therapy in economic transformation: the Hungarian case'. *Communist Economies and Economic Transformation* 3, 439–54.

I. Major 1991b, *Privatisation in Hungary: Principles and Practices* (Stockholm: Stockholm Institute of Soviet and East European Economics Working Paper 20).

I. Major 1991c, *The Hungarian Economy in Transition* (Stockholm: Stockholm Institute of Soviet and East European Economics Working Paper 23).

P. Mariot 1991, 'Spatial assessment of results of the election to the Czechoslovak parliament June 1990'. *Geograficky Casopis* 43, 231–49.

S. Markowksi and S. Jackson 1994, 'The attractiveness of Poland to direct foreign investment'. *Communist Economies and Economic Transformation* 6, 515–35.

C. Mattheisen 1991, *Hungary in the 1990s: Sowing the Seed of Recovery* (London: Economic Intelligence Unit).

B. Milanovic 1992, 'Poland's quest for economic stabilisation 1988–1991: interaction of political economy and economics'. *Soviet Studies* 44, 511–31.

J.P. Morgan 1992, *Investing in Eastern Germany: The Second Year of Unification* (Frankfurt: J.P. Morgan).

B. Mroz 1991/2, 'Poland's economy in transition to private ownership'. *Soviet Studies* 43, 677–88; 44, 6–17.

B. Munske 1995, *The Two Plus Four Negotiations from a German–German Perspective* (Boulder, Colorado: Westview Press).

P. Neckermann 1992, 'What went wrong in Germany after the unification?' *East European Quarterly* 26, 447–69.

T. Nefedova and A. Trejvis 1994, *First Socio-economic Effects of Transformation of Central and Eastern Europe* (Vienna: Osterreichisches Ost- und Sudosteuropa-Institut).

D.M. Nuti 1993, 'Privatisation of socialist economies: general issues and the Polish case' in T. Clarke and C. Pitelis (eds) *The Political Economy of Privatization* (London: Routledge), 373–90.

J. Obrman 1994, 'Sudeten German controversy in the Czech Republic'. *Radio Free Europe/Radio Liberty Research* 3(2), 9–16.

K. Okolicsanyi 1993, 'Hungary plans to introduce voucher privatisation'. *Radio Free Europe/Radio Liberty Research* 2(17), 37–40.

D.L. Olson 1993, 'Dissolution of the state: political parties and the 1992 election in Czechoslovakia'. *Communist and Post-Communist Studies* 26, 301–14.

J. Osmond 1991, 'Germany' in S. White (ed.) *Handbook of Reconstruction in Eastern Europe and the Soviet Union* (London: Longman), 59–111.

J. Osmond (ed.) 1992, *German Unification: A Reference Guide and Commentary* (London: Longman).

M. Osterland 1994, 'Coping with democracy: the reinstitution of local self-government in Eastern Germany'. *European Urban and Regional Studies* 1, 5–18.

S. Padgett 1993, *Parties and Party Systems in the New Germany* (Aldershot: Dartmouth).

T. Palankai 1991, *The European Community and Central European Integration: The Hungarian Case* (New York: Institute for East–West Security Studies).

D. Parker 1993, 'Unravelling the planned economy: privatisation in Czecho-Slovakia'. *Communist Economies and Economic Transformation* 5, 391–404.

J. Pataki 1994, 'Hungary achieves a smooth transition from Antall to Boross'. *Radio Free Europe/Radio Liberty Research* 3(5), 15–21.

J. Pehe 1994, 'Legal difficulties beset the Czech restitution process'. *Radio Free Europe/Radio Liberty Research* 3(28), 6–13.

A. Pickel 1992, 'Jump-starting a market economy: a critique of the radical strategy for economic reform in the light of East German experiences'. *Studies in Comparative Communism* 25, 177–91.

A. Pollert and I. Hradecka 1994, 'Privatisation in transition: the Czech experience'. *Industrial Relations Journal* 25(1), 52–63.

I. Pond 1993, *Beyond the Wall: Germany's Road to Unification* (Washington DC: Brookings Institution).

K.Z. Poznanski 1993a, 'Restructuring of property rights in Poland: a study of evolutionary economics'. *East European Politics and Societies* 7, 395–421.

K.Z. Poznanski (ed.) 1993b, *Stabilization and privatization in Poland: an Economic Evaluation of the Shock Therapy Program* (Dordrecht: Kluwer Academic Publishing).

B. Racz 1991, 'Political pluralism in Hungary: the 1990 elections'. *Soviet Studies* 43, 109–36.

B. Racz 1993, 'The socialist left opposition in Post-Communist Hungary'. *Europe Asia Studies* 45, 647–70.

E. Rajcakova and D. Kusendova 1993, 'The evaluation and the state and development of unemployment in Czecho-Slovakia'. *Acta Facultatis Rerum Naturalium Universitatis Comeniana: Geographia* 32, 271–7.

J. Regulska 1993, 'Democratic elections and political restructuring in Poland 1989–1991' in J. O'Loughlin and H. Van Der Wusten (eds) *The New Political Geography of Eastern Europe* (London: Belhaven Press), 217–34.

G. Revesz 1990, *Perestroika in Eastern Europe: Hungary's Economic Transformation 1945–1988* (Boulder, Colorado: Westview Press).

M. Rhodes 1995, 'National identity and minority rights in the constitutions of the Czech Republic and Slovakia'. *East European Quarterly* 29, 347–69.

X. Richet 1989, *The Hungarian Model: Markets and Planning in a Socialist Economy* (Cambridge: Cambridge University Press).

S. Richter 1992, 'Hungary's changed patterns of trade and their effects'. *Soviet Studies* 44, 965–83.

J. Roesler 1991, 'The rise and fall of the planned economy in the GDR'. *German History* 9(1), 46–51.

J. Roesler 1994, 'Privatisation in Eastern Germany: experience with the Treuhand'. *Europe Asia Studies* 46, 505–17.

A. Rychard 1991, 'The economic change in post-communist Poland: a sociological analysis' in S. Gomulka and C. Lin (eds) *Limits to Reform and Transition in Communist Countries* (Oxford: Oxford University Press).

S. Sabbat-Swidlicka 1994, 'Pawlak builds up peasant power'. *Radio FreeEurope/Radio Liberty Research* 3(24), 13–20.

J. Sachs 1992, 'The economic transformation of Eastern Europe: the case of Poland'. *Economy of Planning* 25, 5–20.

G. Sanford and M. Myant 1991, 'Poland' in S. White (ed.) *Handbook of Reconstruction in Eastern Europe and the Soviet Union* (London: Longman), 149–82.

B. Schlegel 1994, 'Business start-up promotional aid in Hungary: a joint model of the

Deutsche Ausgleichbank and the Hungarian National Bank'. *GeoJournal* 32, 373–9.

I. Schmidt 1991, 'Former GDR communities in radical change'. *International Journal of Urban and Regional Research* 14, 667–75.

T. Schutte 1993, 'Bad debt problems and enterprise restructuring in Eastern Germany'. *Communist Economies and Economic Transformation* 5, 161–86.

N. Shafik 1994, 'Mass privatization in the Czech and Slovak Republics'. *Finance and Development: A Quarterly Publication of the International Monetary Fund and the World Bank* 31(4), 22–4.

A.B. Shingleton *et al.* 1995, *Dimensions of German Unification* (Boulder, Colorado: Westview Press).

H. Siebert 1991, 'German unification: the economics of transition'. *Economic Policy* 13, 287–328.

E. Sik 1994, 'From the multicoloured to the black and white economy: the Hungarian second economy and the transformation'. *International Journal of Urban and Regional Research* 18, 46–70.

B. Slay 1993, 'Evolution of industrial policy in Poland since 1989'. *Radio Free Europe/Radio Liberty Research* 2(2), 21–8.

B. Slay 1994a, *The Polish Economy: Crisis Reform and Transformation* (Princeton, New Jersey: Princeton University Press).

B. Slay 1994b, 'The Polish economy under the Post-Communists'. *Radio Free Europe/Radio Liberty Research* 3(33), 66–76.

G. Smith *et al.* 1992, *Developments in German Politics* (London: Macmillan).

D. Southern 1993, 'Restitution or compensation: the open property question'. *German Politics* 2, 436–49.

D. Stark 1990, 'Privatization in Hungary: from plan to market or from plan to clan'. *East European Politics and Societies* 4, 351–92.

J. Svejnar and M. Singer 1994, 'Using vouchers to privatise an economy: the Czech-Slovak case'. *Economics of Transition* 2, 43–70.

N. Swain 1991, 'Hungary' in S. White (ed.) *Handbook of Reconstruction in Eastern Europe and the Soviet Union* (London: Longman), 114–45.

G.J. Szablowski 1993, 'Governance and competing elites in Poland'. *Governance: International Journal of Policy and Administration* 6, 341–57.

I.P. Szekely and D.M.G. Newbery 1993, *Hungary: An Economy in Transition* (Cambridge: Cambridge University Press).

R. Taras 1995, *Consolidating Democracy in Poland* (Boulder, Colorado: Westview Press).

S. Thomas 1992, 'The political economy of privatization: Poland, Hungary and Czechoslovakia' in C. Clague and G.C. Rausser (eds) *The Emergence of Market Economies in Eastern Europe* (Oxford: Blackwell), 279–96.

I. Tomes 1991, 'Social reform: a cornerstone in Czechoslovakia's new economic structure'. *International Labour Review* 13, 191–8.

H. Tworzecki 1994, 'The Polish parliamentary election of 1993'. *Electoral Studies* 13, 180–5.

A. Tymowksi 1993, 'The unwanted social revolution: Poland in 1989'. *East European Politics and Societies* 7, 169–202.

O. Ulc 1992. 'The bumpy road of Czechoslovakia's velvet revolution'. *Problems of Communism* 41(3), 19–33.

L.L. Wade 1995, 'Searching for voting patterns in post-communist Poland's Sejm elections'. *Communist and Post-Communist Studies* 28, 411–25.

G. Weclawowicz 1996, *Contemporary Poland: Space and Society* (London: UCL Press).

H. Wiesenthal 1994, 'How different is Eastern Germany?' Institute for Human Sciences (Vienna) *Newsletter* 45, 10–3.

C. Wightman and P. Rutland, 1991, 'Czechoslovakia' in S. White (ed.) *Handbook of Reconstruction in Eastern Europe and the Soviet Union* (London: Longman), 31–56.

M.T. Wild 1992, 'From division to unification: regional dimensions of economic change in Germany'. *Geography* 77, 244–60.

J. Winiecki 1992, 'The Polish transition programme: underpinnings, results, interpretations'. *Soviet Studies* 44, 809–36.

S. Wolchik 1993, 'The repluralization of politics in Czechoslovakia'. *Communist and Post-Communist Studies* 26, 412–31.

World Bank 1990, *Poland: Economic Management for a New Era* (Washington DC: World Bank).

V. Zubek 1991, 'Walesa's leadership and Poland's transition'. *Problems of Communism* 40(1–2), 69–83.

V. Zubek 1994, 'The reassertion of the left in Post-Communist Poland'. *Europe Asia Studies* 46, 801–37.

V. Zubek 1995, 'The phoenix out of the ashes: the rise to power of Poland's post-communist SDRP'. *Communist and Post-Communist Studies* 28, 275–308.

# 6

# NATIONAL PROFILES
## Balkan countries

### ALBANIA

Albania's communist government resisted reform and cast the country into a dangerous state of international isolation after the departure of Soviet and Chinese technicians in 1960 and 1978 respectively (Sandstrom and Sjoberg 1991). Fiercely nationalistic and fearful of foreign domination, Albanians found it hard to reconcile their political instincts with the economic reality of continuing external dependence (Biberaj 1990). With the highest rate of population growth in Europe, Albania had to struggle just to stop the very low living standards falling even further behind the average for Europe. Drought during the late 1980s (through a succession of dry winters) reduced agricultural output and also eroded the effectiveness of hydropower projects, while export performance stagnated: at the time trade was transacted mainly with near neighbours (Bulgaria, Italy, Romania and FRY) along with France, Germany and Poland, exchanging minerals, electricity and agricultural produce for raw materials and capital goods. Until May 1990 the country's constitution officially forbade any sort of foreign investment and even credits were ruled out. However, after Hoxha's death in 1985 the country began to move slowly away from the constitutional position of 1976 and money was borrowed to finance foreign trade deficits, although servicing became a problem with the stagnation of the late 1980s (Hall 1994).

### Momentum for revolution

With no sign of economic reform and a lack of external assistance, the outlook for the 1990s was depressing. The plan for 1990 'showed little sign of having been prepared by people with a knowledge of real economics' (Milivojevic 1991, p.7). The fall of N. Ceausescu in Romania sent a shock wave through Albania and activated the country's alienated young people who obtained information through Greek and Italian television broadcasts. There was unrest in Shkoder continuing into the New Year, and other towns (such as Durres, Tirana and Vlore) became involved. The government used the repression of the secret police (*Sigurimi*) and no changes were made until April 1990 when the way was cleared for a resumption of diplomatic relations with the USA and the FSU. President R. Alia's government was very much constrained by conservative elements supporting the Stalinist policies of the Hoxha era and economic reforms had only limited impact (Sjoberg and Wyzan 1991). But peasants were allowed to sell produce from their private plot surpluses on free markets, although the food available from these 200sq.m. plots was very limited and the lack of consumer goods gave the farmers even less incentive. Private enterprise was encouraged in the fields of consumer goods and services but the restrictions on private business made it difficult for any potential entrepreneur to take advantage. The practice of funding enterprises through the state budget was replaced with self-financing from profits and bank credits, although this did not necessarily increase efficiency (Biberaj 1991).

As a result, Albanians continued to demonstrate and some took refuge in foreign embassies in the capital. Alia visited the USA to seek Western support and made a trip to Boston (the centre of Albanian Americans) looking for aid. Subsequently a new electoral law was promulgated and concessions over religious worship were promised, but there was still unrest at the end of 1990 with thousands of ethnic Greeks fleeing across the frontier. The reasons for this movement, prompted by the issue of passports by communist officials, are unclear although it certainly demonstrated that travel was now possible. The Greek government provided only limited hospitality and some 5,000 of the 16,000 migrants subsequently returned, yet emigration did now provide an option for people who despaired of the future within Albania. 'Relinquishing power appeared as dangerous as hanging onto it in Albania in the early 1990s' (Milivojevic 1991, p.5), but a multi-party system of government was announced in December 1990 and radical elements formed a Democratic League of Students and Young Albanian Intellectuals which offered some hope of a peaceful transition. Meanwhile the Ecology Party of Albania arose out of the Committee for Environmental Protection and, more significantly, a Democratic Party (DP) emerged with its own newspaper and electoral programme including land reform. However, the DP failed to dislodge the communists (Party of Labour of Albania (PLA)) in the 1991 election, lacking the transport to reach the villages where an overcrowded rural population was fearful of the consequences of privatisation (Sjoberg 1994).

A prolonged national strike in 1991 led to the removal of PLA hardliners. Since workers were assured of getting four-fifths of their wages in the event of unavoidable lay-offs due to raw material or energy shortages, it was possible to reinterpret this measure to legitimise an escalating series of stoppages until some 0.5mn. people (workers and members of their families) were effectively on strike. This brought half the country's industry to a standstill. Chaos in the countryside combined with disputes over privatisation meant that much cereal land remained unplanted in 1991. Infant malnutrition became a problem and emergency supplies were brought in through Italy's Operation Pelican. Despite tough restrictions against economic refugees, there were two waves of migrating boat people to Bari during 1991 (including Greeks), but many returned while others were repatriated when they could not prove that they were motivated politically rather than economically. A subsequent Albanian-Italian naval agreement prevented further emigration, but the DP was concerned that Italian aid might bolster the PLA government. There was much anarchy, with attacks on people and raids on warehouses, amidst claims of secret police activity to discredit non-PLA politicians. But the DP was successful in the 1992 elections when the party won a landslide majority. Proportional representation just deprived it of a two-thirds majority but S. Berisha (a former communist who became an early advocate of pluralism) won the presidency, with extended powers. The election also heightened polarisation between north and south (with most socialist support in the latter area).

## Democratic party in power

Since 1992 the DP has been governing in coalition with Social Democratic and Republican parties; while the Socialist Party (the former PLA) maintains a strong opposition with the backing of several newspapers allegedly financed by money deposited in the West by communists in the past. There is a strong executive, favoured by the president who retained considerable popularity during the first half of his term of office, although a revised constitution with enhanced presidential powers was turned down in a referendum in 1994. There has been a change in the judiciary, but the new appointees are young and inexperienced so it will take time for a truly independent institution to emerge. There is a difference of view as to whether Albania should look to the USA (with a tendency to exaggerate the potential for US action) or to Europe. NATO has taken an active interest in Albania while declining the country's application for full membership. There has been an agreement on military education and technology with Turkey and military cooperation with several countries including the USA and UK. Albania has also moved closer to the Islamic countries by joining the Organisation of the Islamic Conference (Zanga 1993).

Albania was admitted to the CSCE in 1991 – and later in the same year to the IMF and World Bank. She is also a participating member in the EBRD. Italy agreed a three-year plan for economic cooperation in 1991, acknowledging a special duty for historical and geographical reasons. Albania was included in the Phare programme in 1992 which has been of considerable help for agriculture (Doder 1992). There is also the EU Tempus programme to assist with education and training. The International Development Association financed advisory services concerned with privatisation and economic management. Wide-ranging market reforms (including free market pricing) were planned for 1992 but they have been introduced more slowly than expected (Hall 1993). It seems that 'economic ignorance, ideological single-mindedness and years of relative isolation had rendered the country traumatised and virtually inert in the face of necessary change' (Hall 1994, p. 196). However, there were gains in 1993 with agriculture as the powerhouse despite the lack of fertilisers and pesticides and the neglect of irrigation facilities (Zanga 1994a). While industry grew by 10 per cent in 1993 agriculture registered an impressive 15 per cent increase. This was claimed as a success for the DP's 'social market economy' although the Socialists deplore the high unemployment of some 300,000 people and the severity of budgetary rectitude. They want a more gradual approach to reform, yet weak legitimacy delays reform in any case and increases its cost. Liberalisation of prices has however been accepted, thanks to humanitarian aid and international remittances. 'We must make a dash for reform before the people are overcome with despair at the pain of stabilisation' (Pashko 1993, p. 919).

The markets are well stocked and the profits are helping to modernise the farms. Inflation has been brought down from 300 per cent in 1992 to a projected 30–40 per cent level in 1993. Tirana restaurants and shops that sell imported merchandise are challenging Albanian industry to produce more consumer goods. Investment is crucial, yet the continuing difficulty over a new constitution during 1993–4 (with much dissention among the parties) and the delay in providing a new legal framework is discouraging. There is continuing controversy over restitution since legislation provides for compensation rather than the return of property. Moreover, the climate is soured by the war in Bosnia-Hercegovina that could spill over into Kosovo. This is particularly discouraging for investment in tourism. Efforts have been made to improve relations with Montenegro and Macedonia, but it is difficult to make progress with Serbia on account of the Kosovo, with the possibility of war as a prelude to partition. The issue was not publicly debated in Albania before the revolution since the regime in Kosovo was then more liberal. Today, there is much concern over Kosovo, yet Albania lacks an effective military capability.

## The economy

In the context of foreign investment Albania has much to offer. Albanians leaving the country have helped with cash remittances (US$400mn. in 1992, four times the value of Albania's exports in that year). Unfortunately, there has been little support from Albanians of the diaspora through joint venture capital, but such funding from other quarters is showing interest in Albanian agriculture and there are loans from China tied to farm mechanisation. Investment is encouraged by the natural resources and cheap labour, increasing political stability, liberal investment laws and tax holidays. Reflecting its Muslim inheritance Albania is also looking east, encouraged by the ambivalent Western response to the Bosnian crisis. Albania could act as a bridge between east and west. Agreements with Turkey in 1991 and 1992 were followed by a state visit by Berisha in 1994. There is scope for Turkish investment in mining and tourism, while membership of the Islamic Conference Organisation makes the country eligible for Islamic Development Bank credits. A new hospital in Durres has been supported by the OPEC Fund for International Development and the Islamic Bank. However, this eastern policy has been criticised by the Democratic Alliance Party which prefers a European orientation that will allay Serb fears about Muslim fundamentalism.

Agriculture, minerals and tourism have been identified as priority sectors. Albania has considerable potential for agriculture and food-processing (organic foods). But the engineering industry has been too heavily concerned with the production of low-quality spare parts for machinery of Chinese and FSU origin. Albania is largely self-sufficient in energy (with good potential for hydrocarbons and hydropower) but lack of investment has made it difficult to increase production, while (as noted above) drought has depressed output from hydro-electric stations. Oil is an attractive prospect. Denimex of Germany signed an offshore exploration agreement in 1990 and Agip of Italy would like a concession. Problems of underinvestment have also arisen in mining. Despite rich resources of chromium, copper and nickel, output stagnated in the 1980s. By the end of the decade there was also a slump in chromium output, a major industry with Albania as the third world producer. The whole economy was stagnating and the unions were restive over the lack of investment. However, growth was resumed in 1993: agricultural production increased by 15 per cent and industrial output by 10 per cent. Negotiations are now under way between the state-owned chrome monopoly Albchrome and an Anglo-American group of investors. Some of the country's smaller chrome mines (with less than 160,000t. reserves) are to be privatised; likewise those copper mines with reserves below 4,000t.

'Free zone' economic areas are being set up and seven-year tax holidays are on offer to stimulate investors. Land has been privatised and a building boom is now under way. But the transport system is very underdeveloped and this is bound to constrain the regional spread of economic activity. Moreover, there has been considerable vandalism directed at transport equipment, such as buses and railway rolling-stock, leading to a temporary disruption of services: some track was even torn up on account of land restitution claims. But the number of motor vehicles has increased fourfold as a result of imports between 1991 and 1993: in the latter year there were 61.4,000 cars (18.9ptp) and 85.2,000 other vehicles (buses, trucks, vans and tractors) or 26.2ptp. However there are very great differences between the urban and rural areas (Zanga 1994b). There were 50,500 cars in the urban areas in 1993 (42.9 ptp) and 10,900 in the villages (5.2 ptp). There were 75.9,000 other vehicles in the towns (64.5 ptp) and only 9.3,000 in the villages (4.5 ptp). Tirana alone has 26,000 vehicles of all kinds (102.7 ptp) compared with a national average of

45.0 per thousand. At the time of writing, the EBRD expects 8.1 per cent increase in Albania's GDP in 1995 and a fall in unemployment to 15.8 per cent.

It seemed that Berisha's DP was becoming increasingly divided, although no formal split has occurred and since the domestic situation remained quiet, with no sign of instability, the government carried on to the 1996 election. Relations with Greece have improved following the visit of the Greek foreign minister to Tirana in March 1995: part of a Greek strategy of improving relations with Balkan neighbours. It should safeguard the jobs of some 400,000 Albanians working (often illegally) in Greece through a new work permit system. This resulted in an income of US$450mn. in 1995. Meanwhile, the Socialist Party (former Communist Party) made some progress despite the continued imprisonment of F. Noli and the genocide law banning former senior communist officials. The party can feed off land disputes in the rural areas, corruption and the DP's abuse of power by concentrating patronage within its own ranks. Yet, although Berisha's economic record was good and he enjoyed Western support (US$350mn. in 1995) in return for restraint over Kosovo, he found it necessary to use crude irregularities in the election campaign: harassment of the opposition by the SHIKU (successors of the Sigurimi), intimidation at polling stations and ballot-stuffing. This has produced an overwhelming DP victory but the opposition is now much more disgruntled and the country's international reputation has been tarnished.

## BULGARIA

This year 1989 saw Bulgaria in turmoil through the increasingly erratic communist leadership of T. Zhivkov. Although lacking the extremism of the regime in the neighbouring state of Romania, tension was heightened by reformers campaigning on human rights and environmental issues with the aid of *samizdat* literature. Zhivkov tried to build an East European bloc against perestroika by moving close to FCSFR, FGDR and Romania, while maintaining close ties with China, Cuba and North Korea. There were growing economic problems, despite limited reform in 1988 which allowed for private businesses with up to ten employees. There was also the trauma arising from the continuing pressure against the Turkish minority, forced to accept Bulgarian names. Ethnic Turks in Razgrad began a hunger strike in May and were attacked by the security forces. Protest spread to other towns and the Turkish government opened its border to refugees for almost three months during the summer, which allowed some 300,000 ethnic Turks to leave voluntarily rather than face expulsion. Zhivkov was forced to resign at a combined meeting of the BCP's Politburo and Secretariat in November and was replaced by the former Minister of Foreign Affairs P. Mladenov: the announcement was made on the day after the breaching of the Berlin Wall.

## Democracy

Pluralism followed, with the opposition legalised and the BCP's status as the guiding force in society brought to an end. Exiled Turks were allowed to return and some 200,000 eventually did so; although some communists continued to ferment controversy with demonstrations in Kurdzhali inspired by the notion of 'Bulgaria for the Bulgarians'. The leading offices of state were shared out and by the time the BCP convened a Congress of Renewal in February 1990 Mladenov's role was restricted to head of state. The secret police were disbanded. Moreover, by this time seven non-communist political groups had entered into the Union of Democratic Forces (UDF), a coalition with dissident leader Z. Zhelev as president. The level of public support for the UDF was such that the communists were obliged to bring the group into Round Table discussions, along with the Bulgarian Agrarian National Union (BANU) in March 1990. These provided for the election of a Grand National Assembly to serve, in effect, as both parliament and constitutional assembly. The revamped communist party, the Bulgarian Socialist Party (BSP), formed in April 1990, won 47.1 per cent of the votes in the 1990 elections against 36.2 per cent for the UDF (Troxel 1992). There was 8.0 per cent for the BANU and 6 per cent for the Party of Rights and Freedoms (PRF), essentially a Turkish party which managed to evade the embargo against parties with an overt ethnic or religious inspiration. The elections were a success for the BSP in appealing to urban voters as a party of responsible change, suitably distanced from the years of communism, and in maintaining a hold over the rural population 'whose habits of subordination, developed over the past 45 years, were not easily broken' (Bell 1991, p.20).

However, the ensuing stalemate was broken by a dramatic *faux pas* by Mladenov, overheard by the media proposing the use of tanks against the opposition. Pressure was applied by the democrats through their 'City of Truth', a tented settlement which appeared outside the president's office and eventually forced his resignation. The failure of any BSP candidate to gain the support of the assembly led to the election of Zhelev, the UDF leader (Tzvetkov 1992). By the end of the year a popular president had been joined by a new prime minister heading a coalition government in which BSP ministers were the largest group but not a majority. In economic matters there was a consensus that the problems of obsolescence, stagnant production and foreign indebtedness (to the tune of some US\$10.0bn)needed attention through market reforms, including privatisation. But while the UDF advocated shock therapy, the BSP sought responsible change that would achieve a relatively painless transition. This was electorally effective in 1990 but the programme could not be delivered. There were further falls in output, complemented by shortages of energy and food. A more radical programme was now proposed by the BSP but, although inspired by the UDF philosophy, the latter preferred to see the government fall in order to open the way for a genuine coalition (Izvirski 1993).

The winter of 1990–1 was difficult and the green movement (*Ecoglasnost*) was active in the programme of 'Free Meals for the Poor'. The green politician P. Dimitrov was also president of the coordinating council of the UDF. The UDF became the largest party in late 1991 with Dimitrov as prime minister, the first green party leader to head a European government (Crampton 1993).

The government was reconstructed late in 1992 when the UDF prime minister made further efforts to get the PRF (holding the balance) to join a coalition. Reform was certainly needed but the UDF was seen as confrontational in style, with initiatives taken haphazardly and with inadequate communication. Dimitrov's UDF government fell in 1992 through the partial disintegration of the union and the BSP became the largest party. A government of technocrats was formed under L. Berov, backed in parliament by the BSP and MRF. But it was constantly challenged by UDF motions of no confidence and eventually resigned in 1994 after a brief caretaking government under R. Indjova who tried to get the privatisation programme under way.

Elections later in the same year confirmed forecasts of a political shift, through public disillusionment over the factional rivalries of UDF, in favour of the BSP's younger generation: the leader Z. Videnov or G. Pirinsky of the party's social democratic wing (Waller 1995). Videnov's BSP gained a decisive lead, opening the way for a coalition with the Centrist PRF and the Bulgarian Business Block. The UDF did well in Sofia and the major provincial cities (and generally among the young and educated), but was rejected by the peasantry, who feared radical land reform, and the urban population of the smaller towns, as well as elderly people on fixed incomes who were intimidated by the BSP over their pensions (Engelbreckt 1994). The largest BSP lead over the UDF was in Razgrad, Shumen, Silistra and Turgovishte, reflecting sensitivity over Turks who voted overwhelmingly for the PRF (Slaveykov 1995). The new government has maintained a pro-Western stance, with support for the US-sponsored Partnership for Peace and has not sought to renew close links with Russia (Lefebvre 1994). However, the BSP has been hard pressed to keep its election promises, given the unemployment figure of 20.5 per cent and continuing high inflation. Indeed, governments for the last four years have been weak and only limited reforms have been introduced. So there is little prospect of rapid change. J. Videnov's BSP is slowly formulating policy for economic reform which will include privatisation at the end of 1995, although it is unlikely to be a great success in view of the poor financial state of most of the companies.

## The economy

The Bulgarian economy has been hit by the collapse of the Soviet market which formerly accepted 80 per cent of Bulgarian manufactures. Another blow was the reduction in Soviet oil deliveries, combined with a requirement to pay in hard currency starting at the beginning of 1991 (Jones and Miller 1996). The Gulf crisis also intervened to prevent alternative deliveries from Iraq (running a substantial trade deficit with Bulgaria) (Bristow 1996). Meanwhile, the Kozloduy nuclear power station was scrutinised by environmentalists concerned about safety hazards. Against this background the payment of subsidies to industry (a quarter of national income at the end of 1989) was a crippling burden. Despite its potential, agriculture was weakened by a poor infrastructure and a workforce heavily tilted towards older people (the young people having left for the towns), including many relatively unskilled women workers. The emigration of 70,000 Turks from the Haskovo, Ruse and Varna regions complicated the labour situation in 1989–90 when the state procurement system almost collapsed as farmers withheld supplies, in anticipation of market reforms and high prices. But the collapse of Comecon had a very serious effect in view of the high level of integration (Minassian 1994).

Industrial depression was most evident in the iron and steel industry which depended on imported iron ore and was responsible for much of the pollution in the Sofia area. Steel output collapsed by over 40 per cent in 1991, while electronics and electrical engineering declined by one third. There was a sharp rise in unemployment to 15 per cent. Plovdiv and Montana were regions with highest unemployment in 1991, joined by Ruse and Haskovo in 1992. But, taking a range of criteria into account, there are no major contrasts and there has not been a massive movement to Sofia. Rural western regions seem to have lost, including the wider Sofia area while Sofia city has gained along with Montana, Plovdiv and Varna (Nefedova and Trejvis 1994, p.43). However, in all, 458,000 mainly young, skilled and educated people left the country during the years 1989–91 (Paunov 1993).

## Foreign assistance and investment

Zhelev sought Western help in the latter part of 1990 with gestures of support for the UN position in the Gulf and the promise to remove missiles. Assistance was slow in arriving, but there was some foreign involvement in the economy by the end of the year. The French organisation Club Med was set up to develop tourism while Citroen agreed to cooperate to produce spare parts at Varna and sell passenger cars in the local market. Over the years Bulgaria had done well by comparison with other Balkan countries where the influence of former communists also remains strong. There has been moderation and good neighbourliness from Zhelev (a one-time UDF member who became critical of programmes of both major parties). The Berov government brought some stability through a tight credit policy in 1992. Negotiations with the Paris Club (official lenders) and London Club (commercial bank creditors) reduced a US$8.16bn debt by 47 per cent, with IMF and World Bank support for rescheduling. Furthermore, a trade agreement with Russia has ensured that Bulgaria will be on a main transit route for oil and gas from the Caspian region to the Mediterranean and Southern Europe. Meanwhile there are good prospects for business with the revival of dealings with the FSU. There has been competitiveness through revaluation of the lev. High inflation has continued but zero growth in 1994 should be followed by positive growth in 1995 with rising demand in Germany and FSU.

It is appreciated that foreign investment is needed to increase efficiency and reduce pollution. An extremely liberal foreign investment law was passed in 1991. But the advantages offered were cancelled out by the tax regime which, as the government's own foreign investment commission recognised, denied concessions generally available in other countries. The UK Abbotswell Company has an agreement with Okeanski Ribolov over a British–Bulgarian joint venture for trawling out of Burgas to offshore fisheries in the Falkland Islands and Scotland. Kuwait is providing finance to Bulgaria for a range of projects including poultry breeding, fish-farming and greenhouse construction. In return, Bulgarians will plant shelter belts to arrest the advance of the desert and Balkan Airlines will extend its services to Kuwait City. Moreover, Kuwait will be interested in skilled Bulgarian labour for the construction of some 40,000 residential units over a five-year period. Bulgaria's Glavbolgarstroy has completed a new residential area in the Ukraine for servicemen returning from FGDR. A further contract is being completed in Russia. The Bulgarian–Nigeria joint venture Technoexportstroy will undertake major construction projects in Nigeria (Zloch-Christy 1996).

Foreign investment includes a variety of projects in breweries, food processing, hotels and tourism. The German sports shoe manufacturer Adidas is looking for a deal with a Bulgarian producer in Dobrich in order to penetrate the Bulgarian market. The direct sale of thirty-five of the stronger state companies to foreign and domestic investors has included the US$55mn. purchase of a controlling interest in the trucking company Somat by the German firm Willi Betz. There is also a Bulgarian–German cooperation scheme to set up training centres in five Bulgarian cities for young people working in small businesses. Meanwhile, the US corporation Design Review International bought the Razlog electronics factory, while the Belgian Amilum company invested in the Razgrad maize products factory of Tsarevichni Produkt (turning out maize oil, starch, sugar, glucose and animal feed). South Korean investment is mooted with Daewoo's interest in Bulgarian banks, hotels, cement factories and telecommunications.

Other SOEs should be more attractive for foreign investors once they have been cleared of debt. A privatisation law passed in 1991 had to be repealed because state enterprise managers were abusing their positions by asset-stripping (hiving off assets to private companies owned by themselves). A mass privatisation programme based on the Czech voucher model has been mooted but, in addition to the direct sales already noted, there has been hidden privatisation (with possible mafia links) as private companies are formed to supply SOEs at high prices and receive their production at subsidised prices for resale at market prices. Thus losses are nationalised and profits privatised. This may reflect the influence of former communists, weaknesses in the law and the general inexperience of civil society, as well as profits through smuggling goods into Serbia. The public does not have a high opinion of private capitalists: they seem to reflect the communist stereotype. Former communists have been accused of asset-stripping through their positions in SOEs but it remains to be seen if the BSP will be able to tackle such corruption.

However, under new legislation benefiting from experience elsewhere, SOEs are to be turned into joint stock companies with shares to be sold off to the public later. At least one fifth of privatised enterprises will be retained by government and placed in investment funds to finance security funds. The Bulgarian National Bank has issued 6mn. vouchers worth 30,000 leva each and a further 150,000 worth 100,000 leva each. Bulgarians over the age of 18 may acquire the 30,000 leva vouchers at an initial cost of 1,500 leva with the balance to be paid off in six instalments between 1999 and 2005. Vouchers valued at 100,000 leva will be allocated to meet restitution claims by Bulgarians from whom property was confiscated by the communists. Bulgaria's Centre for Mass Privatisation contemplated dealing with up to 3,000 companies in 1996 instead of the 300–400 originally considered when privatisation was discussed in 1991. The list includes the largest manufacturers like Kremikovtzi steel works and Burgas oil refinery; also hotels and many small wineries and agricultural operations. But by mid-February 1996 only 5.5 per cent of the eligible population had taken part in the privatisation programme. Two-thirds were either not going to buy shares or were undecided, a similar reaction to Romania's situation in 1995. It seems that the government has not given out sufficient information. Consequently only 1,063 enterprises were eventually scheduled for privatisation. Nevertheless, Bulgaria will now need a bankruptcy law and further tax regulations. Bulgaria's GDP was expected to grow by 2.0–2.5 per cent during 1995 with unemployment running at 14.4 per cent (an increase of 1.6 per cent over 1994). Industrial output rose by 4.0 per cent in 1994 (the first annual increase since 1990) and this rate was maintained through 1995: industrial output in January 1996 was 4.6 per cent higher than a year previously. Inflation fell sharply in early 1995, due to a shrinkage of consumer demand, a decline in food prices and a steady exchange rate, but rose later in the year with further volitility in 1996.

## ROMANIA

Romania consistently failed to implement significant economic reform prior to 1989. Despite strikes in Brasov in 1987 and some discontent within the party in the run-up to the fourteenth Communist Party Congress held in November 1989, change was ruled out and the liberalising trends in other

East European countries were deplored (Pecsi 1989). Austerity continued despite declarations that all foreign debts had been paid off. Romania seemed destined for growing isolation once Western banks lost all their influence on policy. In any case, Romanian ambivalence over provisions for human rights agreed in documents emanating from the Vienna CSCE seemed to show that international agreements were not necessarily binding. Hence the revolution in Romania came as a surprise. L. Tokes, a Hungarian priest based in Timisoara, took a defiant stand on human rights and *Securitate* (secret police) intimidation. He refused to move to a new rural parish, to which he was effectively being exiled, and when he was forcibly removed he won support from both Hungarian and Romanian demonstrators. Security forces fired on the crowd and made arrests; yet the party leader N. Ceausescu (in power since 1965 and state president since 1974) felt sufficiently confident to leave for a three-day visit to Iran. However, at a rally in Bucharest immediately after his return, when it was intended that he should demonstrate his authority, he was opposed by a section of the crowd and his failure to cope with the situation was then shown on national television for a critical few seconds before transmission was cut. Demonstrations in Bucharest followed and, crucially, the army refused to support the communist authorities. After Ceausescu and his wife fled from the capital by helicopter and subsequently transferred to a motor vehicle, the couple were apprehended by the army and executed on interim government instructions after a summary trial held in secret in Targoviste.

## The new order

In the days following, the resistance of the *Securitate* was broken and a National Salvation Front (NSF) took over the government. It has been widely rumoured that the security police maintained only token resistance in order to negotiate their status in the new order and that the leading figures on the NSF had prepared a *coup* with Soviet approval. Elements of spontaneity in the initial demonstrations in Timisoara and Bucharest (also in the response by the army) appear genuine. Yet, part of the infrastructure may have already been in place and the revolution has been described as a 'prime candidate for hijacking' (Eyal 1993, p.121). Under the leadership of the interim president I. Iliescu, (a former high-ranking communist official), and prime minister P. Roman (relatively lacking in political experience), the new government quickly abolished many of Ceausescu's most unpopular programmes and promised a token piece of land to every rural dweller. The way was opened for political pluralism but, contrary to initial declarations, the NSF decided that it would remain in being as a political party and contest the elections called for 1990 (Mihut 1994). This caused considerable misgivings when it became apparent that many former communists, along with organisations which had operated under Ceausescu's regime, simply transferred their loyalties to the NSF and then retained solidarity as alternative political parties came into existence (Ronnas 1991a). These included the historic parties (National Liberal Party and National Peasant Party) and a large number of entirely new political organisations (Tismaneanu 1993).

It is a matter for debate how far the former communist establishment manipulated a spontaneous revolutionary movement and retained power through electoral successes (in respect of both the parliament and the presidency) in 1990 and 1992 (Roper 1994b). Not all former communists joined the NSF and, equally, NSF membership included people who were not communist party members in the past. Again, given the size of the old communist party and the extent of *Securitate* surveillance of non-members, it was always going to be difficult for other new parties (made up overwhelmingly of non-communists) to gain immediate political credibility (Verdery and Kligman 1992). Through its control of the levers of power, including the media, the NSF had a major propaganda advantage and came over to the conservative rural electorate as a progressive force in view of its reform credentials including land restitution. Although the authorities may have found it disconcerting that many cooperative farms quickly fell apart as peasant communities unilaterally reclaimed their historic land holdings, the new government was astute enough to recognise the inevitability of this step. They legislated for private peasant farms with a maximum size that would, on the one hand, leave the vast majority of *de facto* restitutions on the right side of the law and, on the other, would allow a large section of the peasantry to own land, at the very least through the symbolic 1ha plots (0.5ha in the case of families who were not members of cooperative farms). When the opposition started to advocate more generous restitution terms for former landowners the NSF was able to hold out the spectre of further expropriation of smallholders (or alternatively of bankruptcy in the face of radical market reforms). So, the NSF has been able to control the rural areas, almost solidly in Moldavia and Wallachia, and this has been the key to its continuing success (Calinescu and Tismaneanu 1991). But the NSF has also worked with nationalist groups which emerged through regional movements like Vatra Romaneasca in Transylvania; organisations which the historic parties condemned as extremist. Spoiled ballots also appear to have favoured the government (Carey 1995).

Well before the revolution it was argued that a post-Ceausescu regime would have to establish a new value system and mobilise the population for renewal (Sampson 1987). The Roman government called for rapid transition to a market economy (Ben-Ner and Montias 1991). Links with the EU developed during 1990, although they were strained by the suppression of dissent and a heightening of inter-ethnic tensions (Demekas and Khan 1991). Romanian–USA relations were even more seriously affected and MFN status was restored only in 1994 (Harrington 1992). Romania has considerable need of Western support, but foreign capital arrived only slowly: US$3.2mn. had been invested in joint ventures by American interests by the end of 1991 compared with US$2.8mn. from Germany, US$2.7mn. from Italy, US$2.4mn. from the UK, US$1.7mn. each from France and the Netherlands, US$1.2mn. from Switzerland and US$1.1mn. from Spain (while another seven countries together invested just over US$5mn.). The capital went into a total of 3,850 joint ventures of which 40 per cent were based in just six areas (451 in Bucharest, 373 in Timisoara, 303 in Constanta, 155 in Cluj, 140 in Brasov and 137 in Sibiu). The Bucharest enterprises especially were relatively highly capitalised.

Despite paying off some US$10bn of foreign debts during the 1980s (by boosting exports while cutting imports and running down the gold and foreign exchange reserves), it was evident that new borrowing would be necessary. The EU Phare Programme assisted the Institute of Technology's Business Incubation Centres, while the UK Know-How Fund also facilitated technology transfer. Furthermore, technological centres with an educational and training role (as well as a remit to develop foreign contacts) were supported by partners such as Washington University. Business has been fostered by new institutions like the Romanian Chamber of Commerce and Romanian Development Agency with responsibilities for stimulating business. Along with family associations and individual operations, private enterprises with up to twenty workers were allowed under a decree in 1990. This was subsequently extended to allow for limited liability companies, while employment limits were removed altogether from the organisations previously sanctioned. Late in 1991 it was reported that there were 120,000 family or single-person units and 41,100,000 companies, of which 6.5 per cent employed more than twenty people and an additional 11.8 per cent employed more than five. However, only 16 per cent were engaged in production: the rest were concerned with trade and other services. The private sector continued to grow in 1992 with the number of companies registered since the revolution passing 400,000. They contributed a quarter of GDP with 45 per cent of retail sales and one-third of imports. Industry remained 90 per cent state-controlled with a further fall in production to score a cumulative decline of 54 per cent over 1989; by contrast, agricultural production was down by only 9 per cent (Isarescu 1992).

Meanwhile, legislation for a new legal framework was brought forward, though it was recognised that there was considerable bureaucratic resistance to change and a shortage of competent people. Subsidies were cut and there were sharp price increases on many goods, notably fuel, although subventions continued on one hundred key items, constituting a major political vested interest. It was revealed that the state was paying out 30bn lei per month in subsidies while the population's total monthly income was only 26bn lei (Nelson 1991, p.196). Meanwhile, the SOEs became autonomous in 1990 as joint stock limited liability companies, in advance of privatisation. Further price liberalisation attracted more protest, notably in November 1990 to coincide with the anniversary of the 1987 Brasov demonstrations against the Ceausescu regime. GDP fell through 1992 and 1993 while inflation reached 200 per cent in 1992 and the budget deficit rose from 1.5 per cent of GDP in 1991 to 3.6 in 1992. Inflation continued at a high level; though with prospects of stabilisation through World Bank support in 1994. Meanwhile, there was a decline in trade with the 28mn.t. of cargo passing through Constanta in 1991 – less than half the 1989 level. But the trade deficit narrowed from US$1.3bn in 1991 to US$0.9bn. in 1992, thanks to a growth of exports (metals, textiles and chemicals). Some 237 enterprises were closed between November 1991 and April 1992.

Misgivings over the brisk pace of reform led the president to replace Roman with the cautious finance minister T. Stolojan and the NSF subsequently split, with the reformist Roman wing retaining the original name while the president's party became the Democratic National Salvation Front (DNSF). The Stolojan cabinet prevented escalation of social tension during the winter months of 1992 and the 1992 elections were then fought on a FDSN platform of very gradual reform (Ionescu 1993a). Iliescu was returned as president while the DNSF became the largest party. A new government was headed by N. Vacaroiu and consisted of DNSF ministers supported by the nationalist parties: the Greater Romania Party (GRP) and the Romanian National Unity Party (RNUP), drawing considerable support from Wallachia and Transylvania respectively (Gallagher 1992). The government was subsequently reorganised in the light of presidential requirements and its name changed again to the Party of Social Democracy in Romania (PSDR) (Ionescu 1994c). The government retains the support of the nationalists because, although they were not represented in the government until two ministers were appointed from the RNUP, they strongly oppose radical market reform that might favour foreign business interests (and also give disproportionate scope for Hungarians and Jews). The GRP, having much in common with the former regime, seeks to rehabilitate the fascist Iron Guard movement of the 1930s (Shafir 1993a).

The Hungarian minority supports its own ethnically based Democratic Union of Hungarians in Romania (DUHR), while the main opposition, the Democratic Convention of Romania (DCR), draws its support overwhelmingly from the towns, especially Bucharest and Transylvanian cities like Brasov and Timisoara (Roper 1994a). The DCR favours more rapid market reform and cuts in subsidies, along with more generous restitution provisions. It has always taken a strong line over excesses in the communist period and is keen to open secret police files. It strengthened its position through the 1992 local elections which brought much success in the large cities, but it has not made headway in the rural areas (Shafir 1992). It will not contemplate links with the government as long as it continues to depend on the support of nationalist parties (Fischer 1992).

Romanian politics continue to give a high profile to the Hungarian minority. The inter-ethnic disturbances in Targu Mures in March 1990 have been interpreted in party political terms as a consequence of the Front's weakness in Transylvania and the need to gain support through the growth of a Romanian nationalist party (Eyal 1993, p.137). Although the rioting was blamed on Hungarians, many people believe it could have been provoked by an organisation close to the former *Securitate* (i.e. the Romanian Service for Information) which may have helped to transport the opposing forces into the town in order to ferment a demonstration. The incident stimulated the GRP to dedicate 1991 to an 'international struggle against Hungarian terrorism' and it was also the inspiration for the creation of the nationalist Vatra Romaneasca organisation from which the RNUP developed, attracting support from Romanians who moved into Transylvania during the Ceausescu years (Gallagher 1994). Strong nationalist rhetoric has emanated from Cluj since the mayoral office was won by a candidate of the RNUP, G. Funar, who now leads the party. Tension has been heightened by controversy over the memorial to King Matthias of Hungary which stands in the main square in the city (Shafir 1994). Alterations to the inscription and threatened removal in the face of archaeological work have been interpreted as hostile gestures to Hungarians who are seeking cultural autonomy (Gallagher 1993). However, the RNUP would not remain in the governing coalition if an inter-state treaty with Hungary gave the Hungarian minority a special status.

Romania has been admitted to the CoE (Shafir and Ionescu 1993) and in 1994 she became the first former Warsaw Pact country to sign up for the NATO Partnership for Peace programme, perhaps reflecting a 'Visegrad Complex': an anxiety to show that Romania is just as European as the Visegrad countries. But it is democratic and economic reforms which count (Ionescu 1994b). Crans Montana Forum fosters economic cooperation between East and West. Their Bucharest conference has given new impetus to Romania's relations with the West (Ionescu 1994e). But there are continuing US reservations over human rights, for the House of Representatives rejected a bilateral trade agreement that sought restoration of MFN status in the wake of a Democratic victory in the presidential election. However, the West European attitude is more pragmatic and sees the inter-ethnic tensions as part of an ongoing political dialogue. However, there is always a danger that continuing deadlock could find outlets in inter-ethnic tensions heightened by the nationalist parties (Rady 1992).

At the time of writing there is discontent with the government, dominated by A. Nastase's left-of-centre PSDR. Although the party has sensed the mood of Romanians who prefer incremental change and 'muddling through', it is clear that this is not a viable long-term policy (Teodorescu 1991). A faster pace of reform is needed but the opposition is not seen as a viable alternative (Ionescu 1991b). There is little affection for intellectuals who have no moral capital for opposition to the communist regime (Harsanyi and Harsanyi 1993). Romanian politics have certainly been weakened by the limited credibility of the intellectuals who reacted passively to Ceausescu's imposition of China-oriented cultural policies. The philosopher C. Noica advocated an isolation syndrome and retreated to Paltinis (a small mountain station near Sibiu) to develop culture rather than fight the system. Although the DCR has gradually increased its effectiveness in media terms, its newspapers are difficult to find in the rural areas, allegedly because of the action of the National Office for Press Distribution which is subordinate to the Ministry of Post and Telecommunications. Meanwhile, it is difficult to explain fully the strength of the PSDR: excuses relate to the control by the old elite and peasant inexperience; yet many peasants vote for GRP and RNUP. It seems that the government finds allies among the peasantry which, despite the trappings of landownership reflected by provisional (and now definitive) titles, does not see itself as a business community. Rather, the peasant group fears higher taxes and even lower net incomes that might lead once again to landlessness even before the euphoria of restitution has begun to dim. The major public services are overmanned by Western standards and the great reorganisation would simply create an unacceptable level of unemployment (widely feared as a threat to stability) (Ionescu 1991a). On balance, people accept market competition, yet they expect government to be protective. 'Most people do not want to replace government control with more seriously-binding contracts that are inflicted by market-related institutions' (Nicolaescu 1993, pp.103–4).

Some Romanians incline towards a strong leader; yet Ceausescu-linked academics seek presidential government by technocrats (Shafir 1993b, 1993d). A division in the Labour Socialist Party, which supports the government, has been reported. One faction is unhappy with support given to the PSDR and a breakaway group could provide alternative policies. Another possibility is that Roman's NSF (now the Democratic Party (DP)) will gain ground. Although it has been criticised by the DCR for its ambivalence over small business and entrepreneurship, the DP hopes for a large coalition extending beyond the DCR, despite the difficulty that will arise in selecting a single presidential candidate (even in the limited context of the DCR). Meanwhile, the DCR has been forced to distance itself from the DUHR in order to win more votes from Romanians in Transylvania, and this should make the prospect of a liaison with Roman's party more attractive. The outcome of the next election may depend on the substance of such a liaison. Meanwhile, there remains a danger that a Latin American model will develop, with a small, rich and corrupt oligarchy ruling a poor nation.

## Privatisation

Privatisation moved only slowly for several years although a law was passed in 1991 to sell off 55 per cent of state equity, leaving a substantial residue in autonomous state corporations operating in strategic areas (power, transport and telecommunications) where government retained the right to sell off directly (Ben-Ner and Montias 1994). In selling equity, 30 per cent was to be allocated to Romanian citizens (obtaining an interest free of charge through private ownership funds) leaving the rest for foreign and domestic investors. A State Ownership Fund (SOF), modelled on Germany's Treuhand, was to deal with privatisation and restructuring, selling one tenth of their equity each year. But the National Privatisation Agency (NPA) moved very slowly despite assistance from Phare in 1991: no enterprise was privatised and no holding companies or Private Ownership Funds (POFs) had been set up by the end of the year. Romanians registered for their 30 per cent stake in July 1992, paying 100 lei for a book of five vouchers (one for each POF). A market then developed for the voucher books with prices soaring to 100,000 lei in Timisoara (though only 4,000 lei in Moldavia). Vouchers were intended to give the population a 30 per cent stake in the 6,600 SOEs with the rest held by the SOF in Bucharest. But the scheme was undermined by unintended speculation in voucher books, public apathy and inflation which prevented significant negoatiation of shares. Meanwhile, foreign investors were being invited to bid by tender for substantial shareholding blocks in forty Romanian companies selected for the purpose by the SOF (Briggs 1993). They included the state airline Tarom and representative companies from all sectors of industry. This represents the second phase of a scheme which began early in 1993 when employees and managers were invited to buy shares in 2,000 small companies.

Up to the end of January 1992 only 293 enterprises had been privatised. It seemed there was a lack of both capital and political will for rapid progress. There were conflicting interests among the various state institutions seeking to control the process: NPA, five separate POFs, the SOF, along with the Council for Economic Coordination and Reform, a proposed Ministry of Restructuring and Privatisation and the Presidency (Daianu 1994). The nomenclature seemed to be influencing the privatisation debate and, given the vested interests protecting state property, the government 'says one thing to the IMF and World Bank and another at home' (Ionescu 1994a, p.34, quoting from the *Financial Times* of 31 December 1993). But others are opposed to accelerated privatisation on the grounds that it will merely share out illusions since many companies are not profitable; also because plans are being launched, with the minimum of public debate, through pressure from the IMF and World Bank setting terms for stabilisation loans (Stan 1995). A new 1994 plan envisaged privatisation of 2,368 mainly small enterprises (though there were 403 medium-sized and thirty-five large enterprises) (Sirbu 1994, p. 497). This introduction of auction bids for the other 40 per cent to be open to foreigners was to accelerate the tempo in 1995, with completion of voucher privatisation by the middle of the year, to be followed by a bankruptcy law. However, although this mass privatisation programme was very ambitious it was always questionable whether the public would be prepared to take it seriously. In the end the timetable drawn up under World Bank pressure could not be achieved and it seems curious that the PSDR government was so confident about privatisation of 3,000 firms before it had managed to get its 1994 legislation through parliament. Although assets were revalued downwards to encourage EMBOs, even this process failed to gain momentum by the end of 1994. The SOF announced that 658 companies had passed into private hands in 1995: less than half the target figure.

The new programme for 1995–6 covered 2,200 large and medium-size enterprises representing all branches of the economy and drawn from all parts of the country. Sixty per cent of equity was available for allocation through non-transferable vouchers (worth US$464mn.). After much initial confusion, over 2.3 million citizens invested their coupons between October 1995 and the end of the year using computers installed in post offices, in anticipation of share certificates being issued by the end of March 1996. More than 70 per cent of citizens participated through investment funds, trust companies and citizens' associations. Perhaps there should have been more industrial units for tender, with money provided by leasing land. But the experience is typical of the 'top-down' privatisation: the enterprises themselves were mostly stagnant, consuming state funds while maintaining an ambivalent stance on privatisation, while the public participated only to the extent of the bills they received. Thus the state could remain the majority shareholder of many private companies. Privatisation included state apartments and state-farms, but again it is possible that arrangements may have been too generous, because in the case of housing there could have been greater use made of cash which would have provided revenue for the state. Following the sale of farms it is likely that parliament will examine arrangements for a market in agricultural land.

Meanwhile, mass privatisation has not been accompanied by significant foreign investment, although holdings can be acquired through the SOF for cash and there were thirty-nine industrial units where 60 per cent of the equity was reserved for foreign buyers. But foreign investors did not have enough time, while some of the firms up for sale were too large for small or medium foreign interests. Some strategic sales have been made by the SOF to foreign investors with the help of the EBRD and EU who have brought in a team led by Creditanstalt. In 1994 a chocolate factory was sold to Kraft Jacobs Suchard and the joint venture with the South Korean car-maker Daewoo was approved; in 1995 the detergent manufacturer Dero was sold to Unilever: more could follow. Some notable greenfield developments have been undertaken, notably the R.J. Reynolds tobacco factory in Bucharest 1995, involving an investment of US$40mn. to produce 480mn. cigarettes per annum. At the same time Romania's privatisation has helped to secure international loans, with a US$280mn. loan negotiated with IBRD in September 1995. IMF did not release the US$265mn. loan due for March 1995 because the Romanian goverment had delayed privatisation and restructuring of the public sector.

Further stock exchange activity may now be expected, following the opening of the Bursa de Valori in Bucharest in 1995 and the privatisation process should roll forwards until all state companies are privatised by the year 2000. Measures are now in place to speed up restructuring, with the risk of some bankruptcies and short-term inter-enterprise debt.

There should be a rationalisation of heavy industry, with closure of the least efficient plant and transfer of production to the more efficient: savings would then finance retraining. Many politicians believe that restructuring will incur heavy social costs but economists believe these fears are exaggerated (Van Frasum *et al.* 1994, p.754). Meanwhile, industry continues to go downhill. There were major strikes and demonstrations in the heavy industrial centre of Resita in 1994 where many people have been forced to leave the town in the face of redundancies and low living standards. The county administration was almost constantly picketed throughout the year on account of late payment of wages, poverty problems and poor services. The engineering works was in a particularly difficult financial position and could not even compete for a contract to refurbish the Iron Gates hydroelectric plant. The government eventually agreed to write off the Resita engineering company's debts. However, Resita is not unique. There are many cases of decline in old industrial centres but especially in eastern agricultural regions with recently opened centres of heavy industry. There is also high unemployment in mining and metallurgy. Better conditions are to be found in lighter industries situated along an axis passing through southern Transylvania to Bucharest and Constanta. Banking restructuring has transformed specialised state banks into commercial banks. More than twenty commercial banks are now functioning. Meanwhile, there is further growth in the private sector which now employs more than a quarter of the 10.5mn. workforce and dominates agriculture now that 85 per cent of the agricultural land has been returned to former owners (Henry 1994). There are more than 0.5mn. private businesses. The private sector contributes 30 per cent of GDP; 55 per cent of retail sales and 30 per cent of foreign trade.

### Investment

The Romanian Development Agency has recognised a succession of investment waves. The first, in 1990–1, involved small and medium projects, followed in 1991–4 by large-scale projects by transnational corporations (ABB, Alcatel, Amoco, Coca-Cola, with its network of bottling plants, Colgate-Palmolive, Shell and Siemens); from 1995 strategic investments by transnational firms will depend on an improved international environment. The EBRD is supporting a joint venture between the American company Purolite International and the Romanian chemical manufacturer Viromet to make resins for water purification. In regional terms investment continues to be highly uneven with the bulk of the foreign capital going to Bucharest and a handful of other urban centres. Transylvanian cities are among the most dynamic in the country, notably Cluj-Napoca which was associated with the Caritas banking scandal (Shafir 1993c). Cluj has a development association; also successful industries like the newly privatised Ursus Brewery with a majority stake by the German brewery Brau und Brunen and Porcelaine Manufacturers, a Romanian–German joint venture which began production in 1990. On the other hand, reports of corruption at the municipal level (especially Bucharest and Cluj) mean that developers may have to go elsewhere.

Romania has tried to create a favourable environment for investment and entrepreneurship, with low wages as a powerful incentive (Nicolescu 1992). A liberal foreign investment law in 1991 was followed by the 'Daewoo Law' in July 1994: an investment law designed expressly to attract the company, well known as a hard bargainer over tax incentives. One hundred per cent foreign ownership of businesses is allowed, with repatriation of profits, tax holidays and exemptions from customs duties. There are attractive resources, including oil (with a production rise in 1993 after steady decline since 1974) and gas. Hydrocarbon exploration opened up to foreign companies in 1990 through production-sharing agreements. UK Enterprise Oil has found gas in the Black Sea. Shell is drilling for gas in Transylvania beneath a salt layer at depths of 1,500m. which is beyond the capacity of Romgaz, operating in shallower fields. Amoco are also prospecting onshore. There is hope for a joint venture with Harbinson & Fisher (Canada) for bottomhole pumps for well-rod pumping. There is also potential for agriculture and tourism. Farm production is increasing again after the years of drought and fertiliser shortage in 1990–2. Some important new trade deals have been started such as Fructexport sending tomato juice to Heinz in the UK for making ketchup. However, agricultural credit is in short supply (Henry 1994). There is a ten-year plan for transport under which Italian firms have formed joint ventures to improve border crossings and 1,000km. of roads. This is part of a US$400mn. programme financed by the World Bank, EBRD and EIB. The Alcatel Group are investing in telecommunications with a joint venture spare parts factory in Timisoara. Romania has construction companies with wide foreign experience: Contransmix has undertaken transport projects in Germany, Greece and Morocco. Foreign investment was US$650.5mn. in 1994 compared with US$621.4mn. for the previous four years together.

A significant achievement has been the creation of a modern central bank by M. Isarescu. The bank has tackled the problem of building reserves, despite delays in reaching agreement with IMF and in returning to international capital markets. An initial lack of tight credit control saw a growth in the money supply by 100 per cent in 1991 and 133 per cent in 1993: hence the annual doubling or trebling in prices, while compensation in wage increases was more limited (especially in the case of the relaxation of price controls in May 1994). There have been frequent strikes, such as the transport strikes of 1994 over wage restrictions, although the overall situation is calm.

But now tighter monetary control of the central bank has won IMF approval and opened the door to standby credits. In 1994 the World Bank approved a US$175mn. loan for the oil industry and delivered the US$180mn. second instalment of a structural adjustment loan. Up to US$400mn. can be lent annually by the World Bank if privatisation and economic reform continue but government has yet to demonstrate its determination to adhere strictly to the conditions. There seems to be a 'tug of war between the IMF and a Romanian government anxious about the social impact of radical economic reform' (Ionescu 1994d, p.24).

However, the Romanian achievement has been considerable, given the scale of the problem and the lack of reform experience. There is an improved macroeconomic climate. Romanians are now being seen as cautious but competent reformers (Sirbu 1994). The budget deficit is on target: below 3.5 per cent of GDP with a target of 2.8 per cent for 1995. Year-on-year inflation fell to 137 per cent in 1994 and rates for 1995 and 1996 are forecast at 48 and 38 per cent respectively (not far from the IMF target of 35 per cent at the end of 1995 seems attainable). Thanks to a substantial growth of exports, a trade deficit of US$305mn. in 1994 (when Bucharest's World Trade Centre opened) should come down to 243mn. in 1995 and 70mn. in 1996 while the increase in GDP of 1.3 per cent in 1993 and 1.5 per cent in 1994 (though below the 5.0 per cent level considered essential for the government to meet its objectives) should climb to 3 per cent in 1995 and 4 per cent in 1996. Industrial production growth of 1.3 per cent in 1993, rising to 3 per cent in 1994, should increase to 4 per cent in 1996.

Romania has gained an international credit rating which facilitated the issue of first post-communist international bonds: a US$150mn. loan arranged in 1995 by Citibank for the National Bank of Romania with the aim of improving foreign currency reserves. Capital markets are crucial for the private sector and borrowing is still too expensive. The EBRD has stakes in three private banks and is expected to participate in privatisation of the Romanian Development Bank due in 1995. The private sector accounted for only 35 per cent of the economy in 1994: a low figure when compared with 55 per cent in Hungary, Poland and Slovakia and 65 per cent in the Czech Republic. However, the privatisation programme should take the proportion to over 50 per cent. There was 3.4 per cent growth in 1994, with the prospect of 4.0 per cent in 1995; but unemployment may reach 14.5 per cent by the end of 1995 if bankruptcy legislation is enacted (industrial employment at the end of 1994 was already 0.81mn. down on the level of 3.16mn. at the end of 1991 (Hall and O'Sullivan 1994). The trade gap widened to US$1.5bn in 1995 because imports surged and annual inflation is estimated at 20 per cent for 1996 (running at 26 per cent late in 1995). On the other hand, the IMF approved an extension to Romania's Stand-By Arrangement for 1996–7. Romania will receive US$400mn. in five disbursements if the programme's conditions are adhered to: current account deficit down from 4.8 per cent of GDP in 1995 to 3.4 per cent by the end of 1996.

Interpretations of events in Romania remain sharply polarised. On the one hand, Romania appears as a refuge for the conservatives with reform restricted to a trickle of relatively insignificant measures which leaves the governing elite (including former communists) in charge of both the economy and the bureaucracy. On this analysis Western help has been misappropriated in order to support the regime of subsidies to non-viable SOEs. On the other hand, it is undeniable that Romania faces massive problems in restructuring the SOEs which were for so long managed without any concern for economic efficiency (Ronnas 1991b) and, given the experience of the Ceausescu years, Romania is understandably wavering in the face of a problematic market economy model (Van Frasum *et al.* 1994). Romanian society seems to have 'relapsed into a political apathy' (Shafir and Ionescu 1994, p.126). There have certainly been improvements in the sense that the terror tactics of the past now appear to be much less in evidence, although the interventions of the 'miners' in Bucharest in 1990 and 1991 are vividly remembered and some see the former *Securitate* elements as a potential threat. Political life is debased by the national government's campaign against mayors who are members of opposition parties; to say nothing of the chronic underfunding of local government. The completion of the first unit at the Cernavoda nuclear power station in 1996 is a considerable morale booster, especially because the additional power should be very helpful in dealing with winter shortages (Ionescu 1993b). At the same time there seems to be a growing awareness of Romania's passageway function, marked by increasing use of the Danube–Black Sea Canal.

## FORMER FEDEREAL REPUBLIC OF YUGOSLAVIA (FFRY)

The very fluid situation in FFRY has arisen primarily through nationalist tensions, but there was also a parallel debate on economic reform running through the 1980s when differences of opinion among the League of Communists of Yugoslavia (LCY) followed national lines and contributed to a crisis in the federal government (Allcock 1991). The B. Mikulic government fell in 1988 because the reform programme was obstructed and the following year a modified programme was considered when A. Markovic, a Croat technocrat, took over the federal premiership. The Markovic Plan was formally launched in 1990 to reform the currency with a new partly convertible dinar replacing the old at a rate of 1 per 10,000 and pegged to the DM at a rate of 7 to 1. The money supply would be controlled and imports liberalised. There would also be regulations for joint ventures to ease access for foreign capital. However, the federal government collapsed in 1990 since the Skupstina ceased to function. Meanwhile any chance of economic reform was undermined by the Serbia's 'Great Bank Robbery' of 1990 which involved rediscounting bank loans and boosting the money supply by one tenth (Dyker 1993a).

The year 1989 saw a sharp polarisation of opinion as the northern republics came out strongly in favour of greater autonomy and liberal reforms. Such a view was projected by the emerging pluralism in Slovenia and Croatia with a Democratic Alliance launched in Ljubljana, while the Movement for a Yugoslav Democratic Initiative appeared in Zagreb. Meanwhile in Serbia reactionary policies were evident in constitutional change to abrogate the status of Kosovo and Vojvodina as autonomous provinces and thereby weaken the position of the Albanian and Hungarian minorities. Equally, Macedonia's nationalist stance, declaring the republic to be the 'national state of the Macedonian nation', was disconcerting to the Albanian and Turkish minorities. It was anomalous that the Serbian leadership under S. Milosevic (who came to power dedicated to defend Serbs and Montenegrans in Kosovo) should oppose the disintegration of FFRY while nevertheless seeking direct rule over the autonomous regions, especially Kosovo with its large Albanian majority. The action against Kosovo, coming on the heels of the dismissal of an Albanian representative (A. Vilasi) from the LCY Central Committee, led to unrest in the province and a rally of Serb support behind Milosevic. Nationalist manifestations took place at the new Cathedral of St Sava in Belgrade and also in Kosovo itself, where the memory of the epic Battle of Kosovo 600 years before emphasised Serb determination to maintain control. There were also strikes by Albanians at Trepca mine and a state of emergency was declared, although Slovenia opposed Serb demands for the army to be sent in and pressed for a conciliatory approach towards the Kosovo Albanians in general and Vilasi in particular (for the Slovene J. Drnovsek was at the head of the Federal State Presidency). With the transfer of administrative jobs from Albanians to Serbs, Albanians built a shadow state with an unofficial president (I. Rugova) who advocated non-violent protest.

The response to the inconsistencies of Serb policy was deepening division within the LCY, reflecting the intensifying rhythm of political activity in the run-up to the republic elections in late 1990 which saw ethnic issues placed firmly in a reform context (Ramet 1995; Zizmond 1992). The protagonists of economic reform and political pluralism were prominent in Slovenia where constitutional changes affirmed the right to secede. When Serb residents in Slovenia were stopped from demonstrating there was a wave of protest from Montenegro and Serbia; by the end of the year many enterprises in Serbia had cut their ties with Slovenia, provoking a Slovene response by withdrawal of contributions to federal funds (Ferfila 1991). The situation continued to deteriorate into 1990 as the Slovenes left the LCY Congress (and subsequently renounced links with the party altogether) after rejection of their plan for eight independent parties. Markovic, who had just presided over the launch of a new, fully convertible currency, declared that FFRY would continue to function with or without the LCY. Divergences along nationalist lines were countered by attempts to bolster support for the federation through a New Movement for Yugoslavia drawing strong support from the military who voiced concern about the direction of Yugoslav politics (Djilas 1991). But the tide of pluralism advanced as more ethnically-based parties passed judgements over the future of the federation (Mrdjen 1993). The LCY in Slovenia was renamed the Party of Democratic Renewal (PDR) and a subsequent LCY plenum failed to attract members from Croatia, Macedonia and Slovenia, while Bosnia's representatives withdrew after the start of the meeting. Meanwhile, with the rotation among the members of the presidency, B. Jovic of Serbia was able to launch a package of measures for a more centralised and less liberal constitution. But he failed to get them adopted. Likewise, Markovic was unable to make headway with his plans for a new all-federation party (Alliance of Reform Forces) to stimulate cooperation by the republics for a reform programme including privatisation of the SOEs. The situation in the various successor states may be discussed with the critical baseline of the republic elections of 1990 in mind (Cohen 1992).

## Bosnia-Hercegovina

A detailed review is impossible because reconstruction is barely under way at the time of writing. As outlined in Chapter 3, the civil war was brought to an end only by the Dayton Agreement at the end of 1995. Although fighting has stopped, many people have been obstructed from moving back to their homes. Both sides were responsible for ensuring that virtually all Serbs left the suburbs of Sarajevo handed over to the Muslim-Croat Federation and even within the federation tension between Muslims and Croats has made it difficult to reunify the city of Mostar, where there is now only a small mixed zone to set against the three Croat and three Muslim districts. Political life in the federation is dominated by the two ethnically-based parties: the Croatian Democratic Union and the Muslim Democratic Action Party of President Izetbegovic. The greatest threat faces the September 1996 elections which are due to take place throughout Bosnia and to create a basis for stable administration that will allow the UN military operation to be gradually wound down. The hardline Bosnian Serb leadership under R. Karadzic has no wish for these elections to take place, wishing to see a complete separation of Republica Srpska from the rest of Bosnia and eventual union with Serbia. Hence the continuing struggle between the leadership in Pale and the more amenable faction under R. Kasagic who will have great difficulty building significant momentum in time for the elections. Basing the elections on the 1991 census (i.e. before ethnic cleansing) creates the possibility of exile administrations for places like Srebrenica, the former Muslim town which the Serbs are now repopulating with refugees from Sarajevo. Meanwhile, reconstruction has barely started, with differences of approach between the

European states (operating the Phare Essential Aid Programme) who favour even-handed assistance to the two parts of the country and the US administration which favours discrimination against the Bosnian Serbs to discourage support for hardliners and to ensure compliance with the Dayton Agreement including a resolution of the outstanding problem over the Brcko Corridor connecting Serb territories in east and west Bosnia.

## Croatia

The political scene has been dominated by F. Tudjman's Croatian Democratic Union (CDU) which won a sweeping victory with its right-wing, nationalistic platform. Tudjman was prominent in the cultural and political revival of Croatia in 1971. He was jailed for his part in the 'Croatian Spring' but visited the US in 1987 and got support for the HDZ, a mass movement in Croatia which gained a majority in the first free parliamentary elections in 1990. However, Croatian Serbs declared autonomy and formed their own Serbian National Council. Serb irregulars were supported by the army prior to its withdrawal from Croatia and the war over Croatian independence was only stopped by UN intervention over about one-third of its territory where the intention was to demilitarise Serb groups within the 'independent enclaves' declared in 1990. They comprised about 12 per cent of the population and consist of ethnic Serbs who boycotted the election (200,000 in UN areas and a similar number in Serbia where of course they did not have the opportunity). There was also a UN presence in the so-called 'pink zone', taken by Serbs after the initial plans had been worked out, where an agreed handover to the Croats was delayed until recovery was possible by military force. The future of the main Serb-held areas remained undecided until 1995. By this time Croatia's military strength had greatly improved and she could operate in concert with a strengthened Bosnian army equipped with anti-tank rockets, heavy mortars and also Orkan multiple rocket launchers. The latter seemed destined for extensive deployment after refurbishment of the Novi Travnik and Vitez munitions factories. Also important were components smuggled from Iran (which jointly developed the system with FYR during the 1980s). This was to pave the way for a massive summer offensive to recapture Krajina (along with extensive territories in northwest Bosnia) and force a handover in Eastern Slavonia by negotiation.

However, although the government was embarrassed by only partial control of all its territory in 1992, Tudjman's CDU was nevertheless successful in the elections of that year. The lead was much smaller and there were gains by both the right-wing Croatian Party of Rights (following the Ustasha) and the main opposition Croatian Social Liberal Party. A split occurred in the CDU in 1994 with the left wing setting up the Croatian Independent Democrats under J. Manolic and S. Mesic; leaving Tudjman with the right wing. Although there was unease over Tudjman's autocratic style the particular reason for the break was the sudden reversal of policy on Bosnia in favour of links with the Muslims (Moore 1994). Nationalism and the independence struggle has naturally eclipsed other issues (Schonfelder 1993). There was a refugee problem, with many Croats seeking sanctuary in Hungary where hospitality was inevitably conditioned by sensitivities over possible ethnic cleansing by Serbs in Vojvodina. At home there was high unemployment through the loss of thousands of jobs in bombed factories; also hyperinflation arising out of the need to finance the war effort. War has also meant the loss of some 200,000 homes.

Croat industrialists want help from the state. A successful stabilisation policy was launched in 1993 but lack of social consensus could lead to protest (Bicanic 1994). An IMF loan is expected in the context of new tax structures and privatisation. Companies have tended to reduce their workforces while adopting a 'wait and see' attitude. There has been little foreign investment, which is serious because enterprises need partners to help with restructuring to develop new products and markets. Most companies do not have the information to properly evaluate the situation: they may not even know who their domestic competitors are. Companies with long-standing Western contacts are in the best situation, for example, clothing factories (Radosevic 1994). The EBRD is considering cooperation with Croatia in pharmaceuticals, petrochemicals, shipbuilding and other sectors with export potential. Privatisation has been slow (Bicanic 1993) but forty Croatian companies have been sold in a debt-for-equity swap that will enable Croatian citizens to draw foreign currency savings, blocked since independence.

Croatia is within the orbit of the IMF (which has endorsed the stabilisation programme of 1993) as well as the World Bank. She will be eligible for further loans as economic restructuring proceeds. However, unemployment reached 16.5 per cent at the end of 1994. Croatia is also on the verge of joining the CoE and the EU Phare programme. Relations with Italy and Slovenia are now good and the oil pipeline from the Adriatic coast was reopened in 1995. Yet although progress has been made by the government of N. Valentic and inflation has been brought under control, the public remained preoccupied by the failure to regain the occupied territories and reports of corruption in high office. There was also dissatisfaction over divisions within the ruling CDU which includes a radical nationalist 'Hercegovina Lobby' as well as a liberal wing opposed to the government's rapid privatisation programme; not to mention the ineffectual hiving off of a splinter group under the leadership of J. Manolic and S. Mesic already noted. Meanwhile, the prospects of the Croatian Peasant Party (CPP) have improved.

But for the Balkan War, Croatia would be close to Slovenia in economic performance, whereas in fact the situation became precarious with the breakaway Serb district of Krajina and the additional burden of people displaced from Serb-occupied areas, to say nothing of the 400,000 refugees from Bosnia. Croatia's aggressive stance in support of a partition of Bosnia-

Hercegovina was favoured by the defence minister G. Susak as a way of achieving a Croat state of Herceg-Bosna based on Mostar. But since the US-brokered Croat–Muslim agreement of 1993 Croatia has been accepted as a member of the international community and the UN has confirmed the integrity of Croatia's borders with the UN Protection Areas as 'Serb-occupied territories'. The Vance-Owen plan for the return of territory to Croatia was a failure and it was with some difficulty that the UN Protection Force was able to renew the mandate that expired in March 1995 since Croatia had sought a withdrawal of all UN forces from Krajina to the international borders. Croatia also wanted more involvement by NATO as opposed to the UN in order to tie the country more closely to the Western alliance.

However, Croatia's prospects were transformed during 1995. In the spring, Croat forces overran the occupied Daruvar/Pakrac area of Western Slavonia and Krajina seemed in danger of being isolated by Croat advances in western Hercegovina. Although most analysts considered that Croatia could recapture all the remaining Serb-occupied territories, the Krajina Serbs still insisted on recognition of their Republika Srpska Krajina (RSK) and the Serbian president Milosevic maintained tacit support. For although the RSK has no prospect for viability outside Croatia the local army provided a useful support for the Serb position in western Bosnia. There was originally an expectation of further conquests along the Adriatic coast which would have made for an economically viable Greater Serb state, but such gains were inconceivable by 1994 and the Serb position in the northwest remained strategically dependent on the Posavina Corridor which was always liable to closure by a determined joint offensive by Bosnians and Croatians. Heavy fighting took place in the Brcko/Orasje area where Serb-controlled territory was almost pinched out between the Croatian border along the Sava in Eastern Slavonia and the northern extremity of Bosnian territory controlled by the Croat/Muslim federation.

President Milosevic hoped that Zagreb would negotiate with RSK over economic matters so that Yugoslav recognition of Croatia could then go ahead and at the same time Belgrade would not concede status to the Krajina Serbs while they continued to rule out reintegration. Yet the Serbs in both Bosnia-Hercegovina and Croatia maintained their pretensions. Krajina Serbs plainly sought a federation of Serb states while Bosnian Serbs aimed at a centralised state for the West Serbian Lands that would eventually unite with Serbia and Montenegro. However, given the close links between Milosevic and the Serb armies in Bosnia and Croatia it always seemed unlikely that events would move far out of his control. Meanwhile, Croatia was under pressure to resolve the conflict in order to expedite investment: the large Croat diaspora in Germany (initially 270,000 but rising to 600,000 as a result of the war) was impatient to return and invest. Yet only a few relatively prosperous areas removed from the fighting (like Istria and the northern Adriatic, along with Medjimurje) could make any progress. There were also parts of Croatia (Dalmatia and Istria) that were seeking greater autonomy; so it was crucial that the occupied territories should be regained and the cohesion of the state secured to a greater extent. In this context an economic agreement between Zagreb and an autonomous Krajina could never be satisfactory because of Croatia's need for effective control to secure communications with the Adriatic.

Tudjman's CDU remains in power following the 1995 elections, but despite military success in Krajina, the party could not maintain even the 1992 level of support, for it was defeated quite decisively in Zagreb and did badly in the towns in general apart from Osijek. This reflects public concern over economic and social problems, despite Tudjman's personal popularity. The CPP of Z.Tomcic is now the main opposition party and there is an effective regional party in Istria (Istrian Democratic Assembly) which will resist centralisation and any attempt by Zagreb to increase its share of the tourist revenue. There is now a brighter prospect of economic growth to take advantage of the country's position between Europe, the Middle East and Asia. Duty-free zones will be established at Adriatic ports. In addition, Croatia could be a springboard for investment in Bosnia-Hercegovina.

## Macedonia

The agenda has been dominated by the struggle by Macedonians to affirm national identity in the face of Albanian, Bulgarian, Greek and Serb designs on their territory (Prevelakis 1996). The creation of a Macedonian Republic in Yugoslavia provided a foundation at a time when Bulgaria refused to recognise the existence of such an ethnic group. And when the republic declared its independence in 1991 the strongest resistance came from Greece where sensitivity over that country's own Macedonian territory resulted in an effective economic blockade, closing access to Thessaloniki and diverting trade through Bulgaria on the Kumanovo–Kjustendil route. This orientation is critically important because Turkey is Macedonia's chief trading partner, while Bulgaria and Turkey were the first countries to recognise Macedonia. Greek hostility arises through fear of a return to Tito-inspired claims over a 'Greater Macedonia'. A change of name was demanded and a stalemate then set in because no alternative was conceivable in Skopje where the nationalistic opposition (the Internal Macedonian Revolutionary Organ-isation (IMRO)) would have resisted any change. A compromise was found in the FYRM formula. Meanwhile, Macedonia suffered through support of the blockade against Serbia, so a valuable market has been lost. There was a further economic burden through the accommodation of 30,000 refugees from Bosnia, controversial to people in Skopje where unemployment has risen and incomes have fallen. West European states announced their intention to establish diplomatic relations with Macedonia at the end of 1993 (Perry 1994). A new currency (the denar) was launched in 1992 and shops were well stocked after a good harvest in that year. But Macedonia was destabilised by the 1992 proposal of the Serb leader Milosevic for a Serbian–Greek confederation. This clearly posed a threat to Macedonia which lay between these two states. A UN package was formulated to overcome the risk of a diplomatic 'black hole' and forestall a Serb invasion which might have followed any move by Macedonian Albanians to enter Kosovo. Good relations were established with a UN Protection Force on the border with Kosovo. But then the Greek Consulate was closed in 1994 over continued use of the name 'Macedonia' and the country has been blockaded ever since.

There were also internal difficulties through the substantial Albanian minority (35 per cent) which seeks accommodation in cultural matters through the status of Albanian as a second national language and creation of an Albanian language university. It is suggested that in Macedonia an ethnically integrated community has the best chance of survival and, although the Macedonians are reluctant to concede equality to the ethnic minorities, Albanians are now participating fully in political life. The Macedonian parties have promoted dialogue not only with the Albanian minority but with Albania proper and also with Kosovo. In 1990 the IMRO combined with the Party for Macedonian National Unity and gained a small lead over the successor to the LCY, leaving the Albanian-supported Party of Democratic Prosperity (PDP) holding the balance. Hence the government of B. Crvenkovski included several Albanians although the cantonising of the country is being resisted. Then a Social Democrat (formerly LCY) government under P. Gosev, allied with the PDP. But, given the critical situation, the three main Macedonian parties came together under the leadership of the Social Democrats and the 1994 elections secured the return of President K. Gligorov. Prime minister Crvenkovski now heads an Alliance for Macedonia government which shares power with the PDP.

This has tended to marginalise the Albanians and relations appear to have deteriorated. But more Albanians have been appointed to the civil service and the police force; there are more Albanian teachers and more time has been found for Albanian radio and television broadcasts. Pressure has come from radical Albanians dissatisfied with progress achieved by moderates in improving minority rights. When a private Albanian university opened in Tetovo (with teachers from Pristina) there was unease that it would become a vehicle for separatism, but initial government insistence on closure has been balanced by tolerance of the teachers operating from their own homes, while Skopje University is catering much more adequately for Albanians. The situation remains tense but the heavy costs of war in Bosnia-Hercegovina and Croatia seemed to reinforce the determination of other Balkan nations to avoid hostilities. And the domino theory that anticipated an extension of hostilities to the Sandzak, Kosovo and Macedonia (whereupon Albania and Greece might confront Bulgaria and Turkey in a Balkan War) now seems less relevant, though still a remote possibility. But there is growing great power rivalry, not only within the Western alliance but between the Western powers and Russia which is not disposed to put pressure on Serbia.

Stabilisation has been successful (Kraft 1995) but foreign debts need rescheduling before an IMF standby loan of US$35mn. can be used. The national currency – denar – was stable during 1994. The government aims to strengthen banking with the privatisation of Stopanska Banka and the support of EBRD to expand commercial banking. And there is a need for a stock exchange if privatisation is going to appear credible to the public, already disadvantaged by a lack of disposable income. Macedonia has already reached agreement with the World Bank over the privatisation of 940 companies during 1995 and has planned for two-thirds of the economy to be in private hands by April 1996. Many small companies were privatised by EMBO but more outside (including international) interest is wanted in the larger companies. There is a need for foreign investment to develop the tobacco industry. British-American Tobacco Industries and Rothmans are interested in MakTabak's cigarette producing capacity. Twenty-five heavy loss-making industries (including the Zelezarnici steel mill near Skopje) were subjected to intensive care before being broken up and sold. This decisive move reflected the political consensus, for there was a risk that unemployment could rise to over 50 per cent by the end of 1995. However, some large companies, such as the Zastava car accessory plant, were split up fairly quickly into smaller profitable units. Some 604 enterprises employing 59,000 workers were privatised in 1994. The Macedonian stock exchange opened in 1995 and was developed with technical assistance from the British Know-How Fund and International Securities Consultancy. There has been an upsurge of interest from foreign business following the lifting of the Greek blockade and Macedonia has been accepted as a member of the Phare Programme.

The end of the Greek embargo should signal the take-off of the Macedonian economy, while the easing of sanctions will bring a boost to trade with Serbia. Macedonia is well placed to do business with neighbours since the languages of Albania, Bulgaria and Serbia are well understood. There is a young, well-educated population to attract investors and a South Korean electronics firm has started production of telecommunications equipment at a state-owned plant at Lake Ohrid. Macedonia is also home to some enterprises which have had to leave Bosnia, such as the Yucan clothing company which has also started business interests in Romania and Ukraine. But the Greek blockade forced the use of air cargo (for which facilities were very poor) and trucking to the West via Bulgaria, Romania and Hungary. Transport links have a high priority, especially the east–west routes to link the Adriatic with the Black Sea. A rail link with Bulgaria is under way and the Bulgarian section should be ready in 1996. There is great potential for tourism in Ohrid, a UNESCO-protected world heritage site. It is unfortunate that Macedonia should have been destabilised by the attempted car bomb assassination of President

Gligorov in 1995. Although he survived and remains in power, the Alliance for Macedonia broke up and Crvenkovsky now heads a Social Democrat administration. For the time being therefore, Gligorov's progressive stance is being maintained and the accommodation for the Albanians continues.

## Slovenia

Slovenia always had an advantage through its low level of dependency on other parts of the federation and its close links with foreign neighbours. Slovenia is particularly close to Austria and rejects the notion of being a Balkan nation (Milanovich 1996). Slovenes have much experience in foreign trade with a reputation as a high quality, reliable supplier of manufactured goods dating back to the days of the Austro-Hungarian empire. Slovenia was FFRY's principal exporter of high-tech manufactures, thanks to such enterprises as Iskra Telecom, an electronics company founded (as Iskra Telematika) in 1946 and now benefiting from investment by Siemens. There is also the major pharmaceutical company Krka exporting to both Eastern and Western Europe (finished products and raw materials respectively) and managing a spa network within the country (Vriser 1992). Slovenia also has a good local infrastructure (banking, transport and insurance) and a legal basis for autarky was established in 1974 with taxation, monetary and fiscal policy delegated to the republic level. By contrast, other parts of Yugoslavia had a weaker economic base. For instance, Vojvodina specialised in agriculture to supply cheap food to Yugoslavia's towns (Bookman 1990). Slovenes saw their contributions to the federal budget squandered, with market reforms coming too late to stop the accentuation of north–south differences. The costs of independence were seen as less than the costs of chaos within Yugoslavia (Cvikl et al. 1993).

In 1986 the liberals in the Slovenian LCY ousted the conservatives and M. Kucan became party president. There was an election boost for independence in 1988 when the military tried to suppress nationalist literature containing evidence of planned militia moves against Slovene liberals. Alternative political parties emerged during the 'Slovene Spring' and tension with Serbia in 1989 pushed Slovenes further towards secession. Elections in Slovenia returned the Demos alliance, with L. Peterle of the Christian Democratic Party being subsequently elected to head the government (Bibic 1993). Also prominent in the coalition were the Democratic Union, the People's Party and the Social Democrats. The Liberal PDR (emerging out of the reformed LCY, as noted above) was the largest single party and Kucan became president. Slovenia declared sovereignty in July 1990: there was a vote for independence through a referendum in September 1990 and after some fighting the Yugoslav army withdrew in October 1991 (Ramet 1993). The Demos were criticised for failing to act decisively over privatisation and this contributed to the collapse of the coalition at the end of 1991, when J.

Drnovsek became interim prime minister. However, due to preoccupation with the Bosnian refugee crisis (as well as constitutional problems and the abortion issue) the privatisation debate was prolonged until the end of the year on the basis of sales and free distribution. The 1992 election saw Kucan retain the presidency while a new five-party coalition was formed under Drnovsek, comprising the main parties opposing the Demos: the PDR (Liberal Democrats) along with some of the previous coalition parties including the Social Democrats and Christian Democrats (Zizmond 1993). Drnovsek's government is secure, although his Liberal Democrats are awkwardly flanked on one side by Peterle's Christian Democrats (gaining ground with their pro-EU stance and a policy of restraint in spending) and the Social Democrats (former LCY) who emphasise social equality.

Slovenia made a success of stabilisation despite a fall in production and a rise in unemployment. Inflation has come down and the tolar is stable, but the trade balance deteriorated between 1992 and 1993 with a decline in exports. Trade with other countries of FRY has fallen steadily since 1990, but links with the EU and the Visegrad states have been consolidated. There has been a radical change on the market because some stimulation seemed necessary to get the economy moving forward. The favourable treatment of minorities is a positive factor, though a nationalist party achieved one-tenth of the votes in 1992 on the grounds that 'Bosnians' and others were taking jobs. There was a revival of retail sales and tourism in 1993, but unemployment continued to grow to 15.4 per cent of the workforce despite the growth of small-scale businesses and self-employed workers. Slovenia is gradually extending the legal framework needed for a free market economy, with a new tax system (1991) and banking law (1993). Laws governing land, forestry and cooperatives were enacted in 1992.

Some 250 companies submitted privatisation proposals for approval by the Slovenian Privatisation Agency. The pharmaceutical firm Lek was the first to float 35 per cent of its stock and the issue was immediately oversubscribed. The matter was complicated by sharp changes in policy. The initial approach was shock therapy (Bicanic 1991). It was decided that there would be no free distribution but that one-tenth of the stock would be sold each year so that people with modest savings could gradually build up a holding. However, it was argued that, in effect, only enterprise managers and foreign capitalists would be able to buy. A revised plan placed half the stock in the hands of employees (10 per cent as a free allocation, 20 per cent for pension funds and 20 per cent reserved for purchase) while the other half was to be used to settle restitution claims (15 per cent) and provide free allocation to Slovenian citizens (35 per cent, with vouchers of increasing value according to age). The process was held up to allow for restitution claims to be submitted until the end of 1993. But this plan was rejected by the representatives of management; a third plan cut out the free distribution and gave greater opportunities for employees and managers.

There was zero growth in Slovenia in 1993 but some industrial restructuring was achieved. Almost 60 per cent of Slovenia's trade was with the EU in 1994. Mura Textiles, which developed from a small workshop in Muraska Sobota in 1925, is a large, modern, export-driven enterprise doing a lot of business in Germany and, like the Gorenje company making domestic appliances in Velenje and the privatised tobacco company in Ljubljana (with skilled low cost labour), is in need of a foreign partner. Bosch Siemens Hausgeraete of Germany is investing in a new electrical appliances factory in a deal that will involve collaboration with Gorenje Nazarje in terms of factory modernisation to increase market penetration in Central and Eastern Europe. The established trading contacts of these companies in areas such as the CIS, FRY and Turkey could be attractive. Foreign investment, although essential, is not popular. Foreign investors cannot be part of joint venture managements which has meant that direct investment has so far been low. The Kranj textile manufacturer Tekstilindus has been bought by Aquasava of Italy. The Austrian manufacturer of hydraulic equipment Huber Palfinger have taken a 30 per cent stake in the Maribor crane manufacturer Metalna (Rojec and Svetlicic 1993). Papirnica Kolicevo cardboard producer has been acquired by Sarrio, the Spanish cardboard manufacturer (part of the Italian Saffa Group). Japan's tyre manufacturer Yokohama have signed a contract with Sava Trade of Kranj who, in addition to their distribution of local products, will sell the Japanese product supplied from a factory in Brescia through stores in Slovenia. The Italian biscuit manufacturer Crich has signed an agreement with the Ljubljana firm of Medex to improve quality and increase production. The growth of business has led to an International Executive Development Centre in Kranj and the formation of the Slovene Association of Entrepreneurs which comprises chambers of commerce, private capital groups and individual business owners, including many from small firms (Bartlett and Prasnikar 1995).

There was a successful courtship of Austria, Germany, Hungary and Italy in the early days of independence, though the USA and some European countries remained ambivalent, seeking a new confederate arrangement for FFRY. There was disruption of trade through the Serb-Croat war and EU sanctions. But 1992 brought a joint Franco-Slovene economic council, an agreement with EFTA and trade talks with other Yugoslav Republics (Zizmond 1993). International representation is inadequate, with some resistance on the part of the international community related to Slovenia's role in breaking up the old federation, calling into question a large number of agreements which many interests (including the USA, NATO and the Third World) would like to maintain. US recognition in 1992 was a milestone although Slovenia would like to see a stronger American role. Negotiation of an association agreement with the EU has been complicated by claims from Italians expelled after the Second World War. Claims in respect of expropriation apply particularly in the areas of Koper (Capodistria) and Piran

(Pirano) adjacent to Trieste and Italy is blocking the association agreement until the matter is resolved. Meanwhile, Slovenia joined the Visegrad Initiative in 1992 and signed a cooperation agreement with the EU in 1993. By the middle of 1993 Slovenia had gained admission to almost all the international financial organisations (with GATT as a major exception) and had negotiated a number of bilateral economic agreements (though these did not cover the world's major economic powers nor Slovenia's major trading partners). Further diversification is needed and this calls for improved conmmunications so that Slovenia can profit from her strategic location at the head of the Adriatic. The European Investment Bank is supporting railway modernisation on the routes between Austria, Croatia and Italy. In mid-1995 the Slovene economy was still performing well. The Krka pharmaceutical concern (the country's largest drugs producer, exporting three-quarters of its output) opened a DM17mn. research and development centre in 1995 for the development of new generic drug products. This follows the company's chemical development department and laboratory for pharmacological kinetics research openedin 1994.

## Yugoslavia

The new, smaller Yugoslavia consists of a Serbian-Montenegran federation in which Serbia is the dominant partner and the country with the major vested interest in the arrangement. Hastily established in 1992, the federation has been described as a virtual *coup* by S. Milosevic because the Titograd parliament decided in 1991 that if the old federation was dissolved then Montenegro would also opt for independence. But Milosevic imposed a range of economic and political pressures to reverse the Montenegran leadership's decision and gain validation through a referendum that was widely boycotted. The present arrangements do not work well because the legal systems of the two countries are incompatible. There is tension over the lack of a significant Montenegran input into policy-making, despite a confederal inspiration which was supposed to make for joint staffing of all state institutions. However, Milosevic's Serbian Socialist Party (SSP) was able to get a federal constitution adopted by the old (largely defunct) federal assembly, helped by the 150,000 Montenegrans in Belgrade who would always oppose independence. The federation president (Montenegran R. Kontic) cooperates closely with Milosevic.

### Serbia

Milosevic's new SSP (developing out of the LCY) eclipses the main rival: V. Draskovic's Movement for Serbian Renewal (MSR) which is nationalistic, conservative and monarchist. Elections in 1993 confirmed the government of the SSP, governing with New Democracy and part of the Democratic Party with opposition from Draskovic's MSR and the Democratic Opposition of Serbia. The prime minister M. Marjanovic is subservient to President

Milosevic who is not looking for a broad-based regime. The war situation made it difficult for opposition parties to make headway without appearing unpatriotic and Draskovic would only go to the point of accepting Croatia's boundaries in the context of a confederation of Croatia Proper and Krajina. Meanwhile, the economy collapsed: Zastava made 13,150 cars each fortnight in 1990 but did not reach this level for the whole year in 1992 when many workers were retained on paid holiday. There are shades of a 'gangster politician' class (Dyker 1993b; Madzar 1993a, 1993b). Stabilisation was attempted (Petkovski *et al.* 1993; Wyzan 1993) and the super dinar was launched in 1994, tied to the DM. President of the central bank D. Avramovic drew up an economic policy based on 'ten commandments' including a balanced budget; price and wage freeze; stimulated exports; control of banks and finance institutions. But there could still be a further round of hyper-inflation (Markotich 1994).

Serbia also faces the complication of Kosovo where Milosevic is deter-mined to maintain Serb control; yet the Albanian population (90 per cent of the total) remains implacably hostile to this arrangement. They voted overwhelmingly for an independent Kosovo but international recognition has not been forthcoming on the grounds that Kosovo was an autonomous region and not a republic. There seems little room for compromise since the moderate policy of the Yugoslav prime minister M. Panic (who proposed an international conference on Kosovo along with the ending of the state of emergency and the reopening of Albanian schools) made no impact on Serb politics where Milosevic remains in the ascendancy. Serbian and Mon-tenegran troops went to Kosovo after they left Macedonia in 1992. There are also Federal Army troops, Serb-dominated police and Serbian irregulars to support authorities in Pristina. Radical Kosovo Serbs want a 'final solution' and Serbia's Democratic Party, led by Z. Djindic, cannot attract support for a policy of equal rights for Kosovo Albanians, Vojvodina Hungarians and Sandzak Muslims. Talks have been held with the Albanian leader Rugova in Kosovo over ending of discriminatory legislation, but Serbs are suspicious, approving direct rule. However, Albania is softening its line on Kosovo (having formerly referred to the territory as the 'Other Half') because it lacks weapons and equipment to intervene and a big influx of refugees could not be handled given the small stocks of food in northern towns (Hall 1994). Meanwhile, Serbia has not been able to settle refugees from Bosnia and Croatia in Kosovo; these people are not really wanted in the Serb heartlands because of the risk of an ultra-nationalist backlash against the settlements in Bosnia and Croatia that President Milosevic has accepted. Serbs may well have to face self-determination in Kosovo in the longer term. At the very least, the international community has a responsibility, with partition as a possible outcome.

Serbia also has a regional problem in the Sandzak where Muslims used to account for more than 60 per cent of a 440,000 population; although a steady exodus to Turkey may have brought the Muslim and Serb populations roughly into balance. Once again, Serbia fears secession, though the Muslim Party of Democratic Action is split into radical and moderate factions under S. Ugljanin and R. Lajik respectively. The local economy has suffered through pervasive police activity which has affected local industry (with its strong Turkish links) and the foreign exchange market. Meanwhile, in Vojvodina the cultural landscape has been influenced by the resettlement of about 100,000 Serbs (out of a total of some 160,000) who fled Krajina after Croatia's 'Operation Storm'. Hungary is concerned about Belgrade's policy of altering Vojvodina's ethnic composition in a situation where the number of Hungarians is falling: 440,000 in 1961 but 340,000 in 1991. Since then more Hungarians have left, possibly 50,000 including draft-dodgers; this results in abandoned houses which are an almost justified target for Krajina refugees. Yet local Hungarians, led by the Association of Hungarians in Vojvodina, find it difficult to coexist with the Krajina Serbs in view of their radical political outlook. Meanwhile, the Democratic Union of Hungarians in Vojvodina seek autonomy for the Novi Sad area although the city itself now has a large Serb majority. Concern arises also from the fact that this inflow of Serbs follows an earlier transfer of some people from Hercegovina and Montenegro in the early post-war years. The earlier colonisation made it possible for Milosevic to launch his drive in 1988 to consolidate Serb control over Vojvodina and by 1990 Vojvodina's autonomy had (like Kosovo's) disappeared.

Overall, Milosevic is in a weak position since he has little to show for the war and he may be preparing a new initiative. He badly needs a new theme to replace a discredited nationalism that devastated the economy and ultimately divided the Bosnian Serbs from Belgrade. So he is anxiously looking for changes in policy appropriate to the removal of sanctions that followed the Dayton agreement. In this he should be supported by his wife M. Markovic who leads the New Left, but other parties might feel that it would be difficult to justify these decisions within Serbia because if negotiations succeed on the basis of the existing frontiers of Bosnia-Hercegovina and Croatia it raises difficult questions about the justification for war in the first place. So, an electoral alliance with opposition parties may be attempted.

### Montenegro

Despite the imposition of federal law and the appearance of pro-Serbian nationalists in cultural institutions, Montenegro, governed since 1989 by M. Bulatovic and his Democratic Party of Socialists (formerly LCY) tries to frame its own policies wherever possible. The economy has been badly hit by sanctions. Major installations like the Zeta Valley aluminium plant and the Niksic steelworks ran at one-fifth of capacity or less, while the port of Bar was almost deserted and the tourist industry virtually eliminated. Efforts were made to revive the maritime fleet, impounded by sanctions, and to establish both a national airline and bank. However, the economy suffered again through the increased vigilance by Italian customs in intercepting smuggled 'Marlboro' cigarettes from the tobacco factory in Podgorica (reverting from Titograd to its traditional name) and also through increased dependence on Romania for smuggled petrol which used to be supplied via Lake Skoder. This reduced Montenegro's capacity to withstand trade sanctions which Belgrade could always threaten in order to obtain compliance.

Talks were held with Croatia to reduce tension in the Prevlaka district which controls access to the Boka Bay naval base and the mouth of the Bay of Kotor, but Belgrade is very much in the driving seat over policy in this area (which Bosnian Serbs would dearly like to control) as well as in Kosovo and the Muslim area of the Sandzak on the Montenegran-Serbian border. Only in relations with Albania does Podgorica have a reasonably free hand, assisted by many Albanian-speaking Montenegrans. However, despite the 'Belgrade Yoke' there is more tolerance in Montenegro, less xenophobia and a stronger opposition through the parliamentary alliance (based on shared anti-communist values) of S. Perovic's Liberal Alliance of Montenegro (which draws some support from the Albanian minority and is strong in provincial centres like Bar, Cetinje and Niksic) and the People's Party of N. Kilibarda which is seeking a new referendum on the status of the country. The Montenegran autocephalous church (abolished in 1921) was restored in 1993 and support for further fighting in support of Serbs fell away as a result of the casualties in the unsuccessful battle for Dubrovnik and subservience to the Serb-dominated federal army. The ruling DPS has been losing ground and seems unlikely to gain a majority in 1996, although it could regain sufficient strength to dominate a coalition. However, an independent Montenegro under LAM leadership is a long-term possibility.

# REFERENCES

J. Allcock 1991, 'Yugoslavia' in S. White (ed.) *Handbook of Reconstruction in Eastern Europe and the Soviet Union* (London: Longman), 258–78.

W. Bartlett and J. Prasnikar 1995, 'Small firms and economic transformation in Slovenia'. *Communist Economies and Economic Transformation* 7, 83–103.

J.D. Bell 1991, 'Bulgaria' in S. White (ed.) *Handbook of Reconstruction in Eastern Europe and the Soviet Union* (London: Longman), 16–28.

A. Ben-Ner and J.M. Montias 1991, 'The introduction of markets in a hypercentralised economy: the case of Romania'. *Journal of Economic Perspectives* 5, 163–70.

A. Ben-Ner and J.M. Montias 1994, 'Economic systems reforms and privatization in Romania' in S. Estrin (ed.) *Privatization in Central and Eastern Europe* (London: Longman), 279–310.

E. Biberaj 1990, *Albania: A Socialist Maverick* (Boulder, Colorado: Westview Press).

E. Biberaj 1991, 'Albania at the crossroads'. *Problems of Communism* 40(5), 1–16.

A. Bibic 1993, 'The emergence of pluralism in Slovenia'. *Communist and Post-Communist Studies* 26, 367–86.

I. Bicanic 1991, 'Privatisation in Yugoslavia's successor states'. *Radio Free Europe/ Radio Liberty Research* 1(22), 43–9.

I. Bicanic 1993, 'Privatisation in Croatia'. *East European Politics and Societies* 7, 422–39.

I. Bicanic 1994, 'Croatia's economic stabilization process'. *Radio Free Europe/Radio Liberty Research* 3(3), 34–9.

M.Z. Bookman 1990, 'The economic basis of regional autarky in Yugoslavia'. *Soviet Studies* 42, 93–109.

D. Briggs 1993, 'Romania: on the starting blocks or running out of steam?' *Business Europa* 1(5), 7–17.

J.A. Bristow 1996, *The Bulgarian Economy in Transition* (Aldershot: Edward Elgar).

M. Calinescu and V. Tismaneanu 1991, 'The 1989 revolution and Romania's future'. *Problems of Communism* 40(1–2), 42–59.

H.F. Carey 1995, 'Irregularities or rigging: the 1992 Romanian parliamentary election'. *East European Quarterly* 29, 43–66.

L.J. Cohen 1992, *Regime Transition in a Disintegrating Yugoslavia* (Pittsburgh: University of Pittsburgh Center for Russian and East European Studies).

R. Crampton 1993, 'Bulgaria' in S. Whitefield (ed.) *The New Institutional Architecture of Eastern Europe* (London: Macmillan), 14–34.

M. Cvikl *et al.* 1993, 'Costs and benefits of independence: Slovenia'. *Communist Economies and Economic Transformation* 5, 295–316.

D. Daianu 1994. 'The changing use of disequilibria during transition: a Romanian perspective' in L. Csaba (ed.) *Privatization, Liberalization and Destruction: Recreating the Market in Central and Eastern Europe* (Aldershot: Dartmouth), 189–215.

D.G. Demekas and M.S. Khan 1991, *The Romanian Economic Reform* (Washington DC: International Monetary Fund).

A. Djilas 1991, *The Contested Country: Yugoslav Unity and Communist Revolution* (London: Harvard University Press).

D. Doder 1992, 'Albania opens the door'. *National Geographic* 182(1), 68–93.

Z. Dovenyi 1992, 'Some historical and geographical aspects of the refugee issue in Hungary' in A. Kertesz and Z. Kovacs (eds) *New Perspectives in Hungarian Geography* (Budapest: Hungarian Academy of Sciences), 171–82.

D.A. Dyker 1993a, 'Yugoslavia' in S. Whitefield (ed.) *The New Institutional Architecture of Eastern Europe* (London: Macmillan), 162–82.

D.A. Dyker 1993b, 'Rump Yugoslavia's new economic policy package'. *Radio Free Europe/Radio Liberty Research* 2(41) 33–6.

K. Engelbreckt 1994, 'Bulgarian political stalemate'. *Radio Free Europe/RadioLiberty Research* 3(25), 20–5.

J. Eyal 1993, 'Romania' in S. Whitefield (ed.) *The New Institutional Architecture of Eastern Europe* (London: Macmillan), 121–42.

B. Ferfila 1991, 'Yugoslavia: confederation or distintegration?' *Problems of Communism* 40(4), 18–30.

M.E. Fischer 1992, 'The new leaders and the opposition' in D.N. Nelson (ed.) *Romania after Tyranny* (Boulder, Colorado: Westview Press), 45–65.

T. Gallagher 1992, 'Electoral breakthrough for Romanian nationalists'. *Radio Free Europe/Radio Liberty* 1(45), 15–20.

T. Gallagher 1993, 'Ethnic tension in Cluj'. *Radio Free Europe/Radio Liberty Research* 2(9), 27–33.

T. Gallagher 1994, 'The rise of the Party of Romanian National Unity'. *Radio Free Europe/Radio Liberty Research* 3(11), 25–32.

D.R. Hall 1993, 'Albania' in F.W. Carter and D. Turnock (eds) *Environmental Problems in Eastern Europe* (London: Routledge), 7–37.

D.R. Hall 1994, *Albania and the Albanians* (London: Pinter), 173–215.

S.G. Hall and J. O'Sullivan 1994, 'Forecasting economies in transition: the case of Romania'. *Economics and Planning* 28, 175–88.

J. Harrington 1992, 'Relations between Bucharest and Washington: an overview 1945–1992'. *Revue Roumaine d'Histoire* 31, 275–89.

D. Harsanyi and N. Harsanyi 1993, 'Romania: democracy and the intellectuals'. *East European Quarterly* 27, 243–60.

D.C. Henry 1994, 'Reviving Romania's rural economy'. *Radio Free Europe/Radio Liberty Research* 3(7), 18–23.

D. Ionescu 1991a, 'Unemployment: Romania's number one social problem'. *Radio Free Europe/Radio Liberty Research* 1(22), 38–42.

D. Ionescu 1991b, 'Romania's uncertain future for economic reform'. *Radio Free Europe/Radio Liberty Research* 1(46), 36–42.

D. Ionescu 1993a, 'Romania's cabinet in search of an economic policy'. *Radio Free Europe/Radio Liberty Research* 2(4), 45–9.

D. Ionescu 1993b, 'Romania's winter of shortages'. *Radio Free Europe/Radio Liberty Research* 2(6), 45–8.

D. Ionescu 1994a, 'Romania's privatisation program: who is in charge?' *Radio Free Europe/Radio Liberty Research* 3(5), 28–34.

D. Ionescu 1994b, 'Romania adjusting to NATO's Partnership for Peace program'. *Radio Free Europe/Radio Liberty Research* 3(9), 43–7.

D. Ionescu 1994c, 'Romanian government reorganised'. *Radio Free Europe/Radio Liberty Research* 3(13), 14–9.

D. Ionescu 1994d, 'Romania's standby agreement with the IMF'. *Radio Free Europe/Radio Liberty Research* 3(18), 19–24.

D. Ionescu 1994e, 'The Crans Montana Forum conference in Bucharest'. *Radio Free Europe/Radio Liberty Research* 3(20), 37–41.

M. Isarescu 1992, 'The prognoses for economic recovery' in D.N. Nelson (ed.) *Romania after Tyranny* (Boulder, Colorado: Westview Press), 149–65.

I. Izvirski 1993, 'Economic reform in Bulgaria 1989–93'. *Communist Economies and Economic Transformation* 5, 519–32.

D.C. Jones and J. Miller 1996, *The Bulgarian Economy: Lessons for Reform During the Early Transition* (Aldershot: Avebury).

E. Kraft 1995, 'Stabilizing inflation in Slovenia, Croatia and Macedonia: how independence has affected macroeconomic policy outcomes'. *Europe Asia Studies* 47, 469–92.

S. Lefebvre 1994, 'Bulgaria's foreign relations in the post-communist era: a general overview and assessment'. *East European Quarterly* 28, 453–70

H. Lydall 1989, *Yugoslavia in Crisis* (Oxford: Clarendon Press).

L. Madzar 1993a, 'Rump Yugoslavia mired in economic problems'. *Radio Free Europe/Radio Liberty Research* 2(39), 45–9.

L. Madzar 1993b, 'The art of the impossible: economic policy in the new Yugoslavia'. *Communist Economies and Economic Transformation* 5, 331–50.

S. Markotich 1994, 'Serbia's new government'. *Radio Free Europe/Radio Liberty Research* 3(17), 8–12.

L. Mihut 1994, 'The emergence of political pluralism in Romania'. *Communist and Post Communist Societies* 27, 411–22.

N. Milanovich 1996, 'Slovenia: the new geopolitical context' in F.W. Carter and H.T. Norris (eds) *The Changing Shape of the Balkans* (London: UCL Press), 25–49.

M. Milivojevic 1991, 'Albania' in S. White (ed.) *Handbook of Reconstruction in Eastern Europe and the Soviet Union* (London: Longman), 3–14.

G. Minassian 1994, 'The Bulgarian economy in transition'. *Europe Asia Studies* 46, 337–51.

P. Moore 1994, 'Changes in the Croatian political landscape'. *Radio Free Europe/ Radio Liberty Research* 3(3), 10–5.

S. Mrdjen 1993, 'Pluralist mobilization as a catalyst for the dismemberment of Yugoslavia' in J. O'Loughlin and H. Van Der Wusten (eds) *New Political Geography of Eastern Europe* (London: Bellhaven Press), 115–31.

T. Nefedova and A. Trejvis 1994, *First Socio-economic Effects of Transformation in Central and Eastern Europe* (Vienna: Osterreichischers Ost- und Sudosteuropa-Institut).

D. Nelson (ed.) 1991, 'Romania' in S. White (ed.) *Handbook of Reconstruction in Eastern Europe and the Soviet Union* (London: Longman), 183–203.

T. Nicolaescu 1993, 'Privatization in Romania: the case for financial institutions' in D.E. Fair and R.J. Raymond (eds) *The New Europe: Evolving Economic and Financial Systems in Eastern Europe* (Dordrecht: Kluwer Academic Publishing).

A. Nicolescu 1992, 'Entrepreneurship in Romania'. *Radio Free Europe/Radio Liberty Research* 1(38), 45–50.

G. Pashko 1993, 'Obstacles to economic reform in Albania'. *Europe Asia Studies* 45, 907–21

M. Paunov 1993, 'Labour market transformation in Bulgaria'. *Communist Economies and Economic Transformation* 5, 213–28.

K. Pecsi 1989, 'The extremist path of economic development in Eastern Europe'. *Communist Economies* 1, 97–109.

D.M. Perry 1994, 'Macedonia from independence to recognition'. *Radio Free Europe/Radio Liberty Research* 3(1), 118–21.

M. Petkovski *et al.* 1993, 'Stabilization efforts in the Republic of Macedonia'. *Radio Free Europe/Radio Liberty Research* 2(3), 34–7.

G. Prevelakis 1996, 'The return of the Macedonian Question' in F.W. Carter and H.T. Norris (eds) *The Changing Shape of the Balkans* (London: UCL Press), 131–55.

S. Radosevic 1994, 'The problem of competitiveness at company level in the former socialist economies: the case of Croatia'. *Europe Asia Studies* 46, 489–503.

M. Rady 1992, *Romania in Turmoil: A Contemporary History* (London: Tauris).

S.P. Ramet 1993, 'Slovenia's road to democracy'. *Europe Asia Studies* 45, 869–86.

S.P. Ramet 1995, *Balkan Babel: The Disintegration of Yugoslavia from the Death of Tito to Ethnic War* (Boulder, Colorado: Westview Press).

M. Rojec and M. Svetlicic 1993, 'Foreign investment in Slovenia: experience, prospects and policy options'. *Communist Economies and Economic Transformation* 5, 103–14.

P. Ronnas 1991a, 'The economic legacy of Ceausescu' in O. Sjoberg and M.L. Wyzan (eds) *Economic Change in the Balkan States* (London: Pinter), 47–68.

P. Ronnas 1991b, 'Romania: ailing state firms may create a road block'. *Radio Free Europe/Radio Liberty Research* 1(17), 85–90.

S.D. Roper 1994a, 'The Romanian party system and the catch-all party phenomenenon'. *East European Quarterly* 28, 519–32.

S.D. Roper 1994b, 'The Romanian revolution from a theoretical perspective'. *Communist and Post Communist Societies* 27, 401–10.

S.L. Sampson 1987, 'Regime and society in Romania'. *International Journal of Romanian Studies* 5(1), 41–51.

P. Sandstrom and O. Sjoberg 1991, 'Albanian economic performance: stagnation in the 1990s'. *Soviet Studies* 43, 931–4.

B. Schonfelder 1993, 'Croatia between reform and post-communist populism'. *Communist Economies and Economic Transformation* 5, 317–30.

M. Shafir 1992, 'Romania's local elections herald a new political map'. *Radio Free Europe/Radio Liberty Research* 1(11), 34–31.

M. Shafir 1993a, 'Growing political extremism in Romania'. *Radio Free Europe/ Radio Liberty Research* 2(14), 18–25.

M. Shafir 1993b, 'Romania and the transition to democracy'. *Radio Free Europe/ Radio Liberty Research* 2(17), 42–8.

M. Shafir 1993c, 'The Caritas affair: a Transylvanian "Eldorado"'. *Radio Free Europe/Radio Liberty Research* 2(38), 23–7.

M. Shafir 1993d, '"A Future or Romania" Group: fish or fowl?' *Radio Free Europe/Radio Liberty Research* 2(49), 9–20.

M. Shafir 1994, 'Ethnic tension runs high in Romania', *Radio Free Europe/Radio Liberty Research* 3(32), 33–40.

M. Shafir and D. Ionescu 1993, 'Romania: political change and economic malaise'. *Radio Free Europe/Radio Liberty Research* 2(1), 108–12.

M. Shafir and D. Ionescu 1994, 'Romania: a crucially unsuccessful year'. *Radio Free Europe/Radio Liberty Research* 3(1), 122–6.

M-C Sirbu 1994, 'Towards a market economy: the Romanian effort'. *East European Quarterly* 28, 471–518.

O. Sjoberg 1994, 'Rural retention in Albania: administrative restrictions on urban-bound migration'. *East European Quarterly* 28, 205–33.

O. Sjoberg and M.L. Wyzan (eds) 1991, *Economic Crisis and Reform in the Balkans: Albania, Bulgaria, Romania and Yugoslavia Facing the 1990s* (London: Pinter).

P. Slaveykov 1995, 'A geographical analysis of the correlation between Bulgarian major political parties'. *GeoJournal* 36, 431–3.

L. Stan 1995, 'Romanian privatization: assessment of the first five years'. *Communist and Post-Communist Studies* 28, 427–35.

A. Teodorescu 1991, 'The future of a failure: the Romanian economy' in O. Sjoberg and M.L. Wyzan (eds) *Economic Change in the Balkan States* (London: Pinter), 69–82.

V. Tismaneanu 1993, 'The quasi revolution and discontents: emerging political pluralism in post-Ceausescu Romania'. *East European Politics and Societies* 7, 309–48.

L. Troxel 1992, 'Socialist persistence in the Bulgarian elections of 1990–1991'. *East European Quarterly* 26, 407–30.

P.S. Tzvetkov 1992, 'The politics of transition in Bulgaria'. *Problems of Communism* 41(3), 34–43.

Y.G. Van Frasum *et al.* 1994, 'Market economy and economic reform in Romania: macroeconomic and microeconomic perspectives'. *Europe Asia Studies* 46, 735–56.

K. Verdery and G. Kligman 1992, 'Romania after Ceausescu: post-communist communism' in I. Banac (ed.) *Eastern Europe in Revolution* (Ithaca, New York: Cornell University Press), 117–47.

I. Vriser 1992, 'Industrialization of Slovenia'. *GeoJournal* 27, 365–70.

M. Waller 1995, 'Making and breaking: factions in the process of party formation in Bulgaria' in R. Gillespie *et al.* (eds) *Factional Politics and Democratization* (London: Frank Cass), 152–67.

M.C. Wyzan 1993, 'Monetary independence and macroeconomic stabilisation in Macedonia: an initial assessment'. *Communist Economies and Economic Transformation* 5, 351–68.

L. Zanga 1993, 'Albania moves closer to the Islamic world'. *Radio Free Europe/Radio Liberty Research* 2(7), 28–31.

L. Zanga 1994a, 'Albania optimistic about economic growth'. *Radio FreeEurope/ Radio Liberty Research* 3(7), 14–17.

L. Zanga 1994b, 'Albanian statistics filling the information void'. *Radio Free Europe/Radio Liberty Research* 3(10), 36–9.

E. Zizmond 1992, 'The collapse of the Yugoslav economy'. *Soviet Studies* 44, 101–12.

E. Zizmond 1993, 'Slovenia: one year after independence'. *Europe Asia Studies* 45, 887–945.

I. Zloch-Christy 1996, *Bulgaria in a Time of Change: Economic and Political Dimensions* (Aldershot: Avebury).

# 7

# RESTRUCTURING IN AGRICULTURE AND INDUSTRY

Agriculture and industry constituted the core of production under communism, since services were hardly valued positively as a means of wealth creation apart from international tourism. There was a massive transfer of labour from agriculture to industry, which achieved rapid rates of growth and attracted the lion's share of the investments made under central planning. Agriculture was widely seen as a 'problem' because plan targets were often missed. Yet farm production increased considerably and the low cost inputs (labour, fertilisers, energy, etc.), along with price subsidies, brought about a high level of intensification which is clearly not being maintained under the transition. Major structural changes are now taking place and industry has lost its privileged position. There is plenty of scope for comparative farming and industry studies to highlight privatisation/restitution arrangements and the role of central government agencies, local authorities and local officials (Turnock 1996). The situation is highly complex, with substantial variations in the thrust of legislation between countries (Braverman *et al.* 1993; Swinnen 1994). Privatisation is taking place and the removal of price controls should stimulate the private farmer in the long run, although for the moment low real wage levels limit the demand for food and some remaining price controls exaggerate the 'price scissors' that sees costs of manufactured goods (including fertiliser and farm machinery) increasing more rapidly than the value of agricultural produce (Brooks *et al.* 1991).

## AGRICULTURE: STRUCTURAL CHANGE

Much greater structural change has occurred in agriculture than in any other sector thanks to the widespread adoption of policies of land 'restitution' to former owners and 'distribution' to the farm workers and the rural population in general (Brooks and Lerman 1994). Both measures were politically necessary, although to differing degrees across the region. Conceptually the restoration of ownership rights enhances the social status of many rural dwellers through a process of 'reagrarisation' and 'embourgoisement' (Manchin and Szelenyi 1985) and it thereby rejects the Stalinist revolutionary

261

ethos (reacting to the aberrations of capitalism) as the conventional road for Eastern Europe. Instead of 'collectivisation' to neutralise the rich peasants (kulaks) and simplify the command structure, the evolutionary process towards a democracy based on ownership of property is resumed after an interruption. However, a selective rediscovery of entrepreneurship in Hungary (Juhasz 1991) leaves open the question whether land should continue to be worked in large units by reformed cooperatives as opposed to small family farms. Where there are good non-agricultural opportunities and perceived benefits through shared use of machinery, cooperation is more likely. Where there are fewer opportunities and labour-intensive agriculture is the main option then individual operation may be preferred. An extreme example of this strategy is hobby farming on very small pieces of land; a development that has been described as 'deagrarisation' (Pavlin 1991).

## Cooperatives

The cooperative farms have also undergone a great change with the removal of the political pressure which was almost entirely responsible for their creation after the Second World War (Csaki and Lerman 1993). Although some form of cooperation is obviously necessary for small farmers, the right to ultimate autonomy over finance and decision-making is naturally desired. There were variations in the extent to which cooperative members exercised control under communism and in FCSFR cooperative members owned their own land and received rents, although the cooperatives asserted the primacy of land users over landowners. But now the owners' interests will have priority and cooperatives are being transformed into Western-style organisations, with some complete breakups and defections by individual members (Swain 1992a). On the other hand, where ownership rights passed to the cooperatives under communism, restitution is now under way. Thinking about optimum farm structures involves values concerning the individual and the community, and the extent of government intervention. It is also central to the wider political debate in which the right wing supports private ownership, a market system and only limited state intervention while the left seeks a continuing role for the cooperatives in the context of an eco-social market economy and heightened government involvement.

Former communist political opinion close to the cooperatives was, of course, against compensation for former owners seeking to retain cooperative farms with only limited leasing of marginal land. Economic efficiency goals might also point to retention of cooperatives with only limited opting out. On the other hand, advocates of 'natural justice' called for full and direct restitution, and the demise of the cooperatives and the principle of restitution became widely implemented due to the pressure of new parties embracing the family farm ideal as a means of bringing a new entrepreneurial stratum into the countryside. The debate has therefore moved on to other issues: will restitution be full or partial; and will it be direct (returning exactly what was lost) or indirect, through allocation of alternative property or financial compensation? Restitution rights vary considerably, although there is a general preference to support smallholders rather than large landowners like the Junker owners in former Prussian territory. In the FGDR, those expropriated through collectivisation since 1953 have got their land back, but not the owners of farms of over 100ha expropriated in 1945 for land reform (though test cases are pending).

Poland has not allowed restitution in cases where peasants were intimidated into selling land to the state at symbolic prices; whereas Hungarian legislation seeks to address this problem. Kulak farms in FCSFR can also be reclaimed under restitution: even small estates of some 300ha. Land reform legislation is often a matter of dispute between political parties and a reluctance to restore substantial holdings to former owners generates uncertainty. In order to enable the largest number of former peasant proprietors to benefit, in addition to realising the distribution of half-hectare holdings to all rural dwellers, Romania's government has imposed a maximum of 10ha (arable equivalent) whereas the opposition Democratic Convention would allow 50ha and thereby accommodate former estate owners (Kideckel 1992). The 10ha limit could be justified in terms of equity but 'its effect was to preclude the recreation of a viable propertied middle class in agriculture, one that might exert certain kinds of pressure on the state' (Verdery 1994, p.1076). The return of woodlands expropriated under nationalisation is also a major issue in mountain regions. Further, there are variations in procedures to turn restitution rights into physical property. In Hungary there has been bidding at land auctions on the basis of vouchers (of value commensurate with each claim) and in respect of land that cooperatives are obliged to make available for restitution claims. Since the price of land has varied according to the value of vouchers being exchanged, supply and demand has been accommodated. On the other hand, in Romania there are no such price mechanisms and despite great flexibility it is simply not possible to meet all claims. Surveys carried out in 500 villages reveal that 25 per cent of salaried farm workers (on state farms and elsewhere) have no land while 26 per cent have less than 1ha; 38 per cent have between 1–3ha; 19 per cent have 3–5ha, and 14 per cent have 5–10ha (Henry 1994).

The net result is that land has been transferred to people who are often too old to farm it, or to heirs in the towns who cannot use the land efficiently. One expert has said that 'there is something perverse' in arrangements that devolve ownership 'to those that are not in a position to farm and for whom the realities of agricultural production are alien' (Swain 1992b, p.17). But there is a strong moral argument in favour of restitution and there is no reason why land allocated to town dwellers should not be worked on a sharecropping basis by people permanently resident in the countryside. In Bulgaria, there are areas where most of the people with claims to land live in towns, while people drafted in by the cooperative management to work the land now find themselves ineligible to own land. In Hungary one-fifth of the land has been allocated on the basis of work performed for the cooperative. Indeed, in Hungary, restitution was initially seen as controversial and less than a quarter of Hungarians thought that land should revert to the pre-communist owners. Ethical fine tuning was needed to balance the injustice of expropriation under communism with the unfairness of leaving people employed by the co-operatives (including many Gypsies in Romania and Turks in Bulgaria) without a significant stake in the land on account of compensation to people living in the towns with little aptitude for farming.

Structural change has also been very disruptive. In parts of Romania peasants unilaterally took over their land and cooperatives therefore collapsed. Despite some attempt at restraint by the police the government recognised the revolutionary nature of the action and framed their restitution programme in order to bring almost all the land seizures within the law; a shrewd political move because it ensured overwhelming support for the government in the rural areas over an opposition which championed restitution in the first place, but on a scale that might have provided for larger estate holdings in conflict with peasant ethos. Where the peasants have waited for the state to act, redistribution has often been slow, with long delays in the issue of definitive titles. Uncertainty has resulted in some land not being worked at all during the year of policy implementation. Moreover, co-ordination which previously operated over quite large areas has collapsed and in Romania irrigation schemes which formerly depended on joint management by cooperative and state farms have broken down. Some specialised stock-rearing units have been divorced from their fodder supplies: in Bulgaria, where socialist farming organisations were dismantled by liquidation committees in 1991, it was not uncommon in the livestock sector for fodder production units to be sold off before the animals were disposed of and for animals to be transferred to small farmers before land was provided for them to be kept on. Moreover, reorganisation of agriculture frequently went ahead on the assumption that peasants are keen to become independent farmers and sever contacts with the cooperatives of the past. For some cooperative systems give poor returns and so provide a motive for private farming (Repassy and Symes 1993). In FGDR, 'Bavarian' attitudes in government have favoured small farms and Treuhand has had only small milk quotas for many of the farms it has been trying to sell off.

Many people receiving land have chosen to retain a system of cooperation, for ownership of small parcels does not preclude leasing or sharecropping arrangements to create larger business units. Thus while Hungary has 5mn.ha owned by some 2.0mn. separate owners, two-thirds of this area is actually worked in the context of large farm structures although further consolidation into functional units is constrained by the lack of a land market and of finance for purchase. So, in practice, compromise has provided for partial restitution (combining the direct and indirect options) and cooperatives are continuing on a reduced scale where the membership so desires. Yet even where cooperatives remain, there is much leasing of land and buildings to businesses which are now run separately (often by companies or by private farmers previously prominent in the cooperative organisation who have decided to opt out). Farming companies rent 97.1 per cent of their land; while other private farms over 100ha rent 85 per cent (with a proportion of two-thirds for all non-company private farms). Altogether, farming companies now occupy 17.1 per cent of the farmland in the Czech Republic and other private farms 18.2 per cent. It is also possible to lease land from state farms which have seen their share of land worked fall from 25.3 to 15.3 per cent.

Yet there is a clear trend towards private farming because, as in Western Europe, there are no overwhelming economic advantages in favour of really large holdings. In the Czech Republic the cooperative share of the total agricultural land fell from 61.4 per cent in 1989 to 49.4 per cent in 1993 and the downward trend continues. There are already very wide size variations for private farms in Eastern Europe because of the choice between farming companies running estates and viable family farms which can employ people full-time and justify ownership of machinery. Some may reach 900ha (with owning and leasing) while others may fall into the 50–100ha range, with the smallest below 5ha. Farms over 100ha (some comprising small estates recovered through restitution in FCS) are particularly rational for the use of machines, but 30–70ha farms can also be viable, specialising in grain and sunflowers. However, mixed 'nostalgia farming' on 15–30ha restitution holdings is satisfactory in the long term, although it may be most suitable for middle-aged people with income from other jobs and access to basic machinery. Strategies seem to vary with age but all peasant households are trying to make rational decisions. Holdings of 10ha can be rewarding where machinery may be acquired cheaply (second-hand from Germany with loans obtained through local contacts) and where crops such as hops can be grown. Machinery and fertilisers are critical areas in view of the high cost of credit but some private farmers have been able to lease land and machinery from the state farms.

Restitution to former landowners means that many of the new owners live in the towns and may only be able to work their small plots of one or two hectares at weekends using traditional methods. At the same time, increasing areas are being taken over by people who want to use rural land for non-agricultural purposes as part of a suburbanising trend, including gardening and hobby farming by the owners of weekend cottages and by younger people from the towns who seek an escape from unemployment in small-scale farming. Pavlin (1991) describes this activity as 'deagrarisation' (rather than 'reagrarisation') because it lies outside conventional farming. Hobby farming should not be despised: not only can there be a useful combination of agriculture and other activities, but farming may recruit talented young people from the towns who may be able to take over holdings owned by fathers or even grandfathers.

A critical issue for the future is the emergence of skilled full-time farmers working viable holdings. The new private farmers may be professional people who played a leading role in the cooperatives and now take full advantage of their skills and contacts. Former managers are well placed to become 'nomenclature farmers' in the event of cooperatives becoming bankrupt. While trying to get good returns for shareholders, they are often ready to acquire property in the event of collapse. They often take over cooperative buildings (an option that is also available to any private farmers when there is surplus space available) because it would be irrational to build in small peasant courtyards. Other qualified professionals may have the confidence to enter farming on their own account. An agronomist may lease cooperative land and provide repair services for agricultural machines (perhaps with an agreement to safeguard jobs in the former cooperative workshops). But there are also cases of partnerships between peasants with complementary skills and who lease state farmland in Poland, with the possibility of buying it at a later stage when restitution issues have been resolved (Harcsa 1993). They may also rent machines (with the intention to buy later if they can) or purchase outright through down payments of one-fifth of the price and instalments for the rest over seven years. Good relations between local peasant families will accelerate the process of putting together small units of land ownership in larger functional units with a pooling of machines and labour. This may happen irrespective of whether the units of ownership derive from existing farms, restitution holdings, land taken out of cooperatives or acquisitions arising through vouchers.

Several factors seem likely to tip the scales in favour of the professionals or alternatively the peasantry (Rose and Tikhomirov 1993). Cooperative leaders are in a strong position when farms are declared bankrupt because of superior knowledge about markets and other aspects of the farming business (Pryor 1992). They can exploit their monopoly of power and information to obtain the best property to launch their own private farm and some might even hasten the bankruptcy scenario. Where cooperatives are very large (including several village communities), the leaders have great informational advantages over the dispersed membership. The leaders are also in a good position where members may be primarily concerned with the working of their own small vineyards: since they have little knowledge of other enterprises and markets they may be happy to leave the technocrats to take over the cooperative buildings and machinery. There are also advantages where the leaders have had the trust of members for successful management in the past, where they live in nearby towns and are not so exposed to close scrutiny in the countryside, and where unemployment makes local workers more dependent on the cooperative management. When the markets are distant and known only to the leaders, their field of action is correspondingly enhanced;

also, where the members are poorly educated and where women are preponderant. Unfavourable historical circumstances such as a high rate of servitude may also have a bearing. And a high level of commuting under communism – leaving the younger people as 'dead hands' at farming – can also weaken the peasants' ability to safeguard their interests.

On the other hand, family solidarity can strengthen the peasants' position and result in farms based on kinship ties or informal networks. Skilled rural workers may have connections through workshop industries which can be beneficial in joint farming and encourage group withdrawal from the cooperative, taking with them an appropriate mix of assets. Tractor drivers can work together on a private farm with the skills to drive and maintain machines. Expertise in agricultural engineering (coping with FSU machines, making spare parts and handling fertilisers and pesticides) may be complemented by wives' knowledge of finance and accounting. People who did well in farming under the communist reforms (for example, in poultry rearing) may have capital to buy land. All these scenarios are more likely to emerge in a well-integrated village community, without too much commuting to divert younger people away from agriculture. It is also important to have a village environment which approves of private enterprise. Perhaps a history of family farming is important. Yet while there could be a return to a family farming tradition after restitution of substantial farms of 200–300ha, descendants of successful pre-communist farmers rarely resume a farming career. Transfer of entrepreneurial values usually occurs outside agriculture, so the continuity theme is weak.

### Reorganisation in the northern countries

Cooperative farm systems were present in FCS, the FGDR and Hungary. Despite orthodox management which inhibited the full use of all the land and labour resources, they offered satisfactory returns, boosted by the additional production from private plots. Restitution and other reforms could now increase uncertainty (Ash 1992), for 'it is naive to expect people who have worked for up to 30 years as operatives in a large production organisation to suddenly become entrepreneurs' (Swain 1992a, p.9). This point is all the more evident in view of limited finance which has been allocated to structural change. So, there is considerable interest in retaining the cooperative system with new 'friendly' structures to replace the highly centralised cooperatives which emerged under communism and with some reduction in labour. In FGDR there is a strong desire to retain the principle of cooperation despite the Bavarian attitude of government that favoured family farms. 'Thus the survival and dominance of large scale cooperatives and farm companies can be said to be despite rather than because of federal government policy' (Wilson 1996, p.160). Alternatively, land could be taken over by partnerships, farming companies or family farms and there is no doubt that interest in private farming is increasing (Young 1993).

Private farming survived under communism on the high ground in Moravia; also in Czech Silesia where the holdings were small and the owners could not be intimidated as kulaks. On the fertile plains private farms were marginalised under communism but some have made a comeback since 1989 because the cooperative members retained land ownership and they can now withdraw at any time in the future (an option which is not possible in a joint stock situation). The cooperative strategy is attractive where the prospects are particularly uncertain, for example, on poor land where agriculture was formerly protected by subsidies (Hudecova and Lostak 1992). Yet the revamped cooperatives no longer have the guarantee of state support and there is always the possibility of bankruptcy if the business is not efficiently run. Embarrassed by debts, cooperatives may have to shed labour and they may eventually collapse altogether. And where they succeed, there is uncertainty over non-agricultural enterprises that may have to close or be transferred to private management. So, it is likely that increasing numbers of small owners will negotiate to take their land out of cooperative management. Of the 52,003 private farms in the Czech Republic in 1993, 53.6 per cent were smaller than 1.0ha and 28.5 per cent were between 1ha and 10ha; while 9.8 per cent were between 10 and 30ha, with 8.1 per cent larger than 30ha. Elderly people and the unemployed are often active on 1–5ha holdings. They produce their own food on small farms, although the small plots are not suitable for livestock.

In Hungary, the cooperatives were particularly successful under communism with 'socialist wage labour', social security and pension rights. Moreover, the farm managers enjoyed considerable autonomy and were able to enter into various arrangements whereby the resources of the cooperative could be used to maximise output from private plots and keep the urban consumer well supplied. The cooperatives attracted young, capable people into management (Swain 1985) and under the New Economic Mechanism private enterprise in farming was closely tied to the equipment and marketing system available to cooperative farms. Thus many country dwellers were active in both the first and second economies which gave them higher living standards and some independence of workplace managers (Persanyi 1990). It is also argued that, despite rising unemployment since the revolution and a fall in incomes, the prospect of an independent smallholding is made unattractive by lack of equipment and business experience (Toth 1992). But the policies of the transition have tended to undermine the cooperatives, because of the disproportionate influence of the ideologically motivated Smallholders Party providing crucial support for the Antall government coalition (Swain 1993c). The Smallholders' Party pressed strongly for a land restitution programme so that beneficiaries might build up viable holdings by a combination of purchase (through vouchers) and by leasing additional land, perhaps from private owners who are urban dwellers and unable to work the land without the complication of commuting.

The law of 1992 gave Hungarian cooperatives a year to decide between three options: (1) to maintain the cooperative, with involvement in purchasing and marketing as well as production; (2) to transform the cooperative into a shareholding company (including shares to outsiders), (3) or to divide the property between the members (Meszaros 1994). Nevertheless, Swain (1993b, p.12) argues that cooperatives should still be actively promoted: 'they have the potential to initiate a cycle of economic growth which might develop more quickly than waiting for the rich farmer to buy out the poor farmer; and dispossessed poor farmers to migrate to the town and swell the urban homeless unemployed.' In 1995 more than 400 of Hungary's 1,300 cooperatives were still functioning, many of them still managed by people who had been in charge through much of the communist period (not just highly qualified people who had moved in during the 1980s). On the other hand, S. Elek (1991) asserts that part-time farming in Hungary is more specialised, modernised and market-oriented than in other parts of Eastern Europe. This is because the last two decades of agricultural policy have given the peasants more market experience and trading skills which will be advantageous in the rebuilding of family farming (Harcsa 1993; Kovach 1991). Moreover, the cooperatives cannot easily maintain the small non-agricultural ventures established under regimes of subsidy to make a very significant contribution to rural employment at the time (Klekner 1992). As in FCS, many of these ancillary ventures have been closed in order to stave off bankruptcy (Varga 1996).

### Reorganisation in the northern countries: the case of Poland

Individual peasant farming was relatively well established and there are nearly a million farms smaller than 5.0ha. Farms still operate a traditional mixed system with a range of different crops and animals (Morgan 1989a, 1989b). Small 'resource-deprived' private farms work 76.5 per cent of the land and supply 76.7 per cent of the production; but they employ 85.3 per cent of the labour while using fertiliser per hectare at only 56 per cent of the state/cooperative sector rate (Klodzinski 1992, p.131). Despite state subsidies for loans to farmers, the use of fertilisers and pesticides remains low (Morgan 1990). Only 250,000 Polish farms are truly commercial but there are a million more on the verge of profitability (for the moment they do not invest and can only maintain what they have). But the restructuring of holdings, with some shedding of labour, is being held back by a return of labour to the land as a result of the decline in industrial production. At the same time a high level of self-sufficiency (increasing since the end of the 1980s) is reducing the countryside to 'an economic and social ghetto' (Morgan 1992, p.147) as worker-farmers fall back on incomes from their small farms alone. This is not good for the food industry over the long term (Mazurski 1991; Pilichowski 1993).

The solution to the problem of labour-shedding in large industries must lie with new factories in the countryside and rural diversification generally. As in other countries, the social problems of agriculture must be solved in the context of a wider social policy. However, there are wide variations in the patterns of choice between part-time farming with ancillary employment and a total separation of agricultural and non-agricultural employment. In the mountains, comparisons emerge between the villages around Jelenia Gora in the Sudeten Mountains, where interest in agriculture is clearly flagging after the demographic upheavals of the post-war era and where considerable areas of lands lie neglected, and those lands around Novy Targ and Zakopane in the Tatra Mountains south of Krakow where agriculture is still valued as a way of life. Here, agriculture is by no means the sole source of income but it is a significant contributor to the budget of extended families which may also be active in manufacturing and tourism. The concept of the 'tourist village' is well illustrated in this area. Such villages have maintained higher rates of population growth than other villages in the Polish Carpathians. They show a reduced level of out-migration by women; and they have more people of productive age. They also have a better infrastructure in terms of commercial and cultural facilities; and above all they show abundant evidence of new house-building including houses of large capacity which can offer rooms to tourists as well as family accommodation for three generations. Tourism integrates closely with agriculture in that catering for visitors can provide an additional outlet for farm produce.

### Restructuring in the Balkan countries

In Romania, most people have insisted on the return of family land at its former site or *vechile amplasamente*. The historic political parties initiated a powerful campaign for restitution which the Salvation Front government probably did not anticipate, but the claims of those who had been both expropriated and imprisoned created a major anti-communist reaction (Verdery 1994, p.1075). Meanwhile, 0.5ha plots were granted where there was land in excess of claims by former owners of up to a maximum of 10ha (arable equivalent); but land commissions might 'create' land by subtracting a fixed percentage from the new holdings of former owners. Even so, because of the demand for a finite amount of land and the complications of illegal occupations and ownership disputes, the restitution process has moved very slowly in some areas. Delay has also arisen through shortcomings in the work of local and county commissions, a lack of surveyors and, in some areas, a lack of adequate documentation. However, a new farm structure is emerging which contrasts continued cooperation (through associations) in lowland areas with a more independent approach, linked with pluriactivity, in the hill and mountain zones. In arable farming areas the complete breakdown of cooperatives is prevented by the lack of machinery on individual farms since there is only one tractor for every sixty-two new landowners (Henry 1994). However, there are some individual farms in the lowlands where the logic 'derives from the availability of adequate family labour, development of intensive farming enterprises and the possibility of substituting animal power (with organic fertiliser) for farm machinery and chemical fertilisers' (Bordanc 1996, p.164).

In the Romanian Carpathians, where the experience with the old co-operatives was particularly difficult, there is certainly a strong desire for independence, and the vested interests of a few families with salaried employment have been insufficient to retain the old organisation. In the mountains peasants have unilaterally reoccupied their ancestral lands (with exchanges where new buildings create complications) and the state has validated this process to the extent of allowing each family restitution of up to a maximum of 10ha. The old cooperative farm buildings often lie abandoned and there are some cases of demolition so that building materials can be salvaged for a variety of purposes. At Suciu de Sus in the northern county of Maramures, demolition occurred in 1991 so that the materials could be used to build a monastery nearby. There can be no doubt about the enthusiasm of many peasants experiencing the euphoria of retrieving their land. Young men from Maramures who previously took seasonal work with woodcutting enterprises are now devoting more time to farming with the result that timber harvesting targets are not being met because of labour shortages. There is some enthusiasm for livestock rearing and there could be good prospects for an increase in the numbers of animals if individual peasants are prepared to collect hay from remote areas which were too expensive for the old cooperative managements to use.

As in Poland, the peasants who find themselves free to plan their own activities tend to concentrate heavily on self-sufficiency in view of the shortcomings of the marketing system at present. The collapse of the cooperatives has meant that there may be no immediate buyer for farm produce (the private buyers who once took the grain surpluses were of course eliminated by the previous communist revolution). So there is scope for small businesses to take care of various aspects of marketing and bulk-buying; also for crop spraying, combine harvesting and butter production (using local milk surpluses). This ensures ample supplies of food for peasant households (with surpluses which pass to family members through private deals) but limits supply to the open market. Only when confidence in the market is restored will there be a stimulus for investment and improvement of infrastructure. Small farms may not be a good basis for future efficiency, so perhaps kinship or neighbourhood arrangements may eventually be made to cope with groups of small, scattered holdings where it is necessary to make long journeys on foot, carrying simple tools to carry out routine tasks. In the mountains, peasants have also to cope with the depredations of wild animals which they are forbidden to hunt.

In Bulgaria privatisation has made slow progress although cooperatives were formally abandoned in 1992 (Buckwell *et al.* 1994; Davidova 1994). Despite forecasts that the restitution process would be completed by the end of 1993 the process extended well into 1995. However, production should pick up when definitive titles have been distributed and a land market can develop (Wyzan and Sjoberg 1992). Shortages of seed, fertiliser and machinery have persisted. Farming in general has become less scientific and there is a general lack of business skills and understanding of a market economy. Only 6 per cent of landholders are thinking of setting up in farming on their own account given the small size of holding and the part-time nature of farming; also the element of inertia deriving from the availability of a cooperative system which 'deprives owners from more long term thinking' about future land markets (Davidova 1994, p.48). Younger farmers are more forward-looking, but there is still a widespread fear of the future and a reluctance to make decisions. Thus farmers who have inherited vineyards, established with regard for Bulgaria's special position for viticulture under Comecon, are not always keen to maintain such an enterprise (Dobreva 1994). They may lease the land to other farmers interested only in the quantity of production, with the result that the production of quality Bulgarian wine is affected. Meanwhile, new cooperatives are taking shape. At Souhindol in central Bulgaria where a cooperative was first created in 1909, the new owners have revamped an organisation that now includes a bakery, a meat-processing plant and vineyards. Vriser (1993) also sees great problems of adjustment for Slovene farmers, a leading class in the inter-war years marginalised by expropriation under communism. Many young people left the land, but now the restitution process is leading to further uncertainty among the 'social farming estates' and cooperatives. In Slovenia's private sector, as elsewhere, there are too many small farmers and not enough holdings that can provide full-time work. Some 5.2 per cent of the land falls to farms smaller than 1ha, while another 35.4 per cent of the land is occupied by farms of between 1 and 5ha, with the additional problem of fragmentation. The smaller holdings call for ancillary employment but this is difficult to find on a permanent basis (Bojnec 1994).

Adjustment is evident in Albania with the abandonment of communist policies of strong rural and upland bias (Zanga 1994). In 1989 brigade ownership of stock was allowed and cooperatives were permitted to sell on open markets. There was also encouragement of private plots on which peasants could rear cattle. But now Albania's 425,000ha of cooperative farmland have been converted into 315,000 private farms and four-fifths of the state farmland has been privatised. Allocating land to the people who were working it (with allowance for the size of each family) was fundamental to peasant support for the new order in Albania (Pata and Osmani 1994).

However, where mountain villages were previously supported by flour deliveries which allowed population to rise way beyond the local agricultural potential (with the local baker a key political figure), there is often insufficient land to support the enlarged communities. So there has been out-migration, with keen competition for farmland as people from the north move to better land near urban areas of Albania. Three years of drought have undermined self-sufficiency in cereals. The 1992 harvest was estimated at 250,000t. when 950,000t were required. The fact that stock breeders want to build up herds means that there are fewer animals for slaughter. Reduction of subsidies is in line with IMF policy of removing wage subsidies and price controls (though with ceilings for bread, cooking oil and sugar).

## The state farms

Many different options are being selected to deal with the relatively highly capitalised state farms (Burger 1993). One viable solution is to transfer the land to large private farming companies: for example, Agrargesellschaften in the FGDR where some are now doing well and where they have good soils suitable for high quality production (such as cereals for brewing) and management has been skilled enough to carry out reorganisation. State farms are being retained in Romania, even where former owners were expropriated by decree. In such cases the interested parties will only receive shares in a farming company and not a land allocation. Moreover, Romanians have found that one way to solve the problem of insufficient land to satisfy restitution claims is to transfer the claim to state farms where it is not necessary for local land commissions to allocate a holding but merely to provide a share of the production, making the financial share-out increasingly fragmented. Thus between 1991 and 1994 Romanian state farms 'became veritable rubber sacks, their capacities stretched in some cases well beyond those implied by the farms' actual surfaces' (Verdery 1994, p.1081). However, retention of large farms may encourage foreign capital, as in Hungary which has some particularly fertile land and a tradition of progressive farming with a relatively favourable structure. However, while buyers may obtain ninety-year leases on large holdings of some 20,000ha (with irrigation facilities and the potential for high-quality dairy and vegetable production) there is also the possibility of obtaining land in smaller blocks (preferably in the range of 800–1,500ha) which will provide viable holdings for individual private farmers with scope for further job creation. In one case the takeover is being linked with a food-processing park and greater tourist provision (including a hotel and facilities for horse riding, golf, shooting and swimming). Employment could eventually exceed the level under the old management (Juhasz 1991).

However, twenty-four of the largest and most technically advanced state farms in Hungary were initially kept in state hands to ensure that expertise in key areas (seed production and maintenance of livestock breeds) would not be dissipated. But the integrated sharecropping cooperatives are required to maintain the biological/genetic base under strict market conditions. One of these key centres is Babolna State Farm which dates back to a Habsburg initiative of 1796: the farm breeds Arab stallions, has a chicken-breeding venture with Arbor Acres of USA, supplies beef and chicken to McDonald's and has trading contacts with FSU, the Middle East and Latin America. Meanwhile, the former Komarom state farm is now a state-owned integrated shareholding cooperative working 5,000ha of arable (1,400ha rented), 800ha of vineyards and an additional area of pasture. This former state farm emerged from the amalgamation of three separate units, although the total area is now somewhat reduced from the level of 6,400ha of arable and employment has been halved from 1,600 to 800. There is high-yield wheat production, dairying, pig-breeding, meat-packing (which draws in pigs from elsewhere and involves some imported meat) and wine-processing. A major market consists of meat which is exported (especially to FSU) and also distributed domestically through the central warehouses of shopping chains. The farm is rationalising its equipment in the context of a vigorous market for second-hand machines. However, the financial situation is insecure, although the remaining state interest could be sold through a share option available for employees at a favourable price.

Another option is piecemeal transfer through restitution or through selling and leasing. In Bulgaria, state farms were broken up so quickly that breeding stock had to be slaughtered when they could not readily be absorbed by small peasant farms. In Poland too there is a policy of piecemeal transfer of state farms to the private sector. Solidarity governments showed a strong interest in privatisation and hence the decision that a State Agricultural Property Agency (SAPA), operating from fifteen regional offices, should administer the State Land Fund, comprising the state farms and also the private holdings of elderly farmers in return for old age pensions. Ideally, leasing or selling units of around 600ha would make a useful contribution to the structure of Polish farming. But progress has been slow in terms of both selling and leasing such land as well as privatising houses. Yet many jobs have been lost in the process since it was deemed preferable to pay welfare benefits than to support unprofitable state farms. Election results in Poland (and elsewhere) from 1993 show that it is politically desirable to place more emphasis on protecting jobs.

The interest in privatisation might be expected to be greatest in former Prussian territories where peasants became freeholders at the beginning of the nineteenth century. However, most of this area constitutes the 'Recovered Territories' where the Germans were expelled and the population largely replaced after 1945 and where state farms were necessarily created in those areas that were not fully resettled. There is less commitment to agriculture than in the more demographically stable parts of the country and younger women especially seem determined to extricate themselves from a small farm lifestyle. Partitioning state farmland may well depend on movement of population back into rural districts of the Recovered Territories. Turning to other parts of the country, it seems that in the corridor lands of inter-war Poland there have been relatively high levels of selling (3.4 per cent of land sold compared with 1.7 per cent in the country as a whole) and leasing (45 per cent of all arable compared with 28 per cent nationally); although it still leaves a large area available.

The Poles had hoped to complete the disposal of state farms by the end of 1995 but this proved to be over-optimistic since the less attractive pieces (left over at the end) were not easily disposed of and the process may not be completed until the end of the decade. Some problems have arisen through delay in drawing up regulations for the land auctions and other transactions. But the main difficulties have been financial. The SAPA requires one-fifth initial payment for sale of land and the balance over three years at a subsidised interest rate of 10 per cent, with similar arrangements for livestock and equipment. But few people have capital to buy land and there is a lack of state funding to help small peasant farmers extend their holdings. There are also difficult financial questions over the provision of additional access roads and buildings that will be needed. Misuse of foreign loans under communism makes government wary of using borrowed money to carry out restructuring operations that will not be directly productive. Another aspect of the situation concerns Poles who lost land in the east when the FSU modified its frontiers in 1945. There is a political argument that they should be compensated through the handing over of state farmland. However, the people affected seem to be more interested in financial compensation than in receiving land in the north and west of the country.

## AGRICULTURE: PRODUCTION, MARKETING AND FINANCE

Agriculture has adapted more readily to the transition than industry, through decline in output in the early 1990s (Table 7.1) and a more simplified enterprise pattern; because fundamentally it 'had no possibility to avoid pressures from reform' (Kraus *et al.* 1994, p.125). Throughout the region there has been a decline in production due to the removal of food subsidies and consequent reduction in demand which, in turn, has discouraged investment. A dip in cereal output, linked with some increased trade dependence, is indicated in Table 7.2. An added problem has been the 'price scissors' for farmers, with prices rising faster for manufactures than for agricultural commodities at farm gate prices. For Hungarian farmers the increases in their cash income have been much smaller than the rising cost of farm inputs: by between a half and one-third if tractors and fertilisers are considered. In Poland there were difficulties because of overall economic policy changes, beginning with the free market for food in 1989. The hyperinflation in Poland in 1989–90 was followed by stabilisation measures which, in conjunction with the withdrawal of food subsidies, obliged consumers to spend higher proportions of household income on food. But due to the prominence of trading companies, market prices increased much more than prices paid to farmers: large farms and processors have benefited from free prices but small farmers have not. Thus farm incomes have not even kept pace with the rise in retail prices for agricultural products. Pressure became more intense with lower subsidies in 1990 and steep rises in energy prices that reduced spending on food. Reduced demand led to lower nutrition standards, while lower income for farmers reduced their demand for manufactures. Until the late 1980s per capita income from farming on small farms was higher than income outside agriculture; but in 1991–3 incomes from farming were 20 per cent lower.

*Table 7.1* Percentage change in agricultural production 1993–6

| Country | 1993 | 1994 | 1995 | 1996[1] | 1997[1] |
| --- | --- | --- | --- | --- | --- |
| Bulgaria | −18.1 | 10.8 | 16.3 | 2.0 | 3.0 |
| The Czech Republic | −0.8 | −2.5 | 4.2 | 3.5 | 3.0 |
| Hungary | −14.7 | 3.0 | 0.0 | 2.0 | 3.0 |
| Poland | 2.4 | −10.7 | 16.1 | −7.0 | 6.0 |
| Romania | 12.4 | 3.0 | 4.9 | 3.0 | 3.0 |
| Slovakia | −12.0 | −3.0 | −8.8 | 3.0 | 3.0 |

*Note* 1 Estimate.
*Source*: Economist Intelligence Unit

Hungary has reported a reduction in consumption of meat and dairy products of 30–40 per cent (with bread becoming a more prominent element in the diet); though levels are expected to rise as the economy improves. The number of pigs has halved due to reduced home consumption and reduced exports. Hungary's cattle population has reduced from 1.25mn. to 0.78mn. and 0.60mn. is likely in the future. Inputs of fertiliser, irrigation water and machinery have been reduced. Reduced stocking in Hungary means farm losses leading to the curtailment of investment and sale of land; reduced labour (with further reductions likely in the future) and fertiliser inputs. Fertiliser use in Poland decreased from 200 to 70kg/ha, with a ten-fold decrease in agrochemicals. Thus, real farm income levels were only maintained by 'a tendency for the extensification of farming operations in the face of declining profitability and market uncertainty' (Morgan 1992, p.147). Marginal areas have been most seriously affected: the reduction in the level of intensification is particularly evident in the frontier region of West Bohemia. Poor soils in northwest Poland also impose constraints in the present economic climate. Meanwhile, there has so far been only a small increase in the average size of holdings.

*Table 7.2*  Cereal production and trade 1980–93

| Country | Domestic production (mn.t) (A) and net trade (B) | | | | | | | | | | | |
| | 1980 | | 1985 | | 1990 | | 1991 | | 1992 | | 1993 | |
| | A | B | A | B | A | B | A | B | A | B | A | B |
|---|---|---|---|---|---|---|---|---|---|---|---|---|
| Albania | 0.87 | -0.01 | 1.05 | .... | 1.04 | +0.15 | 0.49 | +0.24 | 0.42 | +0.54 | 0.61 | +0.65 |
| Bosnia-Hercegovina | – | | – | | – | .... | – | .... | 1.36e | – | 1.26e | – |
| Bulgaria | 8.68 | +0.04 | 7.13 | +0.45 | 7.89 | +0.27 | 8.97 | +0.51 | 6.67 | -0.54 | 5.75 | +0.14 |
| Croatia | – | | – | | | | | | 2.36 | -0.04 | 2.73 | -0.04 |
| FCSFR | 10.74 | +2.05 | 11.77 | +0.39 | 12.49 | +0.05 | 11.94 | -0.17 | 10.20 | -0.12 | | |
| The Czech Republic | – | | – | | – | | | | – | | 6.47 | +0.27 |
| FGDR | 9.64 | +4.01 | 11.64 | +1.72 | 12.33 | +1.27 | – | | | | | |
| Germany | – | | – | | – | | 39.27 | -3.01 | 34.76 | -6.81 | 36.22 | -4.12 |
| Hungary | 13.61 | +0.06 | 14.78 | -2.14 | 12.51 | -0.85 | 15.80 | -1.25 | 9.98 | -4.19 | 9.04 | -2.06 |
| Macedonia | – | | – | | | | | | 0.62 | +0.12 | 0.50 | +0.10 |
| Poland | 18.34 | +7.77 | 23.79 | +2.32 | 28.01 | +1.48 | 27.81 | -0.35 | 19.96 | -0.44 | 23.42 | +2.89 |
| Romania | 20.23 | +1.09 | 23.05 | -0.12 | 17.19 | +1.14 | 19.31 | +1.69 | 12.29 | +1.69 | 15.49 | +2.64 |
| Slovakia | – | | – | | | | | | | | 3.20 | |
| Slovenia | – | | – | | | | | 0.43 | +0.54 | 0.40 | .... | |
| FFYR | 15.27 | +1.11 | 15.84 | -0.77 | 13.66 | +0.79 | 19.18 | -0.85 | | | | |
| Yugoslavia | – | | – | | – | | .... | .... | 6.85 | | 7.66 | .... |

*Note*: + denotes net import, – denotes net export

*Source*: FAO Yearbooks

Several other factors have complicated the farming situation. Demand has been reduced in part by the withdrawal of the Red Army which generated a substantial market in FCSFR, FGDR and Poland. And the textile industry, which used to be a heavy consumer of agricultural raw materials, has been slimmed down. Restitution and other forms of restructuring have led to short-term dislocations. Poor performance in Romania has been attributed to the exhaustion of the peasantry after half a century of central planning, which included coercive production plans for the surviving individual peasant farmers. There have been labour shortages reported in the Czech Republic, leading to the recruitment of seasonal workers from Ukraine. There are also problems with inherited Soviet machinery through frequent breakdowns and heavy fuel consumption. Cuts in stocking levels have arisen through the abandonment of buildings inconveniently situated in relation to the re-structured farm holdings. It is also believed that many animals were illegally exported from Romania for hard currency (leading to a ban on live cattle exports) and this could have affected the breeding stock. Finally, natural hazards, such as drought in Hungary and Romania in 1993, have been compounded by the breakdown of irrigation systems.

## Marketing

Agriculture in Eastern Europe suffers from the poor quality of the infra-structure, including a weak marketing system (Surd 1994). Abandonment of the cooperatives undermined the established system of bulk deliveries to government warehouses and there has been further damage to the socialist food chain through the splitting of the state monopoly trusts organised on a county basis (Stebelsky 1995). The state has usually retained a limited procurement and some produce is still being offered at subsidised prices. But there is increasing private involvement, although it is usually by small operators who cannot transfer surpluses in such a way as to offer farmers reliable outlets (especially for perishable produce like milk and eggs) and provide a steady supply to consumers at stable prices. Farmers are often left with produce they cannot sell while prices to the consumer vary widely through both time and space.

The open market is not yet operating efficiently in Poland although it was technically freed at the beginning of 1990. The bulk of the marketing is still handled by the cooperatives which are now free to determine their own prices. But they have been disappointed by falling consumer demand (through inflation) and have lost the support of some farmers, who found that the cooperatives could not always take their produce because of uncertain demand and the rising costs of marketing (formerly covered by subsidies) as well as the uncertainties. There are still all too few experienced market managers and consequently prices vary quite sharply through both space and time. Even at the county level there are substantial variations in prices. In

Poland in 1990 the highest prices were 36 per cent above the lowest for cereals and 25 per cent in the case of live pigs. The range would have been greater in the case of specific markets and times of the year. Moreover, if individual market prices are taken into account (those relating to around sixty cooperative grain or livestock purchasing points, i.e. markets within each voivodship), the variations would be greater because local shortages are not yet being corrected by transfers from one market to another. The alternative to the cooperative markets is the old independent *wolnorynkowe* (free market) which has been operating for two decades. It handled one-fifth of the total production in 1989 and has since been increasing its influence. Statistics published in Romania show prices for staple commodities ranging up to 30 per cent above and below the average for forty-one administrative centres during the period June 1993 to June 1994. There is much variation over time and only eleven towns had prices consistently above or below the average for all five months covered by the analysis.

An increasing number of private dealers offer a localised service, but they have not yet got the expertise to operate through wider networks that would balance out the surpluses and deficits. They seem to prefer a small turnover with prices as high as possible; so farmers may be left with unsold produce that is nevertheless in short supply in areas just beyond the immediate locality. Clearly, traders must increase their scale of activity so as to interest the larger farmers, including those catering for export markets, who still have little choice but to deal with the cooperative markets. Hopefully this will be no more than a transitional difficulty, for W. Morgan suggests that a futures market might solve the problem of uncertain prices. But in any case 'it will take a long time for a new generation of adequately trained dealers and market managers to be put in place' (Morgan 1992, p.154). Meanwhile, it is evident that the wheat market is relatively stable because of the network of state grain-buying agencies, each operating a near-monopoly in its area (compromised only by some direct sales by farmers to brewers and millers). Prices have fallen slightly in relative terms (exports are not permitted) but there is an assured demand with no competition from imports apart from the Western Food-Aid Package of 1989–90. So farmers are encouraged to increase grain production because of the relatively reliable market, compared with the situation for fruit, milk and vegetables where there has been much uncertainty as well as low prices. Meanwhile, the flower growers in the Warsaw area are setting up their own retail and wholesale businesses with a careful eye on their labour costs, in one case drawing seasonal workers from the ranks of Russian immigrants willing to undertake farm work for lower wages than Poles.

However, even if large marketing organisations were in place, there would remain the critical matter of international trade, complicated by EU regulations (Table 7.3). Significant food deliveries were sent to Eastern Europe by OECD countries to counter the effects of any temporary withdrawal by

*Table 7.3* Net trade in agricultural products 1988–93

| Country | Trade Balance (US$bn.)[1] | | | | | |
| | 1988 | 1989 | 1990 | 1991 | 1992 | 1993 |
|---|---|---|---|---|---|---|
| Albania | +0.12 | +0.14 | +0.28 | +0.37 | +0.44 | +0.43 |
| Croatia | – | – | – | – | –0.14 | +0.76 |
| FCSFR | –0.29 | –0.19 | +1.26 | –0.94 | +1.26 | – |
| The Czech Republic | – | – | – | – | – | –0.37 |
| Germany | –81.23 | –70.67 | –70.04 | –13.25 | –19.81 | –37.59 |
| Hungary | –0.63 | –0.78 | –0.93 | +1.22 | +0.36 | +3.62 |
| Macedonia | – | – | – | – | – | +0.14 |
| Poland | –1.72 | –3.19 | –4.78 | –0.19 | +2.73 | +4.69 |
| Romania | –4.21 | –2.03 | +3.52 | +1.35 | +1.33 | +1.84 |
| Slovenia | – | – | – | – | –0.54 | +0.42 |
| FFYR | +0.56 | +1.44 | +4.58 | +1.16 | – | – |

*Note* 1 + denotes net import; – denotes net export.
*Source*: FAO Yearbooks

peasants from the markets. But such gestures can significantly distort the domestic market. In any case, free trade places small inefficient producers in competition with imports which may be subsidised in some cases. Romania has imported considerable quantities of cereals and sugar and there is now a degree of dependence in order to maintain bread production which would otherwise collapse. Romanian sugar beet growing is also depressed because of the relatively low price of imported sugar. Although Polish potato exports to FSU compete successfully with production from the Czech Republic, the business is unprofitable in the context of falling world prices, though output might be diverted into starch and other potato products. Poland also has a sugar surplus but export is only possible with subsidies. In Hungary, despite good trade relations with FSU and much export of pig meat, trade was adversely affected by EU subsidised exports with deferred payment with which Hungary cannot compete: hence the need to reduce wheat production in Hungary – down from 15mn.t. in 1989–90 to 10–11mn.t. in the mid-1990s. Similar problems have arisen with meat and wine.

### State intervention policies

The state has an important role but there is little enthusiasm in government circles for a protective farm policy which currently provides an effective social safety net for small producers in Western Europe. Hungary and the other countries of Eastern Europe could not afford such a system. Although the Czech Republic and Poland would like to enter EU between 1997 and 2000, while Bulgaria would see 2010 as optimistic, none of the countries can contemplate the high macroeconomic costs that the present Common Agricultural Policy would impose. A rural social policy is needed but it should be separated from agriculture policy. However, there is limited state inter-vention in marketing. In the Czech Republic where there is a need to restructure supply and demand, there is a market fund for the buying and selling of beef, cereals and milk. The system operates when market prices sink below quoted floor prices. There is also limited market intervention through Hungary's Agricultural Market Office in respect of five commodities (maize, wheat, beef, pig meat and milk) when overproduction occurs. Intervention can result in much transport on account of regional price variations. Further, with pig meat, since many pigs are reared on the grain-growing lands of the south, slaughter capacity is in Transdanubia. Slovakia's Agriculture and Food Chamber brings together producers (state farms, cooperatives and private farmers) and processors in a bid to coordinate supply and demand, while there have been some commodity schemes to stop the decline in production arising from the removal of subsidies and price controls and the problems encountered in export markets. Poland has an Agricultural Market Agency to stabilise the farm produce market and protect farmers' incomes. In Slovenia, the government must implement the laws on privat-isation which will break up the large ('state' and 'social') farms (Vriser 1993). However, it is also aware that these large enterprises are important food producers and if the new farm owners are unable to maintain production the domestic market will suffer (Vriser 1996).

International trade is an important issue, for the East could be Europe's granary (Merritt 1991). It may well be considered desirable to stimulate exports to boost farm incomes and improve the balance of payments (Whatmore 1994). The Czech Republic considers it is uneconomic to try and produce more for export because of the need to compete with subsidised exports from other countries including the EU. However, in Hungary, where agriculture is export-led (with a surplus of US$1.5bn in agricultural trade in 1995), the government sees the ability to export as crucial for the balance of payments and has some money for export subsidies. However, over the long term Hungary believes that competitiveness should be stimulated not by subsidies but by comparative advantages (good arable land and skilled farmers). Such a notion would radically alter the situation arising under communism when there were ample subsidies for the less favourable areas and low prices. Farms on the richer lands are not necessarily the most prosperous, given the largely undifferentiated pattern of state and collective farms. In order to maximise comparative advantages there may have to be accelerated structural change and improved marketing. Meanwhile, Poland has 'soft loans' for priority sectors defined (it seems) by tradition: dairying, livestock and wool. It is considered necessary to prevent excessive food imports (forecast at US$400mn. net for 1995). Polish farmers have been stimulated by protection of the domestic sugar beet market through 40 per cent import duties in 1993. At the same time the growth of food exports, including processed food, has been stimulated by income tax exemptions

281

for export-oriented investments. Poland has also identified potential for exports, within an enlarged EU, of apple concentrate, cabbages, onions and potatoes; also food products to the FSU based on new processing technology (Kwiecinski and Quaisser 1993). A Rural Market Agency was set up in 1990 to buy surplus stocks and arrange intervention sales on domestic and foreign markets. It has taken over state reserves and cereal stores (Rowinski 1994). There should be a net food export by the end of 1995 if exports to CIS countries hold up. The Balkan countries are very interested in agricultural exports and a Special Agricultural Corridor has been opened up to expedite the movement of produce to European markets from the Macedonian frontier at Deve Bair and across Bulgaria (Gueshevo-Ruse) and Romania (Giurgiu-Nadlac) to Hungary and Austria.

Should the state intervene further to build confidence in the market and improve other aspects of the farming infrastructure? It has been argued that intervention should be resisted despite the temptations arising from the recent history of central planning and the elaborate arrangements for agriculture in the EU (Karp and Stefanou 1994). The problems of agriculture are not unique to this sector of the economy and financial assistance should arguably be arranged through banks, with governments kept at arm's length. Management of agriculture through production support would certainly consume resources and reduce government flexibility. Currently there is very little credit available for farmers in Poland to expedite the supply of seed, organic fertilisers or pesticides, while irrigation systems are poor. Polish farmers are reluctant to borrow and face high interest rates. Meanwhile, the state is frustrated by the bargaining power of farming unions which prevents effective control of the uses to which preferential loans for agricultural development may be put. Yet it is hardly politically realistic to withdraw from all forms of intervention. Credit in Poland became more expensive after 1990, making the modernization of agriculture and the food economy more difficult. Enterprises which had started investing at the end of the 1980s found themselves in debt traps. So the Rural Market Agency is also trying to stabilise production and protect agricultural incomes. Protection is being offered to Slovene farmers through minimum import prices (Bojnec 1994). This is part of the wider issue of welfare for the farming population (Kapitanski and Anastasova 1994).

There are some loan guarantees and interest rate subsidies, but the total budget for the guarantee fund (which includes research and water management) is strictly controlled. Bank lending is complicated by uncertainty over property rights and high risk. Even in the Czech Republic, productivity gains are needed through higher yields and per capita output which should form an important part of a rural social programme required as a long-term exercise to catch up with the EU performance (Whatmore 1994). When joining the Common Market each country will want the highest quotas it can get and so there will be a political incentive to maintain agricultural production and enter the EU at the top. Progressive dairy farms are installing new Western machinery and crossing the Czech dairy cows with, for example, French Holsteins to increase output, with further improvement to build up a herd of (say) pure bred Holsteins. But this process could be stimulated by low interest loans or loan guarantees. However, this approach could be irrelevant if the CAP changes; underlining the problem of hitting a moving target.

There may also be a case for intervention in the interest of structural change, with legislation to facilitate land leasing and farm consolidation (Henry 1994). There will be difficulties for small family farms in the Czech Republic where, as in Poland, there is no political pressure to get farmers to cooperate or sell out so that more viable units can emerge. Poles appreciate that massive structural change is needed and the change of thirty years in Western Europe will have to be compressed into as little as a decade. Under these circumstances agriculture has to be seen as a social service with a political imperative for land reform. There might also be strategies for the food industry, over which considerable foreign control is now being exerted. In Poland, local authorities also see a need for improved grain quality, artificial insemination, lime distribution, cooperative marketing/wholesaling systems and training in joint ventures. This raises the issue of local authority support for farming. But, despite their autonomy, authorities are swamped and are having to make cuts; meanwhile, development priorities tend to emphasise infrastructure, education and health rather than agriculture. However, there is scope for the private sector in renting out machines and providing other agricultural services. Charges are higher than those levied by the regional cooperatives, but a better service is provided and government could support the creation of a new chain of service companies.

Conservation issues, connected with the concept of sustainability in agriculture, could also justify state intervention programmes (Bettram 1992). Finally, there is an important government role through provision of better social services: while Polish farmers benefit from exemption from income tax (they pay only a small land tax) they get free health care and (since 1977) pensions in respect of holdings larger than 1ha. Limited help may be expected from abroad. There have been gifts of farm machinery to Albania from Germany. Agricultural joint ventures reflect foreign interest in Albanian agriculture. And loans from China have facilitated the import of Chinese farm machinery. But most transactions are likely to be entirely commercial. Maywick of the UK have installed gas brooders at a major Polish broiler producer in Witkovo. The same company has also attracted interest from the Czech Republic and Hungary.

## Changing production patterns

If there is no efficient alternative system of marketing, peasants who are free to plan their own activities will tend to concentrate on self-sufficiency and restrict their marketing to livestock that are relatively easy to dispose of. Maize and potatoes may be given greater emphasis at the expense of sugar beet and fruit growing. Some Romanian farmers have been cutting down fruit trees because they give top priority to self-sufficiency in maize which provides both human food and animal fodder. This policy ensures ample provision of food for peasant households (with surpluses which pass to family members through private deals) but reduces supplies to the open market. There should be a revival through an improved marketing system and a growth in demand as the economy stimulates new farming systems (Doppler 1994). There are some signs of a revival in production. Thus agriculture was prominent at the start of Albania's recovery in 1993. There is less emphasis on cotton, soya beans and tobacco, but more fodder is being prepared and food markets are well stocked with dairy products, meat, fruit and vegetables; also some marijuana which earns profits to rejuvenate private agriculture. Some food is imported from Greece and Macedonia, but Albania should once again become a net exporter (Zanga 1994).

However, there is still a long way to go to restore supplies of fertilisers and pesticides and to renovate irrigation projects that were destroyed or neglected immediately after the Albanian revolution. Land use changes have been highlighted through the 'deagrarisation' reported from the Slovenian littoral (Pavlin 1991, pp.116–17). While livestock rearing has declined there is specialisation in fruit growing, olive growing and viticulture; but the intensively cultivated surfaces coexist with physically similar ground when farmers are working along traditional lines with low levels of intensification and considerable neglect in the case of holdings worked by older people. There is also a general decrease in cattle rearing and in meadow grazing land, while much poor steeply sloping land has been taken out of use. Fishing will continue to play a significant role and East European interests in distant waters are being safeguarded. An unusual case concerns Poland's pollock fishery in international waters in the Sea of Okhotsk which are opposed by Russia (whose territorial waters surround the international zone) on the pretext of falling stocks. Poland retains processing capacity and can export the production. Another opportunity will lie in the Bering Sea when the current fishing ban ends in 1997.

## RURAL DIVERSIFICATION

Major structural change may be anticipated in the future, particularly in the case of the newly created small farms, and those small farms (overwhelmingly in Poland and the FFYR) that were never collectivised under communism. There is the challenge of investment and modernisation to create commercial farmers 'out of a cushioned quasi-subsistence agricultural system' at a time of rising prices and high interest rates (Swain 1992a, p.10). Currently (1995), state farms in Poland average 2,800ha, compared with 6ha for the private sector which employs twenty-five people per 100ha compared with thirteen in the state sector. Yet many of these small units of land ownership cannot constitute viable agricultural holdings in themselves and, in many cases, will have to be leased to cooperatives or private farmers with payment in cash or through a sharecropping arrangement. Even larger functional units are under capitalised because current market prices and land values cannot justify borrowing money at current levels of interest even where farmers have the confidence to contemplate going into debt in order to buy or lease land and machinery. Meanwhile, all decision-makers are to some extent troubled by the stresses in rural society arising out of the land reform which has produced winners and losers.

The bigger farms will certainly succeed where there is good management in regions like the Poznan area of Poland with its successful orchards and greenhouses linked with processing plants (with leasing and cooperative arrangements). Here there are family farms running intensive pig-rearing systems based on farm-grown potatoes, whey and vitamin supplements. But the number of 'real' farms in Poland may come down to 600–800,000, leaving the others as part of the community structure but with diversification through agrotourism. It is expected that the process will develop through a land market and that trends will vary regionally according to economic circumstances generally. Cooperatives may also encounter difficulties. Under communism they did not generate high incomes for their members, but they were heavily subsidised, through the provision of administrative jobs for party members and the writing off of losses when the value of production was insufficient to repay investment capital and the cost of services provided by state-owned machine stations. Much employment was provided in local enterprises started up under the cooperative umbrella which is now, for the most part, abandoned or has transferred to private management. However, even with new forms of cooperation and further intensification, the large numbers presently engaged in agriculture (especially in the Balkans) can hardly be sustained. Privatised farming in Nograd employs only a small proportion of the former agricultural workforce, at a time when many local industrial enterprises have closed and commuting to work in the towns is much reduced (Varga 1996).

Nevertheless, generalisation is difficult and viable holdings could operate anywhere in the range of 5–2,000ha, for some would suggest that small farms can efficiently exploit potential which had remained suppressed under socialism. Therefore, 'it seems reasonable to expect the emergence of private farms of 50–100ha in Romania, Bulgaria and Poland' (Cochrane 1994, p.335). Cooperatives may change to private or corporate farms which should prosper as rising incomes generate more demand. New institutions will be needed to support the private sector, although as demand for land increases the land market (currently depressed by uncertainty over property rights and the low profitability of farming) will reveal the optimum farm size (Kraus *et al.* 1994). Much depends on the wider economic environment. If the new generation cooperatives are well managed and the markets for farm produce (both domestic and international) are stimulative there could be a trend towards a modified cooperative system (led by Hungary with its existing economies of scale and limited traditions of entrepreneurship). Meanwhile, the people most likely to succeed in private farming may be the 'green barons' with modest stocks of capital, managerial experience and agribusiness contacts (Kovacs 1993). On the other hand, if marketing remains difficult and cooperatives are bankrupted, many more private farmers will be 'created by poverty, by the bankruptcy of the collective farms, by unemployment in industry and by the withdrawal of unemployment benefits from those who, after all, have their land to fall back on' (Swain 1993a, p.18). The scenario of rural overpopulation and subsistence agriculture would involve an extension of the situation evident in Poland, Romania and FRY today where the rural infrastructure is often very poor (Surd 1994). Farm units in Croatia have declined more slowly than production, reflecting increased diversification and feminisation. Land is valued on the grounds of sentiment and security (Stambuk 1991).

The most likely scenario is that fewer people will be needed on the land (Table 7.4). Agricultural employment in Eastern Europe is rapidly declining, from about one-fifth in 1990 to one-tenth in 1995, to an anticipated 5 per cent at the turn of the century. In Poland the decline in the farming population has been estimated at between 400,000 and 500,000 people between 1988 and 1993; even so, a further 333,000 are considered to be surplus (Weclawowicz 1996, p.145). In the FGDR labour is down from 884,000 to 208,000 but still needs a further reduction by as much as one half (Bergmann 1992). Regional programmes could accelerate the pace where a lot of manual work could easily be replaced by machinery (Staziak 1989). Hall (1996) has reported significant demographic upheavals in Albania during the early 1990s with some depopulation of mountain regions. This seems to affect some areas of Albanian settlement where large communities were previously subsidised, but where there is now out-migration in the direction of Tirana. Out-migration is reflected in neglect of hillside terracing and irrigation systems installed in the 1960s and 1970s as a result of much labour and investment but is now compromised by a lack of funding for the maintenance of these intensive systems. In the south there has been some emigration by Greeks which reduced the labour available for agriculture. Yet unemployment in other sectors of the economy is inducing more people to stay on the land. So the active rural population could increase through the growth of unemployment in the towns, encouraging young people to return to their villages to work on the family farm. Hence, there is another school of thought (reflecting the ideological inclination of socialist governments) that would try and maintain high levels of employment in the transition through labour-intensive cultivation (including rabbit breeding, fruit growing and the cultivation of mush-

Table 7.4 Agricultural population 1985–94

| Country | Population active in agriculture (in 000s and percentage of the total active population) | | | | | | | | | | | |
| | 1985 | | 1990 | | 1991 | | 1992 | | 1993 | | 1994 | |
|---|---|---|---|---|---|---|---|---|---|---|---|---|
| Albania | 715 | 52.0 | 762 | 48.5 | 756 | 47.7 | 764 | 47.1 | 762 | 46.4 | 758 | 45.7 |
| Bulgaria | 670 | 14.9 | 539 | 12.2 | 519 | 11.8 | 504 | 11.4 | 486 | 11.0 | 464 | 10.6 |
| FCSFR | 906 | 11.1 | 772 | 9.3 | 747 | 9.0 | 727 | 8.7 | – | – | – | – |
| FGDR | 873 | 9.3 | 758 | 8.1 | 736 | 7.9 | – | – | – | – | – | – |
| Hungary | 752 | 14.5 | 590 | 11.5 | 565 | 11.0 | 541 | 10.5 | 517 | 10.0 | 496 | 9.5 |
| Poland | 4676 | 24.4 | 4030 | 20.8 | 3914 | 20.1 | 3806 | 19.5 | 3713 | 18.9 | 3613 | 18.2 |
| Romania | 2839 | 25.0 | 2356 | 20.2 | 2265 | 19.4 | 2154 | 18.6 | 2078 | 17.9 | 1997 | 17.1 |
| FFYR | 2679 | 26.7 | 2254 | 21.7 | 2237 | 20.8 | – | – | – | – | – | – |

Source: FAO Yearbooks

rooms and vegetables) to support continuing part-time work in agriculture. At the same time there is great scope for small businesses in agriculture to take care of crop-spraying, combine harvesting or butter production using local milk surpluses (Kovach 1994a, 1994b).

Hence the need for promotion of the secondary and tertiary sectors in rural areas (Klodzinski 1992). Factories are being built (sometimes using old cooperative farm buildings) but the rate of progress is very slow. In Poland, tackling rural unemployment of up to 2mn. should be the task of the Agency for Modernising and Restructuring Agriculture set up in 1993 which works on domestic funding and foreign aid. It is interested in rural infrastructure (water, sewage and telephones) and food-processing projects. In 1992 Poland launched an 'Opportunities for Rural Areas and Agriculture' programme to provide preferential credits and subsidies. An interesting question is how far Eastern Europe will identify with the Swiss-Bavarian model of relatively small farms combined with a significant rural industry. Families involved in pluriactivity (where farm occupancy is supported by a range of activities, with the flexibility of family labour as the critical issue) have been seen as 'social anomalies' in a world dominated by capital. The economic factors of uneven development and constrained choice may be complemented by a web of social relations supporting an ideological commitment to family-based farming (Marsden 1990). South Moravia shows a tendency towards the dispersal of employment in manufacturing, reinforced by workshops on the former state and cooperative farms. Population was stable during the 1980s even in areas that were not the most favourable for agriculture. Consolidation may eventually create viable family farms (perhaps based on kinship groups) and displace the surplus population into non-agricultural activities (largely based in the towns), but pluriactivity seems effective in the short term under conditions of market constraints, high interest rates and high unemployment. And although the system is presently dictated by poverty it may remain part of the community ethos, especially in mountain regions where there are opportunities for diversification in commerce and agrotourism. Consolidation is more likely to follow the growth of investment in lowland areas (the Czech Republic, Hungary and Poland).

In countries where the private sector is relatively well established, much progress is being made in combining small-scale agriculture with wood-cutting, handicrafts and tourism as in the Polish Carpathians (Pine 1992, 1993, 1994). In this area agrotourism is particularly successful in a number of villages close to the Tatra and Babia Gora. Large modern houses have been built on the strength of increased incomes and the demand for tourist accommodation, while summer visitors generate demand for locally produced food. However, 'population growth and the uncontrolled expansion of the buildings reduce the tourist attractiveness of some areas' (Kurek 1996, p. 196). More thought will have to be given to an ecological agriculture appropriate to local physical conditions and the demand for high-quality organic food in the spas and other leading resorts. In Romania, where the Vacaroiu government is keen to improve agricultural credit to encourage investment and mechanisation, there is a newly established Commission for Mountainous Regions where agronomists displaced by the collapse of the old cooperatives now work as agricultural advisers to each commune in order to encourage farm improvement through better breeding stock (many of the animals reared on the old cooperatives were of very poor quality), improved local food-processing and diversification into activities where investment in the past has been very low. High-quality agricultural produce could include cheese and preserved fruits which are traditional products of Carpathian agriculture. Processing of plums in the Romanian Carpathians yields a brandy – known as 'tuica' – which has many local variations in strength and bouquet. The brandy enters into commerce to a limited extent, yet with promotion and marketing a number of varieties could be sold more widely and the success of Scotch whisky might be to some extent replicated (Muica and Turnock 1996). The potential for agrotourism linked with careful management of the mountains to prevent erosion by both overgrazing and excessive visitor pressure is demonstrated in the Paring Mountains where national park designations may provide the necessary protection in an area opened up to visitors by the expansion of wood-processing and the development of hydroelectricity (Ploaie 1996). Finance for agricultural recovery should highlight extension work to encourage innovation. Rather than extreme specialisation which is highly sensitive to market changes, there should be more regard for peasant inclination towards pluriactivity, maximising income by activities on and off the farm. There is a role for associations, machinery pools and self-help groups. This should be central to extension work and to university courses in agriculture and rural development. But a proper extension service will take a long time to establish on a country-wide basis.

## FOOD-PROCESSING

Eastern Europe has substantial food-processing capacity, but it is in great need of modernisation to improve quality and rationalisation to relate capacity to the needs of a market economy. The transformation is being driven by foreign capital introducing new technology in dairying, sugar-refining, meat-processing, drinks and confectionary. There is US interest in Polish potatoes, with perceived opportunities in commodities as disparate as apples and oilseed. Danone of France is manufacturing dairy products in Bulgaria while Danish firms are interested in the country's meat-processing, a Dutch firm is producing baby foods and Australians are investing in turkey farms. Unilever has purchased the Baja deepfreezing plant: it will improve technology and develop the facilities to sell Hungarian produce. However, small processing units may well appear through domestic initiatives. Farm income can be boosted through non-farm activities and Polish farmers are setting up wholesale and retail trading businesses and food-processing units. One case concerns a meat-processing business near Krakow: an abattoir for pigs had been built and the farm holding extended so as to be self-sufficient in fodder (Morgan 1992, p.146). Additional pigs are brought from neighbouring farms in order to operate the abattoir and processing plant at full capacity. It may also be possible for enterprises to modernise on their own because banks seem happier to lend to food-processors than to farmers because ownership and security are generally clearer. There will be a need to catch up with the West by offering a wider range of good-quality products which can compete against foreign imports and also penetrate Western markets. East European exports are not yet able to compete on quality and packaging; often they require state subsidy to a level of as much as a half (an example being Polish potatoes and potato products). However, in some countries like Hungary the process is well under way. Finally, there is room for state intervention to eliminate excess capacity on a coordinated basis.

## Dairying

Rationalisation is taking place in the Czech Republic because too many plants are now in competition where previously they had their own assured markets. The number of dairies has been reduced by 40 per cent from 170 in 1989 to 102 in 1995; while milk production has declined by the same extent from 4.5 to 2.7 mn.litres through reduced per capita consumption from 250 to 180 litres (and 9 to 5kg. in the case of butter). Although these levels could increase it is considered necessary for dairies to rationalise at 60 per cent of capacity. The result could be still fewer plants, but modern units capable of exporting. Modern dairies are turning out liquid milk, and dairy products including yoghurt and ice-cream with direct delivery to shops. Weaker producers are being weeded out. Slovakia's Milex dairy company in Bratislavahas entered into a joint venture with Schardinger of Austria which now has a two-thirds stake. The quality of milk received from producer cooperatives and state farms has been improved to EU standards, although the quantity is still inadequate to fully utilise the production capacity of 200mn.litres. Milk production throughout Slovakia has fallen from 1.6 to 0.9bn.litres. The problem is one of profitable operation at prices the public can afford. Most companies will not be able to invest in improved technology and a major rationalisation is expected within five years which will greatly reduce the number of plants in favour of the large modern installations that will be able to run at full capacity. This could be done by takeovers with a view to closure, but with retention of the suppliers and customers. However, the domestic markets should improve with additional opportunity for the sale of dairy products in Austria and FSU. Danone, the French yoghurt maker, has acquired the Warsaw-based Wola dairy, adding to its stake in the Mildes dairy in the south of the country. A Dutch food group Nutricia has acquired a 22.5

per cent stake in Hajdutej Tejipari, Hungary's largest regional dairy.

But there is a need for higher standards across the region where milk often fails to meet EU standards. Many producers in Poland do not respect hygiene regulations. Farms were not encouraged in the past to make improvements because cooperatives purchased large amounts regardless of quality. Only a small proportion of milk is supplied to dairies in trucks guaranteeing a proper temperature. Meanwhile, only a quarter of Poland's 700 processing plants meet international standards. The IFC have approved a loan for the development of Poland's dairy industry; aiming at the production of natural yoghurt comparable with high-quality imports. UHT milk is available, but accounts for less than 5 per cent of the market. There is also a problem in the dairy industry in Romania: many underfed neglected dairy cows had to be slaughtered with the collapse of cooperatives. Milk from private farms rarely reaches the market since peasants prefer to sell cream and cheese, which attracts higher prices. It is calculated that Bucharest is supplied with 200,000 litres of milk daily whereas the demand is 250,000 (Henry 1994, p.21). There is a need for better dairy equipment; hence the significance of the UK engineering firm APV in setting up APV Polska in 1994 to supply drying equipment for baby food and powdered milk production; also equipment for liquid milk-processing, yoghurt, cheese and whey products, butter and low-fat spreads, evaporated and condensed products. Equipment is also available for ice-cream, frozen desserts, soups, jams – and ready made meals using the high-tech Ohmic heating system.

## Sugar

Western penetration of the East European sugar industry is evident through the stake of Eastern Sugar (a joint venture between UK's Tate and Lyle and Generale Sucriere of France) in Hungarian and Slovakian beet sugar refining. Zucker Aktiengesellschaft Uclzen Braunschweig have taken a one-third stake in the Czech refiner Rafinirie Cukru Dobrovice from EBRD. There has also been UK (British Sugar) penetration in Poland through acquisition of state sugar factories. Polish sugar producers are likely to decrease from eighty to twenty or thirty. But in 1995 Poland's forty-seven state-run sugar mills were transformed into four state-controlled holding companies which will carry out a revamping exercise: this is attractive to the weaker producers although the holding companies will not necessarily be umbrellas against bankruptcy. Meanwhile, the stronger companies are looking for foreign partners to supply capital and if they succeed their time in the holding company will be relatively short: some mills like Naklo have strong worker loyalty with out-of-hours work to carry out developments. It is part of a strategy of consolidation in the face of Western competition. The industry is over-producing and cannot afford to export the surplus at prevailing world prices. Sugar beet is a popular crop for farmers and yields well. The holding companies will enter into contracts with growers and set milling quotas; they will aim at 1.5mn.t. of production for the home market and 0.3 for export and prevent over-supply hitting domestic prices. Romanian sugar beet-processing is not yet competitive despite some state support (Gavrilescu 1994). Much sugar is imported while the prices offered to domestic sugar beet producers are too low to be stimulative.

## Wine

The wine trade is switching emphasis from the relatively undemanding FSU market of the 1980s to the more discerning West European consumer. East European demand is being served by cheap wine from France and Italy; therefore the East European producers must go upmarket. The Slovenian wine producer Slovenijavino has acquired a US distributor Laureate Imports for its 'Avia' wine and 'Atlantic' mineral water. But Czech wine, which is having difficulty competing against imported wine, also needs modernisation with the launch of new products with improved presentation. Meanwhile, Romanian wine producers came together in 1990 to form Vinexport Trading, breaking away from the former state exporting company Prodexport. They formed a joint venture with interests from Denmark, Germany, The Netherlands and the UK. Exports are now running at some 15mn.litres a year of bottled wine and wine in bulk for blending. State wineries have had to reduce capacity in view of privatisation of vineyards (resulting in more small-scale production) but some retain their own vineyards (Murfatlar, Tarnave/Jidvei and Valea Calugareasca) and have been modernised by the importing of new bottling lines.

The Hungarian wine industry is recovering from a depression linked with Gorbachev's anti-alcohol campaign launched in 1985 and, more significantly, the unification of Germany and the breakup of FSU. In 1992 export volume was only 30 per cent of that in 1989. The Russian market revived in 1992 and the turnaround started in 1993 and 1994 when exports of 0.94mn.hl approached half the 1989 figure of 2.27, but with dollar earnings showing an increase. There has been an improvement in the quality of the wine by using foreign wine-making expertise (reflected by investment in technical improvements and marketing) and restricting yield per vine to 2kg instead of 4.5kg as before. French and Spanish involvement is restoring the reputation of the Tokaj region, in contrast to the 'Bull's Blood' of Eger (marketed in competition by Egervin and Hungarovin) and the products of Gyongyos and Kecskemet promoted by local companies; for instead of the obligation to sell to state wineries, Hungarovin producers can now promote their own wine. Vinarium has also emerged as a marketing consortium of small, high-quality producers in various regions. It now has its own vineyard (along with wine production, bottling and storage equipment) near the lakeside at Balatonbolgar which is 53 per cent owned by the German company Henkel which adopted a marketing strategy in 1992 to focus on Germany, Scandinavia and the UK. Reference should also be made to small businesses which have been returned to private ownership. The Unicum distillery in Budapest has teamed up with an Italian winemaker to build a new wine plant near Lake Balaton producing a quality *Kastely* (estate) brand which will be sold through the Unicum organisation at affordably high prices. There are many small producers emerging from the breakup of state farms in 1992 and the refashioning of the cooperatives (though many also broke up): like the Matravolgye cooperative from Markaz on the slopes of the Matra, the cooperatives take some 4,000t from the 500 members and produces some 30,000hl of wine. As with other small producers, there have been successes in Far Eastern markets and contributions to local tourism through winetasting in the Eger area. Meanwhile, the state wineries have been privatised and Hungarovin, controlled by the German Henkel organisation, is investing in upmarket brands ('Francois' and 'Hungaria') as well as its own 'Egri Bikaver' (Bull's Blood) noted above. However, the state retains control of part of the Tokaj business in order to prevent total disruption, necessary because the privatisation of agricultural land has led to much fallowing of land previously used for vineyards. The local Tokaj trading organisation buys grapes from individual farmers but has used French and Spanish expertise to produce a quality 'Aszu' wine which, hopefully, will establish a reputation for the local product after a three-year maturation period. Indeed, the Spanish organisation Bodegas Oremos has acquired the best vineyards in the region. There is resentment in Tokaj that assets are sold to foreigners because local vintners lack capital; yet international connections mean that the product is better known.

Despite some quality trade by Vinexport (already mentioned), Romania's vineyards have not yet made the same recovery and until recently the emphasis has been on the clearance of vineyards falling under private ownership, along with neglect or destruction of access roads, water pipelines and plants producing pesticides. Almost 1000ha of orchards and vineyards have been affected in Vrancea alone. Viticulture has been embarrassed by higher costs through interest payments (hence the need for the rescheduled debts and subsidised interest rates) and a lack of effective marketing; while duties on imported drinks have been lowered. The very small units of vineyard ownership (averaging 0.29ha) prevent rational management using machinery. The selling price for grapes is very low and so vinification centres are barely working at a quarter of their capacity: some have been forced to close and there is no incentive for new private plants to open. Many farmers prefer to make their own wine and if the quality is indifferent or the business is not profitable they will switch to something else. Some recovery was evident in 1994 when there were 247,000ha of vineyards (225,000 producing grapes for winemaking) compared with 224,000 in 1990. The state wineries are clearly in the best position when they retain their own vineyards, as at Murfatlar, Jidvei and Valea Calugareasca.

## Beer and other beverages

Once again, Western companies are moving into Eastern Europe. There is much activity in Poland where Heineken of the Netherlands and the German companies Anlagenplanung and Braun und Brunnen are making large investments. Heineken have also entered into a joint venture with the Zywiec brewery as their sole Polish partner. Eventually Heineken brands will be produced by Zywiec which is already producing Pepsi-Cola. The UK's Allied Lyons is retailing British beer through its 'John Bull' establishments in the larger Polish cities. Spirits are also seeing changes with the domestic vodka producers in Poland now facing competition from Smirnoff vodka (produced under licence from International Distillers & Vintners by IDV Poland). Elsewhere, Pepsi-Cola hope to be Eastern Europe's leading soft drinks producer by the end of the century. A large investment will take place in both the Czech Republic and Slovakia, following successful programmes in Hungary and Poland. In Prague a manufacturing and bottling plant (in a former munitions factory) is being modernised and a distribution network will follow. In Slovakia there will be six regional distribution centres. The scale of the investment will be similar to K-Mart and the two will comprise the largest investments in the country since 1989.

The brewing industry of the Czech Republic makes an interesting study. Here, the seventy-two breweries were formerly protected through fixed marketing areas for each producer, although Budvar Budweiser and Urquell were exported through the Koospol foreign trade company. Czech brewers are now seeking foreign partners and the leading breweries like Budejovicky Budvar, Jihoceske Pivovary (also based in Ceske Budejovice), Plzensky Prazdroj, Pivovary Radegast, StaroBrno and Starporamen (Prague) are coming to the fore. BrauUnion of Austria has taken a stake in the Brno-based brewery StaroBrno while the UK brewer Bass, in addition to a one-third stake in Starporamen, is bidding for Jihoceske Pivovary against American and Danish competition. Meanwhile, the world's largest brewer Anheuser-Busch wants an ownership stake in Ceske Budejovice's Budvar brewery (licensed holder of the 'Budweiser' trade name in Europe which Anheuser-Busch want to use for their product). However, a merger of the city's two major breweries is another possibility. Ostrava Brewery has expanded its market through purchase of a brewery in Poland where beer is making inroads into a market where spirits were previously dominant.

These moves threaten the small independent breweries which fear a further decline in their market share as competition increases. Total beer output in the Czech Republic fell from 2bn.litres in 1992 to 1.8bn. litres in 1993 (blamed on the increase in taxation) but exports by the leading firms remained steady at 100mn.litres. Thus, while many smaller breweries have lost ground, the leading brewers have increased output with the benefit of foreign investment and experienced marketing staff attracted from the Koospol company. They hope to increase their exports to counter intense competition at home, made worse by the loss of the market in Slovakia where protectionist policies are now in force. Foreign investment can pose a threat to traditional beers, which is why the Anheuser-Busch initiative has not yet succeeded. But the smaller breweries may face severe difficulties unless they can develop niche products (like Pardubice Porter) with export possibilities. Privatisation has brought freedom to compete, but success depends on capital investment which is difficult without foreign partners.

## INDUSTRIAL RESTRUCTURING

The former SOEs have now restructured to meet the needs of a market economy (Jackson and Biesbrouck 1995). There is a continuing heavy shake-out of labour in order to raise productivity and many units with obsolete plant and pollution problems are shutting down altogether (Dittrich *et al.* 1995). This underlines the weakness of growth strategies in the past: concentrating on increases in capacity rather than reinvestment to modernise older plant. There was a dismal performance during 1990 and 1992, but modest growth in Poland in 1992 spread to most other countries during 1993 and 1994 (Table 7.5). Unemployment rose most sharply in the FGDR where labour-intensive industries were suddenly placed in open competition with the more modern capital-intensive plants of West Germany. The textile industry reduced employment from 330,000 to 30,000 by 1992 but the future remains bleak: in Weissenfels both the textile and footwear industries were totally wiped out. And rural textile industries in the Harz Mountains, enlarged in the 1960s to cushion the isolation of the 'closed' frontier zone, were also eliminated. The large chemical complexes of Buna and Leuna near Merseburg have seen employment reduced from some 50,000 to 15,000. The Schwedt oil refinery experienced a sharp fall in production and a decline in employment from 10,000 to 2,500. The newer plant in these complexes has been taken over by private companies, as the Treuhand organisation disposed of the inherited state assets. The problems facing FGDR enterprises are demonstrated very

*Table 7.5* Percentage change in industrial output 1989–96

| Country | 1989 | 1990 | 1991 | 1992 | 1993 | 1994 | 1995 | 1996[1] | 1997[1] |
|---|---|---|---|---|---|---|---|---|---|
| Albania | n.a. | −8.2 | −42.5 | −20.4 | −10.0 | −8.0 | −3.0 | 3.0 | n.a. |
| Bulgaria | −0.2 | −17.5 | −27.8 | −21.9 | −6.3 | 2.9 | 1.7 | 1.0 | 4.0 |
| The Czech Republic | 1.5 | −3.5 | −22.3 | −10.6 | −5.3 | 2.3 | 9.2 | 9.8 | 9.0 |
| Hungary | n.a. | −8.5 | −19.1 | −9.8 | 0.6 | 5.0 | 4.8 | 3.0 | 5.0 |
| Poland | n.a. | −24.2 | −11.9 | 3.9 | 6.2 | 12.1 | 9.4 | 8.5 | 10.0 |
| Romania | −2.1 | −18.8 | −19.6 | −22.0 | 1.3 | 4.6 | 9.4 | 5.0 | 4.5 |
| Slovakia | 1.1 | −2.7 | −21.6 | −13.7 | −13.5 | 7.5 | 7.5 | 3.0 | −3.0 |

*Note* 1 Estimate.
*Source*: EC Directorate General for Employment, Industrial Relations and Social Affairs (EIU)

clearly by the motorcycle manufacturer MZ of Zschopau, where paternalistic management retains the loyalty of a small town workforce. MZ has concentrated on producing simple, cheap and reliable machines previously sought in domestic, East European and FSU markets. But these markets are now less secure, while German reunification means that foreign customers will face higher prices and payment in hard currency. A partner is therefore essential to put money into the business and enable new models to be put into production.

Elsewhere in the FGDR industrial sector Philips Kommunikations Industrie of Nurnberg (a subsidiary of the Dutch multinational) has taken over RFT Fernmeldwerk at Bautzen on the understanding that 350 of the 1,000 jobs will be secure. The company sees a manufacturing base in FGDR as a virtual precondition for getting orders in this part of Germany; there is further benefit through the old company's extensive East European links, for 80 per cent of production was exported. For the moment this is not a major consideration with the sharp fall in demand and the need to pay FGDR manufacturers in hard currency. Meanwhile, a West German company has taken over the pen factory in Bautzen and is reprofiling production to deal with felt-tip pens. In Chemnitz, with its traditions as a producer of textile machinery, a survival mentality is evident at Chemnitzer Webmaschinenbau where Heckert milling machines were once the flagship of the FGDR machine tool industry. A Swiss interest has been attracted and there is now a small product range to secure 500 of the 4,300 jobs formerly available. Innovation has also arrived in Chemnitz through the US lathe manufacturer Niles-Simmons. This reflects Treuhand's links with North America where an office has been opened in New York. The US Mid-West was targeted for its emphasis on sophisticated machine tools and extensive supply chains (which include strong links with Germany). The hope is that companies will be interested in FGDR assets at a time of heavy investment to overhaul the infrastructure. Other cases of American involvement in the FGDR economy include Medtronic, a US maker of heart pacemakers, which has acquired the corresponding FGDR supplier Tur. But despite takeovers and expansion programmes employment has fallen heavily and, at least in the short term, the losses will not be made good by growth in the tertiary sector. Unemployment has been all the greater because recession in western Germany forced a reconsideration of planned investments by firms such as Krupp at Eisenhuttenstadt and Mercedes at the Ahrensdorf (former ITA) truck plant near Berlin.

In turn, Western countries are often attracted to East European industries because, once employment is reorganised, skilled labour is relatively cheap (outside FGDR). FGDR is in competition with East European states which are also looking to Europe and North America for investment. They can offer much lower labour costs, but not always the same level of political stability. Each country has a range of assets which should be particularly attractive to foreign companies. Reorganisation has been relatively slow but the older industrial areas have suffered badly because their outdated plant is no longer competitive; while there may be little experience in diversification because enterprise managers previously discouraged competition within their labour catchments. Foreign investment is therefore very desirable in facilitating technology transfer, higher productivity and improved export performance after the collapse of the FSU left many enterprises without a market (Hitchens *et al.* 1995). In particular, Baltic coast shipbuilders were left holding unsaleable vessels built to Soviet specifications. New markets are being found, not only in Western Europe and North America but also in the Far East and South Africa. And in addition to basic goods like steel, sold at low prices, more sophisticated goods are being turned out, like specialised ships and a range of chemical, engineering and glass products which can be sold through existing market networks developed by the Western owner or partner. At the same time Western companies can build up domestic market share quickly, avoiding import duties which (even with a liberalisation of trade) may still be at 30–40 per cent; and they can build an image as a company assisting economic recovery. They may also see opportunities in the wider markets of Eastern Europe, the CIS and Middle East where East Europeans often have wide experience.

Some expectations have been disappointed in the short term. In Hungary companies that went in quickly, like General Electric and General Motors, find that they underestimated the scale and duration of the recession. In the case of Tungsram (acquired by General Electric), the workforce was cut from 18,000 to 13,000, with 10,000 as the eventual target. Use of realistic accounting procedures produced losses in 1990 and 1991 after showing an initial profit in 1989, so management has been reorganised, with research and development linked closely to production and market needs (Okolicsanyi 1992). Guardian Glass at Oroshaza found that East European orders for float glass were making up only a quarter of the production instead of the half that had been anticipated. Thus more of the output has been sold in the West, in spite of high transport costs arising from a factory location well beyond Hungary's frontier with Austria. But progress in trade liberalisation was underestimated, so that much of the domestic demand can, potentially, be met through imports. Lower import duties certainly facilitate the import of second-hand cars and this reduces the potential for home market sales by Western car manufacturers setting up within the country. However, labour has performed better than was expected and the longer term prospects are good. On the positive side there is also a growth of indigenous small businesses, first encouraged in some communist states in the 1980s as part of a growing 'second economy'. Hungary has had particular success through the spring-board provided by the NEM, but even the countries which retained more centralised economic systems until 1989 are now catching up with successes in business incubation. Small businesses are good for job creation; also for innovation and technological diffusion. They are also helpful in terms of decentralisation because they can operate in rural areas much more easily than large enterprises.

However, there has been quite marked spatial discrimination. The accent is now on competition rather than equity (Hamilton 1982). Some areas are still heavily embedded in the attitudes and ethics of the old regime while modernising regions, embracing much of Slovenia for example (Vriser 1992), are becoming 'disembedded' through links with Western business (Grabher 1994).

Foreign investment tends to be concentrated in capital cities and the more established industrial regions where productivity may be higher (reflecting superior skill and efficiency). The removal of subsidies on transport and power could make it difficult for industries to compete when they are located in the easternmost parts of Eastern Europe on account of former linkage with the FSU. However, situations vary considerably. The Kosice steelworks in eastern Slovakia is doing well, with a reduced workforce (partly redeployed in special steel-making and in steel-using industries established in the vicinity) thanks to a low cost product which benefits from mechanical handling of Ukrainian iron ore pellets (from the new Dolinskaya plant) and coke from Ostrava delivered directly to the mill by broad- and standard-gauge railways respectively. However, most joint venture capital has gone into consumer industries, especially in the capitals and in those provincial cities where there is a depth of industrial experience. However, town centres may be unattractive due to disputes over property ownership and the pressures to develop a stronger central business district. So, many small businesses are appearing on the edge of towns and villages, often concerned with whole-saling and retailing. But some industrial estates are also being promoted where there are technological links with universities. At Brno in the Czech Republic, the local authorities have reached an agreement with Bovis for a business and technology park on the university campus: a site of some 100ha 4.5kms north of the city where 20,000 sq.m. starter units are to be built. Some serviced industrial sites are also becoming available through the abandonment of nuclear power projects: Stendal in FGDR and Zarnowiec in Poland. Large enterprises should be more sensitive towards the feelings of residents – after a privileged status for industry under communism industries should try and 'recompense' the cities for the environmental stress they created in the past. In the future the emphasis will be on intensive rather than extensive development (Potrykowska 1995). Meanwhile, small businesses should bring benefits to small towns and villages where there is potential in food- and wood-processing, engineering (through sub-contracting) and ser-vice industries. Meanwhile, in the rural areas there will be great scope in the privatised service sector and in small-scale food and wood-processing and in tourism.

As regards choosing specific countries there is a clear choice for Western businesses between setting up in every country or concentrating in one place as a base for the whole of Eastern Europe. Unilever has acquired detergent companies in several countries, while Proctor & Gamble concentrated on the FCSFR. In general there are significant north–south differences in terms of specialisation and the volume of investment (Murray 1992). Northern countries have been most favoured because they are perceived as being more stable, with a stronger industrial tradition (including many enterprises with an international reputation) and a more committed workforce. Czech industry also offers the benefit of a particularly central position in Europe. The north also has strong domestic markets, with higher levels of television, washing machine and car ownership. It is possible that difficulties will be encountered in old northern industrial regions and in the more backward areas where both productivity and the quality of production are low. Problems arise in areas of declining mining activity such as the Walbrzych coalfield in Poland. Diversification by light industry and tourism is very necessary. The ideological drive of communism for an even distribution of industry is fading (and some irrationally located industries may be hard hit) but it may be sustained to some extent by the economic rationale of dispersal of small industries aided by modern telecommunications, an important priority in Eastern Europe's modernisation.

## Restructuring in the south

However, discrimination by foreign companies in favour of the northern countries reduces confidence in market forces in the Balkans and results in more interventionist economic strategies which could further discourage outside investment. The situation is not helped by strong political differences over the matter of reform. During its period in office the Union of Democratic Forces in Bulgaria was repeatedly blocked by the Bulgarian Socialist Party (the reformed Communist Party) acting in concert with smaller parties. The uncertainty was bad for the electronics and engineering industries already weakened by the collapse of the FSU market. Alternative outlets were needed in Eastern Europe and Asia, but uncertainty discouraged foreign investment. In addition, corporation tax was high (though concessions were made in individual cases). Privatisation was also very slow, with the first state companies disposed of only in 1993.

Romania's industry suffers from the defects common to all East European SOEs. But competition has been frustrated by the legacy of bizarre calculations for 'value added': calculated on the basis of individual departments within large enterprises (ranging in number between five and eight in extreme cases) so that costs were sometimes pushed above the levels charged by foreign suppliers. Under market conditions customers can import their requirements and this is a powerful stimulus to the erstwhile monopolists to improve their efficiency. But government is supporting industry very heavily in order to protect employment and production has declined more than employment. There is a stimulus to reorganise more radically but this needs capital, which is not available within the country to any extent, or foreign investment which has been slow in arriving. Romanian enterprises also suffer from technological isolation arising out of a low level of integration in the world economy (Popescu 1993).

Investment has been slow to arrive. Initially most interest came from Italy, France, the UK and USA but the Daewoo investment has pushed South Korea into a leading position. It is urgently necessary to find new markets and to reorganise the unprofitable plants. Romania's natural resources are seen as an attraction to foreign investment: hydrocarbons, salt and manganese deposits; also mineral waters, woodlands, farmlands and the tourism potential. Coca-Cola has opened factories in Bucharest and near to the cities of Iasi and Oradea. They are owned by the Greek-Cypriot Levantia Company which is already operating in Bulgaria. But the distribution of major foreign investments (over US$1mn.) is highly uneven. Out of a total of US$532mn. (70 per cent of all foreign investment), over 60 per cent has gone to Bucharest, while urban regions close to the western frontier (historically linked with Central Europe) have attracted almost one-fifth. However, the situation was transformed in 1994 by the decision of the South Korean firm Daewoo to invest US$156mn. at the former Oltcit car factory (now Autombile Craiova). Overnight this gave the southwestern part of the country a share of around one-fifth of the money placed in major investments, leaving the eastern regions (Moldavia and Muntenia outside Bucharest) as the least attractive areas. It is surprising that the Danube is not more highly regarded, although the sanctions against Serbia may colour perceptions of the value of the navigation. In the longer term the advantage of river transport could help the reorganisation of heavy industry at cities like Resita which are reasonably close by.

The south is much preoccupied with the restructuring of the SOEs given the vested interests concerned with their survival coupled with a relatively low level of outside interest. This does not deny the role of second economy entrepreneurs as building blocks of an emergent market economy but suggests that it has been exaggerated and has not yet become a dynamic legitimate private sector (much of the activity arises through moonlighting; moreover, it is often unregistered and dependent on mafia support). The former SOEs now comprise 'recombinant property' lacking both well-defined rights of private property and a reproduction of old forms of state ownership: new property forms are arising which are neither statist nor private. Enterprise managers are using available legislation to establish joint stock and limited liability companies, so that the assets of the former SOEs may now be split into as many as twenty satellite units. This spreads the risk across various organisational forms, appropriate in a situation of great uncertainty. The links with the state are retained through managerial links with high-placed government officials and also through the prominence of State

Property Agencies in shareholding. In the Czech Republic the state-owned banks founded seven of the nine largest investment funds looking after the shareholdings of individual citizens under voucher privatisation. Recombination may help the reorganisation process because the creation of satellites will result in the identification of winners and losers and relatively small loss-makers may be eliminated. Meanwhile, 'some of the semi-autonomous limited liability companies might more likely become targets for takeovers by foreign firms or indigenous private entrepreneurs whose limited means could not acquire properties left integrated within the large state enterprises' (Stark 1993, pp.17–18).

## INDUSTRIAL STRUCTURE

Although all sectors of industry expanded under communism, heavy industry was accorded priority because of its fundamental role in supplying metals, chemicals and building material to the economy as a whole and the military-industrial establishment in particular. But the strategic importance of these branches is no longer unassailable and uncompetitive production of basic manufactures is no longer a virtue. At home consumer demand will focus more on light industries and restructuring may, on the whole, be less painful in this department since many enterprises have attracted foreign capital. Meanwhile, firms that fail to find Western partners often find it hard to compete and maintain market share. The Hungarian state-owned cosmetic and household chemical producer Coala has dropped from a virtual monopoly position in the domestic market to 40 per cent; a lack of advertising at a time when Western products were making deep inroads (thanks to Colgate-Palmolive's promotional work through children's television and education programmes for the schools) left Coala with the lower end of the market where the company can compete on price. Licences have been lost with Beiersdorf of Germany taking back 'Nivea' and other product licences. The range of products has been reduced from 600 to 200 and a new range of 'Heviz' creams (named after the famous spa) has been launched. But it is doubtful if Coala can flourish without foreign investment, for its distribution has been described as chaotic and its market research as rudimentary. However, the Colgate-Palmolive bid of US$35mn. was rejected by Hungary's SPA. Coala could do some contract manufacturing for Western companies wanting to avoid import taxes.

### Light industry

It is possible for East European industries to attract Western orders by attention to quality and a readiness to accept the need for 'downsizing'. The Wega clothing factory in Bielsko-Biala reduced its workforce from 1,000 to 400 and now finds plenty of business with exports accounting for a quarter of production. The textile industry in Lodz experienced serious problems with a fall in employment from 92,300 jobs in 1985 to 70,800 in 1990. The industry was hit by falling demand from the FSU, and greater competition from imports. With a lack of money to finance reorganisation, several mills closed down completely. When privatisation started in Lodz with the clothing firm Prochnik, the flotation was heavily undersubscribed and there was little Western investment. Meanwhile, the workers were hit by the falling value of their wages (with taxes on wage rises above the norm) (Paczka and Riley 1992). And some important new investments were attracted to other locations. However, the Lodz clothing industry has recovered on the basis of private enterprise and a large number of small businesses now attracts buyers from all over Eastern Europe and FSU.

There have been some major changes at the Podhale leather factory built in Nowy Targ in the mid-1950s. Up to 10,000 workers were employed in producing shoes, but the factory collapsed with the closure of Eastern markets and eventually the business went bankrupt. However, permission was given to continue business and some new enterprises have emerged. The local Industrial Development Agency has been able to create a joint venture company with Rolls Royce and additional space has been taken by Adidas. There are now more than forty small businesses, including three producing shoes, and total employment is around 3,000. Meanwhile, the old firm's apartments have been purchased by the tenants while the local authority has taken over the skating rink and swimming pool. And foreign investment is coming into clothing and footwear in other parts of Poland. Beskid tanning works near Bielsko-Biala is on the brink of privatisation and is seeking out foreign investors interested in its supply of leather for shoes, upholstery and fancy goods. In 1992 Levi opened a plant at Plotsk 70km. northwest of Warsaw. Although Lodz was initially the preferred location, the local authority was not entirely effective at a time when the Plotsk authorities came up with an old warehouse complex and offered effective cooperation to secure its refurbishment. Now, 230 staff are producing 1.5mn. pairs of jeans (3mn. in two years), a proportion of which is to be exported to the EU. Problems have been encountered over customs delays in clearing imported cloth from the US and a lack of capital for the purchase of franchises (US$0.2mn., given the up-beat environment the firm requires) and so the company is providing its own outlets.

In FGDR, capital has been injected into the Lusatian textile industry which experienced drastic reductions in employment immediately after the revolution. High-quality textiles are now being produced in Forst, Guben and Spremberg using a new production concept rejecting mass production and concentrating on quality. The Tiroler Loden Corporation of Innsbruck is building on the century-long weaving tradition of Forst through the activity of a subsidiary company (Brandenburgische Tuache) within the old 'Forster' factory. Meanwhile, Gubener Tuchmacher works closely with a Paris-based fashion designer and deals with orders from international fashion houses. There is the possibility that this business could extend to a network of Brandenburg textile companies (Kratke 1995, pp.23–4).

Meanwhile, the wood-processing industry, turning out paper, board and furniture, benefits from good supplies of domestic timber over much of Eastern Europe and the prospect of a strong domestic market. The building materials sector is attracting the attention of foreign investors producing cement and tiles. Moves are being made by Western building materials groups like Braas of Frankfurt and Redland of the UK who favour local production because long-distance transport costs are high, while setting up outlays in Eastern Europe is acceptable because of the low labour costs. Moreover, local production creates its own market which has a capacity for very rapid growth in the years ahead, when markets in the West are expected to be stable or declining. Pol-Float Saint Gobain, the Polish subsidiary of French glass manufacturer Saint Gobain, is spending DM170mn. on an environmentally friendly glassworks at Dabrowa Gornicza; while Pilkington's subsidiary Pilkington Sandomierz is investing Zl400mn. to produce 140,000t of float glass per annum for the domestic market; also windows for the car industry. Marley is producing plastic building products at Szekszard in Hungary and has access to East European markets through the German firm Gemenc-Plast. Foreign investment in modernisation helps to provide a secure future and it also provides investment to solve environmental problems which have become a serious problem as a result of the priority under communism for increases in output regardless of cost. Belgium's Cimenteries CBR acquired a 34 per cent share in Zaklady Cementowo-Wapiennicze Gorazdze near Opole in 1993, a long established producer which developed in an area of small-scale lime burning opened up by the Berlin–Katowice railway and modernised under communism. The owners will carry out further developments including a new limestone plant and transport facilities (a new set of railway wagons to supply larger customers) and have offered an attractive social security package (including share ownership on preferential terms). Atmospheric emissions have been reduced and improvements have been made in Gagolin Village. Western firms are also interested in setting up the production of household items. Philips of the Netherlands have set up joint ventures with Polam Farel for the manufacture of lighting fixtures and with Polam Pila to assemble television sets at Kwidzyn. Grundig of Germany are also to produce television sets at a new factory at Kalisz.

The famous Bohemian glass industry has been reorganised. Sklo Bohemia was privatised in 1993 and the technology has since been updated. Preciosa of Jablonec produces machine-cut glass stones, up to 85 per cent of which are exported: it has done well since privatisation in 1992, diversifying into crystal chandeliers and fashion jewellery. But some new owners have only limited expertise and may not have the propensity to invest, while other factories remain in desperate need of privatisation so that long-term production and marketing can be planned. Crystalex is the leader in non-lead decorative glass production and operates from seven separate factories. Privatisation is under way but the government wants the company to remain in Czech hands, like Sklarny Bohemia which was sold in 1995. A problem for the future is that direct selling by individual glass companies will be constrained because the 'Bohemia Glass' and 'Bohemia Crystal' trademarks are exclusively owned by the state trading company Glassexport: no glass distributed by other companies can carry these logos which are recognised worldwide (though the logo is misused abroad and neither Glassexport nor its member factories have a big enough budget to take legal action). Glassexport is actively promoting its products abroad and has arranged a massive display of products from its associated factories in a castle in Liberec. It will be difficult for a rival to duplicate the marketing system of Glassexport, which must however 'get it right' to ensure that Czech glass retains its world position.

### Heavy industry: the case of metallurgy

In the communist period steel output had to be increased irrespective of cost (see Table 7.6). Attention was given to low-grade natural resources and imports from FSU were secured on favourable terms. Old plants were retained despite their technological backwardness but even the new capacities provided in the 1960s and 1970s require extensive modernisation, including the adoption of the latest converter technology. The Bulgarian steel industry started with the coalfield-based Pernik plant, started in 1934 and enlarged under communism as the labour-intensive 'Lenin' works before the more capital-intensive Kremikovtzi complex was built on a low-grade orefield. The first production of iron was in 1962, followed by steel in 1966 and rolling capacity in 1974. The industry was highly uneconomic due to inadequacy of the domestic ore (which in any case needed enrichment) and the friable nature of the domestic coke supply. But the plant was badly located for imported ore which had to be railed up to 500km. overland after arriving by water at Lom on the Danube (following transfer to barges at Galati) and later at Varna, where ore arrived off the 'Druzhba' ferry from Ukraine. There was also the need for linkage with 'reckless investment in the machine tool, engineering and utilities section' in order to consume the enhanced metal output (Palairet 1995, p.503). Although there was some modernisation with French equipment in the 1970s it was effected 'within a structure rooted in abundant cheap power and labour' (ibid.). Major environmental problems may have sapped the energy and motivation of workers.

Despite low labour costs it is proving impossible to maintain the output levels of the mid-1980s in the context of a market economy with reduced demand from the military and realistic pricing which has undermined some steel-using industries previously exporting goods such as ships and railway rolling-stock. Furthermore, trade with Western Europe has been complicated by allegations of dumping. The EU has therefore raised tariff barriers against East European tube makers in the Czech Republic (Chomutov, Ostrava and Vitkovice) and others in Croatia (Sisak), Hungary (Csepel) and Poland. Eastern Europe's steel industry has also been hit by higher costs for raw materials and energy from the FSU which has both direct and indirect effects. Higher costs in Ukraine (dependent on Russia for energy) will affect ore pellets from the Dolinskaya complex which has replaced five old ore enrichment plants burdened by serious pollution problems. At one stage FCS had to send lorry loads of diesel fuel to Ukraine to encourage the loading of ore wagons. However, there is continuing interest in the plant and of the four countries which joined the FSU in the project only Germany has pulled out because of changed circumstances at Eisenhuttenstadt. Although FCS showed some ambivalence, Slovakia has taken over the interest. Romania is particularly involved and indeed was the largest Eastern European contributor, with 27 per cent of the capital (compared with 51 for the FSU, 14 for FCS, five for FGDR and four for Bulgaria). Some 4,500 Romanians were working on the site in the early 1990s.

*Table 7.6* Crude steel production (mn.t.) 1948–92

| Country | 1948 | 1960 | 1970 | 1980 | 1985 | 1989 | 1990 | 1991 | 1992 |
|---|---|---|---|---|---|---|---|---|---|
| Albania | 0.00 | 0.00 | 0.08 | 0.19 | 0.65 | 0.20 | 0.14 | 0.03 | n.a. |
| Bulgaria | 0.00 | 0.25 | 1.80 | 2.56 | 2.94 | 2.90 | 2.18 | 1.61 | 1.55 |
| FCSFR | 2.62 | 6.77 | 11.48 | 15.22 | 15.04 | 15.46 | 14.88 | – | – |
| The Czech Republic | – | – | – | – | – | – | – | 7.97 | 7.33 |
| FGDR | 0.30 | 3.34 | 5.05 | 7.31 | 7.85 | 7.83 | – | – | – |
| Hungary | 0.77 | 1.89 | 3.11 | 3.77 | 3.54 | 3.26 | 2.92 | 2.04 | n.a. |
| Poland | 1.95 | 6.68 | 11.75 | 18.65 | 15.36 | 12.47 | 11.50 | 9.31 | 8.45 |
| Romania | 0.35 | 1.81 | 6.52 | 13.18 | 13.79 | 14.41 | 9.76 | 7.51 | 5.61 |
| Slovakia | – | – | – | – | – | – | – | 4.11 | 4.99 |
| FFYR | 0.37 | 1.44 | 2.23 | 3.63 | 4.52* | 4.54 | 3.58 | – | – |

*Source*: United Nations Yearbooks

Production has been cut drastically and investments in modernisation have been made with the help of the international financial institutions. Greater efficiency has been possible through modern casting methods and pollution has been reduced by the use of cleaner fuels. And whereas plant closures would make for greatest efficiency, most of the inherited locations have been retained. In FGDR Krupp Stahl bought EKO Stahl Eisenhuttenstadt with the aim of building an electric scrap smelter and hot rolling mill while modernising the existing cold rolling mill. Following the takeover of Hoechst, Krupp is the fifth largest steel-maker in Europe with 10mn.t. raw steel capacity. However, only 2,800 of EKO's 5,750 workers remain, although 1,000 of those displaced were expected to find work in tube, transport and construction units to be built nearby.

There was relatively little reorganisation of the industry prior to 1989, although Czestochowa was modernised in the mid-1980s and is now a Polish leader. In Poland, there is a new holding company to rationalise the industry which has seen production fall to as little as one-third of its 18mn.t. capacity while retaining a workforce of 150,000. At the end of 1992 a US$4.5bn. restructuring plan was worked out by Polish and Canadian experts. Bulk steel production will make more use of scrap, while continuous casting should account for 60 per cent of production at the end of 1996 compared with only 8 per cent in 1992. Production is to concentrate on simple quality products that are required for export markets. Four sectors were identified: flat products, quality steel products, long products and pipes. Only one mill has been privatised but employment has been brought down to 93,000, largely due to the elimination of service and social departments which were transformed into independent companies, though still providing services to the mills. Emissions (particularly gases) have been cut. Huta Katowice is to acquire a continuous casting line from Mannesman and will become the main Polish producer. It has a substantial export business involving more than two-thirds of its 3.7mn.t. output, although much of the trade has been unprofitable hitherto. Katowice is to merge with the former Huta Lenina of Nowa Huta (Krakow) where the investment programme will include electric arcs and scrap-consuming mini-mills.

Meanwhile, a joint venture for quality steel-making has been initiated with EBRD support between Lucchini of Italy (efficient operators of scrap-based steel mills) and Huta Warszawa. The Warszawa-Lucchini US$200mn. modernisation project will protect a workforce of 4,700 and the new strip mill will be linked closely with the needs of the expanding car industry. Toxic emissions from the Warsaw plant will be greatly reduced in the process. Zaklad Wielkopiecowy Szczecin turns out high-quality foundry export, some of which is exported through its own harbour depot. Its financial situation has been improved by hiving off a cement plant that processed the blast furnace slag. Huta Bankowa in Dabrowa Gornicza has been reprofiled to produce forged and rolled products from steel delivered from Huta Katowice. Huta Batory in Chorzow has closed obsolete heavy production departments and is investing in a new electric mill. Assistance is coming from Phare in respect of a scrap steel management programme and the design of new mills. The expectation is that Polish steel output can be maintained at only 11.7 mn.t. and some capacity will have to be closed down: Ostrowiec and Szczecin mills along with parts of Bankowa, Batory, Bobrek and Buczek. Labour is being cut drastically to reduce the workforce from 124,000 in 1992 to 44,000 in 2002.

In the Czech Republic, the industry is being reorganised with external assistance. The United Nations Organisation for Industrial Development is reorganising the steel industry with heavier dependence on scrap, as at Kladno in the Czech Republic (with greater concern for the environment through the change from coal-based smelting of iron ore to steel-making from scrap using natural gas). In Ostrava the leading firms (Vitkovice, Nova Hut and Trinecke Zeleziarny) are being rationalised under a regional development plan through lay-offs and foreign partnerships. Vitkovice concentrates on hot rolled plates and seamless tubes and has set up a gas production subsidiary jointly with a Swedish company; Nova Hut has signed a joint venture agreement with the US and South Korean companies for a mini-mill and is linking with Hayes Wheels International's joint venture with Autokola Nova Hut. Nova Hut is now meeting European quality standards for its tube products and the certificate validating this achievement will bring advantages in exporting to the West. Finally, Trinecke Zeleziarny is looking for foreign finance of a mini-mill. It remains to be seen whether these companies survive independently, with foreign support and diversification, or if mergers will be necessary. Meanwhile, in Slovakia, Kosice's East Slovakian Ironworks (Vychodoslovenske Zeleziarny (VSZ)) has been particularly successful in securing exports to compensate for the loss of markets in the FSU and in the domestic armaments industry. It is a relatively efficient unit because iron ore pellets from Ukraine can be carried by broad gauge railway directly to the furnaces while coking coal transported from Ostrava by standard gauge railway can be mechanically unloaded. There is also a labour cost advantage, especially with the slimming down of the workforce from 19,800 to 11,000. Through joint ventures Kosice has also been able to diversify into tin sheet and dynamo steel; while there has been a growth of local steel-using engineering industries producing for the car industry in Bratislava and also for export. The works is crucially important for Slovakia by virtue of the key role of engineering and armaments industries. More foreign investment will be sought.

In Hungary, production declined from 3.7mn.t. in the mid-1980s to 1.6mn.t. in 1992. Production now concentrates on Dunaujvaros and Diosgyor, along with the smaller plant at Ozd. The latter was initially closed, but the possibility of reopening through a scrap-based mini-mill of 400,000t. capacity to supply the car industry has been realised: an electric arc furnace has been installed by an Italian firm along with a continuous casting facility and a modern rod/wire mill. New technology is also being introduced through Japanese finance at Miskolc. Meanwhile, the UN has also been helping the Bulgarian steel industry to switch to greater use of scrap after energy and raw material shortages reduced production to less than 1.5mn.t. in 1992 (when some contract rolling was undertaken to use idle capacity). In Romania, steel production fell from 14.5mn.t. in 1989 to 5.3mn.t. in 1992 and there is a search for markets in the Middle East. All the producers of the communist period have been retained including the inland units of Hunedoara and Resita as well as the newer plants close to the coast at Calarasi and Galati. It was suggested that Resita should close since its local ores were worked out (the last mine was closed in 1994–5) and the transport of imported ore to western Romania, though acceptable under communism, was not considered to be feasible. However, limited steel-making is based on scrap and the future would appear to lie with special steel-making and engineering, rather than bulk iron and steel production. And since the enterprise owns its water supply and hydro-electrical installations it could derive a modest income from a related tourist industry. This will mean writing off some major investments of the communist period including a modern coke-chemical plant, enlarged just before the revolution in connection with a joint project to use imported Serbian coal and Soviet ore in the production of iron ore pellets for use at both Resita and Smederevo. The venture was undermined by both the decision to stop importing iron ore and the UN trade sanctions against Serbia.

*Steel in traditional markets: shipbuilding and armaments*

The fortunes of the steel industry are very much tied to domestic markets and in this context the shipbuilding industry is a major consideration. In FGDR, Deutsche Maschinen- und Schiffbau has attracted interest from Kvaerner of Oslo with regard to the Warnow and Neptun yards in the Rostock area; and from Braemer Vulkan for the Wismar yard and the diesel engine producer in Rostock. In the process the 45,000 workforce of 1989 was reduced to 30,000 in the aftermath of reunification and only 15,000 may survive over the longer term. Kvaerner paid only a symbolic price of DM1mn. for the Warnow yard with debts and liabilities of old contracts taken over by Treuhand. It was calculated in 1992 that the 8,000 jobs safeguarded at that time would each cost DM820,000 over the three years to 1995.

By contrast, the Szczecin yard in Poland has been attractive to foreign companies because of low costs and short completion times (driven by the high cost of credit). Heavy duty cranes have helped the yard to diversify. There is also potential in the Gdynia yard, modernised at the end of the 1970s with modern cutting/welding equipment and dry docks for tankers. There is scope there for exporting to Western Europe. Meanwhile, the Gdansk yard (threatened with closure in 1988) has been building specialised high-value ships, including reefers for Norway and South Africa and Ro-Ro ferries for Finland. Delivery times have increased, in part because of the large number of orders, and the workforce, which fell to 7,200 in the aftermath of the 1988 closure threat, is now insufficient. Some 1,000 additional workers could be taken on, including Gastarbeiter from St Petersburg. The future may be less secure than at Gdynia and Szczecin (both suitable for privatisation with their efficient layouts and good working conditions), but all Polish yards benefit from low labour costs of $1 per hour. This advantage is being exploited through insistence that customers put money up front.

## Armaments

Reorganising the arms industries of former Warsaw Pact countries has been a major challenge and there has been a great effort to retain employment while developing new products and markets (Sabbat-Swidlicka 1993). Efforts to maximise arms sales could complicate closer political ties with the West, including membership of NATO. There have been different attitudes even within Eastern Europe (Cupitt 1993). FCSFR had a particularly important role as an arms producer but when President Havel favoured a radically altered profile there was opposition from Slovakia where 80 per cent of the federation's defence production was located. There is little doubt that differences of approach contributed to the breakup of the federation in 1993 (Fucik 1991). Locations in Slovakia contributed to regional development in this part of the country and also made good sense in the context of Warsaw Pact forces deployed in the Czech Republic. Hydropower was available, with good communications along the Vah Valley; and close links with the metal-lurgical industry of Ostrava (subsequently in Eastern Slovakia too) (Mladek 1993). Kiss (1993) refers to the Martin–Detva–Dubnica triangle with 30,000 workers producing heavy weaponry under Soviet licence, compared with the largest concentration in the Czech Republic of 10,000 in the Slavcin–Bojkovice–Uherski Brod area of Moravia (Kuznetsov 1994).

Fisher (1993) notes that the Meciar government promised to revive the Slovak arms industry, although constraints are imposed by the need for investment and the challenge of a new market situation. Moreover, other countries moved into the markets when FCSFR first abandoned some types of production. Several of the enterprises which have emerged from the breakup of large armaments suppliers are owned entirely by Slovakia's National Property Fund and have therefore been effectively reintegrated into state ownership (Smith 1995). Currently the government's Defence Military Division represents the interests of twenty-five defence manufacturers. Although there has been some labour-shedding the relatively large workforce is retained through the operation of a four-day week. The result could be a hybrid industrial system which could survive long into the transition period (Szelenyi 1989). There have been some successes. Russia's OBK Yakovlev and NPP Klimov defence plants have joined PSP Bystrica in the production of aircraft engines for the Russian military: RD-35 engines from Bystrica will be installed in Russian JAK130 training aircraft. In the Czech Republic, some arms production continues in cooperation with Slovak enterprises. A new prototype self-propelled air defence system built by Konstruckta Trencin uses the Tatra (Koprivnice) armoured chassis and sensors by Tesla of Pardubice (Clarke 1994). Meanwhile, there is Czech–Polish cooperation over trainer aircraft. The Polish tank producer Bumar of Labedy (Gliwice) has developed a new tank and cooperates with French and Swedish companies over new projects (Tiedtke 1983).

But over the long term conversion is more feasible, although this still needs heavy funding and will involve substantial job losses (Kiss 1993). Furthermore, diversification may not relate closely to the high technical standards of military production. Some cut-backs occurred under central planning when an alternative source of employment was sought through licensing agreements with Western firms in respect of heavy engineering products like bulldozers and diesel engines. Conversion at Martin went ahead in the late 1980s thanks to contracts with Hannomag of Germany for tractors and construction machinery; also with Lombardini of Italy regarding the manufacture and sale of small diesel engines (to East European markets only). Dubnica nad Vahom have arrangements with the Reda Corporation of Oklahoma for technology transfer in respect of drilling pumps. The Meopta optical works have converted successfully to the manufacture of overhead projectors and other optical instruments, while ZTS Dubnica (owned by domestic shareholders) now mainly produces spare parts. In the Czech Republic, Aero Volochody in Prague builds jet trainers while Blanicke Strojirny at Vlasim specialises in tools and small tractors for vineyards. Ceska Zbrojovka at Brno-Adamov turns out machinery and the same firm's Uherski Brod plant (owned by domestic shareholders only) now manufactures hunting guns. In Poland a factory in Swidnik now produces gliders while another at Mielec concentrates on old car replicas for the Scandinavian market.

The Balkan countries are also trying to relaunch their arms industries (Dimitrova 1993). Romaero has won orders for BAC 1–11 aircraft from a US domestic carrier; earlier 1–11s (built since 1982) were for Tarom which is now buying Airbus Industrie A-310s and Boeing 737–300s. The Baneasa factory also continues to build Pilatus Britten-Norman 'Islander' planes, a business that started in 1969. Following the termination of agreements with BAC, Romaero has signed a contract with Boeing to produce wing parts and landing gear for 737s and 757s. But Craiova's Avioane company developed the joint production IAR-93 light jet ground attack/tactical reconnaissance aircraft with FRY. The first plane flew in 1974, but there have been few foreign orders in recent years and heavy lay-offs seem inevitable since the Romanian economy can hardly sustain such capacities. Romania's core armaments factories like the RATMIC installations at Cugir, Mizil and Resita face heavy lay-offs and a switch to civilian production. In Bulgaria there has been a lack of consistency from government and there have been political scandals over illegal arms sales. The industry needs consistent policy and government help over restructuring (Engelbrekt 1993). There have been 'leaps in the dark' without adequate feasibility studies and inadequate resources for conversion, while the context of a revised defence strategy appears to be lacking. All countries are having to reckon with enterprises that are overstaffed and over-equipped with large stocks and specialised machinery installed in order to cope in Former Warsaw Pact emergencies. There is also a desperate search for orders (sometimes involving embargoed countries) by enlarged marketing departments with consequent acceptance of jobs at prices below production costs that may offer few scale economies (Kiss 1995).

## EXPANDING INDUSTRIAL SECTORS: THE MOTOR VEHICLE INDUSTRY

This has been a major beneficiary of Western investment since 1989, thanks to the dual attraction of cheap labour and access to the expanding market in a region with only around 120 cars per thousand people in 1990 compared with 360 in Western Europe (Table 7.7). Indeed, it would appear that Eastern Europe is the latest 'spatial fix' for the global automobile industry (Sadler *et al.* 1993). There was already significant production following rapid expansion between 1965 and 1976 (from 0.25mn. cars to 0.76mn.) through cooperation deals and licensing arrangements with Western companies, especially Citroen, Fiat and Renault. But growth was relatively slow during the 1980s despite attempts to produce specially for the Western market, such as the Skoda 'Favorit' from FCS. Factories were small by Western standards, yet all the East European countries except Albania and Hungary did feature in the production tables. Given the pent-up demand in Eastern Europe, underscored by the priority for rail transport under central planning, a prominent feature of the transition was bound to be a relative expansion in road traffic and a sharp increase in car ownership as the freeing of trade made it possible for both new and used cars to be imported. And despite a relatively slow pace of reform, car-makers have remained impressed by the potential market. Firms are keen to get in behind tariff barriers, with the added

*Table 7.7* Foreign investment in car production to 1996

| Country | Company | Location | Partner | Capacity 000s pa |
|---|---|---|---|---|
| Bulgaria | Rover | Varna | Dary | 10 Maestro |
| Czech Republic | VW | Mlada Boleslav | Skoda | 340 Felicia |
| FGDR | GM(Opel) | Eisenach | AWE | 150 – |
| FGDR | VW | Mosel (Zwickau) | VEB | 250 Golf |
| Hungary | GM | Szentgotthard | Raba | 50 Astra |
| Hungary | Suzuki | Esztergom | Autokonszern[1] | 60 Swift |
| Poland | Daewoo | Lublin | FSL | 50 Nexia |
| Poland | Daewoo | Warsaw | FSO | 220 Espero |
| Poland | Fiat | Bielsko Biala/Tychy | FSM | 240 Cinquecento |
| Poland | Ford | Plonsk | – | 20 Escort |
| Poland | GM(Opel) | Gliwice | – | – |
| Romania | Daewoo | Craiova | Rodae Automobile | 200 Cielo |
| Slovenia | Renault | Novo Mesto | IMV | 100 Five/Clio/Twingo |
| Slovakia | VW | Bratislava | BAZ | 30 Golf/Passat |

*Note* 1 Also Itocha and International Finance Corporation.
*Source*: Trade journals

attraction of low cost labour, suggesting the possibility of car production in the East for export (Hughes 1992). Wage costs of DM4 per hour in Hungary have been compared with DM35 in Germany (Sadler and Swain 1995, p.399).

Up to the time of writing (mid-1996) an additional capacity of some 1.7mn. cars per annum has been announced (mainly by Daewoo, Fiat, General Motors andVolkswagen) and components manufacturers have also moved in. In FGDR where the vehicle company ITA has been radically reorganised, Opel and BMW have taken over the former Wartburg plant at Eisenach and aim to produce 150,000 cars per annum. Volkswagen was keen to move assembly and components manufacture away from high cost locations in the West. Hence the DM4.6bn investment at Mosel, Zwickau with a 5,000 workforce to produce 250,000 cars annually from 1994. The old Trabant factory was converted to manufacture the Volkswagen 'Golf' in 1992 with 2,300 workers compared with the 11,000 employed under the former management. But a new factory has come on stream. Meanwhile, engines are to be produced at Chemnitz (where two-stroke engines, with attendant pollution hazards, were previously made for Trabant cars) and cylinder heads at Eisenach. The company has concentrated a great deal of attention on developing an indigenous supplier network and is cooperating with fifteen component suppliers within Saxony. Training centres were opened at Chemnitz and Zwickau to help the component companies as well as Volkswagen itself.

German companies have also been drawn by the Czech Republic's engineering skills and proximity to the main markets of Eastern Europe; also cheap labour despite cultural similarities. Volkswagen purchased management control of Skoda Mlada Boleslav and initially planned to invest DM9.5bn to produce up to 220,000 additional new cars annually (rising to 460,000 by the year 2000), alongside the production of the Skoda Favorit, while expanding engine production for the Volkswagen range. The plant started building the Felicia in 1994 (resembling the Volkswagen Golf and replacing the Favorit as the flagship model) which has good export potential. Unfortunately, Volkswagen was hit by recession in Western Europe and competition in the East. Reduced duties on cars imported from the EU from 15.2 to 11.4 per cent (part of the Czech Republic's Association Agreement with the EU) meant a loss of market share for Volkswagen; while Lada of Russia and Tavaria of Ukraine started undercutting the Favorit. It is now expected that capacity will rise more slowly to reach 340,000 by the end of the decade, well below the target first announced. Investment will only amount to one-third of the level announced in 1991, with the new engine plant shelved for the time being.

Meanwhile, despite having no stake in car production under communism, on account of specialisation agreements which gave the country a major stake in the production of buses, Hungary has attracted much of the new investment in the early 1990s and is now restarting a tradition established in the 1920s and 1930s. New investment has been stimulated by substantial tax concessions, including ten years' exemption from corporate taxes on profits (provided profits are reinvested). There have also been subsidies in recognition of employment creation and some provision of infrastructure. Emphasis has been placed on workers from rural areas unfamiliar with industrial employment under communist conditions. The result is a high level of flexibility, with wage costs that are low by West European standards. As a result of negotiations which began in 1986 and which include a ten-year tax holiday, Suzuki is making an investment of US$230mn. at Esztergom where a former Soviet Army firing range has direct access to port facilities on the Danube. The plan has been to turn out 15,000 cars in 1993, rising to 50,000 in 1995 and ultimately to 60,000 in 1997. Magyar Suzuki is owned primarily by Suzuki and by Autokonszern, a consortium of about sixty companies, some of which are active in the production of components. In addition to the two 40 per cent holdings, 11 per cent is held by the Japanese finance house Itochu (previously C.Itoh) and 9 per cent by the International Finance Corporation. But Suzuki has increased its stake to 49.9 per cent and Itochu to 15.5 per cent; while Autokonszern's share has fallen back to 30.1 per cent. The project is tailor-made to cover the development of components, building on Comecon's experience. There was an initial target of 60 per cent local content and twenty-five Hungarian companies were selected from a list of over a hundred as a base for Suzuki's drive to improve production standards. Government hopes that as many as 18,000 new jobs will be created, many of them in the northern industrial zones experiencing high unemployment. But it will take some time to build up to this level and Suzuki's stringent quality standards will have to be met. In the meantime parts are coming from Japan. The small Swift car is being produced and there should be 1,100 jobs at the factory when full capacity is reached. It is reported that Suzuki will expand the range of cars produced at Esztergom to include four-wheel drive passenger cars for the Subaru Group.

Another factory, producing 50,000 cars Opel Astra cars each year, was opened in 1992 by General Motors at Szentgotthard, four years after the first contact between the company and the Hungarian government. This is much more of a branch plant, employing an estimated 450 workers and using the team concept matched only by Eisenach. General Motors at Szentgotthard began by importing kits for assembly (mainly from Aspern in Austria) and then had to export the finished cars. However, an engine plant will follow the initial assembly facility. The enterprise is the result of cooperation between General Motors Europe and the Raba Railway Carriage and Machine Factory which dates back to 1980 when Raba produced axles for General Motors plants in Europe. But to facilitate the new venture in 1991 the Hungarian government agreed to pay most of Raba's capital commitment. Szentgotthard has been declared a customs-free zone to facilitate close cooperation with the existing engine plant at Aspern in Austria (just 100km. away) (Okolicsanyi 1992). In addition to the usual service requirements, a 30km. high pressure gas pipeline has been built. And to relieve congestion six extra crossing points along the Austrian–Hungarian border have been opened. Szentgotthard now employs 650 workers assembling Astra hatchbacks and estates and turning out Ecotec 16-valve engines (250,000 per annum with a two-shift working). Although the cars are mainly for the home market (avoiding high import duties), since re-export is hardly economic compared with high-volume plants in Germany, one-fifth of the 1994 production of 12,250 cars went abroad, mainly to Germany, Italy and Turkey due to Szentgotthard's flexibility in making up shortfalls.

In Poland by contrast, there were a number of car and light vehicle factories operating under communism, and these were established links for Western firms to build on. Fiat cooperated with the small car factory (Fabryka Samochodow Malolitrazowych (FSM)) in the 1970s when the successful 126p (known to the Poles as the *maluch* or toddler) was produced at Bielsko-Biala and Tychy and which found much favour on the domestic market. In 1990 Fiat Auto Poland was set up to look after arrangements made in 1987 for the production of a new car, the Cinquecento. The first vehicles appeared the following year and production increased to the target figure of 240,000 cars in 1994.

In addition, 20,000 Fiat Uno cars were produced from kits because Polish demand could not be met from imports, benefiting from the decree that allowed substantial import duty relief on machinery and equipment sent to the factory. Meanwhile, Poland's passenger car factory (Fabryka Samochodow Osobowych (FSO)) was opened in the Zeran district of Warsaw to build the Fiat 125 under licence and from this emerged the Polonez, although it was heavy on fuel and prone to fire. However, in 1990, rather than maintain the links with Fiat, the Polish government sought a greater diversity of Western contacts and General Motors (Opel) set out to modernise the plant by investing US$75mn. for an 80 per cent stake in the joint venture. The main objective was the assembly of Astra cars in a new US$20mn. factory that was to open in 1994 with initial production of 35,000 vehicles, working up to 100–150,000. The components were to be imported in kits: ready-painted car bodies from the Antwerp factory, engines and transmission equipment from Bochum. General Motors also expressed interest in upgrading Polish producers of components with the possibility of supply for other models. There was also talk of a further investment of US$300mn. to develop a new model to revamp the Polonez (now relatively unpopular) with an Opel engine and new suspension. But the company's proposed stake remained small compared with Fiat and only 1,000 of the 19,000 FSO workers were to be engaged on the Astra.

Meanwhile, high tariff levels on imported cars induced Ford to reconsider its investment in a car seat cover factory at Plonsk aimed at the supply of Ford plants throughout Europe. Instead, the company undertook a US$54mn. investment to achieve an annual output of 20,000 Escort cars from kits imported from Belgium, Germany and the UK. Production started in 1995 and included completion of 10,000 Transit vans, employing 250 people with the prospect of contracts with Polish components suppliers. Somewhat later an agreement was reached in 1994 between Peugeot and Lublin's state car and lorry factory (Fabryka Samochodow w Lublinie (FSL)) to assemble the 405 cars: 2,000 in 1993 rising to 10,000 in 1996 using about one-fifth of Polish parts. The French company also intended to assemble light vans. Arrangements were also made for Ukrainian designed Tavaria cars to be assembled in Lodz. However, Daewoo then came on the scene with proposals for both FSL and FSO that were far superior to the deals with Peugeot and GM respectively. Accordingly, the GM and Peugeot agreement was discontinued in 1995. In view of the Daewoo intervention in Warsaw it was reported in 1995 that GM have decided to build a greenfield factory with an investment of US$340mn. to build an initial 72,000 low cost family cars per annum by 1998, rising to 150,000 over the longer term. It is not known if Peugeot have alternative arrangements in mind.

The way has been cleared for Daewoo to follow up its business in Craiova (Romania) by investing up to US$400mn. in Lublin and taking a 70 per cent stake in FSL, looking to an annual production of 50,000 Nexia saloons (possibly the Tico also) and 40,000 trucks by the end of the century. Meanwhile, Daewoo has taken a 60 per cent stake in FSO and is offering alternatives to the ageing Polonez, which will however remain in production as long as there is demand. The Daewoo link is very good news for FSO workers because massive reductions in the workforce of 20,000 seemed inevitable given the fact that other European factories employed only 2,000 to 3,000 workers for a similar volume of production. Daewoo will take the whole workforce to set up a complete production base for 220,000–300,000 cars per annum: this is nearly four times the General Motors target which was related only to assembly, apart from the possibility of engines and gearboxes in the future. Daewoo will train FSO workers on their Nexia and Espero models but production of 40,000 Espero and Tico cars is planned for 1990 and the company is also looking ahead to new generation T100 and J100 cars which will enter production in South Korea in 1996–7.

Thus, it seems clear that investment in Eastern Europe is the latest fashion for car-makers anxious to decentralise away from the high cost core of Europe. The trend is not restricted to European firms because of Suzuki's early interest in Hungary and the recent Daewoo activity in both Poland and Romania. But much will depend on the growth of the East European market and the labour cost advantages of different peripheral areas for Eastern Europe is very much in competition with Iberia (Swain 1992a). At the moment the large size of the Polish home market seems to be a telling factor not only for car production but also for the building of lorries, vans and buses. However, it is noticeable that, as demonstrated by the Hungarian experience, there are sharply contrasting approaches between projects which create classic branch plants, 'enclaves dislocated from local market and regulatory upheaval' and 'relatively locally-embedded production facilities within a European manufacturing system' (Sadler *et al.* 1993, p.348). The latter situation is obviously preferable from the East European angle although the former does have its own attractions in terms of employment and technology transfer and established bases which could be enlarged in the light of continuing cost advantages and local market opportunities. At the same time foreign investment is opening up divisions between East European companies which have found a long-term future through a foreign partner and those which have not. Zastava in Yugoslavia faces an uncertain future while in Romania the Daewoo deal in respect of the Oltcit factory in Craiova leaves the older Dacia plant at Pitesti-Colibasi in a vulnerable position. It is still possible to create new designs although development capital for SOEs may be difficult to find.

There appear to be prospects for small-scale assembly of cars or commercial vehicles where foreign firms are unwilling to contemplate investment in major production facilities. In the Czech Republic, Mercedes are turning out vans at Prague-Letnany and trucks at Jablonec in collaboration with Avia and Liaz respectively, while Renault buses are coming out of Karosa's Vysoke Myto factory. MAN trucks are being built by Raba at Gyor in Hungary while Balkancar are producing trucks for South Korea's Hyundai Corporation. The majority of such deals seem to be clustered in Poland where the prospects for the home market are particularly promising. The German company Neoplan is assembling buses in Bolechow while MAN hopes to build buses at Poznan's military vehicle factory which already assembles MAN truck-tractors. From 1995 Scania has been assembling articulated buses as well as trucks at Slupsk, and Volvo have a factory for buses and trucks in Wroclaw. At the same time there has been a positive response to the situation from Sobieslaw Zasada Centrum (SZC), an importer and service company for Mercedes-Benz products, which has drawn several Polish commercial vehicle factories and components suppliers under its umbrella. The aim is to acquire interests in flagging companies and to undertake investments that will turn them round, with Mercedes technology and the commercial link with the company helping to give the group a competitive edge. Business is not highly profitable at present, but the long-term prospects are good. The initiative began with delivery vans at the military auto plant (Wojskowe Zaklady Motoryzacyjne) at Glowno near Lodz, followed by the assembly of Mercedes 300D passenger cars at Karczew near Warsaw. Special purpose-built truck bodies are produced at Kalisz, while the company has bought into the Star truck-maker at Starachowice (reportedly talking to Navistar International Transport about the production of Navistar lorries in Poland and Star lorries with Navistar engines). But although foreign firms see SZC as being in a strong position with the advantage of privileges from government, there is a danger of intensified competition from the already active Western firms.

# REFERENCES

T.N. Ash 1992, 'East European agriculture at the cross-roads'. *Radio Free Europe/ Radio Liberty Research* 1(4), 33–8.

T. Bergmann 1992, 'The reprivatization of farming in eastern Germany'. *Sociologia Ruralis* 32, 305–16.

G. Bettram 1992, 'Nature conservation and agricultural practices in Slovenia' in A. Gilg *et al.* (eds) *Progress in Rural Planning* Vol. 2 (London: Belhaven Press), 167–75.

S. Bojnec 1994, 'Agricultural reform in Slovenia' in J.F.M. Swinnen (ed.) *Policy and Institutional Reform in Central European Agriculture* (Aldershot: Avebury), 135–68.

F. Bordanc 1996, 'Spatial variations in the progress of land reform in Romania'. *GeoJournal* 38, 161–5.

A. Braverman *et al.* (eds) 1993, *The Agricultural Transition in Central and Eastern Europe and Former USSR* (Washington DC: World Bank).

K.M. Brooks and Z. Lerman 1994, 'Farm reform in the transition economies'. *Finance and Development: A Quarterly Publication of the International Monetary Fund and the World Bank* 31(4), 25–8.

K.M. Brooks *et al.* 1991, 'Agriculture and the transition to the market'. *Journal of Economic Perspectives* 5, 149–61.

A. Buckwell *et al.* (eds) 1994, *The Transformation of Agriculture: A Case Study of Bulgaria* (Boulder, Colorado: Westview Press).

A. Burger 1993, 'Restructuring Eastern Europe's agriculture' in A. Kertesz and S.Z. Kovacs (eds) *New Perspectives in Hungarian Geography* (Budapest: Hungarian Academy of Sciences), 105–13.

D.I. Clarke 1994, 'Eastern Europe's troubled arms industries'. *Radio Free Europe/ Radio Liberty Research* 3(14), 35–43; 3(21), 28–39.

N.J. Cochrane 1994, 'Farm restructuring in Central and Eastern Europe'. *Soviet and Post-Soviet Review* 21, 319–35.

C. Csaki and Z. Lerman 1993, 'Land reform and the future role of cooperatives in agriculture in the former socialist countries of Europe' in C. Csaki and Y. Kislev (eds) *Agricultural Cooperatives in Transition* (Boulder, Colorado: Westview Press), 143–59.

R.T. Cupitt 1993, 'The political economy of arms exports in post-communist societies: the case of Poland and CSFR'. *Communist and Post-Communist Studies* 26, 87–103.

S. Davidova 1994, 'Changes in agricultural policies and restructuring of Bulgarian agriculture: an overview' in J.F.M. Swinnen (ed.) *Policy and Institutional Reform in Central European Agriculture* (Aldershot: Avebury), 31–76.

A. Dimitrova 1993, 'The plight of Bulgaria's arms industry'. *Radio Free Europe/ Radio Liberty Research* 2(7), 48–53.

E.J. Dittrich *et al.* 1995, *Industrial Transformation in Europe: Process and Contexts* (London: Sage).

S. Dobreva 1994, 'The family farm in Bulgaria: tradition and change'. *Sociologia Ruralis* 24, 340–53.

W. Doppler 1994, 'Farming systems approach and its relevance for agricultural development in Central and Eastern Europe' in J.B. Dent and M.J. MacGregor (eds) *Rural and Farming Systems Analysis: European Perspectives* (Wallingford: CAB International), 65–77.

S. Elek 1991, 'Part-time farming in Hungary: an instrument of tacit decollectivisation?' *Sociologia Ruralis* 31, 82–8.

K. Engelbrekt 1993, 'Bulgaria and the arms trade'. *Radio Free Europe/Radio Liberty Research* 2(7), 44–7.

S. Fisher 1993, 'The Slovak arms industry'. *Radio Free Europe/Radio Liberty Research* 2(38), 34–9.

J. Fucik 1991, 'The Czechoslovak armament industry'. *Military Technology* 7, 98–102.

I. Gabor 1991, 'Private entrepreneurship and re-embourgoisement in Hungary'. *Society and Economy* 13, 122–33.

D. Gavrilescu 1994, 'Agricultural reform in Romania: between market priority and the strategies of food security' in J.F.M. Swinnen (ed.) *Policy and Institutional Reform in Central European Agriculture* (Aldershot: Avebury), 169–210.

G. Grabher 1994, 'The disembedded regional economy: the transformation of East German industrial complexes into Western enclaves' in A. Amin and N. Thrift (eds) *Globalization, Institutions and Regional Development in Europe* (Oxford: Oxford University Press), 177–95.

D.R. Hall 1996, 'Albania: rural development, migration and uncertainty'. *GeoJournal* 38, 185–9.

F.E.I. Hamilton 1982, 'Regional policy for Poland: a search for equity'. *Geoforum* 13, 121–32.

I. Harcsa 1993, 'Small scale farming, informal cooperation and the household economy in Hungary'. *Sociologia Ruralis* 33, 105–8.

D.C. Henry 1994, 'Reviving Romania's rural economy'. *Radio Free Europe/RadioLiberty Research* 3(7), 18–23.

D.M.W.N. Hitchens *et al.* 1995, *Competitiveness of Industry in the Czech Republic and Hungary* (Aldershot: Avebury).

H. Hudecova and M. Lostak 1992, 'Privatisation of Czechoslovak agriculture: results of a 1990 sociological survey'. *Sociologia Ruralis* 32, 287–304.

S. Hughes 1992, 'Living with the past: trade unionism in Hungary since political pluralism'. *Industrial Relations Journal* 23, 293–303.

M. Jackson and W. Biesbrouck 1995, *Marketization, Restructuring and Competition in Transition Industries in Central and Eastern Europe* (Aldershot: Avebury).

J. Juhasz 1991, 'Hungarian agriculture: present situation and future prospects'. *European Review of Agricultural Economics* 18, 399–416.

Y. Kapitanski and M. Anastasova 1994, 'Problems of social insurance in the agricultural sector during the transition to a market economy' in F. Grief (ed.) *Die Zukunft der landlichen Infrastruktur in Ostmitteleuropa* (Wien: Schriftenreihe der Bundesanstalt fur Agrarwirtschaft 75), 33–8.

L. Karp and S. Stefanou 1994, 'Domestic and trade policy for Central and East European agriculture'. *Economics of Transition* 2, 345–71.

D.A. Kideckel 1992, 'Peasants and authority in the new Romania' in D.N. Nelson (ed.) *Romania after Tyranny* (Boulder, Colorado: Westview Press), 67–81.

Y. Kiss 1993, 'Lost illusions? defense industry conversion in Czechoslovakia 1989–92'. *Europe Asia Studies* 45, 1045–69.

Y. Kiss 1995, 'Sink or swim?: Central European defence industry enterprises in the aftermath of the Cold War'. *Europe Asia Studies* 47, 787–812.

P. Klekner 1992, 'The role of agriculture in the development of fringe areas' in M. Tikkylainen (ed.) *Development Issues and Strategies in the new Europe* (Aldershot: Gower), 121–30.

M. Klodzinski 1992, 'Processes of agricultural change in Eastern Europe: the example of Poland' in R.M. Auty and R.B. Potter (eds) *Agricultural Change, Environment and Economy* (London: Mansell), 123–37.

L. Kopacka 1994, 'Industry in the transition of Czech society and economy'. *GeoJournal* 32, 207–14.

I. Kovach 1991, 'Rediscovering small scale enterprise in rural Hungary' in S.

Whatmore *et al.* (eds) *Rural Enterprise: Shifting Perspectives on Small Scale Production* (London: Fulton), 78–96.

I. Kovach 1994a, 'Privatization and family farms in Central and Eastern Europe'. *Sociologia Ruralis* 34, 369–82.

I. Kovach 1994b, 'Part-time small-scale farming or a major form of economic pluriactivity in Hungary' in J, Szmatka *et al.* (eds) *East European Societies on the Threshold of Change* (Lampeter: Edwin Mellen Press), 175–92.

D. Kovacs 1993a, 'Political change and the generation effect among agricultural cooperative managers in Hungary'. *Sociologia Ruralis* 33, 100–4.

K. Kovacs 1993, 'The slow transition of Hungarian agriculture'. *Anthropological Journal of European Cultures* 2, 105–27.

S. Kratke 1995, *Where East Meets West: Prospects of the German-Polish Border Region* (Frankfurt/Oder: Europa Universitat Viadrina, Faculty of Cultural Sciences).

J. Kraus *et al.* 1994, 'Agricultural reform and transformation in the Czech Republic' in J.F.M. Swinnen (ed.) *Policy and Institutional Reform in Central European Agriculture* (Aldershot: Avebury), 107–34.

W. Kurek 1996, 'Agriculture versus tourism in rural areas of the Polish Carpathians'. *GeoJournal* 38, 191–6.

E. Kuznetsov 1994, 'Adjustment of Russian defence-related enterprises in 1992–4: macro-economic implications'. *Communist Economies and Economic Transformation* 6, 473–514.

A. Kwiecinski and W. Quaisser 1993, 'Agricultural prices and subsidies in the transformation process of the Polish economy'. *Economic Systems* 17, 125–54.

R. Manchin and I. Szelenyi 1985, 'Theories of family agricultural production in collectivised economies'. *Sociologia Ruralis* 25, 248–68.

T. Marsden 1990, 'Towards the political economy of pluriactivity'. *Journal of Rural Studies* 6, 375–82.

K.R. Mazurski 1991, 'Problems of Polish agriculture' in A. Gilg *et al.* (eds) *Progress in Rural Policy and Planning* Vol. 1 (London: Belhaven Press), 131–9.

G. Merritt 1991, 'The East could become the granary of Europe' in G. Merritt *Eastern Europe and the USSR: The Challenge of Freedom* (London: Kogan Page), 151–68.

S. Meszaros 1994, 'The reform process in Hungarian agriculture: an overview' in J.F.M. Swinnen (ed.) *Policy and Institutional Reform in Central European Agriculture* (Aldershot: Avebury), 77–106.

J. Mladek 1993, 'Localization and development of machine industry in Central Povazie'. *Acta Facultatis Rerum Naturalium Universitatis Comenianae: Geographica* 32, 161–91.

W.B. Morgan 1989a, 'Recent government policy and private agriculture in Poland'. *Resource Management and Optimization* 6, 291–305.

W.B. Morgan 1989b, 'Individual farming and spatial policy in Poland'. *Geographica Polonica* 56, 121–32.

W.B. Morgan 1990, 'Some aspects of recent improvements in the productivity of private agriculture in Poland'. *Geographica Polonica* 57, 99–110.

W.B. Morgan 1992, 'Economic reform, the free market and agriculture in Poland'. *Geographical Journal* 158, 145–56.

R.D. Mueller and J. Mueller 1996, 'Policy concerns in Bulgarian food distribution'. *GeoJournal* 38, 167–74.

N. Muica and D. Turnock 1996, 'The potential for traditional food and drink products in Eastern Europe: fruit processing – especially brandy (tuica) distilling – in Romania'. *GeoJournal* 38, 197–206.

R. Murray 1992, 'Flexible specialisation and development strategy: the relevance for

Eastern Europe' in E. Ernste and V. Mier (eds) *Regional development and Contemporary Industrial Responses* (London: Belhaven Press), 197–218.

T. Nicolescu 1992, 'Entrepreneurship in Romania'. *Radio Free Europe/Radio Liberty Research* 1(38), 45–50.

K. Okolicsanyi 1992, 'Hungary: a car industry is born'. *Radio Free Europe/Radio Liberty Research* 1(19) 26–33.

S. Paczka and R. Riley 1992, 'Lodz textiles in the new Polish economic order'. *Geography* 77, 361–3.

M. Palairet 1995, '"Lenin" and "Brezhnev": steelmaking and the Bulgarian economy 1956–1990'. *Europe Asia Studies* 47, 493–505.

K. Pata and M. Osmani 1994, 'Albanian agriculture: a painful transition from communism to free market challenges'. *Sociologia Ruralis* 24, 71–83.

B. Pavlin 1991, 'Contemporary changes in the agricultural use of land in the border landscape units of the Slovene littoral'. *Geographica Slovenica* 22, 1–119.

M. Persanyi 1990, 'The rural environment in a post-socialist economy: the case of Hungary' in T. Marsden *et al.* (eds) *Technological Change and the Rural Environment* (London: Fulton), 32–52.

A. Pilichowski 1993, 'Poland's agrarian structure: a sociological perspective'. *Sociologia Ruralis* 33, 92–5.

F. Pine 1992, 'Uneven burdens: women in rural Poland' in S. Rai *et al.* (eds) *Women in the Face of Change: The Soviet Union Eastern Europe and China* (London: Routledge), 57–75.

F. Pine 1993, 'The cows and pigs are his, the eggs are mine: women's domestic economy and entrepreneurial activity in rural Poland' in C.M. Hann (ed.) *Socialism: Ideals, Ideologies and Local Practice* (London: Routledge), 227–42.

F. Pine 1994, 'Privatisation in post-socialist Poland: peasant women, work and restructuring of the public sphere'. *Cambridge Anthropology* 17(3), 19–42.

G. Ploaie 1996, 'The impact of tourism and conservation on agriculture in the mountains of Valcea County, Romania'. *GeoJournal* 38, 219–28.

C. Popescu 1993, 'Romanian industry in transition'. *GeoJournal* 29, 41–8.

A. Potrykowska 1995, 'Restructurization, deindustrialization and unemployment in Poland: a case study of Warsaw'. *Geographia Polonica* 64, 19–36.

F.L. Pryor 1992, *The Red and the Green: The Rise and Fall of Collectivised Agriculture in Marxist Regimes* (Princeton: Princeton University Press).

H. Repassy and D. Symes 1993, 'Perspectives on agrarian reform in East Central Europe'. *Sociologia Ruralis* 33, 81–91.

R. Rose and E. Tikhomirov 1993, 'Who grows food in Russia and Eastern Europe?' *Post-Soviet Geography* 34, 111–26.

J. Rowinski 1994, 'Transformation of the food economy in Poland' in J.F.M. Swinnen (ed.) *Policy and Institutional Reform in Central European Agriculture* (Aldershot: Avebury), 211–36.

A. Sabbat-Swidlicka 1993, 'Poland's arms trade faces new conditions'. *Radio Free Europe/Radio Liberty Research* 2(4), 49–53.

D. Sadler and A. Swain 1995, 'State and market in Eastern Europe: regional development and workplace implications of direct foreign investment in the automobile industry in Hungary'. *Transactions Institute of British Geographers* 19, 387–403.

D. Sadler *et al.* 1993, 'The automobile industry and Eastern Europe: new production strategies or old solutions?' *Area* 25, 339–49.

K. Sebestyen 1993, 'Transformation of cooperatives in Hungarian agriculture' in C. Csaki and Y. Kislev (eds) *Agricultural Cooperatives in Transition* (Boulder, Colorado: Westview Press), 301–9.

A. Smith 1995, 'Uneven development and the restructuring of the armanents industry in Slovakia'. *Transactions Institute of British Geographers* 19, 404–24.

M. Stambuk 1991, 'Agricultural depopulation in Croatia'. *Sociologia Ruralis* 31, 281–9.

D. Stark 1993, *Recombinant Property in East European Capitalism* (Princeton, New Jersey: Princeton University Sociology Department/Berlin: Wissenschaftszentrum) Discussion Paper FSI 93–103.

A. Staziak 1989, 'Changes in rural settlement in Poland up to 2000'. *Geographia Polonica* 56, 109–14.

I. Stebelsky 1995, *The Food System in the Post-Soviet Era* (Boulder, Colorado: Westview Press).

V. Surd 1994, 'Critical status of rural Romania' in F. Grief (ed.) *Die Zukunft der landlichen Infrastruktur in Ostmitteleuropa* (Wien: Schriftenreihe der Bundesanstalt fur Agrarwirtschaft 75), 61–7.

N. Swain 1985, *Collective Farms Which Work?* (Cambridge: Cambridge University Press).

N. Swain 1992a, *Eastern Europe and the Global Strategies of Automobile Producers* (Durham: Department of Geography, University of Durham).

N. Swain 1992b, *Transitions from Family to Collective Farming in Post-Socialist Central Europe: A Victory for Politics over Sociology* (Liverpool: University of Liverpool Centre for Central and Eastern European Studies).

N. Swain 1992c, *Transitions from Collective to Family Farming in Post-Socialist Central Europe: Background and Strategies for Change* (Liverpool: University of Liverpool Centre for Central and Eastern European Studies).

N. Swain 1993a, *Transitions to Family Farming in Post-Socialist Central Europe* (Liverpool: University of Liverpool Centre for Central and Eastern European Studies).

N. Swain 1993b, *From Kolkhoz to Genuine Cooperative: Transition Problems in Central European Agriculture* (Liverpool: University of Liverpool Centre for Central and Eastern European Studies).

N. Swain 1993c, *The Smallholders Party Versus the Green Barons: Class Relations in the Restructuring of Hungarian Agriculture* (Liverpool: University of Liverpool Centre for Central and Eastern European Studies).

J.F.M. Swinnen 1994, 'Overview of policy and institutional reform in Central European agriculture' in J.F.M. Swinnen (ed.) *Policy and Institutional Reform in Central European Agriculture* (Aldershot: Avebury), 1–30.

I. Szelenyi 1989, 'Eastern Europe in an epoch of transition towards a socialist mixed economy?' in V. Nee and D. Stark (eds) *Remaking the Institutions of Socialism: China and Eastern Europe* (Stanford, California: Stanford University Press), 208–32.

S. Tiedtke 1983, 'Czechoslovakia' in N. Ball and M. Leitenberg (eds) *The Structure of the Defense Industry: An International Survey* (London: Croom Helm), 181–213.

A. Toth 1992, 'The social impact of restructuring in rural areas of Hungary: disruption of security or an end to the rural socialist middle class?' *Soviet Studies* 44, 1039–43.

D. Turnock 1996, 'Agriculture in Eastern Europe: communism, the transition and the future'. *GeoJournal* 38, 137–49.

S. Varga 1996, 'Changes in Hungary's agrarian sector with special regard to the northern hill region'. *GeoJournal* 38, 181–4.

I. Vasary 1990, 'Competing paradigms: peasant farming and collectivisation in a Balaton community'. *Journal of Communist Studies* 6(2), 163–82.

K. Verdery 1994, 'The elasticity of land: problems of property restitution in Transylvania'. *Slavic Review* 53, 1071–1109.

I. Vriser 1992, 'Industrialization in Slovenia'. *GeoJournal* 27, 365–70.

I. Vriser 1993, 'Agrarian economy in Slovenia', *GeoJournal* 31, 373–7.

I. Vriser 1996, 'The development, present significance and future prospects of agricultural enterprises in Slovenia'. *GeoJournal* 38, 151–6.

G. Weclawowicz 1996, *Contemporary Poland: Space and Society* (London: UCL Press).

C. Wellisz 1992, 'Joint ventures jump-start the Polish automobile industry'. *Radio Free Europe/Radio Liberty Research* 1(33), 28–32.

S. Whatmore 1994, 'Global agro-food complexes and the refashioning of rural Europe' in A. Amin and N. Thrift (eds) *Globalization, Institutions and Regional Development in Europe* (Oxford: Oxford University Press), 46–67.

O. Wilson 1996, 'Emerging patterns of restructured farm businesses in Eastern Germany', *GeoJournal* 38, 157–60.

M.L. Wyzan and O. Sjoberg 1992, 'Agricultural privatisation in Bulgaria and Albania: legal foundations and prospects' (Stockholm Institute of East European Economics Working Paper 61).

C. Young 1993, 'A bitter harvest?: problems of restructuring East Central European agriculture'. *Geography* 78, 69–72.

L. Zanga 1994, 'Albania optimistic about economic growth'. *Radio Free Europe/ Radio Liberty Research* 3(7), 14–7.

# 8

# PROSPECTS FOR THE REGIONS OF EASTERN EUROPE

Under socialism, regional development existed only at the level of ideological proclamations, for, according to Enyedi (1990), progress depended on the haphazard outcome of various sectoral decisions taken by ministries. The stronger regions were restrained by what Dostal and Hampl (1994, p. 204) describe as 'the policy of nivelization of interregional disparities in living standards based on the industrialization campaign [which involved] an extraordinary suppression of any important selective tendencies at the interregional level'. Moreover, although they benefited from low energy costs, maintained by the FSU for the benefit of its allies through the 1980s, the regions of Eastern Europe did not enjoy the post-war economic boom experienced in Western Europe or the high levels of technological innovation which persistently marginalised the smoke-stack industries so strongly encouraged in the east. They had access to relatively undemanding markets in the FSU, but rejected specialisation in preference for a more autarkic approach which required heavy capital borrowings from the West to modernise and diversify exports. But while East European industries supplied each home market (and generated a good deal of pollution in the process), they rarely achieved the levels of efficiency necessary for a rewarding export business. Moreover, although the more dynamic regions were held back, there were still significant variations between regions at the end of the communist period (Tables 8.1 and 8.2).

Investment is now much more dependent on wider global considerations through external scrutiny of Eastern Europe's potentials. The Balkan countries tend to be regarded as relatively risky whereas Poland, Slovakia and Slovenia seem more stable; while the Czech Republic, FGDR and Hungary are particularly attractive. However, while central government can evolve policies best calculated to stimulate growth there is scope for specific responses to opportunities from individual regions which are now free to establish direct contacts with foreign business (Meegan 1994). The stakes are high because the successful regions will become partially 'disembedded' through the development of strong inter-regional linkages and growing dependence on external institutions (Grabher 1992, 1994). But at the same

323

Table 8.1 Regional variations in population age structure 1988

| Country | Child population | | | | Aged population | | | | Working age population | | | |
|---|---|---|---|---|---|---|---|---|---|---|---|---|
| | A | B | C | D | A | B | C | D | A | B | C | D |
| Bulgaria | 21.0 | 22.8 | 18.1 | 4.7 | 21.9 | 30.2 | 16.4 | 13.8 | 57.1 | 61.7 | 49.5 | 11.8 |
| FCSFR | 23.0 | 27.3 | 19.3 | 8.0 | 19.4 | 21.7 | 15.9 | 5.8 | 57.6 | 61.5 | 56.8 | 4.7 |
| FGDR | 19.4 | 22.3 | 17.6 | 4.7 | 16.2 | 19.6 | 12.7 | 6.9 | 64.4 | 67.1 | 62.3 | 4.8 |
| Hungary | n.a. | n.a. | n.a. | n.a. | n.a. | n.a. | n.a. | n.a. | 57.3 | 59.0 | 55.0 | 4.0 |
| Poland | 30.7 | 34.4 | 23.5 | 10.9 | 12.8 | 16.2 | 9.1 | 7.1 | 56.6 | 61.0 | 53.1 | 7.9 |
| Romania | 23.7 | 30.0 | 15.1 | 14.1 | 13.0 | 18.9 | 9.0 | 9.9 | 63.3 | 69.5 | 56.8 | 12.7 |
| FFRY | 25.4 | 29.1 | 21.0 | 8.1 | 10.2 | 13.1 | 7.2 | 5.9 | 64.2 | 65.7 | 62.7 | 3.0 |
| Total | 18.4 | 28.3 | 11.7 | 16.6 | 14.2 | 20.1 | 7.6 | 12.5 | 67.2 | 71.2 | 60.7 | 10.5 |

Note A National average; B Regional maximum; C Regional minimum; D Regional difference. Total excludes Hungary for child and aged population.
Source: Bachtler 1992b, p.41

Table 8.2 Regional variations in employment structure 1988

| Country | Industry | | | | Agriculture | | | | Services | | | |
|---|---|---|---|---|---|---|---|---|---|---|---|---|
| | A | B | C | D | A | B | C | D | A | B | C | D |
| Bulgaria | 46.3 | 51.8 | 41.6 | 10.2 | 19.3 | 26.2 | 1.8 | 24.4 | 34.9 | 53.0 | 28.2 | 24.8 |
| FCSFR | 36.1 | 55.0 | 35.3 | 19.7 | 13.7 | 21.1 | 2.0 | 19.1 | 40.2 | 62.1 | 35.3 | 17.1 |
| FGDR | 47.0 | 58.5 | 30.1 | 28.4 | 10.8 | 26.8 | 1.1 | 25.7 | 42.3 | 63.9 | 35.3 | 28.6 |
| Hungary | 38.6 | 47.8 | 28.2 | 19.6 | 16.0 | 32.3 | 0.7 | 31.6 | 45.5 | 83.6 | 37.8 | 45.8 |
| Poland | 36.4 | 60.9 | 12.0 | 48.9 | 28.9 | 61.3 | 6.0 | 55.3 | 34.2 | 46.6 | 22.7 | 23.9 |
| Romania | 40.2 | 61.4 | 25.8 | 35.6 | 27.9 | 48.1 | 3.8 | 44.3 | 27.0 | 43.1 | 16.8 | 20.1 |
| FFRY | 33.1 | 43.1 | 28.8 | 14.3 | 30.7 | 38.4 | 14.6 | 23.8 | 35.1 | 49.1 | 31.2 | 17.9 |
| Total | 41.1 | 61.4 | 12.0 | 49.4 | 21.0 | 61.3 | 0.7 | 60.6 | 37.0 | 83.6 | 16.8 | 66.8 |

Note A National average; B Regional maximum; C Regional minimum; D Regional difference.
Source: Bachtler 1992b, pp.52–3

time new practices relevant to the market economy should be internalised so that there is local integration through the old second economy transforming itself into a self-sustaining sector able to foster economic growth. On the other hand, the more backward regions may become 'overembedded' and circumscribed by the rationality of the old business environment. Change tends to occur through defensive measures against external threats as institutions seek to insulate themselves from an increasingly threatening environment. New enterprises are not excluded but until they develop on a large scale institutional development will be constrained by a bazaar economy dominated by short-term speculative business (Pedersen 1993).

Local government has a critical role in regional development, given the transfer of power away from the centre (Horvath 1991). Although this process is contested through party politics and much tension is generated over matters of local government finance, Toth (1993) sees a logical evolution towards greater decentralisation and regional autonomy with the trend towards democracy. Local government should therefore become more involved with business and 'first of all it should create the conditions necessary for an increase of capacity utilization within existing places of work' (Weclawowicz 1996, p.151). But it is clear that the regions will be able to take their own initiatives and compete for inward investment (Gorzelak and Kuklinski 1992; Hardy et al. 1995). The tremendous opportunities of the post-Fordist era make the quality of regional leadership all the more critical (Esser and Hirsch 1994). Diversification will be all the greater because ethnicity will exert an influence on the evolution of distinct economic and social profiles.

The capacity of local authorities to influence regional development will depend primarily on their powers and finances (Baldersheim et al. 1996; Osterland 1994). Powers may increase faster than financial capabilities, because it has been shown that although local authorities in Hungary have considerable powers over taxation and development initiatives their real resources are limited. In 1995 the local authorities at Rychnov nad Kneznou took the novel step of raising money through municipal bonds to cover the cost of various local projects including hotel reconstruction and the refurbishment of apartment blocks. But such practices are still very rare although other alternative methods of funding, such as partnership schemes, are being considered. At the same time, public expectations are high and performance is variable. In FGDR, Western conventions over consultation have not yet been taken fully on board and very few people see the local authority as a source of information. Moreover, it may take time to establish priorities, although the Czechs seem to be stressing the importance of environmental protection and public safety, followed by improvement of utilities and social services. Child care and cultural facilities are less important, while housing causes few problems as a result of the repairs carried out since 1989. This consensus between local councils and their electorates makes for a high level of legitimacy, but there is little scope for direct engagement in economic activity. There is also a general lack of managerial skills among council leaders with regard to information and experience as well as familiarity with business law and foreign languages (Lados 1993). There is certainly a need for more enterprise specialists on councils. One way of gaining expertise is by collaboration with local authorities in the West, exemplified by the links between Kosice in Slovakia and Halifax (Nova Scotia) in Canada (Lotz 1992).

Basically, regional development strategies will inevitably be founded on the present industrial structure, though there may be raw material sources that have been neglected under communism and there are also possibilities for the more fertile agricultural areas and regions of tourist potential, including highland regions where the successes of Western 'mountainology' could be repeated (Alden and Boland 1996). Clearly, SOEs should not take a defensive and inflexible view but should be encouraged to participate in the reform process and promote regional cooperation (Smith 1994). Almost certainly, the surviving SOEs will have an important role in the foreseeable future, for despite the many cases of closure there may be 'insular areas that would represent the frameworks for stability of employment in individual areas and in the country as a whole' (Bucek 1992, p.2). As already noted, these 'islets of development' may well be developed by joint ventures linking former SOEs with foreign companies supplying investment capital, new technology and a marketing system; and state governments (especially in the Balkans) may be persuaded to assist with low-interest credits and tax exemptions (Toldy-Osz 1992). Even in the car industry, where a great deal of new investment has been undertaken, the plants are generally rooted into existing large enterprises or sites with important infrastructural advantages relating to the communist military-industrial complex.

Meanwhile, agricultural work must be safeguarded through greater efficiency and competitiveness in export markets. Rey (1994) has raised the importance of reasserting comparative advantage, highlighting the richer areas such as Czech Silesia where small peasant farms persisted under communism, partly because the farms were too small for the peasants to be branded as kulaks. However, the reassertion of the principle of comparative advantage will create difficulty for farmers in poorer regions at a time of reduced subsidies; leading to reduced intensification and a shift from arable to pasture. However, agricultural employment in Eastern Europe is rapidly declining from some 20 per cent in 1990 to 10 per cent in 1995 and an anticipated level of only 5 per cent at the turn of the century. There are also jobs at risk through the abandonment of ancillary businesses previously supported by the cooperatives. Hence the need for promotion of the secondary and tertiary sectors in rural areas (Klodzinski 1992). Some new factories have been built, and Swain (1994, p.9) suggests that run-down or abandoned machine-tractor stations could be transformed into 'embryonic business parks'. An alternative way forward is to adopt the 'Bavarian Model' of pluriactivity more widely (Klekner 1992). Quality products from a system of predominantly organic farming could be handled by an enlarged processing sector. Food-processing, textile and craft industries could be complemented by various forms of rural tourism (Derounian 1995). Agrotourism could make a significant impact in areas where tourism is expanding. Growth is evident on the Polish coast of West Pomerania with clean beaches and attractive lake country; also good communications locally and internationally. Germans and Scandinavians have realised the potential. Berliners are holidaying at the Inskie lake area and on the coast at Miedzyzdroje and Swinoujscie. Seaside properties are being sought in the Oder estuary. This approach could also form a base for sustainable tourism in Albania to follow communism's 'prescriptive approach' to tourism that did at least protect the country from environmentally damaging projects funded by multinational groups. However, successful diversification will call for substantial investment and an educational programme to mobilise the younger people. Significantly, Romania's Agriculture Ministry has created a Commission for Mountainous Regions to promote the principles of mountainology.

## Investment attractiveness: population and settlement

According to the synergetic evaluation of Chalupa (1993), the adaptability of the population will be important in efforts to demonstrate and improve local competitiveness. Population resources are generally favourable for growth, with labour markets that are attractive in terms of skill and motivation as well as cost. Yet there are differences in approach, reflected in levels of ambivalence towards the reform process and foreign economic penetration in particular. Better-educated Poles (especially those who have done well during the transition) are positive about reform, while those with a rural background are the most distrustful. Significantly, negative attitudes are much less apparent in Wroclaw in the west than they are in Lublin in the east, where German business is associated with a modern *Drang nach Osten*. For although foreign penetration is linked with modernisation (new machinery and new technology), a new work ethos of increased productivity and a revitalised economy, it is also associated (rightly or wrongly) with unemployment and the decline of local businesses. However, Poles tend to be very positive about their local situation, despite disillusionment with politics at the national level. They may be opposed to privatisation nationally while accepting it in their own factories; and they may have reservations about German capital in the national economy while welcoming it in their own enterprises (Kuron 1995).

Attitudes will be coloured to some extent by the problems encountered during the transition and these have often been particularly severe in some of the poorer regions. Unemployment is high in Poland's newer industrial regions, especially where there has been a heavy dependence on Soviet orders: textiles and vehicles in the case of Kielce, Lomza and Starachowice. By contrast, rates have been lowest in areas with large, economically well-developed and diversified agglomerations, playing a leading role in the national economy (Czyz 1993, p. 494). It is the latter that tend to be more attractive for inward investment: Warsaw and provincial cities like Gdansk, Krakow, Poznan, Szczecin and Wroclaw. Lodz and Katowice are also attractive to investment because of a very positive attitude to the structural weaknesses encountered since 1989. However, there may be problems of morale and adaptability in weaker regions, like the high unemployment areas of eastern and northern Hungary where social problems may be compounded by a poor environment and infrastructure. So there is a danger that the underdeveloped areas of the communist period will now be further disadvantaged because 'unemployment in these regions may mean the last step in the disintegration of the local societies which is a real danger now' (Dovenyi 1994, p.396). (See map 8.1.)

Ethnicity could also have a bearing on regional potentials through the value systems of specific groups, for 'an emancipational process of nationalities and regions can be expected' (Vaisher 1992, p.397) and this could work to the benefit of regions like Moravia, where there has been greater cultural awareness in recent years. More problematically, there is the possibility of tension in multi-ethnic areas although the extremes reached in some recent Balkan conflicts should not be applied widely (Pehe 1994). Border areas (especially large towns in the northern and western borderland) are likely to attract an ethnically mixed population including Asians and refugees trying to get into Western Europe. This creates instability in the area from which the Germans were expelled: 'a greater part of the population has not identified themselves with their social milieu' (Vaisher 1993, p.171). A relatively low level of adherence to religious cults also indicates 'lower social control' (ibid., p.171), expressed through high levels of crime, divorce, suicide and illegitimacy in the Czech Republic's northern borderland.

A well-integrated settlement hierarchy is also desirable for a spatially diverse pattern of growth. Large 'gateway' settlements are needed to receive inward investment and to accommodate large projects, but close links through the settlement hierarchy with the smaller towns and rural districts can also facilitate a dispersal of investments so that smaller projects are allocated to places lower down the hierarchy. Where central places at the local level are not easily identifiable, as in areas of small farm (*tanya*) settlement in Hungary, or where they are remote from urban centres, as is often the case on the frontiers of Hungary where a new boundary system was imposed after the First World War, development may be restricted. Some remedial action may be possible; for example, through the Czech Republic's 'Programme for Renewal of Rural Municipalities' which has been launched to improve village infrastructure. The Ministry of Agriculture's 'Agrarian Programme' also makes a contribution (as it also does in suburban areas, national parks and in

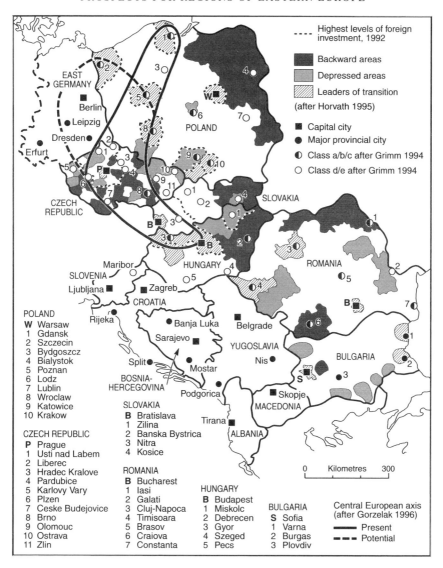

*Map 8.1* Aspects of regional development (after Gorzelak 1996, Grimm *et al.* 1994 and Horvath 1995)

regions with environmental problems) by encouraging farm diversification and environmental improvements such as re-afforestation, enlargement of grasslands and reduced use of chemical fertilisers. Promotion of key villages to urban status could help in the process of creating potential growth points at the district level.

329

It is an important question for the future how far the further decline of employment in agriculture will precipitate a mass migratory movement towards capital cities and regional centres. The alternative is for services and employment to become more widely available in larger nucleated villages or small urban centres so as to allow for resettlement at a more local level. Rural planning in communist Romania aimed at the promotion of some 400 rural communes to urban status and although the plan has now been abandoned the potential for an expanded urban network remains; though without the draconian complement of arbitrary destruction of the smaller villages. Hungarian research suggests that small towns in areas of high unemployment could be transformed by local initiative. A more even urban network could achieve a better regional balance, along with continuing progress in education and growth in the tertiary sector; for this encourages economic activity to be 'more evenly distributed across the country, than would otherwise be dictated by manufacturing and farming activities which rely on natural, local resources and therefore lead to regional variations' (Nemes 1994, p. 367). However, at the present time some of the small towns may lack adequate services, especially those which expanded under socialism without a proper 'small town society' (Csatari 1993). And although no village in Hungary is more than 30 minutes journey from the nearest town there are variations in the quality of transport and services within each small town hinterland (which may be 20-30,000 people, though usually no more than 15,000 for the newer small towns) (Ferenc 1991).

However, whatever development occurs in rural areas is likely to be linked with larger urban centres through supply of farm produce to centrally placed processing units or small manufacturing units which are part of local area networks around technologically strong nuclei such as provincial universities (Musil *et al.* 1995). Such centres had mixed fortunes under communism because although some medium-sized towns benefited from extensive socialist development, through the concentration of industrial projects on the upper echelons of the central place hierarchy, there was also 'under urbanisation' because population did not always increase in proportion to the rapid growth of functions. This was due to inadequate housing which meant an excessive dependence on commuting. Dostal and Hampl (1994, p. 209) also see socialist development as overextensive, leading to a deterioration in living standards in the later years. Some cities in FGDR failed to recover from the collapse of population at the end of the Second World War, especially when they lacked the status of regional centres.

Dynamic centres need good services and additional attractions through their labour catchments and living conditions. Large cities are in competition and the process is being monitored by research in The Netherlands with respect to selected core areas (Van Weesep and Van Der Wusten 1992). Several provincial cities are already demonstrating their gateway functions. Each of the Lander in FGDR has designated a *Modelstadt* to demonstrate improved housing conditions, shopping facilities and office provision (Rueschemeyer 1993; Schmidt 1991). But on a much larger scale, Grimm (1995) has shown Leipzig will improve its position as the commercial centre for the Lander of Sachsen, Sachsen-Anhalt and Thuringen, helped by the enlargement of Halle-Leipzig Airport at Schkeuditz and provision of improved rail connections in addition to the existing autobahn links. The city is regaining its international functions lost under the FGDR regime, apart from the spring and autumn trade fairs which have provided some momentum for the recent expansion (Wiest 1993). In Brno also the dynamism of the trade fair has acted as a catalyst for further growth. Many new events are being staged and the fairground is being linked directly with the motorway system which is to be extended into Austria. The appearance of the city has changed with city centre reconstruction, infrastructure is much improved and foreign banks have established a presence.

Gyor in Hungary, a rapidly growing regional centre close to the Austrian and Slovak borders, has long-standing cultural links with the West (Benke 1995). Already several projects are under way by UK companies: Associated Newspapers, Tesco (through the Global food retail chain) and United Biscuits. The latter has established Eastern Europe's most modern potato crisp factory in an industrial park with good access to the railway and motorway links between Budapest and Vienna. The Austrian transport company Quehenberger has opened a customs clearance and storage centre in the park and a third tenant is the Austrian textile manufacturer Hubor Tricot which intends to open a lingerie plant. A 100,000sq.m. food sub-park is also envisaged. Gyor's success is stimulating smaller communities in the area to draw up their own plans for investment, including golf courses, tourist facilities and restaurants, with encouragement from the Hungarian government's Investment and Trade Development Agency. Lodz in central Poland also has an entrepreneurial spirit and the private sector has absorbed many workers made redundant by the state sector (Griffith 1996). The regional development agency has supported promising companies and has ensured adequate liquidity through buying their invoices and discounting them with local banks. The city has experienced a boom in the clothing industry through small tailoring workshops which supply the Ptak market, held in converted hangars 10km. south of the city and frequented by buyers from Eastern Europe and FSU. There are also blue chip companies like Coats and Wrangler which have set up in the city. Lodz has one of Poland's four management centres (others are in Gdansk, Lublin and Poznan) assisted by the UK Know-How Fund. The Lodz centre (Foundation for the Promotion of Entrepreneurship) hopes to introduce a full management course working closely with the Edinburgh University Business School and sees the possibility of working up the small businesses of Ptak market into larger concerns.

The Polish city of Krakow is another outstanding provincial centre of enterprise, which has seen a dramatic growth in private sector business. There is a highly profitable First Polish American Bank (FPAB) created in 1990 with the support of the Polish-American Enterprise Fund, a private sector business development group backed by the US government. With a sound infrastructure, Krakow is a good place for distribution to the region including the Katowice area, where the FPAB intends to expand its business. There are also international links with Belarus, Hungary, Slovakia and Ukraine. The year 1995 saw the start of investment in improving east–west road links and also the refurbishment of the regional airport of Balice (renamed after Pope John Paul II) in 1995 to accommodate the larger jets used on international services. The environment attractions are boosted not only by the historic centre (recognised by UNESCO in 1978 as being of world importance in terms of cultural heritage) but by the mountain resort of Zakopane and the Biesczady national forest on the Ukrainian border. A Krakow Regional Development Agency has been set up to implement a consistent regional policy of economic restructuring and development throughout the region, with attention to infrastructure in small towns and rural areas.

There is particular optimism over the future prospects of capital cities, especially the northern capitals which may be expected to attach themselves to the West European system: Warsaw with Berlin, Prague with the Central German cities and Budapest with Vienna. They will also contribute to a north–south axis (Berlin–Leipzig–Dresden–Prague–Bratislava–Budapest), linking together several provincial cities which, relatively speaking, lost ground under communism. There can be no doubt about the potential of Budapest in the context of the European metropolitan system (Barta 1993). Previously stranded on the margins of Western Europe as the large centre of a small country, Budapest attracts heavy inward investment, combines proximity to Vienna with a business community with wide experience of FSU and East European markets, an administration positively inclined towards an expanding role for the city and a range of subsidised cultural events. Budapest has a good infrastructure and an urban society which will project the cosmopolitan image of an international metropolis (Enyedi 1994, pp. 399–400). It is also the centre of a dynamic region. Budapest, for northwest Hungary in general, has proved to be an area of innovation. A 'stratum of early entrepreneurs [was] established during the era of the liberalized command economy' of the NEM followed by the joint ventures of recent years (Csefalvay 1994, p. 358). There is good potential in the future not only for Budapest but for the whole Danube axis because while growth will initially affect Budapest and the northwest (with industry, tourism and improved infrastructure} these growth areas could give an impetus to other regions and reduce their high unemployment. But for this to be possible economic growth will have to continue steadily into the next century and agriculture must be stabilised after the upheavals in ownership. Stability is also needed in neighbouring countries and cross-border cooperation should increase.

Prague is also a city of great potential although, despite strong urban traditions, it was perhaps less receptive than Budapest and Warsaw to Western influences during the years of socialism. Prague will certainly develop its gateway role, benefiting from its architecture, tradition and human potential, although its population growth may be rather slow (perhaps reaching 1.5mn. in thirty years) because the breakup of FCSFR means it is no longer the federal capital. Transport will have to be a priority with reconstruction of the airport, high speed railways and motorways to Dresden (for Berlin) and Nurnberg (for Frankfurt and Munich). Industry is characterised by the prominence of engineering and there are persistent manpower problems. Higher productivity and capital intensification should gradually increase the importance of electronics and other high technology branches. International firms have gained a foothold in the capital city and this has resulted in a rapid rise in land and property prices (Sykora and Simonickova 1994). While some space will arise through redundant functions from the communist period (such as trade union offices and army facilities) there will be a large increase in demand for space for industrial parks and the tertiary sector. Flats have been sold for commercial use by their new owners and this will prevent any pronounced suburbanisation of industrial and commercial enterprises. Meanwhile, speculative builders see much potential for housing in some suburban locations (taking account of road schemes) and there has already been growth in towns and villages on the edge of Prague to solve the housing shortage. There is also a likelihood that what are presently second homes will become permanent residences: about one-fifth of second home owners are considering this possibility. Housing pressures will undermine the emphasis on vegetable and flower growing which was prominent in the past.

### Investment attractiveness: transport, power and the environment

Infrastructure was frequently neglected during the communist era when overcrowded public transport used obsolete equipment and there were constant struggles to maintain adequate levels of electricity output during the winter months (Mieczkowski 1978). Subsidised transport under communism encouraged lengthy transport hauls and a relatively dispersed industrial geography, i.e. there was high 'transport absorptiveness' (Taylor 1989). But since 1989 the situation has been changing significantly and a major modal shift has occurred. In three years following reunification, journeys on public transport in FGDR fell by 47 per cent while car registrations rose by 57 per cent (Pucher 1993, 1994). New equipment and technology is being obtained through production licences and outright purchase of Western equipment. There are improvements being made in such areas as ticketing, catering and publicity, often aided by joint ventures with Western companies. A shortage of investment capital limits the rate of change and requires difficult decisions between rival projects and transport modes, while individual movement is constrained by rising costs and the 'softness' of East European currencies which make international travel extremely expensive. Yet over the longer term a radical overhaul of transport, with considerable technological improvement, is inevitable given the marginalisation of the economic infrastructure under central planning. A great increase in movement is likely now that bureaucratic obstacles are being removed and personal freedom enhanced.

At the same time, state-owned transport companies are being privatised with foreign involvement in the appointment of new management and in the development of many new routes and linkages, providing for greater efficiency and profit (Hall 1993a, 1993b). However, there seems to be less scope for privatisation in the short term than for agriculture or manufacturing. West European precedents are not altogether encouraging, while further constraints arise from limitations in both capital generation and spending power within Eastern Europe. Rail privatisation does not appear likely in the foreseeable future although manufacturing and ancillary services can be hived off (McDonald's have taken over the restaurant at the Nyugati station in Budapest) (Hope 1990). International finance might conceivably lead to private rail or road networks, but the best prospects seem to lie with the industrial enterprises rather than the infrastructure. Airlines and railways remain essentially state-owned although some parts of the business (like catering) can certainly be privatised, along with shipping and road haulage, often through EMBO or joint ventures with foreign capital. For example, a number of road haulage companies have arisen through the breakup of CSAD, the state road transport company in FCSFR, while Bulgaria has privatised its road-carrying company Somat.

Transport flows are beginning to show a number of changes against the patterns prior to 1989, particularly the growth of international traffic with Western Europe, given the reorientation of trade and the expansion of cultural links (Michalak and Gibb 1993). Important choices will have to be made and EU Transport Ministers (ECMT 1991) suggest that certain axes will have to be singled out for development rather than have investment geared to wholesale improvement of the inherited networks. This applies most obviously to the railways, where modernisation (and better international cooperation) along transport corridors is needed to provide high speed services (Mellor 1992). Three main east–west corridors are proposed: from the Randstad and Ruhr to Berlin, Warsaw and both Moscow and St Petersburg; from the Rhineland to Vienna and Budapest (also Dresden and Nurnberg to Prague; and from Northern Italy and Austria to Hungary and FFRY (ECMT 1991, p.415). These routes will certainly be needed for rail transport which should maintain a key role for the foreseeable future (Tietze 1990). Although freight traffic has declined both absolutely and relatively, there may be some recovery when industrial production picks up and when Eastern Europe starts to enjoy an enhanced transit role. In addition to east–west movements between FSU and Western Europe, north–south traffic originating in Scandinavia will be expedited by the provision of further 'missing links' on the route through Germany, FCSFR and Hungary en route to the Middle East; with routes through Poland being available if the German roads are saturated (Bianchi 1992). Growth is most likely in FGDR, Hungary and Poland with a further rise in the importance of containers on international and domestic routes. Meanwhile, the recent reduction in freight traffic has meant that motive power and line capacity is available for long-distance domestic and international passenger traffic.

A growth in the relative importance of road transport is already evident, helping to reduce the disparities in the share of transport falling to the roads between East and West at the present time (Roe 1992). At the beginning of the 1990s over half the passenger and freight traffic in Eastern Europe fell to the railways, but it is predicted that in 2010 the roads will carry 87.5 per cent of the traffic in the FGDR (compared with 8.5 for rail) (Kowalski 1993). Much of East European industry has developed on the basis of good rail access through private sidings, but there is always a road alternative and this will become more compelling with new generation factories for light industry built without direct access to rail services. There is a growing volume of international road traffic (both freight and passenger) and this should increase further with more streamlined border formalities and additional crossing points. There has been considerable privatisation of road haulage and of bus services, especially in the northern countries, and further upheaval has occurred through price increases arising from reductions in subsidies and higher energy costs. But to realise the very great potential for road transport, heavy investment will be needed to cope with a backlog of maintenance and to provide more urban bypasses, dual carriageways and motorways. At present, the prominence of agricultural traffic and slow-moving lorries means that average speeds are low by Western standards.

The autobahnen of the FGDR are now being thoroughly renovated and integrated with those of the West through new construction works in the vicinity of the old border at Eisenach and Hof, for example. Moreover, some extensions are planned. Halle could be linked northwards to Magdeburg, Stendal and the Berlin–Rostock motorway; and there could also be connections from Halle to Braunschweig, from Rostock to Hannover; also from Leipzig to Jena direct and thence through Meiningen to Wurzburg. Other countries plan to extend their motorways (Jun and Okolicsanyi 1994). For example, Slovenia wants to develop motorway links both between Austria and Croatia and between Italy and Hungary (Muller 1993). And momentum is building up for completion of the Trans-Europe Motorway (TEM) which dates back to the 1960s with an agreement between ten countries under UN auspices. Some 4,000km. are completed, while 3,000km. are under construction and another 3,000 are at the design stage. With the freeing of trade and progress being made towards the achievement of a CEFTA it will be possible for regions to encourage production relevant to transit routes in which they are involved. Differences in the speed with which transport services are improved could influence the outcome of many competitive struggles involving 'hub status', particularly in Pannonia where the historic importance of Budapest may be reasserted despite the investment in routes from Western Europe to the Balkans passing through FFYR (Erdosi 1992; Kinnear 1992).

An improvement in commercial air travel is essential for the development of business links (Symons 1993). There are now additional flights between Eastern and Western Europe by operators in both parts of the continent. The leading Western airlines are not only increasing services on existing routes but are opening new routes, such as Alitalia's services from Milan and Rome to Berlin, Budapest and Prague. Eastern Europe's former monopoly 'flag carrying' airlines are being privatised and the process should be complete by the end of the century. Furthermore, they are beginning to introduce Western aircraft to replace fleets of fuel-thirsty Soviet aircraft. The process still has a long way to go but it is being accelerated by hire (or second-hand purchase) of Western planes as an alternative to the order of new aircraft which would involve both great expense and delay. Airports are in need of modernisation, as in Prague where British and North American companies are involved in building and operating a new terminal on the former Soviet airfield of Milovice, 30km. northeast of the city with Maglev (magnetic levitation) links to the centre. With a capacity of 4.8mn. passengers, Prague's new airport will be in a strong position to challenge for hub status. More provincial airports are being used by international services and such facilities will greatly enhance the 'gateway' functions of regional centres, as already noted in the case of Krakow. Further competition will also arise in terms of port facilities (Hall 1992), although there is the possibility of coordinated development in the Black Sea theatre (Connelly 1994). Inland waterways will be included in this picture, especially the Danube which is now connected with Western Europe through the Rhine–Main–Danube Canal (Siedenfus 1987).

The poor state of telecommunications was widely seen as a bottleneck to economic development and massive improvements are now under way (Table 8.3). Hungary is benefiting from a US$362mn. EIB loan for improvements in transport and telecommunications (Tiner 1992). Telephone companies in Bulgaria, Hungary and Poland are being separated from post office managements and there is a trend towards privatisation in order to increase foreign investment. At the same time the massive growth of cellular networks in the urban areas is widely appreciated as a boon to indigenous business. Meanwhile, the quality of urban transport is being enhanced by the extension of metro systems, which are available in most of the state capitals and a few provincial cities (Haydock 1995). Buses and tramways are being developed on a selective basis to provide complementary and connecting services. It is likely that tramways will be retained for the most part, but with improvements similar to what has taken place in Western Europe in recent years. There is a need for better interior design with new seats and bright panels as well as

*Table 8.3* Telephone provision 1989–93

| Country | Number of phones (000s) | | | | | Phones per population (000s) | | | | |
|---|---|---|---|---|---|---|---|---|---|---|
| | 1989 | 1990 | 1991 | 1992 | 1993 | 1989 | 1990 | 1991 | 1992 | 1993 |
| Albania | 39 | 40 | 42 | 45 | 49 | 1.2 | 1.2 | 1.3 | 1.3 | 1.4 |
| Croatia | 754 | 823 | 891 | 955 | 1027 | 15.9 | 17.3 | 18.6 | 19.9 | 21.5 |
| Czech Republic | 1557 | 1624 | 1707 | 1819 | 1961 | 15.0 | 15.8 | 16.6 | 17.6 | 19.0 |
| Bulgaria | 1994 | 2175 | 2205 | 2340 | 2300 | 22.2 | 25.2 | 25.7 | 27.5 | 26.3 |
| Germany | 28843 | 31887 | 33560 | 35421 | 36900 | 46.5 | 40.1 | 42.0 | 44.0 | 45.7 |
| Hungary | 916 | 996 | 1128 | 1291 | 1498 | 8.7 | 9.4 | 10.9 | 12.5 | 14.6 |
| Macedonia | 270 | 286 | 290 | 312 | 324 | 12.8 | 13.4 | 13.5 | 14.4 | 14.8 |
| Poland | 3124 | 3293 | 3565 | 3938 | 4419 | 8.2 | 8.6 | 9.3 | 10.3 | 11.5 |
| Romania | 2338 | 2366 | 2443 | 2574 | 2624 | 10.1 | 10.2 | 10.6 | 11.3 | 11.5 |
| Slovakia | 669 | 711 | 759 | 821 | 893 | 12.7 | 13.4 | 14.4 | 15.5 | 16.7 |
| Slovenia | 390 | 422 | 459 | 494 | 516 | 19.8 | 21.1 | 22.9 | 24.7 | 25.9 |
| Yugoslavia | 1585 | 1682 | 1782 | 1873 | 1923 | 15.3 | 16.1 | 16.9 | 17.7 | 18.0 |

*Source*: United Nations 1995, *UN Statistical Yearbook* (40th edn 1993) (New York: United Nations)

improved illumination, insulation, heating, ventilation and passenger information (Forster 1992). Secondary suspension is also needed for greater comfort and reduced damage to track. Germany's 1992 *Verkehrsfinanzierungs-Gesetz* has provided 90 per cent federal grants towards the cost of new cars for the FGDR (compared with only half in the rest of Germany). The Prague railway network will need restructuring with a new station in Holesovice and a container terminal will be needed at Malesice. Bypass facilities for lorries must be improved and warehousing moved to the edge of the city. More use could be made of the waterways through modernisation of the Moldau River.

The developments in transport and telecommunications will have important implications for regional development. Individual cities will be competing for investment to improve their own facilities and to attract new enterprise on the basis of nodal position on the international transport networks (including airports with hub status). The main transit routes, including the lines of communication with the Adriatic, Baltic and Black Sea ports will also attract growth. The expansion of the motorway network is leading to growth areas around the main intersections. Thus the Polish section of TEM (of which only 120km. is built) will intersect at Strykow near Lodz with the motorway from Swiecko to Terespol via Warsaw; also Katowice with the route from Zgorzelec to Medyka. Meanwhile, the Szczecin–Prague motorway, crossing the frontier at Lubawka, is destined to intersect with the latter at Kobierzyce south of Wroclaw. Here the local authority is attracting distribution enterprises starting with the huge Makro cash-and-carry warehouse in 1993 and Cadbury's is now distributing its products throughout Poland. Moreover, the Swedish Ikea company is to build Poland's largest shopping centre (including a furniture store and supermarkets) at this site and there is cooperation with Wroclaw for an agricultural wholesale market. The American food-processor company Cargill is building a starch and gluten factory which will yield various foods, pharmaceuticals and cosmetics. Annual income to the commune (0.3mn.Zl from Cargill and 0.2mn.Zl each from Cadbury and Makro) will go into modernisation: a new health centre, church and school (drawing students from seven villages) as well as improved water, gas, telephones and sewage. Meanwhile, it is expected that growth will occur at Strykow near Lodz, where agricultural land is being sold for development. This should have a positive effect on the future of the Lodz textile and clothing industry.

## Environment

There is, on the face of it, a clear contradiction between seeking to increase investment in production and maintaining environmental quality. Indeed, communist regimes were notoriously unsuccessful at resolving this paradox by effective controls to limit pollution (Carter and Turnock 1993). Large cities were blighted by high levels of air and water pollution, while the surrounding landscape was typically disfigured by the rash of extractive industries and waste tips. Neglect of conservation resulted not only in a loss of landscape quality but serious water shortages (Gergov 1991; Knight 1995). Leipzig suffered from the mining of lignite in the immediate vicinity and experienced the highest level of harmful emissions in the FGDR in 1989. On the other hand, despite polluting industries, Warsaw derived some benefit from the Kampinos National Park (the second largest in Poland), a former royal hunting forest. Now there are reductions in pollution through the closure of some factories, briquetting plants and heating stations, along with improved filtering and waste water-processing at plants which are still operating. In the case of historic buildings and monuments, there is much to be done to rescue buildings and entire architectural groups which in a Western situation would probably have been lost beyond recall through the comprehensive redevelopment ethos of the 1960s and 1970s. There is no doubt about the desire to conserve in the Czech Republic where the drive comes from the president downwards. The problem is to operate an effective system of rehabilitation at a time of ideological change and financial stringency, with a new taxation system only gradually being put together. There is the clean-up in Prague among contaminated derelict buildings, expedited by the growth of small businesses although it is not clear if this will be an effective answer to maintenance problems in general. There are also pressures from developers looking for quick profits and consequently building styles need to be harmonised. Meanwhile, air quality in Prague is now adversely affected by increasing numbers of cars. This leads to pressure for more roads although some projects are opposed locally by the NIMBY syndrome.

There are more specific conservation objectives to safeguard the urban fringes for recreational purposes and general use is being made of green corridor systems through larger grassland, woodland and water surfaces (Csatari 1995). The importance of such corridors will be respected when Prague's transport rings are being considered (Bicik and Stepanek 1994 p. 58) and, well beyond the immediate limits of the built-up area, there is clearly a need to balance ecological and recreational potential at a time of increasing pressure (Bicik 1994). Many protected natural areas are facing a growing influx of tourists, and several of the national parks and reserves are unprepared for such a growth in numbers. However, providing the natural resources of these areas are wisely managed, development may be sustainable. Carrying capacity has proved a useful tool in planning tourism, as well as models of ultimate environmental thresholds. The latter has been applied to the Tatra, where tourism followed the railways at the end of the nineteenth century to rural areas previously concerned with pastoralism and mining. Because of erosion in parts of the Tatra Mountains National Park (established in 1954), some tourist routes are being closed temporarily to allow vegetation to recover, with fences and barriers to reduce further erosion. New forest plantings will create mixed woodland rather than a softwood monoculture. Closure of the mountains at night (eliminating the tourist chalets) and the imposition of a tourist tax to generate income for footpath maintenance are other policies under consideration. There is also a need for more effective control in the development of Zakopane, where few traditional buildings remain and improved infrastructure is needed to cover sewage disposal and diversified tourist facilities for all weathers (Wiska and Hindson 1991). In the Tatra and elsewhere there is also scope for conservation in rural settlements, where the buildings and cultural manifestations offer resources for community-based ecotourism (Pozes 1991).

Such progress is underpinned by more stringent environmental legislation, although there is a continuing discrepancy between eventual aims and short-term achievements (De Bardeleben and Hannigan 1994). 'Although society was assured that a leading priority for the new legislators was saving the environment, in fact very little work was devoted to integrating environmental concerns in the transitional policy framework' (Georgieva 1993, p.73). However, certain principles are now widely accepted: that polluters should be legally responsible for the damage they cause, that standards should be raised, that environment impact should be fundamental in the consideration of new development and that the public should have access to information. Evidently, greater progress is being made in the northern half of the region where there is a relatively developed technical and scientific infrastructure. But within this northern group there are contrasts between the gradualism in Hungary and Poland, where effective environmental movements were active in the 1980s, and FCSFR, where much of the activity necessarily followed on from the velvet revolution (Fisher 1992).

Good progress is being made with Poland's twenty-year environment plan drawn up in 1990 by the country's Environmental Protection Ministry. The standard of sulphur dioxide emissions below 2.9mn.t. was achieved in 1994; likewise the goals for reducing dust and nitrogen oxide emissions and dumping raw sewage (300 modern municipal sewage treatment plants are being built each year). Smog alerts are becoming much rarer in Krakow and Katowice, where mining and heavy industry are no longer so dominant on account of industrial restructuring (Sitnicki *et al.* 1991). It is significant that more responsibility for environmental control is passing to local government so that progressive urban administrations can, to an extent, control their own environment destinies. Burgas in Bulgaria has a Director of Ecology and, as a result, Burgas lays down more demanding standards than apply nationally and these are imposed by local ecological police. Each enterprise has to report energy and material inputs and outputs (Yarnal 1995, p.13). It should also be mentioned that the Director is chairman of the local environmental NGO (Ecoglasnost), which, like other similar organisations across the region, has been effective in projecting public opinion and securing higher environmental standards (Frankland 1995; Stec 1993).

International efforts are being mounted in particularly sensitive areas like the Danube Delta. The need to protect the fauna and the delta landscapes was appreciated before the Second World War and the initial list of nature reserves drawn up in 1940 was increased in 1956 by the Romanian Academy's Natural Monuments Commission. However, conservation work was compromised by the economic development programmes previously described. Since the revolution a Danube Delta Biosphere Reserve of 5,900sq.km. has been created for the delta itself and for the extensive Razim-Sinoie lacustrine complex to the south; also for the sea coast, the Danube channel and the flood plain upstream of Tulcea to Isaccea and Galati. International support has come from UNESCO, the World Conservation Union (IUCN) and the World Wildlife Fund (Gastescu 1993). Cooperation is also developing between the Czech Republic, Germany and Poland in the notorious 'Black Triangle' where pollution levels are at their highest. The situation has eased through the decline in the industrial activity but local inhabitants are impatient for further short-term improvements, though there is a danger that funds may be dissipated in duplicated and uncoordinated activities. Poland is also involved in cooperation with neighbouring countries as part of the 'Green Lungs of Europe' project to coordinate activities in networks of national parks and other protected areas. They have grown out of the earlier 'Green Lungs of Poland' project and include Russia and five other FSU states. Finally, the Baltic Sea Environmental Protection Committee, which dates back to 1960, aims at reducing pollution and creating a taskforce for programme implementation. A new convention agreed in 1994 provides a wider programme to run for twenty years, with more stringent monitoring and action for the 132 hot spots most seriously threatened by pollution.

### Energy and the environment

This is a particularly challenging issue because electricity is essential for growth and indeed its widespread availability through internationally coordinated grid systems is fundamental to a spatially balanced economy. Yet production of power station fuels involves extensive environmental dislocation while the power stations and heating units are themselves notorious sources of pollution through the emission of dust and sulphur dioxide. Eastern Europe is heavily in deficit where energy is concerned (Table 8.4) and this imposes a massive economic burden. At the same time the reduced impact of extractive industries that would be required in the event of self-sufficiency is limited by the severe damage that arises from extensive use of low-grade lignite. Domestic production of oil and gas is significant in some countries, but despite further prospecting there is no likelihood of major change in the

*Table 8.4* Trade dependence for energy 1980–92

| Country | mn.t. coal equivalent | | | | | | | |
|---|---|---|---|---|---|---|---|---|
| | 1980 | | 1990 | | 1991 | | 1992 | |
| | A | B | A | B | A | B | A | B |
| Albania | 3.59 | –0.20 | 3.55 | –0.53 | 2.35 | –0.31 | 1.54 | +0.13 |
| Bulgaria | 10.99 | +22.91 | 13.58 | +23.91 | 12.30 | +18.76 | 12.22 | +15.74 |
| FCSFR | 67.54 | +31.40 | 64.86 | +31.45 | 60.72 | +28.21 | – | – |
| FGDR | 85.42 | +38.18 | 90.80 | +27.73 | – | – | – | – |
| Hungary | 21.89 | +17.47 | 20.61 | +18.12 | 20.16 | +17.46 | 19.05 | +15.09 |
| Poland | 173.83 | +2.92 | 136.55 | +0.53 | 132.13 | +2.97 | 128.86 | +4.46 |
| Romania | 84.19 | +14.54 | 56.82 | +23.12 | 49.41 | +20.98 | 46.15 | +17.28 |
| FFRY | 26.60 | +19.27 | 36.52 | +19.49 | 21.36 | +20.00 | – | – |

*Note* A Domestic production; B Inferred trade (+ denotes net import).
*Source*: United Nations 1995, *UN Statistical Yearbook* (40th Edn 1993) (New York: United Nations)

trade balance. Deficits have been met in the past by deliveries from FSU but since concessionary prices are no longer available and some of the pipelines need repair, there may be a desire to diversify. Western oil companies could get involved through the extension of West European pipelines (Pinder and Simmonds 1993), but oil could also be supplied from the Middle East while gas could come from the same source by tanker or be piped from Norway through Germany or Sweden (Kramer 1990). Poland's energy guidelines to 2010 involve diversification in favour of gas and liquid fuels, but coal will still produce 60 per cent of all electricity in the year 2000 despite the need for modernisation in the mines (Radetzki 1995). Deliveries of gas could come from Russia in view of the proposed pipeline from the Yamal Peninsula to Western Europe but in the interests of energy security Poland may try and increase gas production from the Baltic Sea, and further links with the West European gas distribution would be desirable.

Demand for electricity is falling due to factory closures and higher prices. The gradual introduction of energy-efficient equipment will also reduce pressure to bring new capacity on stream. Indeed, there must be conservation, for 'East European nations cannot afford to keep pouring energy down the drain' (Kats 1991, p.865). Better coordination may also bring useful economies. In 1991 the Visegrad states agreed to coordinate efforts to bring their electricity transmission systems into a Union for the Coordination of Production and Transmission of Energy. This means that in an emergency, power can be imported from the West but under normal conditions the benefits lie in closer contacts for international transfers of energy: thus Poland is likely to sell to Germany on a regular basis. But additional power will be needed in the future and some countries wish to increase output without the burden of increased dependence on imported energy. Hydro sources remain a possibility although high development costs are a disincentive. It is possible that small schemes may be cost-effective in yielding significant amounts of power while contributing to water storage and flood control without the costs of massive relocation of settlement and heavy losses of agricultural land. Bulgaria is carrying out feasibility studies for a series of four dams on the Upper Arda River. Large hydro schemes are usually opposed on environmental grounds, and the one large project recently implemented, where the Danube forms the frontier between Hungary and Slovakia, generated a major international dispute when Hungary pulled out of the project on environmental grounds while Slovakia continued alone (Fitzmaurice 1995; Ostry 1988).

Nuclear power is an attractive solution to the energy supply problem, but there are high initial costs and a sophisticated engineering industry is highly advantageous. Nuclear cooperation between the FSU and Eastern Europe started in the 1960s but led to major controversy after the Chernobyl disaster. Safety standards have now been improved, but consideration of new capacity has been deferred in some cases. The small stations built in FGDR have been closed but the existing stations are being retained in Bulgaria, FCSFR, Hungary and FFRY. In the case of the three countries without any nuclear capacity in 1989, Albania still has no plans but Romania opened the first unit at Cernavoda in 1996 while Poland decided to abandon its Zarnowiec (Gdansk) project (dubbed 'Zarnobyl' by anxious Poles fearing another nuclear disaster). However, despite the hazards perceived by East Europeans and some of their neighbours in Austria and Germany, the nuclear option limits the scale of lignite mining and thermal power station emissions (Kopacka 1994). Of course, despite public unease it is not possible to close down generating plant which is in good working order (Pavlinek *et al.* 1994), but while better filtering equipment is being used at lignite-burning power stations total consumption of lignite may decrease slowly. In FCSFR it is expected that sulphur dioxide emissions will decline to 0.98mn.t. by 1995 on the basis of nuclear power generation and desulphurisation at thermal power stations. Air pollution in the FGDR is being reduced as less lignite is burnt, power plants (some 280 in all) are modernised and some enterprises are closed. The levels of river and lake pollution have also gone down. But the programme will take time and rapid change is taking place in the FGDR to reach EU standards (2,500m.g of sulphur dioxide per cubic meter – one-fifth of the level noted at some power stations at the beginning of the 1990s). Reduced demand for lignite has helped to reduce pollution problems in lignite mining areas and is best resolved through a reduction in both coal output and in power generation. In North Bohemia mining decreased by one-third because of falling demand during the first three years of the transition (to reach 53.4mn.t. in 1992). Mining should end totally in the Usti nad Labem region by 1996 on account of the adverse effect on settlement. But in the region as a whole, production is estimated at 32-45mn.t. at the end of the century.

## Regional policy

Regional aid is being made available to all parts of the FGDR through Gemeinschaftsaufgabe for five years; with additional help for areas particularly affected by structural change. The Hungarian government initiated a Regional Development Fund in 1989 as part of a restructured regional policy (Hajdu and Horvath 1994; Horvath and Hrubi 1992). The Ministry for Environment and Regional Policy coordinates regional and urban development activities generally and supervises development programmes for underdeveloped and depressed areas like Szabolcs-Szatmar-Bereg (Nefedova and Trejvis 1994, p.39). But the help can only address local crises and 'without revitalising and strengthening the role of regional policy, an eventual social and economic disruption of the northern and eastern regions of Hungary seems to be unavoidable' (Nemes 1994, p. 368). The Polish government has been active in establishing special economic zones to attract investment that could boost employment in problem regions. Located in southeast Poland between Sandomierz and Tarnow, Euro-Park Mielec offers ten-year tax holidays, with 50 per cent exemption to follow for another ten. The aim is to diversify the local economy which is heavily bound up with a factory producing aircraft and other transportation equipment. A major attraction is standard and broad gauge rail access which allows direct shipment to both Western Europe and the Far East.

In FCSFR a Regional Planning Decree in 1977 linked the 'balanced and even development of territory' with the central planning system. Problem regions include North Bohemia and Ostrava, where environmental improvements are needed, and Eastern Slovakia (bordering the FSU) where many professional services are in short supply and where better housing and infrastructure was needed. A new Regional Policy Act was drafted in 1992 to support the problem regions looked after by the Ministry for Economic Policy and Development (Kara 1994). Problem regions have now been redefined in the limited context of the Czech Republic. There are some economically weak regions (mainly in Moravia) and others vulnerable to structural change. There are also border areas and regions (mainly in northern Bohemia) with unfavourable environmental conditions. Weak regions are benefiting from programmes to support small and medium-sized firms and a new Czech-Moravian Development Bank has been established for this purpose.

However, strong regional policies are unlikely at the present time because 'the initial priority is clearly to develop strategies at the national level' (Bachtler 1992b, p.135). With a favourable investment climate nationally, regional fortunes could easily change, as in the case of Mlada Boleslav in the Czech Republic where a one-sided industrial structure based on car manufacture has been supported by foreign investment from Volkswagen. However, there seems to be a difference in approach between advocates of efficiency on the one hand and protection on the other. Barta (1992) argues that policy should strengthen the competitiveness of national economies and major cities, while Bachtler (1992a) thinks that regional policy should support potential growth areas that can lead the national restructuring process. He suggests that attention should be given to diversified industrial regions with a relatively good technical and material base. But other opinions favour an emphasis on welfare. Pavlinek (1992) calls for effective regional social policy to deliver education and welfare, including job training and incentives (capital grants, tax exemptions and relocation allowances) to protect the weaker regions. The efficiency approach is likely to predominate in the short term but the regional situation should be carefully monitored. Small businesses will need encouragement to support the large enterprises and develop the service sector, and in rural areas considerable growth could arise from clusters of small and medium-sized enterprises grouped into 'small enterprise spatial systems'. In this way the 'top-down' process of breaking down the SOEs could be complemented by a 'bottom-up' programme to integrate the transformed state enterprises with existing handicraftsmen and family managed workshops (Bianchi 1992).

Some poorer regions may benefit from growth occurring on the edge of large cities, especially Berlin, Budapest, Prague and Warsaw. More space is needed for recreation, for new industrial estates linked with motorways and for residential developments. Some wealthy middle-class families are being encouraged to exchange their city apartments for up-market housing on the urban–rural fringe; for example, at Mysiadlo 15km. from the centre of Warsaw where 136 homes are being individually designed by Canadian and Polish architects. Indeed, Gawryszewski (1992) raises the possibility of significant counter-urbanisation as professionals move to suburban zones with good conditions for high-tech industry. This view is born out by many cases of development following the relaxation of planning controls, contributing to a surge in house-building with increasing contrasts in house size characteristic of gentrified villages in the West. But although pressure may well increase on villages close to large cities, the relatively poor services in rural areas generally will discourage counter-urbanisation in the foreseeable future.

## Cross-border cooperation

Border areas constitute a special problem because the closed frontier of communism created many backward areas where the dangers of instability may be increased by an ethnically mixed population including Asians and refugees trying to get into Western Europe. The easing of border restrictions could be very beneficial in overcoming isolation and enabling the most convenient service centres to be used. Additional border crossings might be provided and telephone links improved. There could also be priority for the growth of small businesses and coordination in environmental matters could be useful in areas like the Oder Valley, where FGDR installed a number of major industrial enterprises (the Eisenhuttenstadt metallurgical complex, the Schwedt oil refinery and several power stations) without considering their impact on Poland (Ciechocinska 1992). Cooperation would be particularly beneficial along Hungary's borders where the imposition of new frontiers after the First World War separated many towns from much of their hinterland (Berenyi 1992). Integration could be enhanced in the Vienna-Bratislava-Gyor area if the logic of a unified city region was no longer being suppressed by closed frontiers (Horvath 1993b). Trieste could also regain some of its former importance.

Tension could be reduced in the Balkans through international support for cross-border cooperation in areas of ethnic tension like Kosovo and Macedonia, where foreign investment along the main international routes could contain xenophobic tendencies (Moore and Schmidt 1994; Troebst 1994), especially the highly destabilising campaigns in support of a Greater Serbia (Markotich 1994a). Development of Trans-Balkan lines of communication between the Adriatic and Black Seas could give all states a vested interest in economic cooperation. The most significant case of cooperation to date is the contact by Italy's Friuli-Venezia Giulia region with Austria and Slovenia (part of a wider collaboration with Hungary and FFRY in the framework of Alps-Adria Working Community. Indeed, Friuli-Venezia Giulia has valuable experience in cooperation with Eastern Europe and stands as a laboratory for evolving policy. On the ethnic front there are reciprocal benefits for Austrians, Italians and Slovenes because Slovenes use Austrian and Italian border towns for shopping while tourist movements flow in the opposite direction. In addition, many Croats from Zagreb have second homes in the Slovenian coastal area, while some Slovenes have property in Croatia's Istrian peninsula. At the present time Slovenia seeks priority improvement of road and rail links with Hungary and other neighbouring countries and wishes to see the transit role of the port of Koper enhanced. She also wants to maximise the opportunities for trade with Germany, as well as Austria and Italy, in competition with the Visegrad countries (Horvath 1993a).

The publication of the European Commission's (1994) report *Europe 2000+* makes this an opportune moment to consider links between the regions of Eastern Europe and the EU. In 1991, the Commission saw border areas disadvantaged at the extremities of transport systems planned on a national basis. Artificially separated from natural hinterlands and handicapped by distorted patterns of commerce and local authority services, the mobility of local inhabitants is further constrained by different languages, tax and welfare systems as well as employment practices. The situation has been particularly difficult in areas adjacent to the closed borders of communist Eastern Europe. But now there is a strong 'cohesion effect' resulting from the transition, especially along such axes as Dresden–Wroclaw, Nurnberg–Prague,

Thessaloniki–Sofia and Trieste–Ljubljana; with good growth potential for the capital cities and other urban towns involved. The EU launched an Interreg programme in 1990-3 for internal borders, which had a bearing on the former Inner German frontier (Buckholz 1994; Ritter and Hajdu 1989). But this is being followed up by Interreg II for 1994-9, financed to the tune of ECU24bn (1992 values) and resourced by Phare money as well. It will include the German, Italian and Greek frontiers with Eastern Europe.

The Euroregion concept has been borrowed from Western Europe where Euroregions were first recognised in the 1960s with the support of the Regional Development Fund and the Council of Europe. A tier of Euroregions now straddle Germany's borders with the Czech Republic and Poland. Neisse covers all three countries while Spree-Neisse-Bobr, Viadrina and Pomerania extend northwards along the Oder–Neisse frontier between Germany and Poland. Elbe-Labe, Erzgebirge and Egrensis straddle the German–Czech border, with Bayrischer Wald including Austrian territory as well. Programmes seek cooperation in culture, training and the environment, along with more developed economic structures underpinned by German investment to take advantage of relatively low labour costs. Investment in the Czech Republic by Austrian and German firms has been encouraged by the free trade zones and innovation centres at Cheb and Ceske Valenice. To boost the technological level of production universities or faculties have been founded in Cheb, Ceske Budejovice and Usti nad Labem. Like Germany's New Lander, northwest Bohemia lies within eight hours' travel of over 80mn. people. There is also much German investment in Szczecin related to imports of building materials, chemicals and timber and also to sailing potential of the Oder estuary (for Swinoujscie is closer to Berlin than Rostock). Diversification in the oil-refining town of Schwedt is taking place through a growth of light industry which could be integrated into an east–west trade corridor over the longer term.

Particular mention may be made of the Viadrina region where the university at Frankfurt (Oder) has been renamed the University of Viadrina. Major commercial functions at Kostrzyn, on the Polish side of the river, have created 1,200 jobs in the town's municipal bazaar because a large German clientele (including many from Berlin) patronises the petrol stations and catering establishments as well as the local market. Kostrzyn is now seen by the government as a future economic zone, with enhanced prospects after the German capital moves back to Berlin. And while German firms are investing in projects that exploit the relatively cheap labour across the frontier there is also the prospect of technical progress through the plan for an industrial complex to develop on both sides of the German–Polish frontier and to link the EKO steelworks of Eisenhuttenstadt with metal industries in Cybinka on the Polish side (Kratke 1995). Just to the east of the region a cluster of special economic zones are being set up around Zielona Gora to attractive economic and financial conditions for investment. The list includes Brody on the

Neisse, close to the Olszyna border crossing, and other places further away where state-owned land has a favourable infrastructure: Babimost close to Zielona Gora airport, Torzym at a major road junction is an environmentally attractive area and Zbaszynek which is a railway junction, is addition to the Former Soviet airfields of Szprotawa and Zagan where buildings and services are already available.

The Neisse Euroregion links the Zittau area of Germany with Liberec in the Czech Republic and Bogatynia in Poland. After contacts were first made at Zittau in 1991, new border crossings were opened and EU support was provided for ecological studies referred to above in references to the Black Triangle. The administrative centre will move around the three countries in rotation. As German investment moves across the borders to take advantage of cheap labour there will be particular advantages for the Liberec area where modernisation of the industrial structure was constrained by the FCSFR policy of expanding the manufacturing base in Slovakia. The reopening of the frontier with Saxony and access to the German market (especially in Berlin) offers a better future for light industry, including glass manufacture and textiles. And Liberec (including the Jablonec area) will have the advantage of adjusting to the West European market without the burden of the communist legacy of heavy industry dominance. Growth will also occur in Poland where the Dresden–Liberec road runs through the Porajow district of Bogatynia. Land belonging to the Agricultural Property Agency is being set aside for development and infrastructure is being provided over 200ha (which could be increased to 700ha). There is the potential for special economic zone status in an area where developments in tourism and financial services would be particularly appropriate. An agricultural commodity exchange is also being opened to act as a large market for wholesale trade with EU countries.

Further to the east the Carpathian Euroregion is a particularly interesting experiment bringing together the frontier districts of Hungary (Debrecen/Miskolc), Poland (Krosno), Slovakia (Kosice) and Ukraine (Mukacevo). Romania is an observer in respect of the Baia Mare area. Local groups in this Carpathian region became active in 1990 and cross-border trade was recognised in treaties between Former Czechoslovakia, Hungary, Poland and Ukraine in 1992. The region was then created in 1993 on the initiative of regional officials with local contacts supported by legal and political advice from central governments. Indeed, the foreign ministers of Hungary, Poland and Ukraine signed a cooperation agreement in Debrecen in 1993 and since then Slovakia has become an associate. The Carpathian Euroregion is one of fifteen projects run by the Institute for East West Studies (IEWS) – an American–European–Japanese NGO set up in 1981. IEWS acts as an 'honest broker' helping to find a 'common language' across the region (Kaliberda 1994). The intention is to pool economic information and improve contact through additional border crossings and better telecommunications. There is a substantial environmental programme through the East Carpathian Bio-sphere Nature Reserve established in 1993 to cover 164,000ha in Poland, Slovakia and Ukraine. There is certainly potential for further projects of this kind, but central governments may be uneasy about initiative in international affairs devolving to local communities, especially where ethnic minorities may be involved.

There are problems of finance with respect to cross-border initiatives because EU money in support of Euroregions is not available for East European countries, although some Interreg and Phare money could be used. However, even if EU money could be used in Eastern Europe there would be difficulties because East European governments see their western regions as being least deserving of support, as many of them lie within the boomerang-shaped growth area extending from northwestern Hungary through western Slovakia, and the Czech Republic into western Poland (Gorzelak 1996, p.128). Naturally, Poland wants resources for the eastern border areas, not for the regions adjacent to Germany where there is a good deal of new enterprise already. By contrast, Poland's eastern border is economically and politically unstable, having entered the market economy with backward agriculture, a low level of urbanisation and poor demographic and transport structure. 'The spontaneous invasion of poor citizens from the FSU and the development of a mafia-like sector of the economy are exacerbating the problem of underdevelopment' (Weclawowicz 1996, p.167). Backwardness may persist for a long time although the unpolluted environment is unusual in Europe's rural landscapes and there will be some growth associated with the main border crossing points like Malaszewice near Terespol in Biala Podlaska province situated on the rail and road routes from Warsaw to Moscow. Even the Carpathian EuroRegion generates some ambivalence because governments are preoccupied with a range of regional problems which are not restricted to border territories. Thus, while seeking growth in the Carpathian region, Hungary hopes that increased transit traffic between the FSU and Italy will have a beneficial effect on the Great Plain and contribute positively to the infrastructure and job creation there.

More fundamentally there is concern over the Euroregion concept because local organisations may appear to take initiatives independently of central governments. There are issues of principle at stake because local groups may not always reflect national interests. So, to control the devolution of power to border communities the Polish government set up a department in 1992 to prepare cross-border agreements. More fundamental objections have been raised over the possibility of a special status for border regions which could be divisive in political as well as economic terms. It has been argued in Poland that the act of 'joining Europe' should involve the whole of each country and not just a small part which, through its special status, creates an element of partition (De Weydenthal 1993). 'The great wealth and economic potential disparity between Germany and the relatively underdeveloped former Regained Territories raises the threat of losing economic and political control to Germany' (Weclawowicz 1996, p.167).

Reactionary opinion has even visualised the dismemberment of the state through the hiving off of peripheral territories. This is an exaggeration of course, because sovereignty is in no way affected and supporters of cross-border cooperation feel that alarmist views flatter the Euroregion concept with a coherence that goes way beyond reality. Yet local agreements may give minority groups disproportionate influence and there is particular sensitivity where Hungarian minorities are concerned because of the possibility of territorial changes in Hungary's favour, where public opinion supports revisions to the Trianon treaty. District councils in Eastern Slovakia have attracted the censure of the Meciar government in linking economic cooperation with cultural policies that imply a common Carpathian heritage. The government in Bratislava evidently fears that the Carpathian Euroregion could be a focus for undesirable political activity on the part of Hungarians living in the area. Romania has similar sensitivities in an area of Satu Mare where Hungarians are still influential. On the other hand, it is true that Euroregions are particularly important for Hungary in view of the difficulties which exist with neighbouring countries over the status of Hungarian minorities (Reisch 1993). Thus it seems that cross-border cooperation in general and Euroregions in particular will be constrained by the wider climate of international relations.

## Regions of the future

What are the effective regions? Any region with its own voice. Most systems have been inherited from communism and are in need of an overhaul; but this will involve difficult decisions (Dostal *et al*. 1992). The president of the Czech Republic wants to create thirteen regions which will allow people to participate more fully in government. But the prime minister (V. Klaus), favouring a society of free citizens, thinks that decentralisation is not conducive to a smooth transition (Pehe 1994). He favours larger regions as those advocated for Hungary based on the cities of Debrecen, Gyor, Kecskemet, Miskolcs, Pecs, Szekesfehervar and Szeged (Toth 1994). Bulgarian reforms also appear to favour a regional approach with nine large regions with a lower tier of 275 small counties. The counties have substantial powers but their situation shows great variations between areas that were marginalised by the centralisation of economic development and those that attracted substantial investments (Christov 1991). But there are clashes in Slovakia between the Meciar government's preference for large city regions and the 'local' unit aspirations of the Hungarian minority, reflecting small areas where Hungarians would be in a majority and where there would also be coherence in functional/commuting terms (Bezak 1990).

Paradoxically, small regions can be controversial where regional autonomy is an issue. In 1992 Croatia introduced a new system of twenty counties (*zupanije*) plus the city of Zagreb (Klemencic 1995). This has some advantages for Istria, where a regional party (the Istrian Democratic Alliance) represents an ethnically mixed population including Albanians, Italians, Serbs and Slovenes as well as Croats. Despite a political culture of tolerance, the party seeks a federal system which would allow more taxation revenue to accrue to the regions and, in the process, would allow Istria to keep much more of its tourist revenue (Markotich 1994b). But there has been opposition to the new administrative arrangements from Dalmatia over the high level of centralisation of government in Zagreb and the division of Dalmatia into four counties: Dubrovnik-Neretva, Sibenik, Split-Dalmatia and Zadar-Knin. The region retains some cohesion through the Association of Communes and a regional Chamber of Commerce (Dominis 1994). The political party Dalmatia Action feels that region is treated by Zagreb in the same insensitive manner which characterised previous relations with Belgrade: hence the slogan 'ZG=BG'. The region enjoyed a *de facto* autonomy between 1990 and 1995 through the isolation of the 'Dalmatian Island' after the Krajina Serbs blocked the Zagreb–Split road in 1990 at the height of the tourist season and subsequently destroyed the Maslenice Bridge in 1991. For a time even the air links were severed and the only safe road route to Zagreb was via the Pag Bridge and ferry crossings.

Much more speculatively, inter-regional cooperation could create 'meso-regions' based on network relationships among urban centres over distances of up to 400km. Based to a certain extent on a common identity, meso-regions might extend into two or three different states and, likewise, any one national territory could comprise overlapping segments of two or three meso-regions. The meso-regions would crystallise around development axes and would be sufficiently integrated to compete at the European level. Lutzky (quoted in Maggi and Nijkamp 1992) has divided Europe into seven regions and shows Eastern Europe involved marginally in 'Baltic Hanse' with opportunities for shipping, shipbuilding and oil refining over an area focusing on the Baltic ports and the lines of communication running inland along the Elbe, Oder and Vistula valleys. There would be a complementary focus along the route from Paris and the Ruhr passing through Berlin and Warsaw to Belarus, the Baltics and Russia (Miklos 1992). Meanwhile, the region would be much more fully involved with the 'Middle-European Capitals' with opportunities for trade, heavy industry and administrative activity along with research and development in the social sciences. This area would focus on the Pannonian Basin with growth along the north–south routes (noted above) and east–west routes from southern France and Northern Italy passing through Slovenia and Hungary to Ukraine (Lvov and Kiev) and Russia. Again, a 'Balkan Take-off' region with opportunities for the production of food and household goods could exploit the axes interconnecting the ports of the Adriatic, Aegean and Black Seas via the Danube, Morava-Vardar and Trans-Dinaric routes. These three regions could together form a middle tier between the 'East Slavian Federation' to the east (with similar opportunities to the Balkan Take-off) and the 'Mediterranean Sunbelt', 'Technology Network West' and 'North Sea Partners' on the western side.

## CONCLUSION

Dramatic change has occurred in Eastern Europe through the cancellation of the Brezhnev Doctrine, and the resulting abandonment of the Communist Party's monopoly of power has resulted in pluralisation restoring political initiative to civil society. The new forces of legitimation, including the churches and NGOs, are helping to create complex party systems, including many small political factions, and new institutions to maintain stability. Economic change has been accentuated by trade shocks associated with the collapse of FSU, the reunification of Germany and the conflict in FFRY. Trade has been diversified and many production enterprises have experienced privatisation and reorganisation, with substantial Western investment. Yet there is a major element of continuity in the power of Russia which must be central to revised security arrangements and also a key factor in economic policy, given the size of the Russian market and the opportunities for the purchase of raw materials. At the domestic level there is also the influence of the reformed communist hierarchies which are now in charge of the region's burgeoning social democracy movement. Although there is no question of a return to communist-style central planning, interventionist economic policies are a credible alternative to free market forces, and hybrid systems seem destined to be a feature of the East European transition for the foreseeable future. Decades of integration into the Soviet camp have left a legacy of ambivalence towards Western economic penetration and heightened sensitivity over ethnic issues and security implications in particular.

There is again a balance sheet to be drawn when the benefits of the transition are considered. Goods and services have become much more freely available and there has been greater freedom for individuals to compete in the economy. But there has also been unemployment and insecurity with a corresponding growth in crime and corruption, often associated with local mafia organisation. Given the reservations over the private sector's ability to create jobs and the scale of foreign investment, reform has been relatively slow in the south where there are still large SOEs dependent on state support. These commitments reduce the state's ability to develop other welfare systems while inflationary pressures linked with government spending tend to reduce real incomes even for those who remain in work. Yet there was a clear consensus for change after the fall of communism and there is a dogged determination to wait for economic conditions to improve. There are signs of greater confidence for investors as the institutional safeguards are put in place. In most countries barely one-tenth of the population would support a return to communism, though the ratings are higher in Bulgaria, Hungary and Slovakia. Yet people are certainly suspicious of politicians and sceptical of the whole political system; perhaps because of revolutionary fervour some of the new parties have been too confrontational. In some countries there is certainly a need for a stronger sense of cultural democracy and a willingness to compromise for the wider good. Yet instability arises to some extent from the material gulf that separates Eastern Europe from the West by a full Kondratieff cycle of between thirty and sixty years given the failure of communist industrialisation to bridge a historic divide. With 'the summit of economic difficulties shifting eastwards and southwards' (Nefedova and Trejvis 1994, p.38), substantial Western economic intervention is needed to prevent a possible 'Peronist' internalisation of economic and demographic problems.

What will be the profile of the new Eastern Europe at the start of the new millennium? There is a choice between open borders with a growth of trade and progressive enlargement of the EU; against a high level of protectionism and limited effectiveness for international organisations. This would have implications for economic planning with foreign investment attracted to the main transit routes, the approaches to major ports and the major airports, as opposed to a more limited autarkic approach with a bias towards strategic industries. In parallel there is the possibility of a growth in foreign capital through joint ventures, foreign-owned banks and regional offices for multi-national companies, and against development based on domestic capital investment related very much to production for home market demand. This would have implications for the development of regional specialisation, positive in the former case but negative in the latter. There are also contrasts between low unemployment with rising welfare provision and low levels of international migration; and an alternative situation where economic stagnation produces high unemployment with low welfare provision and higher levels of out-migration. Such a contrast might be reinforced by contrasting situations regarding social cohesion (the extent of class conflict and class-based political parties), economic restructuring and the resolution of pollution problems.

Politically, there is a choice between national chauvinism, with the orchestration of territorial disputes and intransigence towards ethnic minorities, and a pragmatic approach in which the drawbacks arising from the existing boundaries are minimised by cross-border cooperation and acceptance of internationally sponsored codes of practice in treating minority groups. All this would have implications for the level of defence spending and support for unprofitable strategic industries. Of course, the choices are not simple preferences between two sets of extremes and the outcomes do not rest on the East Europeans alone, for the positive scenario depends on a world order which will be shaped very largely outside the region. Given the turmoil in FFRY the worst scenario is not by any means implausible and there are certainly nationalist parties in other parts of the region that thrive on intolerance. Yet it remains a fact that even in the Balkans most countries are preoccupied with economic and social reconstruction and there is, among the majority, a sense of realism over current problems combined with optimism over future prospects. It is important that such an outlook should be reciprocated by the international community at all levels: international institutions, individual national governments, commercial and private organisations – and even private individuals who at a time of increased mobility can cumulatively propagate a European way to enhance international collaboration.

## REFERENCES

J. Alden and P. Boland 1996, *Regional Development Strategies: A European Perspective* (London: Jessica Kingsley).

J. Bachtler 1992a, 'Regional problems and policies in Central and Eastern Europe'. *Regional Studies* 26, 665–71.

J. Bachtler (ed.) 1992b, 'Socio-economic situation and development of the regions in the neighbouring countries of the Community in Central and Eastern Europe' (Brussels/Luxembourg: Commission of the European Communities Directorate-General for Regional Policies, Regional Development Studies 2).

H. Baldersheim *et al.* 1996, *Local Democracy and the Processes of Transformation in East-Central Europe* (Boulder, Colorado: Westview Press).

G. Barta 1992, 'The changing role of industry in regional development and regional development policy in Hungary'. *Tijdschrift voor Economische en Sociale Geografie* 58, 372–9.

G. Barta 1993, 'Budapest: a Central European metropolis in 2005' (Budapest: Centre for Regional Studies).

E. Benke 1995, 'Gyor in the money'. *Business Europa* 12, 16–23.

I. Berenyi 1992, 'The socio-economic transformation and the consequences of the liberalisation of borders in Hungary' in A. Kertesz and Z. Kovacs (eds) *New Perspectives in Hungarian Geography* (Budapest: Academiai Kiado), 143–57.

A. Bezak 1990, 'Functional urban regions in the settlement system of Slovakia'. *Geograficky Casopis* 42, 57–73.

G. Bianchi 1992, 'Combining networks to promote integrated regional development' in T. Vasko (ed.) *Problems of Economic Transition: Regional Development in Central and Eastern Europe* (Aldershot: Avebury), 89–105.

H. Bicik 1994, 'Contribution to the assessment of changes in land use: an example of the recreational environs of Prague'. *Acta Universitatis Carolinae: Geographica* 29, 21–35

H. Bicik and V. Stepanek 1994, 'Long-term and current tendencies in land use: case study of Prague's environs and Czech Sudetenland'. *Acta Universitatis Carolinae: Geographica* 29, 47–66.

M. Bucek 1992, 'Regional policy of the Slovak Republic in the period of transition' in T. Vasko (ed.) *Problems of Economic Transition: Regional Development in Central and Eastern Europe* (Aldershot: Avebury), 1–17.

H. Buckholz 1994, 'The inner German border: consequences of its establishment and abolition' in C. Grundy-Warr (ed.) *World Boundaries: Eurasia* (London: Routledge), 55–62.

F.W. Carter and D. Turnock (eds) 1993, *Environmental Problems of Eastern Europe* (London: Routledge).

P. Chalupa 1993, 'Synergetic evaluation of regional, social, economic and population processes'. *Katedra Geografie Pedagogicke Fakulty Masarykovy Universzirty Brno* 4, 27–41.

T. Christov 1991, 'The administrative–territorial division of Bulgaria in 1987: some new regional problems'. *Acta Facultatis Rerum Naturalium Universitatis Comeniana* 31, 39–48. In Bulgarian with an English summary.

M. Ciechocinska 1992, 'The paradox of reductions in development in the East-Central European fringe areas' in M. Tikkylainen (ed.) *Development Issues and Strategies in the New Europe* (Aldershot: Gower), 189–209.

D.A. Connelly 1994, 'Black Sea economic cooperation'. *Radio Free Europe/Radio Liberty Research* 3(26), 31–8.

B. Csatari 1993, 'Crisis signs of the Hungarian small towns' in A. Duro (ed.) *Spatial Research and the Social-political Changes* (Pecs: Centre for Regional Research), 97–102.

B. Csatari 1995, 'A special regional environmental-social conflict on the great Hungarian Plain'. *Geograpia Polonica* 64, 167–75.

Z. Csefalvay 1994, 'The regional differentiation of the Hungarian economy in transition'. *GeoJournal* 32, 351–61.

T. Czyz 1993, 'The regional structure of unemployment in Poland'. *Geographia Polonica* 61, 479–96.

J. De Bardeleben and J. Hannigan (eds) 1994, *Environmental Quality and Security After Communism: Eastern Europe and the Soviet Successor States* (Boulder, Colorado: Westview Press).

J.G. Derounian 1995, 'Rural regeneration in Romania'. *Report for the Natural and Built Environment Professions* 5, 4–6.

J.B. De Weydenthal 1993, 'Controversy in Poland over "Euroregions"'. *Radio Free Europe/Radio Liberty Research* 2(16), 6–9.

J.B. de Weydenthal 1994, 'Cross-border cooperation in East Central Europe'. *Radio Free Europe/Radio Liberty Research* 3(2), 32–5.

I. Dominis 1994, 'Dalmatia: a Croatian resource divided'. *Radio Free Europe/Radio Liberty Research* 3(9), 37–42.

P. Dostal and M. Hampl 1994, 'Development of an urban system' in M. Barlow *et al.* (eds) *Territory, Society and Administration: The Czech Republic and the Industrial Region of Liberec* (Amsterdam: University of Amsterdam/Charles University Prague/Czech Academy of Sciences Prague), 191–224.

P. Dostal *et al.* (eds) 1992, *Changing Territorial Administration in Czechoslovakia: International Viewpoints* (Amsterdam: Instituut voor Sociale Geografie).

Z. Dovenyi 1994, 'Transition and unemployment: the case of Hungary'. *GeoJournal* 32, 393–8.

G. Enyedi 1990, 'Private economic activity and regional development in Hungary'. *Geographia Polonica* 57, 53–62.

G. Enyedi 1994, 'Budapest and the European metropolitan integration'. *GeoJournal* 32, 399–402.

F. Erdosi 1992, *Transportation Effects on Spatial Structure of Hungary* (Pecs: Centre for Regional Studies, Hungarian Academy of Sciences).

J. Esser and J. Hirsch 1994, 'The crisis of Fordism and the dimensions of "Post Fordist" regional and urban structure' in A. Amin (ed.) *Post-Fordism: A Reader* (Oxford: Blackwell), 71–98.

European Commission 1994, *Europe 2000+: Cooperation for European Territorial Development* (Luxemburg: Office for Official Publications of the EC).

European Conference of Ministers of Transport (ECMT) 1991, *Prospects for East–West European Transport* (Paris: ECMT Publications).

I. Ferenc 1991, 'Main spatial features and settlement concerns of inland public transport connections in Hungary'. *Foldrajzi Ertezito* 40, 265–95. In Hungarian with an English summary.

D. Fisher 1992, *Paradise Deferred: Environmental Policymaking in Central and Eastern Europe* (London: RIIA).

J. Fitzmaurice 1995, *Damming the Danube: Gabcikovo/Nagymaros and Post-Communist Politics in Europe* (Boulder, Colorado: Westview Press).

B. Forster 1992, 'Updating transforms eastern tram fleets'. *Railway Gazette International* 148, 665–8.

E. Frankland 1995, 'Green revolutions: the role of Green Parties in Eastern Europe's transition 1989-1994'. *East European Quarterly* 29, 315–45.

P. Gastescu 1993, 'The Danube Delta: geographic characteristics and ecological recovery'. *GeoJournal* 29, 57–67.

A. Gawryszewski 1992, 'Spatial population mobility in Poland'. *Geographia Polonica* 59, 41–53.

K. Georgieva 1993, 'Environmental policy in a transition economy: the Bulgarian example' in A. Vari and P. Tamas (eds) *Environment and Democratic Transition: Policy and Politics in Central and Eastern Europe* (Dordrecht: Kluwer Academic Publishing), 67–87.

C. Gergov 1991, 'The use and protection of water resources in Bulgaria' in J. De Bardeleben (ed.) *To Breath Free: Eastern Europe's Environmental Crisis* (Baltimore, Maryland.: Johns Hopkins University Press), 159–73.

G. Gorzelak 1996, *The Regional Dimension of Transformation in Central Europe* (London: Jessica Kingsley).

G. Gorzelak and A. Kuklinski (eds) 1992, 'Dilemmas of regional policies in Eastern and Central Europe' (Warsaw: University of Warsaw European Institute for Regional and Local Development).

G. Grabher 1992, 'Eastern Conquista: the truncated industrialization of East European regions by large West European corporations' in H. Ernste and V. Meier (eds) *Regional Development and Contemporary Industrial Response: Extending Flexible Specialization* (London: Belhaven Press).

G. Grabher 1994, 'The disembedded regional economy: the transformation of East German industrial complexes into Western enclaves' in A. Amin and N. Thrift (eds) *Globalization, Institutions and Regional Development in Europe* (Oxford: Oxford University Press), 177–95.

A. Griffith 1996, 'Lodz: Poland's second city'. *Business Europa* 15, 23–30.

F-D. Grimm *et al.* 1994, *Zentrensysteme ale Trager der Raumenkwicklung in Mittel- und Osteuropa* (Leipzig: Institut der Landerkunde).

F-D. Grimm 1995, 'Return to normal: Leipzig in search for its future position in Central Europe'. *GeoJournal* 36, 319–35.

Z. Hajdu and G. Horvath (eds) 1994, *European Challenges and Hungarian Responses in Regional Policy* (Pecs: Centre for Regional Studies, Hungarian Academy of Sciences).

D.R. Hall 1992, 'East European ports in a restructured Europe' in B.S. Hoyle and D.A. Pinder (eds) *European Port Cities in Transition* (London: Belhaven Press) 98–115.

D.R. Hall 1993a, 'Impacts of economic and political transition on the transport geography of Central and Eastern Europe'. *Journal of Transport Geography* 1, 20–35.

D.R. Hall (ed.) 1993b, *Transport and Economic Development in the New Central and Eastern Europe* (London: Belhaven Press).

S. Hardy *et al.* (eds) 1995, *An Enlarged Europe: Regions in Competition?* (London: Jessica Kingsley).

D. Haydock 1995, 'Berlin five years after: bringing the network up to modern standards'. *European Railway Magazine* 5, 31–8.

R. Hope 1990, 'East journies into the unknown'. *Railway Gazette International* 146, 597–609.

G. Horvath (ed.) 1991, *Regional Policy and Local Governments* (Pecs: Centre for Regional Studies, Hungarian Academy of Sciences).

G. Horvath (ed.) 1993a, *Development Strategies for the Alpine-Adriatic Region* (Pecs: Centre for Regional Studies, Hungarian Academy of Sciences).

G. Horvath 1993b, 'Restructuring and interregional cooperation in Central Europe: the case of Hungary' in R. Cappellin and P.W.J. Batey (eds) *Regional Networks, Border Regions and European Integration* (London: Pion), 157–76.

G. Horvath 1995, 'Economic reforms in East-Central Europe', in S. Hardy *et al.* (eds) *An Enlarged Europe: Regions in Competition?* (London: Jessica Kingsley), 15–52.

G. Horvath and L. Hrubi 1992, *Restructuring and Regional Policy in Hungary* (Pecs: Centre for Regional Studies, Hungarian Academy of Sciences).

D.C. Jones 1991, 'The Bulgarian labour market in transition'. *International Labour Review* 13, 211–26.

J. Jun and K. Okolicsanyi 1994, 'Highway construction in the Visegrad countries'. *Radio Free Europe/Radio Liberty Research* 3(2), 39–46.

A. Kaliberda 1994, 'The interregional association of transborder trade in the "Carpathian Euroregion"' in F. Grief (ed.) *Die Zukunft der landlichen Infrastruktur in Ostmitteleuropa* (Wien: Schriftenreihe der Bundesanstalt für Agrarwirtschaft 75), 199–202.

J. Kara 1994, 'New Czech regional policy' in M. Barlow *et al.* (eds) *Territory, Society and Administration: The Czech Republic and the Industrial Region of Liberec* (Amsterdam: University of Amsterdam/Charles University Prague/Czech Academy of Sciences Prague), 67–83.

G.H. Kats 1991, 'Energy options for Hungary'. *Energy Policy* 19, 855–68.

B. Kinnear 1992, 'Regional development: challenges and problems in Central Europe' in T. Vasko (ed.) *Problems of Economic Transition: Regional Development in Central and Eastern Europe* (Aldershot: Avebury), 63–88.

P. Klekner 1992, 'The role of agriculture in the development of fringe areas' in M. Tikkylainen (ed.) *Development Issues and Strategies in the new Europe* (Aldershot: Gower), 121–30.

M. Klemencic 1995, 'Administrative-territorial division of Croatia'. *GeoJournal* 35, 391–400.

M. Klodzinski 1992, 'Processes of agricultural change in Eastern Europe' in R.M. Auty and R.B. Potter (eds) *Agricultural Change: Environment and Economy* (London: Mansell), 123–37.

G.C. Knight 1995, 'The emerging water crisis in Bulgaria'. *GeoJournal* 35, 415–23.

L. Kopacka 1994, 'The transition of the Czech industry and its energetic and ecological consequences'. *Acta Universitatis Carolinae Geographica* 29, 81–98.

J. Kowalski 1993, 'Transport implications of German unification' in D.R. Hall (ed.) *Transport and Economic Development in the New Central and Eastern Europe* (London: Belhaven Press) 82–92.

J.M. Kramer 1990, *The Energy Gap in Eastern Europe* (Lexington: D.C. Heath).

J.M. Kramer 1995, 'Energy and the environment in Eastern Europe' in J. De Bardeleben and J. Hannigan (eds) *Environmental Security and Quality after Communism* (Boulder, Colorado: Westview Press), 89–104.

S. Kratke 1995, *Where East Meets West: Prospects for the German-Polish Border*

*Region* (Frankfurt/Oder: Europa-Universitat Viadrina, Faculty of Cultural Sciences).

J. Kuron 1995, 'The self-limiting revolution: democratic changes in Poland after 1989'. *Woodrow Wilson Center for East European Studies* January to February 1–3.

M. Lados 1993, 'Enterprises of local town councils in Hungary' in A. Duro (ed.) *Spatial Research and the Social Political Changes* (Pecs: Centre for Regional Studies), 109–15.

J. Lotz 1992, 'The Kosice connection' in T. Vasko (ed.) *Problems of Economic Transition: Regional Development in Central and Eastern Europe* (Aldershot: Avebury), 181–95.

R. Maggi and P. Nijkamp 1992, 'Missing networks and regional development in Europe' in T. Vasko (ed.) *Problems of Economic Transition: Regional Development in Central and Eastern Europe* (Aldershot: Avebury), 29–49.

S. Markotich 1994a, 'Serbian intellectuals promote concept of a "Greater Serbia"'. *Radio Free Europe/Radio Liberty Research* 3(23), 18–23.

S. Markotich 1994b, 'Croatia's Istrian Democratic Alliance'. *Radio Free Europe/Radio Liberty Research* 3(33), 14–19.

R. Meegan 1994, 'A "Europe of the Regions": a view from Liverpool on the Atlantic arc periphery'. *European Planning Studies* 2, 59–80.

R.E.H. Mellor 1992, 'Railways and German unification'. *Geography* 77, 261–4.

W. Michalak and R. Gibb 1993, 'Development of the transport system: prospects for East–West integration' in D.R. Hall (ed.) *Transport and Economic Development in the New Central and Eastern Europe* (London: Belhaven Press) 34–48.

B. Mieczkowski 1978, *Transportation in Eastern Europe: Empirical Findings* (Boulder, Colorado: East European Monographs).

L. Miklos 1992, 'Protecting the environment during regional development' in T. Vasko (ed.) *Problems of Economic Transition: Regional Development in Central and Eastern Europe* (Aldershot: Avebury), 51–62.

P. Moore and F. Schmidt 1994, 'Possible ways out of the deadlock over Kosovo'. *Radio Free Europe/Radio Liberty Research* 3(15), 7–9.

E. Muller 1993, 'Slowenien: Auswirkungen der neuen Eigenstaatlichkeit auf die wirtschaftsgeographische Situation'. *Europa Regional* 1(1), 16–24.

J. Musil *et al.* (eds) 1995, *The Pillars of Central Europe: The Role of Cities in the Process of Transformation* (Aldershot: Avebury).

T. Nefedova and A. Trejvis 1994, *First Socio-economic Effects of Transformation of Central and Eastern Europe* (Vienna: Osterreichisches Ost- und Sudosteuropa Institut).

N. Nemes 1994, 'Regional disparities in Hungary during the period of transition to a market economy'. *GeoJournal* 32, 363–8.

M. Osterland 1994, 'Coping with democracy: the reinstitution of local self-government in Eastern Germany'. *European Urban and Regional Studies* 1, 5–18.

D. Ostry 1988, 'The Gabcikovo-Nagymaros dam system as a case study in conflict of interest in Czechoslovakia and Hungary'. *Slovo: Journal of Contemporary Soviet-East European Affairs* 1(1), 11–24.

P. Pavlinek 1992, 'Regional transformation in Czechoslovakia: towards a market economy'. *Tijdschrift voor Economische en Sociale Geografie* 83, 361–71.

P. Pavlinek *et al.* 1994, 'Demonopolitisation, economic restructuring and the environment in Bulgaria and the Czech Republic' in P. Jordan and E. Tomasi (eds) *Zustand und Perspektiven der Unwelt im ostlichen Europa* (Wien: Peter Lang Europaischer Verlag der Wissenschaften/Wiener Osteuropa Studien), 57–82.

J.S. Pedersen 1993, 'The Baltic region and the new Europe' in R. Cappellin and P.W.J.

Batey (eds) *Regional Networks, Border Regions and European Integration* (London: Pion), 135–56.

J. Pehe 1994, 'Civil society at issue in the Czech Republic'. *Radio Free Europe/Radio Liberty Research* 3(32), 13–18.

D. Pinder and B. Simmonds 1993 'Oil transport: pipelines, ports and the new political climate' in D.R. Hall (ed.) *Transport and Economic Development in the New Central and Eastern Europe* (London: Belhaven Press), 49–66.

M. Pozes 1991, 'Development of rural settlements in the commune of Koper'. *Geographica Slovenica* 22, 114. In Slovenian with an English summary.

J. Pucher 1993, 'Transport revolution in Eastern Europe'. *Transportation Quarterly* 47, 97–114.

J. Pucher 1994, 'Modal shift in Eastern Germany: transportation impacts of political change'. *Transportation* 21, 1–22.

M. Radetzki 1995, *Polish Coal and European Energy Market Integration* (Aldershot: Avebury).

A.A. Reisch 1993, 'Hungarian–Ukrainian relations continue to develop'. *Radio Free Europe/Radio Liberty Research* 2(16), 22–7.

V. Rey (ed.) 1994, *Czechoslovakia: transition, fragmentation, recomposition* (Fontenay-St Cloud: Ens Editions). In French with an English summary.

G. Ritter and J. Hajdu 1989, 'The East–West German border'. *Geographical Review* 79, 326–44.

M. Roe 1992, *East European International Road Haulage* (Aldershot: Avebury).

M. Rueschemeyer 1993, 'East Germany's new towns in transition: a grassroots view of the impact of unification'. *Urban Studies* 30, 495–506.

I. Schmidt 1991, 'Former GDR communities in radical change'. *International Journal of Urban and Regional Research* 14, 667–75.

H.S. Siedenfus 1987, 'From the Rhine-Main-Danube Canal to the Main-Danube connection' in J.F. Tismer *et al.* (eds) *Transport and Economic Development: Soviet Union and Eastern Europe* (Berlin: Duncker u. Humblot), 429–48.

S. Sitnicki *et al.* 1991, 'Opportunities for energy emissions control in Poland'. *Energy Policy* 19, 995–1002.

A. Smith 1994, 'Uneven development and the restructuring of the armaments industry in Slovakia'. *Transactions of the Institute of British Geographers* 19, 404–24.

S. Stec 1993, 'Public participation laws, regulations and practices in seven countries in Central and Eastern Europe: an analysis emphasising impacts on the development of the decision-making process' in A. Vari and P. Tamas (eds) *Environment and Democratic Transition: Policy and Politics in Central and Eastern Europe* (Dordrecht: Kluwer Academic Publishing) 88–119.

N. Swain 1994, 'Agricultural development policy in the Czech Republic: is one really necessary?' *University of Liverpool Centre for Central and East European Studies, Working Papers Rural Transition Series 12*.

L. Sykora and I. Simonickova 1994, 'From totalitarian urban manageralism to a liberalized real estate market: Prague's transformation in the early 1990s' in M. Barlow *et al.* (eds) *Development and Administration of Prague* (Amsterdam: University of Amsterdam/Charles University Prague/Czech Academy of Sciences Prague), 47–72.

L. Symons 1993, 'Airlines in transition to the market economy' in D.R. Hall (ed.) *Transport and Economic Development in the New Central and Eastern Europe* (London: Belhaven Press), 67–81.

Z. Taylor 1989, 'Contemporary trends in the Polish transport system'. *Geographia Polonica* 56, 179–94.

W. Tietze 1990, 'On the modernization of the Central European railnet after the end of division'. *GeoJournal* 20, 325–31.

T. Tiner 1992, 'The changing role of telecommunications in the reconstruction of the city of Budapest' in A. Kertesz and Z. Kovacs (eds) *New Perspectives in Hungarian Geography* (Budapest: Hungarian Academy of Sciences), 185–209.

I. Toldy-Osz 1992, 'Joint ventures in a period of transition to a market economy' in T. Vasko (ed.) *Problems of Economic Transition: Regional Development in Central and Eastern Europe* (Aldershot: Avebury), 211–13.

J. Toth 1993, 'Historical and today's socio-economic conditions of regionalism in Hungary' in A. Duro (ed.) *Spatial Research and the Social-Political Changes* (Pecs: Centre for Regional Studies), 15–28.

J. Toth 1994, 'Urbanization and spatial structure in Hungary'. *GeoJournal* 32, 343–50.

S. Troebst 1994, 'Macedonia: powderkeg defused'. *Radio Free Europe/Radio Liberty Research* 3(4), 33–41.

A. Vaishar 1992, 'Ethnic structure of the Czech Republic in the census of 1991 and its connections'. *Geographica Slovenica* 23, 385–401.

A. Vaishar 1993, 'Ethnic, religious and social problems of frontier districts in the Czech Republic'. *Geographica Slovenica* 24, 167–77.

J. Van Weesep and H. Van Der Wusten 1992, 'Dutch research in Eastern Europe: a new initiative'. *Tijdschrift voor Economische en Sociale Geografie* 83, 418–21.

G. Weclawowicz 1996, *Contemporary Poland: Space and Society* (London: UCL Press).

K. Wiest 1993, 'Die Region Halle-Leipzig: Neugliederung und Kooperationsansatze'. *Europa Regional* 1(2), 1–11.

A. Wiska and J. Hindson 1991, 'Protecting a Polish paradise'. *Geographical Magazine* 63(6), 1–2.

B. Yarnal 1995, 'Bulgaria at a crossroads: environmental impacts of socieconomic change'. *Environment* 37(10), 7–15.

# BIBLIOGRAPHY

## EASTERN EUROPE

J. Adam 1979, *Wage Control and Inflation in Soviet Bloc Countries* (London: Macmillan).

J. Adam 1989, *Economic Reform in the Soviet Union and Eastern Europe since the 1960s* (London: Macmillan).

J. Ambler *et al.* eds. 1985, *Soviet and East European Transport Problems* (London: Croom Helm).

A. Amin and N. Thrist (eds) 1994, *Globalization Institutions and Regional Development in Europe* (Oxford: Oxford University Press).

A.H. Amsden *et al.* 1994, *The Market Meets its Match: Restructuring the Economies of Eastern Europe* (Cambridge, Massachusetts: Harvard University Press).

S. Ardittis 1995, *The Politics of East–West Integration* (London: Macmillan).

D. Arter 1993, *The Politics of European Integration in the Twentieth Century* (Aldershot: Dartmouth).

V.J. Assetto 1988, *The Soviet Bloc in the IMF and the IBRD* (Boulder, Colorado: Westview Press).

S. Ausch 1972, *Theory and Practice of CMEA Cooperation* (Budapest: Academy of Sciences).

J. Bachtler (ed.) 1992, *Socioeconomic Situation and Development of the Regions of the Neighbouring Countries of the Community in Central and Eastern Europe* (Bruxelles/Luxembourg: Commission of the European Communities, Directorate General for Regional Policies, Regional Development Studies 2).

R. Bahro 1978, *The Alternative in Eastern Europe* (London: New Left Books).

E. Bairam 1988, *Technical Progress and Industrial Growth in the USSR and Eastern Europe: An Empirical Study 1961–1975* (Aldershot: Gower).

I. Banac (ed.) 1992, *Eastern Europe in Revolution* (Ithaca, New York: Cornell University Press).

D.L. Bark 1974, *Agreement on Berlin: A Study of the 1970–1972 Quadripartite Negotiations* (Washington DC: American Enterprise Institute).

A. Basch 1944, *The Danube Basin and the German Economic Sphere* (London: Kegan Paul Trench Trubner).

J. Batt 1988, *Economic Reform and Political Change in Eastern Europe: A Comparison of the Czechoslovak and Hungarian Experiences* (London: Macmillan).

J. Batt 1991, *East Central Europe from Reform to Transformation* (London: RIIA/Pinter).

T. Beeson 1982, *Discretion and Valour: Religious Conditions in Russia and Eastern Europe* (Philadelphia, Pennsylvania: Fortress Press).

P. Bender 1972, *East Europe in Search of Security* (Baltimore, Maryland: Johns Hopkins University Press).

R.J. Bennett (ed.) 1989, *Territory and Administration in Europe* (London: Pinter).

R.J. Bennett (ed.) 1993, *Local Government in the new Europe* (London: Belhaven Press).

C. Benson and E. Clay 1993, *Eastern Europe and the Former Soviet Union: Economic Change, Social Welfare and Aid* (London: Overseas Development Institute).

R. Bentley 1984, *Technological Change in the GDR* (Boulder, Colorado: Westview Press).

I. Berend 1990, *The Hungarian Economic Reforms 1953–1988* (Cambridge: Cambridge University Press).

I. Berend and G. Ranki 1974, *Hungary: A Century of Economic Development* (Newton Abbot: David & Charles).

I. Berend and G. Ranki (eds) 1979, *Underdevelopment and Economic growth: Studies in Hungarian Social and Economic History* (Budapest: Academy of Sciences).

I. Berend and G. Ranki 1974, *Economic Development in East Central Europe in the Nineteenth and Twentieth Centuries* (New York: Columbia University Press).

W.H. Berentsen *et al.* (eds) 1989, *Regional Development: Processes and Policies* (Budapest: Hungarian Academy of Sciences).

S. Bergland and J.A. Dellenbrandt (eds) 1991, *The New Democracies in Eastern Europe: Party Systems and Political Cleavages* (Aldershot: Edward Elgar).

G.K. Bertsch and S. Elliott-Gower (eds) 1991, *The Impact of Governments in East–West Economic Relations* (London: Macmillan).

G.K. Bertsch and J.R. McIntyre (eds) 1983, *National Security and Technology Transfer: the Strategic Dimension of East-West Trade* (Boulder, Colorado: Westview Press).

J.F. Besemeres 1980, *Socialist Population Politics: The Political Implications of Demographic Trends in the USSR and Eastern Europe* (White Plains, New York: Sharpe).

S. Bethlen and I. Volgyes 1985, *Europe and the Superpowers: Political, Economic and Military Power in the 1980s* (Boulder, Colorado: Westview Press).

R.R. Betts (ed.) 1950, *Central and Southwestern Europe 1945–1948* (London: RIIA).

D.E. Bierman and J. Laboda 1992, *East Central Europe: The Land and its People in Historical Perspective* (Cincinnati, Ohio: Nordic).

O. Blanchard *et al.* 1991, *Reform in Eastern Europe* (Cambridge, Massachusetts: MIT Press).

M. Bleaney 1988, *Do Socialist Economies Work?: The Soviet and East European Experience* (Oxford: Blackwell).

H. Blommestein and M. Marrese 1991, *Transformation of Planned Economies: Property Rights, Reform and Macroeconomic Stability* (Paris: OECD).

B.R. Bociurkiw and J.W. Strong (eds) 1975, *Religion and Atheism in the USSR and Eastern Europe* (London: Macmillan).

A. Bolitho 1971, *Foreign Trade Criteria in Socialist Countries* (Cambridge: Cambridge University Press).

D.L. Bond 1991, *Trade or Aid?: Official Export Credit Agencies and the Economic Development of Eastern Europe and the Soviet Union* (Boulder, Colorado: Westview Press).

M. Bornstein (ed.) 1973, *Plan and Market: Economic Reform in Eastern Europe* (New Haven, Connecticut: Yale University Press).

M. Bornstein *et al.* (eds) 1981, *East–West Relations and the Future of Eastern Europe: Politics and Economics* (London: George Allen & Unwin).

J.M. van Brabant 1977, *East European Cooperation: The Role of Money and Finance* (New York: Praeger).

362

J.M. van Brabant 1980, *Socialist Economic Integration: Aspects of Contemporary Economic Problems in Eastern Europe* (Cambridge: Cambridge University Press).

J.M. van Brabant 1987, *Adjustment, Structural Change and Economic Efficiency: Aspects of Monetary Cooperation in Eastern Europe* (Cambridge: Cambridge University Press).

J.M. van Brabant 1989, *Economic Integration in Eastern Europe: A Handbook* (London: Harvester/Wheatsheaf).

J.M. van Brabant 1990, *Remaking Eastern Europe: On the Political Economy of Transition* (Dordrecht: Kluwer Academic Publishing).

J.M. van Brabant 1991, *Integrating Eastern Europe into the International Economy: Convertibility Through a Payments Union* (Dordrecht: Kluwer Academic Publishing).

J.M. van Brabant 1992, *Privatizing Eastern Europe: The role of Markets and Ownership in the Transition* (Dordrecht: Kluwer Academic Publishing).

B. Bracewell 1976, *Economic Integration East and West* (London: Croom Helm).

J.C. Brada (ed.) 1976, *Quantitative and analytical studies in East–West relations* (Bloomington, Indiana: Indiana University Press).

J.C. Brada *et al.* 1988, *Economic Adjustment and Reform in Eastern Europe and the Soviet Union* (Durham, North Carolina: Duke University Press).

A. Braun 1990, *The Soviet–East European Relationship in the Gorbachev Era* (Boulder, Colorado: Westview Press).

A. Bromke 1985, *Eastern Europe in the Aftermath of Solidarity* (Boulder, Colorado: Westview Press).

A. Bromke and T. Rakowska-Harmstone (eds) 1972, *The Communist States in Disarray 1965–1971* (Minneapolis, Minnesota: University of Minnesota Press).

A. Bromke and P.E. Uren 1967, *The Communist States and the West* (New York: Praeger).

A. Brown and E. Neuberger (eds) 1968, *International Trade and Central Planning* (Berkeley, California: University of California Press).

C. Brown (ed.) 1994, *Political Restructuring in Europe* (London: Routledge).

J.F. Brown 1966, *The New Eastern Europe* (London: Pall Mall).

J.F. Brown 1975, *Relations Between the Soviet Union and its East European Allies: A Survey* (Santa Monica, California: Rand Corporation).

J.F. Brown 1977, *Eastern Europe's Uncertain Future* (New York: Praeger).

J.F. Brown 1988, *Eastern Europe and Communist Rule* (Durham, North Carolina: Duke University Press).

J.F. Brown 1991, *Surge to Freedom: The End of Communist Rule in Eastern Europe* (Twickenham: Adamantine Press).

W. Brus 1972, *The Market in a Socialist Economy* (London: Routledge & Kegan Paul).

W. Brus and K. Laski 1989, *From Marx to Market: Socialism in Search of an Economic System* (Oxford: Clarendon Press).

P.J. Bryson 1984, *The Consumer Under Socialist Planning: The East German Case* (New York: Praeger).

Z.K. Brzezinski 1961, *The Soviet Bloc* (New York: Praeger).

Z.K. Brzezinski 1967, *The Soviet Bloc: Unity and Conflict* (Cambridge: Cambridge University Press).

J. Bugajski 1992, *Nations in Turmoil: Conflict and Cooperation in Eastern Europe* (Boulder, Colorado: Westview Press).

J. Bugajski and M. Pollack 1989, *East European Fault Lines: Dissent, Opposition and Social Action* (New York: Praeger).

M. Burawoy and L. Lukacs 1992, *The Radiant Past: Ideology and Reality in Hungary's Road to Capitalism* (Chicago: University of Chicago Press).

3R.V. Burks 1961, *The Dynamics of Communism in Eastern Europe* (Princeton, New Jersey: Princeton University Press).

R.F. Byrnes 1980, *United States Policy Towards Eastern Europe and the Soviet Union* (Boulder, Colorado: Westview Press).

G. Calvo and J.A. Frenkel 1991, *Obstacles to Transforming Centrally-planned Economies: The Role of Capital Markets* (Washington DC: IMF).

F.W. Carter (ed.) 1977, *Historical Geography of the Balkans* (London: Academic Press).

F.W. Carter and H.T. Norris (eds) 1996, *The Changing Shape of the Balkans* (London: UCL Press).

F.W. Carter and D. Turnock (eds) 1993, *Environmental Problems in Eastern Europe* (London: Routledge).

F.W. Carter *et al.* 1995, *Interpreting the Balkans* (London: Royal Geographical Society Geographical Intelligence Paper 2).

H.M. Catudal 1978, *The Diplomacy of the Quadripartite Agreement on Berlin: A New Era in East–West Politics* (Berlin: Berlin Verlag).

D. Charles and J. Howells 1992, *Technology Transfer in Europe* (London: Belhaven Press).

D. Chirot (ed.) 1989, *The Origin of Backwardness in Eastern Europe: Economics and Politics from the Middle Ages Until the Early Twentieth Century* (Berkeley, California: University of California Press).

P. Cipkowski 1991, *Revolution in Eastern Europe: Understanding the Collapse of Communism in Poland, Hungary, East Germany, Czechoslovakia, Romania and the Soviet Union* (Chichester: John Wiley).

C.C. Clague and G. Rausser (eds) 1991, *The Emergence of Market Economies in Eastern Europe* (Oxford: Blackwell).

T. Clarke and C. Pitelis (eds) 1993, *The Political Economy of Privatization* (London: Routledge).

E.T. Comisso 1979, *Workers' Control Under Plan and Market Implications of Yugoslav Self-Management* (New Haven, Connecticut: Yale University Press).

W.D. Connor 1979, *Socialism, Politics and Equality: Hierarchy and Change in Eastern Europe and the USSR* (New York: Columbia University Press).

D.M. Crowe and J. Kolsti 1991, *The Gypsies of Eastern Europe* (Armonk, New York: M.E. Sharpe).

L. Csaba 1991, *Eastern Europe in the World Economy* (Cambridge: Cambridge University Press).

L. Csaba (ed.) 1994, *Privatization, Liberalization and Destruction: Recreating the Market in Central and Eastern Europe* (Aldershot: Dartmouth).

C. Csaki and Y. Kislev (eds) 1993, *Agricultural Cooperatives in Transition* (Boulder, Colorado: Westview Press).

B. Csikos-Nagy 1975, *Socialist Price Theory and Price Policy* (Budapest: Academy of Sciences).

J.L. Curry (ed.) 1983, *Dissent in Eastern Europe* (New York: Praeger).

C. Curtis 1978, *The Ides of August: The Berlin Wall Crisis of 1961* (London: Weidenfeld and Nicolson).

C. Cviic 1991, *Remaking the Balkans* (London: RIIA/Pinter).

R. Dahrendorf 1990, *Reflections on the Revolution in Europe* (London: Chatto & Windus).

B. Dallago *et al.* (eds) 1992, *Privatization and Entrepreneurship in Post-Socialist Countries: Economy, Law and society* (London: Macmillan).

N. Davies and A. Polonsky (eds) 1991, *Jews in Eastern Europe and the USSR 1939–1946* (London: Macmillan).

W.P. Davison 1958, *The Berlin Blockade: A study in Cold War Politics* (Princeton, New Jersey: Princeton University Press).

K. Dawisha 1990, *Eastern Europe, Gorbachev and Reform* (Cambridge: Cambridge University Press).

K. Dawisha and P. Hanson (eds) 1981, *Soviet–East European Dilemmas: Coercion, Competition and Consent* (London: Allen & Unwin).

A.H. Dawson (ed.) 1986, *Planning in Eastern Europe* (London: Croom Helm).

B. Deacon *et al.* 1991, *Eastern Europe in the 1990s: Past Developments and Future Prospects for Social Policy* (London: Sage).

B. Deacon *et al.* 1992, *The New Eastern Europe: Social Policy Past, Present and Future* (London: Sage).

A. Decker *et al.* 1992, *Conflict in Urban Development: A Comparison Between East and West Europe* (Aldershot: Avebury).

P. Dembinski 1990, *The Logic of the Planned Economy: The Seeds of Collapse* (Oxford: Clarendon Press).

G. Demko (ed.) 1984, *Regional Development: Problems and Policies in Eastern and Western Europe* (London: Croom Helm).

M. Dewar 1951, *Soviet Trade with Eastern Europe* (London: RIIA).

E.J. Dittrich *et al.* (eds) 1995, *Industrial Transformation in Europe: Process and Contexts* (London: Sage).

M.L. Dockrill 1988, *The Cold War 1945–1963* (London: Macmillan).

M.M. Drachkovitch (ed.) 1982, *East Central Europe: Yesterday, Today, Tomorrow* (Stanford, California: Hoover Institution Press).

J. Drenowski (ed.) 1982, *Crisis in the East European Economy: The Spread of the Polish Disease* (London: Croom Helm).

E.L. Dulles 1972, *The Wall: A Tragedy in Three Acts* (Columbia, South Carolina: University of South Carolina Press).

D.J. Dunn 1987, *Religion and Nationalism in Eastern Europe and the Soviet Union* (London: Lynne Rienner).

D.A. Dyker 1990, *Yugoslav Socialism: Development and Debt?* (London: Routledge).

J.S. Earle *et al.* (eds) 1993, *Privatisation in the Transition to a Market economy* (London: Pinter).

R. East 1992, *Revolution in Eastern Europe* (London: Pinter).

M. Ellman 1989, *Socialist Planning* (Cambridge: Cambridge University Press).

J. Eyal 1989, *The Warsaw Pact and the Balkans: Moscow's Southern Flank* (London: Macmillan).

D.E. Fair and R.J. Raymond (eds) 1993 *The New Europe: Evolving Economic and Financial Systems in Eastern Europe* (Dordrecht: Kluwer Academic Publishing).

Z.M. Fallenbuchl (ed.) 1975, *Economic Development in the Soviet Union and Eastern Europe* (New York: Praeger), 2 vols.

R.B. Farrell (ed.) 1970, *Political Leadership in Eastern Europe and the Soviet Union* (Chicago: Aldine).

J.K. Fedorowicz 1986, *East–West trade in the 1980s: Prospects and Policies* (Boulder, Colorado: Westview Press).

G.R. Feiwel 1971, *Growth and Reforms in Centrally Planned Economies: The Lessons of the Bulgarian Experience* (New York: Praeger).

H. Feis 1967, *Churchill, Roosevelt, Stalin: The War they Waged and the Peace they Sought* (Princeton, New Jersey: Princeton University Press).

F. Fejto 1971, *A History of the People's Democracies: Eastern Europe Since Stalin* (New York: Praeger).

S. Fischer-Galati (ed.) 1963, *Eastern Europe in the Sixties* (New York: Praeger).

S. Fischer-Galati (ed.) 1979, *The Communist Parties of Eastern Europe* (New York: Columbia University Press).

S. Fischer-Galati (ed.) 1981, *Eastern Europe in the 1980s* (Boulder, Colorado: Westview Press).

N. Fodor 1990, *The Warsaw Treaty Organization: A Political and Organizational Analysis* (London: Macmillan).

T. Foldi and T. Kiss (eds) 1969, *Socialist World Market Prices* (Leyden: Sijthoff).

A. Francis and P. Grootings (eds) 1989, *New Technologies and Work: Capitalist and Socialist Perspectives* (London: Routledge).

R.A. Francisco 1980, *Agricultural Policies in the USSR and Eastern Europe* (Boulder, Colorado: Westview Press).

R.A. Francisco *et al.* (eds) 1979, *The Political Economy of Collectivised Agriculture* (New York: Pergamon Press).

A. Fraser 1992, *The Gypsies* (Oxford: Blackwell).

R.A. French and F.E.I. Hamilton (eds) 1979, *The Socialist City: Spatial Structure and Urban Policy* (Chichester: John Wiley).

M. Friedlander (ed.) 1990, *Foreign Trade in Eastern Europe and the Soviet Union* (New York: Praeger).

J. Fullenbach 1981, *European Environmental Policy: East and West* (London: Butterworth).

N. Funk and M. Mueller (eds) 1993, *Gender Politics and Post-communism* (London: Routledge).

H. Gabrisch 1989, *Economic Reforms in Eastern Europe and the Soviet Union* (Boulder, Colorado: Westview Press).

M. Gamarnikov 1968, *New Economic Reforms in Eastern Europe* (Detroit, Michigan: Wayne State University Press).

C. Gati (ed.) 1974, *The Politics of Modernization in Eastern Europe* (New York: Praeger).

C. Gati (ed.) 1976, *The International Politics of Eastern Europe* (New York: Praeger).

R.T. de George and J.P. Scanlon (eds) 1976, *Marxism and Religion in Eastern Europe* (Dordrecht: Reidel).

K. Gerner 1985, *The Soviet Union and Central Europe in the Postwar Era: A Study in Precarious Security* (Aldershot: Gower).

M.J. Gething 1982, *Warsaw Pact Air Power in the 1980s* (London: Arms and Armour Press).

N.V. Gianaris 1982, *The Economies of the Balkan Countries* (New York: Praeger).

M. Glenny 1990, *The Rebirth of History: Eastern Europe in the Age of Democracy* (Harmondsworth: Penguin).

S. Gomulka and C. Lin 1991, *Limits to Reform and Transition in Communist Countries* (Oxford: Oxford University Press).

G. Gorzelak 1996, *The Regional Dimension of Transformation in Central Europe* (London: Jessica Kingsley).

K. Gottstein (ed.) 1992, *Integrated Europe?: Eastern and Western Perspectives of the Future* (Boulder, Colorado: Westview Press).

S.R. Graubard (ed.) 1991, *Eastern Europe, Central Europe, Europe* (Boulder, Colorado: Westview Press).

A. Greenbaum (ed.) 1988, *Minority Problems in Eastern Europe Between the World Wars* (Jerusalem: Hebrew University of Jerusalem).

K. Grzybowski 1964, *The Socialist Commonwealth of Nations* (New Haven, Connecticut: Yale University Press).

A. Gyorgy and J.A. Kuhlman (eds) 1978, *Innovation in Communist Systems* (Boulder, Colorado: Westview Press).

C. Hadjimichalis and D. Sadler (eds) 1995, *Europe at the Margins* (Chichester: John Wiley).

H. Hakovirta 1988, *East–West Conflict and European Neutrality* (Oxford: Clarendon Press).

D.R. Hall (ed.) 1991, *Tourism and Economic Development in Eastern Europe and the Soviet Union* (London: Belhaven Press).

D.R. Hall (ed.) 1993, *Transport and Economic Development in the New Central and Eastern Europe* (London: Belhaven Press).

D.R. Hall and D. Danta (eds) 1996, *Reconstructing the Balkans: A Geography of the new Southeast Europe* (Chichester: John Wiley).

T.T. Hammond (ed.) 1975, *The Anatomy of Communist Takeovers* (New Haven, Connecticut: Yale University Press).

E. Hankiss 1990, *East European Alternatives* (Oxford: Clarendon Press).

F.J. Harbutt 1989, *The Iron Curtain: Churchill, America and the Origins of the Cold War* (Oxford: Oxford University Press).

J.P. Hardt and C.H. McMillan (eds) 1988, *Planned Economies: Confronting the Challenges of the 1980s* (Cambridge: Cambridge University Press).

P. Havlik (ed.) 1990, *Dismantling the Command Economy in Eastern Europe* (Boulder, Colorado: Westview Press).

E.W. Haydon 1976, *Technology Transfer to Eastern Europe: United States Corporate Experience* (New York: Praeger).

D. Heater 1992, *The Idea of European Unity* (Leicester: Leicester University Press).

M.J. Hebbert and J.C. Hansen 1990, *Unfamiliar Territory: The Reshaping of European Geography* (Aldershot: Avebury).

A. Heller and F. Feher 1990, *From Yalta to Glasnost: The Dismantling of Stalin's Empire* (Oxford: Blackwell).

D.R. Herspring and I. Volgyes 1979, *Civil–Military Relations in Communist States* (Boulder, Colorado: Westview Press).

F. Hertz 1947, *The Economic Problem of the Danubian States* (London: Gollancz).

E.A. Hewett 1974, *Foreign Trade Prices in the CMEA* (Cambridge: Cambridge University Press).

M.R. Hill 1983, *East–West Trade: Industrial Cooperation and Technology Transfer – the British Experience* (Aldershot: Gower).

R.J. Hill and J. Zielonka (eds) 1990, *Restructuring Eastern Europe: Towards a New European Order* (Aldershot: Edward Elgar).

H.H. Hoehmann *et al.* (eds) 1976, *The New Economic Systems of Eastern Europe* (Berkeley, California: University of California Press).

G.W. Hoffman 1963, *The Balkans in Transition* (Princeton, New Jersey: Van Nostrand).

G.W. Hoffman (ed.) 1971, *Eastern Europe: Essays in Geographical Problems* (London: Methuen).

G.W. Hoffman 1972, *Regional Development Strategies in Southeast Europe* (New York: Praeger).

G.W. Hoffman and L. Dienes 1985, *The European Energy Challenge: East and West* (Durham, North Carolina: Duke University Press).

H-H. Hohmann *et al.* 1975, *The New Economic Systems of Eastern Europe* (London: Hurst).

C. Holden 1989, *The Warsaw Pact: Soviet Security and Bloc Politics* (Oxford: Blackwell).

F.D. Holzman (ed.) 1987, *The Economics of Soviet Bloc Trade and Finance* (Boulder, Colorado: Westview Press).

R.L. Hutchings 1983, *Soviet-East European Relations: Consolidation and Conflict 1968–1980* (Madison, Wisconsin: University of Wisconsin Press).

M.R. Jackson and J.D. Woodson (eds) 1984, *New Horizons in East–West economic and Business Relations* (Boulder, Colorado: Westview Press).

367

N. Jamgotch 1968, *Soviet–East European Dialogue: International Relations of a New Type?* (Stanford, California: Stanford University Press).

B. Jancar-Webster (ed.) 1993, *Environmental Management in East Central Europe: Response to Crisis* (Armonk, New York: M.E. Sharpe).

B.M. Jankovic 1988, *The Balkans in International Relations* (London: Macmillan).

C. Jeffery and R. Sturm 1993, *Federalism, Unification and European Integration* (London: Frank Cass).

I. Jeffries (ed.) 1981, *The Industrial Enterprise in Eastern Europe* (New York: Praeger).

D. Jeffries 1993, *Socialist Economies and the Transition to the Market: A Guide* (London: Routledge).

L.G. John (ed.) 1975, *EEC Policy Towards Eastern Europe* (Farnborough: Saxon House).

C. Johnson (ed.) 1970, *Change in Communist Systems* (Stanford, California: Stanford University Press).

A.R. Johnson 1977, *Soviet-East European Military Retaliations* (Santa Monica, California: Rand Corporation).

C.D. Jones 1981, *Soviet Influence in Eastern Europe: Political Autonomy and the Warsaw Pact* (New York: Praeger).

P. Joseph (ed.) 1987, *The Economies of Eastern Europe and Their Foreign Trade Relations* (Brussells: NATO Economic Directorate).

B. Kaminski 1991, *The Collapse of State Socialism: The Case of Poland* (Princeton, New Jersey: Princeton University Press).

R.E. Kanet (ed.) 1988, *The Soviet Union, Eastern Europe and the Third World* (Cambridge: Cambridge University Press).

M.C. Kaser 1967, *Comecon: Integration Problems of the Planned Economies* (Oxford: Oxford University Press).

M.C. Kaser (ed.) 1968, *Economic Development for Eastern Europe* (London: Macmillan).

M.C. Kaser and E.A. Radice (eds) 1986, *The Economic History of Eastern Europe 1919–1975* (Oxford: Clarendon Press).

M.C. Kaser and J.G. Zielinski 1970, *Planning in East Europe: Industrial Management by the State* (London: The Bodley Head).

I. Katznelson 1992, *Marxism and the City* (Oxford: Clarendon Press).

D. Kemme 1991, *Economic Transition in Eastern Europe and the Soviet Union: Issues and Strategies* (Boulder, Colorado: Westview Press).

P. Kende and Z. Strmiska 1987, *Equality and Inequality in Eastern Europe* (Leamington Spa: Berg).

M. Keren and G. Ofer 1992, *Trial of Transition: The Economic Transformation of the Post-communist Bloc* (Boulder, Colorado: Westview Press).

S.P. Kertesz (ed.) *East-Central Europe and the World: Developments in the Post-Stalin Era* (Notre Dame, Indiana: University of Notre Dame Press).

R.B. King 1973, *Minorities under Communism: Nationalities as a Source of Tension among Balkan Communist States* (Cambridge, Massachusetts: Harvard University Press).

R.B. King and R.W. Dean (eds) 1974, *East European Perspectives on European Security and Cooperation* (New York: Praeger).

W.R. Kintner and W. Klaiber 1971, *Eastern Europe and European Security* (New York: Dunnellen).

J. Kipp (ed.) 1993, *Central European Security Concerns* (London: Frank Cass).

T. Kiss 1971, *International Division in Open Economies with Special Regard to the CMEA* (Budapest: Academy of Sciences).

368

T. Kiss (ed.) 1973, *The Market of Socialist Economic Integration: Selected Conference Papers* (Budapest: Academy of Sciences).

M. Knell and C. Rider (eds) 1992, *Socialist Economies in Transition* (Aldershot: Edward Elgar).

H. Kohler 1965, *Economic Integration in the Soviet Bloc with an East German Case Study* (New York: Praeger).

W. Kolarz 1946, *Myths and Realities in Eastern Europe* (London: Lindsay Drummond).

G.W. Kolodko 1991, *Hyper-inflation and Stabilization in Post-socialist Economies* (Dordrecht: Kluwer Academic Publishing).

J. Kornai 1990, *The Road to a Free Economy* (New York: Norton).

J. Kornai 1992, *The Socialist System* (Oxford: Oxford University Press).

L.A. Kosinski (ed.) 1974, *Demographic Developments in Eastern Europe* (New York: Praeger).

H.L. Kostanick (ed.) 1977, *Population and Migration Trends in Eastern Europe* (Boulder, Colorado: Westview Press).

J.M. Kovacs and M. Tardos (eds) 1992, *Reform and Transformation in Eastern Europe: Soviet-type Economies on the Threshold of Change* (London: Routledge).

A. Koves 1985, *The CMEA Countries in the World Economy: Turning Inwards or Turning Outwards* (Budapest: Academy of Sciences).

A. Koves 1992, *Central and East European Economies in Transition: The International Dimension* (Boulder, Colorado: Westview Press).

J.A. Kuhlman 1978, *The Foreign Policies of Eastern Europe* (Leyden: Sijthoff).

W. Lamentowicz *et al.* 1990, *Eastern Europe and Democracy: The Case of Poland* (New York: Praeger).

J.R. Lampe (ed.) 1992, *Creating Capital Markets in Eastern Europe* (Baltimore, Maryland: Johns Hopkins University Press).

J.R. Lampe and M.R. Jackson 1982, *Balkan Economic History 1550–1950* (Bloomington, Indiana: Indiana University Press).

D. Lane 1976, *The Socialist Industrial State: Towards a Political Sociology of State Socialism* (London: Allen & Unwin).

E. Laszlo and J. Kurtzman (eds) 1980, *Eastern Europe and the New International Economic Order* (Elmsford, New York: Pergamon Press).

M. Lavigne 1974, *The Socialist Economies of the Soviet Union and Eastern Europe* (London: Martin Robertson).

M. Lavigne 1992, *The Soviet Union and Eastern Europe in the Global Economy* (Cambridge: Cambridge University Press).

J. Le Grand and S. Estrin (eds) 1989, *Market Socialism* (Oxford: Clarendon Press).

P. Lendvai 1968, *Eagles in Cobwebs: Nationalism and Communism in the Balkans* (London: Macdonald).

F. Levcik and J. Stankovsky 1979, *Industrial Cooperation between East and West* (London: Macmillan).

P.G. Lewis (ed.) 1984, *Eastern Europe: Political Crisis and Legitimation* (London: Croom Helm).

P.G. Lewis (ed.) 1992, *Democracy and Civil Society in Eastern Europe* (London: Macmillan).

W.J. Lewis 1982, *The Warsaw Pact: Arms Doctrine and Strategy* (Cambridge, Massachusetts: Institute for Foreign Policy Analysis).

K. Liebreich 1991, *Doing Business in Eastern Europe: Poland, Hungary, Czechoslovakia* (London: BBC Books).

R.H. Linden 1979, *Bear and Foxes: The International Relations of the East European States 1965–1969* (Boulder, Colorado: East European Monographs).

BIBLIOGRAPHY

R.H. Linden 1987, *Communist States and International Change: Romania and Yugoslavia in Comparative Perspective* (London: Allen & Unwin).

M. Lindsay 1992, *The Development of Capital Markets in Eastern Europe* (London: Pinter).

K. London (ed.) 1966, *Eastern Europe in Transition* (Baltimore, Maryland: Johns Hopkins University Press).

J. Lovenduski and J. Woodall 1987, *Politics and Society in Eastern Europe* (London: Macmillan).

M. McCauley (ed.) 1977, *Communist States in Europe 1945–1949* (London: Macmillan).

F. Malino and D. Sorkin (eds) 1991, *From East to West: Jews in a Changing Europe* (Oxford: Blackwell).

P. Marer 1972, *Soviet and East European Trade 1946–1969: Statistical Compendium and Guide* (Bloomington, Indiana: Indiana University Press).

P. Marer 1972, *Postwar Pricing and Price Patterns in Socialist Foreign Trade 1946–1971* (Bloomington, Indiana: IDRC).

P. Marer and J.M. Montias (eds) 1980, *East Europe Integration and East–West Trade* (Bloomington, Indiana: Indiana University Press).

P. Marer and S. Zecchini 1991, *The Transition to a Market Economy* (Paris: OECD), 2 vols.

M. Marrese and S. Richter (eds) 1990, *The Challenge of Simultaneous Economic Relations with East and West* (London: Macmillan).

M. Marrese and J. Vanous 1983, *Soviet Subsidization of Trade with Eastern Europe: A Soviet Perspective* (Berkeley, California: Institute of International Studies).

A. Masnata 1974, *East–West Economic Cooperation: Problems and Solutions* (Aldershot: Gower).

D.S. Mason 1992, *Revolution in East-Central Europe: The Rise and Fall of Communism and the Cold War* (Boulder, Colorado: Westview Press).

V. Mastney 1987, *Soviet-East European Survey 1986–1987* (Boulder, Colorado: Westview Press).

L. Mazurkiewicz 1992, *Human Geography in Eastern Europe and the Soviet Union* (London: Belhaven Press).

Z. Medvedev 1990, *Legacy of Chernobyl* (Oxford: Blackwell).

R.E.H. Mellor 1971, *Comecon: Challenge to the West* (New York: Van Nostrand).

R.E.H. Mellor 1975, *Eastern Europe: A Geography of the Comecon Countries* (London: Macmillan).

G. Merritt 1991, *Eastern Europe and the USSR: The Challenge of Freedom* (London: Kogan Page).

P. Michel 1990, *Politics and Religion in Eastern Europe* (Oxford: Polity Press).

A.A. Michta 1992, *East Central Europe after the Warsaw Pact: Security Dilemmas in the 1990s* (New York: Greenwood Press).

B. Mieczowski 1978, *Transportation in Eastern Europe: Empirical Findings* (Boulder, Colorado: East European Monographs).

B. Mieczowski (ed.) 1980, *Eastern European Transportation Systems and Modes* (The Hague: Nijhoff).

K. Mihailovic 1972, *Regional Development: Experiences and Prospects in Eastern Europe* (The Hague: Mouton).

W.E. Moore 1945, *Economic Demography of Eastern and Southern Europe* (Geneva: League of Nations).

P. Murrell 1990, *The Nature of Socialist Economies: Lessons from East European Foreign Trade* (Princeton, New Jersey: Princeton University Press).

J. Musil 1981, *Urbanization in Socialist Countries* (London: Croom Helm).

370

O.A. Narkiewicz 1981, *Marxism and the Reality of Power 1919–1980* (London: Croom Helm).

O.A. Narkiewicz 1986, *Eastern Europe 1968–1984* (London: Croom Helm).

O.A. Narkiewicz 1990, *Petrification and Progress: Communist Leaders in Eastern Europe 1956–1988* (New York: Harvester/Wheatsheaf).

V. Nec and D. Stark (eds) 1989, *Remaking the Economic Institutions of Socialism* (Stanford, California: Stanford University Press).

T. Nefedova and A. Trejvis 1994, *First Socio-economic Effects of Transformation of Central and Eastern Europe* (Vienna: Osterreichisches Ost- under Sudosteuropa-Institut).

S.S. Nello 1991, *The New Europe: Changing Economic Relations Between East and West* (New York: Harvester/Wheatsheaf).

S.S. Nello 1991, *Eastern Europe and the European Community: A Study in Trade Relations* (New York: Harvester/Wheatsheaf).

D.N. Nelson 1980, *Local Politics in Communist Countries* (Lexington, Kentucky: University Press of Kentucky).

D.N. Nelson (ed.) 1983, *Communism and the Politics of Inequality* (Lexington, Kentucky: Lexington Books).

D.N. Nelson (ed.) 1984, *Soviet Allies: The Warsaw Pact and the Issue of Reliability* (Boulder, Colorado: Westview Press).

D.N. Nelson 1986, *Alliance Behaviour in the Warsaw Pact* (Boulder, Colorado: Westview Press).

D.N. Nelson 1988, *Elite-Mass Relations in Communist Systems* (New York: St Martin's Press).

D.N. Nelson 1991, *The Costs of Demilitarizing Security in the Soviet Union and Eastern Europe* (Koln: Bundesinstitut für Ostwissenschaftliche und Internationale Studien).

P. van Ness (ed.) 1988, *Market Reform in Socialist Societies* (London: Lynne Rienner).

J. O'Loughlin and H. van der Wusten (eds) 1993, *The New Political Geography of Eastern Europe* (London: Belhaven Press).

R.H. Osborne 1967, *East Central Europe* (London: Chatto & Windus).

S.J. Paliwoda 1981, *Joint East-West Marketing and Production Ventures* (Aldershot: Gower).

A. Palmer 1970, *The Lands Between: A History of East-Central Europe Since the Congress of Vienna* (London: Weidenfeld & Nicolson).

L. Pasvolsky 1971, *Economic Nationalism in the Danubian States* (New York: Macmillan).

K. Pecsi 1978, *Economic Questions of Production Integration within the CMEA* (Budapest: Hungarian Scientific Council for World Economy).

K. Petkov and J.E.M. Thirkell 1990, *Labour Relations in Eastern Europe: Organisation, Design and Dynamics* (London: Routledge).

J.G. Pilon 1992, *The Bloody Flag: Post-communist Nationalism in Eastern Europe* (New Brunswick, New Jersey: Rutgers University Press).

J. Pinder 1990, *The European Community and Eastern Europe* (London: RIIA/Pinter).

A. Polonsky 1980, *The Little Dictators: The History of Eastern Europe since 1918* (London: Routledge & Kegan Paul).

K. Post and P. Wright 1989, *Socialism and underdevelopment* (London: Routledge).

H. Poulton 1994, *The Balkans: Minorities and States in Conflict* (London: Minority Rights Group).

N.J.G. Pounds 1969, *Eastern Europe* (London: Longman).

N.J.G. Pounds 1973–9, *Historical Geography of Europe* (Cambridge: Cambridge University Press), 2 vols.

N.J.G. Pounds and N. Spulber 1957, *Resources and Planning in Eastern Europe* (Bloomington, Indiana: Indiana University Press).

K. Poznanski 1992, *Constructing Capitalism: The Reemergence of Civil Society and Liberal Economy in the Post-Communist World* (Boulder, Colorado: Westview Press).

G. Pridham (ed.) 1989, *Securing Democracy: Political Parties and Democratic Consolidation in Southern Europe* (London: Routledge).

F.L. Pryor 1963, *The Communist Foreign Trade System* (London: Allen & Unwin).

M. Radu (ed.) 1981, *Eastern Europe and the Third World: East versus South* (New York: Praeger).

T. Rakowska-Harmstone (ed.) 1979, *Perspectives for Change in Communist Societies* (Boulder, Colorado: Westview Press).

T. Rakowska-Harmstone and A. Gyorgy (eds) 1979, *Communism in East Europe* (Bloomington, Indiana: Indiana University Press).

S.P. Ramet (ed.) 1992, *Adaptation and Transformation in Communist and Post-Communist Systems* (Boulder, Colorado: Westview Press).

C. Ransom 1973, *The European Community and Eastern Europe* (London: Butterworth).

Z. Rau (ed.) 1991, *The Reemergence of Civil Society in Eastern Europe and the Soviet Union* (Boulder, Colorado: Westview Press).

R.A. Remington 1973, *The Warsaw Pact: Case Studies in Conflict Resolution* (Cambridge, Massachusetts: MIT Press).

G. Revesz 1989, *Perestroika in Eastern Europe: Hungary's Economic Transformation 1945–1988* (Boulder, Colorado: Westview Press).

I. Rieder 1991, *Feminism and Eastern Europe* (Dublin: Attic Press).

M. Riff 1992, *The Face of Survival: Jewish Life in Eastern Europe Past and Present* (London: Vallentine Mitchell).

M. Roe 1992, *East European International Road Haulage* (Aldershot: Avebury).

J.M.C. Rollo *et al.* 1990, *The New Eastern Europe: Western Responses* (London: RIIA/Pinter).

M.G. Roskin 1991, *The Rebirth of East Europe* (Englewood Cliffs, New Jersey: Prentice Hall).

J. Rothschild 1989, *Return to Diversity: A Political History of East Central Europe since World War Two* (Oxford: Oxford University Press).

D.S. Rugg 1985, *The World's Landscapes: Eastern Europe* (London: Longman).

J. Rupnik 1986, *Czechoslovakia* (London: Pinter).

B. Sarfalvi (ed.) 1970, *Recent Population Movements in East European Countries* (Budapest: Hungarian Academy of Sciences).

B. Sarfalvi (ed.) 1975, *Urbanization in Europe* (Budapest: Hungarian Academy of Sciences).

C.T. Saunders (ed.) 1980, *East and West in the Energy Squeeze: Prospects for Cooperation* (London: Macmillan).

C.T. Saunders (ed.) 1983, *Regional Integration in East and West* (London: Macmillan).

H.W. Schaefer 1972, *Comecon and the Politics of Integration* (New York: Praeger).

M.E. Schaffer (ed.) 1985, *Technology Transfer and East–West Relations* (London: Croom Helm).

G. Schopflin (ed.) 1970, *Soviet Union and Eastern Europe: A Handbook* (London: Blond).

G. Schopflin (ed.) 1982, *Eastern European Handbook* (London: St Martin's Press).

G. Schopflin and N. Wood (eds) 1989, *In Search of Central Europe* (Oxford: Polity Press).

D.E. Schultz and J.S. Adams (eds) 1981, *Political Participation in Communist Systems* (Elmsford, New York: Pergamon).

H.W. Schwarze 1973, *Eastern Europe in the Soviet Shadow* (New York: Day).

H. Scott 1976, *Women and Socialism: Experiences from Eastern Europe* (London: Allison Busby).

R. Selucky 1972, *Economic Reforms in Eastern Europe* (New York: Praeger).

H. Seton-Watson 1985. *The East European Revolution* (Boulder, Colorado: Westview Press).

A. Shlaim and G.N. Yannopoulos (eds) 1978, *The EEC and Eastern Europe* (Cambridge: Cambridge University Press).

P.S. Shoup (ed.) 1990, *Problems of Balkan Security: Southeastern Europe in the 1990s* (Washington DC: Wilson Center Press).

H. Siebert 1991, *The New Economic Landscape in Europe* (Oxford: Blackwell).

J.A.A. Sillince (ed.) 1990, *Housing Policies in Eastern Europe and the Soviet Union* (London: Routledge).

F. Silnitsky *et al.* 1979, *Communism and Eastern Europe* (Brighton: Harvester).

G.D. Simmonds (ed.) 1977, *The USSR and Eastern Europe in the Era of Brezhnev and Kosygin* (Detroit, Michigan: University of Detroit Press).

J. Simon and T. Gilberg (eds) 1985, *Security Implications of Nationalism in Eastern Europe* (Boulder, Colorado: Westview Press).

W.B. Simons (ed.) 1980, *The Constitutions of the Communist World* (Alphen aan den Rijn: Sijthoff and Noordhoff).

S. Sinanian *et al.* (eds) 1972, *Eastern Europe in the 1970s* (New York: Praeger).

F.B. Singleton (ed.) 1987, *Environmental Problems in the Soviet Union and Eastern Europe* (London: Lynne Rienner).

L. Sirc 1969, *Economic Devolution in Eastern Europe* (New York: Praeger).

O. Sjoberg and M.L. Wyzan (eds) 1991, *Economic Crisis and Reform in the Balkans: Albania, Bulgaria, Roumania and Yugoslavia facing the 1990s* (London: Pinter).

H.G. Skilling 1966, *The Governments of Communist East Europe* (New York: Crowell).

A.H. Smith 1983, *The Planned Economies of Eastern Europe* (London: Croom Helm).

C. Smith and P. Thompson (eds) 1992, *The Labour Process in Eastern Europe and China* (London: Routledge).

M.J. Sodaro and S.L. Wolchik (eds) 1983, *Foreign and Domestic Policy in Eastern Europe in the 1980s: Trends and Prospects* (London: Macmillan).

J. Sokolovsky 1990, *Peasants and Power: State Autonomy and the Collectivisation of Agriculture in Eastern Europe* (Boulder, Colorado: Westview Press).

N. Spulber 1957, *The Economics of Communist Eastern Europe* (Cambridge, Massachusetts: MIT Press).

R.F. Staar 1968, *Aspects of Modern Communism* (Columbia, South Carolina: University of South Carolina Press).

R.F. Staar 1982, *The Communist Regimes in Eastern Europe* (Stanford, California: Hoover Institution Press).

J. Staniszkis 1991, *The Dynamics of Breakthrough in Eastern Europe* (Berkeley, California: University of California Press).

J.P. Stern 1982, *East European Energy and East-West Trade in Energy* (London: Policy Studies Institute).

T. Stoianovich (ed.) 1992, *Balkan Civilisation: The First and Last Europe* (New York: M.E. Sharpe).

G. Stokes (ed.) 1991, *From Stalinism to Pluralism: A Documentary History of Eastern Europe since 1945* (Oxford: Oxford University Press).

B.R. Stokke 1968, *Soviet and East European Trade and Aid in Africa* (New York: Praeger).

J. Story (ed.) 1993, *The new Europe: Politics, Government and the Economy since 1945* (Oxford: Blackwell).

P.F. Sugar 1980, *Ethnic Diversity and Conflict in Eastern Europe* (Santa Barbara, California: ABC-Clio).

P.F. Sugar and I.J. Lederer 1994, *Nationalism in Eastern Europe* (Seattle, Washington: University of Washington Press).

P.F. Sugar *et al.* 1988, *The Problems of Nationalism in Eastern Europe Past and Present* (Washington DC: Smithsonian Institute, Wilson Center).

P. Summerscale 1982, *The East European Predicament: Changing Patterns in Poland, Czechoslovakia and Romania* (Aldershot: Gower).

G. Swain and N. Swain 1993, *Eastern Europe since 1945* (London: Macmillan).

N. Swain 1985, *Collective Farms Which Work?* (Cambridge: Cambridge University Press).

J.F.M. Swinnen 1994, *Policy and Institutional Reform in Central European Agriculture* (Aldershot: Avebury).

R. Szawlowski 1976, *The System of International Organizations of the Communist Countries* (Leyden: Sijthoff).

I. Szelenyi 1983, *Urban Inequalities under State Socialism* (Oxford: Oxford University Press).

I. Szelenyi and R. Manchin 1986, *Peasants, proletarians, entrepreneurs: Transformation of Rural Social Structures under State Socialism* (Madison, Wisconsin: University of Wisconsin).

G. Szell (ed.) 1992, *Labour Relations in Transition in Eastern Europe* (Berlin: Walter de Gruyter).

J. Szmatka *et al.* (eds) 1993, *Eastern European Societies on the Threshold of Change* (Lampeter: Edwin Mellen Press).

J. Tamke 1983, *The People's Republics of Eastern Europe* (London: Croom Helm).

J. Telgarsky and R.J. Struyk 1991, *Towards a Market-Oriented Housing Sector in Eastern Europe: Developments in Bulgaria, Czechoslovakia, Hungary, Poland, Romania and Yugoslavia* (Washington, DC: Urban Institute Press).

S.M. Terry (ed.) 1984, *Soviet Policy in Eastern Europe* (New Haven, Connecticut: Yale University Press).

M. Tikklylainen (ed.) 1995, *Local and Regional Development During the 1990s Transition in Eastern Europe* (Aldershot: Avebury).

V. Tismaneanu 1988, *The Crisis of Marxist Ideology in Eastern Europe: The Poverty of Utopia* (London: Routledge).

J.F. Tismer *et al.* (eds) 1987, *Transport and Economic Development: Soviet Union and Eastern Europe* (Berlin: Osteuropa-Institut an der Frien Universitat Berlin).

R.L. Tokes (ed.) 1979, *Opposition in Eastern Europe* (Baltimore, Maryland: Johns Hopkins University Press).

P. Toma (ed.) 1970, *The Changing Face of Communism in Eastern Europe* (Tucson: University of Arizona Press).

J. Tomaszewski 1989, *The Socialist Regimes of Eastern Europe: Their Establishment and Consolidation 1944–1967* (London: Routledge).

J.F. Triska 1969, *Communist Party States: Comparative and International Studies* (Indianapolis, Indiana: Bobbs-Merrill).

J.F. Triska and P.M. Cocks (eds) 1977, *Political Development in Eastern Europe* (New York: Praeger).

J.F. Triska and C. Gati (eds) 1981, *Blue Collar Workers in Eastern Europe* (London: George Allen & Unwin).

B. Turner *et al.* (eds) 1992, *The Reform of Housing in Eastern Europe and the Soviet Union* (London: Routledge).

D. Turnock 1986, *Studies in Industrial Geography: Eastern Europe* (Folkestone: Dawson).

D. Turnock 1988, *The Making of Eastern Europe from the Earliest Times to 1815* (London: Routledge).

D. Turnock 1989, *Eastern Europe: An Historical Geography 1815–1945* (London: Routledge).

D. Turnock 1989, *The Human Geography of Eastern Europe* (London: Routledge).

I. Vajda and M. Simai (eds) 1971, *Foreign Trade in a Planned Economy* (Cambridge: Cambridge University Press).

T. Vasko (ed.) 1992, *Problems of Economic Transition: Regional Development in Central and Eastern Europe* (Aldershot: Avebury).

R.D. Vine (ed.) 1987, *Soviet-East European Reforms as a Problem for Western Policy* (London: Croom Helm).

I. Volgyes (ed.) 1975, *Comparative Political Socialization: Eastern Europe* (New York: Praeger).

I. Volgyes (ed.) 1975, *Environmental Deterioration in the Soviet Union and Eastern Europe* (New York: Praeger).

I. Volgyes 1978, *Social Deviance in Eastern Europe* (Boulder, Colorado: Westview Press).

I. Volgyes 1979, *The Government and Politics of Eastern Europe* (Lincoln, Nebraska: Cliff's Notes).

I. Volgyes (ed.) 1979, *The Peasantry of Eastern European* (New York: Pergamon), 2 vols.

I. Volgyes 1989, *Politics in Eastern Europe* (Pacific Grove, California: Brooks/Cole Publishing Company).

I. Volgyes and G. Enyedi (eds) 1982, *The Impact of Modernization on Rural Transformation* (New York: Pergamon).

I. Volgyes and M. Volgyes 1970, *Czechoslovakia, Hungary, Poland: The Breadbasket and the Battleground* (Camden, New Jersey: Nelson).

M.E. Volten (ed.) 1990, *Uncertain Futures: Eastern Europe and Democracy* (New York: Praeger).

K-E. Wadekin 1982, *Agricultural Policies in Communist Europe* (The Hague: Nijhoff).

K-E. Wadekin (ed.) 1990, *Communist Agriculture: Farming in the Soviet Union and Eastern Europe* (London: Routledge).

W.W. Wallace and R.A. Clarke 1986, *Comecon Trade and the West* (London: Pinter).

H.G. Wanklyn 1941, *The Eastern Marchlands of Europe* (London: Philip).

P.T. Wanless 1985, *Taxation in Centrally Planned Economies* (London: Croom Helm).

B. Ward 1967, *The Socialist Economy: A Study of Organizational Alternatives* (New York: Random House).

S. Wasowski (ed.) 1970, *East–West Trade and the Technology Gap* (New York: Praeger).

W.A. Welsh (ed.) 1981, *Survey Research and Public Attitudes in Eastern Europe and the Soviet Union* (New York: Pergamon).

S. White (ed.) 1991, *Handbook of Reconstruction in Eastern Europe and the Soviet Union* (London: Longman).

S. White *et al.* 1982, *Communist Political Systems: An Introduction* (London: Macmillan).

S. Whitefield (ed.) 1993, *The New Institutional Architecture of Eastern Europe* (London: Macmillan).

F. Wiener 1976, *The Armies of the Warsaw Pact Nations* (Vienna: Ueberreuter).

J. Wilczynski 1969, *The Economics and Politics of East-West Trade* (London: Macmillan).

J. Wilczynski 1972, *Socialist Economic Development and Reform* (London: Macmillan).

J. Wilczynski 1974, *Technology in Comecon* (New York: Praeger).

J. Wilczynski 1977, *The Economics of Socialism* (London: Allen & Unwin).

P.J. Wiles 1968, *Communist International Economics* (Oxford: Blackwell).

A.J. Williams (ed.) 1994, *Reorganizing Eastern Europe: European Institutions and the Refashioning of Europe's Security Architecture* (Aldershot: Dartmouth).

J. Williamson 1991, *Currency Convertibility in Eastern Europe* (Washington DC: Institute for International Economics).

J. Williamson 1991, *The Economic Opening of Eastern Europe* (Washington DC: Institute for International Economics).

E. Winiecki and J. Winiecki 1992, *The Structural Legacy of Soviet-Type Economy: A Collection of Papers* (London: Centre for Research into Communist Economies).

J. Winiecki 1988, *The Distorted State of Soviet Type Economies* (London: Routledge).

J. Winiecki 1993, *Post Soviet-Type Economies in Transition* (London: Routledge).

T.W. Wolfe 1970, *Soviet Power and Europe 1945–1970* (Baltimore, Maryland: Johns Hopkins University Press).

R.L. Wolff 1956, *The Balkans in our Time* (Cambridge, Massachusetts: Harvard University Press).

A.S. Yergin 1980, *East–West Technology Transfer: European Perspectives* (Beverly Hills, California: Sage Publications).

J.W. Young 1991, *Cold War Europe 1945–1989: A Political History* (London: Routledge).

S.D. Zagoroff *et al.* 1955, *The Agricultural Economy of the Danubian Countries 1935–1945* (Stanford, California: Stanford University Press).

A. Zauberman 1964, *Industrial progress in Poland, Czechoslovakia and East Germany 1937–1962* (Oxford: Oxford University Press).

Z.A.B. Zeman 1991, *The Making and Breaking of Communist Europe* (Oxford: Blackwell).

I. Zloch-Christy 1987, *Debt Problems of Eastern Europe* (Cambridge: Cambridge University Press).

A. Zonoviev 1984, *The Reality of Communism* (London: Gollancz).

A. Zwass 1984, *The Economies of Eastern Europe in a Time of Change* (London: Macmillan).

# ALBANIA

E. Biberaj 1986, *Albania and China: A Study of an Unequal Alliance* (Boulder, Colorado: Westview Press).

E. Biberaj 1989, *Albania: A Nation in Transition* (Boulder, Colorado: Westview Press).

E. Biberaj 1990, *Albania: A Socialist Maverick* (Boulder, Colorado: Westview Press).

G. Bird (ed.) 1992, *Economic Reform in Eastern Europe* (Aldershot: Edward Elgar).

W.E. Griffiths 1962, *Albania and the Sino-Soviet Rift* (Cambridge, Massachusetts: MIT Press).

D.R. Hall 1994, *Albania and the Albanians* (London: Pinter).

H. Hamm 1963, *Albania: China's Beachhead in Europe* (London: Weidenfeld & Nicolson).

R. Marmallaku 1975, *Albania and the Albanians* (London: Hurst).

N.C. Pano 1968, *The People's Republic of Albania* (Baltimore, Maryland: Johns Hopkins University Press).

P.R. Prifti 1978, *Socialist Albania since 1944: Domestic and Foreign Developments* (Cambridge, Massachusetts: MIT Press).

O. Sjoberg 1991, *Rural Change and Development in Albania* (Boulder, Colorado: Westview Press).

O. Sjoberg 1991, *Urbanisation under Central Planning: The Case of Albania* (Uppsala: Uppsala University).

S. Skendi 1957, *East Central Europe Under the Communists: Albania* (New York: Praeger).

J.I. Thomas 1969, *Education for Communism: School and State in the People's Republic of Albania* (Stanford, California: Hoover Institution Press).

# BULGARIA

J.D. Bell 1986, *The Bulgarian Communist Party from Blagoev to Zhivkov* (Oxford: Clio).

J.A. Bristow 1996, *The Bulgarian Economy in Transition* (Aldershot: Edward Elgar).

J.F. Brown 1970, *Bulgaria under Communist Rule* (New York: Praeger).

T. Butler (ed.) 1976, *Bulgaria Past and Present* (Columbus, Ohio: American Association for the Advancement of Slavic Studies).

R.J. Crampton 1987, *A Short History of Modern Bulgaria* (Cambridge: Cambridge University Press).

L.A. Dellin (ed.) 1957, *East Central Europe Under the Communists: Bulgaria* (New York: Praeger).

G.R. Feiwel 1977, *Growth and Reforms in Centrally Planned Economies: The Lessons of the Bulgarian Experience* (New York: Praeger).

D.C. Jones and J. Miller 1996, *The Bulgarian Economy: Lessons for Reform During the Early Transition* (Aldershot: Avebury).

J.R. Lampe 1986, *The Bulgarian Economy in the Twentieth Century* (London: Croom Helm).

R.J. MacIntyre 1988, *Bulgaria: Politics, Economics, Society* (London: Pinter).

W.A. Welsh 1988, *Bulgaria* (Boulder, Colorado: Westview Press).

I. Zloch-Christy 1996, *Bulgaria in a Time of Change: Economic and Political Dimensions* (Aldershot: Avebury).

# FORMER CZECHOSLOVAKIA

M. Barlow *et al.* (eds) 1994, *Development and Administration of Prague* (Amsterdam: University of Amsterdam and Charles University Prague).

M. Barlow *et al.* (eds) 1994, *Territory, Society and Administration: The Czech Republic and the Industrial Region of Liberec* (Amsterdam: University of Amsterdam and Charles University Prague).

J. Bloomfield 1979, *Passive revolution: politics in the Czechoslovak Working Class 1945–1948* (New York: St Martin's Press).

J.F.H. Bradley 1981, *Politics in Czechoslovakia 1945–1971* (Washington DC: University Press of America).

H. Brisch and I. Volgyes (eds) 1979, *Czechoslovakia* (Boulder, Colorado: Westview Press).

J. Bugajski 1987, *Czechoslovakia: Charter 77's Decade of Dissent* (New York: Praeger).

V. Busek and N. Spulber (eds) 1957, *East Central Europe under the Communists: Czechoslovakia* (New York: Praeger).

## BIBLIOGRAPHY

E.J. Czerwinski and J. Piekalkiewicz 1972, *The Soviet Invasion of Czechoslovakia: Its Effects on Eastern Europe* (New York: Praeger).

J. Demek *et al.* 1971, *Geography of Czechoslovakia* (Prague: Academia).

G.R. Feiwel 1968, *New Economic Patterns in Czechoslovakia* (New York: Praeger).

G. Golan 1971, *The Czechoslovak Reform Movement: Communism in Crisis 1962–1968* (Cambridge: Cambridge University Press).

G. Golan 1973, *Reform Rule in Czechoslovakia: The Dubcek Era 1968–1969* (Cambridge: Cambridge University Press).

Z. Hejzlar and V. Kusin (eds) 1975, *Czechoslovakia 1968–1969* (New York: Garland).

P. Hruby 1980, *Fools and Heroes: The Changing Role of Communist Intellectuals in Czechoslovakia* (Oxford: Pergamon).

R.R. James (ed.) 1969, *The Czechoslovak Crisis 1968* (London: Weidenfeld & Nicolson).

J. Kalvoda 1978, *Czechoslovakia's Role in Soviet Strategy* (Washington DC: University Press of America).

K. Kansky 1976, *Urbanization under Socialism: The Case of Czechoslovakia* (New York: Praeger).

K. Kaplan 1986, *The Communist Party in Power: A Profile of Party Politics in Czechoslovakia* (Boulder, Colorado: Westview Press).

K. Kaplan 1987, *The Short March: The Communist Takeover in Czechoslovakia 1945–1948* (London: Hunt).

J. Krejci 1990, *Czechoslovakia at the Crossroads of European History* (London: Tauris).

Z. Krystufek 1981, *The Soviet Regime in Czechoslovakia* (Boulder, Colorado: Westview Press).

V.V. Kusin 1972, *Political Grouping in the Czechoslovak Reform Movement* (New York: Columbia University Press).

V.V. Kusin 1978, *From Dubcek to Charter 77* (New York: St Martin's Press).

M. Myant 1989, *The Czechoslovak Economy 1948–1988: The Battle for Economic Reform* (Cambridge: Cambridge University Press).

M. Myant 1993, *Transforming Socialist Economies: The Cases of Poland and Czechoslovakia* (Aldershot: Edward Elgar).

D.W. Paul 1981, *Czechoslovakia: Profile of a Socialist Republic at the Crossroads of Europe* (Boulder, Colorado: Westview Press).

R.A. Remington (ed.) 1973, *Winter in Prague: Documents on Czechoslovak Communism in Crisis* (Cambridge, Massachusetts: MIT Press).

H. Renner 1989, *History of Czechoslovakia since 1945* (London: Routledge).

H-P. Riese 1979, *Since the Prague Spring* (New York: Vintage Books).

W. Shawcross 1971, *Dubcek* (New York: Simon & Schuster).

D. Short 1986, *World Bibliographical Series: Czechoslovakia* (Oxford: Clio).

M. Simecka 1984, *The Restoration of Order: The Normalization of Czechoslovakia* (London: Verso).

H.G. Skilling 1976, *Czechslovakia's Interrupted Revolution* (Princeton, New Jersey: Princeton University Press).

H.G. Skilling 1981, *Charter 77 and Human Rights in Czechoslovakia* (Winchester, Massachusetts: Allen & Unwin).

H.G. Skilling (ed.) 1990, *Czechoslovakia 1918–1988* (London: Macmillan).

H.G. Skilling and P. Wilson (eds) 1991, *Civic Freedom in Central Europe: Voices from Czechoslovakia* (London: Macmillan).

J.N. Stevens 1985, *Czechoslovakia and the Crossroads: The Economic Dilemmas of Communism in Post-war Czechoslovakia* (Boulder, Colorado: East European Monographs).

N. Stone and E. Strouhal 1989, *Czechoslovakia: Crossroads and Crises 1918–1988* (London: Macmillan).

Z. Suda 1980, *Zealots and Rebels: A History of the Ruling Communist Party of Czechoslovakia* (Stanford, California: Hoover Institution Press).

E. Taborsky 1961, *Communism in Czechoslovakia 1948–1960* (Princeton, New Jersey: Princeton University Press).

A. Teichova 1988, *The Czechoslovak Economy 1918–1980* (London: Routledge).

O. Ulc 1974, *Politics in Czechoslovakia* (San Francisco, California: Freeman).

J. Valenta 1979, *Soviet Intervention in Czechoslovakia 1968: Anatomy of a Decision* (Baltimore, Maryland: Johns Hopkins University Press).

W.W. Wallace 1977, *Czechoslovakia* (London: Benn).

H.G. Wanklyn 1954, *Czechoslovakia: A Geographical and Historical Study* (London: Philip).

B. Wheaton and Z. Kavan 1992, *The Velvet Revolution: Czechoslovakia 1988–1991* (Boulder, Colorado: Westview Press).

S. Wolchik 1991, *Czechoslovakia in Transition: Politics, Economics and Society* (London: Pinter).

I.W. Zartmann 1970, *Czechoslovakia: Intervention and Impact* (New York: New York University Press).

Z. Zeman 1990, *The Masaryks: The Making of Czechoslovakia* (London: Tauris).

P.E. Zinner 1962, *Communist Strategy and Tactics in Czechoslovakia* (New York: Praeger).

## FORMER GDR

R. Bentley 1984, *Technological Change in the GDR* (Boulder, Colorado: Westview Press).

R. Bentley 1991, *Research and Technology in the Former GDR* (Boulder, Colorado: Westview).

P.J. Bryson 1984, *The Consumer under Socialist Planning: The East German Case* (New York: Praeger).

P.J. Bryson et al. 1991, *The End of the East German Economy: From Honecker to Reunification* (London: Macmillan).

M. Burleigh 1990, *Germany Turns Eastwards* (Cambridge: Cambridge University Press).

H.M. Catudal 1978, *The Diplomacy of the Quadripartite Agreement on Berlin: A New Era in East–West Politics* (Berlin: Berlin Verlag).

D. Childs 1983, *The GDR: Moscow's German Ally* (London: Allen & Unwin).

D. Childs et al. 1989, *East Germany in Comparative Perspectives* (London: Routledge).

D. Colleo 1978, *East German Problems Reconsidered* (Cambridge: Cambridge University Press).

C. Curtis 1978. *The Ides of August: The Berlin Wall Crisis of 1961* (London: Weidenfeld & Nicolson).

W.P. Davison 1958, *The Berlin Blockade: A Study of Cold War Politics* (Princeton, New Jersey: Princeton University Press).

M. Dennis 1988, *German Democratic Republic: Politics, Economics and Society* (London: Pinter).

T.H. Elkins 1972, *Germany* (London: Chatto & Windus).

T.H. Elkins and B. Hofmeister 1988, *Berlin: The Spatial Structure of a Divided City* (London: Methuen).

M.T. Foster 1979, *The East German Army: Second in the Warsaw Pact* (London: Allen & Unwin).

R.A. Francisco and R.L. Merritt (eds) 1985, *Berlin Between Two Worlds* (Boulder, Colorado: Westview Press).

M. Freund 1972, *From Cold War to Ostpolitik: Germany and the New Europe* (London: Wolff).

R. Fritz-Bournazel 1988, *Confronting the German question: Germany on the East–West Divide* (Oxford: Berg).

G. Glaessner 1992, *The German Revolution 1989–1990 and German Unification* (London: Pinter).

H. Graml 1991, *The Reichkristallnacht: Anti-Semitism and the Jewish People in the Third Reich* (Oxford: Blackwell).

D. Grosser 1992, *German Unification: The Unexpected Challenge* (Oxford: Berg).

M.D. Hancock and H. Welsh (eds) 1992, *German Unification: Process and Outcomes* (Boulder, Colorado: Westview Press).

A.M. Hanhardt 1986, *German Democratic Republic* (London: Pinter).

D.R. Herspring 1973, *East German Civil–Military Relations* (New York: Praeger).

I. Jeffries and M. Melzer (eds) 1987, *The East German Economy* (London: Croom Helm).

A. Jones 1993, *The New Germany: A Human Geography* (London: Belhaven Press).

K. Kaiser 1969, *German Foreign Policy in Transition* (Oxford: Oxford University Press).

D.M. Keithly 1992, *The Collapse of East German Communism: The Year the Wall Came Down in 1989* (New York: Praeger).

H. Krisch 1981, *The GDR: A Profile* (Boulder, Colorado: Westview Press).

H. Krisch 1985, *The GDR: The Search for Identity* (Boulder, Colorado: Westview Press).

G. Langguth 1990, *Berlin and the 'German Question': The Berlin Policy of the GDR* (Boulder, Colorado: Westview Press).

L.H. Legters (ed.) 1978, *The GDR: A Developed Socialist Society* (Boulder, Colorado: Westview Press).

A.J. McAdams 1985, *East Germany and Detente: Building Authority after the Wall* (Cambridge: Cambridge University Press).

M. McCauley 1983, *The GDR since 1945* (London: Macmillan).

D.A. Macgregor 1989, *The Soviet–East German Military Alliance* (Cambridge: Cambridge University Press).

J. Mander 1979, *Berlin: Hostage for the West* (London: Greenwood).

R.E.H. Mellor 1978, *The Two Germanies: A Modern Geography* (London: Harper & Row).

R.E.H. Mellor 1979, *German Railways: A Study in Historical Geography* (Aberdeen: Aberdeen University Geography Department O'Dell Memorial Monograph 8).

P. Merkl 1974, *German Foreign Policies: West and East* (Santa Barbara, California: Clio).

G. Minnerup 1992, *The German Question in the Age of Perestroika* (London: Pinter).

N.E. Moreton 1978, *East Germany and the Warsaw Alliance* (Boulder, Colorado: Westview Press).

E. Moreton (ed.) 1989, *Germany between East and West* (Cambridge: Cambridge University Press).

B. Munske 1995, *The Two plus Four Negotiations from a German Perspective* (Boulder, Colorado: Westview Press).

D.J. Nelson 1978, *Wartime Origins of the Berlin Dilemma* (Atlanta, Georgia: University of Alabama Press).

J. Osmond (ed.) 1992, *German Unification: A Reference Guide and Commentary* (London: Longman).

S. Padgett 1993, *Parties and Party Systems in the New Germany* (Aldershot: Dartmouth).

A. Pickel 1991, *Radical Transitions: The Survival and Revival of Entrepreneurship in the GDR* (Boulder, Colorado: Westview Press).

I. Pond 1993, *Beyond the Wall: Germany's Road to Unification* (Washington DC: Brookings Institution).

N.J.G. Pounds 1962, *Divided Germany and Berlin* (Princeton, New Jersey: Van Nostrand).

D. Raff 1988, *A History of Germany from the Medieval Empire to the Present* (Oxford: Berg).

A.D. Rotfeld and W. Stutzle 1991, *Germany and Europe in Transition* (Oxford: Oxford University Press).

M. Rueschemeyer and C. Lemke eds. 1989, The quality of life in the GDR (Armonk, New York: M.E. Sharpe).

B. Scharf 1984, *Politics and Change in East Germany: An Evaluation of Socialist Democracy* (London: Pinter).

H.W. Schwarze 1970, *The GDR Today: Life in the Other Germany* (London: Wolff).

A.B. Shingleton *et al.* 1995, *Dimensions of German Unification* (Boulder, Colorado: Westview Press).

T. Sharp 1975, *The Wartime Alliance and the Zonal Division of Germany* (Oxford: Clarendon Press).

N. Simmons 1988, *Berlin: The Dispossessed City* (London: Hamish Hamilton).

J.E. Smith 1961, *The Berlin Question of 1961* (Baltimore, Maryland: Johns Hopkins University Press).

W. Stolper 1960, *The Structure of the East German Economy* (Cambridge, Massachusetts: Harvard University Press).

J.M. Starrels and A.M. Mallinckrodt 1975, *Politics in the German Democratic Republic* (New York: Praeger).

J. Strawson 1974, *Battle for Berlin* (London: Batsford).

J.S. Sutterlin and D. Klein 1989, *Berlin: From Symbol of Confrontation to Keystone of Stability* (New York: Praeger).

R. Tilford (ed.) 1975, *The Ostpolitik and Political Change in Germany* (Farnborough: Saxon House).

A. Tully 1977, *Berlin: Story of a Battle* (London: Greenwood).

H.A. Turner 1987, *The Two Germanies since 1945* (New Haven, Connecticut: Yale University Press).

H.A. Turner 1993, *Germany from Partition to Reunification* (London: Routledge).

D. Verheyen 1991, *The German Question: A Cultural, Historical and Geopolitical Exploration* (Boulder, Colorado: Westview Press).

A. Wagner 1980, *Living in Berlin* (Hove: Wayland).

W. Wagner 1957, *The Genesis of the Oder–Neisse Line: A Study in the Diplomatic Negotiations of World War Two* (Stuttgart: Brentano).

I. Wallace 1987, *World Bibliographical Series: East Germany* (Oxford: Clio).

H.G.P. Wallach 1992, *United Germany: The Past Politics Prospects* (London: Greenwood).

L.L. Whetten 1971, *Germany's Ostpolitik* (Oxford: Oxford University Press).

H. Wiesenthal and A. Pickel 1996, *The Grand Experiment: Contrasting Views on Shock Therapy, Transition theory and the East German Case* (Boulder, Colorado: Westview Press).

G.M. Winrow 1990, *The Foreign Policy of the GDR in Africa* (Cambridge: Cambridge University Press).

R. Woods 1990, *Opposition in the GDR under Honecker 1971–1985* (London: Macmillan).

# HUNGARY

A.A. Balassa 1969, *The Hungarian Experience in Economic Planning* (New Haven, Connecticut: Yale University Press).

I. Bencze and E.V. Tajti 1972, *Budapest: An Industrial Geographical Approach* (Budapest: Hungarian Academy of Sciences).

I. Berend 1990, *The Hungarian Economic Reforms 1953–1988* (Cambridge: Cambridge University Press).

I. Berend and G. Ranki 1974, *Hungary: A Century of Economic Development* (Newton Abbot: David & Charles).

I. Berend and G. Ranki (eds) 1979, *Underdevelopment and Economic Growth: Studies in Hungarian Social and Economic History* (Budapest: Academy of Sciences).

I.T. Berend and G. Ranki 1985, *The Hungarian Economy in the Twentieth Century* (London: Croom Helm).

A. Bozoki and A. Korosenyi 1992, *Post-communist Transition: Emerging Pluralism in Hungary* (London: Pinter).

J.C. Brada and I. Dobozi 1988, *The Hungarian Economy in the 1980s: Reforming the System and Adjusting to External Shocks* (London: JAI Press).

J.C. Brada *et al.* 1993, *Firms Afloat and Firms Adrift: Hungarian Industry and the Economic Transition* (Armonk, New York: M.E. Sharpe).

G. Csepeli and A. Orkeny 1992, *Ideology and Political Beliefs in Hungary: The Twilight of State Socialism* (London: Pinter).

G. Enyedi (ed.) 1976, *Rural Trsnaformation in Hungary* (Budapest: Hungarian Academy of Sciences).

G. Enyedi 1976, *Hungary: An Economic Geography* (Boulder, Colorado: Westview Press).

G. Enyedi and V. Szirmai 1992, *Budapest: A Central European Capital* (London: Belhaven Press).

A. Felkay 1990, *Hungary and the USSR 1956–1988: Kadar's Political Leadership* (New York: Greenwood Press).

Z. Ferge 1980, *A society in the making: Hungarian Social and Societal Policies 1945–1975* (White Plains, New York: M.E. Sharpe).

C. Gati 1986, *Hungary and the Soviet Bloc* (Durham, North Carolina: Duke University Press).

C.M. Hann 1980, *Tazlar: A Village in Hungary* (Cambridge: Cambridge University Press).

P. Hare *et al.* (eds) 1981, *Hungary: A Decade of Economic Reform* (Winchester, Massachusetts: Allen & Unwin).

H-G. Heinrich 1986, *Hungary: politics, Economics and Society* (London: Pinter).

J. Held (ed.) 1980, *The Modernization of Agriculture: Rural Transformation in Hungary* (Boulder, Colorado: Westview Press).

E. Helmrich (ed.) 1957, *East Central Europe under the Communists: Hungary* (New York: Praeger).

O. Hieronymi 1989, *Economic Policies for a New Hungary: Proposals for a Coherent Approach* (Columbus, Ohio: Battelle Press).

J.K. Hoensch 1988, *A History of Modern Hungary 1867–1986* (London: Longman).

A. Horvath and A. Szakolczai 1992, *The Dissolution of Communist Power: The Case of Hungary* (London: Routledge).

T. Huszar *et al.* (eds) 1978, *Hungarian Society and Marxist Sociology in the 1970s* (Budapest: Corvina).

P. Ignotus 1972, *Hungary* (London: Benn).

T. Kabdebo 1980, *World Bibliographical Series: Hungary* (Oxford: Clio).

P.M. Kalla-Bishop 1973, *Hungarian Railways* (Newton Abbot: David & Charles).

B. Kiraly and P. Jones (eds) 1980, *The Hungarian Revolution of 1956 in Retrospect* (New York: Columbia University Press).

J. Kornai 1990, *The Road to a Free Economy: Shifting from a Socialist System – The Example of Hungary* (New York: W.W. Norton).

B. Kovrig 1970, *The Hungarian People's Republic* (Baltimore, Maryland: Johns Hopkins University Press).

B. Kovrig 1979, *Communism in Hungary from Kun to Kadar* (Stanford, California: Hoover Institution Press).

P. Lendvai 1988, *Hungary: The Art of Survival* (London: Tauris).

I. Major 1991, *The Hungarian Economy in Transition* (Stockholm: Stockholm Institute of Soviet and East European Economics Working Paper).

T. Palankai 1991, *The European Community and Central European Integration: The Hungarian Case* (Boulder, Colorado: Westview).

M. Pecsi (ed.) 1964, *Applied Geography in Hungary* (Budapest: Hungarian Academy of Sciences).

M. Pecsi and F. Probald (eds) 1974, *Man and Environment* (Budapest: Hungarian Academy of Sciences).

M. Pecsi and B. Sarfalvi 1964, *A Geography of Hungary* (Budapest: Corvina).

A. Raba and K.E. Schenk (eds) 1987, *Investment System and Foreign Trade Implications in Hungary* (Stuttgart: Gustav Fischer).

J. Radvanyi 1972, *Hungary and the Superpowers: The 1956 Revolution and Realpolitik* (Stanford, California: Hoover Institution Press).

G. Revesz 1990, *Perestroika in Eastern Europe: Hungary's Economic Transformation 1945–1988* (Boulder, Colorado: Westview Press).

X. Richet 1989. *The Hungarian Model: Planning and the Market in a Socialist Economy* (Cambridge: Cambridge University Press).

W.F. Robinson 1973, *The Pattern of Reform in Hungary: A Political Economic and Cultural Analysis* (New York: Praeger).

B. Sarfalvi (ed.) 1969, *Problems in Hungarian Applied Geography* (Budapest: Hungarian Academy of Sciences).

B.Sarfalvi (ed.) 1971, *The Changing Face of the Great Hungarian Plain* (Budapest: Hungarian Academy of Sciences).

W. Shawcross 1974, *Crime and Compromise: Janos Kadar and the Politics of Hungary since the Revolution* (New York: Dutton).

P.F. Sugar 1990, *A History of Hungary* (London: Tauris).

I.P. Szekely and D.M.G. Newbery 1993, *Hungary: An Economy in Transition* (Cambridge; Cambridge University Press).

P.A. Toma and I. Volgyes 1977, *Politics in Hungary* (San Francisco, California: Freeman).

F.A. Vali 1961, *Rift and Revolt in Hungary: Nationalism versus Communism* (Cambridge, Massachusetts: Harvard University Press).

I. Volgyes 1981, *Hungary: A Profile* (Boulder, Colorado: Westview Press).

I. Volgyes 1982, *Hungary: A Nation of Contradictions* (Boulder, Colorado: Westview Press).

I. Volgyes and N. Volgyes 1977, *The Liberated Female: Life, Work and Sex in Socialist Hungary* (Boulder, Colorado: Westview Press).

I. Volgyes *et al.* 1980, *The Modernization of Hungarian Agriculture* (Boulder, Colorado: Westview Press).

## POLAND

C. Abramsky *et al.* (eds) 1986, *The Jews in Poland* (Oxford: Blackwell).

T.P. Alton 1955, *Polish Post-War Economy* (New York: Columbia UP).

V.L. Benes and N.J.G. Pounds 1970, *Poland* (London: Benn).

M. Checinski 1982, *Poland: Communism, Nationalism, Anti-semitism* (New York: Kanz-Cohl).

J. Coutonvidis and J. Reynolds 1986, *Politics of Liberation: Poland 1939–1947* (Leicester: Leicester University Press).

I. Bialecki *et al.* (eds) 1987, *Crisis and Transition: Polish Society in the 1980s* (Leamington Spa: Berg).

J. Bielasiak *et al.* (eds) 1984, *Polish Politics: Edge of an Abyss* (New York: Praeger).

G. Blazyca and R. Rapacki 1991, *Poland into the 1990s* (London: Pinter).

M.K. Ciechocinska and L.S. Graham (eds) 1986, *The Polish Dilemma: Views from Within* (Boulder, Colorado: Westview Press).

J.L. Curry 1990, *Poland's Journalists: Professionalism and Politics* (Cambridge: Cambridge University Press).

M. Dobbs 1981, *Poland Solidarity Walesa* (Oxford: Pergamon).

M.K. Dziewanowski 1976, *The Communist Party of Poland: An Outline of History* (Cambridge, Massachusetts: Harvard University Press).

L. Ebrill *et al.* 1994, *Poland: The Path to a Market Economy* (Washington DC: International Monetary Fund Occasional Paper 113).

G.R. Feiwel 1971, *Problems in Polish Economic Planning* (New York: Praeger).

J.C. Fisher (ed.) 1966, *City and Regional Planning in Poland* (Ithaca, New York: Cornell University Press).

S. Gomulka and A. Polonsky 1990, *Polish Paradoxes* (New Haven, Connecticut: Yale University Press).

A.J. Groth 1972, *People's Poland: Government and Politics* (San Francisco, California: Chandler).

O. Halecki (ed.) 1957, *East Central Europe Under the Communists: Poland* (New York: Praeger).

O. Halecki and A. Polonsky 1983, *A History of Poland* (London: Routledge).

F.E.I. Hamilton 1975, *Poland's Western and Northern Territories* (Oxford: Oxford University Press).

C.M. Hann 1985, *The Village without Solidarity: Polish Peasants in Years of Crisis* (New Haven, Connecticut: Yale University Press).

D. Hills 1988, *Return to Poland* (London: The Bodley Head).

P. Kaminsky 1991, *The Collapse of State Socialism: The Case of Poland* (Princeton, New Jersey: Princeton University Press).

R.E. Kanet and M.D. Simons (eds) 1980, *Policy and Politics in Gierek's Poland* (Boulder, Colorado: Westview Press).

J. Karski 1985, *The Great Powers and Poland 1919–1945: From Versailles to Yalta* (Lanham, Maryland: University Press of America).

M.D. Kennedy 1991, *Professionals, Power and Solidarity in Poland: A Critical Sociology of Soviet-type Society* (Cambridge: Cambridge University Press).

G. Kolankiewicz 1988, *Poland: Politics, Economics and Society* (London: Pinter).

A. Korbonski 1965, *The Politics of Socialist Agriculture in Poland 1945–1960* (New York: Columbia University Press).

A. Kruszewski 1972, *The Oder–Neisse Boundary and Poland's Modernization* (New York: Praeger).

A. Kuklinski (ed.) 1977, *Regional Studies in Poland* (Warsaw: Polish Academy of Sciences).

P. Latawski (ed.) 1991, *The Reconstruction of Poland 1914–1923* (London: Macmillan).

R.C. Lewanski 1984, *World Bibliographical Series: Poland* (Oxford: Clio).

P. Marer and W. Siwinski (eds) 1988, *Creditworthiness and Reform in Poland* (Bloomington: Indiana University Press).

S. Mikolajczyk 1948, *The Rape of Poland: Pattern of Soviet Aggression* (New York: Whittlesey House).

J.M. Montias 1962, *Central Planning in Poland* (New Haven, Connecticut: Yale University Press).

M. Myant 1993, *Transforming Socialist Economies: The Cases of Poland and Czechoslovakia* (Aldershot: Edward Elgar).

S.I. Ploss 1986, *Moscow and the Polish Crises: An Interpretation of Soviet Policies and Intentions* (Boulder, Colorado: Westview Press).

A. Polonsky and B. Drukier 1980, *The Beginning of Communist Rule in Poland* (London: Routledge & Kegan Paul).

A. Polonsky and S. Gomulka (eds) 1989, *Polish Paradoxes* (London: Routledge).

N.J.G. Pounds 1964, *Poland Between East and West* (Princeton, New Jersey: Princeton University Press).

K.Z. Poznanski (ed.) 1993, *Stabilization and Privatization in Poland: An Economic Evaluation of the Shock Therapy Program* (Dordrecht: Kluwer).

A.R. Rachwald 1983, *Poland Between the Superpowers: Security Versus Economic Recovery* (Boulder, Colorado: Westview Press).

P. Raina 1978, *Political Opposition in Poland 1954–1977* (London: Arlington Books).

P. Raina 1981, *Independent Social Movements in Poland* (London: London School of Economics).

W.F. Robinson (ed.) 1980, *August 1980: The Strikes in Poland* (Munich: Radio Free Europe).

G. Sanford 1983, *Poland: Communism in Crisis* (London: Croom Helm).

G. Sanford 1986, *Military Rule in Poland: The Rebuilding of Communist Power 1981–1983* (London: Croom Helm).

G. Sanford 1990, *The Solidarity Congress 1981: The Great Debate* (London: Macmillan).

T. Sharman 1988, *Poland* (London: Columbus Books).

S. Siebel-Achenbach 1991, *Lower Silesia from Nazi Germany to Communist Poland 1943–1948* (London: Macmillan).

K. Slomczynski *et al.* 1979, *Class Structure and Social Mobility in Poland* (White Plains, New York: M.E. Sharpe).

R.F. Staar 1975, *Poland 1944–1962: The Sovietization of a Captive People* (Westport, Connecticut: Greenwood Press).

S. Steion 1982, *The Poles* (London: Collins).

S. Sword (ed.) 1991, *The Soviet Takeover of the Polish Eastern Provinces 1939–1941* (London: Macmillan).

K. Syrop 1982, *Poland in Perspective* (London: Robert Hale).

A. Szczypiorski 1981, *The Polish Ordeal: The View from Within* (London: Routledge).

A. Szymanski 1984, *Class Struggle in Socialist Poland* (New York: Praeger).

R. Taras 1986, *Poland: Socialist State, Rebellious Nation* (Boulder, Colorado: Westview Press).

J. Taylor 1952, *The Economic Development of Poland 1919–1950* (Ithaca, New York: Cornell University Press).

A. Touraine 1983, *Solidarity: The Analysis of a Social Movement Poland 1980–1981* (Cambridge: Cambridge University Press).

M. Vale (ed.) 1981, *Poland: The State of the Republic* (London: Pluto Press).

G. Weclawowicz 1996, *Contemporary Poland: Space and Society* (London: UCL Press).

J. Wedel 1986, *The Private Poland: An Anthropologist's Look at Everyday Life* (New York: Facts on File Publications).

J.B. de Weydenthal 1978, *The Communists of Poland: An Historical Outline* (Stanford, California: Hoover Institution Press).

J. Woodall (ed.) *Policy and Politics in Contemporary Poland* (London: Pinter).
J.G. Zielinski 1973, *Economic Reform of Polish Industry* (Oxford: Oxford University Press).
J. Zielonka 1989, *Political Ideas in Contemporary Poland* (Aldershot: Dartmouth).

# ROMANIA

G.J. Bobango 1979, *The Emergence of the Romanian National State* (Boulder, Colorado: Westview Press).
A. Braun 1978, *Romanian Foreign Policy since 1965* (New York: Praeger).
I.C. Butnaru 1992, *Silent Holocaust: Romania and its Jews* (London: Greenwood).
J.F. Cadzow and A. Ludanyi (eds) *Transylvania: The Roots of Ethnic Conflict* (Kent, Ohio: Kent State University Press).
A. Deletant and D. Deletant 1985, *World Bibliographical Series: Romania* (Oxford: Clio).
E. Dobrescu and I. Blaga 1973, *Structural Patterns of Romanian Economy* (Bucharest: Meridiane).
S. Fischer-Galati (ed.) 1956, *Rumania* (New York: Mid-European Studies Center).
S. Fischer-Galati (ed.) 1957, *East Central Europe Under the Communists: Rumania* (New York: Praeger).
S. Fischer-Galati 1970, *Twentieth-century Romania* (New York: Columbia University Press).
S. Fischer-Galati *et al.* (eds) 1982, *Romania Between East and West* (Boulder, Colorado: Westview Press).
M.E. Fisher 1989, *Nicolae Ceausescu: A Political Biography* (London: Lynne Rienner).
F. Floyd 1965, *Rumania: Russia's Dissident Ally* (London: Pall Mall).
V. Georgescu (ed.) 1985, *Romania: Forty Years 1944–1984* (New York: Praeger).
T. Gilberg 1975, *Modernization in Romania since World War Two* (New York: Praeger).
T. Gilberg 1990, *Nationalism and Communism in Romania: The Rise and Fall of Ceausescu's Personal Dictatorship* (New York: Praeger).
L.S. Graham 1982, *Romania: A Developing Socialist State* (Boulder, Colorado: Westview Press).
G. Ionescu 1964, *Communism in Romania 1944–1962* (Oxford: Oxford University Press).
K. Jowitt 1972, *Revolutionary Breakthroughs and National Development: The Case of Romania 1944–1965* (Berkeley, California: University of California Press).
E.K. Keefe *et al.* 1972, *Area Handbook for Romania* (Washington DC: American University).
R.B. King 1980, *History of the Romanian Communist Party* (Stanford, California: Hoover Institution Press).
A. MacKenzie (ed.) 1985, *Concise History of Romania* (London: Robert Hale).
R-H Markham 1949, *Rumania Under the Soviet Yoke* (Boston, Massachusetts: Meador).
I.M. Matley 1970, *Romania: A Profile* (London: Pall Mall).
J.M. Montias 1967, *Economic Development in Communist Rumania* (Cambridge, Massachusetts: MIT Press).
D.N. Nelson 1980, *Democratic Centralism in Romania* (Boulder, Colorado: East European Monographs).
D.N. Nelson (ed.) 1981, *Romania in the 1980s* (Boulder, Colorado: Westview Press).

D.N. Nelson 1988, *Romania: Politics in the Ceausescu Era* (New York: Gordon & Breach Science Publishers).

D.N. Nelson (ed.) 1991, *Romania after Tyranny* (Boulder, Colorado: Westview Press).

W. Patterson 1994, *Rebuilding Romania: Energy, Efficiency and the Economic Transition* (London: Royal Institute for International Affairs).

M. Pearton 1971, *Oil and the Romanian State* (Oxford: Clarendon Press).

M. Rady 1992, *Romania in Turmoil: A Contemporary History* (London: Tauris).

P. Ronnas 1984, *Urbanization in Romania: A Geography of Social and Economic Change Since Independence* (Stockholm: Stockholm School of Economics).

S. Sampson 1984, *National Integration Through Socialist Planning: An Anthropological Study of a Romanian New Town* (Boulder, Colorado: East European Monographs).

M. Shafir 1985, *Romania: Politics Economy and Society* (London: Pinter).

I. Spigler 1973, *Economic Reform in Rumanian Industry* (Oxford: Oxford University Press).

J. Sweeney 1991, *The Life and Evil Times of Nicolae Ceausescu* (London: Heinemann).

V. Trebici 1976, *Romania's Population and Demographic Trends* (Bucharest: Meridiane).

A.C. Tsantis and R. Pepper 1979, *Romania: The Industrialization of an Agrarian Economy under Socialist Planning* (Washington DC: World Bank).

D. Turnock 1974, *An Economic Geography of Romania* (London: Bell).

D. Turnock 1986, *The Romanian Economy in the Twentieth Century* (London: Croom Helm).

K. Verdery 1983, *Transylvanian Villagers* (Berkeley, California: University of California Press).

S. Verona 1992, *Military Occupation and Diplomacy: Soviet Troops in Romania 1944–1958* (Durham, North Carolina: Duke University Press).

R. Weiner 1984, *Romanian Foreign Policy and the United Nations* (New York: Praeger).

## FORMER YUGOSLAVIA

N. Adizes 1971, *Industrial Democracy Yugoslva Style: The Effect of Decentralization on Organizational Behaviour* (New York: Free Press).

J.B. Allcock and M. Milivojevic (eds) 1990, *Yugoslavia in Transition: Choices and Constraints* (Oxford: Berg).

I. Avsenek 1955, *Yugoslav Metallurgical Industries* (New York: Mid-European Studies Center).

I. Banac 1984, *The National Question in Yugoslavia* (Ithaca, New York: Cornell University Press).

I. Banac 1988, *With Stalin Against Tito: Cominformist Splits in Yugoslav Communism* (Ithaca, New York: Cornell University Press).

N. Beloff 1987, *Tito's Flawed Legacy: Yugoslavia and the West since 1939* (Boulder, Colorado: Westview Press).

G.K. Bertsch 1976, *Values and Community in Multinational Yugoslavia* (New York: Columbia University Press).

R. Bicanic 1973, *Economic Policy in Socialist Yugoslavia* (Cambridge: Cambridge University Press).

J. Bombelles 1968, *The Economic Development of Communist Yugoslavia 1947–1964* (Stanford, California: Hoover Institution Press).

A. Borowiec 1977, *Yugoslavia after Tito* (New York: Praeger).

S.L. Burg 1983, *Conflict and Cohesion in Socialist Yugoslavia: Political Decision Making Since 1966* (Princeton, New Jersey: Princeton University Press).

R.F. Byrnes (ed.) 1957, *East Central Europe Under the Communists: Yugoslavia* (New York: Praeger).

L.J. Cohen 1983, *Political Cohesion in a Fragile Mosaic: The Yugoslav Experience* (Boulder, Colorado: Westview Press).

L.J. Cohen 1987, *Yugoslavia: Tradition and Change in a Multi-ethnic State* (Boulder, Colorado: Westview Press).

L.J. Cohen 1992, *Regime Transition in a Disintegrating Yugoslavia* (Pittsburgh, Pennsylvania: University of Pittsburgh Center for Russian and East European Studies).

M. Crnobrnja 1994, *The Yugoslav Drama* (London: Tauris).

V. Dedijerb 1971, *The Battle Stalin Lost: Memoirs of Yugoslavia 1948–1953* (New York: Viking).

B.D. Denitch 1976, *The Legitimation of a Revolution: the Yugoslav Case* (New Haven, Connecticut: Yale University Press).

A. Djilas 1991, *The Contested Country: Yugoslav Unity and Communist Revolution* (London: Harvard University Press).

D. Dodor 1978, *The Yugoslavs* (New York: Random House).

A.N. Dragnich 1954, *Tito's Promised Land: Yugoslavia* (New Brunswick, New Jersey: Rutgers University Press).

V. Dubey *et al.* 1975, *Yugoslavia: Development with Decentralization* (Baltimore, Maryland: Johns Hopkins University Press).

W.N. Dunn and J. Obradovic 1978, *Workers' Self-management and Organizational Power in Yugoslavia* (Pittsburgh, Pennsylvania: University of Pittsburgh Press).

S. Estrin 1983, *Self-management, Economic Theory and Yugoslav Practice* (Cambridge: Cambridge University Press).

J.C. Fisher 1966, *Yugoslavia: A Multinational State* (San Francisco, California: Chandler House).

J.H. Gapinski *et al.* 1989, *Modelling the Economic Performance of Yugoslavia* (New York: Praeger).

M. Glennie 1992, *The Fall of Yugoslavia* (Harmondsworth: Penguin).

J. Gow 1992, *Legitimacy and the Military: The Yugoslav Crisis* (London: Pinter).

J. Halpern 1972, *A Serbian Village in Historical Perspective* (New York: Holt Reinhart & Winston).

D.B.G. Heuser 1989, *Western Containment Policies Towards Yugoslavia 1948–1953* (London: Routledge).

T. Hocevar 1965, *The Structure of the Slovenian Economy 1848–1963* (New York: Studia Slovenica).

G.W. Hoffman and F.W. Neal 1962, *Yugoslavia: The New Communism* (New York: Twentieth Century Fund).

B. Horvat 1976, *The Yugoslav Economic System: The First Labor-managed Economy in the Making* (New York: M.E. Sharpe).

J. Irvine 1992, *State-building and Nationalism in Yugoslavia: The Communist Party and the Croat Question* (Boulder, Colorado: Westview Press).

B. Jancar 1987, *Environmental Management in the Soviet Union and Yugoslavia: Structure and Regulation in Communist Federal States* (Durham, North Carolina: Duke University Press).

R.J. Kerner (ed.) 1949, *Yugoslavia* (Berkeley, California: University of California Press).

H. Lydall 1984, *Yugoslav Socialism in Theory and Practice* (London: Oxford University Press).

H.Lydall 1989, *Yugoslavia in Crisis* (Oxford: Clarendon Press).

B. McFarlane 1988, *Marxist Regimes: Yugoslavia – politics, Economies, Society* (London: Pinter).

D. Milenkovitch 1971, *Plan and Market in Yugoslav Economic Thought* (New Haven, Connecticut: Yale University Press).

M. Milivojevic *et al.* 1988, *Yugoslav Security Dilemmas* (Oxford: Berg).

A.E.F. Moodie 1945, *The Italo-Yugoslav Boundary: A Study in Political Geography* (London: Philip).

J.H. Moore 1980, *Growth with Self-management: Yugoslav Industrialisation 1952–1975* (Stanford, California: Hoover Institution Press).

S.K. Pavlowitch 1971, *Yugoslavia* (London: Benn).

S.K. Pavlowitch 1988, *The Improbable Survivor: Yugoslavia and its Problems 1918–1988* (London: Hurst).

M.B. Petrovich 1976, *A History of Modern Serbia 1805–1918* (New York: Harcourt Brace Jovanovich).

D. Plestina 1992, *Regional Development in Communist Yugoslavia* (Boulder, Colorado: Westview Press).

M. Radulovic 1948, *Tito's Republic* (London: Coldharbour Press).

S.P. Ramet (ed.) 1985, *Yugoslavia in the 1980s* (Boulder, Colorado: Westview Press).

S.P. Ramet 1992, *Balkan Babel: Politics, Culture and Religion in Yugoslavia* (Boulder, Colorado: Westview Press).

M. Richardson 1995, *Effects of War on the Environment: Croatia* (London: Spon).

A.Z. Rubinstein 1970, *Yugoslavia and the Non-aligned World* (Princeton, New Jersey: Princeton University Press).

S.R. Sacks 1983, *Self-management and Efficiency: Large Corporations in Yugoslavia* (London: George Allen & Unwin).

A. Simic 1973, *The Peasant Urbanites: A Study of Rural–Urban Mobility in Serbia* (New York: Seminar Press).

J. Simmie and J. Dekleva 1991, *Yugoslavia in Turmoil: after Self-management* (London: Pinter).

F.B. Singleton 1970, *Yugoslavia: The Country and its People* (London: Queen Anne Press).

F.B. Singleton and B. Carter 1982, *The Economy of Yugoslavia* (London: Croom Helm).

L. Sirc 1979, *The Yugoslav Economy Under Self-management* (New York: St Martin's Press).

S. Stankovic 1981, *The End of the Tito Era* (Stanford, California: Hoover Institution Press).

P.F. Sugar 1964, *Industrialization of Bosnia-Hercegovina* (Seattle, Washington: University of Washington Press).

M. Thompson 1992, *A Paper House: The Ending of Yugoslavia* (New York: Vintage).

J. Tomasevich 1955, *Peasants, Politics and Economic Change in Yugoslavia* (Stanford, California: Stanford University Press).

J. Vanek 1972, *The Economics of Workers' management: A Yugoslav Case Study* (London: George Allen & Unwin).

W.S. Vucinich 1969, *Contemporary Yugoslavia: 20 Years of Socialist Experiment* (Berkeley, California: University of California Press).

H.M. Wachtel 1973, *Workers' Management and Workers' Wages in Yugoslavia: The Theory and Practice of Participatory Socialism* (Ithaca, New York: Cornell University Press).

D. Wilson 1980, *Tito's Yugoslavia* (Cambridge: Cambridge University Press).

S. Woodward 1987, *Yugoslavia* (London: Pinter).

M.G. Zaninovich 1968, *The Development of Socialist Yugoslavia* (Baltimore, Maryland: Johns Hopkins University Press).

# INDEX

abattoir 289
ABB (Asea Brown Boveri) 207, 237
Abbotswell 227
abortion 16–17, 119–20, 202, 208–9, 250
absorptiveness 39, 41, 333
abuse *see* coercion
Academic Lifeline 166
academics 167
Academy of Sciences 65–6
access/accessibility 6, 12, 27, 55, 88, 143, 146, 160, 164–5, 178, 240, 275, 311
accommodation *see* apartments, hotels and housing
accountability 108, 152–3
accountancy/accounting 149, 194, 198, 267, 297, 301
activity rate 189
Adamec, L. 177
adaptability/adaptation 89, 107, 327–8
Adidas 227, 302
administration/administrative region/administrator 7, 22, 34, 38, 48–9, 58–62, 87–9, 91, 123–4, 126, 154, 157, 167, 183–4, 187, 191, 205, 219, 229–30, 237, 241–2, 261, 274, 279, 285, 300, 332, 340, 348, 351
Adria/Adriatic 5, 7, 40–1, 45–7, 106, 244–6, 248, 252, 338, 346, 351
advertising 301
Aero Volochody 310
affluence *see* prosperity
Africa/Africans 19, 42, 13–14, 227, 238; *see also* South Africa
age/ageing 14, 19, 109
agencies 274, 279, 281–2, 302, 332, 348
agglomeration *see* conurbation

agglomeration economies 52; *see also* economies of scale
Agip 222
Agrargesellschaften 273
agreement 61, 222, 246, 251–2, 310, 335, 341, 348–50; *see also* treaty
agribusiness 286
agricultural adviser 266, 289; *see also* management and professionals
agricultural circle 39; *see also* cooperatives
agricultural–industrial complex or town/agroindustry 38, 58, 64
agricultural land 34–9, 52, 54, 63, 219; *see also* land
agricultural school 56
agriculture 5–8, 24, 34–9, 55, 62–4, 104, 123, 136, 139, 142, 160–1, 164, 189–91, 194, 196, 202, 209, 218, 220–2, 226, 228, 231, 236–8, 249, 261–95, 326, 328–9, 332, 334–5, 338, 343
agrogorod 58
agronomist 289
agrotourism 285, 289, 327
Ahrensdorf 296
aid 91, 94, 102, 104, 121, 162–7, 187, 195, 202–3, 218–21, 223, 226, 228, 230, 243, 279, 282, 288
Airbus Industrie 310
aircraft 39, 41–2, 181, 204–5, 229, 309–10, 336
air defence *see* defence
airfield/airport 43, 47, 51, 203, 331, 348, 353
airline/air transport 235, 248, 255, 334–6, 351
air pollution 62–7; *see also* emissions

investment/investor 9, 16–18, 34,
  36–8, 40–5, 52, 54–5, 62, 84, 87,
  103, 106, 113, 118, 136–8, 144–5,
  149–57, 163–5, 168–9, 178–9,
  181–5, 187–90, 193–4, 196–9,
  204–10, 218–19, 221–2, 226–8, 231,
  235–40, 244–5, 248, 261, 271, 276,
  282, 285–6, 288–9, 294, 297–309,
  311–16, 323, 325, 327–8, 331–2,
  334–5, 344, 346–8, 352–3
investment attractiveness 205, 327–43
investment fund 156, 166, 206, 228,
  236, 301
inward investment *see* investment
iron *see* steel
Iron Curtain 105–6, 191
Iron Gates 42, 44
Iron Guard (Romania) 232
iron ore 40, 226, 298, 304–5
irrigation 5–7, 36–7, 63, 65, 221, 264,
  273, 276, 278, 284, 286
Isaccea 341
Isarescu, M. 238
Iskra Telecom 249
Islam 22, 220
Islamic Development Bank 222
Ismail 93
isolation 43, 99–100, 218, 221, 229,
  234, 245, 345, 351
Israel 161
Istria 120–1, 245–6, 346, 351
Istrian Democratic Assembly 246, 351
ITA 296
Italy 1–3, 32, 96, 105–7, 115, 197, 160,
  163, 218, 220, 222, 231, 238, 244,
  251–2, 255, 292–3, 300, 306–7, 310,
  314, 335–6, 346–7, 349, 351
Iudjova, R. 225
Ivesco 166
Izetbogovic, A. 242

Jablonec 64, 303, 316, 348
Jajce 99
Japan 40, 178, 182, 197, 251, 307, 313
Jaruzelski, W. 84, 200–1, 203
Jaslo 60
Jastrzebie-Zdroj 51
Jean Monnet Project 167
Jelcz 107
Jelenia Gora 5, 64, 270
Jena 189, 332
Jesenice 55
Jews 8, 13, 49, 108, 123, 232

jobs/jobs market/job security 141–3,
  147–8, 155, 180, 185, 187–90, 202,
  223, 250, 266, 296, 302, 308, 310,
  313, 345, 349; *see also* employment
joint company/venture 26, 42–3, 47, 51,
  113, 150, 166, 169, 184, 194, 197,
  200, 221, 231, 236, 238, 240, 251,
  283, 290, 291, 294, 302–3, 326,
  332–4
Jovic, B. 242
J.P. Morgan 207
judiciary/justice 153, 262; *see also*
  legal system
Junker 263

Kadar, J. 84, 191–2
Kalibarda, M. 255
Kaliningrad 1, 103–4
Kalisz 303, 316
Kampinos 339
Karadzic, R. 242
Karkonosze *see* Sudeten Mountains
Karl Marx Stadt *see* Chemnitz
Karlovy Vary 329
Karosa 316
Katowice 52, 65, 207, 303, 328–9, 332,
  338, 340
Kazanlik 36
Kecskemet 49, 169, 199–200, 292, 350
key village 56, 329
Kielce 328
Kiev 194
kindergarten *see* nursery
kinship 22, 111
kiosk 148, 168
Kiszczak, C. 201
Kjustendil 246
Kladno 307
Klaus, V. 179, 181–3, 350
Klodzko 4
K Mart 184, 294
Knin 351
Know-How Programme 165, 197, 231,
  248, 331
knowledge *see* information
Kobanyi Sorgyar 200
Kobierzyce 338
Kolodko, G. 210
Komarom 274
Kombinate 189–90
Komlo 63
Konin 44, 60
Konstrukta Trencin 309

marijuana 284
Marjanovic, M. 252
market/marketing/market share/market
  system 5–7, 13, 27, 23–7, 40, 58, 67,
  87, 89, 103–4, 108, 136–76, 143,
  145, 148–69, 158, 160, 162–4, 166,
  168–9, 178–9, 181, 183, 185, 187–8,
  192, 194–9, 201, 203–4, 206, 219,
  221, 225–7, 228, 230, 232, 234, 236,
  238, 240, 246, 249–50, 262, 264,
  266, 268–71, 276, 278–86, 288–93,
  295, 297, 299–301, 303–4, 309,
  311–16, 323, 326–7, 331, 347–8
Markovic, A. and M. 240–2, 254
marshall law 200
Marshall Plan 25–6, 104
Martin 309–10
Marchland Europe 3
Maribor 329
Maritsa Iztok 43
Masurian Lakeland 37, 44
Matra 293
Marx, K. 49
mass privatisation 206, 209, 227–8,
  235–7; see also privatisation
mass production see production
Matsushita 182
mayor 59, 88, 240; see also local
  government
Mazowiecki, T. 201, 203
meadow 38, 284; see also grazing
meat 6, 161, 198, 272, 274, 276, 280–1,
  284, 281, 289–90
Meciar, V. 89, 179, 185, 309, 350
Mecklenburg-Vorpommern 91, 189
medecinal plants 6
Medgyessy, P. 196
media 23, 117–18, 184, 224, 230; see
  also broadcasting, television etc.
medical services/medicine 16, 102,
  198; see also health service
Medieval 3–4, 6, 92
Mediterranean 6, 9, 227
Medjimurje 245
Medyka 40, 338
Meiningen 335
Mercedes 296, 316
merchant 4, 112, 279
Merseburg 295
Mesic, S. 243–4
meso-region 351
metallurgy/metals 31, 51, 63, 144, 197,
  232, 237, 301, 304–9, 346–7

Metalna 251
metro 43, 336
MFN 178, 230, 233
Miasteczko Slaski 51
middle class 89, 108
Middle East 6, 9, 41, 194, 199, 229,
  246, 274, 297, 307, 335, 342
Mielec 204–5, 310, 344
migrant/migration/migration policy 13,
  17–23, 38, 49–58, 60, 85, 109–16,
  180, 186, 189, 205, 219, 269–70,
  273, 286, 330, 353
Mikolow 51
Mikulic, B. 240
military 5, 7, 16–17, 64, 84–5, 92–4,
  97–104, 115, 118, 121, 126, 180,
  184, 187, 189, 191, 200, 203, 220–1,
  223, 227, 229, 241–3, 245–6, 249,
  253, 255, 309, 313, 333
military-industrial complex/
  establishment 13–14, 29,
  156, 301, 326
militia see military
milk 264, 271, 278, 279, 281, 288,
  290–1; see also dairying
milling/mills 279, 302
Milosevic, S. 97, 99, 241, 245, 247, 252
minerals 5, 31, 58, 218, 222; see also
  by individual commodity
mineral water 292, 300
mining 5, 18, 28, 51, 55, 65, 142–4,
  202, 205, 222, 237, 240, 299, 308,
  339–40, 342; see also by individual
  commodity
ministry see government
minorities 8, 13, 17, 21, 85, 91–2,
  95–103, 108, 120–5, 142, 162,
  184–5, 193, 196, 223, 232–3, 241,
  247, 250, 255, 350
Mir 43
Miskolc 49, 307, 329, 348, 350
Mitteleuropa see Central Europe
mixed economy 54
mixed farming 265, 269
Mizil 310
Mlada Boleslav 181, 311–12, 344
Mladenov, P. 223–4
mobility 9, 39–43, 45, 91, 108, 141,
  144, 162, 219, 330, 346, 354; see
  also transport
Modelstadt 330
modernise/modernisation 7, 14, 22, 24,
  52, 101, 189, 196, 204, 207, 221,